Foundation for Object/Relational Databases

The Third Manifesto

Foundation for Object/Relational Databases

The Third Manifesto

A detailed study of the impact
of objects and type theory
on the relational model of data
including a comprehensive
proposal for type inheritance

C. J. Date

and

Hugh Darwen

ADDISON-WESLEY

An imprint of Addison Wesley Longman, Inc.

Reading, Massachusetts • Harlow, England • Menlo Park, California
Berkeley, California • Don Mills, Ontario • Sydney
Bonn • Amsterdam • Tokyo • Mexico City

Library of Congress Cataloging-in-Publication Data

Date, C.J.
  Foundation for object/relational databases : the third manifesto /
C. J. Date and Hugh Darwen.
     p.   cm.
  Includes bibliographical references and index.
  ISBN 0-201-30978-5 (alk. paper)
    1. Object-oriented databases.   2. Relational databases.
  I. Darwen, Hugh.   II. Title.
  QA76.9.D3D15994   1998
  005.75'6—dc21   98-10364
                                                                CIP

ISBN 0-201-30978-5

Text printed on recycled and acid-free paper.

1 2 3 4 5 6 7 8 9 10–MA–02 01 00 99 98
First printing, June 1998

All logical differences are big differences
—Wittgenstein (attrib.)

———— ♦ ♦ ♦ ♦ ♦ ————

Again I must remind you that
A Dog's a Dog—A CAT'S A CAT
—T. S. Eliot, demonstrating that
logical differences are not
everything, and nor is logic

———— ♦ ♦ ♦ ♦ ♦ ————

We would like to dedicate this book to
philosophers and poets everywhere

Contents

PART II   FORMAL SPECIFICATIONS

PART III   INFORMAL DISCUSSIONS AND EXPLANATIONS

PART IV   SUBTYPING AND INHERITANCE

APPENDIXES

Preface

The Third Manifesto is a detailed proposal for the future direction of data and data-base management systems (DBMSs). Like Codd's original papers on the relational model, it can be seen as an abstract blueprint for the design of a DBMS and the language interface to such a DBMS. In particular, it lays the foundation for what we believe is the logically correct approach to integrating relational and object technologies—a topic of considerable interest at the present time, given the recent appearance in the marketplace of several "object/relational" DBMS products (some-times called *universal servers*). Perhaps we should add immediately that we do not regard the idea of integrating relational and object technologies as "just another fad," soon to be replaced by some other briefly fashionable idea. On the contrary, we think that object/relational systems are in everyone's future—a fact that makes it even more important to get the logical foundation right, of course, while we still have time to do so.

The first version of the *Manifesto* was published informally in early 1994 (though we had been thinking about the idea of such a document for several years prior to that time), and the first "official" version appeared in 1995. Since then we have presented the material in a variety of forms and forums and discussed it with numerous people—indeed, we continue to do so to this day—and we have refined and expanded the original document many, many times. We would like to stress, however, that those refinements and expansions have always been exactly that; nobody has ever shown us that we were completely on the wrong track, and devel-opment of the *Manifesto* has always proceeded in an evolutionary, not a revolution-ary, manner. Now we feel it is time to make the material available in some more permanent form; hence the present book.

One reason we feel the time is ripe for wider dissemination of our ideas is as follows. As already indicated, we see a parallel between the *Manifesto* and Codd's original papers on the relational model; like those papers of Codd's, the *Manifesto* offers a foundation for what (we believe) the database systems of the future ought to look like. Also like those papers of Codd's, however, the *Manifesto* itself is, de-liberately, fairly terse and not all that easy to read or understand. Would it not have been nice to have had a book that documented and explained and justified Codd's ideas, back at the beginning of the relational era? Well, here we are at the beginning of "the object/relational era," and—modesty aside—we believe this book can play a role analogous to that of that hypothetical relational book. To that end, we have been careful to include not only the formal specifications of the *Manifesto* itself (of course), but also a great deal of supporting and explanatory material and numerous detailed examples.

By the way, we should make it clear that our ideas do rest very firmly in the relational tradition. Indeed, we would like our *Manifesto* to be seen, in large part, as a definitive statement of just what the relational model itself consists of at the time of writing* (for it too has undergone a certain amount of evolution over the years). Despite our remarks in the previous paragraph concerning "the object/relational era," therefore, the ideas expressed in the *Manifesto* must not be thought of as superseding those of the relational model, nor do they do so; rather, they use those ideas as a foundation and build on them. We believe strongly that the relational model is still highly relevant to database theory and practice and will remain so for the foreseeable future. Thus, we regard our *Manifesto* as being very much in the spirit of Codd's original work and continuing along the path he originally laid down. To repeat, we are talking evolution, not revolution.

There is another point to be made here, too. Given the current interest in object/relational systems, we can expect to see a flurry of books on such systems over the next few years. However, it is unlikely, if history is anything to go by, that those books will concern themselves very much with general principles or underlying theory; it is much more probable that they will be product-oriented, if not actually product-specific. The present book, by contrast, definitely is concerned with theoretical foundations rather than products; in other words, it allows you to gain a solid understanding of the underlying technology *per se*, thereby enabling you among other things to approach the task of evaluating commercial products from a position of conceptual strength.

While we are on the subject of commercial products, incidentally, we should make it clear that we ourselves have no particular commercial ax to grind. We regard ourselves as independent so far as the marketplace is concerned, and we are not trying to sell any particular product.[†] The ax we do have to grind is that of logical correctness!—we want to do our best to ensure that the industry goes down the right path, not the wrong one.

And in *that* connection, we would like to mention another reason we feel the book is timely: namely, the fact that the SQL standards bodies, both national and international, are currently at work on a proposal called *SQL3* that addresses

---

*Indeed, we even toyed at one time with the idea of calling the book *A Relational Model of Data for Large Shared Data Banks*.

[†]It is true that one of us, Darwen, works for a company that does have a product to sell, but the product in question is not mentioned by name anywhere in this book.

some of the same issues as our *Manifesto* does. An appendix to the present book gives a detailed set of comparisons between our ideas and those of the current SQL3 proposal.

Note: Another body, the Object Database Management Group (ODMG), has also published a set of proposals that, again, address some of the same issues. Another appendix to this book therefore takes a look at the ODMG ideas as well.

Two more special features of the book are the following:

- We define a new and simplified relational algebra, called **A,** which emphasizes rather more than previous algebras have done its firm foundation in predicate logic.

- We also define a database programming language called **Tutorial D,** which realizes the ideas of the *Manifesto* in concrete form and is used as the basis for examples and illustrations throughout the book.

Finally, we should mention one further feature that we believe to be highly significant, and that is our proposal for a model of *subtyping and inheritance*. Many authorities have rightly observed that there is currently no consensus on any such model, and we offer our proposal for consideration in the light of this observation. Indeed, we believe we have some original—and, we also believe, logically sound and correct—thoughts to offer on this important subject. Part IV of the book (five chapters) is devoted to this topic.

STRUCTURE OF THE BOOK

The body of the book is divided into four major parts:

    I. Preliminaries
   II. Formal Specifications
  III. Informal Discussions and Explanations
  IV. Subtyping and Inheritance

Part I sets the scene by explaining in general terms what the *Manifesto* is all about and why we wrote it. It also contains an informal overview of two approaches to building an object/relational system, one of which is (we claim) right and the other wrong. We recommend that you read both of these chapters fairly carefully before moving on to later parts of the book.

Part II is the most formal part. It consists of three chapters:

- Chapter 3 is the *Manifesto* itself—a "no frills" version, with virtually nil by way of illustration or further explanation. (For the benefit of anyone who might have seen earlier drafts of the *Manifesto*, we should explain that this "no frills" version consists essentially of just the formal text from those earlier drafts, with all commentary and suchlike material deleted.)

- Chapter 4 contains the definition, mentioned above, of our new relational algebra ("**A**").

- Chapter 5 defines the language **Tutorial D.** This language, which is (of course) based on the principles laid down in the *Manifesto* and on our new algebra **A,** serves as the basis for examples throughout the remainder of the book. It also serves to suggest what an implementation of the ideas of the *Manifesto* might look like in actual practice.

Note: Most of the material of these three chapters is provided primarily for purposes of reference; it is not necessary, and probably not even a good idea, to study it exhaustively, at least not on a first reading.

Part III is the real heart of the book. It consists of six chapters, one for each of the six sections of the *Manifesto* as defined in Part II. (Again, for the benefit of anyone who might have seen earlier drafts of the *Manifesto*, this part of the book consists essentially of a hugely expanded version of the informal commentary from those earlier drafts.) Each chapter discusses the relevant section of the *Manifesto* in considerable detail, with examples, and thereby explains the motivations and rationale behind the formal proposals of Part II (especially Chapter 3). Note, therefore, that the *Manifesto* itself serves as the organizing principle for this, the major part of the book.

Finally, **Part IV** does for subtyping and inheritance what Parts I, II, and III do for the *Manifesto* proper. It consists of five chapters. Chapter 12 gives an overall introduction to the topic; Chapter 13 gives formal definitions; and Chapter 14 gives informal explanations and discussions of the ideas underlying those formal definitions. Chapter 15 then extends the ideas of Chapters 12–14 to address multiple inheritance, and Chapter 16 then extends those ideas further to take tuple and relation types into account as well.

In addition to the foregoing, there are also several **appendixes:** one defining an alternative version of **Tutorial D** that is based on relational calculus instead of relational algebra, another discussing "subtables and supertables," another containing the text of an interview the present authors gave on the subject of the *Manifesto* in 1994, and so on. In particular, the SQL3 and ODMG comparisons can be found in this part of the book, as already mentioned. The final appendix, Appendix H, gives an annotated and consolidated list of references for the entire book.

Note: While we are on the subject of references to publications, we should explain that throughout the book such references take the form of numbers in square brackets. For example, the reference "[2]" refers to the second item in the list of references in Appendix H: namely, a paper by Malcolm P. Atkinson and O. Peter Buneman entitled "Types and Persistence in Database Programming Languages," published in *ACM Computing Surveys*, Volume 19, No. 2, in June 1987.

Finally, we should say a word about our use of terminology. It is our experience that many of the terms in widespread use in this field are subject to a variety of different interpretations, and that communication suffers badly as a result (examples seem superfluous—you can surely provide plenty of your own). While we have not deliberately used familiar terms in unfamiliar ways, therefore, we have nevertheless found it necessary to introduce our own terminology in certain places. We apologize if this fact causes you any unnecessary difficulties.

INTENDED READERSHIP

Who should read this book? Well, in at least one sense the book is definitely *not* self-contained—it does assume you are professionally interested in database technology and are therefore reasonably familiar with classical database theory and practice. However, we have tried to define and explain, as carefully as we could, any concepts that might be thought novel; in fact, we have done the same for several concepts that really should *not* be novel at all but do not seem to be as widely understood as they ought to be ("candidate key" is a case in point). Thus, we have tried to make the book suitable for both reference and tutorial purposes, and we have indicated clearly those portions of the book that are more formal in style and are provided primarily for reference.

Our intended audience is, therefore, just about anyone with a serious interest in database technology, including but not limited to the following:

- Database language designers and standardizers
- DBMS product implementers and other vendor personnel
- Data and database administrators
- Information modelers and database designers
- Database application designers and implementers
- Computer science professors specializing in database issues
- Database students, both graduate and undergraduate
- People responsible for DBMS product evaluation and acquisition
- People interested in any aspect of the "objects *vs.* relations" controversy, including especially anyone who might be involved in object/relational systems
- People interested in type theory and the topic of type inheritance

For academic readers in particular (students as well as teachers), we should add that what we have tried to do is present the foundations of the database field in a way that is clear, precise, correct, and uncluttered by the baggage—not to mention mistakes—that usually (and regrettably) seem to accompany commercial implementations. Thus, we believe the book provides an opportunity to acquire a firm understanding of that crucial foundation material, without being distracted by irrelevancies. Perhaps we should say too that we believe there are several interesting (and, we hope, self-evident) research projects lurking just below the surface of certain portions of the material.

ACKNOWLEDGMENTS

First of all, we are delighted to be able to acknowledge all of the numerous friends and colleagues who, over the past several years, have given encouragement, participated in discussions, and offered comments (both written and oral) on various drafts of *The Third Manifesto* or portions thereof: John Andrews, Tanj Bennett, Charley Bontempo, Declan Brady, Bob Brown, Rick Cattell, Linda DeMichiel, Vincent Dupuis, Bryon Ehlmann, Mark Evans, Ron Fagin, Oris Friesen, Ric Gagliardi, Ray Gates, Mikhail Gilula, Zaid Holmin, Michael Jackson, Achim Jung, John Kneiling, Adrian Larner, Bruce Lindsay, David Livingstone, Albert Maier, Carl Mattocks, Nelson Mattos, David McGoveran, Roland Merrick, Serge Miranda, Jim Panttaja, Mary Panttaja, Fabian Pascal, Ron Ross, Arthur Ryman, Alan Sexton, Mike Sykes, Stephen Todd, Rick van der Lans, Anton Versteeg, and Fred Wright (and we apologize if we have inadvertently omitted anyone from this list). We would also like to acknowledge the many conference and seminar attendees, far too numerous to mention individually, who have expressed support for the ideas contained herein.

Second, we would like to thank our reviewers Charley Bontempo, Declan Brady, Rick Cattell, David Livingstone, and David McGoveran for their careful and constructive comments on the manuscript.

Third, we are—of course!—deeply indebted to our wives, Lindy Date and Lindsay Darwen, for their unfailing support throughout this project and so many others over the years.

Finally, we are, as always, grateful to our editor, Elydia Davis, and to the staff at Addison-Wesley for their assistance and their continually high standards of professionalism. It has been, as always, a pleasure to work with them.

Hugh Darwen adds: My gratitude to my colleague and friend, Chris Date, goes without saying. However, I would like to comment on something, significant to us, that you possibly haven't noticed. It concerns the book's attribution. In our previous joint productions our names have been linked by the preposition *with,* intended to distinguish the primary author from the contributing assistant. This time around we have thought it more appropriate to use the conjunction *and,* of whose commutativity we Relationlanders are especially conscious! We came to this conclusion despite the fact that, as usual, Chris has done the lion's share of the actual writing. That the writing so faithfully and agreeably records our joint thinking (often painstakingly wrought out) is therefore a source of great pleasure to me, especially in those cases where I can still identify the thinking in question as having arisen from ideas first placed into discussion by myself.

My own thinking has been molded, of course, with the aid of many mentors over the years, including Chris himself. Here I would like to single out just two other people for special mention: Adrian Larner for my relational thinking, and Nelson Mattos for my object-oriented thinking.

Chris Date adds: If Hugh feels he has learned from me over the years, I can assure you (and him) that I have most certainly learned a great deal from him!—a state of affairs for which I will always be grateful. As for the matter of the book's attribution, it is of course true that *The Third Manifesto* is a joint effort, but Hugh should really take the credit for being the original and prime mover on this project: It was he who came up with the idea of the *Manifesto* in the first place, and it was he who wrote the very first draft, early in 1994. Though I should immediately add that our thinking on the matters with which the *Manifesto* deals goes back very much further than that; in some respects, in fact, I think we could claim that it goes all the way back to the beginning of our respective careers in the database field.

C. J. Date
Healdsburg, California
1998

Hugh Darwen
Shrewley, England
1998

PRELIMINARIES

This first part of the book consists of two introductory chapters. Chapter 1 contains important background information, including in particular brief explanations of certain fundamental ideas—e.g., the distinction between *model* and *implementation*—that pervade and underlie the entire *Manifesto* and hence the entire book. Chapter 2 consists of an informal discussion of two candidate approaches, one right and the other wrong, to the crucial question of integrating objects and relations. As noted in the preface, we recommend that you read both these chapters carefully before moving on to later parts of the book.

1

Background and Overview

WHAT IS *THE THIRD MANIFESTO?*

The Third Manifesto is a detailed, formal, and rigorous proposal for the future direction of data and database management systems (DBMSs for short). Like Codd's original papers on the relational model [19–21], therefore, the *Manifesto* can be seen as an abstract blueprint for the design of a DBMS and the language interface to such a DBMS. Among other things, it lays the foundation for what we believe is the logically correct approach to integrating relational and object technologies—a topic of considerable interest and importance at the present time, given the recent appearance in the marketplace of several "object/relational" DBMS products, also known as "universal servers"; see, e.g., references [83], [94], [95], and [110].

Now, in the preface we stressed the point that the *Manifesto* does rest firmly in the classical relational tradition. Of course, we do believe that object technology has important contributions to make to the database management field as well; indeed, our remarks above on object/relational systems were meant to suggest as much. However, we do *not* believe that object database technology is destined to replace relational database technology. We would like to emphasize, therefore, that the ideas expressed in the *Manifesto* are in no way intended to supersede those of the relational model, nor do they do so; rather, they use those ideas as a foundation and build on them. We believe strongly that the relational model is still highly relevant to database theory and practice, and we believe further that it will remain so for the foreseeable future. Thus, we regard our *Manifesto* as being very much in the spirit of

Codd's original work and continuing along the path he originally laid down. We are interested in evolution, not revolution.

Another matter we need to get out of the way right at the outset has to do with our use—or lack thereof, for the most part—of terminology from the object world. The fact is, even the term *object* itself unfortunately does not have a precise and universally agreed interpretation: Sometimes it seems to mean a *value;* sometimes a *variable;* sometimes even a *type;* and there are probably other interpretations as well.* As a label, moreover, it is applied to a wide variety of distinct disciplines: It is used among other things to describe a certain *graphic interface* style, a certain *programming* style, certain *programming languages* (not the same thing as programming style, of course), and certain *analysis* and *design* techniques, as well as a certain approach to what is after all the principal focus of this book, *database management.* And it is quite clear that the term does not mean the same thing in all of these different contexts (see, e.g., the annotation to reference [10] in Appendix H). Moreover, similar criticisms can be made regarding most other object terms as well (*class, method,* and so on). Given this state of affairs, therefore, and given also that we are trying to be very precise in this book (for the most part, at any rate), we prefer to avoid terminology that might be subject to misinterpretation.

And one more preliminary remark (related to the previous one): To repeat, we are, of course, interested in this book in database management specifically. We are therefore interested in—among other things—the applicability of object concepts and technology to database management specifically. *Please understand, therefore, that all remarks made in this book concerning object concepts and technology must be understood in this light.* We offer no opinion whatsoever regarding the suitability of object ideas in any context other than that of database management specifically.

WHY DID WE WRITE IT?

We originally wrote the *Manifesto* because we were concerned about certain trends that we began to observe in the database industry at the time (trends that, we should add, we continue to observe in some circles to this day). Specifically, we were concerned about certain well-publicized but ill-considered attempts to integrate object and relational technologies. Not that there is anything wrong with the idea of such integration *per se,* we hasten to add; the problem lay in the specific manner in which that integration was being attempted.

We were not the first writers to address these issues, of course. Indeed, our *Manifesto* was specifically written to follow—and, we hope, supersede—two previous ones (hence our choice of title):

---

*Sometimes an object is defined to be an *instance,* but that definition merely shifts the question of interpretation on to this new term. In this book, therefore, we tend to avoid the use of "instance" terminology also, except in informal contexts.

- *The Object-Oriented Database System Manifesto* [1]
- *The Third Generation Database System Manifesto* [111]

Like our own *Manifesto,* each of these documents proposes a basis for future DBMSs. However:

- The first [1] essentially ignores the relational model! In our opinion, this flaw is more than enough to rule it out immediately as a serious contender. In any case, it seems to us that it also fails to give firm direction.

- The second [111] does correctly embrace the relational model, but fails to emphasize (or indeed even mention) the hopelessness of continuing to follow a commonly accepted perversion of that model, namely SQL, in fond pursuit of that model's ideals. In other words, it assumes that SQL, with all its faults, is an adequate realization of that model and hence an adequate foundation for the future.

  By contrast, we feel strongly that any attempt to move forward, if it is to stand the test of time, must reject SQL unequivocally. Our reasons for taking this position are many and varied, far too much so for us to spell them out in detail here; in any case, we have described them in depth in many other places (see, e.g., references [28], [46], [48], [62], [73], and [76], among others), and you are referred to those publications for the specifics. Of course, we do realize that SQL databases and applications are going to be with us for a very long time—to think otherwise would be quite unrealistic—and so we do have to pay some attention to the question of what to do about today's SQL legacy. The *Manifesto* therefore does include some specific suggestions in this regard. See Chapter 3, and more particularly Chapter 10, for further discussion of those suggestions.

A more detailed discussion and analysis of the two previous manifestos can be found in the annotation in Appendix H.

BACK TO THE RELATIONAL FUTURE

As just explained, it is a major thesis of the *Manifesto* that we must get away from SQL and back to our relational roots. In other words, we do not believe that SQL is capable of providing the kind of solid foundation we seek. Instead, we believe that any such foundation must be firmly rooted in **The Relational Model of Data,** first presented to the world in 1969 by E. F. Codd in reference [19].*

---

*As noted in the preface, the relational model itself has evolved over time. *The Third Manifesto* is based on the version of the model described in references [51] and [56] but itself can be seen as representing another step in that evolution. For that reason, definitions in the present book should be regarded as superseding those in those earlier publications (in the few cases where they differ). In fact—as mentioned in the preface—we would like our *Manifesto* to be seen, in part, as a definitive statement of just what it is that currently constitutes the relational model (in this connection see in particular Chapter 3, especially the section entitled "RM Prescriptions").

Now, we have already said that we acknowledge the desirability of supporting certain features that have been much discussed in more recent times: to be specific, features that are commonly regarded as aspects of **object orientation.** However, we believe that the features in question are orthogonal to (i.e., independent of) the relational model, and hence that the relational model needs no *extension,* no *correction,* no *subsumption*—and, above all, no *perversion!*—in order for it to be possible to define some language that:

- Is truly relational (unlike SQL);
- Does accommodate those desirable orthogonal features;
- And, finally, can represent the firm foundation we seek.

Let there be such a language, and let its name be **D.** *Note:* No special significance attaches to this choice of name; we use it merely to refer generically to any language that conforms to the principles laid down in the *Manifesto.* Thus, there could be any number of distinct languages all qualifying as a valid **D.**

The *Manifesto* defines a variety of prescriptions and proscriptions that apply to any such **D.** Some of those prescriptions arise from the relational model, and these we call **Relational Model Prescriptions,** abbreviated **RM Prescriptions.** Prescriptions that do not arise from the relational model we call **Other Orthogonal Prescriptions,** abbreviated **OO Prescriptions.** We similarly classify the *Manifesto's* proscriptions into RM and OO categories.

The various prescriptions and proscriptions are itemized and discussed in detail in Parts II and III of this book. The RM Prescriptions and Proscriptions are not negotiable.* Unfortunately, the same cannot quite be said of the OO Prescriptions and Proscriptions, as there is not, at the time of writing, a clear and commonly agreed model for them to be based on (indeed, part of what we are trying to do is precisely to propose such a model). We do believe that certain OO features—namely, those having to do with **user-defined types** and (probably) **type inheritance**—are significant and likely to become more so in the future; however, there is still no consensus on an abstract model, even with respect to these important topics. Thus, we have been forced to provide our own definitions in these areas. And it is only fair to say that inheritance, at least, raises a number of questions that do not yet seem to have been answered satisfactorily in the open literature. As a result, our proposals in this area are necessarily still a little tentative (see Part IV of this book).

In addition to the prescriptions and proscriptions mentioned above, the *Manifesto* includes a series of **Very Strong Suggestions,** also divided into RM and OO categories (again, see Parts II and III of the book).

---

*Some might find this statement excessively dogmatic. All we mean, however, is that prescriptions and proscriptions arising from the relational model are only as negotiable as the pertinent features of the relational model themselves are.

Note: For definiteness, we assume throughout the *Manifesto* and throughout this book that the language **D** is imperative in style.* Like all such languages, therefore, it is based on the four core concepts **type, value, variable,** and **operator.** For example, we might have a type INTEGER; the integer "3" might be a value of that type; N might be a variable of that type, whose value at any given time is some integer value (i.e., some value of that type); and "+" might be an operator that applies to integer values (i.e., to values of that type). See the section "Some Logical Differences" below for further elaboration of these concepts.

By the way, do not infer from our assumption of an imperative style that we discount the possibility of (e.g.) a "functional programming style" **D;** at the time of writing, however, we have not investigated such a possibility in any depth. But we should point out that certain of the prescriptions, proscriptions, and suggestions described in this book would have to be reformulated in the context of a "functional **D.**" For example, a functional **D** would obviously have no need of variables (in the usual programming language sense of that term) at all, and hence would not need any update operators either [86]. (On the other hand, we feel bound to add that a database language that does not allow the database to be updated does not seem very practical.)

SOME GUIDING PRINCIPLES

Throughout our work on *The Third Manifesto* (and other related work, of course), we have tried hard to follow certain guiding principles, of which the most important—indeed, it underlies all the rest—is this:

> **All logical differences are big differences**

The relevance of this maxim, which is due to Ludwig Wittgenstein,[†] is as follows. The relational model is at heart *a formal system*—just as a DBMS is, or an operating system, or indeed any computer program, come to that. Formal systems are what computers are, or can be made to be, good at. And, of course, the basis of any formal system is *logic*. It follows that—with respect to formal systems in general, and with respect to the matters that are the concern of the *Manifesto* in particular—

---

*We have recently observed a distressing tendency to confuse *imperative* with *procedural*. While it is true that all procedural languages are imperative, it is important to understand that the converse (i.e., that all imperative languages are procedural) is false. In particular, **D**—or its relational portion, at any rate— is imperative but not procedural.

[†]At least, we think it is. To our chagrin, however, we have been unable to track the quotation down to its source. We would be grateful to anyone who could enlighten us in this regard.

differences that are logical in nature are very important ones, and we need to pay very careful attention to them.

Incidentally, Wittgenstein's maxim has an interesting corollary: namely, that *all logical mistakes are big mistakes.* Because, of course, a mistake is a difference—a difference between what is right and what is wrong. And we do unfortunately observe a number of logical mistakes that have been made, and still are being made, in the database industry as a whole . . .

We further conjecture that the inverse of Wittgenstein's maxim is true as well: namely, that *all nonlogical differences are small differences*—by which we mean, not that (for example) psychological differences are unimportant in general, but that they *are* unimportant from the point of view of formal systems in particular. In the context of *The Third Manifesto* specifically, therefore, we pay little attention to nonlogical considerations, such as matters of syntax. (Syntax is important from a human factors point of view, of course, and in our design of **Tutorial D**—see Chapter 5— we have naturally tried to favor good syntax over bad. However, we choose not to regard differences that are mere differences in syntax as logical differences, nor as very important ones.)

Another fundamental principle we have tried hard to follow is that of *conceptual integrity* (the term is due to Fred Brooks). In his classic *The Mythical Man-Month* [12], Brooks has this to say:

> . . . conceptual integrity is *the* most important consideration in system design. It is better to have a system omit certain anomalous features [and] to reflect one set of design ideas, than to have one that contains many good but independent and uncoordinated ideas (*italics in the original*).

And writing 20 years later, he adds:

> A clean, elegant programming product must present . . . a coherent mental model . . . [Conceptual] integrity . . . is the most important factor in ease of use . . . **Today I am more convinced than ever.** Conceptual integrity *is* central to product quality (*boldface and italics in the original*).

Perhaps we should elaborate briefly on this question of conceptual integrity. It goes without saying that in order to maintain integrity of concepts, it is of course necessary to *have* some concepts in the first place. Furthermore, the concepts in question had better be carefully chosen ones, preferably few in number, agreed upon by all parties concerned, and indeed agreeable, not disagreeable, in nature. As an obvious example, suppose the "product" in question is a database system specifically and the agreed-upon concepts are those of the relational model; then that system must adhere rigidly to *all* aspects of that model. In particular, it must not sacrifice the conceptual integrity of that model in pursuit of some kind of "simple syntax" goal.

We will have reason to refer to these guiding principles many times over in the pages ahead.

SOME CRUCIAL LOGICAL DIFFERENCES

Following on from the previous section, there are certain crucial logical differences that deserve to be spelled out right away, since they are relevant to just about everything that follows.

Model *vs.* Implementation

The first logical difference we want to discuss is that between *model* and *implementation,* which we define thus:

- A **model** is an abstract, self-contained, *logical* definition of the objects, operators, and so forth, that together constitute the abstract machine with which users interact.* *Note:* The term "objects" here is generic—it is not meant in its object-oriented sense.
- An **implementation** of a given model is the *physical* realization on a real computer system of the components of that model.

As you can see, the distinction between model and implementation is really just a special case—an important special case—of the familiar distinction between logical and physical aspects of a system. And just in case it might not be obvious, we would like to make it clear that our overriding concern throughout the *Manifesto,* and throughout this book, is with *an abstract model* specifically, not with matters of implementation merely (though our informal discussions and explanations do occasionally touch on implementation matters for clarification reasons, especially in Part III). We would also like to make it clear that by "implementation" here we mean implementation of "the system" (i.e., the DBMS) specifically, not of some application that runs on top of that system.

Values *vs.* Variables

The second logical difference we want to elaborate on here is that between *values* and *variables* (where by *variable* we mean a variable in the usual programming language sense; note that it follows from our assumption of an imperative style for the language **D** that we need to deal with variables). Now, you might find it hard to be-

---

*The term *architecture* has sometimes been used with the same meaning. To quote reference [12] once again, "the architecture of a system [is] the complete and detailed specification of the user interface." We prefer *model* over *architecture* because over the years the latter term has grown to acquire a variety of meanings, most of them not very precise.

lieve that people could get confused over the difference between two such simple and fundamental notions. The fact is, however, that it is all too easy to fall into traps in this area. Following Cleaveland [18], therefore, we adopt the following definitions:

- A **value** is an "individual constant" (for example, the individual constant "3"). A value has *no location in time or space.* However, values can be represented in memory by some *encoding,* and of course such encodings do have locations in time and space (see the next paragraph). Note that, by definition, *a value cannot be updated;* for if it could, then after such an update it would not be that value any longer (in general).

- A **variable** is a holder for an encoding of a value. A variable does have a location in time and space. Also, of course, variables, unlike values, can be updated; that is, the current value of the variable in question can be replaced by another value, probably different from the previous one. (Of course, the variable in question is still the same variable after the update.)

Please note very carefully that it is not just simple things like the integer "3" that are legitimate values. On the contrary, values can be arbitrarily complex; for example, a value might be an array, or a stack, or a list, or a geometric point, or a polygon, or an X-ray, or a document, or a fingerprint (and so on). Analogous remarks apply to variables too, of course.

Incidentally, it is worth noting in passing that confusion over the values *vs.* variables distinction seems to be rife in the object world.* For instance, consider the following extract from a tutorial on object databases [116] (the italicized portions in square brackets are comments added by the present authors):

> We distinguish the declared type of a variable from . . . the type of the object that is the current value of the variable [*so an object is a value*] . . . we distinguish objects from values [*so an object is not a value after all*] . . . a **mutator** [is an operator such that it is] possible to observe its effect on some object [*so in fact an object is a variable*].

So what exactly *is* an object? Is it a value? Is it a variable? Is it both? Is it something else entirely? *Note:* As a matter of fact, it is largely because of this confusion over what objects really are that we prefer, both in the *Manifesto* and in the present book, not to use object terminology at all, except in a few very informal contexts.

Values *vs.* Encodings *vs.* Appearances

The next logical difference we want to discuss is the one, touched on in the preceding subsection, between a value *per se* and an *encoding* of that value that happens

---

*Actually, it seems to us that much of the object literature is confused over *all* of the logical differences discussed in this section—logical *vs.* physical, model *vs.* implementation, and value *vs.* encoding *vs.* appearance, as well as the value *vs.* variable difference in particular.

to appear in some particular context. In fact, the very same value—or, rather, encodings of the very same value—can appear in many different contexts simultaneously, and those encodings themselves are not necessarily all the same. For example, the integer value "3" occurs exactly once in the set of integers (there is exactly one integer "3" in the universe, as it were), but any number of variables might simultaneously contain some encoding of that integer as their current value. Furthermore, some of those variables might contain (say) a decimal encoding, and others a binary encoding, of that particular integer. Thus, there is also a logical difference between (a) an *encoding* of a value, on the one hand, and (b) an *appearance* in some context of that encoding of that value, on the other. Moreover, there might even be a logical difference between the encodings appearing in different contexts.

The foregoing remarks notwithstanding, we usually find it convenient—for fairly obvious reasons—to abbreviate "appearance of an encoding of a value" to just "appearance of a value," or (more often) to just "value," so long as there is no risk of ambiguity. Note carefully too that "appearance of a value" is a model concept, whereas "encoding of an appearance" is an implementation concept. For example, users might need to know whether two distinct variables contain appearances of the same value (i.e., whether they "compare equal"), but they do not need to know whether those two appearances use the same encoding.

TOPICS DELIBERATELY OMITTED

There are, of course, many aspects of database management systems that are necessary or at least desirable in practice but have little or nothing to do with the foundation of such systems *per se*. Such aspects include:

- Recovery and concurrency
- Security and authorization
- Stored procedures and triggered actions*
- Support for the development of generic applications (sometimes referred to as a *call-level interface*)
- Scalability and performance issues

and doubtless many other things besides. Now, we do (of course) recognize that such features can be extremely important in practice—in fact, the quality of support for them can make or break a DBMS as a commercial proposition. As already stated, however, such features are indeed not part of the foundation as such; they are therefore not addressed in the *Manifesto,* and they are not discussed in the present book (at least, not very much).

---

*More usually known, somewhat inappropriately, as just *triggers*.

THE THIRD MANIFESTO: A SUMMARY

As already explained, the *Manifesto* consists of a series of prescriptions, proscriptions, and "very strong suggestions," together with proposals for a model of subtyping and type inheritance. For purposes of subsequent reference, and also to give some idea of the *Manifesto's* scope, on the opposite page we show a mnemonic list of those prescriptions, proscriptions, and suggestions. (An analogous list for our inheritance proposals is given in Part IV of this book.) We remind you that "OO" here stands for **Other Orthogonal.**

We close this introductory chapter by confessing that we do feel a little uncomfortable with the idea of calling what is, after all, primarily a technical document a "manifesto." According to *Chambers Twentieth Century Dictionary,* a manifesto is "a written declaration of the intentions, opinions, or motives" of some person or group (e.g., a political party). By contrast, *The Third Manifesto* is—we hope—a matter of science and logic, not mere "intentions, opinions, or motives." Given the historical precedents that led us to write it, however, our title was effectively chosen for us.

RM Prescriptions

1. Scalar types
2. Scalar values are typed
3. Scalar operators
4. Actual *vs.* possible representations
5. Expose possible representations
6. Type generator TUPLE
7. Type generator RELATION
8. Equality
9. Tuples
10. Relations
11. Scalar variables
12. Tuple variables
13. Relation variables (relvars)
14. Real *vs.* virtual relvars
15. Candidate keys
16. Databases
17. Transactions
18. Relational algebra
19. Relvar names, relation selectors, and recursion
20. Relation-valued operators
21. Assignments
22. Comparisons
23. Integrity constraints
24. Relvar and database predicates
25. Catalog
26. Language design

RM Proscriptions

1. No attribute ordering
2. No tuple ordering
3. No duplicate tuples
4. No nulls
5. No nullological mistakes
6. No internal-level constructs
7. No tuple-level operations
8. No composite attributes
9. No domain check override
10. Not SQL

OO Prescriptions

1. Compile-time type checking
2. Single inheritance (conditional)
3. Multiple inheritance (conditional)
4. Computational completeness
5. Explicit transaction boundaries
6. Nested transactions
7. Aggregates and empty sets

OO Proscriptions

1. Relvars are not domains
2. No object IDs

RM Very Strong Suggestions

1. System keys
2. Foreign keys
3. Candidate key inference
4. Transition constraints
5. Quota queries
6. Generalized transitive closure
7. Tuple and relation parameters
8. Special ("default") values
9. SQL migration

OO Very Strong Suggestions

1. Type inheritance
2. Types and operators unbundled
3. Collection type generators
4. Conversion to/from relations
5. Single-level store

2

Objects and Relations

INTRODUCTION

As indicated in the preface and also in Chapter 1, there is a great deal of current interest in the idea of integrating objects and relations. However (and despite the fact that several DBMS vendors have already announced—in some cases, even released—object/relational products), there is, regrettably, some confusion over the question of the right way to perform that integration. Since one of the key technical objectives of *The Third Manifesto* is precisely to provide an answer to this question, it therefore seems worthwhile to devote this early chapter to an informal discussion of some of the issues involved in that integration. That informal discussion, though it *is* only informal, should help to pave the way for a better understanding of the material in Parts II and III of this book.

Now, before we can consider the question of integrating objects and relations in any detail, there is a crucial preliminary question that we need to address, and that is as follows:

> *What concept is it in the relational world that is the counterpart to the concept* object class *in the object world?*

The reason this question is so crucial is that *object class* really is the most fundamental concept of all in the object world—all other object concepts depend on it to a greater or lesser degree. And there are two equations that can be, and have been, proposed as answers to this question:

- domain = object class
- relation = object class*

We now proceed to argue, strongly, that the first of these equations is right and the second is wrong.

WHAT PROBLEM ARE WE TRYING TO SOLVE?

Before we go any further, we should be clear as to what the problem is that we are trying to solve. The basic issue is this: Databases of the future will need to contain much more sophisticated kinds of data than current commercial ones typically do. For example, we might imagine a biological database that includes a BIRD relation like that shown in Fig. 2.1.[†] Thus, what we have to do is find a way of extending—dramatically—the range of possible kinds of data that we can keep in our databases. Of course, we need to be able to manipulate that data, too; in the case of the BIRD relation, for example, we might want to find all birds whose migration route includes Italy:

```
SELECT NAME, DESCR, SONG, VIDEO
FROM   BIRD
WHERE  INCLUDES ( MIGR, COUNTRY ('Italy') ) ;
```

Note: We use SQL as the basis for this example for reasons of familiarity, though in fact—as explained in Chapter 1—the *Manifesto* expressly proscribes it. SQL is not a valid **D.**

So the question we are addressing is this: How can we support new kinds of data within the classical relational framework? Note that we do take it as axiomatic that we want to stay in the relational framework; it would be unthinkable to walk away from so many years of solid relational research and development.

Now, some people might criticize our characterization of the problem as unfair, in that it tends to suggest right away that the solution we advocate ("domain = class") is indeed the right one. Such criticisms miss the point, however, which is that—as so often—to state the problem clearly is to point the way to the right way to solve the problem. Please note too that the arguments that follow do not depend

---

*More precisely, *relvar* = object class (see the section "Relations *vs.* Relvars" later in this chapter). In the original paper [36] on which this chapter is based, we noted that much of the industry was running with the wrong equation, a logical mistake—see Chapter 1—that we referred to informally as **The Great Blunder.**

[†]We follow the convention in Fig. 2.1 (and in similar figures throughout the book) of using *double underlining* to indicate primary key columns—despite the fact that the *Manifesto* does not actually require primary key support! (It does require *candidate* key support; see Chapter 6 for further discussion.)

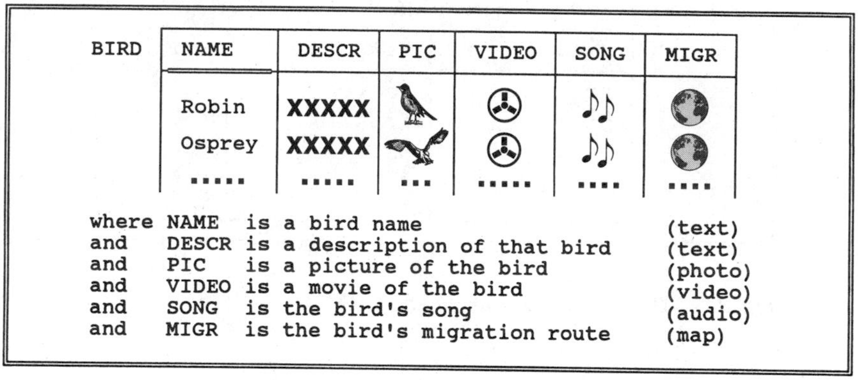

Fig. 2.1   The BIRD relation

in any way on our specific characterization of the problem, nor on the specific example shown in Fig. 2.1.

RELATIONS *VS.* RELVARS

The first thing we need to do is clear up a confusion that goes right back to the beginning of the relational era. Consider the bill of materials relation MMQ shown in Fig. 2.2. As that figure suggests, every relation has two parts, a *heading* and a *body,* where the heading is a set of column-name:domain-name pairs and the body is a set of rows that conform to that heading.* In the case of relation MMQ of Fig. 2.2:

- The column names are MAJOR_P#, MINOR_P#, and QTY (where P# means *part number*);

- The corresponding domain names are P#, P# again, and QTY, respectively;

- Each row includes a MAJOR_P# value (from the P# domain), a MINOR_P# value (also from the P# domain), and a QTY value (from the QTY domain).

Informally, of course, we often ignore the domain-name components of the heading (as indeed we did in the BIRD relation in Fig. 2.1).

A note on terminology: Throughout this book, we prefer the term *relation* to the term *table,* mainly for reasons of precision (see the discussion of RM Prescription 10 in Chapter 6). For similar reasons, we also tend to prefer the terms

---

*One reviewer (David McGoveran) argued that it would be more correct, and preferable, to regard the body alone as the relation proper and the heading not as part of the relation *per se* but as "metadata" that defines the relation *type.*

MMQ	MAJOR_P# : P#	MINOR_P# : P#	QTY : QTY
	P1	P2	5
	P1	P3	3
	P2	P3	2
	P2	P4	7
	P3	P5	4
	P4	P6	8

Fig. 2.2   The bill of materials relation MMQ

attribute and *tuple** to the terms *column* and *row,* except in contexts like the present chapter where we are not trying to be quite so precise.

Now, there is a very important (though perhaps unusual) way of thinking about relations, and that is as follows: Given a relation *R,* the heading of *R* denotes a certain *predicate* (i.e., a truth-valued function), and each row in the body of *R* denotes a certain *true proposition,* obtained from the predicate by substituting certain domain values for the placeholders or parameters of that predicate ("instantiating the predicate"). In the case of relation MMQ, for example, the predicate looks something like this:

part MAJOR_P# contains QTY of part MINOR_P#

(the three parameters are MAJOR_P#, QTY, and MINOR_P#, corresponding of course to the three columns of the relation). And the corresponding true propositions are

part P1 contains 5 of part P2

(obtained by substituting the domain values P1, 5, and P2);

part P1 contains 3 of part P3

(obtained by substituting the domain values P1, 3, and P3); and so on. In a nutshell:

- *Domains* comprise the things we can talk about;
- *Relations* comprise the truths we utter about those things.

It follows that:

- First, domains and relations are both necessary (without domains, we have nothing to talk about; without relations, we cannot say anything).
- Second, domains and relations are *not* the same thing (beware anyone who tries to tell you otherwise!).

---

*Usually pronounced to rhyme with "couple."

In fact, there is a third implication as well, which is that, between them, domains and relations are *sufficient,* as well as necessary—i.e., we do not need anything else, logically speaking.

By the way, there is a nice analogy here (albeit a slightly loose one) that might help you appreciate and remember these important points:

Domains are to relations as nouns are to sentences

Now we can get back to the main theme of the present section (i.e., relations *vs.* relvars). The sad fact is, there has been much confusion historically between relations *per se*—i.e., relation *values*—and relation *variables.* Suppose we say in some programming language:

```
DECLARE N INTEGER ... ;
```

N here is not an integer *per se,* it is an integer *variable* whose *values* are integers *per se*—different integers at different times. In exactly the same way, if we say in SQL:

```
CREATE TABLE R ... ;
```

R here is not a relation (SQL would say "table") *per se,* it is a relation *variable* whose *values* are relations *per se*—different relations at different times. Thus, when we "update R" (e.g., by "inserting a row"), what we are really doing is *replacing the old relation value of R* en bloc *by a new, different relation value.* Of course, it is true that the old value and the new value are somewhat similar—the new one just has one more row than the old one—but conceptually they are different values.

Now, the trouble is, when people talk about relations, very often they really mean relation *variables,* not relations *per se.* But there is a logical difference here!— in fact, it is a special case of the logical difference (and big difference), discussed in the previous chapter, between values and variables in general. And the fact that the distinction is often not clearly made has been a rich source of confusion in the past. For example, the overall value of a given relation (a set of rows, loosely speaking) does not change over time, whereas of course the value of a given relation variable certainly does. And—observing that, like a relation but unlike a relation variable, the overall value of a given *domain* (a set of scalars, again loosely speaking) also does not change over time—some people have proposed that domains and relations are therefore really the same kind of thing (the arguments to the contrary discussed earlier in this section notwithstanding). And then, possibly becoming confused over the difference between relations *per se* and relation variables, those same people have gone on to make matters worse by claiming that domains and relation *variables* are really the same kind of thing. See the section "Relvars *vs.* Object Classes" later in this chapter for a detailed discussion of this latter confusion.

In *The Third Manifesto,* therefore, we have tried very hard to be clear on this point (and the same goes for the rest of this book). Specifically, we have introduced the term **relvar** as a convenient shorthand for *relation variable,* and we have taken care to phrase our remarks in terms of relvars, not relations, when it really is relvars that we mean.

Note: We apologize for the introduction of this new term; the field of computer science in general, and the field of database management in particular, are both awash in far too much terminology as it is (and we have to say in passing that much of that terminology is quite extraordinarily bad). Nevertheless, we find that (a) it is really important to be clear about the distinction between relations *per se* (= relation values) and relation variables, and (b) it saves a lot of writing and a lot of breath to be able to use "relvars" as a shorthand, instead of always having to use the longhand form "relation variables."

DOMAINS *VS.* OBJECT CLASSES

Now we can move on to discuss the equation that we claim is the right one, "domain = class." We begin by observing that, unfortunately, many people have only a rather weak understanding of what domains are all about; typically, they perceive them as just conceptual pools of values, from which columns in relations draw their actual values (to the extent they think about the concept at all, that is). This perception is accurate so far as it goes, but of course it does not really go far enough. The fact is, a domain is nothing more nor less than a *data type* (*type* for short)—possibly a simple system-defined type like INTEGER or CHAR, more generally a user-defined type like P# or QTY in the bill of materials example of Fig. 2.2. Indeed, we can use the terms *type* and *domain* interchangeably (and we will do so from this point forward).

Now, it is important to understand that the data type concept includes the associated concept of the *operators* that can legally be applied to values of the type in question (values of that type can be operated upon *solely* by means of the operators defined for that type). For example, in the case of the (presumably system-defined) type INTEGER:

- The system defines operators "=", "<", and so on, for comparing integers;
- It also defines operators "+", "*", and so on, for performing arithmetic on integers;
- It does *not* define operators "∥" (concatenate), SUBSTR (substring), and so on, for performing string operations on integers; in other words, string operations on integers are not supported.

And if we had a system that supported domains properly (but most do not), then we would be able to define our own domains—say the part number domain, P#. And we would probably define operators "=", "<", and so on, for comparing part numbers. However, we would probably not define operators "+", "*", and so on, which would mean that arithmetic on part numbers would not be supported (why would you ever want to add or multiply two part numbers together?).

Observe, therefore, that we distinguish very carefully between a type (or domain) *per se,* on the one hand, and the *representation* or *encoding* of values of that type inside the system, on the other (another big logical difference here, in fact). For example, part numbers might be represented internally as character strings, but it does not follow that we can perform character string operations on part numbers. Rather, we can perform such operations only if appropriate operators have been defined for the type. And, of course, the operators we define for a given type will depend on the intended *meaning* or *semantics* of the type in question, not on the way values of that type happen to be represented or encoded inside the system; indeed, those internal representations or encodings should be *hidden* so far as the user is concerned.

By now you might have realized that what we have been talking about is what is known in programming language circles as *strong typing*. Different writers have slightly different definitions for this term; as we use it, however, it means, among other things, that (a) every value *has* a type, and (b) whenever we try to perform an operation, the system checks that the operands are of the right types for the operation in question. And note carefully that—as already indicated—it is not just *comparison* operations that we are talking about here (despite the emphasis on comparison operations in much of the database literature). For example, suppose we are given the well-known suppliers-and-parts database,* with relvars S (suppliers), P (parts), and SP (shipments), and consider the following expressions:

```
P.WEIGHT + SP.QTY     /* part weight plus shipment quantity  */
P.WEIGHT * SP.QTY     /* part weight times shipment quantity */
```

The first of these expressions makes no sense, and the DBMS should reject it. The second, on the other hand, does make sense—it denotes the total weight for all parts involved in the shipment. So the operators we would define for weights and quantities would presumably include "*" but not "+".

Observe now that so far we have said nothing at all about the nature of the values that can belong to a domain. In fact, those values can be **anything at all.** We tend to think of them as being very simple (numbers, strings, and so forth), but there is absolutely nothing in the relational model that requires them to be limited to such simple forms.† Thus, we can have domains of audio recordings, domains of maps, domains of video recordings, domains of engineering drawings, domains of legal documents, domains of geometric objects (etc., etc.). The only requirement is that—

---

*See the introduction to Part III of this book for some sample data values for this database.

†Note in particular that—contrary to what is commonly supposed—the relational model requirement that all relvars be in at least *first normal form* does not impose any such limitation. See RM Prescriptions 6 and 7 in Chapters 3 and 6, also references [34] and [56].

to say it one more time—the values in the domain must be manipulable *solely* by means of the operators defined for the domain in question; the internal representation must be hidden.

The foregoing message is so important that we state it again in different words:

> **The question as to what data types are supported is orthogonal
> to the question of support for the relational model**

To sum up, therefore: What we are saying is that, in the relational world, a domain is a data type, system- or user-defined, of arbitrary internal complexity, whose values are manipulable solely by means of the operators defined for the type in question (and whose internal representation is therefore hidden from the user). Now, if we turn to the object world, we find that the most fundamental object concept of all, the *object class,* is a data type, system- or user-defined, of arbitrary internal complexity, whose values are manipulable solely by means of the operators defined for the type in question (and whose internal representation is therefore hidden from the user)* . . . In other words, domains and object classes are **the same thing!** Thus, we have here the key to integrating the two technologies—and, of course, this is exactly the position advocated in *The Third Manifesto.* Indeed, we believe that a relational system that supported domains properly would be able to deal with all of those "problem" kinds of data that (it is often claimed) object systems can handle and relational systems cannot: time-series data, biological data, financial data, engineering design data, office automation data, and so on. Accordingly, we also believe that a true "object/relational" system would be nothing more nor less than a true *relational* system—which is to say, a system that supports the relational model, with all that such support entails.

RELVARS *VS.* OBJECT CLASSES

In the previous section we equated object classes and domains. Many people, however, equate object classes and *relvars* instead (see, e.g., references [5] and [91–93]). We now argue that this latter equation is a serious logical mistake (which is why OO Proscription 1 in the *Manifesto* asserts categorically that *relvars are not domains*). Why might anyone make such a mistake? Well, consider the following simple object class definition, expressed in a hypothetical object language:

---

*Some people might disagree with our characterization here of an object class as a data type (see, e.g., references [5] and [91–93]). We respond to such criticisms by claiming that the disagreement is primarily a matter of terminology: If in some object system the term "object class" does *not* mean a data type, then there has to be some other term in that system that does. We then claim that our remaining arguments are still valid, *mutatis mutandis.*

```
CREATE OBJECT CLASS EMP
     ( EMP#        CHAR(5),
       ENAME       CHAR(20),
       SAL         NUMERIC,
       HOBBY       CHAR(20),
       WORKS_FOR   CHAR(20) ) ... ;
```

EMP#, ENAME, etc., here are *instance variables* (also known as *members* or *attributes*), whose values in any given "instance" of class EMP at any given time together make up the overall value of that instance at that time. *Note:* In a pure object system, those instance variables would be *private*—i.e., they would be part of the representation merely and thus hidden from the user [81].* In the discussion that follows, however, it is necessary to assume that they are *public* instead—i.e., they are definitely *not* hidden (and the system is therefore not "pure").

Now consider the following simple relational—or at least SQL—relvar definition:

```
CREATE TABLE EMP
     ( EMP#        CHAR(5),
       ENAME       CHAR(20),
       SAL         NUMERIC,
       HOBBY       CHAR(20),
       WORKS_FOR   CHAR(20) ) ... ;
```

These two definitions certainly look very similar—and the idea of equating them thus looks very tempting. And certain systems, both prototypes and commercial products, have effectively done just that. So let us take a closer look. . . . More precisely, let us take the CREATE TABLE statement just shown and consider a series of possible extensions to it that (some people would argue) serve to make it more "object-like." *Note:* The discussion that follows is based on a specific commercial product; in fact, it is based on an example in that product's own user documentation. We do not identify that product here, however, since it is not our intent in this book to criticize or praise specific products. Rather, the criticisms we make later in this section apply, *mutatis mutandis,* to *any* system that espouses the "relvar = class" equation.

The first extension is to permit *composite* (i.e., row-valued) *columns;* that is, we allow column values to be rows from some other relvar (or possibly the same relvar). In the example, we might replace the original CREATE TABLE by the following collection of definitions (refer to Fig. 2.3):

```
CREATE TABLE EMP
     ( EMP#        CHAR(5),
       ENAME       CHAR(20),
       SAL         NUMERIC,
       HOBBY       ACTIVITY,
       WORKS_FOR   COMPANY ) ;
```

---

*In which case our hypothetical syntax is not very good (though it *is* realistic), since it mixes together matters that would better be kept separate. To be specific, it mixes type considerations with representation ones.

```
CREATE TABLE ACTIVITY
   ( NAME  CHAR(20),
     TEAM  INTEGER ) ;

CREATE TABLE COMPANY
   ( NAME      CHAR(20),
     LOCATION  CITYSTATE ) ;

CREATE TABLE CITYSTATE
   ( CITY   CHAR(20),
     STATE  CHAR(2) ) ;
```

Explanation: Column HOBBY in relvar EMP is declared to be of type ACTIVITY. ACTIVITY in turn is a relvar of two columns, NAME and TEAM, where TEAM gives the number of players in a team corresponding to NAME; for instance, a possible "activity" might be (Soccer,11). Each HOBBY value is thus actually a *pair* of values, a NAME value and a TEAM value (more precisely, it is a pair of values that currently appear as a row in relvar ACTIVITY). Observe that we have already violated the *Manifesto* dictum that relvars are not domains—the "domain" for column HOBBY is defined to be the *relvar* ACTIVITY. See later for further discussion of this point.

Similarly, column WORKS_FOR in relvar EMP is declared to be of type COMPANY, and COMPANY is also a relvar of two columns, one of which is defined to be of type CITYSTATE, which is another two-column relvar, and so on. In other words, relvars ACTIVITY, COMPANY, and CITYSTATE are all considered to be *types* (or domains) as well as relvars. The same is true for relvar EMP itself, of course.

This first extension is thus roughly analogous to allowing objects to contain other objects, thereby supporting the concept sometimes known as a *containment hierarchy.*

As an aside, we remark that we have characterized this first extension as "columns containing rows" because that is the way advocates of the "relvar = class" equation themselves characterize it (see, e.g., reference [92]). It would be more accurate, however, to characterize it as "columns containing *pointers to* rows"—a

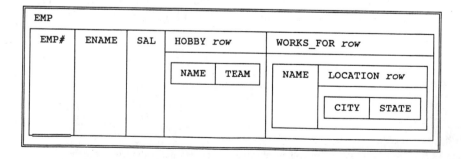

Fig. 2.3   Columns containing (pointers to) rows—deprecated

logical difference that we will be examining in a few moments. (In Fig. 2.3, therefore, we should really replace each of the three occurrences of the term *row* by the term *pointer to row.*)

Remarks analogous to those of the previous paragraph apply to the second extension also, which is to allow *relation-valued columns;* that is, column values are allowed to be *sets* of rows from some other relvar (or possibly the same relvar). For example, suppose employees can have an arbitrary number of hobbies, instead of just one (refer to Fig. 2.4):

```
CREATE TABLE EMP
     ( EMP#        CHAR(5),
       ENAME       CHAR(20),
       SAL         NUMERIC,
       HOBBIES     SET OF ( ACTIVITY ),
       WORKS_FOR   COMPANY ) ;
```

Explanation: The HOBBIES value within any given row of relvar EMP is now (conceptually) a set of zero or more (NAME,TEAM) pairs—i.e., rows—from relvar ACTIVITY. This second extension is thus roughly analogous to allowing objects to contain "aggregate" objects: a more complex version of the containment hierarchy. (We note in passing that in the particular product on which our example is based, those aggregate objects can be *sequences* or *bags* as well as sets *per se.* In case you are unfamiliar with the term, we should explain that a bag—also known as a *multiset*—is like a set, except that it is allowed to contain duplicates.)

The third extension is to permit relvars to have associated *methods* ("method" being the usual object term for an *operator,* for some reason). For example:

```
CREATE TABLE EMP
     ( EMP#        CHAR(5),
       ENAME       CHAR(20),
       SAL         NUMERIC,
       HOBBIES     SET OF ( ACTIVITY ),
       WORKS_FOR   COMPANY )
METHOD RETIREMENT_BENEFITS ( ) : NUMERIC ;
```

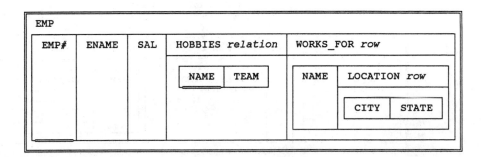

Fig. 2.4 Columns containing sets of (pointers to) rows—deprecated

Explanation: RETIREMENT_BENEFITS is a method that takes a given EMP row as its argument and produces a result of type NUMERIC. The code that implements that method might be written in a language such as C.

The final extension is to permit the definition of *subclasses.* For example (refer to Fig. 2.5):

```
CREATE TABLE PERSON
      ( SS#         CHAR(9),
        BIRTHDATE   DATE,
        ADDRESS     CHAR(50) ) ;

CREATE TABLE EMP
      AS SUBCLASS OF PERSON
      ( EMP#        CHAR(5),
        ENAME       CHAR(20),
        SAL         NUMERIC,
        HOBBIES     SET OF ( ACTIVITY ),
        WORKS_FOR   COMPANY )
METHOD RETIREMENT_BENEFITS ( ) : NUMERIC ;
```

Explanation: EMP now has three additional columns (SS#, BIRTHDATE, and ADDRESS) inherited from PERSON (because each EMP "instance" is a PERSON "instance" as well, loosely speaking). If PERSON had any methods, it would inherit those too. *Note:* Tables PERSON and EMP are examples of what are sometimes called *supertables* and *subtables,* respectively. See Appendix D for further discussion of these concepts.

Along with the definitional extensions sketched above, numerous manipulative extensions are required too, of course—for instance:

- "Path expressions" (e.g., EMP.WORKS_FOR.LOCATION.STATE). Note that such expressions can return scalars or rows or relations, in general; note further that in the latter two cases the components of those rows or relations might

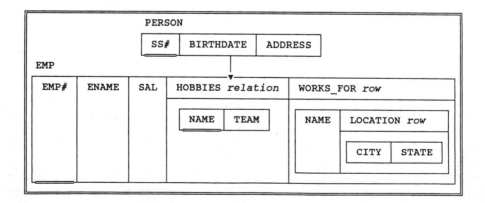

Fig. 2.5   Relvars as superclasses and subclasses—deprecated

themselves be rows or relations in turn (and so on). For example, the expression EMP.HOBBIES.NAME returns a relation.

- Row and relation literals (possibly nested)—e.g.,

```
( 'E001', 'Smith', $50000,
        ( ( 'Soccer', 11 ), ( 'Bridge', 4 ) ),
                        ( 'IBM', ( 'San Jose', 'CA' ) ) )
```

(not meant to be actual syntax).

- Relational comparison operators—e.g., SUBSET, SUBSETEQ, and so on. *Note:* SUBSET here really means "*proper* subset," and SUBSETEQ means "subset" (!).

- Operators for traversing the class hierarchy.*

- The ability to invoke methods within, e.g., SELECT and WHERE clauses (in SQL terms).

- The ability to access individual components within column values that happen to be rows or relations.

So much for a quick overview of how the "relvar = class" equation is realized in practice. So what is wrong with it?

Well, note first of all that a relvar is a *variable* and a class is a *type*. So how can they possibly be the same? (We showed in the section "Relations *vs.* Relvars" earlier that relation *values* and domains are not the same thing; now we see that relation *variables* and domains are not the same thing either.)

This first argument should be logically sufficient to stop the "relvar = class" idea dead in its tracks. However, there is more that can usefully be said, so let us agree to suspend disbelief a little longer . . . Here are some more points to consider:

- The equation "relvar = class" implies the further equations "row = object" and "column = (public) instance variable." Thus, whereas a true object class has methods and no public instance variables [81], a relvar "object class" has public instance variables and only optionally has methods. So, again, how can the two notions possibly be the same?

- There is a major logical difference between the column definitions (e.g.) "SAL NUMERIC" and "WORKS_FOR COMPANY." NUMERIC is a true data type (equivalently, a true, albeit primitive, domain); it places a time-independent constraint on the values that can appear in column SAL. By contrast, COMPANY is *not* a true data type; the constraint it places on the values that can

---

*Care is needed here, too. It might well be the case that a request to retrieve PERSON information together with associated EMP information yields a result that is not a relation—meaning that the vital relational property of *closure* (according to which the result of every relational operation is another relation) has been violated, with potentially disastrous implications [63].

appear in column WORKS_FOR is *time-dependent* (it depends, obviously, on the current value of relvar COMPANY). In fact, as pointed out earlier, the relvar *vs.* domain distinction has been muddied here.

■ We have seen that row "objects" are apparently allowed to contain other such "objects"; for example, EMP "objects" apparently contain COMPANY "objects." But they do not—not really; instead, they contain *pointers** to those "contained objects," and users must be absolutely clear on this point. For example, suppose the user updates some particular COMPANY row in some way (refer back to Fig. 2.3). Then that update will immediately be visible in all EMP rows that "contain" that COMPANY row. *Note:* We are not saying this effect is undesirable, we are only saying it has to be explained to the user. But explaining it to the user amounts to telling the user that the "model" in Fig. 2.3 is incorrect—EMP rows do not contain COMPANY rows, they contain *pointers to* COMPANY rows instead (as already stated).

Here are some further implications and questions arising from this same point:

· Can we insert an EMP row and specify a value for the "contained" COMPANY row that does not currently exist in the COMPANY relvar? If the answer is *yes,* the fact that column WORKS_FOR is defined as being of type COMPANY does not mean very much, since it does not significantly constrain the INSERT operation in any way. If the answer is *no,* the INSERT operation becomes unnecessarily complex—the user has to specify, not just an existing company name (i.e., a foreign key value) as would be required in the analogous relational situation, but an entire existing COMPANY row. Moreover, specifying an entire COMPANY row means, at best, telling the system something it already knows; at worst, it means that if the user makes a mistake, the INSERT will fail when it could perfectly well have succeeded.

· Suppose we want an ON DELETE RESTRICT rule for companies (i.e., an attempt to delete a company must fail if the company has any employees). Presumably this rule must be enforced by procedural code, say by some method *M* (note that relvar EMP has no foreign key to which a declarative version of the rule might be attached). Furthermore, native SQL DELETE operations must now not be performed on relvar COMPANY other than within the code that implements that method *M*. How is this requirement enforced? Analogous remarks and questions apply to other referential actions, of course, such as ON DELETE CASCADE.

· Note too that deleting an EMP row presumably will *not* "cascade" to delete the corresponding COMPANY row, despite the pretense that the EMP row contains that COMPANY row.

---

*Or *object IDs,* to use the object term. See Chapter 9, also references [72] and [74].

It follows from all of the above that we are not exactly talking about the relational model any more. The fundamental data object is no longer a relation containing values, it is a "relation"—actually not a proper relation at all, so far as the relational model is concerned—containing values *and pointers.* In other words, **we have undermined the conceptual integrity of the relational model.** (Refer back to Chapter 1 if you need to refresh your memory regarding "conceptual integrity"; see also reference [72], and Chapter 9 of the present book, for detailed arguments in support of the position that the relational model's conceptual integrity is indeed undermined by pointers.*)

- Suppose we define view V to be the projection of EMP over, e.g., just the column HOBBIES. V is a relvar too, of course, but a derived relvar instead of a base one (EMP is a base relvar).[†] So if "relvar = class" is a correct equation, V is also a class. *What class is it?* Also, classes have methods; *what methods apply to V?*

   Well, "class" EMP had just one method, RETIREMENT_BENEFITS, and that one clearly does not apply to "class" V. In fact, it hardly seems reasonable that *any* methods that applied to "class" EMP would apply to "class" V—and there certainly are no others. So it looks as if (in general) *no methods at all* apply to the result of a projection; i.e., the result, whatever it is, is not really a class at all. (We might *say* it is a class, but that does not make it one!—it will have public instance variables and no methods, whereas we have already observed that a true class has methods and no public instance variables.)

   In fact, it is quite clear that when people equate relvars and classes, it is specifically base relvars they have in mind—they are forgetting about the derived ones. (Certainly the pointers discussed above are pointers to rows in base relvars, not derived ones.[‡]) But to distinguish between base and derived relvars in this way is a mistake of the highest order, because the question as to which relvars are base and which derived is, in a very important sense, arbitrary. For further discussion of this issue, see the discussion of RM Prescription 14 in Chapter 6, also references [66] and [68].

- Finally, *what domains are supported?* Those who espouse the "relvar = class" equation never seem to have much to say about domains, presumably because they cannot see how domains as such fit into their overall scheme. And yet (as we saw in the section "Relations *vs.* Relvars" earlier) domains are essential.

---

*In fact, it seems fitting to refer to this reintroduction of pointers (into the model, that is, as opposed to the implementation) as **The Second Great Blunder** (the first, you will recall, being the wrong equation "relvar = class").

[†]*The Third Manifesto* uses the terms *real* and *virtual* instead of *base* and *derived* (see Parts II and III of this book); we use the more traditional terms here for familiarity.

[‡]Actually the idea of pointers "pointing into" relvars of any kind is a highly dubious proposition anyway. Further discussion of that issue here would take us too far afield, however; see the annotation to reference [72] in Appendix H for more specifics.

The overall message of this section can be summarized as follows. Obviously, systems can be built that are based on the wrong equation "relvar = class"; indeed, some such systems already exist. Equally obviously, those systems—like a car with no oil in its engine, or a house that is built on sand—might even provide useful service, for a while; but they are doomed to eventual failure.

A NOTE ON INHERITANCE

You will probably have noticed that we did briefly mention the possibility of *inheritance* in the previous section but not in the earlier section "Domains *vs.* Object Classes." And you might have concluded that support for inheritance does constitute at least one point in favor of the "relvar = class" equation. Not so, however; we do indeed want to include inheritance as part of our "domain = class" approach, and thus be able to define one domain as a "subdomain" of some other "superdomain." The problem is, however, that (as mentioned in the previous chapter) there does not seem to be a clearly defined and generally agreed *model* of inheritance at the time of writing. As a consequence, *The Third Manifesto* includes *conditional* support for inheritance, along the lines of "If inheritance is supported, then it must be in accordance with some well-defined and commonly agreed model." We do also offer some detailed proposals toward the definition of such a model. See Part IV of this book for an extensive discussion of this topic.

CONCLUDING REMARKS

We have discussed the question of integrating objects and relations. It is our opinion that object technology has exactly one unquestionably good idea, **user-defined types** (which includes user-defined operators). It also has one *probably* good idea, **type inheritance** (though the jury is still out on this one, to some extent). A key technical insight underlying *The Third Manifesto* is that these two ideas are *completely orthogonal to the relational model.* Hence—as we claimed in Chapter 1, and as we have tried to show in the present chapter—we need do *absolutely nothing* to the relational model in order to achieve the object functionality we desire.

To sum up, therefore: What we need is for the vendors to give us **true relational DBMSs** (and note that "true relational DBMSs" does not mean SQL systems) that include **proper domain support,** and we would then have the "object/relational" DBMSs we want. Indeed, an argument can be made that the whole reason that object DBMSs *per se* (as opposed to "object/relational" DBMSs) might seem attractive is precisely the failure on the part of existing SQL vendors to support the relational model adequately. But this fact should not be seen as an argument for abandoning the relational model entirely (or at all!)

PART **II**

FORMAL SPECIFICATIONS

This part of the book is provided primarily for reference; **you probably should not even attempt to read it straight through**—certainly not on a first reading, anyway. Chapter 3 is *The Third Manifesto* itself (the "no frills" version; i.e., it consists simply of the various prescriptions, proscriptions, and very strong suggestions that together constitute the *Manifesto* proper, without any explanatory material at all). Chapter 4 defines our new relational algebra, **A** (which is also "no frills," in a sense); **A** is intended to serve as the foundation for the relational portions of the language **D.** (We remind you that the name **D** refers generically to any language that conforms to the principles of the *Manifesto;* there could thus be any number of distinct languages all qualifying as a valid **D.**) Last, Chapter 5 defines **Tutorial D**—i.e., a **D** defined primarily as a basis for the examples in Part III.

3

The Third Manifesto

RM PRESCRIPTIONS

1. A **scalar data type—scalar type** for short, also known as a **domain**—is a
   named set of scalar values. Scalar types *T1* and *T2* are equal if and only if they
   are in fact the same type (note in particular, therefore, that two scalar types that
   are identical in all respects except for their names are different types). **D** shall
   provide facilities for users to define their own scalar types (*user-defined* scalar
   types); other scalar types shall be provided by the system (*builtin* or *system-
   defined* scalar types). It shall be possible to destroy user-defined scalar types.
   Values of a given scalar type, and variables whose values are constrained to be
   of a given scalar type, shall be operable upon solely by means of the operators
   defined for that scalar type (see RM Prescription 3). For each scalar type and
   each declared possible representation of that type (see RM Prescription 4), those
   operators shall include:

   a. An operator called a *selector* whose purpose is to select an arbitrary value of
      the scalar type in question (again, see RM Prescription 4);

   b. A set of operators whose purpose is to expose the possible representation in
      question (see RM Prescription 5).

   The system-defined scalar types shall include the type **truth value** (containing
   just two values, *true* and *false*). All four monadic and 16 dyadic logical operators shall be supported, directly or indirectly, for this scalar type.

2. All scalar values shall be **typed**—i.e., such values shall always carry with them, at least conceptually, some accompanying identification of the (unique) type to which they belong.

3. **D** shall provide facilities for users to define their own scalar **operators** (*user-defined* scalar operators); other such operators (*builtin* or *system-defined* scalar operators) shall be provided by the system. It shall be possible to destroy user-defined scalar operators, in general (though the operators required by RM Prescription 5 violate this prescription slightly, in that they can be destroyed only by destroying the associated type, and the same might possibly be true of selector operators). Furthermore:

   a. The definition of a given scalar operator shall include a specification of the type of each parameter to that operator, the **declared type** of that parameter. If operator *Op* has a parameter *P* of declared type *T,* then the argument *A* that corresponds to *P* in any given invocation of *Op* shall also be of declared type *T.*

   b. Every scalar operator is either an *update* operator or a *read-only* operator. A scalar **update operator** is one for which at least one argument must be specified by means of a scalar variable reference specifically, not by means of an arbitrary scalar expression, and invocation causes values to be assigned to such arguments (at least potentially); parameters corresponding to such arguments are said to be *subject to update.* A scalar **read-only operator** is a scalar operator that is not a scalar update operator.

   c. Invoking a scalar read-only operator shall return a (scalar) **result.** Invoking a scalar update operator shall not.

   d. The definition of a scalar read-only operator shall include a specification of the type of the result of that operator, the **declared type** of that result.

   e. The definition of a scalar update operator shall include a specification of which parameters to that operator are subject to update. Arguments corresponding to such parameters shall be **passed by reference.** All other scalar update operator arguments, and all scalar read-only operator arguments, shall be **passed by value.**

   f. Let *SX* be a scalar expression. Then *SX* has a **declared type** (more precisely, the result of evaluating *SX* has a declared type), recursively derived in the obvious way from the declared types of the operands of *SX* and the declared types of the results of any subexpressions contained within *SX*.

4. Let *T* be a scalar type, and let *v* be an appearance (in some context) of some value of type *T*. By definition, *v* has exactly one **actual representation** and one or more **possible representations** (at least one, because there is obviously always one that is the same as the actual representation). Actual representations associated with type *T* shall be specified by means of some kind of *storage structure definition language* and shall not be visible in **D** (see RM

Proscription 6). At least one possible representation (not necessarily the same as any actual representation) associated with type T shall be declared as part of the definition of T and hence shall be visible in **D.** For each declared possible representation PR for T, a **selector** operator S shall automatically be defined with the following properties:

a. For definiteness, assume the components of PR (see RM Prescription 5) and the parameters of S each constitute an ordered list. Then the two lists must contain the same number of elements, n say, and the declared types of the ith elements in the two lists ($i = 1, 2, ..., n$) must be identical.

b. Every value of type T shall be produced by some invocation of S.

c. Every (successful) invocation of S shall produce some value of type T.

5. Let some declared possible representation PR for scalar type T be defined in terms of components $C1, C2, ..., Cn$ (each of which has a name and a declared type). Let v be a value of type T, and let $PR(v)$ denote the corresponding possible representation. Then $PR(v)$ shall be **exposed**—that is, a set of read-only and update operators shall automatically be defined such that:

a. For all such values v and for all i ($i = 1, 2, ..., n$), it is possible to "retrieve" (i.e., read the value of) the Ci component of $PR(v)$;

b. For all variables V of declared type T and for all i ($i = 1, 2, ..., n$), it is possible to update V in such a way that if the values of V before and after the update are v and v' respectively, then the corresponding possible representations $PR(v)$ and $PR(v')$ differ at most only in their Ci components.

Such a set of operators shall be provided for each possible representation declared in the definition of T.

6. The type generator **TUPLE** shall be supported. That is, given some tuple heading H (see RM Prescription 9), it shall be possible to use the **generated type** TUPLE$\{H\}$ as the basis for defining (or, in the case of values, selecting):

a. Values and variables of that generated type (see RM Prescriptions 9 and 12);

b. Tuple attribute values and tuple heading attributes of that generated type (again, see RM Prescription 9);

c. Declared possible representation components of that generated type (see RM Prescription 5).

The generated type TUPLE$\{H\}$ is referred to as a **tuple type,** and the name of that type is, precisely, TUPLE$\{H\}$. The terminology of *degree, attributes,* and *headings* introduced in RM Prescription 9 shall apply, *mutatis mutandis,* to that tuple type, as well as to values and variables of that type (see RM Prescription 12). Tuple types TUPLE$\{H1\}$ and TUPLE$\{H2\}$ are equal if and only if $H1 = H2$. The applicable operators shall include operators analogous to the RENAME, *project,* EXTEND, and JOIN operators of the relational algebra (see RM Prescription 18), together with tuple assignment (see RM Prescription 21) and tuple comparisons (see RM Prescription 22); they shall also include (a) a tuple selector operator (see RM Prescription 9), (b) an operator for extracting a specified attribute value from a specified tuple (the tuple in question might be required to be of degree one—see RM Prescription 9), and (c) operators for performing tuple "nesting" and "unnesting."

7. The type generator **RELATION** shall be supported. That is, given some relation heading H (see RM Prescription 10), it shall be possible to use the **generated type** RELATION$\{H\}$ as the basis for defining (or, in the case of values, selecting):

   a. Values and variables of that generated type (see RM Prescriptions 10 and 13);

   b. Tuple attribute values and tuple heading attributes of that generated type (see RM Prescription 9);

   c. Declared possible representation components of that generated type (see RM Prescription 5).

   The generated type RELATION$\{H\}$ is referred to as a **relation type,** and the name of that type is, precisely, RELATION$\{H\}$. The terminology of *degree, attributes,* and *headings* introduced in RM Prescription 10 shall apply, *mutatis mutandis,* to that relation type, as well as to values and variables of that type (see RM Prescription 13). Relation types RELATION$\{H1\}$ and RELATION$\{H2\}$ are equal if and only if $H1 = H2$. The applicable operators shall include the operators of the relational algebra (see RM Prescription 18), together with relational assignment (see RM Prescription 21) and relational comparisons (see RM Prescription 22); they shall also include (a) a relation selector operator (see RM Prescription 10), (b) an operator for extracting a specified tuple from a specified relation (the relation in question might be required to be of cardinality one—see RM Prescription 10), and (c) operators for performing relational "nesting" and "unnesting."

8. The **equality** comparison operator "=" shall be defined for every type. Let expressions $X1$ and $X2$ denote values $v1$ and $v2$, respectively, where $v1$ and $v2$ are of the same type T. Then $X1 = X2$ shall be *true* if and only if $v1$ and $v2$ are in fact the same element of T (i.e., if and only if $X1$ and $X2$ denote the same value). Moreover, let Op be an operator with a parameter P of declared type T. Then, for all such operators Op, if $X1 = X2$ is true, then two (successful) invocations of Op that are identical in all respects except that the argument corresponding to P is specified as $X1$ in one case and $X2$ in the other shall be indistinguishable in their effect. Conversely, if there exists such an operator Op such that two (successful) invocations of Op that are identical in all respects except that the argument corresponding to P is specified as $X1$ in one case and $X2$ in the other are distinguishable in their effect, then $X1 = X2$ shall be *false*.

9. A **tuple value** t (**tuple** for short) is a set of ordered triples of the form $<A,T,v>$, where:

a. *A* is the name of an **attribute** of *t*. No two distinct triples in *t* shall have the same attribute name.

b. *T* is the name of the **type** of attribute *A* of *t*.

c. *v* is a value of type *T*, called the **attribute value** for attribute *A* of *t*.

The cardinality of the set of triples in *t*—equivalently, the number of attributes of *t*—is the **degree** of *t*. The set of ordered pairs *<A,T>* that is obtained by eliminating the *v* (value) component from each triple is the **heading** of *t*; tuple *t* is said to **conform** to that heading (equivalently, *t* is said to be of the corresponding tuple type—see RM Prescription 6), the degree of *t* is said to be the **degree** of that heading, and the attributes and corresponding types of *t* are said to be the **attributes** and corresponding **types** of that heading. Given a tuple heading *H*, a *selector* operator shall be available for selecting an arbitrary tuple conforming to *H*.

10. A **relation value** *r* (**relation** for short) consists of a *heading* and a *body,* where:

    a. The **heading** of *r* is a tuple heading *H* as defined in RM Prescription 9; relation *r* is said to **conform** to that heading (equivalently, *r* is said to be of the corresponding relation type—see RM Prescription 7), and the degree of that heading is said to be the **degree** of *r*. The attributes and corresponding types of *H* are the **attributes** and corresponding **types** of *r*.

    b. The **body** of *r* is a set *B* of tuples, all having that same heading *H;* the cardinality of that body is said to be the **cardinality** of *r*.

    Given a relation heading *H*, a *selector* operator shall be available for selecting an arbitrary relation conforming to *H*.

11. A **scalar variable of type *T*** is a variable whose permitted values are scalars of a specified scalar type *T,* the **declared type** of that variable. **D** shall provide facilities for users to define scalar variables. Defining a scalar variable shall have the effect of initializing that variable to some value—either a value specified explicitly as part of the operation that defines the variable, or some implementation-defined value if no such explicit value is specified.

12. A **tuple variable of type TUPLE{*H*}** is a variable whose permitted values are tuples that conform to a specified tuple heading *H*. The **declared type** of that tuple variable is TUPLE{*H*}. The attributes of *H* are the **attributes** of the tuple variable, the corresponding types are the **declared types** of those attributes, and the degree of *H* is the **degree** of the tuple variable. **D** shall provide facilities for users to define tuple variables. Defining a tuple variable shall have the effect of initializing that variable to some tuple value—either a value specified explicitly as part of the operation that defines the variable, or some implementation-defined value if no such explicit value is specified.

13. A **relation variable—relvar** for short—**of type RELATION{*H*}** is a variable whose permitted values are relations that conform to a specified relation head-

ing *H*. The **declared type** of that relvar is RELATION{*H*}. The attributes of *H* are the **attributes** of the relvar, the corresponding types are the **declared types** of those attributes, and the degree of *H* is the **degree** of the relvar. **D** shall provide facilities for users to define and destroy database relvars (i.e., relvars that belong to the database, as opposed to the application—see RM Prescription 16). **D** shall also provide facilities for users to define application relvars (i.e., relvars that are not database relvars).

14. Database relvars are either *real* or *virtual*. A **virtual relvar** is a database relvar whose value at any given time is the result of evaluating a certain relational expression, specified when the relvar in question is defined. A **real relvar** is a database relvar that is not virtual. Defining a real relvar shall have the effect of initializing that relvar to an empty relation (i.e., a relation of cardinality zero).

15. By definition, every relvar always has at least one **candidate key.** At least one such key shall be defined at the time the relvar in question is defined, and it shall not be possible to destroy all of the candidate keys of a given relvar (other than by destroying the relvar itself).

16. A **database** is a named container for relvars; the content of a given database at any given time is a set of (database) relvars. The necessary operators for defining and destroying databases shall not be part of **D** (in other words, defining and destroying databases shall be done "outside the **D** environment").

17. Each **transaction** shall interact with exactly one database. However, distinct transactions shall be able to interact with distinct databases, and distinct databases shall not necessarily be disjoint. Also, it shall be possible for a transaction to define new relvars, or destroy existing ones, within its associated database (see RM Prescription 13).

18. **D** shall support the usual operators of the **relational algebra** (or some logical equivalent thereof). Specifically, it shall support—directly or indirectly—at least the operators RENAME, *restrict* (WHERE), *project,* EXTEND, JOIN, UNION, INTERSECT, MINUS, (generalized) DIVIDEBY PER, and (generalized) SUMMARIZE PER. All such operators shall be expressible without excessive circumlocution. **D** shall also support the required **relation type inference** mechanism, whereby the heading of the result of evaluating an arbitrary relational expression shall be well defined and known to both the system and the user (see RM Prescription 7).

19. **Relvar names** and **relation selector invocations** shall both be legal relational expressions. **Recursion** shall be permitted in relational expressions.

20. **D** shall provide facilities for defining and destroying read-only operators that are **relation-valued.** The relation that results from invoking such an operator shall be defined by means of a certain relational expression, specified when the operator is defined. That expression shall be allowed to contain parameters; such

parameters shall represent scalar values and shall be permitted wherever scalar selector invocations are permitted. Invocations of such operators shall be permitted within relational expressions wherever relation selector invocations are permitted.

21. **D** shall permit:

    a. (The value of) a scalar expression to be **assigned** to a scalar variable;

    b. (The value of) a tuple expression to be **assigned** to a tuple variable; and

    c. (The value of) a relational expression to be **assigned** to a relvar;

    provided in each case that the source and target types are the same. In addition, **D** shall support a **multiple** form of the assignment operation, in which several individual assignments are performed in some specified sequence as part of a single logical operation.

22. **D** shall support certain **comparison operators,** as follows:

    a. The operators for comparing scalars shall include "=", and possibly "<", ">", etc. (depending on the scalar type in question);

    b. The operators for comparing tuples shall be "=" and "≠" (only);

    c. The operators for comparing relations shall include "=", "≠", "is a subset of" (etc.); and

    d. The operator "∈" for testing membership of a tuple in a relation shall be supported;

    provided in every case except "∈" that the comparands are of the same type, and in the case of "∈" that the tuple and the relation have the same heading.

23. An expression that evaluates to a truth value is called a **logical expression** (also known as a *truth-valued, conditional,* or *boolean* expression). An **integrity constraint** is a logical expression that (a) is named; (b) is, or is logically equivalent to, a closed WFF ("well formed formula") of the relational calculus; and (c) is required to evaluate to *true*. **D** shall provide facilities for defining and destroying integrity constraints. Such constraints shall be classified into **domain** (i.e., **type**), **attribute, relvar,** and **database** constraints, and **D** shall support the **constraint inference** mechanism required by that classification scheme (insofar as feasible).

24. Every relvar has a corresponding **relvar predicate** and every database has a corresponding **database predicate.** Relvar predicates shall be satisfied at statement boundaries. Database predicates shall be satisfied at transaction boundaries.

25. Every database shall include a set of relvars that constitute the catalog for that database. It shall be possible to assign to relvars in the catalog.

26. **D** shall be constructed according to well-established principles of **good language design.**

RM PROSCRIPTIONS

1. **D** shall include no construct that depends on the definition of some ordering for the attributes of a relation. Instead, for every relation *r* expressible in **D,** the attributes of *r* shall be distinguishable by *name*.

2. **D** shall include no construct that depends on the definition of some ordering for the tuples of a relation.

3. For every relation *r,* if *t1* and *t2* are distinct tuples in *r,* then there must exist an attribute *A* of *r* such that the comparison "*A* FROM *t1* = *A* FROM *t2*" evaluates to *false* (where the expressions *A* FROM *t1* and *A* FROM *t2* denote the values for attribute *A* in tuples *t1* and *t2,* respectively).

4. Every attribute of every tuple shall have a value (of the applicable type).

5. **D** shall not forget that relations with no attributes are respectable and interesting, nor that candidate keys with no components are likewise respectable and interesting.

6. **D** shall include no constructs that relate to, or are logically affected by, the "physical" or "storage" or "internal" levels of the system.

7. There shall be no tuple-at-a-time operations on relvars or relations.

8. **D** shall not include any specific support for "composite domains" or "composite attributes," since such functionality can more cleanly be achieved, if desired, through the type support already prescribed.

9. "Domain check override" operators are *ad hoc* and unnecessary and shall not be supported.

10. **D** shall not be called SQL.

OO PRESCRIPTIONS

1. **D** shall permit **compile-time type checking.**

2. If **D** permits some type *T'* to be defined as a **subtype** of some **supertype** *T,* then such a capability shall be in accordance with some clearly defined and generally agreed model.

3. If **D** permits some type *T'* to be defined as a subtype of some other type *T,* then *T'* shall not be prevented from additionally being defined as a subtype of some other type that is neither *T* nor any supertype of *T* (unless the requirements of OO Prescription 2 preclude such a possibility).

4. **D** shall be **computationally complete.** That is, **D** may support, but shall not require, invocation from so-called "host programs" written in languages other than **D.** Similarly, **D** may support, but shall not require, the use of other programming languages for implementation of user-defined operators.

5. Transaction initiation shall be performed only by means of an explicit **"begin transaction"** operator. Transaction termination shall be performed only by means of a **"commit"** or **"rollback"** operator; commit must always be explicit, but rollback can be implicit (if and only if the transaction fails through no fault of its own). If transaction *TX* terminates with commit ("normal termination"), changes made by *TX* to the applicable database shall be committed. If transaction *TX* terminates with rollback ("abnormal termination"), changes made by *TX* to the applicable database shall be rolled back.

6. **D** shall support **nested transactions**—i.e., it shall permit a *parent* transaction *TX* to initiate a *child* transaction *TX'* before *TX* itself has terminated, in which case:

   a. *TX* and *TX'* shall interact with the same database (as is in fact required by RM Prescription 17).

   b. *TX* is not required to suspend execution while *TX'* executes (though it is allowed to do so). However, *TX* shall not be allowed to terminate before *TX'* terminates; in other words, *TX'* shall be wholly contained within *TX*.

   c. Rollback of *TX* shall include the rolling back of *TX'* even if *TX'* has terminated with commit. In other words, "commit" is always interpreted within the parent context (if such exists) and is subject to override by the parent transaction (again, if such exists).

7. Let *AggOp* be an **aggregate** operator, such as SUM. If the argument to *AggOp* happens to be empty, then:

   a. If *AggOp* is essentially just shorthand for some iterated dyadic operator *Op* (the dyadic operator is "+" in the case of SUM), and if an identity value exists for *Op* (the identity value is 0 in the case of "+"), then the result of that invocation of *AggOp* shall be that identity value;

   b. Otherwise, the result of that invocation of *AggOp* shall be undefined.

OO PROSCRIPTIONS

1. Relvars are not domains.

2. No value shall possess any kind of ID that is somehow distinct from the value *per se.*

RM VERY STRONG SUGGESTIONS

1. **D** should provide a mechanism according to which values of some specified candidate key (or certain components thereof) for some specified relvar are supplied by the system. It should also provide a mechanism according to which an arbitrary relation can be extended to include an attribute whose values (a) are

unique within that relation (or within certain partitions of that relation), and (b) are once again supplied by the system.

2. **D** should include some declarative shorthand for expressing **referential constraints** (also known as **foreign key** constraints).

3. Let *RX* be a relational expression. By definition, *RX* can be thought of as designating a relvar, *R* say—either a user-defined relvar (if *RX* is just a relvar name) or a system-defined relvar (otherwise). It is desirable, though not always entirely feasible, for the system to be able to **infer the candidate keys** of *R,* such that (among other things):

   a. If *RX* constitutes the defining expression for some virtual relvar *R′*, then those inferred candidate keys can be checked for consistency with the candidate keys explicitly defined for *R′* and—assuming no conflict—become candidate keys for *R′;*

   b. Those inferred candidate keys can be included in the information about *R* that is made available (in response to a "metaquery") to a user of **D.**

   D should provide such functionality, but without any guarantee (a) that such inferred candidate keys are not proper supersets of actual candidate keys, or (b) that such an inferred candidate key is discovered for every actual candidate key.

4. **D** should support **transition constraints**—i.e., constraints on the legal transitions that a given relvar or database can make from one value to another.

5. **D** should provide some shorthand for expressing **quota queries.** It should not be necessary to convert the relation concerned into (e.g.) an array in order to formulate such a query.

6. **D** should provide some shorthand for expressing the **generalized transitive closure** operation, including the ability to specify generalized *concatenate* and *aggregate* operations.

7. **D** should permit the parameters to user-defined operators (including in particular relation-valued operators—see RM Prescription 20) to be **tuples or relations** as well as scalars.

8. **D** should provide some kind of **special values** mechanism for dealing with "missing information."

9. **SQL** should be implementable in **D**—not because such implementation is desirable in itself, but so that a painless migration route might be available for current SQL users. To this same end, existing SQL databases should be convertible to a form that **D** programs can operate on without error.

OO VERY STRONG SUGGESTIONS

1. Some form of **type inheritance** should be supported (in which case, see OO Prescriptions 2 and 3). In keeping with this suggestion, **D** should not support **coercions** (i.e., implicit type conversions).

2. Operator definitions should be **logically distinct** from the definitions of the types of their parameters and/or results, not "bundled in" with any of those latter definitions (though selectors and the operators required by RM Prescription 5 might be regarded as exceptions to this suggestion).

3. "Collection" type generators, such as **LIST, ARRAY,** and **SET,** as commonly found in languages supporting rich type systems, should be supported.

4. Let C be a collection type generator other than RELATION. Then a **conversion** operator, say C2R, should be provided for converting values of a given generated C type to relations, and an inverse operator, say R2C, should also be provided, such that:

   a. $C2R(R2C(r)) = r$ for every expressible relation r;

   b. $R2C(C2R(c)) = c$ for every expressible value c of that generated C type.

5. **D** should be based on a **single-level storage** model.

4

A New Relational Algebra

INTRODUCTION

In this chapter, we propose a new relational algebra that we call **A**. The name **A** is a doubly recursive acronym: It stands for *ALGEBRA,* which in turn stands for *A Logical Genesis Explains Basic Relational Algebra.* As this expanded name suggests, **A** has been designed in such a way as to emphasize, perhaps more clearly than has been the case with previous algebras, its close relationship to and solid foundation in the discipline of first-order logic.* In addition, the abbreviated name **A** has pleasing connotations of beginning, basis, foundation, simplicity, and the like—not to mention that it is an obvious precursor to **D.**

The algebra **A** differs from Codd's original algebra [19–21] in four principal respects:

- Cartesian product (TIMES) is replaced by a natural join operator that, appealing to its counterpart in predicate logic, we choose to call simply ◄AND►. The original TIMES becomes merely a special case of ◄AND►.

    Note: We adopt the convention of using solid arrowheads ◄ and ► to delimit **A** operator names, as in ◄AND►, in order to distinguish those operators from their counterparts in both predicate logic and **Tutorial D** (see the next chapter).

---

*For a good reference on logic, see, e.g., McCawley [99].

Also, do not be misled by the name; the ◄AND► operator of **A** is, of course, a *relational* operator (it yields a result that is a relation), whereas its predicate logic counterpart *and* is a *logical* operator (it yields a result that is a truth value). Analogous remarks apply to the **A** operators ◄OR► and ◄NOT► as well (see the two paragraphs immediately following).

- UNION is replaced by a more general ◄OR► operator that does not require its operands to have the same heading. The original UNION becomes merely a special case of ◄OR►.

- We include a relational complement operator, ◄NOT►. The availability of ◄NOT► allows us to drop *difference* (MINUS), which becomes merely a special case of ◄AND► and ◄NOT► combined.

- We are able to dispense with *restrict* (WHERE), and also the EXTEND and SUMMARIZE operators that were added to the original algebra by several authors (the present writers included), since these operators all become further special cases of ◄AND►.

In addition to ◄AND►, ◄OR►, and ◄NOT►, **A** includes three operators called ◄RENAME►, ◄REMOVE►, and ◄COMPOSE►, which are discussed in the next section but one. It also includes a *transitive closure* operator, ◄TCLOSE►, which is discussed in the final section of this chapter.

MOTIVATION AND JUSTIFICATION

In this section we explain our reasons for developing **A** and justify the departures from Codd's algebra identified in the previous section. Our explanations and notation are deliberately not too formal (formal definitions appear in a later section). In particular, we show tuples not as sets of <attribute name, type name, value> triples, as the full formal apparatus of Chapter 3 would require, but as simple parenthesized commalists of values (see Chapter 5 for an explanation of the term "commalist"). For example, we use the expression (EX,DX) to mean a 2-tuple in which EX denotes a certain employee and DX a certain department.

Since we often appeal in what follows to ideas from predicate logic, using natural language predicates as examples, a brief note on the terminology we use in that connection is in order:

- First, we refer to the variables that appear in such predicates as **placeholders.** For example, in the predicate "Employee E works in department D," E and D are placeholders. *Note:* Placeholders are thus *logic* variables, not variables in the sense of a programming language, which is why we prefer to use a different term.

- Second, we follow custom in using Greek derivatives involving the suffix *-adic* when referring to the number of placeholders in a predicate, but Latin ones involving the suffix *-ary* when referring to the degree of a relation. For example, the predicate "Employee E works in department D" is dyadic, while a relation corresponding to that predicate—see the discussion of RM Prescription 10 in Chapter 6—is binary.

The algebra **A** has been motivated by certain general objectives, as follows:

- For psychological reasons, we sought a collection of operators with immediate counterparts in logic and with less reliance on set theory in their nomenclature. We feel that relational theory is better taught and understood this way; indeed, we have been dismayed at the widespread poor understanding in the database community at large of the logical foundations of relational theory, and we think it likely that this poor understanding has contributed to the deficiencies we observe in available relational (or would-be relational) technology.

- Previous algebras have had more than one operator corresponding to logical *and.* We thought this apparent redundancy worth looking into, with a view to eliminating it.

- We wanted all of the relational operators of **Tutorial D** to be mappable to expressions in **A,** for convenience and also for our own satisfaction (and we would strongly recommend that the same be true for any "industrial strength" **D** too). Full details of the mappings in question are deferred to Chapter 5, but some idea of what is involved can be found in later sections of the present chapter as well.

We now proceed to justify the four principal respects in which **A** differs from previous algebras.

Dispensing with TIMES

In logic, when two predicates are connected by *and,* attention must be paid to the names of the placeholders. Any placeholder name that appears in both predicates must be understood to stand for the same thing when it consequently appears more than once in the resulting predicate. For example, consider the natural language predicates "Employee E works in department D" and "Employee E works on project J." The *and* of these two predicates yields a triadic predicate, not a tetradic one— namely, "Employee E works in department D and employee E works on project J." This latter predicate can perhaps be abbreviated to just "Employee E works in department D and on project J," to stress the fact that we cannot substitute some particular employee for the E that works in department D without at the same time substituting that very same employee for the E that works on project J. This observation regarding placeholder names lies at the very heart of the well known *natural join* operator, and of course that operator is the ◄AND► of the algebra **A.**

As for the classical TIMES operator, it is of course just a special case of join (◄AND► in **A**). More precisely, TIMES corresponds to the *and* of two predicates that have no placeholders in common—for example, "Employee E works in department D and project J has budget B." TIMES as such can thus be discarded.

We return for a moment to the predicate "Employee E works in department D and on project J" in order to make another point. As already noted, that formulation of the predicate is really an abbreviation. Now, it might be abbreviated still further, to just "Employee E works in department D on project J"; however, that further abbreviation could lead to the erroneous conclusion that project J is somehow "in" department D. In reference [20], Codd characterized this kind of error as *the connection trap,* but it has since become known, at least in some circles, as the *join* trap instead—rather unfairly, we feel, since it is not unique to join in particular, nor to relational operators in general. In fact, it was precisely Codd's point in reference [20] that the error is more likely to arise in a nonrelational context than it is in a relational one.

Dispensing with UNION

We can combine natural language predicates with *or* as well as *and.* Thus, there is a ternary relation corresponding to the triadic predicate "Employee E works in department D or employee E works on project J." If employee EX works in department DX, then (EX,DX,J) is a tuple in the body of this relation for all possible projects J, regardless of whether employee EX actually works on project J (and regardless of whether there is even a project J in the company at this time). Likewise, if employee EX works on project JX, then (EX,D,JX) is a tuple in the body of this relation for all possible departments D, regardless of whether employee EX actually works in department D (and regardless of whether there is even a department D in the company at this time).

Just as we introduce ◄AND► as the **A** counterpart of *and,* therefore, we introduce ◄OR► as the **A** counterpart of *or.* As for the classical UNION operator, it is of course just a special case of ◄OR►. More precisely, UNION corresponds to the *or* of two predicates that have exactly the same placeholders—for example, "Employee E works in department D or employee E is on loan to department D." UNION as such can thus be discarded.

Note: We do not concern ourselves here with the computational difficulties that might arise from our generalization of Codd's UNION, because at this point we are only defining an algebra. Various safety mechanisms can be and normally are imposed in practice to circumvent such difficulties. For similar reasons, we also do not concern ourselves with the high degree of redundancy that most relations produced by ◄OR► will exhibit.

Dispensing with MINUS

Let WORKS_IN be a relation with attributes E and D, where E is an employee and D is a department, and let the corresponding predicate be "Employee E works in department D." Then the *logical complement* (◄NOT►) of this relation has a body that consists of all possible tuples of the form (E,D) such that it is not the case that employee E works in department D. *Note:* Computational difficulties arise here again as they did with ◄OR►, but again we need not concern ourselves with them at this point.

To see that MINUS can now be discarded, consider the following example. Let WORKS_IN be as above; let WORKS_ON be a relation with attributes E and J, where J is a project; and let the predicate corresponding to WORKS_ON be "Employee E works on project J." Now consider the unary relation corresponding to the monadic predicate "Employee E works in some department but works on no project at all." In Codd's algebra, we could obtain this relation by projecting both WORKS_IN and WORKS_ON over their E attributes and then taking the appropriate difference. In **A,** we first project WORKS_ON over E (see the next section for a discussion of projection), and then we take the ◄NOT► of that projection; the corresponding predicate is "There does not exist a project such that employee E works on that project." This relation can then be joined ("◄AND►ed") with WORKS_IN and the result projected over E to obtain the desired final result.

Dispensing with *restrict* (WHERE), EXTEND, and SUMMARIZE

Restrict (WHERE), EXTEND, and SUMMARIZE all require certain **operators** to be invoked as part of their execution. In the case of *restrict,* the operators in question return values (actually truth values) that are used to disqualify certain tuples from appearing in the result relation; in the case of EXTEND and SUMMARIZE, they return values that are used as the basis for defining certain attributes of the result relation.

It occurred to us that it made sense, and could possibly be useful, to **treat such operators as relations.** Consider an operator *Op* that is in fact a scalar function (a scalar function is an operator that returns exactly one result, where that result is a scalar value). Suppose *Op* has n parameters. Then *Op* can be treated as a relation with $n + 1$ attributes, one for each parameter and one for the result. The attributes corresponding to the parameters clearly form a candidate key for this relation; however, that candidate key is not necessarily the only one. For example, let PLUS be a relation with attributes X, Y, and Z, each of type INTEGER, corresponding to the scalar function "+" of integer arithmetic and to the predicate "X + Y = Z." Then each of {X,Y}, {Y,Z}, and {Z,X} is a candidate key for relation PLUS; further, that relation contains exactly one 3-tuple (X,Y,Z) for every possible combination of X, Y, and Z values that satisfies the predicate.

Note: By analogy with relvars (see Chapters 2 and 3), we might regard a relation like PLUS as a "relcon" or relation *constant:* It is named, like a relvar, but unlike a relvar it has a value that does not change over time. Observe, therefore, that the candidate keys discussed in the previous paragraph are candidate keys for a relation constant, not a relation variable.

Let us take a closer look at what is going on here. A scalar function is a special case of a relation, of course, as the PLUS example illustrates. More precisely, *any* relation can be regarded as an operator that maps from some subset of its attributes to the rest; and, if the mapping in question is a *functional* (i.e., many-to-one) mapping specifically, then the relation can be regarded as a function. In fact, since a set of n elements has 2^n subsets, a relation of degree n can be regarded as representing 2^n different operators, of which some will be functions and some not (in general). For example, PLUS can be regarded among other things as an operator that maps from Z to X and Y—but of course that particular mapping is not a functional one (the functional dependencies $Z \rightarrow X$ and $Z \rightarrow Y$ do not hold), and the corresponding operator is thus not a function.

We now claim that, given the fact that operators can be treated as relations, and given also the availability of the **A** operators ◄AND►, ◄REMOVE►, and ◄RENAME► (the latter two still to be discussed, of course), it is indeed the case that we can dispense with *restrict,* EXTEND, and SUMMARIZE. We will justify this claim in the next section but one.

◄REMOVE►, ◄RENAME►, AND ◄COMPOSE►

◄REMOVE►

◄REMOVE► is the **A** counterpart to the existential quantifier of predicate logic. It corresponds to Codd's *project.* However, it differs from *project* in that it specifies, not an attribute to be projected over, but rather an attribute to be "projected away"; it is equivalent to projecting the relation in question over all of its attributes except the one specified. Our motivation for this inversion, so to speak, with respect to Codd's *project* is a psychological one—projecting a relation with (say) attributes X and Y over X is equivalent to existentially quantifying over Y. Thus, e.g., the projection of WORKS_IN over E corresponds to the natural language predicate "There exists some department D such that employee E works in department D." We feel that ◄REMOVE► is psychologically closer to our foundation in logic than *project* is. *The Third Manifesto,* however, explicitly requires the language **D** not to arbitrate in this matter; rather, projection over specified attributes and projection over all except specified attributes are required to be equally easy to express.

◄RENAME►

◄RENAME► (meaning, specifically, "rename some *attribute* of some relation") is another primitive operator in **A.** Such an operator is essential in any concrete syntax for relational expressions in which attributes are distinguished by name (as they are in **A,** of course).

◄COMPOSE►

In addition to the five operators discussed so far—◄AND►, ◄OR►, ◄NOT►, ◄REMOVE►, and ◄RENAME►—we have allowed ourselves the luxury (some might think) of including a "macro" operator called ◄COMPOSE►. ◄COMPOSE► is a combination of ◄AND► and ◄REMOVE►, in which attributes common to the "◄AND►ed" relations are subsequently "◄REMOVE►d." *Note:* The name ◄COMPOSE► is meant to be suggestive of the fact that relational composition is a natural generalization of *functional* composition. For those who might not be familiar with this latter notion, we should explain that the composition of two functions $f(\ldots)$ and $g(\ldots)$, in that order, is the function $f(g(\ldots))$.

Codd did in fact include a relational composition operator in his earliest papers [19–20] but for some reason subsequently discarded it; we find it useful in support of our desire to treat operators as relations. To be specific, it turns out that a certain degenerate form of composition can be used to simulate the expression of operator invocations, as will be seen in the next section.

Closing Remarks

It should be clear that **A** is relationally complete [21]. Previous algebras have needed six operators for this purpose (typically RENAME, *restrict, project,* TIMES, UNION, and MINUS); we have reduced that number to five. Moreover, thanks to our observation that operators can be treated as relations, we have also avoided the need for EXTEND and SUMMARIZE; indeed, these operators might have been added needlessly in the past, simply for lack of that observation.

Points arising:

- As a matter of fact **A** is "more than" relationally complete, in the sense that its unconstrained ◄OR► and ◄NOT► operators permit the definition of relations that cannot be defined in previous algebras. The point is purely academic, c. course, since as already noted the ◄OR► and ◄NOT► operations will *not* be totally unconstrained in practice, in order to avoid certain computational problems that would otherwise arise.

- We do not actually need both ◄AND► and ◄OR► in order to achieve relational completeness, thanks to De Morgan's Laws. For example, A ◄AND► B is identically equal to ◄NOT► ((◄NOT► A) ◄OR► (◄NOT► B)), so we could dispense with ◄AND► if we included both ◄NOT► and ◄OR►. We could even collapse ◄NOT► and ◄OR► into a single operator, ◄NOR► ("neither A nor B"; equivalently, "not A and not B"). Equally well, of course, we could dispense with ◄OR► and collapse ◄AND► and ◄NOT► into a single operator, ◄NAND► ("not A or not B"). Overall, therefore, we could if desired reduce our algebra to just three operators: ◄RENAME►, ◄REMOVE►, and either ◄NOR► or

◄NAND► (plus the ◄TCLOSE► operator, to be discussed in the final section of this chapter).

Of course, we are not suggesting that all of the various operators that we claim can be dispensed with should in fact *be* dispensed with in the concrete syntax of **D**—they are useful and convenient shorthands, generally speaking, and as a matter of fact RM Prescription 18 of our *Manifesto* expressly requires that they ("or some logical equivalent thereof") be supported. But we do suggest that such operators be explicitly defined *as* shorthands, for reasons of clarity and simplicity among others [33].

TREATING OPERATORS AS RELATIONS

In this section we elaborate on our idea of treating operators as relations. Consider the relation PLUS once again, with attributes X, Y, and Z, each of type INTEGER, corresponding to the predicate "X + Y = Z." Let TWO_AND_TWO be the (unique) relation whose body consists of just the single 2-tuple

```
{ < X, INTEGER, 2 >, < Y, INTEGER, 2 > }
```

(we now revert to something closer to the formal notation for tuples—i.e., as sets of <attribute name, type name, value> triples—introduced in Chapter 3). Then the expression

```
TWO_AND_TWO ◄COMPOSE► PLUS
```

yields the relation whose body consists of the single 1-tuple

```
{ < Z, INTEGER, 4 > }
```

Observe, therefore, that we have effectively invoked the "+" operator with arguments X = 2 and Y = 2 and obtained the result Z = 4.* Of course, that result is still embedded as an attribute value inside a tuple inside a relation (like all operators of **A,** ◄COMPOSE► always returns a *relation*); if we want to extract that result as a pure scalar value, we will have to go beyond **A** *per se* and make use of the operators (required by RM Prescriptions 7 and 6, respectively) for (a) extracting a specified tuple from a specified relation and (b) extracting a specified attribute value from a specified tuple. In **Tutorial D** terms, for example, these extractions can be performed as follows:

```
Z FROM ( TUPLE FROM ( result ) )
```

---

*Note that the result has a name, Z. We are currently investigating the implications of this fact for the language **D.**

where *result* stands for the result of evaluating the **A** expression TWO_AND_TWO ◄COMPOSE► PLUS.

In other words, while it is certainly true that any given operator can be treated as a relation, it will still be necessary to step outside the confines of the algebra *per se* in order to obtain the actual result of some invocation of that operator. For present purposes, however, we are interested only in treating operators as relations *within a pure relational context;* such a treatment allows us to explain the classical relational operation EXTEND, for example, in a purely relational way (i.e., without having to leave the relational context at all), as we now proceed to show.

Consider the expression

```
TWO_AND_TWO ◄AND► PLUS
```

(this expression is the same as before, except that we have replaced ◄COMPOSE► by ◄AND►). The result is a relation whose body consists of just the single 3-tuple

```
{ < X, INTEGER, 2 >, < Y, INTEGER, 2 >, < Z, INTEGER, 4 > }
```

It should be clear, therefore, that the original **A** expression is logically equivalent to the following **Tutorial D** *extension:*

```
EXTEND TWO_AND_TWO ADD X + Y AS Z
```

This example should thus be sufficient to suggest how we can indeed dispense with EXTEND, as claimed.

Moreover, that very same expression TWO_AND_TWO ◄AND► PLUS is logically equivalent to the following **Tutorial D** *restriction:*

```
PLUS WHERE X = 2 AND Y = 2
```

This same example should thus also be sufficient to suggest how we can dispense with *restrict,* again as claimed.

As for SUMMARIZE, it is well known that any given summarization can be expressed in terms of EXTEND instead of SUMMARIZE *per se* (though the details are a little complicated; see Chapter 5 or the discussion of RM Prescription 18 in Chapter 6 for examples). It follows that we can dispense with SUMMARIZE as well.

Before we leave this section, we would like to stress the point that it is not only operators that are scalar functions specifically that can be treated as relations. Consider the following examples:

- An example of an operator that is scalar but not a function is SQRT ("square root"), which, given a positive numeric argument, yields two distinct results; e.g., SQRT(4.0) returns both +2.0 and –2.0.

- An example of an operator that is a function but not scalar is ADDR_OF ("address of"), which, given an employee E, returns the address of that employee as a collection of four values (STREET, CITY, STATE, and ZIP).

Again we take a closer look (briefly). First, SQRT. SQRT can obviously be treated as a relation with attributes X and Y (say), each of type RATIONAL.* However, that relation is not a function because the functional dependency X → Y does not hold—for example, the tuples (4.0,+2.0) and (4.0,–2.0) both appear. (By contrast, the functional dependency Y → X does hold; SQRT *can* be regarded as a function if it is looked at in the inverse—i.e., "square of"—direction.) Observe that the relation contains:

- For $x = 0$, exactly one tuple with X = $x;$
- For $x > 0$, exactly two tuples with X = $x;$
- For $x < 0$, no tuples at all with X = x.

It follows from the foregoing that the expression

```
SQRT ◄COMPOSE► { { < X, RATIONAL, 4.0 > } }
```

effectively represents an invocation of the SQRT operator, but—in contrast to the situation in conventional programming languages—the invocation in question returns *two results*. More precisely, it produces a (unary) relation with the following body:

```
{ { < Y, RATIONAL, +2.0 > },
  { < Y, RATIONAL, -2.0 > } }
```

(If desired, we could now extract each of the two tuples separately from this result, and then go on to extract each of the two scalar values +2.0 and –2.0 separately from those tuples.) One implication of this example is that a relational language such as **D** could reasonably include an extended form of EXTEND that (unlike the traditional EXTEND) is not necessarily guaranteed to produce exactly one output tuple from each input tuple.

Now we turn to ADDR_OF. This operator too can obviously be treated as a relation, this one having attributes E, STREET, CITY, STATE, and ZIP, where attribute E forms a candidate key. *Note:* The other four attributes might form a candidate key as well, if no two employees ever live at the same address (in which case the ADDR_OF relation would correspond to the inverse function that also happened to apply). Of course, the name ADDR_OF would be a little questionable if such were the case; EMP_AT might be just as appropriate, EMP_ADDR perhaps more so. The issue is merely psychological, of course.[†]

It follows from the foregoing that the expression

```
{ { < E, EMPLOYEE, e > } } ◄COMPOSE► ADDR_OF
```

(where *e* stands for some employee) effectively represents an invocation of the ADDR_OF operator, but—in contrast to the situation in conventional programming

---

*Throughout this book, we use the more accurate RATIONAL in place of the more familiar REAL.

[†]Analogous remarks apply to the SQRT example, where the name is again not very appropriate if the relation is looked at in the inverse ("square of") direction.

languages—the invocation in question returns a *nonscalar result.* One implication of this example is that a relational language such as **D** could reasonably include an extended form of EXTEND that (unlike the traditional EXTEND) is not necessarily guaranteed to produce just one additional attribute.

FORMAL DEFINITIONS

We now proceed to give formal definitions for the **A** operators discussed up to this point. First we explain our notation (which is based on that introduced in Chapter 3, of course, and—unlike that of previous sections—is now meant to be completely precise). Let r be a relation, let A be the name of an attribute of r, let T be the type of attribute A, and let v be a value of type T. Then:

- The heading Hr of r is a set of ordered pairs of the form $<A,T>$, one such pair for each attribute A of r. By definition, no two pairs in that set can contain the same attribute name A.

- Let tr be a tuple that conforms to Hr; i.e., tr is a set of ordered triples of the form $<A,T,v>$, one such triple for each attribute A of Hr.

- The body Br of r is a set of such tuples tr. Note that (in general) there will be some such tuples tr that conform to Hr but do not appear in Br.

The rest of our notation is meant to be self-explanatory.

Observe that a heading is a set, a body is a set, and a tuple is a set. A member of a heading is an ordered pair of the form $<A,T>$; a member of a body is a tuple; and a member of a tuple is an ordered triple of the form $<A,T,v>$. Observe too that every subset of a heading is a heading, every subset of a body is a body, and every subset of a tuple is a tuple.

Now we can define the operators *per se.* Each of the definitions that follow consists of (a) a formal specification of the restrictions, if any, that apply to the operands of the operator in question, (b) a formal specification of the heading of the result of that operator, and (c) a formal specification of the body of that result, followed by (d) an informal discussion of the formal specifications.

- Let s be ◄NOT► r.

```
Hs  =  Hr

Bs  =  { ts : exists tr ( tr ∉ Br and ts = tr ) }
```

The ◄NOT► operator yields the complement s of a given relation r. The heading of s is the heading of r. The body of s contains every tuple with that heading that is not in the body of r.

- Let s be r ◄REMOVE► A. It is required that there exist some type T such that $<A,T> \in$ Hr.

```
Hs  =  Hr minus { <A,T> }

Bs  =  { ts : exists tr exists v
                ( tr ε Br and v ε T and <A,T,v> ε tr and
                                 ts = tr minus { <A,T,v> } ) }
```

The ◄REMOVE► operator yields a relation *s* formed by removing a given attribute *A* from a given relation *r*. The operation is equivalent to taking the projection of *r* over all of its attributes except *A*. The heading of *s* is the heading of *r* minus the pair *<A,T>*. The body of *s* contains every tuple that conforms to the heading of *s* and is a subset of some tuple of *r*.

■ Let *s* be *r* ◄RENAME► *(A,B)*. It is required that there exist some type *T* such that *<A,T>* ∈ H*r* and that there exist no type *T* such that *<B,T>* ∈ H*r*.

```
Hs  =  ( Hr minus { <A,T> } ) union { <B,T> }

Bs  =  { ts : exists tr exists v
                ( tr ε Br and v ε T and <A,T,v> ε tr and·
                                 ts = ( tr minus { <A,T,v> } )
                                       union { <B,T,v> } ) }
```

The ◄RENAME► operator yields a relation *s* that differs from a given relation *r* only in the name of one of its attributes, which is changed from *A* to *B*. The heading of *s* is the heading of *r* except that the pair *<A,T>* is replaced by the pair *<B,T>*. The body of *s* consists of every tuple of the body of *r*, except that in each such tuple the triple *<A,T,v>* is replaced by the triple *<B,T,v>*.

■ Let *s* be *r1* ◄AND► *r2*. It is required that if *<A,T1>* ∈ H*r1* and *<A,T2>* ∈ H*r2*, then *T1 = T2*.

```
Hs   =  Hr1 union Hr2

Bs   =  { ts : exists tr1 exists tr2
                ( ( tr1 ε Br1 and tr2 ε Br2 ) and
                                 ts = tr1 union tr2 ) }
```

The ◄AND► operator is relational *conjunction,* yielding a relation *s* that in previous literature has been referred to as the *natural join* of the two given relations *r1* and *r2*. The heading of *s* is the union of the headings of *r1* and *r2*. The body of *s* contains every tuple that conforms to the heading of *s* and is a superset of both some tuple in the body of *r1* and some tuple in the body of *r2*. We remark that the ◄AND► operator might logically be called the *conjoin.*

■ Let *s* be *r1* ◄OR► *r2*. It is required that if *<A,T1>* ∈ H*r1* and *<A,T2>* ∈ H*r2*, then *T1 = T2*.

```
Hs   =  Hr1 union Hr2

Bs   =  { ts : exists tr1 exists tr2
                ( ( tr1 ε Br1 or tr2 ε Br2 ) and
                                 ts = tr1 union tr2 ) }
```

The ◄OR► operator is relational *disjunction,* being a generalization of what in previous literature has been referred to as *union* (in the special case where the given relations *r1* and *r2* have the same heading, the result *s* is in fact the union in the traditional sense of those two relations). The heading of *s* is the union of the headings of *r1* and *r2.* The body of *s* contains every tuple that conforms to the heading of *s* and is a superset of either some tuple in the body of *r1* or some tuple in the body of *r2.* We remark that the ◄OR► operator might logically be called the *disjoin.*

Finally, we define the "macro" operator ◄COMPOSE►. Let *s* be *r1* ◄COMPOSE► *r2* (where *r1* and *r2* are as for ◄AND►). Let the attributes common to *r1* and *r2* be *A1, A2, ..., An* ($n \geq 0$). Then *s* is defined to be the result of the expression

```
( r1 ◄AND► r2 )  ◄REMOVE► An ... ◄REMOVE► A2 ◄REMOVE► A1
```

Note that when $n = 0$, *r1* ◄COMPOSE► *r2* is the same as *r1* ◄AND► *r2,* which is in turn the same as *r1* TIMES *r2* in Codd's algebra.

TRANSITIVE CLOSURE

The algebra **A** departs from Codd's original algebra in one further respect: namely, it includes an explicit *transitive closure* operator, ◄TCLOSE►. In order to explain how that operator works, we consider the bill of materials relation MM shown in Fig. 4.1 (a repeat of Fig. 2.2 from Chapter 2, except that now we ignore the attribute QTY). That relation is an example of what is sometimes called a *digraph relation,* because it can be represented as a graph of nodes and directed arcs (see Fig. 4.2).

Note: It is sometimes more convenient from an intuitive point of view to convert a digraph such as that of Fig. 4.2 into a pure hierarchy with possibly repeated nodes. Fig. 4.3 shows a hierarchic version of the digraph of Fig. 4.2. The two graphs are information-equivalent, of course.

MM	MAJOR_P# : P#	MINOR_P# : P#
	P1	P2
	P1	P3
	P2	P3
	P2	P4
	P3	P5
	P4	P6

Fig. 4.1   Relation MM

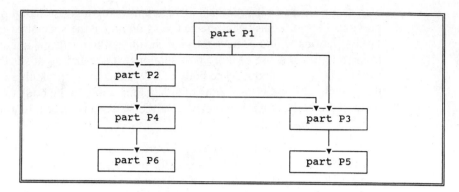

Fig. 4.2   Graph of relation MM

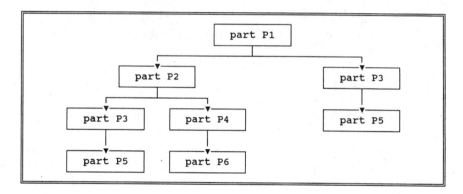

Fig. 4.3   Graph of relation MM as a hierarchy

Now, since MM is specifically a *binary* relation, we can apply the transitive closure operation to it. We define that operation as follows.

- Let r be a binary relation with attributes X and Y, both of the same type T. Then the *transitive closure* of r, ◀TCLOSE▶ r, is a relation r^+ with heading the same as that of r and body a superset of that of r, defined as follows: The tuple

```
{ < X, T, x >, < Y, T, y > }
```

appears in r^+ if and only if it appears in r or there exists a sequence of values $z1$, $z2$, ..., zn (all of type T) such that the tuples

```
{ < X, T, x  >, < Y, T, z1 > }
{ < X, T, z1 >, < Y, T, z2 > }
      . . . . . . . . . . . . . . .
{ < X, T, zn >, < Y, T, y  > }.
```

all appear in *r*. (In other words, the "*(x,y)*" tuple appears only if there is a path in the graph from node *x* to node *y*, loosely speaking. Note that the body of r^+ necessarily includes the body of *r* as a subset.)

Fig. 4.4 shows the transitive closure of relation MM.

MAJOR_P# : P#	MINOR_P# : P#
P1	P2
P1	P3
P2	P3
P2	P4
P3	P5
P4	P6
P1	P4
P1	P5
P1	P6
P2	P5
P2	P6

Fig. 4.4   Transitive closure of MM

The transitive closure operation is important in connection with the *part explosion* problem—i.e., the problem of finding all components, at all levels, of some specified part—and similar "recursive query" problems.

5

Tutorial D

INTRODUCTION

Tutorial D is a computationally complete programming language with fully integrated database functionality. It is deliberately not meant to be industrial strength; rather, it is a "toy" language, whose primary purpose is to serve as a teaching vehicle (in fact, of course, it is intended to serve as a basis for illustrating and explaining the ideas of *The Third Manifesto* specifically). As a consequence, many features that would be required in an industrial strength language are intentionally omitted. For example, there is no support for any of the following:

- Sessions and connections
- Any form of communication with the outside world (input/output facilities, etc.)
- Exception handling and feedback information

(In the case of this last omission, however, we should at least say that we expressly do not want a form of exception handling support that requires the user to pass a feedback argument to be set by each operator invocation; such an approach would effectively force every operator to become an update operator! Rather, we advocate some kind of SIGNAL mechanism, perhaps along the lines supported by the *Persistent Stored Modules* feature of the current SQL standard, PSM [76,87].)

For obvious reasons, there is also no support for any of the items listed in the section "Topics Deliberately Omitted" in Chapter 1 (security and authorization, triggered actions, a call-level interface, and so forth). Nor is there any support for subtyping and inheritance; however, possible extensions to deal with these particular topics are introduced in Part IV of this book (see Chapters 14–16).

In addition to the above, many minor details, both syntactic and semantic, that would require precise specification in an industrial strength language have also been ignored. For example, details of the following are all omitted:

- Legal language characters, legal identifiers, scope of names, etc.
- Reserved words (if any), comments,* delimiters, newline markers, etc.
- Operator precedence rules (except for one or two rather important ones)
- "Obvious" syntax rules (e.g., "distinct parameters to the same operator must have distinct names")

On the other hand, the language *is* meant to be well designed, as far as it goes. Indeed, it must be!—for otherwise it would not be a valid **D**. RM Prescription 26 requires that every **D** be constructed according to well-established principles of good language design, and this requirement implies that arbitrary restrictions such as those documented in references [46], [48], [73], and [76], and all other *ad hoc* concepts and constructs, are absolutely prohibited. And, of course, no such restrictions or *ad hoc* concepts or constructs are to be found in **Tutorial D** (or, at least, such is our belief).

As already noted, **Tutorial D** is computationally complete, meaning that entire applications can be written in the language; in other words, it is not just a "data sublanguage" that relies on some host language to provide the necessary computational capabilities. In accordance with the assumptions spelled out in Chapter 1, moreover, it is also, like most programming languages currently in widespread use, imperative in style—though it is worth mentioning that the "data sublanguage" portion, being based as it is on relational algebra, can in fact be regarded as a functional language when considered in isolation. In practice we would hope that this portion of the language would be implemented in an interactive form as well as in the form of a programming language *per se;* i.e., we support *the dual-mode principle* as described in, e.g., reference [55].

As just indicated, **Tutorial D** is also a relational language, at least insofar as its database support is concerned. In certain respects, however, it can be regarded as an object language as well. For one thing, it is based on the single-level storage idea (see OO Very Strong Suggestion 5). More important, it supports what is probably the most fundamental feature of object languages: namely, it allows users to *define their own types.* And since there is no reliance on a host language, there is no "impedance mismatch" between the types available inside the database and those available outside; thus, there is no need to map between the arbitrarily complex types used in the database and the probably rather simple builtin types provided by some

---

In our examples we show comments as text strings bracketed by "/" and "*/" delimiters.

conventional host language. (In other words, we agree with the object community's complaint that there is a serious problem in trying to build an interface between a database involving user-defined types and a conventional programming language.) For example, if the database contains a data value of type POLYGON, then that value can be assigned to a local variable also of type POLYGON; there is no need to break it down into (say) a sequence of numbers representing the X and Y coordinates of the vertices of the polygon in question. Altogether, therefore, it seems fair to characterize **Tutorial D** as a true "object/relational" language.

Tutorial D has of course been explicitly designed to support all of the prescriptions and proscriptions of *The Third Manifesto* as defined in Chapter 3. It deliberately does not support all of the "very strong suggestions" mentioned in that chapter, however (though possible extensions to deal with such matters are considered briefly in Chapters 10 and 11, *q.v.*). Moreover, the language is also deliberately not meant to be *minimal* in any sense—it includes numerous features that are really just shorthand for certain combinations of others (this remark applies especially to its relational support, as will be seen). However, it is at least true that the shorthands in question are explicitly designed to *be* shorthands [33]; i.e., the redundancies are deliberate, and are included for usability reasons.

While we are on the subject of relational support, incidentally, there is another point to be made. It is of course well known that relational algebra and relational calculus are logically equivalent, implying that either can serve as well as the other as a basis for a concrete language [21, 56]. It is also well known that an algebraic style is intuitively preferable to a calculus style for some tasks, while the opposite is true for others. For definiteness, we have used an algebraic style for **Tutorial D;** for interest, however, we sketch the outlines of an alternative calculus-based version in Appendix A.

The bulk of what follows consists of a BNF grammar for **Tutorial D.** The grammar is defined by means of what is essentially standard BNF notation, except for certain simplifying extensions of our own which we now explain. Let <*xyz*> denote an arbitrary syntactic category (i.e., anything that appears on the left hand side of some BNF production rule). Then:

- The expression <*xyz list*> denotes a sequence of zero or more <*xyz*>s in which each pair of adjacent <*xyz*>s is separated by at least one space.

- The expression <*xyz commalist*> denotes a sequence of zero or more <*xyz*>s in which each pair of adjacent <*xyz*>s is separated by a comma (as well as zero or more spaces).

- The expression <*ne xyz list*> (where *ne* stands for "nonempty") denotes an <*xyz list*> that contains at least one <*xyz*>.

- The expression <*ne xyz commalist*> is defined analogously.

We should perhaps stress the fact that braces "{" and "}" in our grammar stand for themselves—i.e., they are symbols in the language being defined, not (as they usually are) symbols of the metalanguage. Also, all syntactic categories of the form *<... name>* are defined to be *<identifier>*s, barring explicit production rules to the contrary; the category *<identifier>* in turn is terminal and is not defined further here. Finally, some of the production rules are accompanied by a prose explanation of certain additional syntax rules and/or the corresponding semantics (but only in those cases where such explanations seem necessary).

TYPES AND EXPRESSIONS

```
<type>
    ::=    <scalar type>
       |   <tuple type>
       |   <relation type>

<scalar type>
    ::=    <scalar type name>
       |   SAME_TYPE_AS ( <scalar exp> )

<tuple type>
    ::=    <tuple type name>
       |   SAME_TYPE_AS ( <tuple exp> )

<relation type>
    ::=    <relation type name>
       |   SAME_TYPE_AS ( <relation exp> )

<exp>
    ::=    <scalar exp>
       |   <tuple exp>
       |   <relation exp>

<with exp>
    ::=    WITH <ne name intro commalist> : <exp>
```

The *<with exp>* is a *<scalar exp>*, *<tuple exp>*, or *<relation exp>* according as the specified *<exp>* is a *<scalar exp>*, *<tuple exp>*, or *<relation exp>*. The individual *<name intro>*s are executed in sequence as written. The semantics of the overall *<with exp>* are defined to be those of a version of *<exp>* in which each occurrence of each introduced name is replaced by the text of the corresponding expression (see the production rule immediately following). In general, of course, those replacing expressions will involve further occurrences of introduced names; the replacement process is therefore performed repeatedly until no such occurrences remain.

Note: SQL3 includes a similar feature [76,87]. Moreover, SQL3 also allows its analog of an *<exp>* in this context to include occurrences of its own introduced name, thereby supporting recursive expressions (of a kind).* It might prove desirable to incorporate such a feature into **Tutorial D** also, though we note

---

*The SQL3 support is actually more general than this brief description might suggest. See reference [87] for more details.

that (a) **Tutorial D** already permits user-defined operators to be recursive, and (b) in the case of relations specifically, it also provides transitive closure (TCLOSE) as a builtin operator.

```
<name intro>
    ::=    <exp> AS <introduced name>
```

The *<introduced name>* can be used wherever a *<scalar exp>*, *<tuple exp>*, or *<relation exp>* is permitted, according as the specified *<exp>* is a *<scalar exp>*, *<tuple exp>*, or *<relation exp>*.

SCALAR DEFINITIONS

```
<scalar type name>
    ::=    <builtin scalar type name>
        |  <user scalar type name>

<builtin scalar type name>
    ::=    BOOLEAN
         | INTEGER
         | RATIONAL
         | CHARACTER | CHAR
```

Support for the builtin scalar type BOOLEAN (including the usual operators NOT, AND, OR, etc., and literals TRUE and FALSE) is required by RM Prescription 1. Support for the builtin scalar types INTEGER, RATIONAL,* and CHARACTER (abbreviated CHAR) is also provided for convenience, with specifics as follows:

- INTEGER (signed integers): literals expressed as an optionally signed decimal integer; usual arithmetic and comparison operators, with usual notation

- RATIONAL (signed rational numbers): literals expressed as an optionally signed decimal number mantissa (including a decimal point), optionally followed by the letter E and an optionally signed decimal integer exponent (examples: 5., 5.0, 17.5, –5.3E+2); usual arithmetic and comparison operators, with usual notation

- CHARACTER or CHAR (varying length character strings): literals expressed in the usual way, as sequences of characters enclosed in single quotes; usual character string manipulation and comparison operators, with usual notation— "‖" (concatenate), SUBSTR (substring), etc.

In practice, of course, we would expect a variety of other builtin scalar types— BIT, DATE, TIME, etc.—to be supported too. We omit them from **Tutorial D** for simplicity.

---

*As noted in Chapter 4, throughout this book we use the more accurate RATIONAL in place of the more familiar REAL.

Incidentally, note that we explicitly do not propose support for types such as, e.g., CHAR(5) (meaning character strings of either maximum or exact length five characters). Rather, we take the position that the type here is simply CHAR, and the specification "(5)" is a constraint on the use of that type in some particular context. One desirable consequence of this approach is that if variables X and Y are defined as, say, CHAR(5) and CHAR(6), respectively (not valid **Tutorial D** syntax), then comparisons between X and Y are legal—i.e., they do not violate the requirement of RM Prescription 22 that the comparands must be of the same type.

```
<user scalar type def>
    ::=    TYPE <user scalar type name>
               <ne possrep def list>
           [ <scalar type constraint> ]
```

Note: Regarding what are sometimes called *ordered* or *ordinal* types—i.e., types for which the operator "<" makes sense—see the discussion of RM Prescription 3 in Chapter 6.

```
<possrep def>
    ::=    POSSREP [ <possrep name> ]
                   ( <ne possrep component def commalist> )
```

POSSREP here stands for *possible representation* (see RM Prescription 4). The *<possrep name>* can be omitted only if the *<possrep def>* is the only such within the applicable *<user scalar type def>;* for such a *<possrep def>,* a *<possrep name>* is assumed that is identical to the corresponding *<user scalar type name>.* Each *<possrep def>* causes "automatic" definition of:

- A scalar selector corresponding to that *<possrep def>.* The name of that scalar selector is the specified or implied *<possrep name>.* We assume the obvious syntax for *<scalar selector inv>*s (i.e., scalar selector invocations), *viz.* the applicable *<scalar selector name>* followed by a nonempty parenthesized commalist of arguments, where the *i*th argument is an expression of the same type as the *i*th *<possrep component>.*

- A set of THE_ operators (including THE_ pseudovariables), one for each *<possrep component>* of that *<possrep def>.* Each such operator or pseudovariable has a name of the form THE_*C,* where *C* is the corresponding *<possrep component name>.* The syntax for such THE_ operator and pseudovariable invocations is given in the section "Scalar Operations," later.

Note: Here and elsewhere in this book we use expressions of the form *definition of an X causes "automatic" definition of a Y* to mean that (a) whatever agency— possibly the system, possibly some human user—is responsible for supplying the definition of the X in question is also responsible for supplying the definition of the corresponding Y, and further that (b) until that Y definition has been supplied, the process of defining that X cannot be considered complete.

```
<possrep component def>
    ::=    [ <possrep component name> ] <type>
```

The *<possrep component name>* can be omitted only if the *<possrep component def>* is the only such within the applicable *<possrep def>; for such a *<possrep component def>*, a *<possrep component name>* is assumed that is identical to the corresponding *<possrep name>*.

```
<scalar type constraint>
    ::=    CONSTRAINT ( <bool exp> )
```

The *<bool exp>* must not mention any variables; however, the *<user scalar type name>* from the containing *<user scalar type def>* can be used—in this context only—to denote an arbitrary value of the scalar type in question.

```
<user scalar op def>
    ::=    OPERATOR <user scalar op name>
                   ( <parameter def commalist> )
                   <returns or updates def> ;
                   <statement>
           END OPERATOR
```

In practice, it would probably be desirable to support an "external" format of *<user scalar op def>* as well. Syntactically, such a *<user scalar op def>* would include, not a *<statement>* as above, but rather a reference to some external file in which the code that implements the operator can be found (possibly written in some different language). It might also be desirable to support a format of *<user scalar op def>* that includes neither a *<statement>* nor an external reference; such a format would define merely what Chapter 14 calls a "specification signature" for the operator in question, and the implementation code would then have to be defined elsewhere. Splitting operator definitions into separate pieces in this way is likely to prove particularly useful if type inheritance is supported (again, see Chapter 14).

Analogous remarks apply to *<user tuple op def>* and *<user relation op def>, q.v.*

```
<parameter def>
    ::=    <parameter name> <scalar type>

<returns or updates def>
    ::=    <returns def> | <updates def>
```

Operators defined with an *<updates def>* are update operators and must be invoked by explicit *<call>*s; operators defined with a *<returns def>* are read-only operators and must not.

```
<returns def>
    ::=    RETURNS ( <scalar type> )
```

Note: **Tutorial D** does not currently support read-only operators that are not functions (see the final portion of the section "Treating Operators as Relations" in Chapter 4). Nor does it currently support the concept of named results (again, see Chapter 4). It does, however, support read-only operators that return tuple or relation results (see *<user tuple op def>* and *<user relation op def>,* later).

```
<updates def>
    ::=   UPDATES ( <ne parameter name commalist> )

<scalar var def>
    ::=   VAR <scalar var name> <scalar type>
                                    [ INIT ( <scalar exp> ) ]
```

If the INIT specification appears, the scalar variable is initialized to the value of the specified *<scalar exp>;* otherwise, it is initialized to an implementation-defined value.

```
<user scalar op drop>
    ::=   DROP OPERATOR <user scalar op name>

<user scalar type drop>
    ::=   DROP TYPE <user scalar type name>
```

TUPLE DEFINITIONS

```
<tuple type name>
    ::=   TUPLE { <heading> }

<heading>
    ::=   <attribute name and type commalist>

<attribute name and type>
    ::=   <attribute name> <type>

<tuple var def>
    ::=   VAR <tuple var name> <tuple type>
                                    [ INIT ( <tuple exp> ) ]
```

If the INIT specification appears, the tuple variable is initialized to the value of the specified *<tuple exp>;* otherwise, it is initialized to an implementation-defined value.

```
<user tuple op def>
    ::=   OPERATOR <user tuple op name>
                ( <parameter def commalist> )
                RETURNS ( <tuple type> ) ;
                <statement>
          END OPERATOR
```

Note: **Tutorial D** goes further than the *Manifesto* here, in that the *Manifesto* does not actually require support for user-defined read-only operators that are tuple-valued. We include such support in the interests of completeness.

```
<user tuple op drop>
    ::=   DROP OPERATOR <user tuple op name>
```

RELATIONAL DEFINITIONS

```
<relation type name>
    ::=    RELATION { <heading> }

<relation var def>
    ::=    <database relation var def>
                            <candidate key def list>
         | <application relation var def>
                            <candidate key def list>
```

A *<relation var def>* defines a relation variable, of course. In practice it might be desirable to provide a way of defining relation constants also (see Chapter 4). *Note:* Specifying an empty *<candidate key def list>* is legal only if the *<relation var def>* involves a *<relation exp>* (i.e., the *<relation var def>* is a *<virtual relation var def>* or specifies a *<relation type>* of the form SAME_TYPE_AS (*<relation exp>*); specifying such an empty *<candidate key def list>* is equivalent to specifying a *<ne candidate key def list>* that contains exactly one *<candidate key def>* for each candidate key that can be inferred by the system for the result of the specified *<relation exp>* (see the discussion of RM Very Strong Suggestion 3 in Chapter 10).

```
<database relation var def>
    ::=    <real relation var def>
         | <virtual relation var def>
```

A *<database relation var def>* defines a database relvar (i.e., one that is "persistent" and is to be part of the database); in other words, it causes an entry to be made in the catalog. Note, however, that neither databases nor catalogs are explicitly mentioned anywhere in the syntax of **Tutorial D.**

```
<real relation var def>
    ::=    VAR <relation var name> REAL <relation type>

<candidate key def>
    ::=    KEY { <attribute name commalist> }
```

We use the unqualified keyword KEY to refer to a candidate key specifically, for simplicity. Regarding *primary* keys, see the discussion of RM Prescription 15 in Chapter 6.

```
<virtual relation var def>
    ::=    VAR <relation var name> VIRTUAL <relation exp>

<application relation var def>
    ::=    VAR <relation var name> <scope> <relation type>
```

An *<application relation var def>* defines either a "local" relvar (i.e., one that is not part of the database at all) or a "global" relvar (i.e., the application's perception of some data that does belong to the database).

```
<scope>
    ::=    LOCAL | GLOBAL
```

```
<user relation op def>
    ::=   OPERATOR <user relation op name>
                ( <parameter def commalist> )
                RETURNS ( <relation type> ) ;
                <statement>
          END OPERATOR
```

Note: **Tutorial D** goes further here than the *Manifesto* does, in that it permits the definition of a user-defined, relation-valued operator to be of arbitrary generality, instead of insisting that it be limited to a relational expression.

```
<user relation op drop>
    ::=   DROP OPERATOR <user relation op name>

<constraint def>
    ::=   CONSTRAINT <constraint name> ( <bool exp> )
```

The *<bool exp>* must not mention any variables other than relvars. *Note:* We could relax this rule if we wanted to support constraints involving scalar and tuple variables as well as relvars, of course.

```
<constraint drop>
    ::=   DROP CONSTRAINT <constraint name>

<relation var drop>
    ::=   DROP VAR <relation var name>
```

The *<relation var name>* must denote a database relvar, not an application one.

SCALAR OPERATIONS

```
<scalar exp>
    ::=   <scalar selector inv>
      |   <scalar var ref>
      |   <THE_ op inv>
      |   <scalar op inv>
      |   <attribute extractor inv>
      |   <agg op inv>
      |   <with exp>
      |   <introduced name>
      |   ( <scalar exp> )
```

Numeric expressions, character string expressions, and in particular boolean expressions—i.e., *<bool exp>*s—are all *<scalar exp>*s, and we assume the usual syntax in each case. The following are also *<scalar exp>*s:

■ A special form of *<bool exp>*, IS_EMPTY (*<relation exp>*), which returns TRUE if the body of the relation denoted by *<relation exp>* contains no tuples and FALSE otherwise;

■ CAST expressions of the form CAST_AS_*T* (*<scalar exp>*), where *T* is a scalar type and *<scalar exp>* denotes a scalar value to be converted ("cast") to that type;

■ IF-THEN-ELSE and CASE expressions of the usual form.

For the syntax of *<scalar selector inv>,* see *<possrep def>* in the section "Scalar Definitions" earlier.

```
<scalar var ref>
    ::=    <scalar var name>
         | <THE_ pv inv>

<THE_ pv inv>
    ::=    <THE_ pv name> ( <scalar var ref> )
```

We include this production rule in this section because we expect most *<THE_ pv inv>*s in practice to designate scalar variables. In fact, however, a *<THE_ pv inv>* can designate a scalar, tuple, or relation variable, depending on the type of the *<possrep component>* being accessed.

```
<THE_ op inv>
    ::=    <THE_ op name> ( <scalar exp> )
```

We include this production rule in this section because we expect most *<THE_ op inv>*s in practice to denote scalar values. In fact, however, a *<THE_ op inv>* can denote a scalar, tuple, or relation value, depending on the type of the *<possrep component>* being accessed.

```
<scalar op inv>
    ::=    <builtin scalar op inv>
         | <user scalar op inv>

<builtin scalar op inv>
    ::=    ... the usual possibilities

<user scalar op inv>
    ::=    <user scalar op name> ( <argument commalist> )
```

Every argument must be of the same type as the parameter to which it corresponds. *Note:* The same is true for *<builtin scalar op inv>*s too, of course, and analogous remarks apply to *<tuple op inv>*s and *<relation op inv>*s also—unless the operator in question is either "overloaded" or "generic" (see Chapter 6). An example of an overloaded operator is "+", which applies to both integers and rational numbers; an example of a generic operator is JOIN, which applies to any pair of relations whatsoever (so long as attributes with the same name have the same type, of course).

```
<argument>
    ::=    <scalar exp>

<attribute extractor inv>
    ::=    <attribute name> FROM <tuple exp>
```

We include this production rule in this section because we expect most attributes in practice to be scalar. In fact, however, an *<attribute extractor inv>* can evaluate to a scalar, a tuple, or a relation, depending on the type of the attribute in question.

```
<agg op inv>
    ::=    <agg op name> ( <relation exp> [, <attribute ref> ] )
```

If the *<agg op name>* is COUNT, *<attribute ref>* is irrelevant and must be omitted; otherwise, it can be omitted if and only if the *<relation exp>* denotes a relation of degree one, in which case the sole attribute of the result of *<relation exp>* is assumed by default.

```
<agg op name>
    ::=    COUNT | SUM | AVG | MAX | MIN

<attribute ref>
    ::=    <attribute name>
       |   <THE_ pv name> ( <attribute ref> )

<scalar assign>
    ::=    <scalar var ref> := <scalar exp>
```

The scalar variable identified by *<scalar var ref>* and the scalar value denoted by *<scalar exp>* must be of the same scalar type.

```
<scalar comp>
    ::=    <scalar exp> <scalar comp op> <scalar exp>
```

The scalar values denoted by the two *<scalar exp>*s must be of the same scalar type. Scalar comparisons are a special case of the syntactic category *<bool exp>*.

```
<scalar comp op>
    ::=    = | ≠ | ... etc. (depending on type)
```

TUPLE OPERATIONS

```
<tuple exp>
    ::=    <tuple selector inv>
       |   <tuple var ref>
       |   <THE_ op inv>
       |   <tuple op inv>
       |   <attribute extractor inv>
       |   <tuple extractor inv>
       |   <with exp>
       |   <introduced name>
       |   ( <tuple exp> )

<tuple selector inv>
    ::=    TUPLE { <tuple component commalist> }

<tuple component>
    ::=    <attribute name> <exp>

<tuple var ref>
    ::=    <tuple var name>
       |   <THE_ pv inv>

<tuple op inv>
    ::=    <builtin tuple op inv>
       |   <user tuple op inv>
```

```
<builtin tuple op inv>
    ::=    <tuple project>
         | <other builtin tuple op inv>
```

Note: Although we generally have little to say regarding operator precedence, we find it convenient to assign a high precedence to tuple projection in particular. This fact accounts for the foregoing production rule. An analogous remark applies to relational projection also (see the next section).

```
<tuple project>
    ::=    <tuple exp>
                  { [ ALL BUT ] <attribute name commalist> }
```

The *<tuple exp>* must not be an *<other builtin tuple op inv>* (in order to avoid ambiguity).

```
<other builtin tuple op inv>
    ::=    <tuple rename> | <tuple join> | <tuple extend>
         | <tuple wrap> | <tuple unwrap>

<tuple rename>
    ::=    <tuple exp> RENAME <ne renaming commalist>
```

The *<tuple exp>* must not be an *<other builtin tuple op inv>*. The individual *<renaming>*s are executed in sequence as written.

```
<renaming>
    ::=    <attribute name> AS <attribute name>
         | PREFIX <character string literal>
               AS <character string literal>
         | SUFFIX <character string literal>
               AS <character string literal>
```

For the syntax of *<character string literal>*, see *<builtin scalar type name>*. The *<renaming>* PREFIX '*a*' AS '*b*' causes all attributes of the applicable tuple or relation whose name begins with the characters of *a* to be renamed such that their name now begins with the characters of *b* instead. The *<renaming>* SUFFIX '*a*' AS '*b*' is defined analogously. Note that (of course) a *<character string literal>* can denote an empty character string.

```
<tuple join>
    ::=    <tuple exp> JOIN <tuple exp>
```

The *<tuple exp>*s must not be *<other builtin tuple op inv>*s. If the tuples denoted by those *<tuple exp>*s have any attribute names in common, then the corresponding attribute values must be the same.

```
<tuple extend>
    ::=    EXTEND <tuple exp> ADD <ne extend add commalist>
```

The *<tuple exp>* must not be an *<other builtin tuple op inv>*. The individual *<extend add>*s are executed in sequence as written.

```
<extend add>
   ::=    <exp> AS <attribute name>
```

The *<exp>* is allowed to include an *<attribute ref>* wherever a *<scalar selector inv>* is allowed.

```
<tuple wrap>
   ::=    <tuple exp> WRAP <ne wrapping commalist>
```

The *<tuple exp>* must not be an *<other builtin tuple op inv>*. *Note:* See the discussion of RM Prescription 6 in Chapter 6 (also the final section of the present chapter) for an explanation of both *<tuple wrap>* and *<tuple unwrap>*.

```
<wrapping>
   ::=    ( [ ALL BUT ] <attribute name commalist> )
                             AS <attribute name>
```

```
<tuple unwrap>
   ::=    <tuple exp> UNWRAP <ne unwrapping commalist>
```

The *<tuple exp>* must not be an *<other builtin tuple op inv>*.

```
<unwrapping>
   ::=     <attribute name>
```

The specified attribute must be of some tuple type.

```
<user tuple op inv>
   ::=    <user tuple op name> ( <argument commalist> )
```

```
<tuple extractor inv>
   ::=    TUPLE FROM <relation exp>
```

The *<relation exp>* must denote a relation of cardinality one.

```
<tuple assign>
   ::=    <tuple var ref> := <tuple exp>
       |  <tuple update>
```

In the first format, the tuple variable identified by *<tuple var ref>* and the tuple value denoted by *<tuple exp>* must be of the same tuple type.

```
<tuple update>
   ::=    UPDATE <tuple var ref>
                 <ne attribute update commalist>
```

The individual *<attribute update>*s are executed in sequence as written.

```
<attribute update>
   ::=    <attribute ref> := <exp>
       |  <tuple update>
       |  <relation update>
```

In the first format, *<attribute ref>* and *<exp>* must be of the same type; also, *<exp>* is allowed to include an *<attribute ref>* wherever a *<scalar selector inv>* is allowed.

```
<tuple comp>
    ::=    <tuple exp> <tuple comp op> <tuple exp>
       |   <tuple exp> IN <relation exp>
```

In both formats, the values denoted by the two comparands must have the same heading. Tuple comparisons are a special case of the syntactic category *<bool exp>*.

```
<tuple comp op>
    ::=   =  |  ≠
```

RELATIONAL OPERATIONS

Note: For "safety" reasons, **Tutorial D** deliberately does not support the generalized ◄OR► and ◄NOT► operators of the algebra **A** as defined in Chapter 4. Of course, it does support the traditional UNION and MINUS operators in their place.

```
<relation exp>
    ::=    <relation selector inv>
       |   <relation var ref>
       |   <THE_ op inv>
       |   <relation op inv>
       |   <with exp>
       |   <introduced name>
       |   ( <relation exp> )

<relation selector inv>
    ::=    RELATION [ { <heading> } ] { <tuple exp commalist> }
       |   TABLE_DEE
       |   TABLE_DUM
```

Every tuple denoted by some *<tuple exp>* in the *<tuple exp commalist>* must have the same heading, and that heading must be exactly the one defined by *<heading>* if *<heading>* is specified. If *<heading>* is not specified, the *<tuple exp commalist>* must not be empty. TABLE_DEE and TABLE_DUM are shorthand for the relation selector invocations RELATION{}{TUPLE{}} and RELATION{}{}, respectively (see Chapters 6 and 7 for further explanation).

```
<relation var ref>
    ::=    <relation var name>
       |   <THE_ pv inv>

<relation op inv>
    ::=    <builtin relation op inv>
       |   <user relation op inv>

<builtin relation op inv>
    ::=    <project>
       |   <other builtin relation op inv>

<project>
    ::=    <relation exp>
                   { [ ALL BUT ] attribute name commalist> }
```

The *<relation exp>* must not be an *<other builtin relation op inv>*.

```
<other builtin relation op inv>
    ::=    <rename> | <where> | <union> | <intersect> | <minus>
         | <join> | <compose> | <semiminus> | <semijoin>
         | <divide> | <extend> | <summarize> | <tclose>
         | <wrap> | <unwrap> | <group> | <ungroup>

<rename>
    ::=    <relation exp> RENAME <ne renaming commalist>
```

The *<relation exp>* must not be an *<other builtin relation op inv>*. The individual *<renaming>*s are executed in sequence as written.

```
<where>
    ::=    <relation exp> WHERE <bool exp>
```

The *<relation exp>* must not be an *<other builtin relation op inv>*. The *<bool exp>* is allowed to include an *<attribute ref>* wherever a *<scalar selector inv>* is allowed. *Note:* The *<where>* operator includes the restriction operator of classical relational algebra as a special case.

```
<union>
    ::=    <relation exp> UNION <relation exp>
```

The *<relation exp>*s must not be *<other builtin relation op inv>*s, except that either or both can be another *<union>*.

```
<intersect>
    ::=    <relation exp> INTERSECT <relation exp>
```

The *<relation exp>*s must not be *<other builtin relation op inv>*s, except that either or both can be another *<intersect>*.

```
<minus>
    ::=    <relation exp> MINUS <relation exp>
```

The *<relation exp>*s must not be *<other builtin relation op inv>*s.

```
<join>
    ::=    <relation exp> JOIN <relation exp>
```

The *<relation exp>*s must not be *<other builtin relation op inv>*s, except that either or both can be another *<join>*. *Note:* If the relations denoted by those *<relation exp>*s have no attribute names in common, the *<join>* degenerates to a Cartesian product. We choose not to provide any distinct syntax for this special case.

```
<compose>
    ::=    <relation exp> COMPOSE <relation exp>
```

The *<relation exp>*s must not be *<other builtin relation op inv>*s, except that either or both can be another *<compose>*. *Note:* If the relations denoted by those *<relation exp>*s have no attribute names in common, the *<compose>* degenerates to a *<join>* (and that *<join>* in turn degenerates to a Cartesian product).

```
<semiminus>
    ::=    <relation exp> SEMIMINUS <relation exp>
```

The *<relation exp>*s must not be *<other builtin relation op inv>*s. See the final section of this chapter for the semantics of *<semiminus>*.

```
<semijoin>
    ::=    <relation exp> SEMIJOIN <relation exp>
```

The *<relation exp>*s must not be *<other builtin relation op inv>*s. See the final section of this chapter for the semantics of *<semijoin>*.

```
<divide>
    ::=    <relation exp> DIVIDEBY <relation exp> PER <per>
```

The *<relation exp>*s must not be *<other builtin relation op inv>*s.

```
<per>
    ::=    <relation exp>
       |  ( <relation exp>, <relation exp> )
```

The *<relation exp>*s must not be *<other builtin relation op inv>*s. *Note:* Reference [35] defines two distinct "divide" operators that it calls the Small Divide and the Great Divide, respectively. In **Tutorial D,** a *<divide>* in which the *<per>* consists of just one *<relation exp>* is a Small Divide, a *<divide>* in which it consists of a parenthesized commalist of two *<relation exp>*s is a Great Divide. See the final section of this chapter, also the discussion of RM Prescription 18 in Chapter 6, for further explanation.

```
<extend>
    ::=    EXTEND <relation exp> ADD <ne extend add commalist>
```

The *<relation exp>* must not be an *<other builtin relation op inv>*. The individual *<extend add>*s are executed in sequence as written.

```
<summarize>
    ::=    SUMMARIZE <relation exp> PER <relation exp>
                        ADD <ne summarize add commalist>
```

The *<relation exp>*s must not be *<other builtin relation op inv>*s. The individual *<summarize add>*s are executed in sequence as written. *Note:* The SUMMARIZE supported by **Tutorial D** is the generalized version of that operator defined in reference [56]. See the final section of this chapter, also the discussion of RM Prescription 18 in Chapter 6, for further explanation.

```
<summarize add>
    ::=    <summary> AS <attribute name>

<summary>
    ::=    <summary type> [ ( <scalar exp> ) ]
```

The optional *<scalar exp>* and enclosing parentheses can be omitted only if the *<summary type>* is COUNT (see below). Observe that *<summary>* and *<agg*

op inv> are not the same thing! *Note:* It might be desirable in practice to extend the syntax of *<summary>* such that, e.g., a *<summary>* of the form

```
( MAX ( X ) - MIN ( Y ) ) / 2
```

would be legal. The precise syntax rules for such an extension are rather complicated, however, and not directly relevant to our main purpose; we therefore omit them here.

```
<summary type>
    ::=    COUNT | COUNTD | SUM | SUMD | AVG | AVGD | MAX | MIN
```

The "D" ("distinct") in COUNTD, SUMD, and AVGD means "eliminate redundant duplicate values before performing the aggregation."

```
<tclose>
    ::=    TCLOSE <relation exp>
```

The *<relation exp>* must not be an *<other builtin relation op inv>*. Furthermore, it must denote a relation of degree exactly two, and the two attributes of that relation must have the same type.

```
<wrap>
    ::=    <relation exp> WRAP <ne wrapping commalist>
```

The *<relation exp>* must not be an *<other builtin relation op inv>*. *Note:* See the discussion of RM Prescription 7 in Chapter 6 (also the final section of the present chapter) for an explanation of both *<wrap>* and *<unwrap>*.

```
<unwrap>
    ::=    <relation exp> UNWRAP <ne unwrapping commalist>
```

The *<relation exp>* must not be an *<other builtin relation op inv>*.

```
<group>
    ::=    <relation exp>
           GROUP ( [ ALL BUT ] <attribute name commalist> )
           AS <attribute name>
```

The *<relation exp>* must not be an *<other builtin relation op inv>*. *Note:* See the discussion of RM Prescription 7 in Chapter 6 (also the final section of the present chapter) for an explanation of both *<group>* and *<ungroup>*.

```
<ungroup>
    ::=    <relation exp> UNGROUP <attribute name>
```

The *<relation exp>* must not be an *<other builtin relation op inv>*. The attribute identified by the *<attribute name>* must be of some relation type.

```
<user relation op inv>
    ::=    <user relation op name> ( <argument commalist> )
```

```
<relation assign>
    ::=    <relation var ref> := <relation exp>
         |  <relation insert>
         |  <relation update>
         |  <relation delete>
```

In the first format, the relation variable identified by *<relation var ref>* and the relation value denoted by *<relation exp>* must be of the same relation type. An analogous remark applies to *<relation insert>* also (see below).

```
<relation insert>
    ::=    INSERT INTO <relation var ref> <relation exp>

<relation update>
    ::=    UPDATE <relation var ref> [ WHERE <bool exp> ]
                        <ne attribute update commalist>
```

The *<bool exp>* is allowed to include an *<attribute ref>* wherever a *<scalar selector inv>* is allowed. "For each tuple to be updated" (speaking *very* loosely!), the individual *<attribute update>*s are executed in sequence as written. Refer to the discussion of RM Prescription 21 in Chapter 6 for further explanation.

```
<relation delete>
    ::=    DELETE <relation var ref> [ WHERE <bool exp> ]
```

The *<bool exp>* is allowed to include an *<attribute ref>* wherever a *<scalar selector inv>* is allowed.

```
<relation comp>
    ::=    <relation exp> <relation comp op> <relation exp>
```

The relation values denoted by the two *<relation exp>*s must be of the same relation type. Relation comparisons are a special case of the syntactic category *<bool exp>*.

```
<relation comp op>
    ::=    = | ≠ | < | ≤ | > | ≥
```

In this context the operators "≤" and "<" denote "subset of" and "proper subset of," respectively; the operators "≥" and ">" denote "superset of" and "proper superset of," respectively.

RELATIONS AND ARRAYS

The Third Manifesto prohibits tuple-at-a-time retrieval from a relation (analogous to FETCH via a cursor in SQL). However, **Tutorial D** does allow a relation to be converted into an *array* (of tuples), so an effect analogous to such "tuple-at-a-time retrieval" can be obtained by first performing such a conversion and then iterating over the resulting array. But we deliberately adopt a very conservative approach to this part of the language. A fully orthogonal **D** would support arrays as "first-class citizens"—implying support for a general ARRAY type generator, and array variables, and array expressions, and array assignment, and array comparisons, etc., etc. However, to include such extensive support in **Tutorial D** would complicate the language unduly and very likely obscure many of our main points. For simplicity, therefore, we include only as much array support here as seems absolutely necessary; moreover, most of that support is deliberately somewhat special-cased. Note in particular that we choose not to include a syntactic category called *<array type name>*.

```
<array var def>
    ::=    VAR <array var name> ARRAY OF <tuple type>
```

Let *AV* be a **Tutorial D** array variable. The value of *AV* at any given time is a one-dimensional array containing zero or more tuples. If it contains at least one, the lower bound is one. Let the values of *AV* at times *t1* and *t2* be *a1* and *a2,* respectively. Then *a1* and *a2* need not necessarily contain the same number of tuples (so the upper bound varies with time). Note that the only way *AV* can acquire a new value is by means of a *<relation get>* (see below); in practice, of course, additional mechanisms will also be necessary (or at least desirable), but we choose not to specify any such mechanisms here.

```
<relation get>
    ::=    LOAD <array var name> FROM <relation exp>
                                    <sequence item commalist>
```

The tuple type associated with the array designated by *<array var name>* and the relation type of the relation denoted by *<relation exp>* must have the same heading.* If the *<sequence item commalist>* is empty, the target array is loaded in an implementation-defined sequence. *Note:* Although this operation is really an assignment (of a kind), we deliberately choose not to use assignment syntax for it in **Tutorial D** because it effectively involves an implicit type conversion (also known as a *coercion*) from a relation type to an array type, and—in accordance with OO Very Strong Suggestion 1—we do not wish to consider the question of such conversions for assignments in general.

```
<sequence item>
    ::=    <direction> <attribute name>
```

A useful extension in practice might be to permit *<scalar exp>* in place of *<attribute name>* here.

---

*It would be possible, and perhaps desirable, to permit the heading of the target array to be *some projection* of the heading of the specified relation. Such a feature could permit the sequence in which tuples were loaded into the array to be defined in terms of attributes whose values were not themselves to be retrieved—thereby allowing, e.g., retrieval of employee numbers and names in salary sequence without at the same time actually retrieving those salaries.

```
<direction>
    ::=   ASC | DESC

<relation set>
    ::=   LOAD <relation var ref> FROM <array var name>
```

The tuple type associated with the array denoted by *<array var name>* and the relation type of the relvar designated by *<relation var ref>* must have the same heading. Again we deliberately avoid the use of assignment syntax, for the same kind of reason as before. Note that the specified array must not include any duplicate tuples (which means that *<relation set>* is *not* the general "array to relation" conversion operator suggested by our *Manifesto*—see the discussion of OO Very Strong Suggestions 3 and 4 in Chapter 11—since it does not work for all arrays).

We also need a new kind of *<tuple exp>:*

```
<tuple exp>
    ::=   ... all previous possibilities, together with:
        | <array var name> ( <subscript> )

<subscript>
    ::=   <integer exp>
```

We omit the details of *<integer exp>*s here, except to note that an *<integer exp>* is of course a numeric expression and thus a special case of the syntactic category *<scalar exp>*.

Finally, we also need an *<array cardinality>* operator (a special case of the syntactic category *<integer exp>* just mentioned):

```
<array cardinality>
    ::=   COUNT ( <array var name> )
```

STATEMENTS

```
<statement>
    ::=   <statement body> ;

<statement body>
    ::=   <previously defined statement body>
        | <assignment>
        | <begin transaction> | <commit> | <rollback>
        | <with> | <call> | <return> | <case> | <if>
        | <do> | <while> | <leave> | <no op>
        | <compound statement body>

<previously defined statement body>
    ::=   <user scalar type def> | <user scalar type drop>
        | <tuple type def> | <relation type def>
        | <user scalar op def> | <user scalar op drop>
        | <user tuple op def> | <user tuple op drop>
        | <user relation op def> | <user relation op drop>
        | <scalar var def> | <tuple var def> | <relation var def>
        | <relation var drop>
        | <constraint def> | <constraint drop>
        | <array var def> | <relation get> | <relation set>

<assignment>
    ::=   <ne assign commalist>
```

A **Tutorial D** *<assignment>* corresponds to the *multiple* form of assignment required by RM Prescription 21. The individual *<assign>*s are executed in sequence as written.

```
<assign>
    ::=     <scalar assign>
        |   <tuple assign>
        |   <relation assign>

<begin transaction>
    ::=   BEGIN TRANSACTION
```

Nested transactions are supported (see OO Prescription 6); thus, it is legal to issue BEGIN TRANSACTION while a transaction is already in progress. The effect is to suspend execution of the transaction in progress and to begin a new ("child") transaction. COMMIT or ROLLBACK terminates execution of the transaction most recently begun, thereby reinstating the suspended "parent" transaction (if any) as the current one.

```
<commit>
    ::=   COMMIT

<rollback>
    ::=   ROLLBACK

<with>
    ::=   WITH <ne name intro commalist>
```

A *<with>* statement simply introduces shorthand names that can be used to simplify the formulation of subsequent statements.

```
<call>
    ::=   CALL <user scalar op name> ( <argument commalist> )

<return>
    ::=   RETURN [ ( <exp> ) ]

<case>
    ::=   CASE ;
            <ne when def list>
          [ ELSE <statement> ]
          END CASE

<when def>
    ::=   WHEN <bool exp> THEN <statement>

<if>
    ::=   IF <bool exp> THEN <statement>
                        [ ELSE <statement> ]
          END IF

<do>
    ::=   [ <statement name> : ]
          DO <scalar var ref> :=
            <integer exp> TO <integer exp> ;
            <statement>
          END DO
```

```
<while>
    ::=     [ <statement name> : ]
            WHILE <bool exp> ;
                <statement>
            END WHILE

<leave>
    ::=     LEAVE <statement name>
```

A variant of *<leave>* that merely terminates the current iteration of the loop and begins the next might also be useful in practice.

```
<no op>
    ::=     ... an empty string

<compound statement body>
    ::=     BEGIN ; <ne statement list>  END
```

SYNTAX SUMMARY

In this section we present all of the **Tutorial D** production rules in alphabetical order, for ease of subsequent reference. Please note, however, that language features defined (or merely hinted at, in some cases) in previous sections in simple prose form instead of by means of formal production rules are not included. For one example, the boolean operator IS_EMPTY is not mentioned. For another, a production rule for *<scalar selector inv>* is also not included.

```
<agg op inv>
    ::=     <agg op name> ( <relation exp> [, <attribute ref> ] )

<agg op name>
    ::=     COUNT | SUM | AVG | MAX | MIN

<application relation var def>
    ::=     VAR <relation var name> <scope> <relation type>

<argument>
    ::=     <scalar exp>

<array cardinality>
    ::=     COUNT ( <array var name> )

<array var def>
    ::=     VAR <array var name> ARRAY OF <tuple type>

<assign>
    ::=     <scalar assign>
          | <tuple assign>
          | <relation assign>

<assignment>
    ::=     <ne assign commalist>

<attribute extractor inv>
    ::=     <attribute name> FROM <tuple exp>
```

```
<attribute name and type>
    ::=    <attribute name> <type>

<attribute ref>
    ::=    <attribute name>
        |  <THE_ pv name> ( <attribute ref> )

<attribute update>
    ::=    <attribute ref> := <exp>
        |  <tuple update>
        |  <relation update>

<begin transaction>
    ::=    BEGIN TRANSACTION

<builtin relation op inv>
    ::=    <project>
        |  <other builtin relation op inv>

<builtin scalar op inv>
    ::=    ... the usual possibilities

<builtin scalar type name>
    ::=    BOOLEAN
        |  INTEGER
        |  RATIONAL
        |  CHARACTER | CHAR

<builtin tuple op inv>
    ::=    <tuple project>
        |  <other builtin tuple op inv>

<call>
    ::=    CALL <user scalar op name> ( <argument commalist> )

<candidate key def>
    ::=    KEY { <attribute name commalist> }

<case>
    ::=    CASE ;
               <ne when def list>
           [ ELSE <statement> ]
           END CASE

<commit>
    ::=    COMMIT

<compose>
    ::=    <relation exp> COMPOSE <relation exp>

<compound statement body>
    ::=    BEGIN ; <ne statement list>  END

<constraint def>
    ::=    CONSTRAINT <constraint name> ( <bool exp> )

<constraint drop>
    ::=    DROP CONSTRAINT <constraint name>

<database relation var def>
    ::=    <real relation var def>
        |  <virtual relation var def>

<direction>
    ::=    ASC | DESC
```

```
<divide>
    ::=     <relation exp> DIVIDEBY <relation exp> PER <per>

<do>
    ::=     [ <statement name> : ]
            DO <scalar var ref> :=
                <integer exp> TO <integer exp> ;
                <statement>
            END DO

<exp>
    ::=     <scalar exp>
        |   <tuple exp>
        |   <relation exp>

<extend>
    ::=     EXTEND <relation exp> ADD <ne extend add commalist>

<extend add>
    ::=     <exp> AS <attribute name>

<group>
    ::=     <relation exp>
                GROUP ( [ ALL BUT ] <attribute name commalist> )
                AS <attribute name>

<heading>
    ::=     <attribute name and type commalist>

<if>
    ::=     IF <bool exp> THEN <statement>
                        [ ELSE <statement> ]
            END IF

<intersect>
    ::=     <relation exp> INTERSECT <relation exp>

<join>
    ::=     <relation exp> JOIN <relation exp>

<leave>
    ::=     LEAVE <statement name>

<minus>
    ::=     <relation exp> MINUS <relation exp>

<name intro>
    ::=     <exp> AS <introduced name>

<no op>
    ::=     ... an empty string

<other builtin relation op inv>
    ::=     <rename> | <where> | <union> | <intersect> | <minus>
        |   <join> | <compose> | <semiminus> | <semijoin>
        |   <divide> | <extend> | <summarize> | <tclose>
        |   <wrap> | <unwrap> | <group> | <ungroup>

<other builtin tuple op inv>
    ::=     <tuple rename> | <tuple join> | <tuple extend>
        |   <tuple wrap> | <tuple unwrap>

<parameter def>
    ::=     <parameter name> <scalar type>
```

```
<per>
    ::=    <relation exp>
         | ( <relation exp>, <relation exp> )

<possrep component def>
    ::=    [ <possrep component name> ] <type>

<possrep def>
    ::=    POSSREP [ <possrep name> ]
                    ( <ne possrep component def commalist> )

<previously defined statement body>
    ::=    <user scalar type def> | <user scalar type drop>
         | <tuple type def> | <relation type def>
         | <user scalar op def> | <user scalar op drop>
         | <user tuple op def> | <user tuple op drop>
         | <user relation op def> | <user relation op drop>
         | <scalar var def> | <tuple var def> | <relation var def>
         | <relation var drop>
         | <constraint def> | <constraint drop>
         | <array var def> | <relation get> | <relation set>

<project>
    ::=    <relation exp>
                    { [ ALL BUT ] <attribute name commalist> }

<real relation var def>
    ::=    VAR <relation var name> REAL <relation type>

<relation assign>
    ::=    <relation var ref> := <relation exp>
         | <relation insert>
         | <relation update>
         | <relation delete>

<relation comp>
    ::=    <relation exp> <relation comp op> <relation exp>

<relation comp op>
    ::=    = | ≠ | < | ≤ | > | ≥

<relation delete>
    ::=    DELETE <relation var ref> [ WHERE <bool exp> ]

<relation exp>
    ::=    <relation selector inv>
         | <relation var ref>
         | <THE_ op inv>
         | <relation op inv>
         | <with exp>
         | <introduced name>
         | ( <relation exp> )

<relation get>
    ::=    LOAD <array var name> FROM <relation exp>
                                     <sequence item commalist>

<relation insert>
    ::=    INSERT INTO <relation var ref> <relation exp>

<relation op inv>
    ::=    <builtin relation op inv>
         | <user relation op inv>
```

```
<relation selector inv>
    ::=    RELATION [ { <heading> } ] { <tuple exp commalist> }
         | TABLE_DEE
         | TABLE_DUM

<relation set>
    ::=    LOAD <relation var ref> FROM <array var name>

<relation type>
    ::=    <relation type name>
         | SAME_TYPE_AS ( <relation exp> )

<relation type name>
    ::=    RELATION { <heading> }

<relation update>
    ::=    UPDATE <relation var ref> [ WHERE <bool exp> ]
                        <ne attribute update commalist>

<relation var def>
    ::=    <database relation var def>
                            <candidate key def list>
         | <application relation var def>
                            <candidate key def list>

<relation var drop>
    ::=    DROP VAR <relation var name>

<relation var ref>
    ::=    <relation var name>
         | <THE_ pv inv>

<rename>
    ::=    <relation exp> RENAME <ne renaming commalist>

<renaming>
    ::=    <attribute name> AS <attribute name>
         | PREFIX <character string literal>
               AS <character string literal>
         | SUFFIX <character string literal>
               AS <character string literal>

<return>
    ::=    RETURN [ ( <exp> ) ]

<returns def>
    ::=    RETURNS ( <scalar type> )

<returns or updates def>
    ::=    <returns def> | <updates def>

<rollback>
    ::=    ROLLBACK

<scalar assign>
    ::=    <scalar var ref> := <scalar exp>

<scalar comp>
    ::=    <scalar exp> <scalar comp op> <scalar exp>

<scalar comp op>
    ::=    = | ≠ | ... etc. (depending on type)
```

```
<scalar exp>
    ::=    <scalar selector inv>
        |  <scalar var ref>
        |  <THE_ op inv>
        |  <scalar op inv>
        |  <attribute extractor inv>
        |  <agg op inv>
        |  <with exp>
        |  <introduced name>
        |  ( <scalar exp> )

<scalar op inv>
    ::=    <builtin scalar op inv>
        |  <user scalar op inv>

<scalar type>
    ::=    <scalar type name>
        |  SAME_TYPE_AS ( <scalar exp> )

<scalar type constraint>
    ::=    CONSTRAINT ( <bool exp> )

<scalar type name>
    ::=    <builtin scalar type name>
        |  <user scalar type name>

<scalar var def>
    ::=    VAR <scalar var name> <scalar type>
                                    [ INIT ( <scalar exp> ) ]

<scalar var ref>
    ::=    <scalar var name>
        |  <THE_ pv inv>

<scope>
    ::=    LOCAL | GLOBAL

<semijoin>
    ::=    <relation exp> SEMIJOIN <relation exp>

<semiminus>
    ::=    <relation exp> SEMIMINUS <relation exp>

<sequence item>
    ::=    <direction> <attribute name>

<statement>
    ::=    <statement body> ;

<statement body>
    ::=    <previously defined statement body>
        |  <assignment>
        |  <begin transaction> | <commit> | <rollback>
        |  <with> | <call> | <return> | <case> | <if>
        |  <do> | <while> | <leave> | <no op>
        |  <compound statement body>

<subscript>
    ::=    <integer exp>

<summarize>
    ::=    SUMMARIZE <relation exp> PER <relation exp>
                            ADD <ne summarize add commalist>
```

```
<summarize add>
    ::=    <summary> AS <attribute name>

<summary>
    ::=    <summary type> [ ( <scalar exp> ) ]

<summary type>
    ::=    COUNT | COUNTD | SUM | SUMD | AVG | AVGD | MAX | MIN

<tclose>
    ::=    TCLOSE <relation exp>

<THE_ op inv>
    ::=    <THE_ op name> ( <scalar exp> )

<THE_ pv inv>
    ::=    <THE_ pv name> ( <scalar var ref> )

<tuple assign>
    ::=    <tuple var ref> := <tuple exp>
         | <tuple update>

<tuple comp>
    ::=    <tuple exp> <tuple comp op> <tuple exp>
         | <tuple exp> IN <relation exp>

<tuple component>
    ::=    <attribute name> <exp>

<tuple comp op>
    ::=    = | ≠

<tuple exp>
    ::=    <tuple selector inv>
         | <tuple var ref>
         | <THE_ op inv>
         | <tuple op inv>
         | <attribute extractor inv>
         | <tuple extractor inv>
         | <with exp>
         | <introduced name>
         | ( <tuple exp> )
         | <array var name> ( <subscript> )

<tuple extend>
    ::=    EXTEND <tuple exp> ADD <ne extend add commalist>

<tuple extractor inv>
    ::=    TUPLE FROM <relation exp>

<tuple join>
    ::=    <tuple exp> JOIN <tuple exp>

<tuple op inv>
    ::=    <builtin tuple op inv>
         | <user tuple op inv>

<tuple project>
    ::=    <tuple exp>
                    { [ ALL BUT ] <attribute name commalist> }

<tuple rename>
    ::=    <tuple exp> RENAME <ne renaming commalist>
```

```
<tuple selector inv>
    ::=    TUPLE { <tuple component commalist> }

<tuple type>
    ::=    <tuple type name>
        |  SAME_TYPE_AS ( <tuple exp> )

<tuple type name>
    ::=    TUPLE { <heading> }

<tuple unwrap>
    ::=    <tuple exp> UNWRAP <ne unwrapping commalist>

<tuple update>
    ::=    UPDATE <tuple var ref>
                  <ne attribute update commalist>

<tuple var def>
    ::=    VAR <tuple var name> <tuple type>
                                      [ INIT ( <tuple exp> ) ]

<tuple var ref>
    ::=    <tuple var name>
        |  <THE_ pv inv>

<tuple wrap>
    ::=    <tuple exp> WRAP <ne wrapping commalist>

<type>
    ::=    <scalar type>
        |  <tuple type>
        |  <relation type>

<ungroup>
    ::=    <relation exp> UNGROUP <attribute name>

<union>
    ::=    <relation exp> UNION <relation exp>

<unwrap>
    ::=    <relation exp> UNWRAP <ne unwrapping commalist>

<unwrapping>
    ::=    <attribute name>

<updates def>
    ::=    UPDATES ( <ne parameter name commalist> )

<user relation op def>
    ::=    OPERATOR <user relation op name>
                  ( <parameter def commalist> )
                    RETURNS ( <relation type> ) ;
                    <statement>
              END OPERATOR

<user relation op drop>
    ::=    DROP OPERATOR <user relation op name>

<user relation op inv>
    ::=    <user relation op name> ( <argument commalist> )
```

```
<user scalar op def>
    ::=    OPERATOR <user scalar op name>
                    ( <parameter def commalist> )
                    <returns or updates def> ;
                    <statement>
           END OPERATOR

<user scalar op drop>
    ::=    DROP OPERATOR <user scalar op name>

<user scalar op inv>
    ::=    <user scalar op name> ( <argument commalist> )

<user scalar type def>
    ::=    TYPE <user scalar type name>
                <ne possrep def list>
           [ <scalar type constraint> ]

<user scalar type drop>
    ::=    DROP TYPE <user scalar type name>

<user tuple op def>
    ::=    OPERATOR <user tuple op name>
                    ( <parameter def commalist> )
                    RETURNS ( <tuple type> ) ;
                    <statement>
           END OPERATOR

<user tuple op drop>
    ::=    DROP OPERATOR <user tuple op name>

<user tuple op inv>
    ::=    <user tuple op name> ( <argument commalist> )

<virtual relation var def>
    ::=    VAR <relation var name> VIRTUAL <relation exp>

<when def>
    ::=    WHEN <bool exp> THEN <statement>

<where>
    ::=    <relation exp> WHERE <bool exp>

<while>
    ::=    [ <statement name> : ]
           WHILE <bool exp> ;
                <statement>
           END WHILE

<with>
    ::=    WITH <ne name intro commalist>

<with exp>
    ::=    WITH <ne name intro commalist> : <exp>

<wrap>
    ::=    <relation exp> WRAP <ne wrapping commalist>

<wrapping>
    ::=    ( [ ALL BUT ] <attribute name commalist> )
                            AS <attribute name>
```

MAPPING THE RELATIONAL OPERATIONS

As noted in the introduction, many—in fact, almost all—of the builtin relational operators in **Tutorial D** are really just shorthands. In this section we justify this remark by showing how the operators in question map to those of the relational algebra **A** defined in Chapter 4. Recall that **A** has the following operators (in alphabetical order): ◄AND►, ◄COMPOSE►, ◄NOT►, ◄OR►, ◄REMOVE►, ◄RENAME►, and ◄TCLOSE► (not all primitive).

We now proceed to discuss the relational operators of **Tutorial D** one by one. The notation is intended to be self-explanatory, by and large. One general point: Whenever we refer to, e.g., A as a common attribute of two relations *R1* and *R2,* we mean that *R1* and *R2* both have an attribute of that name A, and further that the two attributes in question are both of the same type.

Renaming: The **Tutorial D** *<rename>*

```
R RENAME A AS B
```

is semantically equivalent to the **A** expression

```
R ◄RENAME► (A,B)
```

Other **Tutorial D** *<rename>* formats are just shorthand for repeated application of the format shown above.

Transitive closure: The **Tutorial D** *<tclose>*

```
TCLOSE R
```

is semantically equivalent to the **A** expression

```
◄TCLOSE► R
```

Projection: The **Tutorial D** *<project>*

```
R { ALL BUT A }
```

is semantically equivalent to the **A** expression

```
R ◄REMOVE► A
```

Other **Tutorial D** *<project>* formats are readily defined in terms of the format shown above.

Join: The **Tutorial D** *<join>*

```
R1 JOIN R2
```

is semantically equivalent to the **A** expression

```
R1 ◄AND► R2
```

The **Tutorial D** *<intersect>* *R1* INTERSECT *R2* is just that special case of *R1* JOIN *R2* in which *R1* and *R2* have the same heading, so the ◄AND► operator of **A** takes care of INTERSECT as well.

Compose: The **Tutorial D** *<compose>*

    R1 COMPOSE R2

is semantically equivalent to the **A** expression

    R1 ◄COMPOSE► R2

Union: The **Tutorial D** *<union>*

    R1 UNION R2

(where *R1* and *R2* have the same heading) is semantically equivalent to the **A** expression

    R1 ◄OR► R2

Difference: The **Tutorial D** *<minus>*

    R1 MINUS R2

(where *R1* and *R2* have the same heading) is semantically equivalent to the **A** expression

    R1 ◄AND► (◄NOT► R2)

Semidifference: The **Tutorial D** *<semiminus>*

    R1 SEMIMINUS R2

is semantically equivalent to the **Tutorial D** expression

    (R1 { A, B, ..., C } MINUS R2 { A, B, ..., C }) JOIN R1

(where *A, B, ..., C* are all of the attributes common to *R1* and *R2*). Since this latter expression involves only operators that have already been shown to be expressible in **A,** it follows that semidifference can also be expressed in **A.**

Semijoin: The **Tutorial D** *<semijoin>*

    R1 SEMIJOIN R2

is semantically equivalent to the **Tutorial D** expression

    R1 JOIN R2 { A, B, ..., C }

(where *A, B, ..., C* are all of the attributes common to *R1* and *R2*), and can therefore be expressed in **A.**

Division: The **Tutorial D** *<divide>*

    R1 DIVIDEBY R2 PER R3

(a Small Divide) is shorthand for the **Tutorial D** expression

    R1 { A1 }
        MINUS ((R1 { A1 } JOIN R2 { A2 })
                    MINUS R3 { A1, A2 }) { A1 }

(where *A1* is the set of attributes common to *R1* and *R3* and *A2* is the set of attributes common to *R2* and *R3*), and can therefore be expressed in **A.**

Likewise, the **Tutorial D** *<divide>*

```
R1 DIVIDEBY R2 PER ( R3, R4 )
```

(a Great Divide) is shorthand for the **Tutorial D** expression

```
( R1 { A1 } JOIN R2 { A2 } )
    MINUS ( ( R1 { A1 } JOIN R4 { A2, A3 } )
              MINUS ( R3 { A1, A3 }
                      JOIN R4 { A2, A3 } ) ) { A1, A2 }
```

(where *A1* is the set of attributes common to *R1* and *R3*, *A2* is the set of attributes common to *R2* and *R4*, and *A3* is the set of attributes common to *R3* and *R4*), and can therefore be expressed in **A.**

Extension: As in Chapter 4, let PLUS be a relation constant with heading

```
{ X INTEGER, Y INTEGER, Z INTEGER }
```

and with body consisting of all tuples such that the Z value is equal to the sum of the X and Y values. Then the **Tutorial D** *<extend>*

```
EXTEND R ADD A + B AS C
```

(where we assume without loss of generality that *A* and *B* are attributes of *R*,* of type INTEGER) is semantically equivalent to the **Tutorial D** expression

```
R JOIN ( PLUS RENAME X AS A, Y AS B, Z AS C )
```

and can therefore be expressed in **A.** Analogous equivalents can be provided for all other forms of *<extend>* (including forms in which the *<exp>* in the *<extend add>* is tuple- or relation-valued). For example, the **Tutorial D** expression

```
EXTEND R ADD TUPLE { A A, B B } AS C
```

is semantically equivalent to the **Tutorial D** expression

```
R JOIN S
```

where *S* is a relation with heading

```
{ A TA, B TB, C TUPLE { A TA, B TB } }
```

containing exactly one tuple for each possible combination of *A* and *B* values, in which the *C* value is exactly the corresponding *(A,B)* tuple (*TA* and *TB* here being the types of attributes *A* and *B,* respectively).

Restriction: Let ONE be a relation constant with heading

```
{ X INTEGER }
```

---

*If they are not, we can effectively make them so by means of appropriate joins. An analogous remark applies to many of our examples; for brevity, we choose not to make it every time.

and with body consisting of a single tuple, with X value one. Then the **Tutorial D** *<where>*

```
R WHERE A = 1
```

(where *A* is an attribute of *R* of type INTEGER) is semantically equivalent to the **Tutorial D** expression

```
R JOIN ( ONE RENAME X AS A )
```

and can therefore be expressed in **A.**

Now let GT be a relation constant with heading

```
{ X INTEGER, Y INTEGER }
```

and with body consisting of all tuples such that the X value is greater than the Y value. Then the **Tutorial D** *<where>*

```
R WHERE A > B
```

(where *A* and *B* are attributes of *R* of type INTEGER) is semantically equivalent to the **Tutorial D** expression

```
R JOIN ( GT RENAME X AS A, Y AS B )
```

and can therefore be expressed in **A.**

An analogous definition can be provided for the expression *R* WHERE *A* < *B* and all other simple restrictions. As for *<where>* expressions involving the logical operators AND, OR, and NOT (e.g., *R* WHERE *A* > *B* OR *C* < *D*), they can be defined as intersections, unions, or differences (respectively) of simple restrictions. Hence, all *<where>* expressions can be mapped to **A.**

Summarization: The **Tutorial D** *<summarize>*

```
SUMMARIZE R1 PER R2 ADD agg ( exp ) AS Z
```

(where *R2* has attributes *A*, *B*, ..., *C* and *R1* has the same attributes and possibly more) is semantically equivalent to the **Tutorial D** expression

```
( EXTEND R2 ADD
  R1 JOIN RELATION { TUPLE { A A, B B, ..., C C } } AS Y,
  agg' ( ( EXTEND Y ADD exp AS X ) { X }, X ) AS Z )
{ ALL BUT Y }
```

(where *agg'* is identical to *agg* unless *agg* is COUNTD, SUMD, or AVGD, in which case *agg'* is COUNT, SUM, or AVG, respectively, and where the projection over *X* in the third line is included only if *agg* is COUNTD, SUMD, or AVGD), and can therefore be expressed in **A.**

Wrapping and unwrapping: The **Tutorial D** *<wrap>*

```
R WRAP ( A, B, ..., C ) AS X
```

is shorthand for the **Tutorial D** expression

```
( EXTEND R ADD TUPLE { A A, B B, ..., C C } AS X )
                                    { ALL BUT A, B, ..., C }
```

and can therefore be expressed in **A.** Likewise, the **Tutorial D** *<unwrap>*

```
R UNWRAP X
```

is shorthand for the **Tutorial D** expression

```
( EXTEND R ADD A FROM X AS A,
               B FROM X AS B,
               ......
               C FROM X AS C ) { ALL BUT X }
```

(where A, B, ..., C are all the attributes of X), and can therefore also be expressed in **A.**

   Grouping and ungrouping: Let relation R have attributes A, B, ..., C, D, E, ..., F. Then the **Tutorial D** *<group>*

```
R GROUP ( D, E, ..., F ) AS X
```

is shorthand for the **Tutorial D** expression

```
( EXTEND R
  ADD RELATION { TUPLE { TR R } } ,
      RELATION { TUPLE { D D, E E, ..., F F } } AS TX ,
      TR COMPOSE TX AS X )
{ A, B, ..., C, X }
```

(where TR and TX are attribute names not already appearing in R), and can therefore be expressed in **A.** Likewise, the **Tutorial D** *<ungroup>*

```
R UNGROUP X
```

(where R has attributes A, B, ..., C, and X, and X in turn is a relation-valued attribute with attributes D, E, ..., F) is shorthand for the **Tutorial D** expression

```
( EXTEND ( R COMPOSE T )
  ADD A FROM Y AS A, B FROM Y AS B, ..., C FROM Y AS C )
{ A, B, ..., C, D, E, ..., F }
```

where T is a relation with heading

```
{ X RELATION { D, E, ..., F }, Y TUPLE { D, E, ..., F } }
```

and with body containing every possible tuple such that the Y value (a tuple) is a member of the body of the X value (a relation). Thus it follows that the original *<ungroup>* can be expressed in **A.**

PART III

INFORMAL DISCUSSIONS AND EXPLANATIONS

In many ways, the chapters that follow are really the heart of the book. There are six of them, one for each of the six sections of the *Manifesto* itself:

6. RM Prescriptions
7. RM Proscriptions
8. OO Prescriptions
9. OO Proscriptions
10. RM Very Strong Suggestions
11. OO Very Strong Suggestions

We remind you once again that throughout the body of this book the abbreviation OO stands for **Other Orthogonal.**

Each chapter contains one section for each prescription, proscription, or suggestion, as applicable. (As a consequence, the chapters vary in length considerably; Chapter 6 in particular is very long.) Each section begins by repeating the formal statement from Chapter 3 of the relevant prescription or proscription or suggestion, shown in italics in order to set it off from the discussions and examples that follow.

The examples are expressed in **Tutorial D,** of course, but for the most part they should be fairly self-explanatory—you should not need to study Chapter 5 in depth in order to understand them (though you should probably take at least a quick look at it).

Note: Most of those examples are based on the familiar suppliers-and-parts database. For convenience, we give a set of sample values for that database here (see Fig. III.1). Corresponding data definitions can be found in Chapter 6.

S	S#	SNAME	STATUS	CITY
	S1	Smith	20	London
	S2	Jones	10	Paris
	S3	Blake	30	Paris
	S4	Clark	20	London
	S5	Adams	30	Athens

P	P#	PNAME	COLOR	WEIGHT	CITY
	P1	Nut	Red	12	London
	P2	Bolt	Green	17	Paris
	P3	Screw	Blue	17	Rome
	P4	Screw	Red	14	London
	P5	Cam	Blue	12	Paris
	P6	Cog	Red	19	London

SP	S#	P#	QTY
	S1	P1	300
	S1	P2	200
	S1	P3	400
	S1	P4	200
	S1	P5	100
	S1	P6	100
	S2	P1	300
	S2	P2	400
	S3	P2	200
	S4	P2	200
	S4	P4	300
	S4	P5	400

Fig. III.1   The suppliers-and-parts database: sample values (attribute type names omitted for simplicity)

With respect to Chapter 7, incidentally ("RM Proscriptions"), you might notice that several of the proscriptions in question are logical consequences of the *pre*-scriptions described in Chapter 6. In view of the many unfortunate mistakes we observe in the design of the language SQL, however, we felt it necessary to spell out some of those consequences explicitly in the *Manifesto* (and in this book), by way of clarification.

One last point: In general, the *Manifesto* is intended to be open-ended. That is, anything not explicitly prescribed is permitted, unless it is explicitly *pro*scribed; likewise, anything not explicitly proscribed is permitted too, unless it clashes with something explicitly *pre*scribed.

RM Prescriptions

RM PRESCRIPTION 1: SCALAR TYPES

*A **scalar data type**—**scalar type** for short, also known as a **domain**—is a named set of scalar values. Scalar types* T1 *and* T2 *are equal if and only if they are in fact the same type (note in particular, therefore, that two scalar types that are identical in all respects except for their names are different types).* **D** *shall provide facilities for users to define their own scalar types (user-defined scalar types); other scalar types shall be provided by the system (builtin or system-defined scalar types). It shall be possible to destroy user-defined scalar types. Values of a given scalar type, and variables whose values are constrained to be of a given scalar type, shall be operable upon solely by means of the operators defined for that scalar type (see RM Prescription 3). For each scalar type and each declared possible representation of that type (see RM Prescription 4), those operators shall include:*

    a. *An operator called a* selector *whose purpose is to select an arbitrary value of the scalar type in question (again, see RM Prescription 4);*

    b. *A set of operators whose purpose is to expose the possible representation in question (see RM Prescription 5).*

*The system-defined scalar types shall include the type **truth value** (containing just two values,* true *and* false*). All four monadic and 16 dyadic logical operators shall be supported, directly or indirectly, for this scalar type.*

———— ♦♦♦♦♦ ————

Domains have always been a fundamental ingredient in the relational model (despite the fact that, so far as implementations are concerned, they have been honored more in the breach than the observance). In fact, of course, as explained in Chapter 2, a domain is nothing more nor less than a *data type* (*type* for short), and we prefer this latter term—though we do also use the term *domain* from time to time, treating the two as interchangeable. *Note:* The terms *domain* and *type* as we define them are indeed interchangeable, but the terms *domain* and *scalar type* are not; a domain can also be what we call a *generated* type, and the particular generated types we prescribe are not scalar (see below). Also, the term *object class*—*class* for short—is sometimes used in place of *domain* or *type;* as noted in Chapter 1, however, we prefer not to use object terminology at all, except informally.

It follows from the foregoing that the term *type* covers both scalar and nonscalar types. In practice, however, we often use just *type,* unqualified, to mean a scalar type specifically or a nonscalar type specifically or both, as the context demands, so long as there is no risk of ambiguity.

We refer generically to values of some scalar type as *scalar values* (*scalars* for short, or just *values* if there is no risk of ambiguity). By the same token, we refer generically to variables whose values are constrained to be scalars as *scalar variables* (or just *variables* if there is no risk of ambiguity). Note, however, that the actual representation—i.e., the physical or internal encoding—of such "scalar" values and variables can be arbitrarily complex; for example, a given scalar value might have an actual representation consisting of an array of stacks of lists of character strings, in appropriate circumstances. We adopt the scalar terminology merely in order:

- To distinguish the types in question from certain generated types, especially *tuple* and *relation* types (see RM Prescriptions 6–7 and 9–10), and possibly others as well (see OO Very Strong Suggestions 3–4); also

- To distinguish values and variables of the types in question from values and variables of those generated types.

Note carefully, however, that no matter how complex their actual representation might be, scalar types have *no user-visible components.** (Actual representations are an implementation matter, of course, not something that is of concern to the model.) By contrast, generated types—at least the ones we prescribe, *viz.,* tuple and relation types—certainly do have user-visible components; more specifically, they both involve a set of user-visible *attributes* (see RM Prescriptions 6 and 7).

Scalar types can be either user- or system-defined ("builtin"). We require that at least one builtin scalar type be supported, namely the—absolutely fundamental!—type **truth value** (referred to in **Tutorial D** as BOOLEAN); for definiteness, we assume

---

*Do not be misled by the fact that scalar types do have "possible representations" and those possible representations in turn do have components that are user-visible (see RM Prescription 4 for further explanation). *Note:* Given that they have no user-visible components, scalar types might be said to be "atomic." We do not use such terminology, however, because it has led to too much misunderstanding in the past (on our own part as much as anyone else's, we hasten to add); instead, we concentrate on our improved understanding of the true nature of *first normal form* [34] (see RM Prescription 10).

that support for that type includes (though is not limited to) the operators NOT, AND, and OR and the literals TRUE and FALSE. As noted in Chapter 5, we also assume for the purposes of this book that the builtin scalar types INTEGER, RATIONAL, and CHARACTER (abbreviated CHAR) are supported as well, with appropriate operators and literals in each case.

Now we turn to user-defined scalar types. Here are some **Tutorial D** examples. First we consider the suppliers-and-parts database. Let us assume that attributes supplier status, supplier city, and part city in that database are defined in terms of *builtin* types, not user-defined ones (the attribute definitions in question are shown in the section on RM Prescription 13 later in this chapter). Here then are the necessary user-defined types for the other attributes in that database:

```
TYPE S# POSSREP ( CHAR ) ;

TYPE P# POSSREP ( CHAR ) ;

TYPE NAME POSSREP ( CHAR ) ;

TYPE COLOR POSSREP ( CHAR ) ;

TYPE WEIGHT POSSREP ( RATIONAL ) ;

TYPE QTY POSSREP ( INTEGER ) ;
```

Explanation: Type S# (supplier numbers) has just one *declared possible representation* ("POSSREP"), the name of which is—by default—also S#. (Possible representations are discussed in detail later, under RM Prescriptions 4 and 5.) That possible representation in turn has just one component, the name of which is—again by default—the same as that of the possible representation, namely S# again. And since that component is defined to be of type CHAR, and since we have not specified any *type constraint* for type S# (see RM Prescription 23), the set of valid supplier numbers is, precisely, the set of all values that can be represented by character strings.

Type P# (part numbers) is similar to type S#; note, however, that S# and P# are different types, even though they have essentially the same declared possible representation, because they have different names. Types NAME, COLOR, WEIGHT, and QTY are also all somewhat similar.

Here are some more examples (note carefully that they are still all examples of *scalar* types specifically, even the last one):

```
TYPE LENGTH POSSREP ( RATIONAL ) ;

TYPE POINT
     POSSREP POINT ( X RATIONAL, Y RATIONAL )
     POSSREP POLAR ( R RATIONAL, THETA RATIONAL ) ;

TYPE ELLIPSE
     POSSREP ( A LENGTH, B LENGTH, CTR POINT ) ;

TYPE POLYGON
     POSSREP ( VERTICES
              RELATION { V# INTEGER, VERTEX POINT } ) ;
```

Explanation: Type LENGTH is again somewhat analogous to the types we have already seen (S#, P#, etc.). Type POINT differs from the previous examples, however, in that it has two distinct declared possible representations—one, POINT, consisting of Cartesian coordinates X and Y, and the other, POLAR, consisting of polar coordinates R and THETA. In practice, it is only if a given type has two or more declared possible representations, as in this example, that it is necessary to give those possible representations explicit names. Again, see RM Prescriptions 4 and 5 for a detailed discussion of possible representations.

Type ELLIPSE differs from the previous examples in that its declared possible representation—named ELLIPSE by default—involves user-defined types instead of builtin ones. *Note:* Components A, B, and CTR of that possible representation correspond to the major semiaxis *a,* the minor semiaxis *b,* and the center *ctr,* respectively, of the ellipse in question. We assume for simplicity that ellipses are always oriented such that their major axis is horizontal and their minor axis vertical (implying that *a, b,* and *ctr* together do indeed constitute a valid possible representation).

Finally, type POLYGON differs from the previous examples in that the sole component, VERTICES, of its declared possible representation (which is named POLYGON by default) is *relation-valued* (see RM Prescription 7). That is, a given polygon might possibly be represented by a relation containing one tuple for each vertex of the polygon in question; that tuple would contain a vertex number (a value of type INTEGER), together with the corresponding vertex itself (a value of type POINT). To repeat, however, polygons are still *scalar values* as far as we are concerned, even though they have a fairly complicated possible representation.

A note on terminology: User-defined data types (UDTs for short) are sometimes called *abstract* data types (ADTs) in the literature; we prefer not to use this term, however, in part because we believe a good argument could be made that *all* types are (or should be) "abstract," in the sense that their representation is hidden.* We remark in passing that the literature often uses both of the terms UDT and ADT very sloppily, treating them as if they meant sometimes a value, sometimes a variable, of the type in question, rather than the type *per se.* The following examples are quite typical: "Rows can contain ADTs"; "ADTs are passed by reference"; "How can we replicate UDTs?"; "Caching of UDTs is done close to the application"; "Object/relational databases allow UDTs in columns"; "ADTs are mutable"; and so on (all of these quotes are taken from a recent conference [114]; we omit the precise sources in order to protect the guilty). We remind you that it is its support for UDTs that is the basis for our claim that **D** is an object language as well as a relational one. In fact, as noted in Chapter 5, we see **D** as a full "object/relational" language.

---

*The term *abstract type* is unfortunately also used (though not by us) to mean something quite different—namely, a type such that every value of the type in question must also be a value of some proper subtype of that type (and a type that is not abstract in this sense is then called a *concrete* type). Such matters are discussed and explained further in Part IV of this book.

Here now is an example of destroying a user-defined scalar type:

```
DROP TYPE POLYGON ;
```

Note: Although we do not explicitly prescribe such a thing, we do not mean to preclude the possibility that **D** might usefully include some kind of "alter type" operator as a shorthand.

By the way, the point is worth stressing that the operation of defining a type does not actually create the corresponding set of values. As explained in Chapter 1, values—and hence *sets* of values, *a fortiori*—have no location in time or space; conceptually, the set of values in question already exists, and always will exist. Thus, all the "define type" operation (the TYPE statement, in **Tutorial D**) does is introduce a *name* by which that set of values can be referenced. Likewise, the "destroy type" operation (the DROP TYPE statement, in **Tutorial D**) does not actually destroy the corresponding set of values, it merely drops the name that was introduced by the corresponding "define type" operation.

Now, we have already explained that the actual representation of scalar values and variables is always *hidden from the user* (equivalently, scalar types have no user-visible components). This hiding of actual representations—which is important for reasons of data independence [77–78], of course—is implied by the fact that (as we will see under RM Prescription 3) values and variables of a given type can be operated upon solely by means of the operators defined for that type. In other words, we draw a sharp distinction between *types* as such, on the one hand, and *actual representations* or *internal encodings* of values and variables of those types, on the other. (We discussed this point in some detail in Chapter 2, as you might recall.)

Finally, it is worth pointing out that to a user who merely makes use of some user-defined type—as opposed to the user who is actually responsible for defining or implementing that type—the type in question behaves in most respects just like a builtin one.

RM PRESCRIPTION 2: SCALAR VALUES ARE TYPED

*All scalar values shall be **typed**—i.e., such values shall always carry with them, at least conceptually, some accompanying identification of the (unique) type to which they belong.*

———— ♦ ♦ ♦ ♦ ♦ ————

This prescription merely insists that there be no such thing as a "typeless" scalar value—every scalar value must be a value of some scalar type. In other words, if *v* is a scalar value, then *v* can be thought of as carrying around with it a kind of flag that announces "I am an integer" or "I am a supplier number" or "I am an ellipse" (etc., etc.). Note that, by definition, any given value:

- Will always be of exactly one type (except possibly if type inheritance is supported—see Part IV of this book), and
- Can never change its type.

It follows further from the first of these points that distinct types are always *disjoint*, meaning they have no values in common (again, except possibly if type inheritance is supported—see Part IV of this book).

Note: It follows still further that all of the foregoing points concerning scalar values apply, *mutatis mutandis*, to tuple and relation values also, since tuple and relation values are ultimately made up out of scalar values. See RM Prescriptions 6 and 7.

RM PRESCRIPTION 3: SCALAR OPERATORS

D shall provide facilities for users to define their own scalar **operators** *(user-defined scalar operators); other such operators (builtin or system-defined scalar operators) shall be provided by the system. It shall be possible to destroy user-defined scalar operators, in general (though the operators required by RM Prescription 5 violate this prescription slightly, in that they can be destroyed only by destroying the associated type, and the same might possibly be true of selector operators). Furthermore:*

a. *The definition of a given scalar operator shall include a specification of the type of each parameter to that operator, the* **declared type** *of that parameter. If operator* Op *has a parameter* P *of declared type* T, *then the argument* A *that corresponds to* P *in any given invocation of* Op *shall also be of declared type* T.

b. *Every scalar operator is either an* update *operator or a* read-only *operator. A scalar* **update operator** *is one for which at least one argument must be specified by means of a scalar variable reference specifically, not by means of an arbitrary scalar expression, and invocation causes values to be assigned to such arguments (at least potentially); parameters corresponding to such arguments are said to be* subject to update. *A scalar* **read-only operator** *is a scalar operator that is not a scalar update operator.*

c. *Invoking a scalar read-only operator shall return a (scalar)* **result.** *Invoking a scalar update operator shall not.*

d. *The definition of a scalar read-only operator shall include a specification of the type of the result of that operator, the* **declared type** *of that result.*

e. *The definition of a scalar update operator shall include a specification of which parameters to that operator are subject to update. Arguments corresponding to such parameters shall be* **passed by reference.** *All other scalar update operator arguments, and all scalar read-only operator arguments, shall be* **passed by value.**

> *f. Let* SX *be a scalar expression. Then* SX *has a **declared type** (more precisely,
> the result of evaluating* SX *has a declared type), recursively derived in the ob-
> vious way from the declared types of the operands of* SX *and the declared types
> of the results of any subexpressions contained within* SX.

---------   ♦♦♦♦♦   ---------

The purpose of this prescription is, of course, to define the salient features of scalar
operators. A scalar operator as we define the term is an operator that returns a scalar
result or updates a scalar variable. Not all operators are scalar ones, of course, but
we adopt the obvious convention that the unqualified term *operator* refers to a scalar
operator specifically, unless the context demands otherwise.

Like scalar types, scalar operators can be either user- or system-defined
("builtin"):

- *Builtin* operators are defined, necessarily, only in connection with builtin types.
  In accordance with the assumptions articulated under the discussion of RM Prescription 1 earlier, examples of builtin operators include the boolean operators
  NOT, AND, OR, etc. (these operators are actually prescribed); the comparison
  operators "=", "<", etc. (the "=" operator is prescribed also—see RM Prescription 8); the arithmetic operators "+", "*", etc.; the character string opera-
  tors "||" (concatenate), SUBSTR (substring), etc.; and so on.

- *User-defined* operators, by contrast, can be defined in connection with either
  builtin types or user-defined ones (or a mixture, of course). *Note:* The fact that
  an operator with a given name already exists does not preclude the possibility
  that another operator might be defined with the same name but different parameter and/or result declared types; indeed, RM Prescription 8 actually requires
  one such operator ("=") to be defined for *every* type, and RM Prescription 21
  requires another (":="). In some circumstances (especially if type inheritance
  is supported), it might even be possible to *override* an existing operator, by
  defining another operator with the same name and parameter and result declared types but with different semantics; e.g., it might be possible to override
  a builtin LOG operator to return natural logarithms instead of logarithms to base
  10 (say). For obvious reasons, we recommend that this feature be used with all
  due caution.

Here is an example of a user-defined scalar operator definition involving only
builtin types:

```
OPERATOR ABS ( Z RATIONAL ) RETURNS ( RATIONAL ) ;
   RETURN ( CASE
                WHEN Z ≥ 0.0 THEN +Z
                WHEN Z < 0.0 THEN -Z
            END CASE ) ;
END OPERATOR ;
```

The operator ABS ("absolute value") is defined in terms of just one parameter, Z, of declared type RATIONAL, and returns a result of that same declared type. It is a *read-only* operator, meaning that no invocation ever tries to update its own argument (it merely "reads" that argument). Here is an example of an expression—an IF-THEN-ELSE expression, as it happens—that includes an ABS invocation:

```
IF ABS ( A - B ) + C > D * E THEN F ELSE G END IF
```

Here is another example of a user-defined scalar operator definition, this one involving some user-defined types:

```
OPERATOR DIST ( P1 POINT, P2 POINT ) RETURNS ( LENGTH ) ;
   RETURN ( WITH THE_X ( P1 ) AS X1 ,
                 THE_X ( P2 ) AS X2 ,
                 THE_Y ( P1 ) AS Y1 ,
                 THE_Y ( P2 ) AS Y2 :
           LENGTH ( SQRT ( ( X1 - X2 ) ** 2
                         + ( Y1 - Y2 ) ** 2 ) ) ) ;
END OPERATOR ;
```

The operator DIST ("distance") is defined in terms of two parameters P1 and P2, both of declared type POINT, and returns a result of declared type LENGTH. Like ABS, it is a read-only operator, meaning that no invocation ever tries to update either of its arguments. It uses the operators THE_X and THE_Y (see RM Prescription 5) to obtain the X and Y coordinates of the two points in question, which it then uses to compute the required distance. Note:

- Our use of WITH to introduce shorthand names for certain expressions;

- Our assumption that a SQRT ("square root") operator is available (of course, we assume that operator returns a positive root, not a negative one!);

- Our use of the LENGTH *selector* operator (see RM Prescription 4). In the example, the LENGTH selector invocation can be thought of as taking the result of the SQRT invocation—a rational number, presumably—and in effect converting it to a value of type LENGTH.

Here is an example of an expression that includes an invocation of DIST:

```
DIST ( K2, K9 ) < 100.0
```

A couple more examples:

```
OPERATOR EQ ( P1 POINT, P2 POINT ) RETURNS ( BOOLEAN ) ;
   RETURN ( THE_X ( P1 ) = THE_X ( P2 ) AND
            THE_Y ( P1 ) = THE_Y ( P2 ) ) ;
END OPERATOR ;
```

EQ is the required "=" comparison operator for type POINT (see RM Prescription 8). Observe that the expression within the RETURN is a logical (truth-valued) one; observe too that that expression makes use of the *builtin* "=" operator for type RATIONAL. For simplicity, we will assume from this point forward that the usual infix notation "=" can be used for the equality operator (for all types, not just type

RATIONAL and not just type POINT). We choose to ignore the details of how such an infix notation might be specified in practice, since it is basically just a matter of syntax.

```
OPERATOR LT ( Q1 QTY, Q2 QTY ) RETURNS ( BOOLEAN ) ;
    RETURN ( THE_QTY ( Q1 ) < THE_QTY ( Q2 ) ) ;
END OPERATOR ;
```

LT is the "<" operator for type QTY. Again, we will assume from this point forward that the usual infix notation can be used for this operator (for all "ordered types," not just for type QTY; see Chapter 5 for an explanation of the term "ordered type").

Here now is an example of an *update* operator definition:

```
OPERATOR REFLECT ( P POINT ) UPDATES ( P ) ;
    THE_X ( P )   :=   - THE_X ( P ) , /* multiple assignment -- */
    THE_Y ( P )   :=   - THE_Y ( P ) ; /* see RM Prescription 21 */
END OPERATOR ;
```

The REFLECT operator effectively moves the point with Cartesian coordinates (x,y) to its mirror image position $(-x,-y)$. Thus, it is defined in terms of a single parameter P, of declared type POINT, and, when invoked, it updates the argument corresponding to that parameter appropriately. As in previous examples, we use THE_X and THE_Y operators to "read" the X and Y coordinates of the point in question; we also use THE_X and THE_Y *pseudovariables* (see RM Prescription 5) to *update* those coordinates. Note that invoking REFLECT does not return a result (there is no RETURN statement within the operator definition); such an invocation thus does not have a value and is not a scalar expression. Instead, the invocation must be performed by means of an explicit CALL statement (or something logically equivalent)—for example:

```
CALL REFLECT ( K7 ) ;
```

Finally, here is an example of destroying a user-defined scalar operator:

```
DROP OPERATOR REFLECT ;
```

Points Arising from the Foregoing Examples

- Observe first that there is a significant logical difference between (a) the *formal operands* or *parameters* in terms of which a given operator is defined and (b) the *actual operands* or *arguments* that are passed to any given invocation of that operator. (This difference becomes especially significant if type inheritance is supported. See Part IV of this book.)

- When an operator is invoked, argument and parameter types must match. More precisely (as RM Prescription 3 in fact states), the declared type of each argument must be the same as the declared type of the corresponding parameter (except possibly if type inheritance is supported; again, see Part IV of this book).

- Another important logical difference is that between *update* and *read-only* operators. Although we speak loosely of operators applying to both values and variables, the one kind of operator that, by definition, cannot be applied to a value is—as noted in Chapter 1—one that *updates* that value; such operators apply, by definition, to variables, not values. Thus, read-only operators apply to values (in particular, they apply, harmlessly, to the values that happen to be the current values of variables); update operators, by contrast, apply very specifically to variables only (i.e., the arguments corresponding to parameters that are subject to update must be, very specifically, variables).

- As a consequence of the previous point, when an update operator is invoked, arguments corresponding to parameters that are subject to update—i.e., arguments corresponding to parameters that are named in the UPDATES specification—must be expressly specified as variables, not as arbitrary expressions, and the invocation causes values to be assigned to those variables (at least potentially). By contrast, other arguments (and all arguments to read-only operator invocations) can be specified as arbitrary expressions; by virtue of the next point below, values will definitely *not* be assigned to those arguments.

- Arguments corresponding to parameters that are subject to update are always *passed by reference,* implying that operations on those parameters really are operations on the corresponding arguments (and implying in particular that assigning a value to such a parameter really assigns a value to the corresponding argument). By contrast, all other arguments are *passed by value,* implying that operations on the corresponding parameters are really operations on "dummy" (system-created) arguments that have been given the same values as the genuine arguments.* Assigning a value to a parameter that corresponds to a dummy argument is thus fairly pointless, since it has no lasting effect (in particular, it has no effect on the genuine argument).

- Because invoking a scalar read-only operator returns a scalar result—equivalently, because such an invocation has a scalar value—such an invocation constitutes a special case of a scalar expression. It can therefore appear wherever a scalar selector invocation (or, more loosely, a scalar literal) can appear: in particular, as an argument to another scalar operator invocation. Scalar expressions of arbitrary complexity can thus be constructed by nesting scalar read-only operator invocations.

- Since the system knows the declared types of all parameters to, and all results from, all scalar operators (all scalar *read-only* operators in particular), it follows that the system also knows precisely which scalar expressions are legal (in the

---

*We are defining a *model* here, of course. If the implementation can determine that no attempt will in fact be made to update such arguments, then it is free to pass them by reference instead (and it might prefer to do so, for performance reasons).

sense that they cannot possibly give rise to any type errors). Further, it also knows the type of the result of every such legal expression. As noted in RM Prescription 3, we refer to that type as the *declared type* of the scalar expression in question.

- Because invoking an update operator does not return a result—equivalently, because such an invocation does not have a value—such an invocation should be thought of as a *statement* (typically, as in **Tutorial D,** a CALL statement), not as an expression. In particular, therefore, it cannot appear as an argument to another operator invocation.

The reason we require update operator invocations not to have a value is to avoid the possibility of apparently read-only expressions producing side effects (and we require arguments other than those corresponding to parameters that are subject to update to be passed by value, not reference, for the same reason). For suppose, contrariwise, that we were able to redefine our "absolute value" operator ABS (say) in such a way as not only to return the absolute value of its argument, as before, but also to update that argument to set it to that absolute value. Then (e.g.) executing the IF statement

```
IF ABS ( X ) > 3.0 THEN ... ;    /* *** ILLEGAL !!! *** -- if */
END IF ;                         /* ABS is an update operator */
```

would have the side effect of updating the variable X. We might even imagine a database retrieval operation having the side effect of updating the database!

We conclude this section with some remarks on terminology:

- First, we remark that the read-only *vs.* update distinction, though introduced in the context of scalar operators in particular, applies to other kinds of operators also, of course (see in particular RM Prescription 20).

- Second, update operators and read-only operators are sometimes called *mutators* and *observers* respectively, but we do not use these latter terms. Operators in general are also sometimes called *methods,* but we do not use this term either, except very informally.

- Third, read-only operators in particular are sometimes called *functions.* We prefer not to use this term either, for the following reasons. First of all, a function— strictly speaking—is a many-to-one mapping from argument values to result values (and hence a read-only operator is indeed a function). The trouble is, the term *function* is often used, loosely, as a synonym for *operator* (indeed, it was used that way in the first "official" version of this *Manifesto* [38]), and thus taken to include update operators as well. But an update operator is not a function, because (a) there is no result value, and (b) at least one of its arguments must be, very specifically, a variable, instead of just a value. Moreover, read-only operators might in fact not be functions either, if we were to allow them to return more than one result (as discussed in Chapter 4).

Finally, it is worth pointing out that to a user who merely makes use of some user-defined operator—as opposed to the user who is actually responsible for defining or implementing that operator—the operator in question behaves in most respects just like a builtin one.

RM PRESCRIPTION 4: ACTUAL *VS.* POSSIBLE REPRESENTATIONS

Let T *be a scalar type, and let* v *be an appearance (in some context) of some value of type* T. *By definition,* v *has exactly one **actual representation** and one or more **possible representations** (at least one, because there is obviously always one that is the same as the actual representation). Actual representations associated with type* T *shall be specified by means of some kind of* storage structure definition language *and shall not be visible in **D** (see RM Proscription 6). At least one possible representation (not necessarily the same as any actual representation) associated with type* T *shall be declared as part of the definition of* T *and hence shall be visible in* ***D.*** *For each declared possible representation* PR *for* T, *a **selector** operator* S *shall automatically be defined with the following properties:*

a. *For definiteness, assume the components of* PR *(see RM Prescription 5) and the parameters of* S *each constitute an ordered list. Then the two lists must contain the same number of elements,* n *say, and the declared types of the* ith *elements in the two lists (*i *= 1, 2, ...,* n*) must be identical.*

b. *Every value of type* T *shall be produced by some invocation of* S.

c. *Every (successful) invocation of* S *shall produce some value of type* T.

It is convenient to begin our explanation of this prescription by taking a brief (albeit informal) look at object systems. Now, it is well known that, at least when they first appeared, such systems had difficulty over *ad hoc* query and related matters. And the reason for that state of affairs was, of course, that objects could be accessed only by means of predefined "methods" (i.e., operators); *ad hoc* query access and predefined "method" access are conflicting concepts, almost by definition. For example, suppose objects of class POINT have an associated operator GET_X to "get" (i.e., read or retrieve) their X coordinate, but no analogous GET_Y operator. Then even the following simple queries—

- Get the Y coordinate of point P
- Get all points on the X axis
- Get all points with Y coordinate less than five

(and many others like them)—obviously cannot be handled; in fact, they cannot even be stated.

We note, however, that one operator that must be defined for every class is what in the *Manifesto* we call a *selector* operator. (The more usual object term is *constructor,* and we will return to this small point of terminology at the end of the present section.) The purpose of a selector operator is to "select"—i.e., *specify*—a particular object of the class in question. For example, consider the following **Tutorial D** code fragment:

```
VAR X RATIONAL INIT ( +4.0 ) ;
VAR Y RATIONAL INIT ( -3.0 ) ;
VAR P POINT ;

P  :=  POINT ( X, Y ) ;
```

The effect of this code fragment is, of course, to set the variable P to contain (an appearance of) a particular POINT value—namely, the point with Cartesian coordinates (4.0,–3.0).* And the expression on the right hand side of the assignment is, precisely, an invocation of a selector for class POINT; its effect is, precisely, to select the point with the specified Cartesian coordinates.

Observe, therefore, that the parameters to a given selector S together constitute—necessarily—a possible representation PR for objects of the pertinent class C. In the example, Cartesian coordinates X and Y constitute a possible representation for points. Of course, this fact does not mean that points are *actually* represented by Cartesian coordinates inside the system; it merely means, to repeat, that Cartesian coordinates are a *possible* representation. The actual representation might be Cartesian coordinates, or polar coordinates, or something else entirely.

Observe further that if an operator analogous to the GET_X operator discussed above is provided for *every component* of the possible representation *PR,* then objects of class *C* can be accessed for retrieval purposes just as if *PR* were the *actual* representation and that actual representation were exposed to the user. In other words, *ad hoc* queries and similar operations can now be performed on objects of class *C* after all. In the example, if GET_X and GET_Y operators are both available for points, then arbitrary queries (etc.) involving points now become possible.

Note: It is usual in contexts such as the one at hand to speak not just of GET_ operators alone, but rather of GET_ and SET_ operators. SET_ operators are the update analogs of GET_ operators (GET_ operators are read-only, of course[†]). In the

---

*For the benefit of readers who might be familiar with object systems, we should perhaps emphasize that in our model the variable P really does contain a point as such, not a "reference to" or "object ID of" such a point. See the discussion of OO Proscription 2 in Chapter 9.

[†]Actually, they might not be—it depends on how they are defined. For example, if we define GET_X in terms of just one parameter, of type POINT, then certainly it "reads" its argument and does not update it. But we might define it in terms of *two* parameters, of types POINT and RATIONAL respectively, in which case it would "read" its POINT argument and update its RATIONAL argument (which would have to be specified as a variable, of course, not as a general expression).

case of points, for example, operators SET_X and SET_Y might be provided to update the X and Y coordinates, respectively, of a specified POINT variable. And, of course, just as the provision of GET_ operators for all components of some possible representation makes arbitrary queries possible, so the provision of SET_ operators for all components of some possible representation makes arbitrary updates possible too.

In view of the foregoing, we decided in the *Manifesto* to insist on some appropriate discipline. To be more specific (and now reverting to our more usual and more precise terminology), RM Prescription 4 insists that:

- The definition of a scalar type must include at least one *declared possible representation* for values of that type. *Note:* It is certainly possible for values of a given type to have more than one possible representation (think of points—or even integers, come to that, which can be represented in decimal, or binary, or a variety of other ways). It is also possible for values of a given type to have a possible representation that is not declared, though it goes without saying that such representations are of little interest so far as we are concerned. In fact, we might as well adopt the convention (and we will) that from this point forward the unqualified term *possible representation* always refers to a *declared* possible representation specifically, barring explicit statements to the contrary.

- Declaring a possible representation automatically causes the definition of a corresponding selector (and selectors cannot be defined in any other way). Note, therefore, that selectors and possible representations are in one-to-one correspondence with each other; in fact, selector parameters and possible representation components are in one-to-one correspondence, too (see, e.g., the POINT example earlier). In **Tutorial D,** moreover, we adopt the obvious convention of giving the selector and the corresponding possible representation the same name, to underscore their "hand in glove" relationship (though they *are* logically distinct concepts).

And RM Prescription 5, *q.v.,* goes on to insist that GET_ and SET_ operators, or something logically equivalent, be provided for every component of every possible representation. *Note:* Actually (as you will already have noticed from examples in the previous section), we prefer what we call "THE_ operators" to GET_ and SET_ operators *per se,* for reasons to be explained under RM Prescription 5. In an attempt to avoid confusion, however, we will stay with the GET_ and SET_ terminology for the rest of the present section.*

---

*Observe that—in contrast to the situation found in some object systems—the semantics of GET_ and SET_ operators (or, rather, our THE_ operator analogs thereof) are *prescribed by the model.* Unlike other operators, therefore, they cannot be overridden. *Note:* Analogous remarks apply to selector operators also (but see the final section of Appendix C).

System-Defined Types

We have been making a tacit assumption so far in this section that the scalar types we are dealing with are all user-defined. What about builtin types? Well, it is certainly possible to imagine some builtin types that would comply with everything we have said in this section so far. For example, suppose we had a builtin type COMPLEX ("complex numbers"). Then:

- A possible representation for complex numbers might consist of a pair of rational numbers, one for the "real" component x and the other for the "imaginary" component y of the complex number in question.

- The corresponding selector might take the form

```
COMPLEX ( x, y )
```

  where x and y are numeric (rational) expressions.

- The corresponding "GET_ and SET_" operators might look like this:

```
GET_X ( z )
GET_Y ( z )
SET_X ( z, x )
SET_Y ( z, y )
```

  where z is a complex number expression (for GET_X and GET_Y) or variable (for SET_X and SET_Y), and x and y are numeric (i.e., rational) expressions.

(As an aside, we remark that DATE and TIME in SQL [76,87–89] serve as examples of builtin types for which (a) a possible representation, (b) a selector operator, albeit a limited one, and (c) "GET_" operators—though not "SET_" operators—are all defined. Though we should perhaps add that the "possible" representations for SQL dates and times are really rather close to the *actual* ones; SQL is, unfortunately, often unclear on the distinction between types and representations.)

What about a simpler builtin type, such as INTEGER? Well, here the requirements of RM Prescription 4 (and RM Prescription 5) are satisfied almost trivially. In the case of INTEGER, for example:

- The system defines a format for writing integer literals, probably (as in **Tutorial D**) as optionally signed decimal numbers. By definition, that format can be regarded as a possible representation for integer values.

- That possible representation has no components (well, no interesting components, anyway; i.e., it is not made up of any components that are smaller than itself and are of some different type). Thus, the corresponding selector has no parameters—which means it effectively reduces to nothing more nor less than an integer literal. (A literal can be regarded as a special case of a selector invocation, of course, but not all selector invocations are literals, in general.)

- "GET_ and SET_" operators are required, in general, for each possible representation component. But since there are no such components in the case at hand, no "GET_ and SET_" operators are needed (or provided) either.

Type Definers *vs.* Type Implementers

We return to the example of the user-defined type POINT in order to discuss some further issues. Here first is a **Tutorial D** definition of that type (repeated from the section on RM Prescription 1):

```
TYPE POINT
    POSSREP POINT ( X RATIONAL, Y RATIONAL )
    POSSREP POLAR ( R RATIONAL, THETA RATIONAL ) ;
```

It is convenient to distinguish, informally, between *type definers* and *type implementers.* In the example at hand, the type *definer* has declared two possible representations, POINT and POLAR. Hence there will exist two corresponding selector operators (with the same names as the possible representations, in **Tutorial D**): POINT, which lets the user supply Cartesian coordinates X and Y as two RATIONAL values and returns the appropriate POINT value, and POLAR, which lets the user supply polar coordinates R and THETA as two RATIONAL values and (again) returns the appropriate POINT value.

Suppose now that the Cartesian coordinates representation is in fact the actual one (though there is no need, in general, for an actual representation to be identical to any of the declared possible ones). Then the system will provide certain highly protected operators—not part of **D**—that effectively expose that actual representation, and the *type implementer* will use those operators to implement the necessary POINT and POLAR selectors. For example:

```
OPERATOR POINT ( X RATIONAL, Y RATIONAL ) RETURNS ( POINT ) ;
   BEGIN ;
      VAR P POINT ;
      P.X  :=  X ;          /* assign to actual representation */
      P.Y  :=  Y ;          /* assign to actual representation */
      RETURN ( P ) ;
   END ;
END OPERATOR ;

OPERATOR POLAR ( R RATIONAL, THETA RATIONAL ) RETURNS ( POINT ) ;
   RETURN ( POINT ( R * COS ( THETA ), R * SIN ( THETA ) ) ) ;
END OPERATOR ;
```

Note: We show the definition of the POINT selector in (pseudo) **Tutorial D** for expository reasons, but it could not be written in that language in practice; for one thing, it makes use of the "highly protected operators that are not part of **D**" (represented in the foregoing code via dot qualification). By contrast, the definition of the POLAR selector could, and probably should, be expressed in **D,** more or less as shown. Note that the POLAR definition makes use of the POINT selector, as well as the (presumably builtin) operators SIN and COS.

It follows from the foregoing that the type implementer (but not the type definer, and certainly not the type user) must effectively be aware of the actual representation.

One final comment on this example: We have tacitly been assuming that the two possible representations for points, Cartesian coordinates and polar coordinates, are completely interchangeable. In practice, however, they are not—not quite; owing to practical limitations on the size of rational numbers on any real computer, there will always be certain points that can be represented by Cartesian coordinates and not by polar coordinates. However, we see this problem as an implementation problem merely; it is analogous to problems that have always been with us regarding such matters as the largest and smallest numbers that can be represented in different floating point formats.

Miscellaneous Issues

We close this section with a number of miscellaneous points having to do with actual *vs.* possible representations and the associated notion of selectors.

- Although actual representations are not very relevant to the *Manifesto* or this book, it might help to stress the point (already mentioned in Chapter 1) that if *v1* and *v2* are distinct appearances of values of type *T*, there is no requirement that the actual representations of *v1* and *v2* be of the same form. For instance, one appearance of a certain integer might have a decimal actual representation and another—possibly of the very same integer—a binary actual representation. We remark, however, that in such a situation the system would have to know how to convert between the actual representations in question, in order to be able to implement assignments and comparisons correctly.

- In accordance with RM Proscription 6—see Chapter 7—actual representations (as opposed to possible ones) are not visible in **D.** Instead, as RM Prescription 4 requires, they are specified by means of some logically distinct "storage structure definition language," details of which are beyond the scope of both the *Manifesto* and this book.

- It is an open question as to whether any scalar type *T* can have a declared possible representation that is defined, directly or indirectly, in terms of *T* itself. More precisely, let *T* be a scalar type. Let *S1, S2, ...* be a sequence of sets defined as follows:

  S1 = the set of declared types for all components of all declared possible representations for *T*

> Si = the set of declared types for all components of all declared possible representations for all types in $S(i-1)$ $(i > 1)$

Then the question is whether there must exist some value n $(n > 0)$ such that every type in the set Sn is system-defined.

> *Note:* Character strings (type CHAR) provide a simple example of a type for which the answer to the foregoing question might possibly be no. Every character string consists of either an empty string or a character followed by a character string; we might therefore wish to declare a possible representation for type CHAR that reflects exactly this state of affairs. Note the inherently *disjunctive nature* of any such possible representation. Let *PR* be such a representation for type CHAR, therefore, and let *S* be the (unique) selector corresponding to *PR*. Given the requirement—see the paragraph immediately following—that every individual character string must be obtainable by some invocation of *S*, it follows that the disjunction in question must be incorporated into the definition of *PR per se*. That is, it would not be acceptable (even if it were possible) to declare one possible representation for the empty string and another for nonempty strings.

- Now turning to selectors: Note first that selector operators are read-only, by definition. Further, RM Prescription 4 requires (reasonably) that if *S* is a selector for type *T*, then every value of type *T* must be obtainable by some invocation of *S*, and no invocation of *S* must ever yield a value not of type *T*.

- We note that it is possible for two apparently distinct invocations of the same selector *S* to yield the same value of type *T*. As a trivial example, the expressions "3.0" and "3.00" both yield the same numeric value, three. See the section on RM Prescription 8 later in this chapter for further discussion of this point.

- RM Prescription 3 states that "it shall be possible to destroy user-defined scalar operators." However, selectors might be felt to violate this prescription slightly, in that it is possible to destroy such an operator only by destroying the corresponding possible representation (which in practice might mean destroying the associated type itself).

Finally, we come to the promised note on terminology. As indicated earlier, the term "constructor" is sometimes used in place of our *selector* (especially in object systems). We prefer our term because we regard the operation as, precisely, one of *selecting* an existing value from some specified set of values, not as somehow "constructing" such a value. For example, the expression "3" can be regarded as an invocation of a selector operator that selects the value three from the set of integers (i.e., from type INTEGER). It certainly does not "construct" that value.

Perhaps we should add that the term "constructor" is also sometimes used (again, especially in object systems) to mean an operator that allocates storage for a variable. We do not prohibit such operators. Within a database, however, the only variables we permit are, very specifically, *relation* variables (see RM Prescriptions 13 and 16). In the case of variables in databases, therefore:

- The only "constructor" we permit is, specifically, the operator that *defines* a database relation variable;

- Importantly, those database relation variables—unlike "objects" in typical object systems—are always *named;*

- Hence, we still prefer not to use the "constructor" terminology, in order to avoid confusion.

RM PRESCRIPTION 5: EXPOSE POSSIBLE REPRESENTATIONS

Let some declared possible representation PR *for scalar type* T *be defined in terms of components* C1, C2, ..., Cn *(each of which has a name and a declared type). Let* v *be a value of type* T, *and let* PR(v) *denote the corresponding possible representation. Then* PR(v) *shall be* **exposed**—*that is, a set of read-only and update operators shall automatically be defined such that:*

a. *For all such values* v *and for all* i (i = *1, 2, ...,* n), *it is possible to "retrieve" (i.e., read the value of) the* Ci *component of* PR(v);

b. *For all variables* V *of declared type* T *and for all* i (i = *1, 2, ...,* n), *it is possible to update* V *in such a way that if the values of* V *before and after the update are* v *and* v′ *respectively, then the corresponding possible representations* PR(v) *and* PR(v′) *differ at most only in their* Ci *components.*

Such a set of operators shall be provided for each possible representation declared in the definition of T.

We have already discussed the basic motivation behind this prescription in the previous section; in the present section, we discuss the specific syntax used in **Tutorial D** in this connection. Now, in Chapter 1 we said we did not regard syntax in general as being very important; however, we do have to use *some* syntax to illustrate our ideas, and in the particular case at hand the **Tutorial D** syntax has been very carefully designed to support just the semantics we desire, no more and no less. Indeed, it is that "careful design" that accounts for our use of THE_ operators instead of the more conventional GET_ and SET_ operators. And, of course, it is specifically those THE_ operators that we wish to discuss here.

First of all, then, let *PR* be (as above) a possible representation for scalar type *T,* and let *PR* have components *C1, C2, ..., Cn.* Define THE_*C1*, THE_*C2*, ...,

THE_*Cn* to be a family of operators such that, for each *i* (*i* = 1, 2, ..., *n*), the operator THE_*Ci* has the following properties:

- Its sole parameter is of declared type *T*.

- If an invocation of the operator appears in a "source" position (in particular, on the right hand side of an assignment), then it returns the *Ci* component of its argument. (More precisely, it returns the value of the *Ci* component of the possible representation *PR*(*v*) of its argument value *v*.)

- If an invocation of the operator appears in a "target" position (in particular, on the left hand side of an assignment), then:

   - First, that argument must be explicitly specified as a scalar variable, not as an arbitrary scalar expression.

   - Second, the invocation acts as a **pseudovariable,** which means that it actually *designates*—rather than just returning the value of—the *Ci* component of its argument. (More precisely, it designates the *Ci* component of the possible representation *PR*(*V*) of its argument variable *V;* here we are extending our "*PR*(*v*)" notation in a slight and obvious way.)

      Note: The term *pseudovariable* is taken from PL/I (the substring operator SUBSTR provides a PL/I example). Note, however, that PL/I pseudovariables cannot be nested, but THE_ pseudovariables can, as we will see below. In other words, we do regard pseudovariable invocations as references to variables, implying among other things that they can appear as arguments to other such invocations.

Here is an example:

```
TYPE TEMPERATURE POSSREP CELSIUS ( C RATIONAL ) ;

VAR TEMP TEMPERATURE ;
VAR CEL  RATIONAL ;

CEL  :=  THE_C ( TEMP ) ;
THE_C ( TEMP ) :=  CEL ;
```

The first of these two assignments assigns the temperature denoted by the current value of the TEMPERATURE variable TEMP, converted if necessary to degrees Celsius, to the RATIONAL variable CEL; the second uses the current value of the RATIONAL variable CEL, considered as a temperature in degrees Celsius, to update the TEMPERATURE variable TEMP appropriately. The operator THE_C thus effectively exposes the "degrees Celsius" possible representation for temperatures, for both read-only and update purposes. However, this possible representation is not necessarily an actual representation; e.g., temperatures might actually be represented in degrees Fahrenheit, not degrees Celsius. *Note:* We remark here as an aside that some writers have suggested extending the type notion to include explicit support for units such as degrees Celsius *vs.* degrees Fahrenheit (etc.). We do not preclude such support, but regard it as orthogonal and secondary to our main purpose with the *Manifesto.*

Here is a slightly more complex example:

```
TYPE POINT POSSREP ( X RATIONAL, Y RATIONAL ) ;
                    /* Cartesian coordinates -- corresponding */
                    /* selector is named POINT by default    */

VAR Z RATIONAL ;
VAR P POINT ;

Z   :=  THE_X ( P ) ;
THE_X ( P )  :=  Z ;
```

The first of these two assignments assigns the X coordinate of the point denoted by the current value of the POINT variable P to the RATIONAL variable Z. The second uses the current value of the RATIONAL variable Z to update the X coordinate of the POINT variable P (speaking a trifle loosely). The operators THE_X and THE_Y thus effectively expose the "Cartesian coordinates" possible representation for points, for both read-only and update purposes; again, however, this possible representation is not necessarily the same as any corresponding actual representation.

And one more example, building on the previous one (LINESEG here stands for *line segments*):

```
TYPE LINESEG POSSREP ( BEGIN POINT, END POINT ) ;
                    /* begin and end points -- corresponding */
                    /* selector is named LINESEG by default  */

VAR Z RATIONAL ;
VAR LS LINESEG ;

Z   :=  THE_X ( THE_BEGIN ( LS ) ) ;
THE_X ( THE_BEGIN ( LS ) )  :=  Z ;
```

The first of these two assignments assigns the X coordinate of the begin point of the current value of LS to the variable Z. The second uses the current value of Z to update the X coordinate of the begin point of the variable LS (note the pseudovariable nesting in this second assignment). The operators THE_BEGIN and THE_END thus effectively expose the "begin and end points" possible representation for line segments—yet again, for both read-only and update purposes. Once again, however, this possible representation is not necessarily the same as any corresponding actual representation.

We now observe that THE_ pseudovariables are logically unnecessary! Consider the "updating" assignment from the first of the three examples above:

```
THE_C ( TEMP )  :=  CEL ;
```

This assignment, which uses a pseudovariable, is logically equivalent to the following one which does not:

```
TEMP  :=  CELSIUS ( CEL ) ;         /* invoke CELSIUS selector */
```

Similarly, the updating assignment in the second example was as follows:

```
THE_X ( P )  :=  Z ;
```

Here is a logical equivalent that does not use a pseudovariable:

```
P  :=  POINT ( Z, THE_Y ( P ) ) ;    /* invoke POINT selector */
```

Third example:

```
THE_X ( THE_BEGIN ( LS ) )  :=  Z ;
```

Logical equivalent:

```
LS  :=  LINESEG ( POINT ( Z, THE_Y ( THE_BEGIN ( LS ) ) ,
                 THE_END ( LS ) ) ;
```

In other words, pseudovariables *per se* are not strictly necessary in order to support the kind of component-level updating we are discussing here. However, the pseudovariable approach does seem intuitively more attractive than the alternative (for which it can be regarded as a shorthand); moreover, it becomes even more attractive—though still not *logically* necessary—if type inheritance is supported (see Chapter 14). Note that it also provides a higher degree of imperviousness to changes in the syntax of the corresponding selector (e.g., the LINESEG selector, in the third example above).*

Note: RM Prescription 21 (*q.v.*) requires support for *multiple* assignment. Thus, for example, the multiple assignment

```
THE_BEGIN ( LS )  :=  NEW_BEGIN ,
THE_END   ( LS )  :=  NEW_END   ;
```

might be used to update both the begin and end points of the line segment variable LS in a single operation. (In fact, we have already seen another example of multiple assignment, in the section on RM Prescription 3.)

Now we can explain why we prefer our THE_ operators over the more traditional GET_ and SET_ operators. The basic point is that THE_ pseudovariable invocations can be nested, whereas SET_ operator invocations cannot (recall that SET_ operators are update operators, meaning among other things that—in our model, at any rate, but for good reasons!—invocations of such operators do not have a value). For example, a "SET_ operator" analog of the following updating assignment—

```
THE_X ( THE_BEGIN ( LS ) )  :=  Z ;
```

—would have to look something like this:

```
P  :=  GET_BEGIN ( LS ) ;
CALL SET_X ( P, Z ) ;
CALL SET_BEGIN ( LS, P ) ;
```

This example shows why we prefer THE_ *pseudovariables* to SET_ operators. For symmetry, therefore, we also prefer THE_ *operators* to GET_ operators (although

---

*It might also be easier to implement efficiently.

here we are really talking about a purely syntactic issue, not a logical difference, since GET_ operators, unlike SET_ operators, can be nested).*

While we are considering matters of syntax, by the way, there are a couple of additional points we should mention. First, the fact that we require THE_ operators (or something logically equivalent to THE_ operators) to be provided for every component of every declared possible representation does not mean, of course, that users cannot define additional operators of their own that look like THE_ operators. For example, we might define an operator for type ELLIPSE called THE_CIRCUMFERENCE, even though CIRCUMFERENCE is not a component of any declared possible representation for ellipses. However, that operator is clearly not one of the THE_ operators required by RM Prescription 5. For simplicity, therefore, we take the term "THE_ operator" from this point forward to mean, specifically, one of the operators that RM Prescription 5 does require.

Second, we should say that a more user-friendly way of meeting the requirements of the present prescription might use some kind of *dot qualification syntax.* Here are some examples (revised versions of certain of the examples shown earlier):

```
Z   :=  LS.BEGIN.X ;

LS.BEGIN.X  :=  Z ;

LS  :=  LINESEG ( POINT ( Z, LS.BEGIN.Y ), LS.END ) ;

P.X  :=  NEW_X, P.Y  :=  NEW_Y ;
```

In this book, however, we will stay with our THE_ notation. (In fact, of course, it would be rather confusing if we were to use dot qualification syntax in the way just suggested, because we have already used it for another purpose—namely, to denote the special operators that provide access to actual representations—and we will be doing so again in just a moment.)

A Note on Implementation

Consider type POINT once again. Suppose that (as in the subsection "Type Definers *vs.* Type Implementers" in the section on RM Prescription 4, earlier) the type definer has specified polar coordinates as a possible representation for points, but the type implementer has chosen Cartesian coordinates as the actual representation. As already explained, the system will provide certain highly protected operators, not part of **D,** that effectively expose that actual representation; thus, the type implementer can (and will) use those operators to implement the necessary THE_ operators. (More precisely, the implementer will implement the *read-only* versions of those operators. The *update* or pseudovariable versions require no special work on

---

*Unless GET_ operators too are defined to be update operators, a possibility noted in an earlier footnote.

the part of the implementer, since as we have seen they are logically just shorthand.) Here, for example, are possible implementations for the THE_ operators that apply to type POINT:

```
OPERATOR THE_X ( P POINT ) RETURNS ( RATIONAL ) ;
   RETURN ( P̄.X ) ;              /* access actual representation */
END OPERATOR ;

OPERATOR THE_Y ( P POINT ) RETURNS ( RATIONAL ) ;
   RETURN ( P̄.Y ) ;              /* access actual representation */
END OPERATOR ;

OPERATOR THE_R ( P POINT ) RETURNS ( RATIONAL ) ;
   RETURN ( S̄QRT ( THE_X ( P ) ** 2 + THE_Y ( P ) ** 2 ) ) ;
END OPERATOR ;

OPERATOR THE_THETA ( P POINT ) RETURNS ( RATIONAL ) ;
   RETURN ( ĀRCTAN ( THE_Y ( P ) / THE_X ( P ) ) ) ;
END OPERATOR ;
```

Note: We show the definitions of THE_X and THE_Y in (pseudo) **Tutorial D** for expository reasons, but they could not be written in that language in practice (for one thing, they make use of the "highly protected operators that are not part of **D**"— represented once again via dot qualification). By contrast, the definitions of THE_R and THE_THETA could, and probably should, be expressed in **D,** more or less as shown. Note that those definitions make use of THE_X and THE_Y, as well as the (presumably builtin) operators SQRT and ARCTAN.

Again it follows that the type implementer (but not the type definer, and certainly not the type user) must effectively be aware of the actual representation.

We close this section with a couple of miscellaneous items. First, regarding the implications of RM Prescription 5 for *builtin* types, refer to the previous section. Second, RM Prescription 3 states that "it shall be possible to destroy user-defined scalar operators." However, THE_ operators might be felt to violate this prescription slightly, in that they can be destroyed only by destroying the corresponding possible representation (which in practice might mean destroying the associated type itself).

RM PRESCRIPTION 6: TYPE GENERATOR *TUPLE*

*The type generator **TUPLE** shall be supported. That is, given some tuple heading* H *(see RM Prescription 9), it shall be possible to use the **generated type** TUPLE{H} as the basis for defining (or, in the case of values, selecting):*

a. *Values and variables of that generated type (see RM Prescriptions 9 and 12);*

b. *Tuple attribute values and tuple heading attributes of that generated type (again, see RM Prescription 9);*

c. *Declared possible representation components of that generated type (see RM Prescription 5).*

*The generated type TUPLE{H} is referred to as a **tuple type,** and the name of that type is, precisely, TUPLE{H}. The terminology of degree, attributes, and headings introduced in RM Prescription 9 shall apply, mutatis mutandis, to that tuple type, as well as to values and variables of that type (see RM Prescription 12). Tuple types TUPLE{H1} and TUPLE{H2} are equal if and only if H1 = H2. The applicable operators shall include operators analogous to the RENAME, project, EXTEND, and JOIN operators of the relational algebra (see RM Prescription 18), together with tuple assignment (see RM Prescription 21) and tuple comparisons (see RM Prescription 22); they shall also include (a) a tuple selector operator (see RM Prescription 9), (b) an operator for extracting a specified attribute value from a specified tuple (the tuple in question might be required to be of degree one—see RM Prescription 9), and (c) operators for performing tuple "nesting" and "unnesting."*

The main reason the *Manifesto* talks about tuples at all is because it *has* to talk about both relations and scalars, and tuples are the logical middle ground—relations are made out of tuples, and tuples are made out of scalars (loosely speaking). Thus, since we obviously need to support both relation values and variables and scalar values and variables, it would seem artificial not to support tuple values and variables as well. That said, however, we should probably say too that we do not expect tuple values and variables to play much of a part in any real application of **D** *except* in that "logical middle ground" kind of way. In particular, we should probably remind you that we do not permit either tuple or scalar variables within a database.

RM Prescription 6 depends heavily on RM Prescription 9, where the concept of a tuple is precisely defined. For present purposes, however, we simply assume—reasonably enough, given our intended readership!—that the notion is well understood, and content ourselves for the most part with an explanation of the *tuple type generator* concept specifically.* Consider the following example:

```
VAR ADDR TUPLE { STREET CHAR,
                 CITY   CHAR,
                 STATE  CHAR,
                 ZIP    CHAR } ;
```

This statement defines a tuple variable called ADDR, of type

```
TUPLE { STREET CHAR, CITY CHAR, STATE CHAR, ZIP CHAR }
```

—an example of a *generated (tuple) type*. Each of the name:type combinations

```
STREET : CHAR
CITY   : CHAR
STATE  : CHAR
ZIP    : CHAR
```

---

*Type generators are also known as type *constructors;* we use the term "type generator" in the *Manifesto* in order to avoid confusion with the constructor operators of object systems already discussed under RM Prescription 4.

is an *attribute* of that tuple type, and the set of all such attributes taken together is the *heading* of that tuple type. The cardinality of that set—four, in the example— is the *degree* of that tuple type. And, of course, the tuple variable ADDR is also said to have these same attributes, heading, and degree, and so are all possible values of that variable. *Note:* The attributes in the example all happen to have the same de- clared type, CHAR, but of course different attributes can have different declared types, in general.

Observe that **Tutorial D** deliberately does not provide a separate "define tuple type" operator. One reason—not the only one—for this omission is that such an op- erator would presumably involve the introduction of a name for the tuple type in question (i.e., a name over and above the name TUPLE{…} that it already has). And such additional names would complicate other aspects of our proposal: the question of when two tuple types are equal, for example. For such reasons, we permit tuple types to be defined only implicitly—typically as part of the operation that defines a tuple variable, as in the foregoing example.

RM Prescription 6 also requires support for "operators analogous to the RENAME, *project,* EXTEND, and JOIN operators of the relational algebra." Here are some examples that are (we trust) mostly self-explanatory:

```
ADDR RENAME ZIP AS POSTCODE        /* tuple attribute renaming */

ADDR RENAME PREFIX 'ST' AS 'G'        /* ditto, prefix variant */

ADDR { STATE, ZIP }                        /* tuple project */

EXTEND ADDR                                /* tuple extend */
        ADD NAME ('Clark Kent') AS NAME

ADDR JOIN                                  /* tuple join */
        TUPLE { NAME NAME ('Clark Kent'), COUNTRY 'USA' }
```

In the case of tuple join, if the tuples to be joined together have any attributes in common, then each such common attribute must have the same value in both tu- ples (and if they have no common attributes, the tuple join effectively becomes a kind of "tuple Cartesian product" or "tuple concatenate"—it concatenates two given tuples to produce another one). Note too that tuple extend is really just a special case of tuple join.

Here now is an example of a tuple assignment:

```
ADDR  :=  TUPLE { STREET 'One Jacob Way',
                  CITY   'Reading',
                  STATE  'Massachusetts',
                  ZIP    '01870' } ;
```

The expression on the right hand side of this assignment is an example of a *tuple se- lector invocation* (in fact, of course, it is just a tuple literal).

Note: The tuple variable referenced on the left hand side of a tuple assignment and the tuple denoted by the tuple expression on the right hand side must be of ex- actly the same tuple type—meaning they must have the same attribute names, and corresponding attributes must be of the same type in turn (see RM Prescription 21). Analogous remarks apply to tuple comparisons also (see RM Prescription 22).

The following example illustrates the required *attribute extractor* operator, which extracts an individual attribute value from a tuple:

```
VAR STATE_VAR CHAR ;

STATE_VAR  :=  STATE FROM ADDR ;
```

In practice it might be more user-friendly to employ some kind of dot qualification syntax here, thereby writing, e.g., "ADDR.STATE" instead of "STATE FROM ADDR" on the right hand side of the assignment. It might even be desirable to extend that syntax to allow, e.g., expressions of the form A.B.C.D (where A is a tuple variable with a tuple-valued component B—see below—and B has a tuple-valued component C and C has a tuple-valued component D). In this book, however, we will stay with our FROM notation.

As the foregoing discussion suggests, we do explicitly permit tuples (and relations) to include attributes whose values are tuples. The operators that apply to those included tuples are precisely those operators of **D** that apply to tuple values. Here is an example:

```
VAR NADDR TUPLE { NAME NAME,
                  ADDR TUPLE { STREET CHAR,
                               CITY   CHAR,
                               STATE  CHAR,
                               ZIP    CHAR } } ;
```

Note the logical difference between this tuple variable (NADDR) and the following one (BADDR):

```
VAR BADDR TUPLE { NAME   NAME,
                  STREET CHAR,
                  CITY   CHAR,
                  STATE  CHAR,
                  ZIP    CHAR } ;
```

Variable BADDR has five attributes; variable NADDR, by contrast, has only two.

A note on tuple type inference: One important advantage of the tuple type naming scheme prescribed in the *Manifesto—viz.*, that tuple type names be of the form TUPLE{...}—is that it facilitates the task of determining the type of the result of an arbitrary tuple expression. For example, consider the following tuple expression (a tuple projection):

```
BADDR { NAME, ZIP }
```

This particular expression evaluates to a tuple that is derived from the current value of BADDR by projecting away attributes STREET, CITY, and STATE. And the tuple type of that derived tuple is, precisely,

```
TUPLE { NAME NAME, ZIP CHAR }
```

Analogous remarks apply to all possible tuple expressions.

WRAP and UNWRAP operators: Consider the following tuple types:

```
TUPLE { NAME NAME, STREET CHAR, CITY CHAR,
                   STATE  CHAR, ZIP  CHAR }

TUPLE { NAME NAME, ADDR TUPLE { STREET CHAR, CITY CHAR,
                               STATE  CHAR, ZIP  CHAR } }
```

Let us refer to these two tuple types as *TT1* and *TT2*, respectively. Now let BADDR and NADDR be tuple variables of types *TT1* and *TT2*, respectively (as before). Then:

- The expression

```
BADDR WRAP ( STREET, CITY, STATE, ZIP ) AS ADDR
```

takes the current value of BADDR and "wraps" the STREET, CITY, STATE, and ZIP components of that value, to yield a single tuple-valued ADDR component. The result of the expression is thus of type *TT2*, and so (e.g.) the following assignment is valid:

```
NADDR  :=  BADDR WRAP ( STREET, CITY, STATE, ZIP ) AS ADDR ;
```

- The expression

```
NADDR UNWRAP ADDR
```

takes the current value of NADDR and "unwraps" the (tuple-valued) ADDR component of that value, to yield four scalar components STREET, CITY, STATE, and ZIP. The result of the expression is thus of type *TT1*, and so (e.g.) the following assignment is valid:

```
BADDR  :=  NADDR UNWRAP ADDR ;
```

Together, the WRAP and UNWRAP operators thus provide the tuple "nest" and "unnest" capabilities required by RM Prescription 6. *Note:* We refer to those capabilities as nesting and unnesting instead of wrapping and unwrapping in RM Prescription 6 because nesting and unnesting are the terms most commonly used in the literature in this context. We prefer our wrap/unwrap terminology, however, because the nest/unnest terminology carries too much unwanted baggage with it (see in particular the remark concerning "NF^2 relations" in the next section).

RM PRESCRIPTION 7: TYPE GENERATOR
RELATION

*The type generator **RELATION** shall be supported. That is, given some relation heading H (see RM Prescription 10), it shall be possible to use the **generated type** RELATION{H} as the basis for defining (or, in the case of values, selecting):*

a. Values and variables of that generated type (see RM Prescriptions 10 and 13);

b. *Tuple attribute values and tuple heading attributes of that generated type (see RM Prescription 9);*

c. *Declared possible representation components of that generated type (see RM Prescription 5).*

*The generated type RELATION{H} is referred to as a **relation type,** and the name of that type is, precisely, RELATION{H}. The terminology of* degree, attributes, *and* headings *introduced in RM Prescription 10 shall apply,* mutatis mutandis, *to that relation type, as well as to values and variables of that type (see RM Prescription 13). Relation types RELATION{H1} and RELATION{H2} are equal if and only if* H1 = H2. *The applicable operators shall include the operators of the relational algebra (see RM Prescription 18), together with relational assignment (see RM Prescription 21) and relational comparisons (see RM Prescription 22); they shall also include (a) a relation selector operator (see RM Prescription 10), (b) an operator for extracting a specified tuple from a specified relation (the relation in question might be required to be of cardinality one—see RM Prescription 10), and (c) operators for performing relational "nesting" and "unnesting."*

——— ♦♦♦♦♦ ———

It should be clear that this prescription follows the same general pattern as RM Prescription 6; the discussions below therefore parallel those in the previous section. We begin with an example:

```
VAR PQ ... RELATION { P# P#, TOTQ QTY } ... ;
```

(The ellipses "…" indicate that portions of the definition have been omitted because they are not germane to the present discussion.) This statement defines a relation variable or *relvar* called PQ, of type

```
RELATION { P# P#, TOTQ QTY }
```

—an example of a *generated (relation) type.* Each of the name:type combinations

```
P#   : P#
TOTQ : QTY
```

is an *attribute* of that relation type, and the set of all attributes taken together is the *heading* of that relation type. The cardinality of that set—two, in the example—is the *degree* of that relation type. And, of course, the relation variable PQ is also said to have these same attributes, heading, and degree, and so are all possible values of that variable.

Observe that **Tutorial D** deliberately does not provide a separate "define relation type" operator, for much the same reasons that it does not provide an explicit "define tuple type" operator. In other words, we permit relation types to be defined only implicitly—typically as part of the operation that defines a relation variable, as in the foregoing example.

RM Prescription 7 also requires support for the operators of the relational algebra. We defer discussion of those operators to the section on RM Prescription 18, later.

Here is an example of an assignment to relation variable PQ:

```
PQ   :=   SUMMARIZE SP PER P { P# } ADD SUM ( QTY ) AS TOTQ ;
```

What this assignment does, loosely speaking, is assign to relvar PQ a relation consisting of part numbers and corresponding total shipment quantities (see the discussion of SUMMARIZE under RM Prescription 18, later).

Here is another example:

```
PQ   :=   RELATION { TUPLE { P# P#('P1'), TOTQ QTY( 600) } ,
                     TUPLE { P# P#('P5'), TOTQ QTY( 500) } ,
                     TUPLE { P# P#('P2'), TOTQ QTY(1000) } ,
                     TUPLE { P# P#('P4'), TOTQ QTY( 500) } ,
                     TUPLE { P# P#('P3'), TOTQ QTY( 400) } ,
                     TUPLE { P# P#('P6'), TOTQ QTY( 100) } } ;
```

The expression on the right hand side of this assignment is an example of a *relation selector invocation* (in fact, of course, it is just a relation literal).

Note: The relvar referenced on the left hand side of a relational assignment and the relation denoted by the expression on the right hand side must be of exactly the same relation type—meaning they must have the same attribute names, and corresponding attributes must be of the same type in turn (see RM Prescription 21). Analogous remarks apply to relational comparisons also (see RM Prescription 22).

The following example illustrates the required *tuple extractor* operator, which extracts an individual tuple from a relation:

```
VAR PQ_TUPVAR TUPLE { P# P#, TOTQ QTY } ;

PQ_TUPVAR   :=   TUPLE FROM ( PQ WHERE P# = P# ('P1') ) ;
```

In **Tutorial D,** the relation from which the tuple is to be extracted must be of cardinality one (i.e., it must contain just the tuple to be extracted, no more and no less).

Note that we permit relations (and tuples) to include attributes whose values are relations. (However, we explicitly do not espouse NF^2—"NF squared"—relations as described in, e.g., reference [105] because they involve major extensions to the classical relational algebra, extensions that we find unnecessary.) The operators that apply to those included relations are, precisely, those operators of **D** that apply to relation values. Here is an example:

```
VAR SPQ ... RELATION { S# S#,
                       PQ RELATION { P#   P#,
                                     TOTQ QTY } ... } ... ;
```

Note the logical difference between this relvar (SPQ) and the following one (SPT):

```
VAR SPT ... RELATION { S#   S#,
                       P#   P#,
                       TOTQ QTY } ... ;
```

Relvar SPT has three attributes; relvar SPQ, by contrast, has only two.

A note on relation type inference: Just as the tuple type naming scheme discussed in the previous section facilitates the task of determining the type of the result of an arbitrary tuple expression, so the relation type naming scheme discussed above facilitates the task of determining the type of the result of an arbitrary relational expression. For example, consider the following expression (a relational projection):

```
SPT { S#, P# }
```

This particular expression evaluates to a relation that is derived from the current value of relvar SPT by projecting away attribute TOTQ. And the relation type of that derived relation is, precisely,

```
RELATION { S# S#, P# P# }
```

Analogous remarks apply to all possible relational expressions.

WRAP and UNWRAP operators: The WRAP and UNWRAP operators introduced in the previous section in connection with tuples generalize to relations in the obvious way. We omit the details here.

GROUP and UNGROUP operators: Consider the following relation types:

```
RELATION { S# S#, P# P#, TOTQ QTY }
```

```
RELATION { S# S#, PQ RELATION { P# P#, TOTQ QTY } ... }
```

Let us refer to these two relation types as *RT1* and *RT2*, respectively. Now let SPT and SPQ be relvars of types *RT1* and *RT2*, respectively (as before). Then:

- The expression

```
SPT GROUP ( P#, TOTQ ) AS PQ
```

(which might be read as "group SPT by S#," S# being the sole attribute of SPT not mentioned in the GROUP specification) yields a relation defined as follows. First, the heading looks like this:

```
{ S# S#, PQ RELATION { P# P#, TOTQ QTY } }
```

In other words, the heading consists of a relation-valued attribute PQ (where PQ in turn has attributes P# and QTY), together with all of the other attributes of SPT (of course, "all of the other attributes of SPT" here means just attribute S#). Second, the body contains exactly one tuple for each distinct S# value in SPT (and it does not contain any other tuples). Each tuple in that body consists of the applicable S# value (*s,* say), together with a PQ value (*pq,* say) obtained as follows:

- Each SPT tuple is replaced by a tuple (*x,* say) in which the P# and TOTQ components have been wrapped into a tuple-valued component (*y,* say).

- The *y* components of all such tuples *x* in which the S# value is equal to *s* are "grouped" into a relation, *pq,* and a result tuple with S# value equal to *s* and PQ value equal to *pq* is thereby generated.

The overall result is thus of type *RT2,* and so (e.g.) the following assignment is valid:

```
SPQ  :=  SPT GROUP ( P#, TOTQ ) AS PQ ;
```

■ The expression

```
SPQ UNGROUP PQ
```

yields a relation defined as follows. First, the heading looks like this:

```
{ S# S#, P# P#, TOTQ QTY }
```

In other words, the heading consists of attributes P# and TOTQ (derived from attribute PQ), together with all of the other attributes of SPQ (*viz.,* just attribute S#). Second, the body contains exactly one tuple for each combination of a tuple in SPQ and a tuple *pq* in the PQ value within that SPQ tuple (and it does not contain any other tuples). Each tuple in that body consists of the applicable S# value (*s,* say), together with P# and TOTQ values (*p* and *tq,* say) obtained as follows:

- Each SPQ tuple is replaced by a set of tuples, one such tuple (*x,* say) for each tuple in the PQ value in that SPQ tuple. Each such tuple *x* contains an S# component (*s,* say) equal to the S# component from the SPQ tuple in question and a tuple-valued component (*pq,* say) equal to some tuple from the PQ component from the SPQ tuple in question.

- The *pq* components of each such tuple *x* in which the S# value is equal to *s* are unwrapped into separate P# and TOTQ components (*p* and *tq,* say), and a result tuple with S# value equal to *s,* P# value equal to *p,* and TOTQ value equal to *tq* is thereby generated.

The overall result is thus of type *RT1,* and so (e.g.) the following assignment is valid:

```
SPT  :=  SPQ UNGROUP PQ ;
```

Together, the GROUP and UNGROUP operators thus provide the relation "nest" and "unnest" capabilities required by RM Prescription 7. Again we prefer our own terminology over the more conventional nest/unnest terminology, however.

RM PRESCRIPTION 8: EQUALITY

*The **equality** comparison operator "=" shall be defined for every type. Let expressions X1 and X2 denote values v1 and v2, respectively, where v1 and v2 are of the same type T. Then X1 = X2 shall be* true *if and only if v1 and v2 are in fact the same element of T (i.e., if and only if X1 and X2 denote the same value). Moreover, let Op be an operator with a parameter P of declared type T. Then, for all such operators Op, if X1 = X2 is* true, *then two (successful) invocations of Op that* *are identical in all respects except that the argument corresponding to* P *is specified as* X1 *in one case and* X2 *in the other shall be indistinguishable in their effect. Conversely, if there exists such an operator* Op *such that two (successful) invocations of* Op *that are identical in all respects except that the argument corresponding to* P *is specified as* X1 *in one case and* X2 *in the other are distinguishable in their effect, then* X1 = X2 *shall be* false.

──── ♦♦♦♦♦ ────

This prescription should be mostly self-explanatory, but we give an example to illustrate the part concerning operator invocations. Let CH2 and CH3 be the character string literals

   `'AB'`

and

   `'AB '`

respectively (note the trailing space character in CH3). Further, let type CHAR be defined in such a way that the comparison CH2 = CH3 gives *true* (in other words, CH2 and CH3 are regarded as denoting the same character string). Then the operator CHAR_LENGTH ("character string length") must be such that the comparison CHAR_LENGTH (CH2) = CHAR_LENGTH (CH3) also gives *true*.* (We remark in passing that SQL fails to support RM Prescription 8 on precisely this example, among others.)

Conversely, if CHAR_LENGTH (or any other operator on character strings) yields a different result depending on whether it is invoked on CH2 or CH3, then the comparison CH2 = CH3 must give *false,* by definition.

Note carefully that the foregoing remarks apply to THE_ operators in particular, a fact that has some important consequences, as we now explain.

- First, let type *T* have a possible representation *PR* that involves a component *C*. Let *X1* and *X2* denote values of type *T*. If THE_*C(X1)* ≠ THE_*C(X2)*, then *X1* ≠ *X2* as explained above, and hence *X1* and *X2* denote distinct values. It follows that no value of type *T* can possibly be represented in two distinct ways using the same possible representation *PR*.

- It further follows that certain possible representations must therefore be regarded as being held in some **canonical form.**

In order to illustrate these points, let us suppose that type RATIONAL is not builtin and we therefore wish to define such a type for ourselves. One possible

---

*Furthermore, the concatenate operator "‖" must be such that the expressions CH3‖CH2 and CH2‖CH3 give the same result, which implies that the character strings 'AB AB' and 'ABAB' must be considered equal, which further implies that embedded (as well as trailing) spaces are meaningless for this particular character string data type.

representation we might consider is pairs of integers, representing the numerator and denominator of the rational value in question:

```
TYPE RATIONAL POSSREP ( N INTEGER, D INTEGER )
              CONSTRAINT ( THE_D ( RATIONAL ) > 0 ) ;
```

(See RM Prescription 23 for an explanation of the CONSTRAINT specification.) However, this definition is inadequate as it stands, because it would allow, e.g., (3,2), (6,4), (9,6), ... all as equally valid possible representations of the rational number "1.5" (thereby violating the first of the two points spelled out above). Thus, we need to extend the constraint specification as follows:

```
TYPE RATIONAL POSSREP ( N INTEGER, D INTEGER )
              CONSTRAINT ( THE_D ( RATIONAL ) > 0 AND
                          COPRIME ( THE_N ( RATIONAL ) ,
                                    THE_D ( RATIONAL ) ) ;
```

We are assuming the existence of an operator COPRIME that returns *true* if its two integer arguments have no common factors other than the value one and *false* otherwise. The effect, conceptually, is that the only legal possible representation for (e.g.) the rational number "1.5" is the canonical form (3,2). In other words, although the RATIONAL selector invocations

```
RATIONAL ( 3, 2 )
RATIONAL ( 6, 4 )
RATIONAL ( 9, 6 )
```

(and many others like them) are all legal and all yield the same value, that value is conceptually represented in the canonical form (3,2) in every case. (Note that it will be the responsibility of the type implementer to ensure that these invocations do in fact all yield the desired result and do not cause any type constraint violations.) Thus, if (e.g.) the operator THE_N is applied to any of the selector invocations shown, it will always return the integer value three.

The data type TIME provides another good example of a type for which distinct selector invocations might yield the same value. For example, the (hypothetical) selector invocations TIME ('10:00 am PST') and TIME ('6:00 pm GMT') might very well denote the same absolute time.

Incidentally, it follows from RM Prescription 8 that "=" is a *polymorphic* operator, inasmuch as it applies to operands of many different types (in fact, of *every* type). The particular kind of polymorphism in question is sometimes called *ad hoc* polymorphism [13] (other kinds exist, as we will see elsewhere in this book, but they are beyond the scope of the present discussion). It is also known as *overloading*. We remark that if *Op* is a polymorphic operator (of any kind), then it is possible, or even probable, that several versions—i.e., several distinct implementations—of *Op* will exist under the covers.

Following on from the previous point, we now observe that the possibility of overloading "=" still further to operate between values of different types—thereby supporting equality comparisons between, e.g., integers and rational numbers, or US dollars and UK sterling (etc.)—is not precluded.* In **Tutorial D,** however, we assume that the operator is not overloaded in this way, but instead requires its operands always to be of exactly the same type (except possibly if type inheritance is supported—see Chapter 14). Indeed, it is our opinion that *coercions,* if supported (see OO Very Strong Suggestion 1), constitute a better approach to the problem of comparisons between values of different types. *Note:* The term *coercion* simply means *implicit conversion between types.*

RM PRESCRIPTION 9: TUPLES

*A **tuple value** t (**tuple** for short) is a set of ordered triples of the form <A,T,v>, where:*

a. *A is the name of an **attribute** of t. No two distinct triples in t shall have the same attribute name.*

b. *T is the name of the **type** of attribute A of t.*

c. *v is a value of type T, called the **attribute value** for attribute A of t.*

*The cardinality of the set of triples in t—equivalently, the number of attributes of t—is the **degree** of t. The set of ordered pairs <A,T> that is obtained by eliminating the v (value) component from each triple is the **heading** of t; tuple t is said to **conform** to that heading (equivalently, t is said to be of the corresponding tuple type—see RM Prescription 6), the degree of t is said to be the **degree** of that heading, and the attributes and corresponding types of t are said to be the **attributes** and corresponding **types** of that heading. Given a tuple heading H, a selector operator shall be available for selecting an arbitrary tuple conforming to H.*

————— ♦♦♦♦♦ —————

The purpose of this prescription is simply to pin down the notion of *tuple* precisely. Essentially, a tuple is a set of triples of the form *<A,T,v>* (not **Tutorial D** syntax), where *A* is an attribute name, *T* is the corresponding type name, and *v* is the corresponding value (and no two triples in the set have the same *A* component).[†] Thus, a tuple can be pictured as in this example:

MAJOR_P# : P#	MINOR_P# : P#	QTY : QTY
P2	P4	7

---

*In other words, we prescribe the semantics of "=" in the case where the comparands are of the same type but not otherwise.

[†]We note in passing that—at least in the absence of type inheritance (see Part IV)—*T* is in fact implied by *v,* by virtue of RM Prescription 2.

The attribute names here are MAJOR_P#, MINOR_P#, and QTY; the corresponding type names are P#, P# again, and QTY; and the corresponding values are P#('P2'), P#('P4'), and QTY(7) (for simplicity, these values have been abbreviated to just P2, P4, and 7, respectively, in the picture). The degree of this tuple is three. Its heading is the set of attributes—i.e., pairs—of the form $<A,T>$ (not **Tutorial D** syntax) obtained by eliminating the v (value) component from each triple:

MAJOR_P# : P#	MINOR_P# : P#	QTY : QTY

A given tuple is said to *conform* to a given heading if its heading is identical to the given one (equivalently, it is said to be of a given *tuple type* if its heading is identical to the heading of that given type—see RM Prescription 6).

Note, incidentally, that (by definition) every tuple contains exactly one value for each of its attributes. Note too that (again by definition) no tuple contains anything extra, over and above the prescribed $<A,T,v>$ triples. In particular, there are no "hidden" components that can be accessed only by invocation of some special operator instead of by regular attribute name references, or that cause invocations of the regular operators on tuples (or relations) to have irregular effects. Thus, for example, there are no hidden *tuple IDs* or *object IDs* as are sometimes proposed to allow something to retain its so-called identity even across changes to all of its visible parts (see the discussion of OO Proscription 2 in Chapter 9). Similarly, there are no hidden *timestamps* as have been proposed for the support of "temporal databases" in reference [107].*

RM Prescription 9 also requires support for tuple selectors, and hence for tuple literals. However, we have already discussed these requirements under RM Prescription 6.

Incidentally, observe that tuples, and hence tuple headings, of degree zero are legal (indeed, they are required by RM Proscription 5, which is discussed in the next chapter). We refer to such a tuple—in fact, there is exactly one such!—as the *0-tuple*.

Finally, note that no tuple heading can be defined, directly or indirectly, in terms of itself. More precisely, let H be a tuple heading. Define a sequence of sets *S1, S2,* ... as follows:

$S1$ = the set of declared types for all attributes of H that are declared to be of some tuple or relation type

Si = the set of declared types for all attributes of all types in $S(i-1)$ that are declared to be of some tuple or relation type ($i > 1$)

Then there must exist some value n ($n > 0$) such that every type in the set Sn is system-defined. In other words, no tuple heading H can have a tuple- or relation-valued attribute of type TUPLE{H} or RELATION{H}, or a tuple- or relation-

---

*In fact, any such hidden components would constitute a violation of *The Information Principle* (see the discussion of RM Prescription 16 later in this chapter).

valued attribute for which some attribute of the tuple or relation type in question is of type TUPLE{*H*} or RELATION{*H*}, or … (etc., etc.).

RM PRESCRIPTION 10: RELATIONS

*A **relation value** r (**relation** for short) consists of a* heading *and a* body, *where:*

a. *The **heading** of r is a tuple heading* H *as defined in RM Prescription 9; relation r is said to **conform** to that heading (equivalently, r is said to be of the corresponding relation type—see RM Prescription 7), and the degree of that heading is said to be the **degree** of r. The attributes and corresponding types of* H *are the **attributes** and corresponding **types** of r.*

b. *The **body** of r is a set* B *of tuples, all having that same heading* H; *the cardinality of that body is said to be the **cardinality** of r.*

Given a relation heading H, *a selector operator shall be available for selecting an arbitrary relation conforming to* H.

———— ♦♦♦♦♦ ————

It should be clear that this prescription follows more or less the same pattern as RM Prescription 9; just as the purpose of RM Prescription 9 was to pin down the notion of *tuple* precisely, so the purpose of the present prescription is to pin down the notion of *relation* precisely. The discussions below therefore parallel those in the previous section, to some extent.

Essentially, a relation consists of a *heading* and a *body,* where the heading is a tuple heading as defined in RM Prescription 9 and the body is a set of tuples that conform to that heading. A relation can thus be pictured as a table, as in this example:*

MAJOR_P# : P#	MINOR_P# : P#	QTY : QTY
P1	P2	5
P1	P3	3
P2	P3	2
P2	P4	7
P3	P5	4
P4	P6	8

---

*The example is basically a repeat of Fig. 2.2 in Chapter 2. Incidentally, we can now explain why we prefer *relation* over *table* as the term for the basic data construct in the relational model. *Relation* has a precise (and somewhat abstract) definition; *table,* by contrast, does not. (It could be given one, of course, but any such definition would always run the risk of being misunderstood, owing to the familiar but fuzzy meaning—or meanings, plural—that the term already has.) Thus, a table in the relational world can best be thought of as *a concrete picture of an abstract idea* (*viz.,* a relation as such). And that picture, convenient though it is in informal contexts, does unfortunately suggest some things that are not true; for example, it clearly suggests that the tuples of the relation are in a certain top to bottom order, which of course is not the case.

The attributes, their types, and the degree of this relation are all inherited in the obvious way from the heading. The cardinality (i.e., the number of tuples in the body) is seven. A given relation is said to *conform* to a given heading if its heading is identical to the given one (equivalently, it is said to be of a given *relation type* if its heading is identical to the heading of that given type—see RM Prescription 7). Note that (again by definition) every relation contains exactly one value for each of its attributes in each tuple in its body; in other words, every relation is, by definition, in *first normal form*—even though we allow relations to include attributes whose values are tuples or relations, as we have already seen.

RM Prescription 10 also requires support for relation selectors, and hence for relation literals. However, we have already discussed these requirements under RM Prescription 7.

Relations and Their Interpretation

Let *r* be a relation with heading

```
{ <A1,T1>, <A2,T2>, ..., <An,Tn> }
```

and let *t* be a tuple of the form

```
{ <A1,T1,v1>, <A2,T2,v2>, ..., <An,Tn,vn> }
```

(i.e., *t* conforms to the heading of *r*). Then we observe that:

- The heading of *r* can be regarded as a predicate—i.e., a truth-valued function, with parameters *A1, A2, ..., An* of the indicated types; and
- The tuple *t* can be regarded as an *instantiation* of that predicate—i.e., a *proposition,* obtained by substituting the argument values *v1, v2, ..., vn* for those parameters. (A *proposition* in logic is something that evaluates to either *true* or *false,* categorically.)

Furthermore, we subscribe to the *Closed World Assumption,* according to which:

- If *t* appears in the body of *r,* then it is a *true instantiation* of the predicate (i.e., the corresponding proposition is considered to be *true*);
- Conversely, if *t* does not appear in the body of *r,* then it is a *false* instantiation (i.e., the corresponding proposition is considered to be *false*).

We discussed this interpretation of relations in some detail in Chapter 2 (in the section entitled "Relations *vs.* Relvars"). Here we just remind you of the salient points from that discussion. Consider the following heading once again:

MAJOR_P# : P#	MINOR_P# : P#	QTY : QTY

The predicate here is: *Part MAJOR_P# (a value of type P#) contains quantity QTY (a value of type QTY) of part MINOR_P# (a value of type P# again);* note, therefore, that the predicate is, informally, **what the relation means.** And here once again is a tuple that conforms to this heading:

MAJOR_P# : P#	MINOR_P# : P#	QTY : QTY
P2	P4	7

The proposition (or predicate instantiation) here is: *Part P2 contains quantity 7 of part P4.* And if the tuple actually appears in the relation, we take this proposition to be *true;* otherwise, we take it to be *false.*

   Note: We will revisit and elaborate on this question of predicates under RM Prescription 24, later.

Miscellaneous Issues

We close this section with a couple of miscellaneous points:

- First, note that relations, and hence relation headings, of degree zero are legal (indeed, they are required by RM Proscription 5, which is discussed in the next chapter). In fact, there are exactly two such relations—one whose body contains just one tuple (the 0-tuple, of course), and one whose body contains no tuples at all. Following references [27] and [31], we refer to these two relations as TABLE_DEE and TABLE_DUM, respectively. We note that these two relations can be interpreted as *true* and *false,* respectively.

- Second, no relation heading can be defined, directly or indirectly, in terms of itself. (This point follows immediately from the fact that a relation heading is just a tuple heading; as we have already seen under RM Prescription 9, no tuple heading can be defined, directly or indirectly, in terms of itself.)

RM PRESCRIPTION 11: SCALAR VARIABLES

*A **scalar variable of type** **T** is a variable whose permitted values are scalars of a specified scalar type* T, *the **declared type** of that variable. **D** shall provide facilities for users to define scalar variables. Defining a scalar variable shall have the effect of initializing that variable to some value—either a value specified explicitly as part of the operation that defines the variable, or some implementation-defined value if no such explicit value is specified.*

This prescription does not seem to require much in the way of further explanation. We therefore content ourselves with repeating some of the scalar variable definitions already shown in earlier examples (with the minor addition of an INIT specification, in the case of the point variable P):

```
VAR X RATIONAL INIT ( +4.0 ) ;
VAR Y RATIONAL INIT ( -3.0 ) ;

VAR TEMP TEMPERATURE ;

VAR P POINT INIT ( POINT ( +4.0, -3.0 ) ) ;
VAR LS LINESEG ;
```

RM PRESCRIPTION 12: TUPLE VARIABLES

A ***tuple variable of type TUPLE{H}*** *is a variable whose permitted values are tuples that conform to a specified tuple heading* H. *The **declared type** of that tuple variable is* TUPLE{H}. *The attributes of* H *are the **attributes** of the tuple variable, the corresponding types are the **declared types** of those attributes, and the degree of* H *is the **degree** of the tuple variable.* **D** *shall provide facilities for users to define tuple variables. Defining a tuple variable shall have the effect of initializing that variable to some tuple value—either a value specified explicitly as part of the operation that defines the variable, or some implementation-defined value if no such explicit value is specified.*

———— ♦♦♦♦♦ ————

Again we content ourselves with showing a few examples (note the comments in each case):

```
VAR ADDR TUPLE              /* note explicit initialization */
        { STREET CHAR,
          CITY    CHAR,
          STATE   CHAR,
          ZIP     CHAR }
        INIT ( TUPLE { STREET '', CITY '', STATE '', ZIP '' } ) ;

VAR NADDR TUPLE            /* note tuple-valued component */
        { NAME NAME,
          ADDR TUPLE { STREET CHAR,
                       CITY    CHAR,
                       STATE   CHAR,
                       ZIP     CHAR } } ;

VAR NADDRS TUPLE          /* note relation-valued component */
        { NAME  NAME,
          ADDRS RELATION { STREET CHAR,
                           CITY    CHAR,
                           STATE   CHAR,
                           ZIP     CHAR } ... } ;

VAR NADDRS TUPLE                    /* note the LOC (location) */
        { NAME  NAME,               /* attribute of the ADDRS  */
          ADDRS RELATION { STREET CHAR,   /* attribute is of */
                           CITY    CHAR,   /* a user-defined  */
                           STATE   CHAR,   /* type, POINT     */
                           ZIP     CHAR,
                           LOC     POINT } ... } ;
```

RM PRESCRIPTION 13: RELATION VARIABLES (RELVARS)

*A **relation variable—relvar** for short—of type **RELATION{H}** is a variable whose permitted values are relations that conform to a specified relation heading H. The **declared type** of that relvar is RELATION{H}. The attributes of H are the **attributes** of the relvar, the corresponding types are the **declared types** of those attributes, and the degree of H is the **degree** of the relvar. **D** shall provide facilities for users to define and destroy database relvars (i.e., relvars that belong to the database, as opposed to the application—see RM Prescription 16). **D** shall also provide facilities for users to define application relvars (i.e., relvars that are not database relvars).*

——— ♦♦♦♦♦ ———

In the interests of **logical data independence** [78], we draw a sharp distinction between relvar definitions as understood by the system (i.e., relvar definitions as kept in the catalog—see RM Prescription 25) and relvar definitions as understood by a given application. In other words, there are two sets of definitions, one in the application and one in the catalog; the former set represents the application's perception of the database, the latter represents the database "as it really is." Thus, if it subsequently becomes necessary to change the structure of the database "as it really is," logical data independence is preserved by changing the *mapping* between the two sets of definitions (the mapping in question, of course, being done outside the application, though presumably still within the overall **D** environment).

Here then are some examples of relvar definitions in **Tutorial D** (for simplicity, we assume that all required types have already been defined). First the suppliers, parts, and shipments relvars from the suppliers-and-parts database:

```
VAR S REAL RELATION { S#      S#,
                      SNAME   NAME,
                      STATUS  INTEGER,
                      CITY    CHAR }
               KEY { S# } ;

VAR P REAL RELATION { P#      P#,
                      PNAME   NAME,
                      COLOR   COLOR,
                      WEIGHT  WEIGHT,
                      CITY    CHAR }
               KEY { P# } ;

VAR SP REAL RELATION { S#  S#,
                       P#  P#,
                       QTY QTY }
               KEY { S#, P# } ;
```

These first three examples should be more or less self-explanatory, except perhaps for the REAL specifications, which mean that the relvars are real as opposed to virtual (see RM Prescription 14), and the KEY specifications, which are discussed under RM Prescription 15. Relvars S, P, and SP are now part of the database (i.e., they are described by entries in the catalog).

```
VAR NADDRLOC REAL RELATION { ID    INTEGER,
                             NAME NAME,
                             ADDR TUPLE { STREET CHAR,
                                          CITY   CHAR,
                                          STATE  CHAR,
                                          ZIP    CHAR },
                             LOC  POINT }
                  KEY { ID } ;
```

This example illustrates both (a) a tuple-valued attribute, ADDR, and (b) an attribute, LOC, that is of a user-defined scalar type (POINT).

```
VAR PQ LOCAL RELATION { P#   P#,
                        TOTQ QTY }
              KEY { P# } ;
```

This statement defines a relvar that is local to the application instead of being part of the database (it is basically a repeat of the definition given under RM Prescription 7 earlier, but now shown complete).*

```
VAR SV GLOBAL RELATION { S#    S#,
                         SNAME NAME,
                         CITY  CHAR }
               KEY { S# } ;
```

This statement defines the application's perception of some data (presumably a projection of the suppliers relvar) that is supposed to exist in the database.

```
VAR SSP GLOBAL RELATION { S#     S#,
                          SNAME  NAME,
                          STATUS INTEGER,
                          CITY   CHAR,
                          P#     P#,
                          QTY    QTY }
                KEY { S#, P# } ;
```

This statement also defines the application's perception of some data that is supposed to exist in the database—presumably the join of suppliers and shipments on supplier numbers.

```
VAR MYRV LOCAL SAME_TYPE_AS ( S JOIN SP ) ;
```

The application relvar MYRV is defined to be of the same type as—i.e., to have the same heading as—the result of the relational expression S JOIN SP. It is also defined to have exactly the candidate keys that can be inferred by the system for that result (see the discussion of RM Very Strong Suggestion 3 in Chapter 10). *Note:* In **Tutorial D,** the ability to define a variable as being of the same type as the result of some

---

*We note that one reviewer (David McGoveran) felt there was no need for such local relvars.

expression is not limited to relation variables only but applies to scalar and tuple variables too (see Chapter 5).

Finally, here is an example of destroying a relvar:

```
DROP VAR SP ;
```

The specified relvar must be a database relvar (in **Tutorial D** terms, its definition must have specified either REAL or VIRTUAL, not LOCAL or GLOBAL). *Note:* Although we do not explicitly prescribe such a thing, we do not mean to preclude the possibility that **D** might usefully include some kind of "alter relvar" operator as a shorthand (analogous to ALTER TABLE in SQL).

RM PRESCRIPTION 14: REAL *VS.* VIRTUAL RELVARS

Database relvars are either real *or* virtual. *A **virtual relvar** is a database relvar whose value at any given time is the result of evaluating a certain relational expression, specified when the relvar in question is defined. A **real relvar** is a database relvar that is not virtual. Defining a real relvar shall have the effect of initializing that relvar to an empty relation (i.e., a relation of cardinality zero).*

———— ♦♦♦♦♦ ————

First, a note on terminology: Real and virtual relvars correspond to what are known in common parlance as "base relations" and "views," respectively. We prefer our terms because they capture the essential idea better and relate better to other areas of computer science. (Of course, *real* here does not necessarily imply *physically stored!*)

Now, we have already seen several examples of real relvar definitions in the previous section. Here by contrast are a couple of virtual relvar definition examples:

```
VAR PART_CITIES VIRTUAL P { P#, CITY }
                    /* projection of parts on P# and CITY */
                    KEY { P# } ;

VAR COLOCATED VIRTUAL S JOIN P
                    /* join of suppliers and parts on CITY */
                    KEY { S#, P# } ;
```

Note: If the KEY specifications were omitted in these examples, the relvars would be considered to have whatever candidate keys could be inferred by the system from the specified relational expressions. See the discussion of RM Very Strong Suggestion 3 in Chapter 10.

Now, it is important to understand that, like real relvars, virtual relvars are *variables,* and hence updatable by definition. The point is therefore worth stressing that, contrary to what has traditionally been thought, such relvars (or "views") are in fact *always* updatable, barring integrity constraint violations [55,79]. Space unfortunately does not permit a detailed explanation of this point here; we content ourselves with a few general remarks and a sketch of an example that should suffice to give the general idea.

- As we will see under RM Prescription 24, every relvar has an associated *relvar predicate,* which is (loosely) the logical AND of all integrity constraints that apply to the relvar in question. It is an unshakable principle—indeed, we sometimes refer to it as *The Golden Rule*—that no statement is ever allowed to leave any relvar with a value that causes its relvar predicate to be violated.

- Note carefully too that, by virtue of the *constraint inference* mechanism to be discussed under RM Prescription 23, the foregoing remarks apply to virtual relvars as well as real ones; in other words, "views" too have predicates that they are never allowed to violate. For example, let virtual relvar *RC* be defined as the union of two real relvars *RA* and *RB*. Let the predicates for *RA* and *RB* be *PA* and *PB,* respectively. Then the predicate for *RC, PC* say, is *(PA)* OR *(PB)*.

- Suppose now that the user tries to "insert a tuple" *t* into that "union view" *RC.* * Then *t* must satisfy the predicate *PC = (PA)* OR *(PB)*; hence, it must satisfy *PA* or *PB* (or both). If it satisfies *PA,* it is inserted into *RA;* if it satisfies *PB,* it is inserted into *RB;* and if it satisfies both predicates, it is inserted into both relvars, of course. In every case, the net effect is that the user's "union view update" request has been honored appropriately.

Thus we see that, taken together, *relvar predicates* and *constraint inference* are the key to the relvar updating mechanism (for real relvars as well as virtual ones; again, see RM Prescriptions 23 and 24). For further information, see references [55] and [79].

Incidentally, it is well known, but worth emphasizing nonetheless, that virtual relvars serve two rather different purposes. A user who actually *defines* a virtual relvar *R* is, obviously, aware of the relational expression *RX* from which values of that relvar are obtained; such a user can use the name *R* wherever the expression *RX* is intended, but such uses are basically just shorthand. A user who is merely informed that relvar *R* exists and is available for use, on the other hand, is typically *not* aware of the expression *RX;* to such a user, in fact, relvar *R* should look and behave exactly like a real relvar.

Following on from this point, it is also worth emphasizing that the question as to which relvars are real and which virtual is somewhat arbitrary. For example, let *RA, RB,* and *RC* be relvars with values (at some particular time) *ra, rb,* and *rc,*

---

*Actually there is no such thing as an operation that "inserts a tuple," thanks to RM Proscription 7 (see Chapter 7). We talk in such terms here only to make the example a little easier to follow from an intuitive standpoint.

respectively. If it is true for all time that the values *ra, rb,* and *rc* at the time in question are such that *ra* and *rb* are projections of *rc* and *rc* is the join of those projections, then either (a) *RA* and *RB* could be real and *RC* virtual, or (b) *RC* could be real and *RA* and *RB* virtual. It follows that there must be no arbitrary and unnecessary distinctions—concerning, e.g., updatability in particular—between real and virtual relvars. We refer to this fact as *The Principle of Interchangeability* (of real and virtual relvars).

RM PRESCRIPTION 15: CANDIDATE KEYS

*By definition, every relvar always has at least one **candidate key**. At least one such key shall be defined at the time the relvar in question is defined, and it shall not be possible to destroy all of the candidate keys of a given relvar (other than by destroying the relvar itself).*

——— ♦♦♦♦♦ ———

It is convenient to begin with a precise definition of the term "candidate key." Let *K* be a set of attributes of relvar *R*. Then *K* is a *candidate key* for *R* if and only if it possesses both of the following properties:*

- *Uniqueness:* No legal value of *R* ever contains two distinct tuples with the same value for *K*.
- *Irreducibility* (also known as *nonredundancy*): No proper subset of *K* has the uniqueness property.

Note: Historically, it has been usual to insist that, at least in the case of real relvars, there be a distinguished candidate key called the *primary key.* We agree that this discipline might be useful in practice, but we do not insist on it (and **Tutorial D** does not support it), because we regard the idea of making one candidate key somehow "more equal than the others" as a psychological issue merely [65]. Of course, we do not prohibit it either, in appropriate circumstances.

To repeat, every relvar has at least one candidate key. In the case of a virtual relvar, explicit specification of such keys is optional, because (as mentioned in the previous section) the system should be able to infer them for itself; in other cases, at least one such key must be explicitly specified at the time the relvar is defined (unless SAME_TYPE_AS is used in that relvar definition as illustrated in the section on RM Prescription 13). Now, we have already seen several examples of relvars having just one such key. Here are a few examples that involve more than one.

---

*Observe that our definition applies to *relvars* specifically. As noted in Chapter 4, an analogous notion can be defined for relation *values* (and hence relation constants) as well (see, e.g., reference [56]), but relvars are the important case.

```
VAR TAX_BRACKETS REAL RELATION { LOW          MONEY,
                                 HIGH          MONEY,
                                 PERCENTAGE RATIONAL }
                    KEY { LOW }
                    KEY { HIGH }
                    KEY { PERCENTAGE } ;

VAR MARRIAGES REAL RELATION { HUSBAND          NAME,
                              WIFE             NAME,
                              DATE_OF_MARRIAGE DATE }
/* assuming no polyandry or polygyny and no couple marrying  */
/* each other more than once ...                             */
                    KEY { HUSBAND, DATE_OF_MARRIAGE }
                    KEY { DATE_OF_MARRIAGE, WIFE }
                    KEY { WIFE, HUSBAND } ;

VAR PLUS REAL RELATION { X INTEGER, Y INTEGER, Z INTEGER }
                    /* X + Y = Z */
                    KEY { X, Y }
                    KEY { Y, Z }
                    KEY { Z, X } ;
```

As noted in Chapter 4, this last example might better be regarded as a relation *constant* rather than a relation variable—its value does not change over time—and it might be desirable in practice to provide some special syntax for defining such relation constants explicitly.

RM PRESCRIPTION 16: DATABASES

> A ***database*** *is a named container for relvars; the content of a given database at any given time is a set of (database) relvars. The necessary operators for defining and destroying databases shall not be part of **D** (in other words, defining and destroying databases shall be done "outside the **D** environment").*

We begin by stressing the point that databases, as we use the term, are a purely logical concept; how they map to physical storage is implementation-defined. In the extreme case, a single **D** database could be physically distributed across any number of disparate computers, running any number of disparate DBMSs, at any number of mutually remote sites. We have two major reasons for wanting to introduce such a concept into the *Manifesto:*

- To draw a boundary between data that is "persistent" and data that is not;
- To draw a boundary between data that is accessible to a given transaction and data that is not.

First, regarding *persistence:* Databases (and nothing else) are defined to be "persistent," meaning—loosely—that their lifetime is greater than that of the typical transaction or application execution; more precisely, once an update has been applied to a database and committed, that update is guaranteed never to be rolled back.* Note carefully, therefore, that since the only kind of variable we permit within a database is, very specifically, the relvar, the only kind of variable that might possess the property of persistence is the relvar. Thus, we reject the object world dictum—see, e.g., references [1–2] and [111]—that "persistence should be orthogonal to type," for reasons explained in detail in reference [70]. *Note:* As we have already seen, relvars can exist that are not database relvars (i.e., that do not belong to any database). Such relvars are of course not persistent.

Second, regarding *accessibility:* Any given transaction is defined to interact with exactly one database, meaning that (a) every database relvar accessed by that transaction belongs to the same database, and hence *a fortiori* that (b) every database relvar mentioned within a given relational expression must be part of the same database (see RM Prescriptions 17 and 18). Thus, if database *DB* is the database associated with transaction *TX,* then *TX* must not mention any relvar *R* that is part of some distinct database *DB'* and not part of database *DB*.

Note: It follows that database relvar names must be unique within their containing database. This is one reason why we insist that database definition and destruction be done "outside the **D** environment"—for if not, we would need a scope within which *database* names were unique, which would simply push the naming issue out to another level. In practice, of course, database definition and destruction will presumably be done by means of some kind of system-provided utilities (and the user might even think of those utilities, harmlessly, as in fact being part of the overall "**D** environment").

Observe that we do not prescribe a mechanism for making and breaking the necessary connections between transactions and databases. In practice, such operations will presumably be performed by means of some kind of CONNECT and DISCONNECT statements. The reason we do not prescribe any such mechanism is simply that, in practice, such mechanisms involve far too many concepts—clients, servers, processes, sessions, "DBMS instances," and many other things—that are beyond the purview of the *Manifesto per se.*

We remark that, by insisting on the database relvar as the only kind of variable permitted inside the database, we are subscribing to Codd's *Information Principle.* Codd has stated this principle in various forms and various places over the years; indeed, he has referred to it on occasion as the *fundamental* principle of the relational model. It can be stated thus [72]:

> *All information in the database at any given time must be cast explicitly in terms of values in relations and in no other way*

---

*Except possibly as noted under OO Prescription 6 (see Chapter 8).

In his book [22], Codd gives a number of arguments in support of this principle (arguments with which we concur, of course). And he goes on to point out that one consequence of the principle is that all interrelating between different parts of the database must be "achieved by comparisons of values." In other words, Codd is arguing here against *pointers* or "object IDs"! See the discussion of OO Proscription 2 in Chapter 9.*

One last point: The first "official" version of this *Manifesto* [38] drew a distinction between databases *per se* and database *variables* (analogous to the distinction between relations *per se* and relation variables). It also introduced the term *dbvar* as shorthand for "database variable." While we still believe this distinction to be a valid one, we found that it had little direct relevance to other aspects of the *Manifesto*. We therefore decided, in the interests of familiarity, to revert to more traditional terminology.

RM PRESCRIPTION 17: TRANSACTIONS

*Each **transaction** shall interact with exactly one database. However, distinct transactions shall be able to interact with distinct databases, and distinct databases shall not necessarily be disjoint. Also, it shall be possible for a transaction to define new relvars, or destroy existing ones, within its associated database (see RM Prescription 13).*

This prescription seems to need little in the way of elaboration. Just one point: A database that contains only real relvars might be regarded as a "real" database. Individual transactions, however, will interact with a "user" database that (in general) contains a mixture of real and virtual relvars, where the relvars in question all belong to, or are ultimately derived from, the same real database. Of course, the objective of logical data independence implies that, from the point of view of the transaction concerned, any given "user" database should look and behave just like a real one as far as the user is concerned. In other words, every relvar in that "user" database should look and behave just like a real relvar[†]—which implies further that the choice as to which database is "real" is somewhat arbitrary, so long as all choices are information-equivalent: *The Principle of Interchangeability* in another guise (see RM Prescription 14).

---

*We note in passing that SQL violates *The Information Principle* in a variety of ways; see, for example, the discussion of RM Proscriptions 1, 3, and 4 in Chapter 7.

[†]Apart possibly from virtual relvars defined by the user in question, where the user is of course aware of the fact that the relvars in question are indeed virtual.

RM PRESCRIPTION 18: RELATIONAL ALGEBRA

> *D* *shall support the usual operators of the* **relational algebra** *(or some logical equiv-*
> *alent thereof). Specifically, it shall support, directly or indirectly, at least the oper-*
> *ators RENAME, restrict (WHERE), project, EXTEND, JOIN, UNION, INTERSECT,*
> *MINUS, (generalized) DIVIDEBY PER, and (generalized) SUMMARIZE PER. All*
> *such operators shall be expressible without excessive circumlocution.* *D* *shall also*
> *support the required* **relation type inference** *mechanism, whereby the heading of the*
> *result of evaluating an arbitrary relational expression shall be well defined and*
> *known to both the system and the user (see RM Prescription 7).*

—— ♦♦♦♦♦ ——

We assume you are already familiar with most of the operators mentioned in this prescription (in any case, formal definitions were given in Chapters 4 and 5); the only ones that might be worth elaborating on here are the generalized versions of DIVIDEBY and SUMMARIZE. Before getting into details of those operators, how-ever, we offer a few comments on other aspects of this prescription.

First, it is worth pointing out that the operators of the relational algebra are *generic,* in the sense that—loosely speaking—they work for arbitrary relations. (Contrast the situation with *user-defined* operators, relational or otherwise, in **Tu-torial D,** whose parameters are defined to be of certain specific types and whose arguments are required to match those types exactly.) In fact, the operators of the relational algebra are generic precisely because they are associated with a *type generator—viz.,* RELATION—rather than with some specific scalar type such as INTEGER or ELLIPSE or some specific generated tuple or relation type.

Second, note that RM Prescription 18 requires that the operators "be express-ible without excessive circumlocution." We recognize that this requirement is not particularly precise, but it is hard to make it more so. We mean it to imply among other things that:

- Existential and universal quantification should be equally easy to express. Here, for example, are **Tutorial D** formulations of the queries "Get supplier num-bers for suppliers who supply at least one London part" and "Get supplier num-bers for suppliers who supply every London part" (note that these two queries do conceptually involve existential and universal quantification, respectively):

```
S { S# } JOIN    ( P WHERE CITY = 'London' ) { P# } JOIN SP
S { S# } DIVIDEBY ( P WHERE CITY = 'London' ) { P# } PER  SP
```

- Projection over specified attributes and projection over all but specified attrib-utes should be equally easy to express. Here, for example, are **Tutorial D** for-mulations of the queries "Get supplier numbers for all current suppliers" and "Get everything except supplier number for all current suppliers":

```
S { S# }

S { ALL BUT S# }
```

Third, the required support for *relation type inference* has already been discussed (briefly) under RM Prescription 7.

DIVIDEBY PER

Codd's original divide required the divisor and dividend relations to be such that the heading of the divisor was a subset of that of the dividend [21]. Subsequently, Todd introduced a more general divide that applied to any pair of relations whatsoever [113].* Unfortunately, both of these operators suffered from certain problems over empty relations; moreover, it turned out that Todd's divide was in fact not just an extended version of Codd's—they were really two different operators. In reference [35], therefore, the present authors proposed (a) a generalized version of Codd's divide (which we called the *Small Divide*) and (b) a generalized version of Todd's divide (which we called the *Great Divide*) that overcame the "empty relation" difficulties. We now briefly explain these generalized operators, with examples.

First, the Small Divide. Consider the query "Get suppliers who supply all purple parts" (the point of this example is that, given our usual sample data, the set of purple parts is empty). Let PP stand for the expression

```
( P WHERE COLOR = COLOR ('Purple') )
```

Using Codd's divide, then, we might write:

```
SP { S#, P# } DIVIDEBY PP { P# }
```

However, this expression misses suppliers who supply no parts at all, even though—logically speaking—such a supplier does supply all purple parts (because, as is well known, "FORALL x (*cond*)" always evaluates to *true* if there are no x's, regardless of what the condition *cond* happens to be). By contrast, the following expression is guaranteed to give the right answer in all cases:

```
S { S# } DIVIDEBY PP { P# } PER SP { S#, P# }
```

This expression is defined to be shorthand for the following:

```
S { S# } MINUS ( ( S { S# } JOIN PP { P# } )
                        MINUS SP { S#, P# } ) { S# }
```

Or equivalently, using WITH and introduced names to break the overall expression down, conceptually, into a sequence of steps (and now showing the definition of PP too, as *p*):

---

*Except that attributes with the same name in the two relations must be of the same type (as for join, of course).

```
WITH ( P WHERE COLOR = COLOR ('Purple') ) { P# } AS p ,
     ( S { S# } JOIN p ) AS q ,
     ( q MINUS SP { S#, P# } ) { S# } AS r :
S { S# } MINUS r
```

Now, we have made a tacit assumption here that the dividend and the divisor have disjoint headings—*dend* and *dor,* say—and the PER relation has a heading—*per,* say—that is the union of *dend* and *dor.* But it is a simple matter to extend the definition to allow *dend, dor,* and *per* to be any headings whatsoever, thereby permitting the foregoing example to be simplified to just

```
S DIVIDEBY PP PER SP
```

Because (a) the only common attribute for S and SP is S# and (b) the only common attribute for SP and PP is P#, this expression can easily be defined in such a way as to be semantically equivalent to the earlier version.

We turn now to the Great Divide. Suppose we are given an extended version of suppliers-and-parts that looks like this (in outline):

```
S    { S#, ... }
SP   { S#, P# }                    /* ignore other attributes */
P    { P#, ..., COLOR, ... }
PJ   { P#, J# }                    /* ignore other attributes */
J    { J#, ... }
```

("J" here stands for "projects," and relvar PJ indicates which parts are used in which projects). Now consider the query "Get S#-J# pairs such that supplier S# supplies all red parts used in project J#." Let RPJ stand for the expression

```
( PJ JOIN ( P WHERE COLOR = COLOR ('Red') ) )
```

Using Todd's divide, then, we might write

```
SP { S#, P# } DIVIDEBY RPJ { P#, J# }
```

This expression is defined to yield a relation with heading {S#,J#} and with body consisting of all tuples (*s,j*) such that a tuple (*s,p*) appears in SP for *all* tuples (*p,j*) appearing in PJ. *Note:* We deliberately depart from our formal notation for tuples here, for reasons of intuitive simplicity.

It should not be necessary to go into great detail to persuade you that, like Codd's divide, Todd's divide suffers from problems—worse problems, in fact—over empty relations. For example, the expression shown above misses (*s,j*) tuples where the supplier *s* supplies no parts or the project *j* uses no red parts. By contrast, the following expression is guaranteed to give the right answer in all cases:

```
S { S# } DIVIDEBY J { J# }
            PER ( SP { S#, P# }, RPJ { P#, J# } )
```

This expression is defined to be shorthand for the following:

```
( S { S# } JOIN J { J# } )
    MINUS ( ( S { S# } JOIN RPJ { P#, J# } )
            MINUS ( SP { S#, P# }
                    JOIN RPJ { P#, J# } ) ) { S#, J# }
```

(Converting this expression into an equivalent "step-at-a-time" version using WITH and introduced names is left as an exercise for the reader.)

Once again, however, we have made a tacit assumption here—this time to the effect that the dividend and the divisor have disjoint headings *dend* and *dor,* say, and the PER relations have headings *per1* and *per2,* say, such that *dend* is the difference between *per1* and *per2* (in that order) and *dor* is the difference between *per2* and *per1* (in that order). Again, however, it is a simple matter to extend the definition to allow *dend, dor, per1,* and *per2* to be any headings whatsoever, thereby permitting the foregoing example to be simplified to just

```
S DIVIDEBY J PER ( SP, RPJ )
```

Because (a) the only common attribute for S and SP is S#, (b) the only common attribute for SP and RPJ is P#, and (c) the only common attribute for RPJ and J is J#, this expression can easily be defined in such a way as to be semantically equivalent to the earlier version.

Note: It is worth pointing out that expressions involving either the Small Divide or the Great Divide can always be replaced by logically simpler—though sometimes lengthier—expressions involving *relation comparisons* instead (see RM Prescription 22). For example, here is another formulation of the query "Get suppliers who supply all purple parts":

```
S WHERE ( ( SP RENAME S# AS X ) WHERE X = S# ) { P# } ≥
        ( P WHERE COLOR = COLOR ('Purple') ) { P# } )
```

("≥" here stands for "is a superset of"; we have omitted the final projection over supplier numbers for simplicity, since it would probably not be wanted in practice anyway).

SUMMARIZE

Like the original versions of divide, the original version of SUMMARIZE [24] runs into trouble over empty relations. For example, the expression

```
SUMMARIZE SP BY ( S# ) ADD COUNT AS NP      /* NP = number of */
                                            /* parts supplied */
                                            /* by supplier S# */
```

misses suppliers who supply no parts at all, even though it might be expected that such a supplier should appear in the result with an NP value of zero. By contrast, the following expression gives a result that does include such suppliers:

```
SUMMARIZE SP PER S { S# } ADD COUNT AS NP
```

This expression is defined to be shorthand for the following:

```
( EXTEND S { S# }
         ADD ( ( SP RENAME S# AS X ) WHERE X = S# ) AS Y,
               COUNT ( Y ) AS NP )
{ S#, NP }
```

Step-at-a-time version:

```
WITH ( S { S# } ) AS t1 ,
     ( SP RENAME S# AS X ) AS t2 ,
     ( EXTEND t1 ADD ( t2 WHERE X = S# ) AS Y ) AS t3 ,
     ( EXTEND t3 ADD COUNT ( Y ) AS NP ) AS t4 :
t4 { S#, NP }
```

In general, the expression

```
SUMMARIZE A PER B ADD summary AS Z
```

is defined as follows:

- First, *B* must be of the same (relation) type as some projection of *A;* i.e., every attribute of *B* must be an attribute of *A*. Let the attributes of that projection (equivalently, of *B*) be *A1, A2, ..., An*.

- The heading of the result consists of the attributes *A1, A2, ..., An* plus the new attribute *Z*.

- The body of the result consists of all tuples *t* such that *t* is a tuple of *B* extended with a value for the new attribute *Z*. That new *Z* value is computed by evaluating *summary* over all tuples of *A* that have the same values for *A1, A2, ..., An* as does tuple *t*.

The crucial difference between this revised SUMMARIZE and the original version is that the result has the same cardinality as *B*.

Points arising:

- If the set "all tuples of *A* that have the same values for *A1, A2, ..., An* as does tuple *t*" is empty, *summary* will be applied to an empty set of values (see the discussion of OO Prescription 7 in Chapter 8).

- If *B* is not just of the same type as some projection of *A* but actually *is* such a projection, as in, e.g.,

```
SUMMARIZE SP PER SP { S# } ADD COUNT AS NP
```

then the generalized version of SUMMARIZE degenerates to the original version (it has different syntax—in the example, "PER SP{S#}" would have been "BY (S#)" in the original version—but the effect is the same).

Observe in particular that with this revised form of SUMMARIZE, the operation

```
SUMMARIZE SP PER TABLE_DEE      /* see RM Prescription 19 */
          ADD COUNT AS NSHIP    /* re TABLE_DEE          */
```

will "work"—i.e., will return the "correct" answer, zero—even if SP is empty (more precisely, it will return a relation with one attribute, called NSHIP, and one tuple, containing an NSHIP value of zero). The original SUMMARIZE, by contrast, will return an empty result in this situation.

RM PRESCRIPTION 19: RELVAR NAMES, RELATION SELECTORS, AND RECURSION

Relvar names and *relation selector invocations* shall both be legal relational expressions. *Recursion* shall be permitted in relational expressions.

———— ◆ ◆ ◆ ◆ ◆ ————

In **Tutorial D,** relvar names and relation selector invocations are indeed both legal relational expressions. A relvar name, *R* say, simply denotes the relation that is the current value of the relvar in question. As for relation selector invocations, the **Tutorial D** syntax basically consists of the keyword RELATION followed by a parenthesized commalist of tuple expressions. Here are a couple of examples (the first is a repeat of one shown earlier in the discussion of RM Prescription 7):

```
RELATION { TUPLE { P# P#('P1'), TOTQ QTY( 600) } ,
           TUPLE { P# P#('P5'), TOTQ QTY( 500) } ,
           TUPLE { P# P#('P2'), TOTQ QTY(1000) } ,
           TUPLE { P# P#('P4'), TOTQ QTY( 500) } ,
           TUPLE { P# P#('P3'), TOTQ QTY( 400) } ,
           TUPLE { P# P#('P6'), TOTQ QTY( 100) } }

RELATION { TUPLE { S# SX, P# PX, QTY QX * 3 } ,
           TUPLE { S# SY, P# PY, QTY QY * 7 } }
```

Tutorial D also provides two special shorthands, TABLE_DEE and TABLE_DUM. TABLE_DEE is shorthand for the following relation selector invocation:

```
RELATION { } { TUPLE { } }
```

And TABLE_DUM is shorthand for the following relation selector invocation:

```
RELATION { } { }
```

Note: The first pair of braces in each of these expressions denotes an empty relation heading (it can be omitted from the TABLE_DEE expansion but not the TABLE_DUM expansion!). Refer back to the discussion of RM Prescription 10 for further explanation.

As for recursion: First of all, we do have direct support for the transitive closure operator, of course (TCLOSE in **Tutorial D**). We also have the ability to define recursive operators of our own. Here is an example:

```
OPERATOR EXPLODE ( XY RELATION { X P#, Y P# } )
         RETURNS ( RELATION { X P#, Y P# } ) ;
   RETURN
      ( WITH ( XY UNION ( ( ( XY COMPOSE
                            ( XY RENAME Y AS Z, X AS Y ) )
             RENAME Z AS Y ) ) AS TTT :
          IF TTT = XY THEN TTT          /* unwind recursion     */
          ELSE EXPLODE ( TTT )          /* recursive invocation */
          END IF ) ;
END OPERATOR ;
```

Suppose we are given a relation MM with the following heading:

```
{ MAJOR_P# P#, MINOR_P# P# }
```

Then the EXPLODE invocation

```
EXPLODE ( MM RENAME MAJOR_P# AS X, MINOR_P# AS Y )
```

computes the transitive closure of MM *without* using the builtin operator TCLOSE. *Note:* We make no claim that EXPLODE is very efficient (but it can surely be improved). More to the point, we do assume (in accordance with RM Very Strong Suggestion 7, *q.v.*) that user-defined operators are allowed to take relation-valued parameters such as XY.

We remind you too that in Chapter 5 we mentioned the possibility of writing recursive "WITH expressions." Using such a feature, we might express the transitive closure of MM (again without using the builtin TCLOSE operator) as follows:

```
WITH ( ( MM RENAME MAJOR_P# AS X, MINOR_P# AS Y )
         UNION
         ( ( ( ( MM RENAME MAJOR_P# AS Y, MINOR_P# AS Z )
               COMPOSE TRANCLO ) RENAME Z AS Y )
       AS TRANCLO :
TRANCLO
```

RM PRESCRIPTION 20: RELATION-VALUED OPERATORS

*D shall provide facilities for defining and destroying read-only operators that are **relation-valued.** The relation that results from invoking such an operator shall be defined by means of a certain relational expression, specified when the operator is defined. That expression shall be allowed to contain parameters; such parameters shall represent scalar values and shall be permitted wherever scalar selector invocations are permitted. Invocations of such operators shall be permitted within relational expressions wherever relation selector invocations are permitted.*

———— ♦♦♦♦♦ ————

We begin with an example:

```
OPERATOR PQO () RETURNS ( RELATION { P# P#, TOTQ QTY } ) ;
   RETURN ( SUMMARIZE SP PER P { P# }
                       ADD SUM ( QTY ) AS TOTQ ) ;
END OPERATOR ;
```

Note that operator PQO has no parameters, so an invocation looks like this:

```
PQO ()
```

Here is a moderately complicated example of a relational expression involving two such invocations ("Get pairs of part numbers, *px* and *py* say, such that the total quantity for *px* is greater than that for *py*"):

```
( ( ( PQO () RENAME P# AS PX, TOTQ AS TQX )
      JOIN
    ( PQO () RENAME P# AS PY, TOTQ AS TQY ) )
      WHERE TQX > TQY ) { PX, PY }
```

And here is an example of a *parameterized* relation-valued operator definition:

```
OPERATOR TQP ( PZ P# ) RETURNS ( RELATION { TOTQ QTY } ) ;
   RETURN ( ( PQO () WHERE P# = PZ ) { TOTQ } ) ;
END OPERATOR ;
```

Note that the definition of operator TQP makes use of the previously defined operator PQO. Here is an example of its use:

```
VAR P1_TOTQ QTY ;

P1_TOTQ  :=  TOTQ FROM ( TUPLE FROM ( TQP ( P# ('P1') ) ) ) ;
```

Finally, here is an example of destroying such an operator:

```
DROP OPERATOR TQP ;
```

Note: **Tutorial D** includes support for user-defined, read-only, *tuple*-valued operators too, on the grounds that it would seem artificial to exclude them (even though they are not explicitly prescribed by the *Manifesto*).

RM PRESCRIPTION 21: ASSIGNMENTS

D shall permit:

   a. *(The value of) a scalar expression to be **assigned** to a scalar variable;*

   b. *(The value of) a tuple expression to be **assigned** to a tuple variable; and*

   c. *(The value of) a relational expression to be **assigned** to a relvar;*

*provided in each case that the source and target types are the same. In addition, **D** shall support a **multiple** form of the assignment operation, in which several individual assignments are performed in some specified sequence as part of a single logical operation.*

Of course, we have seen many examples of assignment in this chapter already; however, there is quite a lot more that needs to be said on the topic.

First, note that, like the equality operator "=", the assignment operator ":=" is *overloaded* (or *polymorphic*), inasmuch as it applies to operands of many different types (in fact, of *every* type).

Next, consider the assignment

```
target  :=  source ;
```

RM Prescription 21 assumes that *source* and *target* are of the same type, for reasons discussed in Chapter 11 (under OO Very Strong Suggestion 1). In practice, however, it might be feasible, and desirable, to relax this requirement somewhat and insist only that it must at least be possible to coerce—i.e., implicitly convert—the value of *source* to the type of *target*.* That is, it might be possible to support, e.g., assignment of an INTEGER value to a RATIONAL variable, as in the following example:

```
VAR I INTEGER ;
VAR R RATIONAL ;

R  :=  I ;                  /* I coerced to type RATIONAL (?) */
```

Or (more simply):

```
R  :=  3 ;                  /* instead of "R := 3.0 ;" -- (?) */
```

As noted in Chapter 5, however, in **Tutorial D** we adopt the conservative position that *source* and *target* are *not* allowed to be of different types. Of course, we do permit *explicit* type conversion or "cast" operations, as in this example:

```
R  :=  CAST_AS_RATIONAL ( I ) ;
```

Note: We use syntax of the form CAST_AS_*T* (...), rather than CAST (... AS *T*), because this latter format would raise "type TYPE" issues—e.g., what is the type of operand *T?*—that we prefer to avoid. We remark too that a more general operator of the form CAST_AS_SAME_TYPE_AS (*Y*,*X*), which casts the result of expression *X* to the type of the result of expression *Y,* might prove useful in practice.

Turning now to *relational* assignments specifically: Such assignments are fundamentally the only means by which a relvar can be updated. However, this fact does not preclude the provision of shorthands such as the familiar INSERT, UPDATE, and DELETE operators, and of course we do provide such shorthands in **Tutorial D.** Here are some examples. First, INSERT:

```
INSERT INTO PQ ( SUMMARIZE SP PER P { P# }
                     ADD SUM ( QTY ) AS TOTQ ) ;
```

(PQ here is a relvar with attributes P# and TOTQ—see the discussion of RM Prescription 13, earlier.) We define the semantics of this INSERT as follows:

- The relational expression SUMMARIZE ... AS TOTQ is evaluated, to yield relation *pq,* say.

---

*In other words, we prescribe the semantics of ":=" in the case where the source and target are of the same type but not otherwise.

- The following assignment is executed:

```
PQ  :=  PQ UNION pq ;
```

- Let the cardinality of PQ after the INSERT be a, let the corresponding cardinality before the INSERT be b, and let the cardinality of pq be c. If $a \neq b + c$, the INSERT is undone, and an exception is raised.

The intent of the cardinality check is to ensure that INSERT always has *exactly* the requested effect (i.e., it inserts exactly the set of tuples constituting the body of the relation that is the value of the specified relational expression, no more and no less).*

Here now is an example of DELETE:

```
DELETE SP WHERE S# = S# ('S4') OR S# = S# ('S5') ;
```

Semantics:

- The expression SP WHERE S# = S# ('S4') OR S# = S# ('S5') is evaluated, to yield relation *sp,* say.
- The following assignment is executed:

```
SP  :=  SP MINUS sp ;
```

- Let the cardinality of SP after the DELETE be a, let the corresponding cardinality before the DELETE be b, and let the cardinality of sp be c. If $a \neq b - c$, the DELETE is undone, and an exception is raised.

Note: You might be wondering how it could ever be the case here that $a \neq b - c$ (since the set of tuples the user is requesting be deleted is always some subset of the set of tuples in the target relvar). However, one way such an exception could occur is as follows. Suppose the target relvar is virtual (i.e., it is a "view"). Then deleting one tuple from that "view" might have the side effect of causing other tuples to be deleted from that "view" as well (in the absence of the cardinality check, that is). Note too that this effect can occur even in the absence of support for triggered actions—consider, for example, an attempt to delete just the tuple (S1,...,P1,...) from the Cartesian product of suppliers and parts. Of course, if triggered actions are supported, then the effect can occur in other ways as well.

Here finally is an UPDATE example:

```
UPDATE P WHERE WEIGHT < WEIGHT ( 15 )
              CITY  := 'Paris' ,
              COLOR := COLOR ('Blue') ;
```

---

*We prescribe the cardinality check in order to conform to the semantics of INSERT as usually understood, but of course it would be possible (if preferred) to define the operation in such a way as *not* to require that check. Analogous remarks apply to DELETE and UPDATE, *q.v.*

Semantics:

- The following assignment is executed:

```
P   :=  WITH ( P WHERE WEIGHT < WEIGHT ( 15 ) ) AS old ,
             ( old RENAME PREFIX '' AS 'OLD' ) AS t1 ,
             ( EXTEND t1 ADD COLOR ( 'Blue' ) AS NEWCOLOR,
                            'Paris' AS NEWCITY ) AS upd ,
             ( upd { ALL BUT OLDCOLOR, OLDCITY }
                     RENAME PREFIX 'OLD' AS '',
                            PREFIX 'NEW' AS '' ) AS new :
             ( P MINUS old ) UNION new
```

- Let the cardinality of P after the UPDATE be *a* and let the corresponding cardinality before the UPDATE be *b*. If *a* ≠ *b*, the UPDATE is undone, and an exception is raised.

For convenience, **Tutorial D** also provides a tuple UPDATE operator. Here is an example:

```
UPDATE ADDR ZIP := '95448' ;
```

Of course, the tuple UPDATE operator too is only shorthand. The example just shown is equivalent to:

```
ADDR   :=   TUPLE { STREET FROM ADDR,
                    CITY   FROM ADDR,
                    STATE  FROM ADDR,
                    ZIP    '95448' } ;
```

In practice, UPDATE operations can become quite complex. For example, consider the following relvar (repeated from the section on RM Prescription 13):

```
VAR NADDRLOC REAL RELATION { ID     INTEGER,
                             NAME NAME,
                             ADDR TUPLE { STREET CHAR,
                                          CITY   CHAR,
                                          STATE  CHAR,
                                          ZIP    CHAR },
                             LOC  POINT }
                             KEY { ID } ;
```

Here is a possible UPDATE on this relvar:

```
UPDATE NADDRLOC WHERE ID = 12345
                THE_X ( LOC ) := 7.2,
                UPDATE ADDR ZIP := '95448' ;
```

In other words, **Tutorial D** necessarily permits (a) the use of THE_ pseudo-variables (possibly nested) within an UPDATE and (b) a tuple or relation UPDATE nested within another such UPDATE (if the applicable attribute is tuple- or relation-valued). *Exercise for the reader:* Give a relational assignment that is equivalent to the foregoing UPDATE.

Multiple assignment: The principal reason for wanting to be able to perform several—presumably interrelated—assignments as a single operation is to ensure that integrity checking is not done until all of the assignments in question have been executed.* For example, suppose that the suppliers relvar S is subject to the integrity constraint that suppliers S2 and S3 must have total status 40 (for some strange reason). Then each of the following assignments will fail (we use the UPDATE shorthand for convenience):

```
UPDATE S WHERE S# = S# ('S2') STATUS := 15 :

UPDATE S WHERE S# = S# ('S3') STATUS := 25 ;
```

However, the following *multiple* assignment will succeed (again we use the UPDATE shorthand):

```
UPDATE S WHERE S# = S# ('S2') STATUS := 15 ,
UPDATE S WHERE S# = S# ('S3') STATUS := 25 ;
```

The foregoing example shows multiple assignment on a single target relvar. Here by contrast is an example with two distinct targets:

```
DELETE S  WHERE S# = S# ('S1') ,
DELETE SP WHERE S# = S# ('S1') ;
```

As these examples suggest, the multiple assignment feature implies that there is no logical need for "deferred" (COMMIT-time) integrity checking (see RM Prescriptions 23 and 24). However, such deferred checking might nevertheless still be desirable for usability reasons, and the *Manifesto* therefore permits it.

Note finally that assignment is the only update operator actually prescribed by the *Manifesto* (and we remind you that assignment itself is required only because of our assumption—discussed in Chapter 1—that **D** is imperative in style). However, additional update operators, either system- or user-defined, are of course not precluded.

RM PRESCRIPTION 22: COMPARISONS

*D shall support certain **comparison operators**, as follows:*

a. *The operators for comparing scalars shall include "=", and possibly "<", ">", etc. (depending on the scalar type in question);*

b. *The operators for comparing tuples shall be "=" and "≠" (only);*

c. *The operators for comparing relations shall include "=", "≠", "is a subset of" (etc.); and*

d. *The operator "∈" for testing membership of a tuple in a relation shall be supported;*

---

*Performance might be a reason, too.

provided in every case except "∈" that the comparands are of the same type, and in the case of "∈" that the tuple and the relation have the same heading.

——— ♦♦♦♦♦ ———

RM Prescription 22 assumes that comparands are of the same type (or, in the case of "∈", have the same heading) for essentially the same reason that RM Prescription 21 assumes that the source and target in an assignment are of the same type. In practice, however, it might be feasible, and desirable, to relax this requirement somewhat and insist only that it must at least be possible to coerce—i.e., implicitly convert— one comparand to the type of the other, thereby permitting (e.g.) comparisons between integers and rational numbers. In **Tutorial D,** however, we adopt the same conservative position as we did with regard to assignment and require comparands to be of exactly the same type, except for "IN comparisons" (the **Tutorial D** version of "∈ comparisons"), which are something of a special case. In fact, of course, the comparison "*t* IN *r*" is equivalent to the comparison "*rt* ≤ *r*"—where *rt* is a relation containing just tuple *t* and "≤" stands for "is a subset of"—from which fact the type compatibility rules for such comparisons can be immediately inferred.

   We give only two examples here, both involving a relational comparison specifically (since you might perhaps not be familiar with such comparisons). The first is a formulation of the query "Get parts supplied by all suppliers":

```
P WHERE ( ( SP RENAME P# AS Y ) WHERE Y = P# ) { S# } = S { S# }
```

The second is a repeat of an example from the section on RM Prescription 18 ("Get suppliers who supply all purple parts"):

```
S WHERE ( ( SP RENAME S# AS X ) WHERE X = S# ) { P# } ≥
         ( P WHERE COLOR = COLOR ('Purple') ) { P# } )
```

RM PRESCRIPTION 23: INTEGRITY CONSTRAINTS

*An expression that evaluates to a truth value is called a **logical expression** (also known as a truth-valued, conditional, or boolean expression). An **integrity constraint** is a logical expression that (a) is named; (b) is, or is logically equivalent to, a closed WFF ("well formed formula") of the relational calculus; and (c) is required to evaluate to true. **D** shall provide facilities for defining and destroying integrity constraints. Such constraints shall be classified into **domain** (i.e., **type**), **attribute**, **relvar**, and **database** constraints, and **D** shall support the **constraint inference** mechanism required by that classification scheme (insofar as feasible).*

——— ♦♦♦♦♦ ———

We begin by briefly explaining the prescribed integrity constraint classification scheme. Following references [55] and [79], we divide integrity constraints (*constraints* for short) into database, relvar, attribute, and type constraints. Basically:

- A *database* constraint specifies the legal values for a given database;
- A *relvar* constraint specifies the legal values for a given relvar;
- An *attribute* constraint specifies the legal values for a given attribute;
- A *type* constraint specifies the legal values for a given type. *Note:* "Type" here really means a *scalar* type specifically. Tuple and relation types are subject to type constraints too, of course, but those constraints are (ultimately) just a logical consequence of the type constraints that apply to the scalar types in terms of which those tuple and relation types are (ultimately) defined.

In all cases, the constraint must be "logically equivalent to a closed WFF of the relational calculus" ("WFF" here stands for *well formed formula*). What this means is just that, given values for the relvars (if any) involved in the constraint, the constraint must be such as to evaluate to *true* or *false* unequivocally; in other words, it must not mention any variables (except for the pertinent relvars themselves, of course, and this exception applies only to relvar and database constraints). Of course, if it evaluates to *false,* the constraint is violated, and the operation that caused the violation is canceled (in its entirety).

Type Constraints

It is convenient to discuss (scalar) type constraints first. Here is a simple example, the type constraint for type S# (supplier numbers):

```
TYPE S# POSSREP ( CHAR )
        CONSTRAINT ( SUBSTR ( THE_S# ( S# ), 1, 1 ) = 'S' AND
                     CHAR_LENGTH ( THE_S# ( S# ) ) ≤ 5 ) ;
```

As explained in Chapter 5, a scalar type constraint is allowed to make use of the applicable type name to denote an arbitrary value of the type in question. Thus, this example constrains supplier numbers to be such that they can be represented by a character string of no more than five characters, of which the first must be an "S". Any expression that is supposed to evaluate to a supplier number but does not in fact yield a value that satisfies this constraint will fail.

Let us generalize from this first example. It should be clear that, ultimately, the only way *any* expression can yield a value of type *T* is by means of some invocation of some selector for type *T;* hence, the only way any such expression can violate the type constraint on *T* is if the selector invocation in question does so. It follows that *type constraints can always be thought of, at least conceptually, as being checked during the execution of some selector invocation.* As a consequence, we can say that type constraints are checked *immediately,* and hence that no variable can ever be assigned a value that is not of the appropriate type. (And we remark further that these remarks apply even when we are "in the middle of" some multiple assignment; in other words, while multiple assignment operations cause integrity checking in general to be deferred to the end of the operation, type constraint checking in particular is not deferred in this sense. It is *never* legal for a selector invocation to produce a value that fails to satisfy the applicable type constraint.)

As you can see from this first example, a type constraint is logically just a specification of the values that belong to the type in question. In **Tutorial D,** therefore, we bundle such constraints with the definition of the type in question, and we identify them by means of the applicable type name (and it follows that a type constraint can be destroyed only by destroying the type itself).

Note: POSSREP specifications represent an *a priori* constraint on the type, of course. Moreover, an obvious shorthand would permit the user to specify (e.g.)

```
TYPE S# POSSREP ( CHAR ( 5 ) ) ;
```

instead of

```
TYPE S# POSSREP ( CHAR )
        CONSTRAINT ( CHAR_LENGTH ( THE_S# ( S# ) ) ≤ 5 ) ;
```

Here is another example of a type constraint:

```
TYPE POINT
    POSSREP POINT ( X RATIONAL, Y RATIONAL )
    CONSTRAINT ( ABS ( THE_X ( POINT ) ) ≤ 100.0 AND
                 ABS ( THE_Y ( POINT ) ) ≤ 100.0 ) ;
```

The type checking here is done, conceptually, during execution of invocations of the POINT selector. Note the use of the user-defined operator ABS (see the examples under RM Prescription 3 near the beginning of this chapter).

Here is a third example:

```
TYPE ELLIPSE
    POSSREP ( A LENGTH, B LENGTH, CTR POINT )
    CONSTRAINT ( THE_A ( ELLIPSE ) ≥ THE_B ( ELLIPSE ) ) ;
```

Suppose variable E is declared to be of type ELLIPSE, and its current value has a major semiaxis of length five and a minor semiaxis of length four. Now consider the assignment:

```
THE_B ( E )  :=  LENGTH ( 6.0 ) ;
```

This assignment will fail, of course, but it is not the assignment *per se* that is in error. Instead, the error is inside a selector invocation once again (even though no such invocation is directly visible in the assignment), because—as we saw in the section on RM Prescription 5 earlier in this chapter—the assignment shown is really shorthand for the following:

```
E := ELLIPSE ( THE_A ( E ), LENGTH ( 6.0 ), THE_CTR ( E ) ) ;
```

And it is the selector invocation on the right hand side that fails (at run time, too, be it noted).

We close this subsection with a fourth example (deliberately a rather complicated one):

```
TYPE POLYGON
    POSSREP ( VERTICES RELATION { V# INTEGER, VERTEX POINT } )
    CONSTRAINT
    ( COUNT ( THE_VERTICES ( POLYGON ) ) =
      COUNT ( THE_VERTICES ( POLYGON ) { V# } )
      AND
      COUNT ( THE_VERTICES ( POLYGON ) ) =
      COUNT ( THE_VERTICES ( POLYGON ) { VERTEX } )
      AND
    ( THE_VERTICES ( POLYGON ) RENAME V# AS N ) { N } =
      INTEGERS ( 1, COUNT ( THE_VERTICES ( POLYGON ) ) ) ) ;
```

Explanation: Note first of all that (as explained in our earlier discussion of RM Prescription 1) type POLYGON here is still a *scalar* type, despite the fact that it has a possible representation that involves a *relational* component, called VERTICES. The CONSTRAINT specification consists of three separate constraints all ANDed together. The first constrains values of type POLYGON to be such that no two tuples in the VERTICES relation have the same vertex number (V#); the second constrains values of type POLYGON analogously to be such that no two tuples in the VERTICES relation have the same vertex (VERTEX). As for the third, the general intent is to ensure that if polygon p has n vertices, then the VERTICES relation for p contains exactly n tuples, and the V# values in those tuples are exactly 1, 2, ..., n (and so the third constraint in fact subsumes the first). It works like this:

- First, following reference [26], we assume we have a builtin, read-only, relation-valued operator called INTEGERS (though as a matter of fact we do not have to rely on this assumption, because we can always write a relational expression that yields a relation that is identical to the INTEGERS invocation result we need):

```
OPERATOR INTEGERS ( A INTEGER, B INTEGER )
        RETURNS ( RELATION { N INTEGER } ) ;
    ... ;
END OPERATOR ;
```

  The expression INTEGERS(a,b)—where we assume for simplicity that $a \leq b$—yields a relation with just one attribute (also of type INTEGER) called N. The body of that relation contains one tuple for each integer from a to b inclusive, each such tuple containing just the integer in question, and no other tuples.

- The expression

```
COUNT ( THE_VERTICES ( POLYGON ) )
```

  yields, for any given polygon p, a count of the number of vertices of p—n, say (a value of type INTEGER).

- It follows that the right hand comparand in the third constraint is a relation containing just the integers 1 to *n,* loosely speaking (and the single attribute of that relation is called N).

- The left hand comparand

```
( THE_VERTICES ( POLYGON ) RENAME V# AS N ) { N }
```

in that third constraint is also a relation with one attribute called N, and it contains the distinct V# values for polygon *p.*

- Thus, that third constraint overall specifies that the V# values for polygon *p* are precisely the integers 1 to *n,* as required.

Attribute Constraints

An attribute constraint is basically just a statement to the effect that a specified attribute is of a specified type.* For example, consider the following relvar definition once again:

```
VAR NADDRLOC REAL RELATION { ID   INTEGER,
                             NAME NAME,
                             ADDR TUPLE { STREET CHAR,
                                          CITY   CHAR,
                                          STATE  CHAR,
                                          ZIP    CHAR },
                      LOC  POINT }
                      KEY { ID } ;
```

In this relvar:

- Values of attribute ID are constrained to be of type INTEGER;

- Values of attribute NAME are constrained to be of type NAME;

- Values of attribute ADDR are constrained to be of a certain tuple type (values of which are constrained in turn by the type constraints that apply to the attributes of that tuple type); and

- Values of attribute LOC are constrained to be of type POINT.

In other words, we bundle attribute constraints in **Tutorial D** with the definition of the attribute in question, and we identify the constraint by means of the corresponding attribute name. (It follows that an attribute constraint can be destroyed

---

*We concentrate here on constraints on *attributes* specifically because the primary emphasis in our *Manifesto* is on data in the database (i.e., data in database relvars) rather than local data. However, constraints exactly analogous to attribute constraints apply to scalar and tuple variables and to attributes of tuple variables (all of which are necessarily local), and to local relvars and attributes of local relvars as well. (Likewise, constraints analogous to relvar and database constraints might be defined for local data too. However, we do not discuss such a possibility any further in this book.)

only by destroying the attribute itself.) *Note:* In principle, any attempt to introduce an attribute value into the database that is not a value of the relevant type will simply be rejected. In practice, however, such a situation should never arise, so long as the system in fact enforces the *type* constraints described in the previous subsection.

Relvar Constraints

A relvar constraint is a constraint on an individual relvar (it is expressed in terms of the relvar in question only and does not mention any others). Here are some examples (note the constraint names RC1, ..., RC5):

```
CONSTRAINT RC1 ( IS_EMPTY ( S WHERE STATUS < 1
                            OR     STATUS > 100 ) ) ;
```

("supplier status must be in the range 1 to 100 inclusive").

```
CONSTRAINT RC2 ( IS_EMPTY ( S WHERE CITY = 'London'
                            AND     STATUS ≠ 20 ) ) ;
```

("suppliers in London must have status 20").

```
CONSTRAINT RC3 ( COUNT ( S ) = COUNT ( S { S# } ) ) ;
```

("S# is a candidate key for suppliers"; the more familiar notation "KEY {S#}" might be regarded as shorthand for this longer formulation).

```
CONSTRAINT RC4 ( IF NOT ( IS_EMPTY ( P ) ) THEN
                    COUNT ( P̄ WHERE COLOR = COLOR ('Red') ) > 0
                 END IF ) ;
```

("if there are any parts at all, at least one of them must be red").

For our final example, we return to the relvar SPQ from the section on RM Prescription 7:

```
VAR SPQ ... RELATION { S# S#,
                       PQ RELATION { P#   P#,
                                     TOTQ QTY } ... } ... ;

CONSTRAINT RC5 ( COUNT   ( SPQ UNGROUP PQ ) =
                 COUNT ( ( SPQ UNGROUP PQ ) { S#, P# } ) ) ;
```

("within any SPQ tuple, no two distinct tuples in the PQ value have the same part number"; we are relying here on the fact that attribute S# forms a candidate key for relvar SPQ).

As the foregoing examples suggest, a relvar constraint can be arbitrarily complex, so long as it refers to just one relvar.

Relvar constraints are always checked "immediately" (i.e., at the end of every statement that might cause them to be violated). Thus, any statement that attempts to assign a value to a given relvar that violates any relvar constraint for that relvar will effectively just be rejected.

Here is an example of destroying a relvar constraint:

```
DROP CONSTRAINT RC3 ;
```

Database Constraints

A database constraint is a constraint that interrelates two or more distinct relvars. Here are some examples (note the constraint names):

```
CONSTRAINT DBC1 ( IS_EMPTY ( ( S JOIN SP )
                            WHERE STATUS < 20
                            AND   QTY > QTY ( 500 ) ) ) ;
```

("no supplier with status less than 20 can supply any part in a quantity greater than 500").

```
CONSTRAINT DBC2 ( SP { S# } ≤ S { S# } ) ;
```

("every supplier number in the shipments relvar also exists in the suppliers relvar"; recall that we use "≤" to denote the "subset of" operator). Since S# is a candidate key for suppliers, this constraint is basically the necessary *referential* constraint from shipments to suppliers; i.e., S# is a foreign key for shipments that refers to suppliers.

```
CONSTRAINT DBC3 ( SP { P# } = P { P# } ) ;
```

("every part must have at least one shipment"). *Note:* Of course, it is also the case that every shipment must have exactly one part, by virtue of the fact that P# is a candidate key for parts and there is a referential constraint from shipments to parts; we have not bothered to show this latter constraint here.

Database constraints are checked at end-of-transaction (i.e., COMMIT time); if any such check fails, the transaction is rolled back. *Note:* We have already remarked (in our discussion of RM Prescription 21) that the multiple assignment feature implies that there is no logical need for COMMIT-time integrity checking, but we permit it for usability reasons.

Here is an example of destroying a database constraint:

```
DROP CONSTRAINT DBC3 ;
```

Constraint Inference

In the past, integrity constraints have typically been thought of as applying to "real" data (i.e., real relvars and real databases) only. In *The Third Manifesto,* by contrast, we regard them—in accordance with *The Principle of Interchangeability* discussed under RM Prescription 14—as applying to "virtual" data (e.g., virtual relvars) as well. For example, let virtual relvar LS ("London suppliers") be defined as follows:

```
VAR LS VIRTUAL
      S WHERE CITY = 'London'
      KEY { S# } ;
```

This relvar inherits all of the constraints that apply to relvar S (as well as being subject to a constraint of its own to the effect that the CITY value must be London). In particular, it inherits the constraint that S# values are unique (and hence the explicit specification KEY {S#} is logically unnecessary; we have provided it mainly just to allow the system to check that it is not in conflict with information that is available to it anyway, thanks to the constraint inference rules).

For more specifics on constraint inference as it applies to each of the relational algebra operators, see the next section.

Note: There are known to be certain limits on the degree to which constraint inference might be feasible in practice (see, e.g., references [7] and [96]). This fact accounts for the slightly hesitant tone of the final portion of RM Prescription 23, which requires only that "**D** shall support . . . constraint inference . . . *insofar as feasible.*"

RM PRESCRIPTION 24: RELVAR AND DATABASE PREDICATES

*Every relvar has a corresponding **relvar predicate** and every database has a corresponding **database predicate**. Relvar predicates shall be satisfied at statement boundaries. Database predicates shall be satisfied at transaction boundaries.*

———— ♦♦♦♦♦ ————

We believe the concepts of *relvar predicate* and *database predicate* to be both crucial and fundamental. Unfortunately, they are also concepts that have been very much overlooked in the past, and we therefore amplify them slightly here. Loosely speaking, a relvar predicate is the logical AND of all relvar constraints that apply to the relvar in question,* and a database predicate is the logical AND of all database constraints and all relvar constraints that apply to the database in question. Also:

- To say that relvar predicates shall be satisfied at statement boundaries is to say that no statement—in particular, no assignment statement—shall leave any relvar in a state that violates its own predicate (*"The Golden Rule"*). *Note:* RM Prescription 24 thus implies that it shall not be possible to update a "view"— i.e., a virtual relvar—in such a way as to violate the definition of that "view." In other words, such relvars shall always be subject to what SQL calls the CASCADED CHECK OPTION [76,87–89].

---

*Relvar constraints and predicates were referred to as *table* constraints and predicates in reference [79] (where the concepts originated) and as *relation* constraints and predicates in references [38] and [55].

- To say that database predicates shall be satisfied at transaction boundaries is to say that no transaction shall leave the corresponding database in a state that violates its own predicate.

Now we focus our attention on relvar predicates specifically. The fact is, there are really two distinct predicates associated with any given relvar, which might be called the *external* and the *internal* predicate, respectively. The difference between them is this:

- The *external* predicate for a given relvar is, loosely, *what that relvar means to the user;* it is typically rather informal, and it is not understood by the system. When we said in our discussion of RM Prescription 10 that a relation heading could be regarded as a predicate, we were talking, tacitly, about the *external* predicate. For instance, the external predicate for the bill of materials example discussed under RM Prescription 10 is (to repeat from that discussion) something like this: *Part MAJOR_P# contains quantity QTY of part MINOR_P#.* But there is no way the system can possibly have any understanding of (for example) what it means for one part to "contain" another; only the user can understand such a notion. *Note:* An external predicate is sometimes called an *interpretation.*

- The *internal* predicate, by contrast, is *what the relvar means to the system;* it is formal, and it *is* understood by the system (as well as by the user). In other words, the internal predicate is what RM Prescription 24 means by the term "relvar predicate"—*viz.,* the logical AND of all relvar constraints that apply to the relvar in question. In the case of the bill of materials example, the relvar predicate might specify that the combination of MAJOR_P# and MINOR_P# is a candidate key, and that QTY values are positive and less than 20 (say), and probably other things besides.

In a nutshell, therefore: The interpretation or external predicate represents the user-understood meaning, the internal or relvar predicate represents the system-understood "meaning." And, of course, it is the internal or relvar predicate that serves as the criterion for acceptability of updates against the relvar in question. In other words (and this point cannot be emphasized too strongly), it is *predicates,* not *names,* that represent the semantics of the data in question.

Now, in the previous section we touched on the question of *constraint inference.* It should be obvious that, more generally, it is *predicates* that are inferred, not just individual constraints. The following example is a modified version of one we gave in our discussion of RM Prescription 14:

- Let *RC* = *RA* UNION *RB*, where *RA* and *RB* are relational expressions denoting relations with the same heading. Let the predicates for *RA* and *RB* be *PA* and *PB*, respectively. Then the predicate for *RC*, *PC* say, is (*PA*) OR (*PB*).

Here in outline are the predicate inference rules for the most important of the other relational operators. The notation is meant to be self-explanatory (mostly).

- `RA JOIN RB : (PA) AND (PB)`

- `RA MINUS RB : (PA) AND NOT (PB)`

- `RA WHERE cond : (PA) AND (cond)`

- `RA { X } : PX` (where *PX* is derived from *PA* by existentially quantifying over all of the attributes not retained in the projection—see Chapter 4)

- `EXTEND RA ADD exp AS X : (PA) AND (X = exp)`

- `RA RENAME X AS Y : PA'` (where *PA′* is derived from *PA* by replacing all references to *X* by references to *Y*)

Finally, a word on database predicates. The principal point here is simply that, just as every relvar has an associated system-understood meaning (the *relvar predicate* for that relvar), so every database has an associated system-understood meaning too—the *database predicate* for that database, which we define to be, precisely, the logical AND of all database constraints and all relvar constraints that apply to the database in question. Now, we stated above that "database predicates shall be satisfied at transaction boundaries." In fact, however, it might be possible, and desirable, to insist on the stronger requirement that database predicates, like relvar predicates, be satisfied at *statement* boundaries. See the discussion of multiple assignment under RM Prescription 21.

RM PRESCRIPTION 25: CATALOG

*Every database shall include a set of relvars that constitute the **catalog** for that database. It shall be possible to assign to relvars in the catalog.*

———— ♦♦♦♦♦ ————

Note that—as is in fact required by RM Prescriptions 16 and 17—we regard the catalog as part of the database it describes, not as a separate database in its own right. It follows that the catalog must be self-describing. As for the requirement that "it shall be possible to assign to relvars in the catalog": All this means is that it must be possible for suitably authorized users to update the catalog appropriately. We deliberately do not attempt to spell out the structure of the catalog in detail here.

RM PRESCRIPTION 26: LANGUAGE DESIGN

*__D__ shall be constructed according to well-established principles of **good language design.***

———— ♦♦♦♦♦ ————

As with RM Prescription 18 (where we required the operators of the relational algebra to be "expressible without excessive circumlocution"), we recognize that this prescription is not very precise as it stands, but it is difficult to make it more so. The general intent is simply that **D** should avoid the many design errors we observe in the language SQL (see, e.g., references [46], [48], [73], and [76], among others). To quote reference [45]:

> There are well-established principles for the design of languages, but little evidence that SQL has been designed in accordance with any such principles [slightly reworded].

Examples of such principles include *generality, parsimony, completeness, similarity, extensibility, openness,* and especially *orthogonality* (this list is taken from reference [8]; a somewhat similar list can be found in reference [33]). In connection with the last of these, *orthogonality,* we would like to say that we agree strongly with the following remarks from reference [104]:

> Most languages are too big and intellectually unmanageable. The problems arise in part because the language is too restrictive; the number of rules needed to define a language increases when a general rule has additional rules attached to constrain its use in certain cases. (Ironically, these additional rules usually make the language *less* powerful.) . . . *Power through simplicity, simplicity through generality, should be the guiding principle* [italics in the original].

See also the remarks on *conceptual integrity* in Chapter 1. The net effect is that (as noted in Chapter 5) arbitrary restrictions such as those documented in references [46], [48], [73], and [76], and all other *ad hoc* concepts and constructs, are absolutely prohibited in the design of **D.**

7

RM Proscriptions

RM PROSCRIPTION 1: NO ATTRIBUTE ORDERING

D shall include no construct that depends on the definition of some ordering for the attributes of a relation. Instead, for every relation r expressible in D, the attributes of r shall be distinguishable by name.

———— ♦♦♦♦♦ ————

By definition, the attributes of a relation—at least as that term is used in the relational model—are unordered, left to right.* And in *The Third Manifesto,* by virtue of several of the RM Prescriptions taken together, every attribute of every relation is indeed distinguishable by name. To be more specific, every relation in **D** is obtained by evaluating some relational expression, and the rules for such expressions are such as to guarantee that the desired property is satisfied. For let *RX* be such an expression. Then:

- If *RX* consists of a relation selector invocation, then the attribute names are specified, implicitly or explicitly, as part of that invocation.

---

*The relations of the relational model are not quite the same as mathematical relations, which do have a left to right ordering to their attributes [50].

171

- If *RX* consists of a relvar name, then the attribute names are specified explicitly as part of the definition of the relvar in question—unless either (a) the relvar in question is virtual or (b) SAME_TYPE_AS is used in its definition (as illustrated in the section on RM Prescription 13 in Chapter 6). In these latter two cases the attribute names are inferred by means of the prescribed relation type inference mechanism from the relevant relational expression.

- If *RX* consists of an invocation of a user-defined relation-valued operator, the attribute names are specified explicitly as part of the definition of the operator in question.

- If *RX* consists of an invocation of some builtin relational operator, then the attribute names are inferred by means of the prescribed relation type inference mechanism.

- If *RX* consists of some combination of the foregoing cases, then the attribute names are inferred by appropriate repeated application of these rules.

Despite all of the foregoing, we still feel it worthwhile to state RM Proscription 1 explicitly, owing to the mistakes we observe in SQL in this connection (mistakes, in fact, that imply that SQL tables are not true relations). Among other things, the proscription implies:

- No more anonymous attributes, as in SQL's SELECT A + B FROM R;

- No more duplicate attribute names, as in SQL's SELECT A, A FROM R and SELECT R1.A, R2.A FROM R1, R2;

- No more ordering-dependent shorthands, as in SQL's SELECT * FROM R and INSERT INTO R VALUES (...);

- No more hidden "tuple ID" or timestamp attributes, as in some of today's SQL implementations.

Note: As you might have noticed, **Tutorial D** does rely on a left to right ordering for matching up arguments and parameters in operator invocations, and some people might feel this fact in itself constitutes a violation of the spirit, if not the letter, of RM Proscription 1. To such critics we plead guilty as charged—we are surely entitled to a *little* inconsistency—and appeal to traditional language practice as our justification (or excuse).

RM PROSCRIPTION 2: NO TUPLE ORDERING

D shall include no construct that depends on the definition of some ordering for the tuples of a relation.

———— ♦♦♦♦♦ ————

By definition, the tuples of a relation are unordered, top to bottom. Of course, this fact does not mean that such an ordering cannot be imposed for, e.g., presentation purposes; however, it does mean that the effect of imposing such an ordering is to convert the relation into something that is not a relation (typically a one-dimensional array of tuples—see the discussion of RM Proscription 7 later in this chapter).

RM PROSCRIPTION 3: NO DUPLICATE TUPLES

For every relation r, *if* t1 *and* t2 *are distinct tuples in* r, *then there must exist an attribute* A *of* r *such that the comparison "*A *FROM* t1 = A *FROM* t2*" evaluates to* false *(where the expressions* A *FROM* t1 *and* A *FROM* t2 *denote the values for attribute* A *in tuples* t1 *and* t2, *respectively).*

———— ◆◆◆◆◆ ————

By definition, relations do not contain duplicate tuples. Yet SQL does permit duplicate "tuples" in its tables—another reason why SQL tables are not true relations [29]. In the *Manifesto,* by contrast, duplicate tuples are absolutely, categorically, and unequivocally outlawed. What we tell you three times is true.

RM PROSCRIPTION 4: NO NULLS

Every attribute of every tuple shall have a value (of the applicable type).

———— ◆◆◆◆◆ ————

By definition, relations do not contain "nulls" (nulls are not values!)—see RM Prescriptions 9 and 10. SQL, however, does permit nulls in its tables (yet another reason why SQL tables are not true relations). In the *Manifesto,* by contrast, nulls are absolutely, categorically, and unequivocally outlawed. So too therefore is many-valued logic (see the discussion of RM Very Strong Suggestion 8 in Chapter 10).

RM PROSCRIPTION 5: NO NULLOLOGICAL MISTAKES

D shall not forget that relations with no attributes are respectable and interesting, nor that candidate keys with no components are likewise respectable and interesting.

———— ◆◆◆◆◆ ————

Nullology is the study of the empty set [31] (it has nothing to with nulls!). Now, sets *per se* are ubiquitous in the relational world; for example, a relation has both a set of attributes and a set of tuples. And, since the empty set is certainly a set, it follows that wherever **D** permits sets in general to appear, it should permit empty sets in particular to appear as well. Two important special cases are (a) relations with no attributes and (b) candidate keys with no components.

■ *Relations with no attributes:* As noted under RM Prescription 10 in Chapter 6, there are exactly two relations with no attributes (and hence exactly two possible values of a relvar with no attributes): one containing just one tuple (the 0-tuple), the other containing no tuples at all. We call these two special relations TABLE_DEE and TABLE_DUM, respectively. What makes them so special is their *meanings,* which are simply *true* and *false,* respectively. TABLE_DEE in particular is *the identity with respect to join;** i.e., the join of any relation *r* with TABLE_DEE is simply *r*. Thus, TABLE_DEE plays a role with respect to the operators of the relational algebra analogous to the role of zero with respect to addition (or the role of one with respect to multiplication) in ordinary arithmetic. Note in particular that it follows that *the join of no relations at all* is TABLE_DEE (just as the sum of no numbers at all is zero).

■ *Candidate keys with no components:* Since (as we have just seen) relvars with no attributes are legal, candidate keys with no components ("empty keys") must be legal too, *a fortiori.* Certainly such a key is the only candidate key—the only *possible* candidate key!—for a relvar with no attributes; but other relvars (i.e., relvars with at least one attribute) can have empty keys, too. In fact, to say that relvar *R* has an empty key is to say, precisely and possibly usefully, that legal values of *R* contain at most one tuple [31]. *Note:* If relvar *R* has an empty key, then that empty key is the *only* candidate key for *R* (why?).

At the time of writing, SQL does not support either relations with no attributes or candidate keys with no components.

Note: These omissions are not the only nullological mistakes in SQL, but they are perhaps the most egregious. Others include incorrect treatment—in a variety of ways—of relations with no tuples (see, e.g., references [59], [61], and [73]), and inconsistent treatment—again in a variety of ways—of dyadic relational operations when the relations in question have no common attributes (see, e.g., reference [76]).

----

*Of course, join degenerates to Cartesian product if the operands have no attributes in common. It follows *a fortiori* that join degenerates to Cartesian product if either operand is TABLE_DEE or TABLE_DUM.

RM PROSCRIPTION 6: NO INTERNAL-LEVEL CONSTRUCTS

D shall include no constructs that relate to, or are logically affected by, the "physical" or "storage" or "internal" levels of the system.

This proscription is a logical consequence of the strong separation we insist on between model and implementation (it should be obvious that allowing implementation considerations to show through at the model level undermines physical data independence [77], and it can adversely affect portability and intersystem operability, too). Here are some specific corollaries of this prescription:

- The necessary mapping between (a) relvar definitions as understood by a given application and (b) relvar definitions as understood by the system (see the discussion of RM Prescription 13 in Chapter 6) is performed by means of some logically distinct mapping language and is not visible to the application in question.

- The *Manifesto* (like the relational model) deliberately does not say which database relvars are physically stored and which not. In particular, it expressly does *not* say that real ones are stored and virtual ones not; indeed, it would be quite inappropriate to do so, given that—as noted under RM Prescription 14 in Chapter 6—the choice as to which relvars are real and which virtual is somewhat arbitrary (*"The Principle of Interchangeability"*).

- RM Prescription 4 refers to "some kind of storage structure definition language." RM Prescription 6 implies that the statements of that language—in particular, the mappings of databases to physical storage—must be cleanly separable from everything in **D.**

- As discussed at several points in Chapter 6, the storage structure definition language mentioned in RM Prescription 4 is used to define (among other things) actual representations of scalar values and variables. Those actual representations are thus hidden from the user—i.e., they are not visible in **D.** Analogous remarks apply to tuple and relation values and variables, of course, as well as to scalar ones.

In connection with this last point, however, recall from Chapter 6 that the system must effectively expose actual representations to *type implementers,* in order to enable those implementers to implement the necessary selectors and THE_ operators. However, the operators that expose those actual representations are highly protected and not part of **D,** and those actual representations are certainly not visible to *users* of the types in question—not even to the *definers* of those types, in general.

RM PROSCRIPTION 7: NO TUPLE-LEVEL OPERATIONS

There shall be no tuple-at-a-time operations on relvars or relations.

———— ♦♦♦♦♦ ————

The idea that the operators of the relational algebra—which are, of course, all read-only operators, by definition—work on *relations* (i.e., on sets of tuples, not on individual tuples *per se*) is widely understood and appreciated. What is not so widely understood or appreciated is the idea that the same is true for relational *update* operators also—i.e., relational assignments, also relational INSERT, UPDATE, and DELETE operators, if supported [66]. Tuple-at-a-time updates on a relvar (analogous to UPDATE and DELETE via a cursor in SQL) are thus categorically prohibited.* Tuple-at-a-time retrieval from a relation (analogous to FETCH via a cursor in SQL) is prohibited too; however, an analogous effect can be obtained, if desired, by converting the relation in question to (e.g.) an array of tuples and iterating over that array. Here is an example, expressed in **Tutorial D:**

```
VAR I INTEGER ;
VAR SX S# ;
VAR QX QTY ;
VAR SQA ARRAY OF TUPLE { S# S#, QTY QTY } ;

LOAD SQA
FROM  ( SP WHERE P# = P# ('P1') ) { S#, QTY } ASC S# ;

DO I := 1 TO COUNT ( SQA ) ;
   BEGIN ;
      SX  :=  S#  FROM SQA(I) ,           /* "fetch" ith S# */
      QX  :=  QTY FROM SQA(I) ;           /* and QTY values */
      /* now process SX and QX */
   END ;
END DO ;
```

RM PROSCRIPTION 8: NO COMPOSITE ATTRIBUTES

D shall not include any specific support for "composite domains" or "composite attributes," since such functionality can more cleanly be achieved, if desired, through the type support already prescribed.

———— ♦♦♦♦♦ ————

---

*Indeed, we saw in the discussion of multiple assignment in Chapter 6 that certain tuple-at-a-time updates—if they could even be expressed—would necessarily fail.

It is sometimes suggested—see, for example, reference [22]—that it should be possible somehow to combine, say, attributes S# and P# from the shipments relvar SP into a single *composite* attribute, S#_P# say. Reference [67] argues against this idea, strongly. It does not seem appropriate, or necessary, to repeat all of the arguments from reference [67] here; suffice it to say that the kind of "composite attribute" support typically proposed mixes together all kinds of notions that would be better kept separate. (We remark in passing that SQL gets into a mess in this general area too, over what it calls "row constructors" [76,87–89].) As RM Proscription 8 suggests, the functionality in question can effectively be achieved anyway, if truly desired, by means of the type support prescribed elsewhere in *The Third Manifesto*.

RM PROSCRIPTION 9: NO DOMAIN CHECK OVERRIDE

> *"Domain check override" operators are* ad hoc *and unnecessary and shall not be supported.*

———— ♦ ♦ ♦ ♦ ♦ ————

"Domain check override" [22] is a flawed attempt to provide some—by no means all!—of the functionality provided by the *strong typing* mechanism prescribed by *The Third Manifesto* (refer to the section "Domains *vs.* Object Classes" in Chapter 2 if you need to refresh your memory regarding the term *strong typing*). It is thus, as RM Proscription 9 states, *ad hoc* and unnecessary. *Note:* Space precludes a detailed explanation of the "domain check override" concept here, but basically it is meant to allow (for example) joins to be done even when the join attributes are defined on different domains. Unfortunately, however, the whole idea is based on a failure to make a clear distinction between types and representations; indeed, the concept simply does not stand up at all under proper scrutiny. For further explanation, see reference [64].

RM PROSCRIPTION 10: NOT SQL

> **D** *shall not be called SQL.*

———— ♦ ♦ ♦ ♦ ♦ ————

Little seems necessary by way of elaboration here . . . We are merely trying to "head off at the pass" certain marketing tricks—not without precedent—that we suspect might be tried if some version of **D** were ever to become a commercial reality.

8

OO Prescriptions

OO PRESCRIPTION 1: COMPILE-TIME TYPE CHECKING

*D shall permit **compile-time type checking.***

———— ♦♦♦♦♦ ————

By this prescription, we mean merely that—insofar as feasible—it shall be possible to check at compilation time that no type errors can occur at run time. Of course, this requirement does not preclude the possibility of "compile and go" or interpretive implementations. *Note:* Compile-time type checking is also known as *static* type checking. We remark that support for inheritance seems to imply a need to relax the static type checking requirement somewhat (see Part IV of this book, especially Chapter 14).

OO PRESCRIPTION 2: SINGLE INHERITANCE (CONDITIONAL)

*If **D** permits some type T′ to be defined as a **subtype** of some **supertype** T, then such a capability shall be in accordance with some clearly defined and generally agreed model.*

———— ♦♦♦♦♦ ————

Despite the fact that languages and products that support some kind of inheritance do already exist (and have done for some time), and despite the fact that inheritance has been talked about for many years in books and articles and presentations, there is still no consensus on a formal, rigorous, and abstract inheritance *model.* To quote a recent paper [112]:

> The basic idea of inheritance is quite simple . . . [and yet, despite] its central role in current object systems, inheritance is still quite a controversial mechanism . . . [a] comprehensive view of inheritance is still missing.

We therefore believe it would be foolhardy to try to incorporate an inheritance mechanism into a *foundation* for database systems—which is what *The Third Manifesto* is supposed to be—at this point in time; rather, we believe we should try to reach agreement on an abstract model first. Detailed ideas toward such a model are presented in Part IV of this book.

We speculate that one reason for this state of affairs—i.e., the fact that an inheritance model is still lacking—is that inheritance was first introduced in the context of *software engineering;* i.e., it was more of an implementation idea than a theoretical one, intended primarily to simplify certain aspects of software development and maintenance (see, e.g., references [10] and [90]). Its application to, and attempted incorporation into, an abstract *theory of data* came later. If this speculation is correct, then there is a parallel that can usefully be drawn with the early development of database systems in general. The early hierarchic and network database systems can be seen as attempts to impose a thin layer of abstraction over certain implementation techniques that were in wide use at the time—but those systems never really succeeded in making the clear distinction between model and implementation that we now perceive as so important. Indeed, that distinction was not properly made until 1969, when the relational model—a true, abstract, implementation-independent *model* (or theory) of data—was first defined. Analogously, we see at least some of the current inheritance "models" not as true models *per se,* but merely as attempts to abstract just a little from certain current implementation techniques (and again we observe a failure to make a clear distinction between model and implementation). And, to repeat, we do want a true implementation-independent inheritance model *first,* before we are prepared to attempt to incorporate any inheritance ideas into our *Manifesto.*

OO Prescription 2 therefore sets the scene by requiring that **if** it is possible to define type T' as a *subtype* of supertype T—implying that type T' is to *inherit* certain properties from type T—**then** such a capability must be based on some "clearly defined and generally agreed" inheritance model. In other words, our support for inheritance is *conditional.*

Note: Earlier versions of the *Manifesto* went on to say:

> It is our hope that such a "clearly defined and generally agreed model" will indeed someday be found. The term "generally agreed" is intended to imply that the authors of this *Manifesto,* among others, shall be in support of the model in question. Such support shall not be unreasonably withheld.

These remarks were, regrettably, much misunderstood; we thought it was obvious that they were meant to be tongue in cheek, but not everyone saw them that way . . . Be that as it may, we were at least sincere in hoping that a good inheritance model could and would be found. To that end, we included in earlier versions of the *Manifesto* an appendix containing some preliminary proposals for a type inheritance model (and Part IV of the present book grew out of that appendix, of course).

We should say a word too regarding the distinction between single and multiple inheritance. Briefly (and somewhat loosely), *single* inheritance means that each subtype has a single supertype, and hence inherits properties from just that one type; *multiple* inheritance means that a subtype can have two or more supertypes, and hence can inherit properties from two or more types. Again, these ideas are elaborated (considerably) in Part IV.

We note finally that support for inheritance, whether single or multiple, implies certain extensions to the definitions (given in Chapter 3 and amplified in Chapter 6) of scalar, tuple, and relation values and scalar, tuple, and relation variables. As mentioned under OO Prescription 1 above, it also seems to imply a need to relax the static type checking requirement somewhat. Refer to Part IV of this book for further discussion.

OO PRESCRIPTION 3: MULTIPLE INHERITANCE (CONDITIONAL)

> *If **D** permits some type* T′ *to be defined as a subtype of some other type* T, *then* T′ *shall not be prevented from additionally being defined as a subtype of some other type that is neither* T *nor any supertype of* T *(unless the requirements of OO Prescription 2 preclude such a possibility).*

———— ♦♦♦♦♦ ————

This prescription merely does for multiple inheritance what the previous one did for single inheritance. Again, for further discussion see Part IV of the book (primarily Chapter 15).

OO PRESCRIPTION 4: COMPUTATIONAL COMPLETENESS

> ***D** shall be **computationally complete**. That is, **D** may support, but shall not require, invocation from so-called "host programs" written in languages other than **D**. Similarly, **D** may support, but shall not require, the use of other programming languages for implementation of user-defined operators.*

———— ♦♦♦♦♦ ————

The general intent of this prescription is twofold:

- It must be possible to write entire applications in **D,** instead of having to use one language for database access and another for general computation. In other words, we do not endorse the "embedded data sublanguage" approach adopted in SQL (we do not prohibit it, either, but we do insist that users should have the option of not having to use it).

    Note: Over the years, the idea that users should not have to use an embedded data sublanguage in order to access the database has been proposed by many people, including one of the present authors [43]. As noted in Chapter 5, one important consequence of that idea is that we can avoid the problem of "impedance mismatch" (see, e.g., reference [109]) between the types available inside the database and those available outside; i.e., there is no need to map between the (arbitrarily complex) types used inside the database and the (probably rather simple) types provided by some host language.

- It must be possible to use **D** to write the code that implements user-defined operators, instead of having to resort to using some other language for this purpose.

    Note: Several examples of operator definitions written in **Tutorial D** were shown in Chapter 6 (see, e.g., the discussion of RM Prescription 3). However, we did note in that chapter that definitions of certain operators—specifically, those selectors and THE_ operators that make use of the highly protected operators that expose actual representations—*cannot* be written entirely in **D,** since those protected operators are themselves not part of **D.** Further, we note that the ability to write operator definitions in some other language leads to the possibility of writing programs in **D** that invoke operators provided by some third party (e.g., operators included in an "off the shelf" function library).

We should add that we do not intend this prescription to undermine such matters as optimizability. Nor do we intend it to be a recipe for the use of procedural constructs such as loops to subvert the system's support for declarative queries and the like. Rather, the point is that computational completeness will be needed (in general) for the implementation of user-defined operators anyway, and to be able to implement such operators in **D** itself might well be more convenient than having to make excursions into some other language—excursions that in any case are likely to cause severe problems for optimizers. We do recognize that it might prove necessary in practice to prohibit the use of certain **D** features outside the code that implements such operators (so long as such a prohibition does not too severely restrict what can be done by a "free standing" application—i.e., one that does not require invocation from some program written in some other language).

OO PRESCRIPTION 5: EXPLICIT TRANSACTION BOUNDARIES

*Transaction initiation shall be performed only by means of an explicit **"begin transaction"** operator. Transaction termination shall be performed only by means of a **"commit"** or **"rollback"** operator; commit must always be explicit, but rollback can be implicit (if and only if the transaction fails through no fault of its own). If transaction TX terminates with commit ("normal termination"), changes made by TX to the applicable database shall be committed. If transaction TX terminates with rollback ("abnormal termination"), changes made by TX to the applicable database shall be rolled back.*

◆◆◆◆◆

Once again we are trying with this prescription to avoid certain mistakes we observe in the design of SQL. To be specific:

- SQL has no explicit "begin transaction" operator at the time of writing;* instead, a transaction is begun implicitly whenever the application executes a "transaction initiating" statement while no transaction is currently in progress. One consequence of this omission is that there is no obvious way to provide "transaction wide" information—for example, isolation level information [85]—that is specific to just one transaction. *Note:* **Tutorial D** does not directly address isolation level or similar matters at all, of course, but it does at least provide the explicit BEGIN TRANSACTION operator that is needed as a basis for addressing them. (Perhaps we should add that, regarding isolation level specifically, the only level we would *want* to support—i.e., the only one we would regard as logically correct—would be whatever level is defined to provide total isolation. All other levels have the potential for causing logical mistakes.)

- SQL allows transactions to terminate implicitly as well, in which case—to quote reference [76]—"the system . . . automatically executes either a ROLLBACK or a COMMIT . . . it is implementation-dependent which" (!). Incidentally, *implementation-dependent* is defined by the SQL standard to mean "possibly differing between SQL-implementations, but not specified by this International Standard and not required to be specified . . . for any particular SQL-implementation." So whether the system executes a COMMIT or a ROLLBACK might not even be documented! It could even change from release to release.

---

*An explicit "begin transaction" operator is included in the currently proposed follow-on to the existing SQL standard called SQL3 (see Appendix E). Further problems will arise if that operator actually makes it into the standard, however, precisely because it will still have to be possible—for reasons of backward compatibility—to begin transactions implicitly as well.

As for the explanations in this prescription of normal *vs.* abnormal termination: The objective here is simply to spell out the fact that databases, and therefore relvars contained within databases, possess the property of *persistence*. In fact, as indicated in our discussion of RM Prescription 16 in Chapter 6, database relvars are the *only* variables to possess this property.

OO PRESCRIPTION 6: NESTED TRANSACTIONS

*D shall support **nested transactions**—i.e., it shall permit a* parent *transaction* TX *to initiate a* child *transaction* TX′ *before* TX *itself has terminated, in which case:*

  a. TX *and* TX′ *shall interact with the same database (as is in fact required by RM Prescription 17).*

  b. TX *is not required to suspend execution while* TX′ *executes (though it is allowed to do so). However,* TX *shall not be allowed to terminate before* TX′ *terminates; in other words,* TX′ *shall be wholly contained within* TX.

  c. *Rollback of* TX *shall include the rolling back of* TX′ *even if* TX′ *has terminated with commit. In other words, "commit" is always interpreted within the parent context (if such exists) and is subject to override by the parent transaction (again, if such exists).*

Note: The remarks in this section are based on material that originally appeared in reference [55].

The nested transaction idea can be thought of as a generalization of the familiar notion of *savepoints* [85]. Savepoints allow a transaction to be organized as a *sequence* of actions that can be rolled back individually (loosely speaking); nesting, by contrast, allows a transaction to be organized, recursively, as a *hierarchy* of such actions. In other words:

  ■ BEGIN TRANSACTION is extended to support subtransactions (i.e., if BEGIN TRANSACTION is issued when a transaction is already running, it starts a *child* transaction).

  ■ COMMIT "commits" but only within the relevant *parent* scope (if this transaction is a child).

  ■ ROLLBACK undoes work back to the start of this particular subtransaction (including child, grandchild, etc., transactions, even if these latter transactions terminated with commit).

Note that nested transactions will be awkward to implement—from a purely syntactic point of view!—in a language like SQL that lacks an explicit BEGIN TRANSACTION statement (see the previous prescription): There has to be *some* explicit way of indicating that an inner transaction is to be started, and marking the point to roll back to if that inner transaction fails.

OO PRESCRIPTION 7: AGGREGATES AND EMPTY SETS

Let AggOp *be an* **aggregate** *operator, such as SUM. If the argument to* AggOp *happens to be empty, then:*

a. *If* AggOp *is essentially just shorthand for some iterated dyadic operator* Op *(the dyadic operator is "+" in the case of SUM), and if an identity value exists for* Op *(the identity value is 0 in the case of "+"), then the result of that invocation of* AggOp *shall be that identity value;*

b. *Otherwise, the result of that invocation of* AggOp *shall be undefined.*

———— ♦♦♦♦♦ ————

SQL certainly falls down on the foregoing prescription in connection with the aggregate operators SUM and AVG (in fact, we would argue that it falls down on the aggregate operators MAX and MIN as well [61]). To be specific, SQL defines the sum of an empty set to be null, whereas in fact that sum should be zero; it also defines the average of an empty set to be null, whereas in fact an empty set simply *has* no average (any attempt to request such an average is in error).

Note: It is worth mentioning in passing that COUNT can be regarded as a special case of SUM. Thus, for example, the expression

```
COUNT ( S )
```

is logically equivalent to the following expression:

```
SUM ( EXTEND S ADD 1 AS ONE, ONE )
```

(both of these are valid **Tutorial D** expressions). It follows that—of course—the COUNT of an empty set is zero too (and SQL does get this one right, even though it gets SUM wrong in general).

9

OO Proscriptions

It might be helpful to remark by way of introduction to this chapter that the two OO Proscriptions described in what follows amount, precisely, to a requirement that the two *Great Blunders* identified in Chapter 2 be avoided.

OO PROSCRIPTION 1: RELVARS ARE NOT DOMAINS

Relvars are not domains.

———— ♦♦♦♦♦ ————

In other words, we categorically reject the equation "relvar = class" advocated by, e.g., references [91–93]. (A relvar is a variable. A domain is a type. Variables are not types.)

For an extended discussion of this issue, see Chapter 2.

OO PROSCRIPTION 2: NO OBJECT IDS

No value shall possess any kind of ID that is somehow distinct from the value per se.

———— ♦♦♦♦♦ ————

This proscription means that we reject the object notion of "object IDs," at least insofar as that notion might apply to values. As a consequence, we also reject:

- The notion that other "objects" might make use of such IDs in order to share values, and
- The notion that users might have to "dereference" such IDs, either explicitly or implicitly, in order to obtain values. (The term *dereferencing* refers to the operation of following a pointer to an "object" to get to the "object" pointed to.)

Note: We also reject the concept of hidden "tuple IDs" (as noted in Appendix E and elsewhere, some writers seem to equate that concept with object IDs).

Observe carefully that this proscription does not prohibit *variables* (of any kind) from having IDs that are "somehow distinct from" the variable *per se*. On the contrary: Variables do need some identity that is distinct from their value, and that identity is provided, precisely and sufficiently, by their *name*.

Observe further that this proscription also does not prohibit the existence of *types* whose values are names of variables, since such names are certainly values. For example, "operating system file names" is a legal type, and so is "database relvar names"; thus, it is legal for, e.g., a relvar to have an attribute whose values are such names. (Indeed, relvars with attributes whose values are database relvar names will certainly be needed in the catalog.) To what extent **D** should provide any corresponding dereferencing operators is a question that requires further study, however; in **Tutorial D** we adopt the conservative position that no such operators are provided at all. The following observations are pertinent:

- First of all, a type whose values are names of variables is logically equivalent to a type whose values are *pointers*. If we permit such types, therefore, we run the risk of backsliding into the kind of pointer free-for-all found in prerelational systems—with its attendant looping, and pointer chasing, and lack of proper end user access, and so on and so forth—and *that* state of affairs is definitely something we want to avoid. (Indeed, "object IDs" in general are logically nothing but pointers and do lead directly to such a state of affairs, which is one important reason for rejecting them. See reference [72].)
- On the other hand, we cannot *prevent* users from defining a type whose values are variable names. And perhaps there is no need to. For consider:
  - The only variables **D** allows *within the database* are, very specifically, database relvars. Hence, the only "pointers" to *database* data that might be allowed in **D** are, very specifically, *database relvar names*.
  - As far as data in the database is concerned, therefore, the only kind of dereferencing **D** might need is an operation that would allow a database relvar to be specified, not directly by means of its name, but indirectly by means of a variable whose value is that name. In SQL terms, for example, such a facility might mean that, in place of the familiar SELECT * FROM R, the user would

be able to say SELECT * FROM V, where V is a program variable whose *value* is the required name R.

- As far as data in the database is concerned, therefore, support in **D** for "pointers" and dereferencing does *not* constitute a return to the kind of pointer free-for-all mentioned (and objected to) above.

■ The foregoing remarks notwithstanding, we now observe that if **D** were to support a mechanism akin to the PREPARE and EXECUTE capabilities of "dynamic SQL" or (perhaps better) the analogous **Prepare** and **Execute** capabilities of the SQL Call-Level Interface [76,87–89], dereferencing as such would be unnecessary anyway. *Note:* For the benefit of readers who might not be familiar with these SQL features, we should explain that PREPARE (or **Prepare**) allows a source language statement—possibly a dynamically constructed source language statement—to be compiled at run time, and EXECUTE (or **Execute**) then allows the compiled version of such a statement to be executed. We remark that (as hinted in Chapter 1) an industrial strength **D** will certainly require some such mechanism in order to allow the construction of applications that support *ad hoc* interactions on the part of the end user.

We observe in passing that the heavy reliance of object systems on object IDs—i.e., on pointers—lends weight to our belief that such systems are designed primarily *by* programmers *for* programmers. The relational model, by contrast, explicitly recognizes that the primary purpose of databases is to serve end users rather than application programmers (though this objective does not rule out the possibility of their serving application programmers too, of course). For this reason, Codd very deliberately excluded pointers from the relational model when he first defined it. Here is his rationale for doing so [22]:

> It is safe to assume that all kinds of users [including end users in particular] understand the act of comparing values, but that relatively few understand the complexities of pointers. The relational model is based on this fundamental principle . . . [The] manipulation of pointers is more bug-prone than is the act of comparing values, even if the user happens to understand the complexities of pointers.

It is therefore sad to see that many object/relational products—even those that embrace the right equation "domain = class" rather than the wrong one "relvar = class"—do permit (nay, encourage) the use of pointers within "relations" ("relations" in quotes because those "relations" are in fact not relations at all, in the sense understood by the relational model). And the pointers in question are, of course, not mere database relvar names, as above, but genuine "object ID"-style pointers. This is backsliding with a vengeance!—it seriously undermines the conceptual integrity of the relational model, and it needs to be resisted, firmly.

10

RM Very Strong Suggestions

RM VERY STRONG SUGGESTION 1:
SYSTEM KEYS

D should provide a mechanism according to which values of some specified candidate key (or certain components thereof) for some specified relvar are supplied by the system. It should also provide a mechanism according to which an arbitrary relation can be extended to include an attribute whose values (a) are unique within that relation (or within certain partitions of that relation), and (b) are once again supplied by the system.

— ◆◆◆◆ —

Caveat: We should make it clear at the outset here that RM Very Strong Suggestion 1 involves a number of issues (especially language design issues) that are not yet fully resolved. The discussion that follows should therefore be regarded not as a definitive statement, but rather just as notes toward the kind of functionality we feel is desirable. Note that the functionality in question is not included in **Tutorial D,** though we do believe it would be useful in an industrial strength language.

With that caveat out of the way, we now observe that (as the text of the suggestion indicates) we are really talking about two separate but related ideas here; in fact, there are really several more or less interrelated concepts involved. We begin with the familiar notion of *default values,* which can be loosely explained as follows.

Let *R* be a relvar, and let *R* have an attribute *A* of type *T*. If attribute *A* is defined to have a default value *d* (a value of type *T,* of course), then it is at least syntactically legal to specify tuples for insertion into *R* that do not include an explicit *A* component; such tuples are conceptually extended with an *<A,T,d>* triple before the actual insertion is done. For example, suppose attribute STATUS of the suppliers relvar S is defined to have default 10, perhaps as follows (hypothetical syntax):*

```
VAR S REAL RELATION { S#      S#,
                      SNAME   NAME,
                      STATUS  INTEGER DEFAULT 10,
                      CITY    CHAR }
                  KEY { S# } ;
```

Then the following INSERT might be legal:

```
INSERT INTO S RELATION { TUPLE { S#    S# ('S6'),
                                 SNAME NAME ('Lopez'),
                                 CITY 'Madrid' } } ;
```

And the tuple that is actually inserted looks like this:

```
TUPLE { S#      S# ('S6'),
        SNAME   NAME ('Lopez'),
        STATUS  10,
        CITY    'Madrid' }
```

A relational assignment analog of the foregoing INSERT might look as follows:

```
S   :=  S UNION RELATION { TUPLE { S#      S# ('S6'),
                                   SNAME   NAME ('Lopez'),
                                   STATUS DEFAULT ( S, STATUS ),
                                   CITY   'Madrid' } } ;
```

We are assuming here that the operator invocation DEFAULT (S,STATUS) returns the default value of the specified attribute (STATUS) of the relation denoted by the specified relational expression (S).

Next, we suggest an extension to the foregoing mechanism according to which default values are provided by invoking some system function, instead of being defined explicitly as part of the attribute definition. Suppose, for example, that relvar READING contains a set of instrument readings taken during the course of some experiment. Then that relvar might very well include an attribute called READING#, defined as follows:

```
READING# INTEGER DEFAULT SERIAL
```

---

*Not very good syntax, either, since it mixes up the default specification with the relation type specification.

SERIAL here is the name of a system function, with semantics as follows:

- Let the very first INSERT into the READING relvar involve n tuples. Then those tuples will be given READING# values 1, 2, ..., n (in some unspecified order).

- Let some subsequent INSERT into the READING relvar involve p tuples. Then those tuples will be given READING# values $N + 1, N + 2, ..., N + p$ (in some unspecified order), where N is the highest READING# value previously assigned.*

For simplicity, we assume—though the assumption is perhaps not 100 percent necessary—that if SERIAL or any other system function is specified, then the attribute in question *must* obtain its values via the default mechanism; i.e., "the attribute is nonupdatable" (again, speaking somewhat loosely). We also assume that a means exists for a suitably skilled and authorized user (perhaps the database administrator) to define such system functions. Note that those functions will probably not be conventional user-defined operators in the sense of RM Prescription 3. For one thing, they might require access to certain environment variables that are not directly available to a conventional user of **D.** For another, they typically involve certain "hidden arguments" (i.e., arguments not mentioned explicitly when the operator is invoked); for example, one hidden argument to SERIAL is the highest value N previously assigned.

Here now are some additional examples of system functions that could be useful in appropriate circumstances (see references [25] and [29] for further discussion):

- *SERIAL within some scope:* For example, the relvar ORDER_LINE might include an ORDER# attribute whose values are provided by some business process, together with a LINE# attribute defined thus:

```
LINE# INTEGER DEFAULT SERIAL WITHIN ORDER#
```

- *NOW:* This function provides "the time now" (perhaps as a time or timestamp value, perhaps as an integer, perhaps as a character string, depending on the type of the attribute in question).

- *USERID:* This function provides the user ID of the user inserting the tuples in question.

---

*We remark that these SERIAL values might be thought of as *tuple IDs;* note, however, that those tuple IDs are not hidden from the user, as they are in certain of today's SQL systems. We point out too that there is an element of unpredictability involved in using the SERIAL function. For example, if we insert three tuples into an empty relvar, all in a single operation, we cannot say which tuple gets which ID—we know only that they get IDs 1, 2, and 3 in some unspecified order.

To get back to RM Very Strong Suggestion 1 specifically, the applicability of all of the above to candidate keys should be obvious. For example, the complete definition of the ORDER_LINE relvar might look like this:

```
VAR ORDER_LINE REAL RELATION { ORDER#  CHAR,
                               LINE#   INTEGER DEFAULT SERIAL
                                               WITHIN ORDER#,
                               ITEM#   CHAR,
                               QTY     QTY,
                               ........ }
                     KEY { ORDER#, LINE# } ;
```

We turn now to the second principal part of RM Very Strong Suggestion 1. The basic idea is as follows: We would like to be able to tag the tuples of the result of an arbitrary relational expression in such a way that the tuples remain distinct from one another, even if we project away the attributes that would otherwise have made them distinct. Such a feature would be useful in our proposed support for SQL migration (see the discussion of RM Very Strong Suggestion 9 later in this chapter).

Now, you can probably see right away that we might be able to achieve the foregoing effect if we were allowed to invoke system functions like SERIAL just as if they were ordinary scalar operators—in EXTEND, for example. The trouble is, however, that (as already noted) those functions are *not* ordinary scalar operators, because they typically involve certain hidden arguments. Instead, therefore, we suggest the introduction of a new relational operator, TAG. Here is an example of its use:

```
( SP TAG WITHIN ( S# ) AS P#_SERIAL ) { ALL BUT P# }
```

Given our usual sample data, one possible result of evaluating this expression is shown in Fig. 10.1 (the result is not unique, in general, because TAG, like SERIAL, involves some degree of unpredictability).

S#	QTY	P#_SERIAL
S1	300	1
S1	200	5
S1	400	3
S1	200	4
S1	100	6
S1	100	2
S2	300	1
S2	400	2
S3	200	1
S4	200	3
S4	300	1
S4	400	2

Fig. 10.1   TAG example: one possible result

Explanation: The TAG operation tags tuples of the relation resulting from evaluation of a specified relational expression (the relational expression in the example is just SP, and so the resulting relation is simply the current value of relvar SP, of course). The specification WITHIN (S#) means that those tags are to be unique within distinct S# values (and we assume for simplicity that they start from one for each such S# value; of course, we could extend the definition of the TAG operator to allow the user to specify a different starting value). Thus, the overall result of the TAG operation in the example has attributes S#, P#, QTY, and P#_SERIAL (this last one due to the AS P#_SERIAL specification). We then project away the P# attribute to obtain a result such as that shown in Fig. 10.1. Note that the cardinality of the projection is necessarily the same as that of SP, whereas the same would not be true, in general, if we did not retain attribute P#_SERIAL.

RM VERY STRONG SUGGESTION 2: FOREIGN KEYS

D should include some declarative shorthand for expressing **referential constraints** *(also known as* **foreign key** *constraints).*

──── ♦♦♦♦♦ ────

RM Prescription 23 requires support for the definition (and of course enforcement) of what might be called "general" integrity constraints—i.e., relvar and database constraints of potentially arbitrary complexity. And since a referential constraint is really just a special case of such a general relvar constraint (or database constraint, more likely), it must of course be capable of formulation as a general constraint. Here, for example, is a **Tutorial D** formulation (repeated from Chapter 6) of the referential constraint from shipments to suppliers:

```
CONSTRAINT DBC2 ( SP { S# } ≤ S { S# } ) ;
```

(recall that the symbol "≤" here means "is a subset of").

RM Very Strong Suggestion 2 simply recognizes that it might be desirable to provide some more user-friendly special-case syntax for referential constraints. For example:

```
VAR S  REAL RELATION { S# S#, ... } KEY { S# } ;

VAR SP REAL RELATION { S# S#, ... } KEY { S#, P# }
          FOREIGN KEY { S# } REFERENCES S { S# } ;
                    /* constraint name deliberately dropped */
```

At least such special-casing does provide explicit syntax for a pragmatically important concept, *foreign key,* that is not otherwise mentioned in the *Manifesto* (or in **Tutorial D,** come to that). It also provides a place to attach declarative specifications of certain "referential actions"—cascade delete, etc.—if such specifications are considered desirable,* without necessarily having to get into the business of supporting triggered actions in full generality.

As in SQL [76,87–89], allowing one candidate key for a given relvar to be designated as *primary* could simplify (slightly) the specification of any matching foreign keys:

```
VAR S  REAL RELATION { S# S#, ... } PRIMARY KEY { S# } ;

VAR SP REAL RELATION { S# S#, ... } KEY { S#, P# }
          FOREIGN KEY { S# } REFERENCES S ;
                  /* references primary key of S by default */
```

A couple of final points:

- Note that we do indeed allow foreign keys to reference any candidate key, instead of—as historically—requiring them to reference a primary key specifically [65]. In fact, as noted in Chapter 6, we do not prescribe any explicit support at all for primary keys as such, since we regard the idea of making one candidate key primary (and thus somehow "more equal than the others") as a psychological issue merely.

- Referential constraints are usually thought of as applying to real relvars only. In the *Manifesto,* by contrast, we regard them as applying to virtual relvars as well (*The Principle of Interchangeability* at work once again).

RM VERY STRONG SUGGESTION 3: CANDIDATE KEY INFERENCE

Let RX *be a relational expression. By definition,* RX *can be thought of as designating a relvar,* R *say—either a user-defined relvar (if* RX *is just a relvar name) or a system-defined relvar (otherwise). It is desirable, though not always entirely feasible, for the system to be able to* **infer the candidate keys** *of* R, *such that (among other things):*

a. *If* RX *constitutes the defining expression for some virtual relvar* R′, *then those inferred candidate keys can be checked for consistency with the candidate keys explicitly defined for* R′ *and—assuming no conflict—become candidate keys for* R′.

b. *Those inferred candidate keys can be included in the information about R that is made available (in response to a "metaquery") to a user of* **D.**

---

*We remind you that the ability to update several relvars in a single operation (see the discussion of multiple assignment under RM Prescription 21 in Chapter 6) implies that there is no logical need to be able to specify such actions. However, it might still be desirable to support such a capability for usability or other pragmatic reasons.

D should provide such functionality, but without any guarantee (a) that such inferred candidate keys are not proper supersets of actual candidate keys, or (b) that such an inferred candidate key is discovered for every actual candidate key.

—— ♦ ♦ ♦ ♦ ♦ ——

If *K* is a candidate key for relvar *R,* then:

- Because of the candidate key *uniqueness* property, the functional dependence (FD) *K* → *A* holds for every attribute *A* of *R;*
- Because of the candidate key *irreducibility* property, there is no proper subset *K′* of the attributes of *K* such that the FD *K′* → *A* holds for every attribute *A* of *R.*

Refer to the discussion of RM Prescription 15 in Chapter 6 if you need to refresh your memory regarding the precise definitions of the uniqueness and irreducibility properties of candidate keys.

By way of an example, let *R* be the shipments relvar SP and *K* its sole candidate key {S#,P#}. Then:

- It is the case that every attribute of SP is functionally dependent on the combination of attributes {S#,P#};
- It is not the case that every attribute of SP is functionally dependent on something less than that full combination of attributes. (To be specific, QTY is not, though S# and P# both are.)

It follows from the foregoing that, if we know the FDs that hold for a given relvar, we can determine the candidate keys for that relvar: They are, precisely, those irreducible combinations of attributes *K* such that the FD *K* → *A* holds for every attribute *A* of the relvar in question [96]. Hence, in order to determine the candidate keys for the result of some relational expression *RX,* we need to determine the corresponding FDs. In other words, we need an *FD inference mechanism,* which—assuming we know the FDs that hold in the "base" or real relvars—will let us infer the FDs that hold in the result of evaluating an arbitrary expression involving those real relvars. (And, of course, we do know the FDs that hold in the real relvars, because they will have been defined as part of the corresponding relvar predicates.) Such an inference mechanism is presented in reference [30].

Note: Candidate key inference is in fact a special case of constraint inference in general, support for which is required by RM Prescription 23. We mention candidate keys explicitly here because of their pragmatic importance, and also because it might be desirable to use the special-case inferencing mechanism described in reference [30] instead of a more general mechanism that works for *all* constraints. As noted in our discussion of RM Prescription 23 in Chapter 6, however, there are known to be intrinsic limits on the degree to which such inferencing might be feasible in practice [7], which is why we admit both of the following possibilities:

- The inference mechanism might in fact find *proper superkeys* rather than true candidate keys. (A *superkey* is a superset—not necessarily a proper superset—of a candidate key; in other words, a superkey satisfies the uniqueness property but not necessarily the irreducibility property. A *proper* superkey is a superkey that definitely does not satisfy the irreducibility property.)

- Also, the inference mechanism might fail to discover certain candidate keys entirely.

Implementations can thus compete with one another over their degree of success at inferring candidate keys.

RM VERY STRONG SUGGESTION 4: TRANSITION CONSTRAINTS

> *D should support **transition constraints**—i.e., constraints on the legal transitions that a given relvar or database can make from one value to another.*

——— ♦♦♦♦♦ ———

Here is an example ("no supplier's status must ever decrease"):

```
CONSTRAINT TRC1
        ( IS_EMPTY
          ( ( ( S' { S#, STATUS } RENAME STATUS AS STATUS' )
                JOIN S { S#, STATUS } )
              WHERE STATUS' > STATUS ) ) ;
```

Explanation: We introduce the convention that a primed relvar name, such as S′ in the example, is understood to refer to the corresponding relvar as it was *prior to the update under consideration.* The constraint in the example can thus be understood as follows: If (a) we join together (over supplier numbers) the relation that is the value of relvar S before the update and the relation that is the value afterwards, and (b) we pick out the tuples in that join for which the old status value is greater than the new one, then (c) the final result must be empty. (Since the join is over supplier numbers, any tuple in the result of the join for which the old status value is greater than the new one would represent a supplier whose status had decreased.)

Note: Constraint TRC1 is a *relvar* transition constraint (it applies to just a single relvar, namely suppliers), and the checking is therefore immediate. Here by contrast is an example of a *database* transition constraint ("the total quantity of any given part, taken over all suppliers, can never decrease"):

```
CONSTRAINT TRC2
   ( IS_EMPTY
     ( ( ( SUMMARIZE SP' PER S'{ S# } ADD SUM ( QTY ) AS SQ' )
         JOIN
           ( SUMMARIZE SP  PER S { S# } ADD SUM ( QTY ) AS SQ ) )
       WHERE SQ' > SQ ) ) ;
```

Constraint TRC2 is a database transition constraint (it involves two distinct relvars, suppliers and shipments); the checking is therefore deferred, and the primed relvar names S′ and SP′ are taken to mean relvars S and SP as they were at BEGIN TRANSACTION.

The concept of transition constraints has no meaning for type or attribute constraints.

RM VERY STRONG SUGGESTION 5: QUOTA QUERIES

*D should provide some shorthand for expressing **quota queries.** It should not be necessary to convert the relation concerned into (e.g.) an array in order to formulate such a query.*

———— ♦♦♦♦ ————

A *quota query* is a query that specifies a desired limit, q say, on the cardinality of the result*—for example, the query "Get the three heaviest parts." Here is a possible **Tutorial D** formulation of this example:

```
WITH ( P RENAME WEIGHT AS WX ) AS t1 ,
     ( P RENAME WEIGHT AS WY ) AS t2 ,
     ( EXTEND t1
       ADD COUNT ( t2 WHERE WY > WX )
       AS #_HEAVIER ) AS t3 :
t3 WHERE #_HEAVIER < 3
```

Given our usual sample data, the result consists of parts P2, P3, and P6.

Quota queries are quite common in practice. Now, such queries can be formulated in terms of our usual relational algebra operators, as we have just seen; however, such formulations do tend to be rather roundabout and cumbersome. It therefore seems worthwhile to consider the possibility of providing some shorthand for them. Following reference [69], therefore, we suggest extending **Tutorial D** to support a new form of relational expression—more precisely, a new form of *<other builtin relation op inv>*—called a *<quota>*, thus:

```
<quota>
    ::=    <relation exp> <quota def>
```

Note: The *<relation exp>* must not be an *<other builtin relation op inv>*.

```
<quota def>
    ::=    QUOTA ( <integer exp>, <ne sequence item commalist> )
```

———————————

*Though the actual result cardinality can be either more or less than q, as we will see.

We remind you of the syntax of *<sequence item>* (repeated from Chapter 5):

```
<sequence item>
    ::=    <direction> <attribute name>

<direction>
    ::=    ASC | DESC
```

Using this syntax, the query "Get the three heaviest parts" can be formulated as

```
P QUOTA ( 3, DESC WEIGHT )
```

Explanation: The *<relation exp>* here, which denotes the relation from which the result is to be drawn, is simply P. The desired result cardinality limit is three. DESC WEIGHT means "for the purposes of filling the desired quota, conceptually sequence part tuples by descending weight" (of course, there is no implication that the system must perform a physical sort in order to obtain the desired result). In other words, the *<quota>* is asking for the three tuples of P that come first according to that sequencing. The expression overall is defined to be shorthand for an expression of the following form:

```
( EXTEND ( P RENAME WEIGHT AS WX )
  ADD COUNT ( ( P RENAME WEIGHT AS WY ) WHERE WY > WX )
  AS #_HEAVIER )
WHERE #_HEAVIER < 3
```

(where the names WX, WY, and #_HEAVIER are arbitrary, of course).

Note: Given our usual sample data, this expression does indeed yield a result relation of exactly three tuples. However, if (say) part P4 had weight 18 instead of 14, it would yield four tuples, not three; and if there were currently only two parts altogether instead of six, it would (necessarily!) yield only two tuples. See reference [69] for further discussion of such matters.

Here is another example, this time one that uses a *<quota>* nested inside another relational expression:

```
( ( S { STATUS } ) QUOTA ( 2, ASC STATUS ) ) JOIN S
```

("Get all suppliers whose status is one of the two smallest"; given our usual sample data, the two smallest status values are 10 and 20, and so the result consists of suppliers S1, S2, and S4). The expression representing the first operand to the join here denotes a relation with one attribute, called STATUS, that contains the two smallest supplier status values. The join then yields a relation containing exactly those suppliers having one of those two status values. *Note:* In order to convince yourself of the usefulness of the *<quota>* shorthand, you might like to try formulating this same query in SQL.

We observe that the *<quota>* shorthand also facilitates the formulation of many other kinds of "statistical" queries. For example:

```
S QUOTA ( COUNT ( S ) / 10 , DESC STATUS )
```

("Get the top 10 percent of suppliers"; by "the top 10 percent" here, we mean those suppliers whose status is greater than that of the other 90 percent, loosely speaking).

Following reference [69] again, we also suggest another useful shorthand, of which this expression is an example:

```
NTH_SMALLEST ( P, 3, WEIGHT )
```

("Get all parts whose weight is exactly the third smallest"; the third smallest weight in our sample data is 17, so the result consists of parts P2 and P3). Again, you might like to try formulating this query in SQL to see just how useful the proposed shorthand is. In relational algebra terms, the NTH_SMALLEST invocation just shown is defined to be shorthand for an expression of the following form:

```
( ( EXTEND P
    ADD MAX ( ( EXTEND
                   ( ( P { WEIGHT } ) QUOTA ( 3, ASC WEIGHT ) )
                   ADD COUNT
                   ( ( P { WEIGHT } ) QUOTA ( 3, ASC WEIGHT ) )
                   AS N )
                   WHERE N = 3, WEIGHT )
       AS NTH )
    WHERE WEIGHT = NTH ) { ALL BUT NTH }
```

(where the names N and NTH are arbitrary). What we are suggesting, therefore, is extending **Tutorial D** again to support another new form of relational expression—more precisely again, a new form of *<other builtin relation op inv>*—thus:

```
<nth smallest>
    ::=    NTH_SMALLEST ( <relation exp>, <integer exp>,
                                      <attribute name> )
```

with semantics as just outlined. Of course, NTH_LARGEST should be supported too:

```
<nth largest>
    ::=    NTH_LARGEST ( <relation exp>, <integer exp>,
                                     <attribute name> )
```

We close this section by stressing the point that the constructs we have suggested—*<quota>*, *<nth smallest>*, and *<nth largest>*—are indeed all just shorthand; the advantages, though considerable from a pragmatic point of view, are nevertheless advantages of usability merely.

RM VERY STRONG SUGGESTION 6: GENERALIZED TRANSITIVE CLOSURE

*D should provide some shorthand for expressing the **generalized transitive closure** operation, including the ability to specify generalized* concatenate *and* aggregate *operations.*

——— ♦♦♦♦♦ ———

Tutorial D does include an explicit transitive closure operator, TCLOSE (the **Tutorial D** counterpart of the **A** operator ◄TCLOSE►). Unfortunately, however, TCLOSE by itself does not seem to be adequate for dealing with all possible "recursive queries," as we now explain.

It is convenient to begin by repeating—but amplifying—some of the transitive closure discussion from Chapter 4. Consider once again the bill of materials relation MMQ shown in Fig. 10.2 (a repeat of Fig. 2.2 from Chapter 2). As explained in Chapter 4, we can refer to that relation as a *digraph relation,* because it can be represented as a directed graph of nodes and directed arcs; the nodes are named and possibly labeled (see later), the arcs are directed and (again) possibly labeled. For example, in the particular case of the graph for relation MMQ (see Fig. 10.3):

- Each node is named for a particular part;
- There is an arc from node *Pi* to node *Pj* if and only if part *Pi* contains part *Pj* as an immediate component;
- Each arc is labeled with the corresponding quantity;
- The nodes are unlabeled.

MMQ	MAJOR_P# : P#	MINOR_P# : P#	QTY : QTY
	P1	P2	5
	P1	P3	3
	P2	P3	2
	P2	P4	7
	P3	P5	4
	P4	P6	8

Fig. 10.2   Relation MMQ

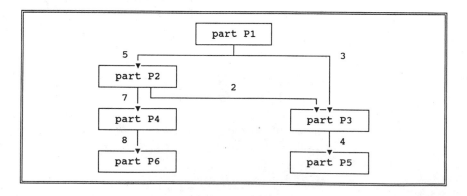

Fig. 10.3   Graph of relation MMQ

As noted in Chapter 4, it is often convenient to replace a directed graph such as that of Fig. 10.3 by a pure hierarchy with possibly repeated nodes, as in Fig. 10.4. The two graphs are information-equivalent, of course.

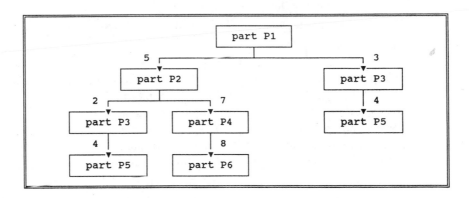

Fig. 10.4   Graph of relation MMQ as a hierarchy

Now, in Chapter 4 we explained how ◄TCLOSE► could be applied to what was effectively the projection of relation MMQ over MAJOR_P# and MINOR_P# (Fig. 10.5 shows the result). And we claimed that ◄TCLOSE► was important in connection with the *part explosion* problem—i.e., the problem of finding all components, at all levels, of some specified part. For example, consider the problem of "exploding" part P2. Here is a **Tutorial D** formulation of this query:

```
( ( TCLOSE ( MM { MAJOR_P#, MINOR_P# } ) )
           WHERE MAJOR_P# = 'P2' ) { MINOR_P# }
```

The trouble is, what we really need is something a little more general than just ◄TCLOSE► *per se*. Consider the query "What is the total quantity of part P5 that is

MAJOR_P# : P#	MINOR_P# : P#
P1	P2
P1	P3
P2	P3
P2	P4
P3	P5
P4	P6
P1	P4
P1	P5
P1	P6
P2	P5
P2	P6

Fig. 10.5   Transitive closure of MMQ { MAJOR_P#, MINOR_P# }

needed to make part P1?" Inspection of either Fig. 10.3 or Fig. 10.4 will quickly show that the answer is 52:

- For each path from node P1 to node P5, we *multiply* the quantities that are the arc labels along that path;
- Then we *add* together all the products so obtained.

Refer to Fig. 10.6.

In practice, it turns out that what is often wanted is not just a simple part explosion as such but, rather, a *gross requirement*—which is, loosely speaking, a combination of the "part explosion" and "total quantity" queries. In other words, we want a listing of all the parts that go to make up a given part, together with the corresponding total quantities. Following reference [82], therefore, we define a *generalized* version of the transitive closure operation that is intended to address problems of this general nature. The operator takes four operands:

- A relation of nodes and node labels (see below)
- A relation of directed arcs and arc labels
- A *concatenate* operator
- An *aggregate* operator

In our example, Operand 1 is the parts relation (not explicitly mentioned in the foregoing discussion); Operand 2 is relation MMQ; Operand 3 is " * "; and Operand 4 is "+". The operation returns a ternary relation with heading

`{ X T, Y T, Z C }`

where X and Y are "node" attributes and are inherited from Operand 2 (note that they have the same type T), Z represents the computed value obtained by following all paths from node X to node Y and applying the *concatenate* and *aggregate* operators appropriately, and C is the type of that computed value. The body of the result contains a tuple for every path, direct or indirect, in the Operand 2 graph.

Note: It so happens that there are no node labels in the bill of materials example, but such is not always the case. For example, consider an airline schedule. Here the nodes denote cities, the node labels are minimum connection times, the arcs

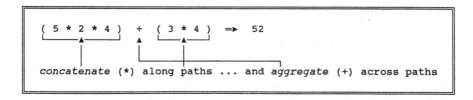

Fig. 10.6 Total quantity of part P5 in part P1

denote flights, and the arc labels are departure and arrival times. Note moreover that the bill of materials graph is *acyclic,* but the airline schedule graph is not! If there can be cycles in the graph, the *concatenate* operator must be defined to take care of them somehow; for example, in the airline schedule example, it must reject routes that visit the same city twice.

RM VERY STRONG SUGGESTION 7: TUPLE AND RELATION PARAMETERS

> ***D*** *should permit the parameters to user-defined operators (including in particular relation-valued operators—see RM Prescription 20) to be* ***tuples or relations*** *as well as scalars.*

——— ♦♦♦♦♦ ———

For simplicity, the discussion that follows concentrates on relations rather than tuples. The points are all applicable to tuples as well, of course, *mutatis mutandis.*

The first point to make is that this suggestion is in fact subject to two distinct interpretations, one of which is much simpler than the other. The first is merely that it should be possible for users to define operators in terms of parameters of some specific relation type. For example:

```
OPERATOR MORE_X_THAN_Y ( X RELATION { S# S# }, Y RELATION { P# P# } )
                                               RETURNS ( BOOLEAN )
            RETURN ( COUNT ( X ) > COUNT ( Y ) ) ;
        END OPERATOR ;
```

Here is a sample invocation of this operator (recall that we require arguments to have *exactly* the same type as the parameters they correspond to):

```
IF MORE_X_THAN_Y ( S { S# }, P { P# } )
   THEN /* there are more suppliers than parts */
     ... ;
END IF ;
```

Tutorial D does not currently support this first interpretation, but it would be a trivial matter to extend it to do so (in fact, we assumed such support was available when we discussed recursive user-defined operators under RM Prescription 19 in Chapter 6).

The more interesting (and more difficult) interpretation, however, is the second, and that is that it would be nice if users could define their own *generic* relational operators. Recall from Chapter 6 that the builtin relational operators are generic, meaning that they work for all relations (loosely speaking). The operator JOIN, for example, applies to any pair of relations whatsoever; there is no question of the relations in question having to conform to certain specific relation types (except of course that attributes with the same name must be of the same type). As was also pointed out in Chapter 6, operators such as JOIN are generic precisely because they are associated with a type generator—namely, RELATION—instead of with some specific relation type; they therefore apply to every specific relation type that is defined by means of that type generator.*

By way of an example, suppose **Tutorial D** did not include direct support for the Great Divide. Then, if the present Very Strong Suggestion were implemented, it would be easy enough for users to define a generic Great Divide operator of their own. User-defined aggregate operators provide another example (the builtin aggregate operators—SUM, MAX, and so on—are also generic in the foregoing sense); for instance, it might be possible to define a MEDIAN operator in this way.

We have no concrete suggestions to offer regarding user-defined generic operator support at this time, because we believe the issue requires further study.

RM VERY STRONG SUGGESTION 8: SPECIAL ("DEFAULT") VALUES

*D should provide some kind of **special values** mechanism for dealing with "missing information."*

———— ♦♦♦♦♦ ————

The "special values" referred to here have more usually been called *default* values in the past. However, the term "default values" is misleading, inasmuch as it suggests an interpretation that was not intended: namely, that the value in question occurs so frequently that it might as well be the default (see RM Very Strong Suggestion 1). Rather, the intent is simply to use an appropriate special value, distinct from all regular values of the attribute in question, when no regular value can be used. For example, if regular values of the attribute HOURS_WORKED are all nonnegative integers, the special value "?" might be used to mean that no regular value is known for some reason. Note that the type of attribute HOURS_WORKED in this example is thus *not* just integers.

Following reference [71], therefore, we suggest some further extensions to **Tutorial D.** First of all, we add a new SPECIALS definition to <*user scalar type def*>,[†] thus:

---

*Generic operators thus constitute another kind of polymorphism (we considered *overloading* or *ad hoc* polymorphism in Chapter 6, and we will be discussing *inclusion* polymorphism at some length in Part IV of this book).

[†]Analogous extensions will be required for tuple and relation types also. We omit the details here.

```
<user scalar type def>
    ::=    TYPE <user scalar type name>
               <ne possrep def list>
           [ CONSTRAINT ( <bool exp> ) ]
           [ SPECIALS ( <special def commalist> ) ]

<special def>
    ::=    <identifier> <special value>
```

The *<identifier>* is an arbitrary identifier, chosen by the type definer (see the discussion of RM Prescription 4 in Chapter 6), and the *<special value>* is a literal of the scalar type being defined. Each *<special def>* causes automatic definition of:

- A niladic operator of the form *special_T* (), where *special* is the specified *<identifier>* and *T* is the type in question, which returns the associated special value;

- A monadic operator of the form IS_*special* (*<scalar exp>*), where *special* is the specified *<identifier>* and the *<scalar exp>* must be of the type in question, which returns TRUE if that *<scalar exp>* evaluates to the associated special value and FALSE otherwise.

Here is an example:

```
TYPE HOURS                              /* type for HOURS_WORKED */
     POSSREP ( CHAR )
     CONSTRAINT ( IS_UNK ( HOURS ) OR
                  IS_NONNEG_INTEGER ( HOURS ) )
     SPECIALS ( UNK HOURS ('?') )
```

In this example, the identifier UNK was presumably chosen because it suggests the interpretation "unknown." Informally, we can say that the semantics of this *<special def>*—as intended by the HOURS definer, and as understood by the HOURS user but *not* by the system—are that the special value HOURS ('?') is to be used when no regular value is known to be the right one. *Note:* For the purposes of the example, we have assumed the availability of an operator IS_NONNEG_INTEGER, which returns TRUE if its argument represents a number of hours that is a nonnegative integer and FALSE otherwise.

Note further that the *<special def>* UNK HOURS ('?') for type HOURS causes automatic definition of:

- An operator of the form UNK_HOURS (), which returns the value HOURS ('?'), and

- An operator of the form IS_UNK (*<scalar exp>*)—where the *<scalar exp>* must be of type HOURS—which returns TRUE if that *<scalar exp>* evaluates to UNK_HOURS () and FALSE otherwise.

Analogous remarks apply to all *<special def>*s. For example, we might define another special value for type HOURS representing (say) "not applicable"—e.g., NA HOURS ('!').

We also propose an operator—another new form of *<other builtin relation op inv>*—for "filtering out" tuples that contain special values:

```
<filter and cast>
    ::=   FILTER_AND_CAST_AS_<scalar type name>
                    ( <relation exp>, <attribute name > )
```

The specified attribute must be of scalar type. The result of the *<filter and cast>* is defined to be a relation with:

- A heading the same as that of the relation denoted by the *<relation exp>,* except that the type corresponding to *<attribute name>* in that heading is the specified scalar type;
- A body consisting of those tuples of the relation denoted by the *<relation exp>* in which the specified attribute contains a value that can be cast to the specified scalar type, except that the values of that attribute in those rows are replaced by their counterparts in that specified type.

For example, let relvar EMP include an attribute HOURS_WORKED. Then the expression

```
FILTER_AND_CAST_AS_INTEGER ( EMP, HOURS_WORKED )
```

yields a result with the same heading as EMP, except that the type of attribute HOURS_WORKED in that result is INTEGER, and with the same body as EMP, except that EMP tuples in which the HOURS_WORKED value is any HOURS special value are eliminated.

Following reference [32], we also suggest two additional relational operators, LEFT JOIN and RIGHT JOIN, the intent of which is to support a "respectable" version of *outer join* (i.e., one that does not involve nulls). For example:

```
S LEFT JOIN SP FILL ( P# UNK_P# (), QTY UNK_QTY () )
```

(we assume here that suitable "UNK" special values have been defined for types P# and QTY). Given our usual sample data, this expression evaluates to a relation that is identical to the result of S JOIN SP, except that it additionally contains the following tuple:

S#	SNAME	STATUS	CITY	P#	QTY
S5	Adams	30	Athens	??	???

(where the question marks stand for the relevant special values). *Note:* For simplicity, we have omitted the type names from the heading of this tuple.

Here then is the syntax for *<left join>* and *<right join>* (both additional cases of the general construct *<other builtin relation op inv>*):

```
<left join>
    ::=    <relation exp> LEFT JOIN <relation exp>
                      FILL ( <ne tuple component commalist> )

<right join>
    ::=    <relation exp> RIGHT JOIN <relation exp>
                      FILL ( <ne tuple component commalist> )
```

Note: The *<relation exp>*s must not be *<other builtin relation op inv>*s.

RM VERY STRONG SUGGESTION 9: SQL MIGRATION

*SQL should be implementable in **D**—not because such implementation is desirable in itself, but so that a painless migration route might be available for current SQL users. To this same end, existing SQL databases should be convertible to a form that **D** programs can operate on without error.*

———— ♦♦♦♦ ————

We reject SQL as a long-term foundation for the future. However, we are not so sanguine as to think that SQL will disappear; rather, it is our hope that (some) **D** will be sufficiently superior to SQL that it will become the database language of choice—by a process of natural selection—and SQL will become "the database language of last resort." In fact, we see a parallel with the world of programming languages, where COBOL has never disappeared (and never will); but COBOL has become "the programming language of last resort" for developing applications, because preferable alternatives exist. We see SQL as a kind of database COBOL, and we would like some **D** to become a preferable alternative to it.

As the foregoing paragraph makes clear, however, we do realize that SQL databases and applications are going to be with us for a very long time—to think otherwise would be quite unrealistic—and so we do have to pay some attention to the question of what to do about today's SQL legacy; hence the present "strong suggestion."

Please understand that the suggestion in question does not mean that **D** needs to be a proper superset of SQL. Rather, it means that it should be possible to write a frontend layer of **D** code on top of the true relational functionality of **D** that will accept SQL operations against converted SQL data, and will give the results that those SQL operations would given if they had been executed against the original unconverted SQL data. We believe it should be possible to construct such a frontend without contravening any of the prescriptions and proscriptions laid down in the *Manifesto*. (Analogous remarks apply to the recommendation that SQL databases be convertible to **D** form, of course.) In fact—noting that **D** is computationally complete, and noting too that SQL frontends already exist for many nonSQL databases—we see no reason to doubt the feasibility of producing a frontend such as the one under consideration (i.e., one that is (a) written in **D** and (b) supports SQL access to **D** databases).

Of course, we would not want a **D** database, even one that is really just a converted SQL database, to be accessible only via SQL; rather, we would like it to be available for use "in native **D** mode" as well. To that end, it is important for anyone involved in the development of an SQL frontend to bear the following goals in mind:

- First (to repeat), users must be able to make direct use of **D** for *ad hoc* queries and for developing new applications on the **D** version of the database.

- That **D** database should not be encumbered with material placed there solely to support the SQL frontend. Such material, having no obvious bearing on the enterprise the database is intended to serve, might cause undue confusion for **D** users.

- SQL users should not be deprived of the benefits of the **D** optimizer. Such deprivation would arise, for example, if the SQL frontend used **D** as a mere access method, instead of mapping high level SQL expressions into equally high level **D** expressions.

We should add that it will almost certainly not be possible to achieve these goals 100 percent, though we do think they should be strongly striven for. The fact is, there are certain features in SQL that (as far as we can see) could only be accurately implemented in an SQL frontend for **D** if **D** in turn contained analogous features of its own—and the features in question are either ones we explicitly proscribe or ones that would constitute blatant violations of *conceptual integrity* (and such violations are prohibited by RM Prescription 26). We hope and believe that the SQL features in question are so pathological that uses of them will be sufficiently few and far between for it to be acceptable for such uses to be worked around on a case-by-case basis.* Examples that come to mind are:

- Extended character set support (user-defined character sets, collations, translations, and so forth)

- View updating where the effects prescribed by SQL are logically incorrect (in particular, updating on views for which WITH CASCADED CHECK OPTION is not specified)

- The SQL statement SET CONSTRAINTS (whether a constraint is "immediate" or "deferred" is specified declaratively in **D,** not procedurally)

- The SQL expression SELECT A, A FROM T (which selects the same column twice without performing any kind of column renaming)

---

*We should add that we are somewhat skeptical as to whether the features in question are supported in existing SQL frontends either (or even in SQL DBMSs, in some cases).

Let us get back to the main thread of our discussion. We now proceed to offer a few practical suggestions for implementing the desired SQL frontend. Of course, it goes without saying that our suggestions come nowhere near to being a complete design for such a frontend—they are only "notes toward" such a design—but they do address certain questions that come to mind almost immediately when our RM Proscriptions, in particular, are considered in this context.

First of all, we assume that the process of converting an SQL database to a **D** analog is "direct," in the sense that (a) every SQL base table maps to a **D** real relvar, and (b) every column in such a base table maps to an attribute in the corresponding relvar. Under that assumption, of course, we are immediately confronted with the possibility that the base table in question might contain duplicate rows or nulls or both. Direct support for these features is expressly prohibited in **D** by RM Proscriptions 3 and 4, so what is to be done? This question is the topic of the two subsections immediately following.

Duplicate Rows

An SQL base table permits duplicate rows if and only if no candidate key is declared for it, via PRIMARY KEY or UNIQUE. Given such a base table *BT,* then, the **D** relvar *RV* corresponding to it will have to have an extra attribute (i.e., one not corresponding to any column in *BT*) that can serve as the necessary candidate key. That candidate key can be declared to have DEFAULT SERIAL (meaning that it is in fact a "system key"), if **D** supports RM Very Strong Suggestion 1 as discussed earlier in this chapter. The SQL frontend can now support certain SQL INSERT operations by mapping them directly into **D** INSERTs; since values for the extra attribute are provided by the system, no corresponding attribute is needed in the relation to be inserted, and of course there *is* no corresponding column in the SQL table to be inserted into.

Unfortunately, if *BT* permits duplicate rows, it follows that any table *IT* to be inserted into *BT* might contain duplicate rows as well. Let *IR* be the **D** relation corresponding to *IT*. Like *RV,* therefore, *IR* will need an extra attribute (i.e., one over and above those corresponding to the columns of *IT*). Our suggested TAG relational operator can be used to provide that extra attribute; if we are not careful, however, we could now be faced with a situation in which each of *IR* and *RV* has an attribute that has no counterpart in the other. And even if we are careful to ensure the extra attributes do correspond (i.e., they have the same name—*X,* say—and same type in both *IR* and *RV*), there is still the problem that, in general, the *X* values provided for *IR* by TAG will clash with the *X* values already present in *RV*. *Note:* We are assuming here that TAG generates *X* values that start again from one every time it is invoked; the clash occurs because *X* is supposed to be a candidate key for *RV*. One solution to this problem is to extend TAG to allow the user to specify a different starting value on different invocations, a possibility mentioned under RM Very Strong Suggestion 1.

We also need to address the problem of *naming* the systematically generated attributes that have no corresponding SQL columns. Happily, SQL expressly prohibits column names that begin with an underscore; assuming **D** has no such prohibition, therefore, we have here the basis of an obvious way to avoid naming clashes. What is more, the same approach could also simplify the task of the SQL frontend in hiding the extra attributes from its users.

We also need to consider the question of duplicate rows that are *dynamically generated*—i.e., the question of those SQL operators that can generate duplicate rows even when the operands to those operators are themselves duplicate-free. The operators in question are (a) SELECT without DISTINCT, (b) VALUES, and (c) UNION ALL.

- SELECT without DISTINCT and VALUES can both be implemented by using our suggested TAG operator and having the frontend discard attributes generated by TAG on presentation of final results.

- The same treatment is not suitable for UNION ALL, but here an easy solution lies in merely adding a constant attribute to the **D** relations corresponding to the SQL tables that are the operands of the UNION ALL. For example, the SQL expression

```
SELECT * FROM T1
UNION CORRESPONDING ALL
SELECT * FROM T2
```

can be mapped to the **Tutorial D** expression

```
( EXTEND T1 ADD 1 AS _EXTRA )
UNION
( EXTEND T2 ADD 2 AS _EXTRA )
```

Again, of course, the frontend would have to discard the extra attribute on presentation of the final result.

Nulls

Nulls in SQL are hard to explain. There are many reasons for this state of affairs, but one important one is that, despite the fact that in SQL circles they are often explicitly called null *values,* SQL nulls are (at least arguably) not values at all but "marks" [22]. However (and regardless of whether or not you agree with this position), the fact is that nulls will have to map to values in **D,** because **D** certainly does not embrace any such peculiar concept as a "mark." With this point in mind, therefore, we offer the following observations:

- The builtin SQL type INTEGER is not the same as the builtin type of that name typically found in conventional programming languages (and a similar observation applies to all of the other builtin types in SQL). The reason is that, as the SQL standard puts it, "the null value . . . is a member of every SQL data type" [87].

- **D** requires support for the builtin type **truth value** (BOOLEAN in **Tutorial D**). The current SQL standard does not explicitly support such a type at all (though it does support expressions—e.g., in WHERE clauses—that return values of such a type). *Note:* SQL3, the proposed follow-on to the current standard, does support a type it calls BOOLEAN, but that type is not at all the same as the prescribed truth-valued type of **D**. See Appendix E for further details.

- The SQL equality comparison operator "=" is not the same as the equality comparison operator found in conventional programming languages. In particular, it is not the same as the equality comparison operator "=" required in **D.**

- The other scalar operators of SQL, where they have apparent counterparts in conventional programming languages, are not the same as those apparent counterparts. For example, the SQL operators "+" and "||" (concatenate) are not the usual "+" and "||" operators. Indeed, the types of the operands of those operators are not the usual types, as already noted above.

These four points, we suggest, crystallize the problems (or, at least, the major problems) arising from nulls that confront the implementer of an SQL frontend. Now we make some observations regarding **D** that might point to ways of addressing those problems.

- As noted in the introduction to this part of the book, the *Manifesto* is intended to be open-ended; i.e., anything not explicitly prescribed is permitted, unless it is explicitly *pro*scribed, and anything not explicitly proscribed is permitted too, unless it clashes with something explicitly *pre*scribed. In particular, therefore, there are no proscribed types, and there are no proscribed operators (generally speaking). Nor do we have any prescriptions or proscriptions concerning concrete syntax, *modulo* RM Prescription 26.

- As a consequence of the foregoing point, **D** is at least theoretically permitted to have (e.g.) an operator called "+" that is not the normal operator of that name. A similar remark applies to "=". That said, however, we venture to suggest that to use such names for SQL-like perversions of the operators they normally stand for would be counter to the spirit of **D**. A similar remark applies to the names of builtin types, such as INTEGER and BOOLEAN (as well as all the other familiar ones—CHARACTER, BIT, DATE, TIME, and so on).

- But if **D** had a builtin type called INTEGER that *was* the same as the type of that name found in conventional programming languages, it could certainly also have another type (builtin or otherwise) called SQL_INTEGER, with the same properties as the SQL type called INTEGER. A similar remark applies to other builtin types.

- Likewise, if **D** had "=" as its operator for equality comparison, it could also have another operator (perhaps "*sql=*") for the corresponding but different SQL operator. A similar remark applies to other SQL scalar operators.

In other words, we would expect **D** to have first claim on the usual names for the most familiar types and operators, but to provide counterparts (or allow the user to define counterparts) to all the corresponding but different SQL types and operators, with names that are different from those of SQL for those counterparts.

Now suppose SQL base table T has a column I of (SQL) type INTEGER. Suppose too that when base table T is mapped to **D** relvar T, column I becomes attribute I, of type SQL_INTEGER. We now point out certain consequences of the foregoing observations (using **Tutorial D** syntax, as and where appropriate).

- The SQL expression

```
SELECT * FROM T WHERE I < 10
```

maps to the **Tutorial D** expression

```
T WHERE ( I sql< 10 ) = SQL_BOOLEAN ( 'TRUE' )
```

We explain this mapping as follows. First of all, the SQL "<" operator maps to a **Tutorial D** analog of that operator ("*sql<*"). Since this latter operator does *not* yield values of the **Tutorial D** type BOOLEAN, we must operate on its result with some operator that does—namely, the **Tutorial D** equality comparison operator ("="). Let the **Tutorial D** type corresponding to operators such as *sql<* (and, in particular, *sql=*) be SQL_BOOLEAN, with values SQL_BOOLEAN ('TRUE'), SQL_BOOLEAN ('FALSE'), and SQL_BOOLEAN ('UNKNOWN'). In the example, then, the right hand comparand in the WHERE clause is specified as an invocation of the selector corresponding to that type. In general, in fact, the SQL WHERE clause "WHERE *cond*" will map to the **D** WHERE clause "WHERE (*SQL_cond*) = SQL_BOOLEAN ('TRUE')" (where *SQL_cond* is the mapped version of *cond,* of course).

- The SQL expression

```
SELECT DISTINCT I, J, ..., K FROM T
```

can be mapped more directly into just

```
T { I, J, ..., K }
```

This straightforward mapping is possible because SQL reverts to the normal programming language treatment of equality in places where its usual treatment is impossible to apply in any sensible or meaningful way.

- The SQL frontend will certainly require SQL_INTEGER to be an "ordered type" (i.e., a type for which the operator "<" is defined—see the discussion of RM Prescription 3 in Chapter 6), because the INTEGER type of SQL is ordered in this sense. Thus, the **Tutorial D** expression

```
T WHERE I < SQL_INTEGER ('20')
```

might be legal. Whether the result of that expression includes those tuples of T for which the I value is SQL_INTEGER ('NULL') will depend, of course, on how the operator "<" is defined for type SQL_INTEGER.

- The result of the **Tutorial D** expression

```
T WHERE I ≠ SQL_INTEGER ('20')
```

certainly does include those tuples of T for which the I value is SQL_INTEGER ('NULL'), unlike its SQL counterpart

```
SELECT * FROM T WHERE I <> 20
```

(The symbol "<>" here is SQL syntax for "not equals.") We venture to suggest that—at least in some cases—**D** expressions involving tables derived from null-infested SQL databases will give results that are more intuitively acceptable than those of SQL expressions.

The foregoing proposals, it has to be said, might make it difficult to meet our goal of making the converted SQL database usable "in native **D** mode." At the same time, we are aware that some SQL database administrators today implement a "null-free" policy (at least insofar as it is possible to steer clear of nulls in SQL), and it would be a shame for users of such databases to have to put up with any inconvenience arising from a migration strategy that takes nulls into account. For databases that have been implemented under a null-free policy, therefore, we believe it should be possible to map the builtin types and operators of SQL directly to their obvious counterparts in **D** and deal "manually" with any SQL expressions that make use of operators that generate nulls dynamically (e.g., outer joins and aggregations over empty sets).

We now turn to certain other SQL idiosyncrasies that will require special attention in the SQL frontend.

SQL Column Names *vs.* D Attribute Names

The following SQL peculiarities will need to be addressed.

- There is more than one way of referring to a column in SQL expressions. For example, the SQL expression

```
SELECT T1.C FROM T AS T1
```

is equivalent to the SQL expression

```
SELECT C FROM T AS T1
```

As a consequence, the result of the first expression yields a table whose sole column is named C and not T1.C. Hence (e.g.) the following SQL expression is not legal:

```
SELECT T2.T1.C FROM ( SELECT T1.C FROM T AS T1 ) AS T2
```

It follows that if **D** adopts the simple approach to attribute naming and refer-encing used in **Tutorial D** (an approach we would certainly recommend for consideration by other **D** designers), then the mapping of SQL FROM clauses will be nontrivial. However, the **Tutorial D** support for systematic renaming of all attributes could be useful in this connection. For example, the SQL FROM clause

```
FROM T1, T2
```

could be mapped to

```
( T1 RENAME PREFIX '' AS 'T1_' )
JOIN
( T2 RENAME PREFIX '' AS 'T2_' )
```

This mapping would avoid the problem that arises when T1 and T2 have columns of the same name. Of course, there would be obvious consequences for mapping other parts of the overall SQL expression that contained the FROM clause in question.

■ The SQL expression

```
SELECT A + B FROM T
```

yields a table with an "anonymous column." The SQL standard actually requires such columns to acquire unpredictable but unique column names, so the SQL frontend to **D** could perhaps simply follow the standard's prescription in this re-spect. Our previous suggestion concerning attribute names beginning with un-derscores could be of help here.

■ The SQL expression

```
SELECT * FROM T1
UNION
SELECT * FROM T2
```

cannot in general be mapped to

```
T1 UNION T2
```

(why not?). Thus, it might be necessary to rename attributes so that correspond-ing attributes in the operands of the union have the same name. Unfortunately, this fact implies that the SQL-to-**D** database conversion process will have to keep some record of SQL column definition order, because there will (of course) be no attribute ordering in **D.** (In fact, such a record will be needed for several other reasons anyway—e.g., supporting SELECT * or INSERT when no column names are specified.)

Character String Comparisons

As noted in Chapter 6, it is possible in SQL for the character strings

`'AB'`

and

`'AB '`

to be treated as equal; to be specific, they are treated as equal if PAD SPACE applies to the applicable collating sequence [76,87–89]. In effect, PAD SPACE means that trailing space characters are implicitly trimmed before the comparison is done. That implicit trimming will have to be made explicit in **D.**

Cursors

Cursor operations can be implemented as follows.

- OPEN causes the target relation to be copied into an array (probably with some appropriate locking), as in the *<relation get>* operation of **Tutorial D** (see Chapter 5).
- If "the cursor is updatable" [76], then each row in that array will have to include, either explicitly or implicitly, some candidate key value for the corresponding row from the underlying real relvar.
- FETCH is straightforward.
- UPDATE or DELETE WHERE CURRENT can be simulated by means of a **D** UPDATE or DELETE WHERE, using the appropriate candidate key value. If the cursor is a scroll cursor, however, (a) UPDATE WHERE CURRENT must cause the corresponding array row to be updated too; (b) DELETE WHERE CURRENT must cause the corresponding array row to be deleted too and must also "close up the gap" in that array.

11

OO Very Strong Suggestions

OO VERY STRONG SUGGESTION 1: TYPE INHERITANCE

*Some form of **type inheritance** should be supported (in which case, see OO Prescriptions 2 and 3). In keeping with this suggestion, **D** should not support **coercions** (i.e., implicit type conversions).*

———— ♦♦♦♦♦ ————

As noted in Chapters 1 and 6, we do believe that type inheritance is important, and we would very much like to support it—but not before it is fully understood! That is why the *Manifesto* currently supports it only conditionally, saying (in effect) in OO Prescriptions 2 and 3 that "If inheritance is supported, it must be according to some good inheritance *model*." At the same time, of course, we do not want to do anything now that might preclude extension to include proper inheritance support later. For this reason, OO Very Strong Suggestion 1 suggests that coercions (i.e., implicit type conversions) be prohibited.* Here we explain why we adopt this rather conservative position. Essentially, the argument goes like this:

———————

*And in fact we do currently prohibit them—see RM Prescriptions 3, 21, and 22 (regarding argument/parameter matching, assignment, and comparisons, respectively).

219

- Type inheritance means among other things that, if we define (say) type CIRCLE to be a *subtype* of *supertype* ELLIPSE, then:

  - By definition, every circle is also an ellipse.

  - Therefore, any code that works for ellipses should also work for circles (because circles *are* ellipses), even if type CIRCLE had not been defined at the time the code in question was written.

  - In other words, it should be possible to invoke that code and pass it a circle instead of an ellipse and have it still work.

  - Thus, wherever an ellipse is expected, it should be possible to substitute a circle—*The Principle of (Value) Substitutability* (see Chapters 13 and 14 for further discussion of this principle).

- Even if a circle is substituted for an ellipse in this way, it is required *that it remain a circle and retain its circle-specific properties* (e.g., the property of having a radius).

- If passing a circle when an ellipse was expected were to cause that circle to be coerced to type ELLIPSE, then it would cease to be a circle and would lose its circle-specific properties (ellipses in general do not have a radius, for example).

- Therefore—it is claimed—coercions undermine the objective of substitutability; hence the present "very strong suggestion."

We should say, however, that it is our feeling that such claims require more study; that is, we think it might be both possible and desirable to relax the prohibition against coercions at some future time. See Chapter 14 for further discussion of this issue.

We feel bound to say too that it is also our feeling that good type design will tend to reduce the number of type conversions needed anyway, implicit or otherwise. For example, consider temperatures. A good design would involve a single TEMPERATURE type and operators to expose a Celsius representation, a Fahrenheit representation, and so on (see the discussion of RM Prescription 5 in Chapter 6). A bad design would involve different types—CELSIUS, FAHRENHEIT, and so on—and hence many conversion operators also.

Note: Of course, coercions—i.e., implicit conversions—are possible in general only in those cases where *explicit* conversions are also possible.* Thus, if no explicit conversion operator has been defined to convert from type T' to type T, values of type T' probably *cannot* be coerced to type T. (We mention this rather obvious point only because it becomes significant if type inheritance is supported. If type T' is defined to be a subtype of type T, then it is probable that values of type T' will never be coerced to type T, precisely because no corresponding explicit conversion operator will have been defined. Our reservations, hinted at above, regarding claims that value substitutability is undermined if coercions are permitted are founded on this observation. Again, refer to Chapter 14 for further discussion.)

---

*Except possibly for the case where the types involved are both system-defined; an ill-designed language might conceivably support coercions, but no explicit conversions, between such types.

OO VERY STRONG SUGGESTION 2: TYPES AND OPERATORS UNBUNDLED

*Operator definitions should be **logically distinct** from the definitions of the types of their parameters and/or results, not "bundled in" with any of those latter definitions (though selectors and the operators required by RM Prescription 5 might be regarded as exceptions to this suggestion).*

In object systems, operators ("methods") are typically bundled in with types ("classes"), meaning that the definition of any given operator is made part of the definition of some type. In the examples in the section on RM Prescription 3 in Chapter 6, for instance, we might have made the definition of the operator REFLECT—which, you will recall, effectively moves the point with Cartesian coordinates (x,y) to its mirror image position $(-x,-y)$—part of the definition of the type POINT.

But suppose we were to define an operator PERP_DIST that computes the perpendicular distance of some point from some line. Should PERP_DIST be bundled with type POINT, or with type LINE? Whichever it is, why? What are the implications? As another example, consider the operator "*", which might be used (among other things) to multiply a velocity by a time to give a distance. Which type does "*" belong to? VELOCITY? TIME? Perhaps DISTANCE? Surely the only sensible answer is "None of the above." In other words, the idea of an operator being bundled in with some type works just fine so long as the operator in question takes exactly one operand (as REFLECT does). But as soon as it takes two or more (as PERP_DIST and "*" do), a degree of arbitrariness, artificiality, asymmetry, and awkwardness inevitably creeps in.

So let us step back for a moment. Why are operators bundled in with types anyway, in object systems? One answer to this question seems to be that those operators need (or might need) *privileged access:* access, that is, to the *internal representation* of instances of the type in question. *Note:* We are using the fuzzy term "instances" here as a convenient shorthand for "values and/or variables."

But we already have a mechanism for dealing with privileged access, namely the *security* mechanism.* Would it not be better, therefore, to unbundle operators from types, and instead use the security mechanism to control which operators are allowed access to which types (more accurately, access to the internal representation

---

*Of course, we are talking about *database* systems specifically here. Programming systems typically do not have a security mechanism, and this lack perhaps accounts for the approach typically taken by object systems. Note too that we do not in fact prescribe a security mechanism for **D**! We justify this omission by noting that security is not a *foundation* consideration and thus not a matter of concern for the *Manifesto* as such. However, we do naturally assume that any industrial strength **D** will include appropriate security support.

of instances of those types)? We believe it would (and we have followed this approach in **Tutorial D,** of course). To be specific, we believe such a scheme would have the advantages that:

- Operators could be permitted privileged access to the internals of instances of any number of types, instead of being limited to just one.
- The arbitrariness, artificiality, asymmetry, and awkwardness inherent in the bundling scheme would be eliminated.

Furthermore, support for such a scheme also implies that:

- **D** will not need to support the concept, found in some object systems, that operators have a *distinguished* or *receiver* or *target* operand. (In a typical object system, if operator *Op* is bundled with type *T,* then *Op* is invoked by "sending a message" to a specific *target operand*—namely, an instance of type *T*. That target operand is, typically, given special treatment, both syntactic and semantic. In **D**, by contrast—assuming this suggestion is implemented—all operands can be treated uniformly. See Chapter 14 for further discussion.)
- **D** will also not need to support either the concept of *protected instance variables* or the concept of *friends.* (See reference [80] for an explanation of these concepts. Basically, they are both *ad hoc* techniques for getting around the limitation that one operator is permitted privileged access to instances of only one type.)

As already indicated, we believe the problem all such notions are intended to address is better solved by judicious application of the system's security mechanism. In fact, the problem in question degenerates to nothing more than that of deciding which operators shall be entitled to make use of which of the "highly protected operators that are not part of **D**" (see the discussion of RM Prescription 4 in Chapter 6).

OO VERY STRONG SUGGESTION 3: COLLECTION TYPE GENERATORS

*"Collection" type generators, such as **LIST, ARRAY,** and **SET,** as commonly found in languages supporting rich type systems, should be supported.*

A *collection* can be defined as a grouping together of an arbitrary number of elements into a single object (using the word "object" here in its general sense, not in its special object-oriented sense). The elements are usually required all to be of the same type; in other words, collections are usually required to be *homogeneous.*

Now, object systems typically support several different type generators for generating collection types: LIST, ARRAY, SET, BAG, and so on. And we agree that lists, arrays, and so on can be useful in appropriate circumstances, and we do therefore suggest that they be supported. However, we also strongly suggest that, if supported, they effectively be just shorthand!—see OO Very Strong Suggestion 4 below. In other words, the present suggestion is very definitely not meant to undermine the *Manifesto's* position that the only kind of variable with "persistence" (i.e., the only kind of variable permitted in the database) is, very specifically, the database relvar.

Note: Support for the collection type generator RELATION is required by RM Prescription 7. Support for additional type generators, if any, should follow the same general pattern.

Incidentally, the arrays supported in **Tutorial D** are deliberately not intended to be the completely general arrays that proper support for an ARRAY type generator would require. For one thing, they are required to be arrays of *tuples* specifically; moreover, it is not permitted for two distinct tuples within the same array to be identical. Our rationale for adopting this position was given in Chapter 5.

OO VERY STRONG SUGGESTION 4: CONVERSION TO/FROM RELATIONS

*Let C be a collection type generator other than RELATION. Then a **conversion** operator, say C2R, should be provided for converting values of a given generated C type to relations, and an inverse operator, say R2C, should also be provided, such that:*

a. $C2R(R2C(r)) = r$ for every expressible relation r;

b. $R2C(C2R(c)) = c$ for every expressible value c of that generated C type.

———— ♦♦♦♦♦ ————

Consider an object system that supports, say, the type generators LIST and ARRAY, and consider the object SP that is—or denotes, rather—the collection of all shipments. Then SP might be implemented either as a list or as an array, and users will have to know which it is (because the access operators will differ accordingly). One consequence of this state of affairs is that, contrary to conventional wisdom, object systems might very well provide less data independence than relational systems do. For example, suppose the implementation of the object SP is changed from a list to an array.* What are the implications for existing code that accesses that object?

We see, therefore, that support for a variety of collection type generators (at the *model* level, as opposed to the implementation level) has the potential to undermine data independence. Needless to say, it also has the effect of complicating the model

---

*Note too that such a change will typically occur in an object system *for performance reasons.* Ideally, therefore, it should not affect anything *except* performance, but in practice it probably will.

considerably, because the model now contains more constructs than it would otherwise. Furthermore, it complicates *use* of the model as well, because it leads to a variety of design alternatives, without, perhaps, good guidelines as to how to make the right choice among those alternatives in any given situation.

For at least these three reasons, therefore, we suggest very strongly that any given generated collection type should be essentially just shorthand for some relation type (possibly some set of relation types).* That is, values and variables of the generated type in question should be defined in terms of relations and relvars, and operations on those values and variables should be defined in terms of operations on those relations and relvars. If these objectives are met, then:

- Data independence is obviously enhanced, because there is no longer any *performance* reason for changing the user's perception of some collection from (say) a list to an array.

- In fact, choosing among alternative designs becomes a purely psychological decision—there is no *logical* reason for preferring (say) an array over a list.

We conclude this section by repeating from the previous section the point that **Tutorial D** arrays are deliberately not intended to be the completely general arrays that proper support for an ARRAY type generator would require. For that reason, we made no attempt in Chapter 5 to define the general conversions that the present suggestion is asking for. Again, our rationale for adopting this position was given in Chapter 5.

OO VERY STRONG SUGGESTION 5: SINGLE-LEVEL STORE

*D should be based on a **single-level storage** model.*

The concept of a "single-level storage model" was proposed—under the name of *direct reference*—by one of the present authors as far back as 1976 [43], and it is supported by most object systems today (though not by the current crop of "object/relational" DBMSs, because those DBMSs are based on SQL). The general idea is simply that there should be no unnecessary differences between data in the database and data not in the database;[†] in other words, access to database data and

---

*If such were not the case, of course, the system would be in violation of *The Information Principle* (see the discussion of RM Prescription 16 in Chapter 6). It goes without saying that object systems do violate that principle, more or less by definition.

[†]There is, of course, a *necessary* difference, *viz.* that between persistence and nonpersistence. There might be a *performance* difference, too. However, neither of these differences should be confused with a difference over levels of storage *per se.*

access to nondatabase data should look the same. And in **Tutorial D,** of course, it does. For example, a **Tutorial D** scalar expression can reference an attribute value within some tuple within some relation, and it makes no difference whether the relation in question is in the database or "in main memory." Thus, e.g., the following is a valid IF statement:

```
IF CITY FROM ( TUPLE FROM ( S WHERE S# = S# ('S1') ) ) =
   CITY FROM ( TUPLE FROM ( P WHERE P# = P# ('P1') ) )
   THEN ... ;
END IF ;
```

Note in particular, therefore, that there is no notion in **Tutorial D** that database data must be "copied into main memory" before it can be processed. The net effect is that it makes no logical difference whether a given piece of data resides in main memory, online secondary storage, tertiary backup storage, etc. What is important is whether it is in the database or not.

PART IV

SUBTYPING AND INHERITANCE

Essentially, this part of the book does for subtyping and inheritance what Parts I, II, and III do for the *Manifesto* proper. Thus, Chapter 12 corresponds to Part I (it contains an overall introduction to the topic); Chapter 13 corresponds to Part II (it contains formal definitions); and Chapter 14 corresponds to Part III (it contains extended but informal explanations and discussions of those formal definitions). Chapter 15 then considers the possibility of extending the subtyping and inheritance ideas discussed in the three prior chapters to include support for multiple inheritance as well. Finally, Chapter 16 goes on to take tuple and relation types into account too.

12

Preliminaries

INTRODUCTION

As noted in our discussion of OO Prescriptions 2 and 3 in Chapter 8, there is currently no consensus on a formal, rigorous, and abstract—"clearly defined and generally agreed"—inheritance model (which is why those prescriptions are conditional, of course). In this part of the book, we offer our own attempt at such a model: an attempt that, naturally, we would like the community at large to consider as a contender for such a "clearly defined and generally agreed" model.

We should probably start by considering the question of why this topic is worth investigating in the first place. There are at least two possible answers to this question:

- First, the ideas of subtyping and inheritance do seem to arise naturally in the real world. That is, it is not at all unusual to encounter situations in which all values of a given type have certain properties in common, while some of those values have additional special properties of their own. For example, all ellipses have an area, while some ellipses—specifically, those that happen to be circles—have a radius as well. Thus, subtyping and inheritance look as if they might be useful tools for "modeling reality."

- Second, if we can recognize such general patterns (patterns of subtyping and inheritance, that is) and build intelligence regarding them into our application and system software, we might be able to achieve certain practical economies. For example, a program that works for ellipses might work for circles too, even if it was originally written with no thought for circles at all (perhaps type CIRCLE had not even been defined at the time the program was written).

Now, much of the existing literature on this subject seems to be concerned primarily with the second of these points rather than the first; i.e., it seems to be concerned with inheritance as a mechanism that might be useful in designing, building, and using (and reusing) *programs.* In other words, it is (as already noted in Chapter 8) interested in inheritance primarily as it applies to *software engineering.* Our own major interest, by contrast, is on the first point rather than the second; i.e., we are interested in inheritance as a conceptual tool that might be useful in designing, building, and using (and reusing) *data structures.* In other words, we are concerned with inheritance as **a model of reality**—or, at least, certain aspects of reality—just as the relational model can be thought of as a model of certain aspects of reality. To put it yet another way, we are interested (as always!) in the possibility of defining *an abstract model,* not in matters of implementation merely.

Incidentally—and presumably as a consequence of the software engineering emphasis mentioned in the preceding paragraph—little work seems to have been done, or at any rate published, on any such abstract inheritance model (despite the fact that there are plenty of *implementations,* including several that are commercially available). This state of affairs accounts for the dearth of references in this part of the book, of course.

Caveat: Before going any further, we should warn you that this whole area is considerably more complex than might at first have been expected. The trouble is, although "the basic idea of inheritance is quite simple" [112], the devil is in the details: You have to study the topic in its entirety (and, we might add, extremely closely and carefully) in order to get properly to grips with it and to appreciate the fact that it is not at all as straightforward as it might seem at first sight. All of which goes some way, perhaps, to justify the undue length of this part of the book (especially Chapter 14).

One last introductory point: The subject of type inheritance has a lot to do with data in general, of course, but not much to do with *persistent* or database data in particular (i.e., there is little or nothing about inheritance that applies to persistent data only). For simplicity, therefore (and despite our remarks in Chapter 1 regarding the general focus in this book on data*base* management specifically), the examples in this part of the book are all expressed in terms of local data instead of database data. (Support for inheritance does have certain implications for relational data and relational operations, of course, but even those implications apply just as much to local data as they do to database data.)

TOWARD A TYPE INHERITANCE MODEL

As the previous section indicates, we use the term *inheritance* to refer to that phenomenon according to which we can sensibly say, for example, that every circle is an ellipse, and hence that all properties that apply to ellipses in general apply to—i.e., are **inherited by**—circles in particular. For example, every ellipse has an area, and therefore every circle has an area too. In the usual terminology of the field, we say we have two types, ELLIPSE and CIRCLE, such that ELLIPSE is a **supertype** of CIRCLE and CIRCLE is a **subtype** of ELLIPSE; we also say (somewhat loosely) that all properties that apply to the supertype apply *a fortiori* to the subtype. Of course, the converse is not true: The subtype will have properties of its own that do not apply to the supertype (again speaking somewhat loosely). For example, circles have a radius, while ellipses in general do not.

(As an aside, we note that some writers—see, e.g., references [1], [102], and [116], among others—have suggested that there are many *kinds* of inheritance that overlap in various ways and yet are all distinct from one another. Certainly it is the case that you can find definitions in the literature of terms such as "inheritance" and "subtype" that are not the same as ours. *Caveat lector.*)

A point arises here that beginners sometimes find a little confusing and is therefore worth spelling out explicitly: namely, that a subtype has a *sub*set of the values but a *super*set of the properties. For example, the subtype CIRCLE contains a subset of the values of the supertype ELLIPSE, but an individual circle has all of the properties of an ellipse and more besides. *Note:* For exactly such reasons, some writers prefer to avoid the "sub and super" terminology and talk of *descendants* and *ancestors* instead (see, e.g., reference [90]); however, we think this latter nomenclature has problems of its own, and choose to stay with the "sub and super" terminology.

By the way, it should be understood that *constraints* are properties too, of a kind, and are therefore inherited too (where by the term "constraints" we mean *type* constraints specifically). Thus, e.g., any constraint that applies to ellipses in general also applies, necessarily, to circles in particular (for if it did not, then some circles would not be ellipses). For example, if ellipses are subject to the constraint that the length of their major semiaxis a must be greater than or equal to that of their minor semiaxis b, then this same constraint must be satisfied by circles also. (For circles, of course, a and b coincide in the radius r, and the constraint is satisfied trivially.)

Now, it is important in this context (as in all others!) to distinguish carefully between *values* and *variables*. When we say that every circle is an ellipse, what we mean, more precisely, is that every circle *value* is an ellipse *value*. We certainly do not mean that every circle *variable* is an ellipse *variable*—i.e., that a variable of declared type CIRCLE is a variable of declared type ELLIPSE, and hence can contain a value that is an ellipse and not a circle. In other words, **inheritance applies to values, not variables** (speaking somewhat loosely once again)—although naturally there are implications for variables too, as will be seen.*

SINGLE *VS.* MULTIPLE INHERITANCE

As explained in Chapter 8, there are two broad "flavors" of type inheritance, single and multiple. Loosely speaking, *single* inheritance means that each subtype has just one

---

*We conjecture that much of the confusion we observe in this whole area (and there is a lot of it) is due precisely to a failure to distinguish properly between values and variables.

supertype and inherits properties from just that one type, while *multiple* inheritance means that a subtype can have any number of supertypes and inherits properties from all of them. Obviously, the former is (or should be) a special case of the latter.

Now, we do believe that support for multiple inheritance will ultimately prove desirable. Our strategy, however, has been to construct a sound model of single inheritance first, and then to extend that model to incorporate multiple inheritance subsequently. Our reason for adopting this perhaps rather conservative approach is that even single inheritance raises many tricky questions; it therefore seemed reasonable to try to find good answers to those questions first, before having to concern ourselves too much about the additional complexities of multiple inheritance. Of course, we did try not to build anything into our model of single inheritance that might have precluded later extension to deal with multiple inheritance too, and it is a measure of our cautious optimism regarding our model that it does seem to extend gracefully to deal with the multiple case. But readers must be the judge here, of course.

Be that as it may, the structure of the next three chapters reflects this historical development:

- Chapter 13 presents a series of detailed technical proposals **("IM Proposals")**, 26 of them altogether, that together constitute a basis—we believe—for the kind of robust inheritance model we are seeking, at least for the single inheritance case.

- Chapter 14 then discusses each of those 26 proposals in depth, with detailed examples. *Note:* Chapters 13 and 14 thus essentially do for our inheritance model what Parts II and III of the book as a whole do for *The Third Manifesto* proper—just as the present chapter does for that inheritance model what Part I does for the *Manifesto* proper, come to that. Indeed, you might already have noticed that Chapters 12–14 have names that parallel those of Parts I–III.

- Chapter 15 then goes on to extend the model discussed in Chapters 13 and 14 to incorporate multiple inheritance support. However, Chapter 15 must still be regarded as slightly tentative at this time.

As for the final chapter, Chapter 16, see the section immediately following. *Note:* We should also mention that the final section of Appendix C includes the outline of a possible adjustment to our model that, if it proves feasible, will have the effect of improving—in fact, simplifying—our overall scheme slightly.

SCALARS, TUPLES, AND RELATIONS

We stated earlier that *inheritance applies to values, not variables.* We were, however, making a tacit assumption at that point that the term "values" meant *scalar* values specifically. Of course, such values can have an actual representation or internal structure that is arbitrarily complex, as explained under RM Prescription 1 in Chapter 6; thus, for example, ellipses and circles might both legitimately be regarded as scalar values in suitable circumstances (as we already know). More to the point, however, inheritance has implications for nonscalar values—i.e., tuple and relation values—too, since such nonscalar values are built up out of scalar values. But we obviously cannot even begin to talk sensibly about those implications until we have pinned down what subtyping and inheritance mean for scalar values specifically.

Until further notice, therefore, we take the unqualified term *value* to mean a *scalar* value specifically. By the same token, of course, we take the unqualified terms *type, subtype, supertype,* and *variable* to mean *scalar* types, subtypes, supertypes, and variables specifically too, until further notice.* *Note:* "Until further notice" here really means "throughout Chapters 13–15." We will consider nonscalar types—more specifically, we will consider tuple and relation types—in Chapter 16.

As you know, scalar values in general can be operated upon solely by means of the operators defined for the applicable scalar type; in other words, such values have no structure (no structure visible to the user, that is—they do have *internal* structure, as already noted, but that structure is part of the implementation, not the model, and it is hidden from the user). It follows that when we talk as we did earlier of inheritance of "properties," what we mean, primarily, is inheritance of *operators.* We certainly do not mean inheritance of *structure.* (More precisely, we mean inheritance of *read-only* operators specifically, thanks to our position that inheritance applies to values, not variables—though once again, of course, there are implications for variables too.) For example, when we say that every circle has an area because every ellipse has an area, what we mean is that subtype CIRCLE **inherits an operator,** AREA say, from supertype ELLIPSE. In other words, we are interested in what is sometimes called **behavioral** inheritance, not **structural** inheritance.†

Turning now to tuple and relation types: As noted earlier, the notions of scalar subtyping and inheritance do have implications for tuples and relations, because tuples and relations are ultimately constructed out of scalar components. For example, a relation with an attribute of type ELLIPSE might include some tuples in which the value corresponding to that attribute is specifically a circle, not "just an ellipse." In Chapter 16, we consider the question of what is involved in

---

*Our approach to inheritance is thus very different from that taken by certain other writers (and indeed found in certain products), which involves something called "subtables and supertables" (tables are not scalar). It is our position that subtables and supertables, whatever else they might be, are *not* an example of type inheritance as such (see the section "Relvars *vs.* Object Classes" in Chapter 2 for a brief example involving subtables and supertables, and Appendix D for an extended discussion of the issue).

†The term *structural inheritance* refers to inheritance of internal structure (i.e., inheritance of actual representations); as such, it is properly an implementation matter, not part of the model. Of course, we certainly do not preclude such inheritance, but, to repeat, it has nothing to do with the model. (We note, however, that much of the inheritance literature, especially in the object world, does tend to assume that inheritance means—or at least includes—inheritance of actual representations; it further tends to assume that operators depend on those actual representations. We regard this state of affairs as more evidence of confusion over the distinction between model and implementation.)

extending our inheritance model to take tuple and relation types into account as well. Like Chapter 15, however, that chapter must still be regarded as slightly tentative at this time.

SUMMARY

As explained above, we define our inheritance model—at least for the case of scalar types, with single inheritance only—in Chapter 13 by means of a series of 26 detailed technical proposals **("IM Proposals").** For purposes of subsequent reference, and also to give some idea of the scope of our inheritance model, on the opposite page we show a mnemonic list of those proposals.

One final point: We adopt the convention throughout much of this part of the book that types T' and T are such that type T' is a subtype of type T (equivalently, type T is a supertype of type T'). You might find it helpful to think of T and T' as ELLIPSE and CIRCLE, respectively, barring explicit statements to the contrary.

1. Types are sets
2. Subtypes are subsets
3. "Subtype of" is reflexive
4. Proper subtypes
5. "Subtype of" is transitive
6. Immediate subtypes
7. Single inheritance only
8. Global root types
9. Type hierarchies
10. Subtypes can be proper subsets
11. Types disjoint unless one a subtype of the other
12. Scalar values (extended definition)
13. Scalar variables (extended definition)
14. Assignment with inheritance
15. Comparison with inheritance
16. Join etc. with inheritance
17. TREAT DOWN
18. TREAT UP
19. Logical operator IS_T(SX)
20. Relational operator RX:IS_T(A)
21. Logical operator IS_MS_T(SX)
22. Relational operator RX:IS_MS_T(A)
23. THE_ pseudovariables
24. Read-only operator inheritance and value substitutability
25. Read-only parameters to update operators
26. Update operator inheritance and variable substitutability

13

Formal Specifications

INTRODUCTION

In this chapter, we simply state the 26 IM Proposals that go to make up our model*
of subtyping and inheritance, with little or no attempt at discussion or further explanation. The material is provided primarily for reference; you probably should not
even attempt to read it straight through (at least, not on a first reading).

We remind you that throughout this chapter (and Chapters 14 and 15) we are
concerned with scalar types only, and hence that the unqualified terms *type, subtype, supertype, value,* and *variable* refer to scalar types, subtypes, supertypes, values, and variables specifically. We remind you too that throughout this chapter and
the next we are concerned with single inheritance only (see IM Proposal 7). Finally,
we remind you that the symbols T and T' are used generically to refer to a pair of
types such that T' is a subtype of T (equivalently, such that T is a supertype of T').
As noted at the end of Chapter 12, you might find it helpful to think of T and T' as
ELLIPSE and CIRCLE, respectively.

---

*Our base model, at any rate—but we do regard the proposals of Chapters 15 and 16 as part of our
model, too (they are 100 percent compatible with the base model, of course).

IM PROPOSALS

1. T and T' are indeed both types; in other words, each is a named set of values.

2. Every value in T' is also a value in T (i.e., the set of values constituting T' is a subset of the set of values constituting T). In other words, if value v is of type T', it is also of type T.

3. T and T' are not necessarily distinct. In other words, every type is both a subtype and a supertype of itself.

4. If and only if types T and T' are distinct, T' is said to be a **proper** subtype of T, and T is said to be a **proper** supertype of T'.

5. Every subtype of T' is also a subtype of T. Every supertype of T is also a supertype of T'.

6. If and only if T' is a proper subtype of T and there is no type that is both a proper supertype of T' and a proper subtype of T, then T' is said to be an **immediate** subtype of T, and T is said to be an **immediate** supertype of T'.

7. Every proper subtype T' has exactly one immediate supertype T.

8. At least one type must be a **global root** type, i.e., a type that has no immediate supertype (unless the given set of types is empty).

9. Let TH be a graph of nodes and directed arcs from one node to another in which:

   a. Each node is given the name of a type.

   b. Let T and T' be two nodes. Then there is at most one directed arc from node T to node T'; in fact, there is such an arc if and only if type T is an immediate supertype of type T'.

   c. If the graph includes any nodes at all, then exactly one has no corresponding immediate supertype node.

   Then TH is said to be a **type hierarchy.** If TH includes any nodes at all, then the (unique) node with no immediate supertype node is called the **local root** node, and the type corresponding to that node is called the **local root** type, with respect to type hierarchy TH.

10. Let T be a type that has at least one proper subtype. Then, in general, values can exist that are of type T and not of any proper subtype of T.

11. If $T1$ and $T2$ are distinct global root types, or distinct immediate subtypes of the same supertype, then they are disjoint (in other words, no value v is of both type $T1$ and type $T2$).

12. Let scalar value v be of type T. If and only if no proper subtype T' of type T exists such that v is also of type T', then T is said to be the **most specific** type for (or of) v.

13. Let scalar variable V be declared to be of type T (i.e., T is the *declared type* for V—see RM Prescription 11). Because of value substitutability (see IM Proposal 24), the value v assigned to V at any given time can have any subtype T' of type T as its most specific type. We can therefore model V as a named ordered triple of the form $<DT,MST,v>$, where:

    - The name of the triple is the name of the variable (V in the example).
    - DT is the name of the declared type for variable V.
    - MST is the name of the **most specific type**—also known as the **current** most specific type—for, or of, variable V.
    - v is a value of most specific type MST—the **current value** for, or of, variable V.

    We use the notation $DT(V)$, $MST(V)$, $v(V)$ to refer to the DT, MST, v components, respectively, of (our model of) scalar variable V. Note that it must always be the case that $MST(V)$ is some subtype—not necessarily a proper subtype—of $DT(V)$. Note too that $MST(V)$ and $v(V)$ change with time, in general; in other words, the phrase "most specific type of variable V" refers to the most specific type of the *current value* of V, not to the most specific type that values of V are ever permitted to have. Note finally that $MST(V)$ is in fact implied by $v(V)$, by virtue of IM Proposals 2, 7, 11, and 12 taken in concert.

14. Let SX be a scalar expression. The notation $DT(V)$, $MST(V)$, $v(V)$ introduced under IM Proposal 13 can be extended in an obvious way to refer to the declared type $DT(SX)$, the current most specific type $MST(SX)$, and the current value $v(SX)$, respectively, of SX—where "declared type" is as explained in RM Prescription 3 and is known at compilation time, and "current most specific type" and "current value" refer to the result of evaluating SX and are therefore not known until run time, in general. Now consider the assignment

    ```
    V   :=  SX ;
    ```

    (where V is a scalar variable). $DT(SX)$ must be a subtype of $DT(V)$, otherwise the assignment is illegal (this is a compile-time check). If the assignment is legal, its effect is to set $MST(V)$ equal to $MST(SX)$ and $v(V)$ equal to $v(SX)$.

15. Consider the comparison

    ```
    SY  =  SX
    ```

    (where SY and SX are scalar expressions). $DT(SX)$ must be a subtype of $DT(SY)$ or *vice versa,* otherwise the comparison is illegal (this is a compile-time check). If the comparison is legal, its effect is to return *true* if $MST(SY)$ is equal to $MST(SX)$ and $v(SY)$ is equal to $v(SX)$, *false* otherwise.

16. Let rx and ry be relations with a common attribute A, and let the declared types of A in rx and ry be $DT(Ax)$ and $DT(Ay)$, respectively. Consider the join of rx

and *ry* (necessarily over *A,* at least in part). *DT*(*Ax*) must be a subtype of *DT*(*Ay*) or *vice versa,* otherwise the join is illegal (this is a compile-time check). If the join is legal, assume without loss of generality that *DT*(*Ay*) is a subtype of *DT*(*Ax*). Then the declared type of *A* in the result is *DT*(*Ax*).

Analogous remarks apply to union, intersection, and difference operators: In every case, (a) corresponding attributes of the operands must be such that the declared type of one is a subtype of the declared type of the other, and (b) the declared type of the corresponding attribute in the result is the less specific of the two (where by the *less specific* of two types *T* and *T*′, one of which is a subtype of the other, we mean whichever is the supertype).

17. For every type *T,* an operator of the form

    `TREAT_DOWN_AS_T ( SX )`

    (or logical equivalent thereof) should be supported, where *SX* is a scalar expression and *T* is a subtype of *DT*(*SX*) (this is a compile-time check). We refer to such operators generically as "TREAT DOWN" operators; their semantics are as follows. First of all, *MST*(*SX*) must be a subtype of *T* (this is a run-time check, in general). Assuming this condition is satisfied, then:

    a. If the TREAT DOWN invocation appears in a "source" position (in particular, on the right hand side of an assignment), then the invocation yields a scalar result, *SR* say, with *DT*(*SR*) equal to *T, MST*(*SR*) equal to *MST*(*SX*), and *v*(*SR*) equal to *v*(*SX*).

    b. If the TREAT DOWN invocation appears in a "target" position (in particular, on the left hand side of an assignment), then, first, the invocation acts as a pseudovariable, which means that it actually *designates* its argument *SX* (more accurately, it designates a version of *SX* for which *DT*(*SX*) is equal to *T* but *MST*(*SX*) is unchanged); second, that argument *SX* must be specified as a scalar variable specifically, not as an arbitrary scalar expression.

18. For every type *T,* an operator of the form

    `TREAT_UP_AS_T ( SX )`

    (or logical equivalent thereof) should be supported, where *SX* is a scalar expression and *T* is a supertype of *DT*(*SX*) (this is a compile-time check). We refer to such operators generically as "TREAT UP" operators; their semantics are as follows.

    a. If the TREAT UP invocation appears in a "source" position (in particular, on the right hand side of an assignment), then the invocation yields a scalar result, *SR* say, with *DT*(*SR*) and *MST*(*SR*) both equal to *T* and *v*(*SR*) equal to *v*(*SX*).

    b. If the TREAT UP invocation appears in a "target" position (in particular, on the left hand side of an assignment), then, first, *T* and *DT*(*SX*) must be identical (this is a compile-time check); second, the invocation acts as a pseudovariable, which means that it actually *designates* its argument *SX* (more accurately, it designates a version of *SX* for which *DT(SX)* and *MST(SX)* are both equal to *T*); third, that argument *SX* must be specified as a scalar variable specifically, not as an arbitrary scalar expression.

19. For every type *T,* a logical operator of the form

```
IS_T ( SX )
```

(or logical equivalent thereof) should be supported, where *SX* is a scalar expression. *DT(SX)* must be a supertype of *T* (this is a compile-time check). The overall expression is defined to yield *true* if *SX* is of type *T, false* otherwise.

20. For every type *T,* a relational operator of the form

```
RX : IS_T ( A )
```

(or logical equivalent thereof) should be supported. Here *RX* is a relational expression and *A* is an attribute of the relation—*r,* say—denoted by that expression. The declared type *DT(A)* of *A* must be a supertype of *T* (this is a compile-time check). The value of the overall expression is defined to be a relation with:

a. A heading the same as that of *r,* except that the declared type of attribute *A* in that heading is *T;*

b. A body consisting of those tuples of *r* in which attribute *A* contains a value of type *T,* except that the declared type of attribute *A* in each of those tuples is *T.*

21. For every type *T,* a logical operator of the form

```
IS_MS_T ( SX )
```

(or logical equivalent thereof) should be supported, where *SX* is as under IM Proposal 19. *DT(SX)* must be a supertype of *T* (this is a compile-time check). The overall expression is defined to yield *true* if the current most specific type of *SX* is *T, false* otherwise.

22. For every type *T,* a relational operator of the form

```
RX : IS_MS_T ( A )
```

(or logical equivalent thereof) should be supported, where *RX* and *A* are as under IM Proposal 20, and (also as under IM Proposal 20) *r* is the relation denoted by *RX*. The declared type *DT(A)* of *A* must be a supertype of *T* (this is a compile-time check). The value of the overall expression is defined to be a relation with:

a. A heading the same as that of *r,* except that the declared type of attribute *A* in that heading is *T;*

b. A body consisting of those tuples of *r* in which attribute *A* contains a value of most specific type *T,* except that the declared type of attribute *A* in each of those tuples is *T.*

23. For every component of every declared possible representation of every type, a THE_ pseudovariable (or logical equivalent) should be supported, with semantics as explained in Chapter 6.

24. Let *Op* be a read-only operator, let *P* be a parameter to *Op,* and let *T* be the declared type for *P*. Then the most specific type of the argument value *v* corresponding to parameter *P* in some invocation of *Op* can be **any subtype** *T'* of *T*. In other words, the read-only operator *Op* applies to values of type *T* and therefore, necessarily, to values of type *T'*—*The Principle of* **(Read-only) Operator Inheritance.** It follows that such operators are *polymorphic,* since they apply to values of several different types—*The Principle of* **(Read-only) Operator Polymorphism.** And it further follows that wherever a value of type *T* is permitted, a value of any proper subtype *T'* of *T* is also permitted—*The Principle of* **(Value) Substitutability.**

25. Let *Op* be an update operator and let *P* be a parameter to *Op* that is not subject to update. Then *Op* behaves as a *read-only* operator so far as *P* is concerned, and all aspects of IM Proposal 24 therefore apply, *mutatis mutandis.**

26. Let *Op* be an update operator, let *P* be a parameter to *Op* that is subject to update, and let *T* be the declared type for *P*. Then it might or might not be the case that the current most specific type of the argument variable *V* corresponding to parameter *P* in some invocation of *Op* can be a proper subtype *T'* of type *T*. It follows that for each such update operator *Op* and for each parameter *P* to *Op* that is subject to update, it is necessary to state explicitly for which subtypes *T'* of the declared type *T* of parameter *P* operator *Op* is inherited—*The Principle of* **(Update) Operator Inheritance.** Update operators are thus only conditionally polymorphic—*The Principle of* **(Update) Operator Polymorphism.** If *Op* is an update operator and *P* is a parameter to *Op* that is subject to update and *T'* is a subtype of the declared type *T* of *P* for which *Op* is inherited, then by definition *Op* can be invoked with an argument variable *V* corresponding to parameter *P* that is of current most specific type *T'*—*The Principle of* **(Variable) Substitutability.**

---

*Except for "result covariance" (because update operators do not return a result). See the discussion of IM Proposal 24 in Chapter 14 for an explanation of the concept of result covariance.

14

Informal Discussions and Explanations

INTRODUCTION

In this chapter, we elaborate on the IM Proposals presented for scalar types and single inheritance in Chapter 13. Throughout the chapter, therefore, we adopt the same conventions as we did in Chapter 13, namely as follows:

- The terms *type, subtype,* and *supertype,* unqualified, refer to scalar types specifically. Likewise, the unqualified terms *value* and *variable* refer to scalar values and variables specifically.

- The symbols T and T' are used generically to refer to a pair of types such that T' is a subtype of T—equivalently, such that T is a supertype of T'.

We now introduce a running example that we will use to illustrate most of the points to be made in this chapter (indeed, we will refer to it repeatedly throughout the rest of the book, appendixes included). Refer to Fig. 14.1. As that figure indicates, the example involves a collection of geometric types—PLANE_FIGURE, ELLIPSE, CIRCLE, POLYGON, and so on—each of which is (in accordance with RM Prescription 1) a named set of values. For example, there is a set of values

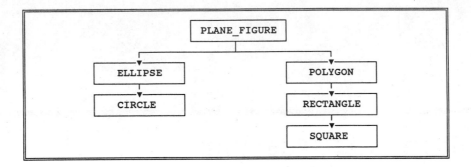

Fig. 14.1 Type hierarchy example

named ELLIPSE, and every value in that set is some specific ellipse.* The types are arranged into what is called a *type hierarchy.*

The type hierarchy concept should be more or less self-explanatory. The type hierarchy of Fig. 14.1, for example, is meant to show, among other things, that type RECTANGLE is a subtype of type POLYGON, which means that all rectangles are polygons, but the converse is not true (some polygons are not rectangles). Further, it also means that all properties that apply to polygons in general apply to—i.e., are **inherited** by—rectangles in particular, but the converse is not true (rectangles have properties of their own that do not apply to polygons in general). *Note:* Recall from Chapter 12 that "properties" here essentially means *operators* and *type constraints;* thus, operators and type constraints that apply to polygons apply to rectangles *a fortiori* (because a rectangle *is* a polygon), but some operators and type constraints that apply to rectangles do not apply to mere polygons.

We will have more to say regarding the type hierarchy concept under IM Proposal 9, more regarding operator inheritance specifically under IM Proposals 24 and 26, and more regarding type constraint inheritance specifically under IM Proposal 2.

Now, **Tutorial D** as defined in Chapter 5 deliberately included no explicit support for inheritance. However, we do need a way of telling the system which types are subtypes of which others (i.e., a way of defining type hierarchies), so let us extend

---

*More precisely, it is an ellipse at *some location in the plane* (we assume for the sake of the example that two geometric figures that are at different locations but are otherwise identical are distinct). Note too that, for example, the set ELLIPSE contains *all possible* ellipses and is therefore in principle infinite. In practice, of course, there will be implementation restrictions in effect that make the set finite after all (and so the unqualified name ELLIPSE is perhaps slightly inappropriate; something like S_ELLIPSE—"S" for *supportable*—might be better). The point is not important for present purposes, however.

the **Tutorial D** syntactic category *<user scalar type def>* to include a SUBTYPE_OF specification, thus enabling us to write (for example):

```
TYPE PLANE_FIGURE ... ;

TYPE ELLIPSE
     POSSREP ( A LENGTH, B LENGTH, CTR POINT )
     SUBTYPE_OF ( PLANE_FIGURE ) ... ;

TYPE CIRCLE
     POSSREP ( R LENGTH, CTR POINT )
     SUBTYPE_OF ( ELLIPSE ) ... ;
```

(and so on). Now the system knows, for example, that CIRCLE is a subtype of ELLIPSE, and hence that operators and type constraints that apply to ellipses in general apply to circles in particular.

A note on the POSSREP specifications for ELLIPSE and CIRCLE: For simplicity, we assume as we did in Chapter 6 that ellipses are always oriented such that their major axis is horizontal and their minor axis vertical. Thus, ellipses might possibly be represented by their semiaxes a and b (and their center). By contrast, circles might possibly be represented by their radius r (and their center).

We now remark that every possible representation for ellipses is—necessarily, albeit implicitly—a possible representation for circles too,* because circles *are* ellipses (in other words, we might regard possible representations as further "properties" that are inherited by subtypes from supertypes). However:

- That inherited possible representation is clearly only a possible representation for circles *inasmuch as* circles are ellipses; it cannot cater for aspects of circles that are circle-specific, such as the radius (at least, not directly).

- That inherited possible representation is not a *declared* one, in the sense of Chapter 6 (see the discussion of RM Prescription 4 in that chapter), because to say it was "declared" would lead to a contradiction between IM Proposals 23 and 26, *q.v.* Thus, to say that type CIRCLE inherits a possible representation from type ELLIPSE is only a *façon de parler*—it does not carry any formal weight.

To pursue these two points just a moment longer: It will often be the case in practice that type T' does have a possible representation—an explicitly declared possible representation, that is—that is similar but not identical to some explicitly declared possible representation for type T. This fact suggests that some syntactic shorthand for declaring a possible representation for type T' (along the lines of "same as possible representation *PR* for type T minus component(s) x plus component(s) y") could be convenient in practice. However, we see this issue as a purely syntactic one and secondary to our main purpose.

---

*Of course, the converse is not true—i.e., a possible representation for circles is not necessarily a possible representation for ellipses.

To get back to the example *per se,* we would like to make it clear that our choice of an example that is slightly academic in flavor (as our geometric example obviously is) is deliberate. Some people might object that it is a little unrealistic, inasmuch as geometric figures—polygons and rectangles and so forth—are not the kind of thing we normally expect to find in a typical commercial database. In fact, however, there are several advantages to such an example, the main one being that the semantics of the various types involved are (or should be) crystal clear to everyone. We can therefore avoid the kind of unproductive debates that tend to arise when "fuzzier" examples are chosen. For example, suppose we had chosen an example involving a type BOOK. Are two copies of the same book two instances of that type or only one? What if the two copies are of different editions? What if one is a translation of the other? Is a journal a book? Is a magazine? And so on.

One final introductory point: It would be remiss of us not to point out that the type hierarchy concept does give rise to some thorny practical problems. For example, what should happen if we try to drop type ELLIPSE? Should there be a way to "alter" or rename type ELLIPSE without dropping it? Should it be possible to introduce a new type between types ELLIPSE and CIRCLE? If so, what are the implications? Such questions must clearly be answered in any real implementation, but we do not regard them as issues that affect our base model *per se,* and we do not address them further in this book.

Without further ado, we now proceed to discuss our IM Proposals in detail.

IM PROPOSAL 1: TYPES ARE SETS

T *and* T′ *are indeed both types; in other words, each is a named set of values.*

———— ◆ ◆ ◆ ◆ ◆ ————

IM Proposal 1 simply asserts that subtypes and supertypes are indeed both types (and therefore named sets of values). One consequence is that subtypes can have lower-level subtypes of their own, and supertypes can have higher-level supertypes of their own (as of course we already know).

IM PROPOSAL 2: SUBTYPES ARE SUBSETS

Every value in T′ *is also a value in* T *(i.e., the set of values constituting* T′ *is a subset of the set of values constituting* T*). In other words, if value* v *is of type* T′*, it is also of type* T.

———— ◆ ◆ ◆ ◆ ◆ ————

It follows from IM Proposal 2 that to say that value v is of type T does not preclude the possibility that v is also of type T'. For example, to say that e is an ellipse does not preclude the possibility that e is also a circle. In fact, to say that v is of type T means, precisely, that the *most specific* type of v (see IM Proposal 12) is *some subtype* of T (see IM Proposals 3–5).

It further follows that if v is of type T', the operators that apply to v are (by definition) all of the operators that apply to values of type T', and those operators include (by definition) all of the operators that apply to values of type T. For example, if AREA is an operator that applies to values of type ELLIPSE, then AREA is also (by definition) an operator that applies to values of type CIRCLE. In other words (loosely): **Operators associated with type T are inherited by type T'.**

Here by way of example are some of the operators that—we will assume—apply to values of type ELLIPSE, and hence to values of type CIRCLE also. *Note:* In practice the various THE_ operators will be defined "automatically" as a consequence of the corresponding possible representation declarations, as explained in Chapter 6. We show explicit definitions here for purposes of subsequent reference.

```
OPERATOR THE_A ( E ELLIPSE ) RETURNS ( LENGTH ) ;
   /* "the a semiaxis of" */ ... ;
END OPERATOR ;

OPERATOR THE_B ( E ELLIPSE ) RETURNS ( LENGTH ) ;
   /* "the b semiaxis of" */ ... ;
END OPERATOR ;

OPERATOR THE_CTR ( E ELLIPSE ) RETURNS ( POINT ) ;
   /* "the center of" */ ... ;
END OPERATOR ;

OPERATOR AREA ( E ELLIPSE ) RETURNS ( AREA ) ;
   /* "area of"; note that AREA is both the name of the  */
   /* operator and the name of the type of the result    */
   /* (meaning it is probably the name of the            */
   /* corresponding selector too) ... such punning might */
   /* or might not be legal in a real D (?)              */
   ... ;
END OPERATOR ;
```

And here is an operator that applies to values of type CIRCLE but not to values of type ELLIPSE:

```
OPERATOR THE_R ( C CIRCLE ) RETURNS ( LENGTH ) ;
   /* "the radius of" */ ... ;
END OPERATOR ;
```

It further follows from IM Proposal 2 that if v is of type T', then v must satisfy all of the constraints that apply to values of type T (as well as all of the constraints that apply to values of type T' specifically).* To repeat an example from Chapter 12,

---

*Here and throughout the rest of this part of the book we take the unqualified term "constraint" to mean a type constraint specifically, barring explicit statements to the contrary.

if *c* is a circle (and hence an ellipse), and if ellipses are subject to the constraint that the length of their major semiaxis *a* must be greater than or equal to that of their minor semiaxis *b,* then that same constraint must be satisfied by *c* (as indeed it is, of course, trivially, because in the case of a circle the semiaxes *a* and *b* coincide in the radius *r*). In other words (loosely): **Constraints associated with type *T* are inherited by type *T'*.**

Here then are the definitions of types ELLIPSE and CIRCLE, now extended to include the type constraints just mentioned:

```
TYPE ELLIPSE
    POSSREP ( A LENGTH, B LENGTH, CTR POINT )
    SUBTYPE_OF ( PLANE_FIGURE )
    CONSTRAINT ( THE_A ( ELLIPSE ) ≥ THE_B ( ELLIPSE ) ) ;

TYPE CIRCLE
    POSSREP ( R LENGTH, CTR POINT )
    SUBTYPE_OF ( ELLIPSE )
    CONSTRAINT ( THE_A ( CIRCLE ) = THE_B ( CIRCLE ) ) ;
```

Now, in our discussion of RM Prescription 2 in Chapter 6, we said that if *v* is a scalar value, it can be thought of as carrying around with it a kind of flag that announces "I am an integer" or "I am a supplier number" or "I am an ellipse" (etc., etc.). Now we see that, conceptually speaking, it might have to carry around several distinct flags—e.g., "I am an ellipse" *and* "I am a circle."

We also said in Chapter 6 that different types are disjoint "except possibly if type inheritance is supported." Now we see that two types are definitely not disjoint if one is a subtype of the other. See IM Proposal 7 for further discussion of this point.

Finally, we remark that IM Proposal 2 implies that it makes no sense for the type hierarchy to contain any *cycles.* For suppose, contrariwise, that types *A* and *B* were each subtypes of the other (a cycle of length two). Then the set of values constituting *A* would be a subset of the set of values constituting *B* and *vice versa;* likewise, the set of operators that applied to values of type *A* would be a subset of the set of operators that applied to values of type *B* and *vice versa,* and the set of constraints that applied to values of type *A* would be a subset of the set of constraints that applied to values of type *B* and *vice versa.* In other words, *A* and *B* would effectively be identical, except for their names; so they might as well be collapsed into a single type. And, of course, an analogous argument applies to cycles of any length. From this point forward, therefore, we will simply prohibit them.

IM PROPOSAL 3: "SUBTYPE OF" IS REFLEXIVE

T *and* T' *are not necessarily distinct. In other words, every type is both a subtype and a supertype of itself.*

———— ♦ ♦ ♦ ♦ ♦ ————

This IM Proposal and the next three all have to do with matters of terminology. IM Proposal 3 in particular simply recognizes that it is convenient to regard any given type *T* as both a subtype and a supertype of itself. This convention has the effect of simplifying the formulation of many of the proposals and rules that we will be discussing later in this chapter (and in the next two chapters as well). Thus, for example, "ELLIPSE is a subtype of ELLIPSE" is a true statement, and so is "ELLIPSE is a supertype of ELLIPSE."

Note: To say that a given dyadic logical or conditional operator *Op* is *reflexive* merely means that "*x Op x*" is *true* for all *x*. Thus, e.g., "=" is reflexive, and so is "is a subtype of." By contrast, "<" and ">" are not.

IM PROPOSAL 4: PROPER SUBTYPES

If and only if types T *and* T′ *are distinct,* T′ *is said to be a **proper** subtype of* T, *and* T *is said to be a **proper** supertype of* T′.

——— ♦♦♦♦♦ ———

Following on from IM Proposal 3, IM Proposal 4 introduces some terminology for talking about subtypes and supertypes when the types in question are in fact distinct. In terms of our geometric example, we can say that (e.g.) CIRCLE is a proper subtype of ELLIPSE. (By virtue of IM Proposal 5, *q.v.*, it is also a proper subtype of PLANE_FIGURE.) It is also a subtype of CIRCLE, but not a proper one. Likewise, PLANE_FIGURE is a proper supertype of both ELLIPSE and CIRCLE; it is also a supertype of PLANE_FIGURE, but not a proper one.

Note: By definition, actual representations (of appearances of values) are not relevant to our model. Despite this fact, it is still important, in order to gain a good understanding of inheritance in general, to appreciate the point that if type *T′* is a proper subtype of type *T,* then there is no requirement that (a) actual representations of appearances of values of type *T′,* and (b) actual representations of appearances of values of type *T,* be of the same form.* For example, let *T′* be CIRCLE and *T* be ELLIPSE. Then we have already seen under IM Proposal 1 that those types might have different *possible* representations—and, of course, it might well be the case (though it is certainly not *necessarily* the case) that those possible representations are the actual ones too.

By the way, it is interesting to note that if type *T′* is a proper subtype of type *T* and the actual representations of appearances of values of types *T′* and *T* are indeed of different forms, the system does *not* need to be explicitly told how to convert

---

*In fact, as explained in the discussion of RM Prescription 4 in Chapter 6, it is not even a requirement that actual representations of distinct appearances of values of the *same* type be of the same form.

between those actual representations, because it will always know how to "treat" values of type *T'* as if they were values of type *T*. See IM Proposal 18 ("TREAT UP") for further explanation.

IM PROPOSAL 5: "SUBTYPE OF" IS TRANSITIVE

Every subtype of T' *is also a subtype of* T. *Every supertype of* T *is also a supertype of* T'.

IM Proposal 5 simply says that a subtype of a subtype is a subtype and a supertype of a supertype is a supertype. Thus, for example, RECTANGLE is a subtype of PLANE_FIGURE, and PLANE_FIGURE is a supertype of RECTANGLE.

Note: To say that a given dyadic logical or conditional operator *Op* is *transitive* merely means that, for all *x, y,* and *z,* "*x Op y*" and "*y Op z*" implies "*x Op z*". Thus, e.g., "=" is transitive, and so is "is a subtype of." By contrast, "≠" and "is disjoint from" are not.

IM PROPOSAL 6: IMMEDIATE SUBTYPES

If and only if T' *is a proper subtype of* T *and there is no type that is both a proper supertype of* T' *and a proper subtype of* T, *then* T' *is said to be an **immediate** subtype of* T, *and* T *is said to be an **immediate** supertype of* T'.

In terms of our running example, IM Proposal 6 says that, e.g., CIRCLE is an immediate subtype of ELLIPSE, and ELLIPSE is an immediate supertype of CIRCLE. CIRCLE is also a subtype of PLANE_FIGURE, but not an immediate one; equivalently, PLANE_FIGURE is a supertype of CIRCLE, but not an immediate one.

IM PROPOSAL 7: SINGLE INHERITANCE ONLY

Every proper subtype T' *has exactly one immediate supertype* T.

IM Proposal 7 simply confirms that (as explained in Chapter 12) we limit our attention for the time being to single inheritance only. Refer to Chapter 15 for a discussion of multiple inheritance.

We remark that it is the single inheritance assumption that makes it possible to talk unambiguously of type *hierarchies* as such. We remark too that (of course) the assumption does not prohibit a proper *super*type from having any number of immediate *sub*types—PLANE_FIGURE, for example, has two.

IM PROPOSAL 8: GLOBAL ROOT TYPES

*At least one type must be a **global root** type, i.e., a type that has no immediate supertype (unless the given set of types is empty).*

——— ♦♦♦♦♦ ———

IM Proposal 8 simply states that, so long as we have at least one type, then we must have at least one *global root* type, i.e., a type with no proper supertypes (and hence with no immediate supertype in particular). Observe that the existence of such a type is assured—assuming the given set of types is nonempty—by the fact that type hierarchies do not contain any cycles. In our running example, PLANE_FIGURE is the sole global root type.

Note: We do not assume that there is exactly one global root type; equivalently, we do not assume that there is just one type hierarchy. We remark, however, that— by virtue of IM Proposal 11, *q.v.*—if there is more than one global root type, we could always invent some kind of "system" type that is an immediate supertype for all of them, thereby tying all of the separate type hierarchies together into a single such hierarchy.* Thus, there would be no loss of generality in assuming just one global root type.

IM PROPOSAL 9: TYPE HIERARCHIES

Let TH *be a graph of nodes and directed arcs from one node to another in which:*

a. *Each node is given the name of a type.*

b. *Let* T *and* T′ *be two nodes. Then there is at most one directed arc from node* T *to node* T′; *in fact, there is such an arc if and only if type* T *is an immediate supertype of type* T′.

c. *If the graph includes any nodes at all, then exactly one has no corresponding immediate supertype node.*

---

*Some commercial object systems come ready equipped with such a type, often called OBJECT (because "everything is an object"). We will be discussing an important special case of such a system type, called *alpha,* in Chapter 16.

Then TH *is said to be a* **type hierarchy.** *If* TH *includes any nodes at all, then the (unique) node with no immediate supertype node is called the* **local root** *node, and the type corresponding to that node is called the* **local root** *type, with respect to type hierarchy* TH.

The purpose of IM Proposal 9, of course, is to make the type hierarchy notion more precise. We should immediately make it clear, however, that type hierarchies *per se* are not really part of our inheritance model; they are merely an intuitively convenient way of depicting subtype/supertype relationships. Indeed, type hierarchies play a role in our inheritance model analogous to that played by *tables* in the relational model: Tables *per se* are not really part of the relational model, they are merely an intuitively convenient way of depicting relations (which are).

Be that as it may, let *TH* be a type hierarchy as defined above. Then:

- Any graph *G* obtained from *TH* by choosing the node corresponding to some type *T* as a local root and deleting (a) all nodes not corresponding to some subtype *T'* of *T,* and (b) all arcs emanating from those nodes, is also a type hierarchy.

- Further, any graph obtained from the graph *G* just defined by deleting a node is also a type hierarchy, provided that deletion of a node is always accompanied by deletion of (a) the arc entering into that node and (b) each corresponding immediate subtype node.*

By way of example, Fig. 14.2 shows a few of the many type hierarchies that can be obtained from that of Fig. 14.1. *Note:* In fact, there are exactly 22 distinct type hierarchies that can be obtained from the type hierarchy of Fig. 14.1 (exercise for the reader).

The *local root* types for the three type hierarchies in Fig. 14.2 are PLANE_FIGURE, RECTANGLE, and CIRCLE, respectively. Observe that a global root type is certainly a local root type (in several distinct type hierarchies, in general), but some local root types are not global root types (again in general).

Note: We should mention in passing that type hierarchies are known by a variety of different names, the following among them:

---

*By contrast, if (a) *TH* is a type hierarchy with local root *T,* and (b) type *T* is an immediate supertype of type *T'* and type *T'* is an immediate supertype of type *T''* (and we assume for simplicity that type *T'* is an immediate supertype of no types other than type *T''*), and (c) *G* is the graph obtained from *TH* by deleting node *T'* and coalescing the arc connecting nodes *T* and *T'* and the arc connecting nodes *T'* and *T''* into a single arc connecting nodes *T* and *T''*, then (d) we adopt the conservative position that *G* is *not* a type hierarchy (at least, not one that can be derived from *TH*), on the grounds that it causes *T''* to lose some of its inheritance (as it were). For example, the graph that contains just nodes POLYGON and SQUARE from Fig. 14.1 (with a single connecting arc) is not a type hierarchy that can be derived from that figure.

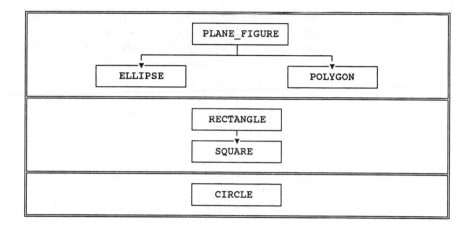

Fig. 14.2   Some of the 22 type hierarchies that can be derived from the type hierarchy of Fig. 14.1

- *Class hierarchies* (on the grounds that types are sometimes called classes, especially in the object world)
- *Generalization hierarchies* (on the grounds that, e.g., an ellipse is a generalization of a circle)
- *Specialization hierarchies* (on the grounds that, e.g., a circle is a specialization of an ellipse)
- *Inheritance hierarchies* (on the grounds that, e.g., circles inherit properties from ellipses)
- *ISA hierarchies* (on the grounds that, e.g., every circle "IS A" ellipse)

In this book, however, we will stay with the term "type hierarchy." We remark that type hierarchies as such will certainly be inadequate if and when we extend our model to support multiple inheritance (see Chapter 15), and possibly even if we do not (see IM Proposal 11).

IM PROPOSAL 10: SUBTYPES CAN BE PROPER SUBSETS

Let T *be a type that has at least one proper subtype. Then, in general, values can exist that are of type* T *and not of any proper subtype of* T.

———— ♦♦♦♦ ————

IM Proposal 10 simply means that we do not require that every value have as its most specific type—see IM Proposal 12—a type that has no proper subtypes (sometimes called a *leaf* type).* In terms of our running example, values can exist whose most specific type is, e.g., ELLIPSE and not CIRCLE (in the real world, some ellipses are not circles). To put matters another way, we do not insist that ELLIPSE have another proper subtype called NONCIRCLE and that every value of type ELLIPSE have either CIRCLE or NONCIRCLE as its most specific type. Of course, we do not prohibit such an arrangement, either, but we do observe that it would have the effect of turning ELLIPSE into a "dummy type" (a concept we will be discussing in just a moment), a state of affairs that might not be desirable in practice.

So type *T'* can be a proper subset of type *T*—but *must* it be? Well, on the face of it, it does seem reasonable to assume that if *T'* is a proper sub*type* of *T,* it is also a proper sub*set* of type *T* (for otherwise there could not possibly be any properties that applied to type *T'* that did not also apply to type *T*). In fact, however, it turns out that such an assumption has little operational significance for the rest of our model, and so we do not make it; but it seems likely that no harm would result from imposing such a requirement in practice.

Following on from the foregoing, we should mention that some inheritance schemes might be regarded as violating IM Proposal 10 (at least in spirit), in the sense that they explicitly include support for certain special types that are not—in fact, are not allowed to be—the most specific type of any value at all. Such a type *must* have proper subtypes, and every value of the type *must* be a value of one of those subtypes. It is worth taking a few moments to consider some of the implications of this idea.

As mentioned in Chapter 6 (in a footnote), a type that is not allowed to be the most specific type of any value at all is sometimes called an *abstract* type (or sometimes a "noninstantiable" type, on the grounds that it has no "instances"). A type that is not abstract in this sense is then called a *concrete* type. We prefer not to use this terminology, however, because it clashes with the abstract data type terminology already introduced (or at least mentioned) in Chapter 6. For present purposes, therefore, let us agree to refer to a type that is not allowed to be the most specific type of any value at all as a *dummy* type, and a type that is not a dummy type in this sense as a *regular* type. (More precisely, a type is a dummy type *if and only if* it is not allowed to be the most specific type of any value at all.)

Why might it be desirable to define a dummy type? The major reason is that it provides a way of specifying certain operators that apply to several different regular types, all of them proper subtypes of the dummy type in question. Such an operator must then be *explicitly specialized*—i.e., an appropriate *version* of the operator must be defined (see IM Proposal 24)—for each of those regular subtypes.† For

*More precisely, a leaf type is a type that has no *nonempty* proper subtypes. See the discussion of the special type *omega* in Chapter 16.

†Except perhaps if the dummy type has a regular supertype, a possibility we are still investigating.

example, PLANE_FIGURE might well be a dummy type in this sense; so too might be the system-provided global root type "often called OBJECT" mentioned (in a footnote) under the discussion of IM Proposal 8.

To fix our ideas, let us assume that type PLANE_FIGURE is indeed a dummy type, and let operator AREA be defined at the PLANE_FIGURE level. To invent some syntax on the fly:

```
TYPE PLANE_FIGURE DUMMY ;                    /* dummy type */

OPERATOR AREA ( PF PLANE_FIGURE ) RETURNS ( AREA ) ;
    /* this operator must be explicitly specialized for */
    /* type POLYGON, type ELLIPSE, and so on, because   */
    /* its parameter PF is of a dummy type ... no        */
    /* implementation code is provided at this level     */
END OPERATOR ;
```

Note that a dummy type:

- Has no values that are not also values of some proper subtype (as already explained);

- Cannot be a leaf type;

- Cannot be the target type in a TREAT UP operation (see IM Proposal 18).

We remark that the DUMMY specification on type PLANE_FIGURE is logically shorthand for a certain type constraint (along the lines of "every value of type PLANE_FIGURE is either a value of type ELLIPSE or a value of type POLYGON"). However, we should perhaps point out that specifying DUMMY explicitly will let the system know *at compilation time* that the type in question is a dummy one, whereas specifying just the equivalent type constraint will (in all probability) mean it will not be aware of this fact until run time.

We close this section with the observation that some systems use the dummy type notion as a way of providing *type generator* functionality. For example, RELATION might be a dummy type in such a system (with generic operators JOIN, UNION, and so forth), and every specific relation type would then be a proper (and regular) subtype of that dummy type. *Note:* We do not adopt such an approach in *The Third Manifesto* because we certainly do not want our support for type generators to require support for type inheritance. (We remark too that the approach seems to imply that specific— i.e., explicitly specialized—implementation code must be provided for each specific join, each specific union, and so forth: surely not a very desirable state of affairs!)

IM PROPOSAL 11: TYPES DISJOINT UNLESS ONE A SUBTYPE OF THE OTHER

If T1 *and* T2 *are distinct global root types, or distinct immediate subtypes of the same supertype, then they are disjoint (in other words, no value* v *is of both type* T1 *and type* T2).

IM Proposal 11 simply states that (e.g.) no geometric figure can be both an ellipse and a polygon. At first sight, such a restriction does seem both intuitive and reasonable; unfortunately, however, there are many situations where it is not reasonable at all (see Chapters 15 and 16). Indeed, it is clear that the restriction will definitely have to be relaxed if multiple inheritance is supported, and possibly even if it is not. For the time being, however, we choose to invoke *The Principle of Cautious Design* [49] and stay with the disjointness requirement as currently articulated in this IM Proposal.

Incidentally, one reason for requiring such disjointness is that it avoids certain *operator invocation ambiguities* that might otherwise occur. For suppose, contrariwise, that some value *v* could be of both type *T1* and type *T2,* neither of which was a subtype of the other. Suppose further that an operator named *Op* had been defined for type *T1* and another operator with the same name *Op* had been defined for type *T2* (in other words, *Op* had been *overloaded*—see IM Proposal 13). Then an invocation of *Op* with argument *v* would be ambiguous.*

Note: It follows *a fortiori* from the disjointness requirement that if

- *TH1* and *TH2* are type hierarchies with distinct local root types, neither of which is a subtype of the other, and
- Types *T1* and *T2* belong to *TH1* and *TH2* respectively, then
- *T1* and *T2* are disjoint.

In other words, type hierarchies with disjoint local root types are themselves disjoint. For example, a type hierarchy rooted at type ELLIPSE and a type hierarchy rooted at type POLYGON will necessarily be disjoint—no value can be both of some type from one of these two hierarchies and of some type from the other.

It further follows *a fortiori* that distinct leaf types are disjoint.

---

*We remark in passing that such ambiguities do not arise over constraints. For if constraint *C1* has been defined for type *T1* and constraint *C2* has been defined for type *T2,* and if constraints *C1* and *C2* conflict, then it simply means that types *T1* and *T2* must be disjoint after all (because no value *v* can possibly satisfy both *C1* and *C2*).

IM PROPOSAL 12: SCALAR VALUES (EXTENDED DEFINITION)

Let scalar value v *be of type* T. *If and only if no proper subtype* T′ *of type* T *exists such that* v *is also of type* T′, *then* T *is said to be the **most specific** type for (or of)* v.

———— ♦♦♦♦♦ ————

The definition of **scalar value** needs some extension if type inheritance is supported—basically because such a value can now be of more than one type. However, it is necessarily the case that such a value has exactly one *most specific* type, by virtue of IM Proposal 11 (and it might continue to be the case even if the prohibitions of IM Proposal 11 are relaxed somewhat in order to support multiple inheritance—see Chapter 15). For example, a given value might have types PLANE_FIGURE, POLYGON, and RECTANGLE, but not SQUARE, in which case the most specific type would be, precisely, RECTANGLE. In fact, it follows from IM Proposals 7, 11, and 12 taken together that if scalar value *v* is of most specific type *T*, then the set of types possessed by *v* is, precisely, the set consisting of all supertypes of *T* (a set that includes *T* itself, of course). In other words, *v* is of every type that is a member of this set and is of no type that is not a member of this set.

IM PROPOSAL 13: SCALAR VARIABLES (EXTENDED DEFINITION)

Let scalar variable V *be declared to be of type* T *(i.e.,* T *is the declared type for* V— *see RM Prescription 11). Because of value substitutability (see IM Proposal 24), the value* v *assigned to* V *at any given time can have any subtype* T′ *of type* T *as its most specific type. We can therefore model* V *as a named ordered triple of the form* <DT,MST,v>, *where:*

- *The name of the triple is the name of the variable (*V *in the example).*
- DT *is the name of the declared type for variable* V.
- MST *is the name of the **most specific type**—also known as the **current** most specific type—for, or of, variable* V.
- v *is a value of most specific type* MST—*the **current value** for, or of, variable* V.

We use the notation DT(V), MST(V), v(V) *to refer to the* DT, MST, v *components, respectively, of (our model of) scalar variable* V. *Note that it must always be the case that* MST(V) *is some subtype—not necessarily a proper subtype—of* DT(V). *Note too that* MST(V) *and* v(V) *change with time, in general; in other words, the phrase "most specific type of variable* V*" refers to the most specific type of the current* *value of* V, *not to the most specific type that values of* V *are ever permitted to have. Note finally that* MST(V) *is in fact implied by* v(V), *by virtue of IM Proposals 2, 7, 11, and 12 taken in concert.*

───── ♦♦♦♦♦ ─────

Like the definition of *scalar value,* the definition of **scalar variable** also needs some extension if type inheritance is supported—basically because such a variable is permitted to have a value that is of *any subtype* of the declared type of the variable in question. For example, let scalar variable E be defined as follows:

```
VAR E ELLIPSE ;
```

At run time, then, the current value of variable E can have any subtype of ELLIPSE (including, of course, ELLIPSE itself) as its most specific type. Thus, the current value might be a circle instead of "just an ellipse" (such a possibility is intuitively reasonable, of course, since a circle *is* an ellipse). Note, therefore, that we must now be extremely careful to distinguish the two important types that apply to any given variable: the *declared* type, which does not change over time, *vs.* the *current most specific* type, which does (in general). Of course, the second of these will always be some subtype—not necessarily proper—of the first.

Note further that if type *T* is the current most specific type of variable *V,* then every proper supertype of type *T* is also a "current type" of variable *V.*

We have now laid sufficient groundwork to introduce two important concepts that pervade the topic of type inheritance, *polymorphism* and *substitutability.* Formal discussion of these topics is deferred to IM Proposals 24–26, but explaining them informally here should help you understand several of the other topics we need to consider before we can get to those formal discussions.

First of all, the very notion of inheritance implies that if *T'* is a subtype of *T,* then all operators that apply to values of type *T* apply to values of type *T'* too. For example, if AREA(*e*) is legal, where *e* is an ellipse, then AREA(*c*), where *c* is a circle, must be legal too. Note, therefore, that there is another important distinction we must be very careful over: namely, the distinction between the *parameters* in terms of which a given operator is defined, with their *declared* types, and the corresponding *arguments* to some invocation of that operator, with their *actual* types. In the AREA(*c*) example just quoted, AREA is defined in terms of a parameter of declared type ELLIPSE, but the actual type of the argument *c* is CIRCLE.

Recall now that ellipses and circles, at least as we defined them under IM Proposal 1, have different possible representations:

```
TYPE ELLIPSE POSSREP ( A LENGTH, B LENGTH, CTR POINT ) ... ;

TYPE CIRCLE  POSSREP ( R LENGTH, CTR POINT ) ... ;
```

It is conceivable, therefore, that two different versions of the AREA operator will have to exist under the covers, one that makes use of the ELLIPSE possible representation and one that makes use of the CIRCLE possible representation. To repeat, it is conceivable—but it is *not* absolutely necessary: Since (a) the code that implements AREA for type ELLIPSE will have been written in terms of the ELLIPSE possible representation, and (b) that possible representation must be a possible representation for CIRCLE too (though, as noted in the introduction to this chapter, not a *declared* one), it follows that (c) that code should work for circles too.* To be more specific, the area of a general ellipse is πab, while the area of a circle is πr^2. Thus, the code that implements the ELLIPSE version of AREA will presumably invoke THE_A and THE_B, and that code will certainly work for a circle. However, the type definer or implementer might prefer—for a variety of reasons—to define a distinct version of AREA that is specific to circles and invokes THE_R instead.

To pursue this last point a moment longer: In fact, it might be desirable to have two versions of the operator anyway (even if the possible representations are the same), for reasons of efficiency. Consider polygons and rectangles, for example; the algorithm that computes the area of a general polygon will certainly work for a rectangle, but for rectangles a much more efficient algorithm—multiply the height by the width—is available.

Of course, it makes no logical difference to the user how many versions of AREA exist under the covers; to the user there is just one AREA operator, which works for (say) ellipses and therefore for circles too, by definition. In other words, AREA is *polymorphic:* It can take arguments of different types on different invocations.

Now, we have met the concept of polymorphism before (e.g., in our discussion of the equality and assignment operators in Chapter 6). It is not a new idea—SQL, for example, already has polymorphic operators ("=", "+", "||", and many others), and in fact so do most other languages. However, there is no inheritance, as such, involved in these examples; they are all instances of what is sometimes called *overloading* polymorphism. The kind of polymorphism exhibited by the AREA operator, by contrast, is known as *inclusion* polymorphism, on the grounds that the relationship between (e.g.) circles and ellipses is basically that of set inclusion [13]. For obvious reasons, we take the unqualified term "polymorphism" in what follows to mean inclusion polymorphism specifically, barring explicit statements to the contrary.[†]

A helpful way of characterizing the difference between overloading and inclusion polymorphism is as follows:

- *Overloading* polymorphism means we have several distinct operators with the same name (and the user does need to know that the operators in question are in fact distinct, with distinct—though preferably similar—semantics).

---

*Note, however, that the ELLIPSE version of the code will not work for circles too if it is written in terms of the *actual* ELLIPSE representation instead of a possible one, and the actual representations for types ELLIPSE and CIRCLE differ. The practice of implementing operators in terms of actual representations is thus clearly contraindicated. Code defensively!

[†]As noted in Chapter 10, the usual relational operators—join and so forth—exhibit yet another kind of polymorphism that might be called *generic* polymorphism.

■ *Inclusion* polymorphism means we have one operator with several distinct versions under the covers (but the user does not need to know that the versions in question are in fact distinct—to the user, there is just the one operator).

Note: These matters are explained more fully under IM Proposal 24, but we elaborate on them slightly here for purposes of future reference (despite the fact that we recognize that our elaboration might not make very much sense at this juncture). Briefly, for overloading polymorphism, the distinct operators will each have their own distinct *specification signature* (for otherwise there would be ambiguity; two operators with the same name and same specification signature would be indistinguishable). For inclusion polymorphism, by contrast, the single operator will—necessarily!—have just one specification signature, but each under-the-covers version of that operator will have its own *version* signature. Refer to IM Proposal 24 for further discussion.

The trouble is, as we will see under IM Proposal 24, there can be no guarantee with inclusion polymorphism that the various versions under the covers do in fact all implement the same operator!—i.e., distinct versions might have distinct *semantics*. If they do, of course, we do not have true inclusion polymorphism any longer, we have overloading polymorphism instead, and it is our position that such an implementation is in violation of our model. But you should be aware that such violations can certainly arise in practice, and are even argued by some writers to be desirable. Once again, see IM Proposal 24 for further discussion.*

Back to inclusion polymorphism specifically. What are the implications of this idea for the user? Consider the following example. Suppose we need to display some diagram, made up of squares, circles, ellipses, etc. Without polymorphism, the code—or pseudocode, rather—for this task will look something like this:

```
FOR EACH x ∈ DIAGRAM
   CASE ;
      WHEN IS_SQUARE ( x ) THEN CALL DISPLAY_SQUARE ... ;
      WHEN IS_CIRCLE ( x ) THEN CALL DISPLAY_CIRCLE ... ;
      .....
   END CASE ;
```

(See IM Proposal 19 for an explanation of the operators IS_SQUARE, IS_CIRCLE, etc.) With polymorphism, by contrast, the code is much simpler and more succinct:

```
FOR EACH x ∈ DIAGRAM CALL DISPLAY ( x ) ;
```

Explanation: DISPLAY here is a polymorphic operator. The version of DISPLAY that works for values of type T will be defined (in all probability) at the time type T is defined *and will be made known to the system at that time.* At run time,

---

*The situation is further confused by the fact that, regrettably, much of the literature actually uses the term *overloading* to refer to inclusion polymorphism anyway.

then, when the system encounters the DISPLAY invocation with argument *x,* it will have to determine the current most specific type of *x* and then invoke the version of DISPLAY that is appropriate to that most specific type (a process known as *run-time binding*). In other words, polymorphism effectively means that CASE expressions and CASE statements that would otherwise have had to appear in the user's source code are *moved under the covers;* the system performs those CASE operations in the user's behalf.

Note in particular the implications of the foregoing for program maintenance. Suppose, for example, that a new type TRIANGLE is defined—another immediate subtype of POLYGON—and hence that the diagram to be displayed can now additionally include triangles. Without polymorphism, every program that contains a CASE operation such as the one shown above will now have to be modified to include code of the form

```
WHEN IS_TRIANGLE ( x ) THEN CALL DISPLAY_TRIANGLE ... ;
```

With polymorphism, however, no such modifications are needed.

Because of examples like the foregoing, polymorphism is sometimes characterized, a little colorfully, as "allowing old code to invoke new code"; that is, a program *P* can effectively invoke some version of an operator *Op* that did not even exist (the version, that is) at the time *P* was written. Thus, we have—at least potentially— what is usually called *code reuse:* The very same program *P* might be usable on data that is of a type *T* that, to repeat, did not even exist at the time *P* was written.*

Turning now to *substitutability:* This concept is really just the concept of polymorphism already discussed, looked at from a slightly different perspective. We have seen, for example, that if AREA(*e*) is legal, where *e* is an ellipse, then AREA(*c*), where *c* is a circle, must be legal too. In other words, wherever the system expects an ellipse, we can always substitute a circle instead.† More generally, wherever the system expects a value of type *T,* we can always substitute a value of type *T′* instead—*The Principle of (Value) Substitutability* (see IM Proposal 24).

We remark finally that the notions of polymorphism and substitutability, important though they are in practice, are both logically implied by the notion of type inheritance—they are not, logically speaking, completely separate concepts. In other words, if the system supports type inheritance, it *must* support polymorphism and substitutability as well, *a fortiori* (for if it did not, then it would not be supporting type inheritance, by definition).

---

*Certainly the code of program *P* is being reused here. The code that implements operator *Op* under the covers might or might not be reused; for example, the code that implements the AREA operator for ellipses might or might not be reusable for circles, as we saw earlier.

†Observe in particular, therefore, that if some relation *r* has an attribute *A* of declared type ELLIPSE, some of the *A* values in *r* might be circles instead of mere ellipses. Likewise, if type *T* has a possible representation that involves a component *C* of declared type ELLIPSE, then for some values *v* of type *T* the operator invocation THE_*C*(*v*) might—or, more likely, will—return a value of type CIRCLE.

IM PROPOSAL 14: ASSIGNMENT WITH INHERITANCE

Let SX *be a scalar expression. The notation* DT(V), MST(V), v(V) *introduced under IM Proposal 13 can be extended in an obvious way to refer to the declared type* DT(SX), *the current most specific type* MST(SX), *and the current value* v(SX), *respectively, of* SX—*where "declared type" is as explained in RM Prescription 3 and is known at compilation time, and "current most specific type" and "current value" refer to the result of evaluating* SX *and are therefore not known until run time, in general. Now consider the assignment*

```
V  :=  SX ;
```

(where V *is a scalar variable).* DT(SX) *must be a subtype of* DT(V), *otherwise the assignment is illegal (this is a compile-time check). If the assignment is legal, its effect is to set* MST(V) *equal to* MST(SX) *and* v(V) *equal to* v(SX).

———— ♦♦♦♦♦ ————

Consider the following example:

```
VAR E ELLIPSE ;
VAR C CIRCLE ;

C  :=  CIRCLE ( ... ) ;        /* initialize C to some circle */

E  :=  C ;          /* note appeal to substitutability on RHS */
```

The first assignment here assigns some circle value to variable C (the expression on the right hand side of that assignment is an invocation of the CIRCLE selector). The second assignment then copies that circle value from variable C to variable E. After that second assignment, then, the current most specific type of E is CIRCLE, not ELLIPSE (the *declared* type, of course, is still ELLIPSE). Thus, whereas assignment *without* inheritance* requires the same type on both sides, assignment *with* inheritance means that:

- The declared type *DT(SX)* of the expression on the right hand side can be any subtype of the declared type *DT(V)* of the variable on the left hand side.
- The most specific type *MST(SX)* of the value denoted by the expression on the right hand side can be any subtype of the declared type *DT(V)* of the variable on the left hand side. (In fact, of course, it must be some subtype of the declared type *DT(SX)* of the expression on the right hand side, and so is some subtype of *DT(V)* *a fortiori*.)
- The variable *V* on the left hand side acquires its new most specific type (as well as its new value) from the value denoted by the expression *SX* on the right hand side.

---

*And, in accordance with OO Very Strong Suggestion 1, without coercions.

Note carefully, therefore, that what does *not* happen is that the value of the expression on the right hand side gets converted to the declared type of the variable on the left hand side. For if such a conversion did occur, *the value would lose its most specific properties* (loosely speaking). In the case at hand, for example, we would not be able to ask for the radius of E—more precisely, the radius of the circle that is now the current value of E—because the circle would have been converted to an ellipse, and ellipses that are not circles do not have a radius.

(*Note:* You might possibly see a problem here, and indeed there is one: namely, the operator THE_R—"the radius of "—cannot legally be applied to a variable such as E whose declared type is ELLIPSE, not CIRCLE. IM Proposal 17 addresses this issue.)

To continue with the example:

```
VAR A AREA ;

A  :=  AREA ( E ) :
```

What happens now is the following:

- First, the system performs compile-time type checking on the expression AREA(E), as required by OO Prescription 1; the check succeeds, because E is of declared type ELLIPSE and the single parameter to AREA is of declared type ELLIPSE also (just to remind you, the definition of the AREA operator was given as one of the examples in the section on IM Proposal 2).

- Second, the system discovers at run time that the current most specific type of E is CIRCLE; it therefore invokes the version of AREA that applies to circles (i.e., it performs the "run-time binding" process mentioned in the previous section).

The fact that it is the circle version of AREA that is invoked might or might not be relevant to the user; it definitely will be, if the most specific type of the result of the operation depends on whether it is the circle version or the ellipse version that is invoked. Note, however, that this state of affairs—i.e., the fact that the user might effectively have to know which version of AREA is invoked—does *not* undermine our earlier claim to the effect that, so far as the user is concerned, there is really just one operator. See IM Proposal 24 for further discussion of this particular issue.

One last point: For definiteness, we have been making the assumption throughout this section (and IM Proposal 14 itself makes the same assumption) that, in accordance with OO Very Strong Suggestion 1, the assignment operator ":=" has not been overloaded in such a way as to permit $DT(SX)$ *not* to be a subtype of $DT(V)$, thereby effectively requiring coercion of $v(SX)$ to the type, declared or current most specific, of V.* IM Proposal 14 will clearly need some extension if that assumption is jettisoned.

---

*Such overloading might permit, e.g., the assignment of a UK sterling value to a variable of declared type US dollars, with implicit currency conversion from sterling to dollars. You might care to reflect on some of the complexities involved in such an overloading, bearing in mind in particular the fact that currency conversion rates vary with time.

IM PROPOSAL 15: COMPARISON WITH INHERITANCE

Consider the comparison

```
SY  =  SX
```

(where SY and SX are scalar expressions). DT(SX) must be a subtype of DT(SY) or vice versa, otherwise the comparison is illegal (this is a compile-time check). If the comparison is legal, its effect is to return true *if MST(SY) is equal to MST(SX) and* v(SY) *is equal to* v(SX), false *otherwise.*

———— ♦♦♦♦ ————

Consider the following example:

```
VAR E ELLIPSE ;
VAR C CIRCLE ;

IF E = C THEN ... ;          /* note appeal to substitutability */
END IF ;
```

The comparison "E = C" here will give *true* (in **Tutorial D** terms, it will evaluate to TRUE) if and only if the current value of variable E (a) is a circle—i.e., is of type CIRCLE—and (b) is in fact the same circle as the current value of variable C.

In general, the situation with respect to equality comparisons is analogous to that with respect to assignments. That is, whereas equality comparison *without* inheritance* requires the same type on both sides, equality comparison *with* inheritance means that:

- The declared type *DT(SX)* of the expression on the right hand side can be any subtype of the declared type *DT(SY)* of the expression on the left hand side (or *vice versa*).

- The most specific type *MST(SX)* of the value denoted by the expression on the right hand side can be any subtype of the most specific type *MST(SY)* of the value denoted by the expression on the left hand side (or *vice versa*).

- The comparison will definitely give *false* if the current most specific types of the comparands are different (a difference in type is a logical difference!), but will give *true* if those most specific types are the same *and* the values are the same too.

The rules for less-than comparisons, greater-than comparisons, and so on—for types where those comparisons are defined—follow the same general pattern as those for equality comparisons, of course (except that it might not be necessary to insist that the most specific types be the same for the comparison to give *true*).

———————

*And, in accordance with OO Very Strong Suggestion 1, without coercions.

Note: For definiteness, we have been assuming (as IM Proposal 15 itself does) that, in accordance with OO Very Strong Suggestion 1, the equality comparison operator "=" has not been overloaded in such a way as to permit the comparands to be of different types, neither of which is a subtype of the other, thereby effectively requiring coercion of $v(SY)$ to the type, declared or current most specific, of SX or coercion of $v(SX)$ to the type, declared or current most specific, of SY.* IM Proposal 15 will clearly need some extension if that assumption is jettisoned.

We remark that if coercions are *not* permitted, even such a simple comparison as

```
R = I    /* e.g., 3.0 = 3 : EITHER ILLEGAL OR FALSE ?!?!? */
```

(where the current most specific types of R and I are RATIONAL and INTEGER respectively) will either (a) always be illegal (if INTEGER is not a subtype of RATIONAL) or (b) always give *false* (otherwise). This state of affairs might be seen as an argument in favor of permitting coercions. To elaborate:

- If INTEGER is *not* a subtype of RATIONAL:
  - The concept of value substitutability does not arise (i.e., integers cannot be substituted for rationals);
  - Therefore the idea of converting integers to rationals seems useful;
  - Therefore it seems reasonable to assume that an operator to perform such conversions will have been defined;
  - Therefore no harm is done by invoking that conversion operator implicitly in an INTEGER-to-RATIONAL comparison (or in an INTEGER-to-RATIONAL assignment). In particular, value substitutability is not undermined because, as already noted, the concept simply does not apply.
- On the other hand, if INTEGER *is* a subtype of RATIONAL:[†]
  - Integers can be substituted for rationals (i.e., the concept of value substitutability does apply);
  - Therefore there is little point in defining an operator to convert integers to rationals (after all, integers would *be* rationals already);
  - Therefore it seems reasonable to assume that no such operator will have been defined;
  - Therefore the question of invoking such an operator implicitly does not arise, meaning that (again) value substitutability is not undermined.

Refer to the section on OO Very Strong Suggestion 1 in Chapter 11 for further discussion of this issue.

---

*Such overloading might permit, e.g., a comparison to be performed between a UK sterling amount and a US dollar amount, with implicit currency conversion either way. Again, you might care to meditate on some of the complexities involved in such an overloading.

[†]We remark in passing that if types INTEGER and RATIONAL are in fact subtype and supertype as suggested here, then they provide a good example of a situation where the actual representation of the subtype will almost certainly differ from that of the supertype.

IM PROPOSAL 16: JOIN ETC. WITH INHERITANCE

Let rx *and* ry *be relations with a common attribute* A, *and let the declared types of* A *in* rx *and* ry *be* DT(Ax) *and* DT(Ay), *respectively. Consider the join of* rx *and* ry *(necessarily over* A, *at least in part).* DT(Ax) *must be a subtype of* DT(Ay) *or vice versa, otherwise the join is illegal (this is a compile-time check). If the join is legal, assume without loss of generality that* DT(Ay) *is a subtype of* DT(Ax). *Then the declared type of* A *in the result is* DT(Ax).

Analogous remarks apply to union, intersection, and difference operators: In every case, (a) corresponding attributes of the operands must be such that the declared type of one is a subtype of the declared type of the other, and (b) the declared type of the corresponding attribute in the result is the less specific of the two (where by the less specific *of two types* T *and* T′, *one of which is a subtype of the other, we mean whichever is the supertype).*

———— ♦♦♦♦ ————

IM Proposal 16 should be easy enough to understand as stated, but it does have one slightly counterintuitive implication that is worth spelling out explicitly. It applies to all of the operators mentioned except union. Consider the relations RX and RY shown in Fig. 14.3; note that the sole attribute A in RX is of declared type ELLIPSE and its counterpart A in RY is of declared type CIRCLE. *Note:* We adopt the convention in the figure that values of the form Ei are ellipses that are not circles and values of the form Ci are circles. Most specific types are shown in lower case italics.

Now consider the join of RX and RY, RJ say (again, see Fig. 14.3). Clearly, every A value in RJ will necessarily be of type CIRCLE (because any A value in RX whose most specific type is merely ELLIPSE cannot possibly "compare equal" to any A value in RY). Thus, it might be thought that the declared type of attribute A in RJ should be CIRCLE, not ELLIPSE. But consider the following:

- Since RX and RY each have A as their sole attribute, RX JOIN RY reduces to RX INTERSECT RY, and so the rule regarding the declared type of the result attribute for JOIN must reduce to the analogous rule for INTERSECT.

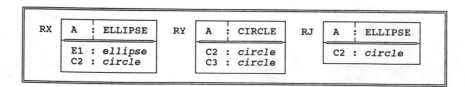

Fig. 14.3   Join with inheritance (example)

■ RX INTERSECT RY in turn is logically equivalent to RX MINUS (RX MINUS RY). Let the result of the second operand here—i.e., RX MINUS RY—be RZ. Then it is clear that:

- RZ will include some A values of most specific type ELLIPSE, in general, and so the declared type of attribute A in RZ must be ELLIPSE.

- The original expression thus reduces to RX MINUS RZ, where the declared type of attribute A in both RX and RZ is ELLIPSE, and hence yields a final result in which the declared type of attribute A must obviously be ELLIPSE once again.

■ It follows that the declared type of the result attribute for INTERSECT, and therefore for JOIN too, must indeed be as stated.

The foregoing discussion takes care of RX MINUS RY, too. What about RY MINUS RX? Clearly, every A value in the result of this latter expression will be of type CIRCLE, and so again it might be thought that the declared type of A in that result should be CIRCLE, not ELLIPSE. However, noting that RX INTERSECT RY is also logically equivalent to RY MINUS (RY MINUS RX), we can quickly see that specifying the declared type of A in the result of RY MINUS RX to be CIRCLE leads to a contradiction. It follows that the declared type of the result attribute for MINUS too must indeed be as stated.

Finally, consider RX UNION RY. Here it should be obvious that the result will include some A values of most specific type ELLIPSE, in general, and so the declared type of attribute A in that result must necessarily be ELLIPSE. Thus, the declared type of the result attribute for UNION too must be as stated (but in the case of UNION this situation can hardly be described as counterintuitive).

IM PROPOSAL 17: TREAT DOWN

For every type T, *an operator of the form*

```
TREAT_DOWN_AS_T ( SX )
```

(or logical equivalent thereof) should be supported, where SX is a scalar expression and T *is a subtype of* DT(SX) *(this is a compile-time check). We refer to such operators generically as "TREAT DOWN" operators; their semantics are as follows. First of all,* MST(SX) *must be a subtype of* T *(this is a run-time check, in general). Assuming this condition is satisfied, then:*

a. *If the TREAT DOWN invocation appears in a "source" position (in particular, on the right hand side of an assignment), then the invocation yields a scalar result,* SR *say, with* DT(SR) *equal to* T, MST(SR) *equal to* MST(SX), *and* v(SR) *equal to* v(SX).

b. *If the TREAT DOWN invocation appears in a "target" position (in particular, on the left hand side of an assignment), then, first, the invocation acts as a pseudovariable, which means that it actually designates its argument* SX *(more accurately, it designates a version of* SX *for which* DT(SX) *is equal to* T *but* MST(SX) *is unchanged); second, that argument* SX *must be specified as a scalar variable specifically, not as an arbitrary scalar expression.*

──── ♦♦♦♦♦ ────

Consider the following example (a partial repeat of the example from the earlier discussion of IM Proposal 14):

```
VAR E ELLIPSE ;
VAR C CIRCLE ;

C  :=  CIRCLE ( ... ) ;

E  :=  C ;
```

As explained under IM Proposal 14, what does *not* happen here is that the circle value of C gets converted to type ELLIPSE—because if such a conversion were to occur, then we would no longer be able to ask for the radius of the circle that is now the current value of E. Suppose now that we do want to ask for that radius. We might try:

```
VAR L LENGTH ;

L  :=  THE_R ( E ) ; /* invoke "the radius of" : TYPE ERROR! */
```

The right hand side of the assignment here gives a compile-time type error, because variable E is of declared type ELLIPSE and THE_R does not apply to values of type ELLIPSE. *Note:* If the compile-time type check were not done, we would get a *run-time* type error instead—which is worse—if the current value of E at run time were only an ellipse and not a circle. In the case at hand, of course, we do know that the value at run time will be a circle; the trouble is, we know this, but the compiler does not.

TREAT DOWN is intended to address such situations. The correct way to obtain the radius in the example is as follows:

```
L  :=  THE_R ( TREAT_DOWN_AS_CIRCLE ( E ) ) ;
```

The expression TREAT_DOWN_AS_CIRCLE(E) is defined to have declared type CIRCLE, so the compile-time type checking now succeeds. Then, at run time:

- If the current value of E is indeed of type CIRCLE, then the overall expression does correctly return the radius of that circle. More precisely, the TREAT DOWN invocation yields a result, CC say, with (a) *DT*(CC) equal to CIRCLE, because of the "_AS_CIRCLE" specification, (b) *MST*(CC) equal to *MST*(E), which is CIRCLE also in the example, and (c) *v*(CC) equal to *v*(E); then (d) the expression "THE_R(CC)" is evaluated, to give the desired radius (which can then be assigned to L).

- However, if the current value of E is only of type ELLIPSE, not CIRCLE, then the TREAT DOWN fails on a run-time type error.

The broad intent of IM Proposal 17 is thus to ensure that run-time type errors can occur only in the context of a TREAT DOWN invocation (but see Assignments 2 and 3 below, also IM Proposal 26, for further discussion of this point).

Note: Suppose CIRCLE in turn had a proper subtype, COLORED_CIRCLE say.* Then the current value of variable E at some given time might be of most specific type COLORED_CIRCLE instead of just CIRCLE. If it is, then the TREAT DOWN invocation

```
TREAT_DOWN_AS_CIRCLE ( E )
```

will succeed, and will yield a result, CC say, with (a) *DT*(CC) equal to CIRCLE, because of the "_AS_CIRCLE" specification, (b) *MST*(CC) equal to COLORED_CIRCLE, because COLORED_CIRCLE is the most specific type of E, and (c) v(CC) equal to v(E). In other words (loosely): TREAT DOWN always leaves the most specific type alone, it never makes it less specific than it was before.

Here are some more examples. Suppose we have the following variables:

```
VAR E ELLIPSE ;
VAR C CIRCLE ;
VAR L LENGTH ;
```

Suppose further that the current value of E is of type CIRCLE (more precisely, *MST*(E) is some subtype of CIRCLE). Now consider the operators THE_A ("the *a* semiaxis of"), THE_B ("the *b* semiaxis of"), and THE_R ("the radius of"). Note that:

- For read-only purposes, THE_A and THE_B apply to type ELLIPSE and hence to type CIRCLE too.

- For update purposes, by contrast, they apply *only* to type ELLIPSE (see IM Proposal 26 for an explanation of this point).

- THE_R applies only to type CIRCLE, for both read-only and update purposes.

---

*Examples like this one are commonly quoted in the industry. We feel bound to say, however, that we find the idea of colored circles being somehow a special case of circles in general a little unconvincing. After all, "colored circles" must by definition be *images* (perhaps on a display screen), while circles in general are not images but *geometric figures*. Thus, it seems to us more reasonable to regard COLORED_CIRCLE not as a subtype of CIRCLE, but rather as a completely separate type with a possible representation in which one component is of type CIRCLE and another is of type COLOR. (What is more, it is not the case that our declared possible representation for circles is a possible representation for colored circles too, a fact that strongly suggests that colored circles are not circles in the same sense that, e.g., circles are ellipses.) We will stay with the subtype/supertype interpretation of colored circles and circles for now, however, since the issue of which interpretation is better is somewhat tangential to our main point, but we will have more to say regarding this issue in the final section of Appendix C, *q.v.*

Then the following assignments will have the indicated effects (we have numbered those assignments for purposes of reference).

```
1. THE_R ( E )   :=   LENGTH ( 5.0 ) ;
```

Here a compile-time type error occurs because THE_R does not apply to type ELLIPSE. *Note:* More precisely, the error occurs because the declared possible representation for type ELLIPSE has no R component; recall from Chapter 6 that assignment to a THE_ pseudovariable in general is shorthand for an assignment in which the target is the applicable variable and the source is the result of some invocation of the applicable selector, and the applicable selector in turn is defined in terms of parameters that correspond to components of the applicable possible representation. See IM Proposal 23 for further discussion of this shorthand question.

```
2. THE_R ( TREAT_DOWN_AS_CIRCLE ( E ) )   :=   LENGTH ( 5.0 ) ;
```

Note first that the argument to THE_R on the left hand side here is of declared type CIRCLE (observe the use of a TREAT DOWN reference as a nested pseudovariable). Assume for the moment that *MST*(E) is exactly CIRCLE, not some proper subtype of CIRCLE. Then the assignment will set the value of E to be a circle with radius five (and with center unchanged, i.e., equal to THE_CTR(E) as it was prior to the assignment). *MST*(E) will still be CIRCLE after the update.

Now assume (as we did earlier) that CIRCLE has a proper subtype COLORED_CIRCLE, and the current value of E is of most specific type COLORED_CIRCLE instead of just CIRCLE. Then:

- If THE_R applies to colored circles for update purposes (which it probably does—see IM Proposal 26), then Assignment 2 will set the value of E to be a colored circle with radius five (and with center unchanged, i.e., equal to THE_CTR(E) as it was prior to the assignment). Note, therefore, that *MST*(E) will still be COLORED_CIRCLE after the update.

- If on the other hand THE_R does *not* apply to colored circles for update purposes, a run-time type error will occur.

```
3. THE_A ( E )   :=   LENGTH ( 5.0 ) ;
```

Assuming once again that (as stated) the current value of E is of type CIRCLE, this assignment will cause a run-time type error, because THE_A does not apply to type CIRCLE for update purposes (see IM Proposal 26). If, on the other hand, the current value of E were of most specific type ELLIPSE, the assignment would set the value of E to be an ellipse with *a* semiaxis five (and with *b* semiaxis and center unchanged, i.e., as they were prior to the assignment).

We remark that it would probably prove convenient in practice to support a new kind of relational expression* of the form

---

*And a tuple expression analog, too, and corresponding tuple and relational pseudovariables.

```
RX TREAT_DOWN_AS_T ( A )
```

Here *RX* is a relational expression, *A* is an attribute of the relation denoted by that expression, and *T* is a type. The overall expression is defined to be shorthand for the following:

```
( ( EXTEND ( RX ) ADD ( TREAT_DOWN_AS_T ( A ) ) AS A' )
                             { ALL BUT A } ) RENAME A' AS A
```

(where *A'* is an arbitrary name not already appearing as an attribute name in the result of evaluating *RX*).

We remark finally that a slightly more general form of TREAT DOWN (both operator and pseudovariable versions) could prove useful in practice:

```
TREAT_DOWN_TO_SAME_TYPE_AS ( SY, SX )
```

(where *SX* and *SY* are scalar expressions such that $DT(SY)$ is a subtype of $DT(SX)$). We define the semantics of this expression to be identical to those of the expression

```
TREAT_DOWN_AS_T ( SX )
```

where *T* is $DT(SY)$. The obvious relational expression analog should be supported too:

```
RX TREAT_DOWN_TO_SAME_TYPE_AS ( SY, A )
```

IM PROPOSAL 18: TREAT UP

For every type T, *an operator of the form*

```
TREAT_UP_AS_T ( SX )
```

(or logical equivalent thereof) should be supported, where SX *is a scalar expression and* T *is a supertype of* DT(SX) *(this is a compile-time check). We refer to such operators generically as "TREAT UP" operators; their semantics are as follows.*

a. *If the TREAT UP invocation appears in a "source" position (in particular, on the right hand side of an assignment), then the invocation yields a scalar result,* SR *say, with* DT(SR) *and* MST(SR) *both equal to* T *and* v(SR) *equal to* v(SX).

b. *If the TREAT UP invocation appears in a "target" position (in particular, on the left hand side of an assignment), then, first,* T *and* DT(SX) *must be identical (this is a compile-time check); second, the invocation acts as a pseudovariable, which means that it actually designates its argument* SX *(more accurately, it designates a version of* SX *for which* DT(SX) *and* MST(SX) *are both equal to* T); *third, that argument* SX *must be specified as a scalar variable specifically, not as an arbitrary scalar expression.*

———— ♦♦♦♦♦ ————

Consider the following example (a repeat of the example from the discussion of IM Proposal 15):

```
VAR E ELLIPSE ;
VAR C CIRCLE ;

IF E = C THEN ... ;
END IF ;
```

As explained under IM Proposal 15, the comparison "E = C" here will give *false*—in **Tutorial D** terms, it will evaluate to FALSE—if the current most specific types of E and C are different, even if the current *values* of those two variables are the same (i.e., even if $v(E) = v(C)$). For example, suppose E and C have been assigned values as follows:

```
E  :=  ELLIPSE ( LENGTH ( 5.0 ), LENGTH ( 5.0 ),
                               POINT ( 0.0, 0.0 ) ) ;

C  :=  CIRCLE  ( LENGTH ( 5.0 ), POINT ( 0.0, 0.0 ) ) ;
```

Thus, variable E denotes the ellipse with semiaxes *a* and *b* both equal to five and center the origin, while variable C denotes the circle with radius five and center the origin. These two values are indeed "the same," loosely speaking, and yet if $MST(E) \neq MST(C)$ the comparison will still give *false* (as noted under IM Proposal 15, two values cannot possibly be "the same" in our model if they are not of the same type).

Now, we might try:

```
IF TREAT_DOWN_AS_CIRCLE ( E ) = C THEN ... ; END IF ;
```

If the current value of E is not of type CIRCLE, however, the TREAT DOWN invocation here will raise a run-time type error (even if $a = b$). By contrast, a run-time type error cannot possibly occur with the following:

```
IF E = TREAT_UP_AS_ELLIPSE ( C ) THEN ... ; END IF ;
```

Furthermore, the comparison will now give *true* if the current value of E is only of most specific type ELLIPSE, not CIRCLE (just so long as $v(E)$ is equal to $v(C)$). More precisely, what happens is this: First, the TREAT UP invocation yields a result, EE say, with (a) $DT(EE)$ equal to ELLIPSE, because of the "_AS_ELLIPSE" specification, (b) $MST(EE)$ also equal to ELLIPSE, again because of the "_AS_ELLIPSE" specification, and (c) $v(EE)$ equal to $v(C)$; then (d) the comparison "E = EE" is performed. The net effect (in the example) is that two ellipses are compared.

Continuing with the example, we now point out, however, that in accordance with IM Proposal 15, the very same comparison

```
E = TREAT_UP_AS_ELLIPSE ( C )
```

will give *false* if the current value of E is of type CIRCLE!—even if the corresponding comparison "E = C" would have given *true*. By contrast, the following version is guaranteed to give *true* in all cases (just so long as $v(E)$ is equal to $v(C)$), and is therefore the only "safe" form of the comparison:

```
TREAT_UP_AS_ELLIPSE ( E ) = TREAT_UP_AS_ELLIPSE ( C )
```

Incidentally, note the point, implicit in the foregoing discussion, that a value that is only of type ELLIPSE—i.e., a value of most specific type ELLIPSE—might actually correspond to a circle "in the real world." The reason is that values in our model are of the type we *say* they are, via the corresponding selector; thus, for example, an invocation of the ELLIPSE selector returns a value of type ELLIPSE, not CIRCLE, even if the *a* and *b* semiaxes of that ELLIPSE value are equal. In other words, to define CIRCLE to be a subtype of ELLIPSE is to divide the set of real-world ellipses into those that the system knows are circles *vs.* those that it does not—*not* into those that are circles *vs.* those that are not. Hence the system *will* probably know that if some value is of type CIRCLE, it must satisfy the constraint that its semiaxes *a* and *b* are equal—indeed, we stated this constraint explicitly in our CIRCLE type definition earlier, in the section on IM Proposal 2—but it will *not* know that a value of most specific type ELLIPSE whose semiaxes *a* and *b* are equal should "really" be of type CIRCLE.

Perhaps we should take a moment to explain why we adopt this rather conservative position. After all, the alternative—that the system should know that (e.g.) an ellipse whose semiaxes *a* and *b* are equal should really be a circle—does seem intuitively more attractive ("the more knowledge the system has, the better" is a good general rule). This latter alternative is sometimes called *specialization by constraint;** we exclude it from our model (at least at the time of writing) for a number of reasons, not the least of which is that other attempts to define an inheritance model seem to have usually done likewise. However, we should add that we are actively investigating the possibility of revising our model slightly to include support for specialization by constraint at some future time. Space precludes detailed examination of this topic here; see the final section in this chapter, also Appendix C, for a more comprehensive discussion.

Back to TREAT UP *per se*. Now, we saw in the previous section that the assignment

```
THE_A ( E )  :=  LENGTH ( 5.0 ) ;
```

will fail on a run-time type error if the current value of E is of type CIRCLE, because THE_A does not apply to type CIRCLE for update purposes (see IM Proposal 26). By contrast, the assignment

```
THE_A ( TREAT_UP_AS_ELLIPSE ( E ) )  :=  LENGTH ( 5.0 ) ;
```

---

*We note that other writers use this term to mean something quite different (see, e.g., reference [116]).

will succeed, regardless of whether the current value is of type CIRCLE or merely of type ELLIPSE. In fact, this latter assignment can be regarded as shorthand for the following *multiple* assignment:

```
E                := TREAT_UP_AS_ELLIPSE ( E ) ,
THE_A ( E )  :=  LENGTH ( 5.0 ) ;
```

(The most specific type of E after this assignment will be ELLIPSE, regardless of what it was before.) In other words, we can avoid certain run-time type errors by judicious use of TREAT UP as a pseudovariable. Note carefully, however, that the specified target type *T* and the declared type *DT*(*SX*) of the argument *SX* must be identical when TREAT UP is used in this fashion (why?).

We further observe that TREAT UP is the key to the problem of changing the current most specific type of some variable *V* from *T1* to *T2* (say), where the declared type of *V* is some common supertype *T* (say) of *T1* and *T2* (note that—in accordance with IM Proposal 11—T1 and T2 must be disjoint). For example, suppose we extend the type hierarchy of Fig. 14.1 to include another type NONCIRCLE (an immediate subtype of ELLIPSE, like CIRCLE), and suppose once again that E is a variable of declared type ELLIPSE. Suppose further that *MST*(E) is NONCIRCLE (so THE_A(E) ≠ THE_B(E); this condition is a constraint on noncircles, in fact).* Now consider the following multiple assignment operation (we have numbered the steps for purposes of subsequent reference). *Note:* For the sake of the example, we assume that (a) as in Chapter 6, CAST_AS_*T*—CAST for short—is the explicit type conversion operator for conversion to type *T,* (b) CASTs from ellipses to circles and from ellipses to noncircles have in fact been defined, and (c) they have been given "sensible" semantics! With regard to point (c) here, by the way, note that the semantics of TREAT are *prescribed by the model;* those of CAST, by contrast, are up to the implementer.

```
1. E             :=  TREAT_UP_AS_ELLIPSE ( E ) ,
2. THE_A ( E )   :=  some value ,
3. E             :=  ( IF THE_A ( E )  =  THE_B ( E )
4.                        THEN CAST_AS_CIRCLE ( E )
5.                        ELSE CAST_AS_NONCIRCLE ( E )
6.                     END IF ) ;
```

Explanation: Step 1 ensures that the current value of E is "only" of type ELLIPSE (i.e., its current most specific type is ELLIPSE); Step 2 then updates the a semiaxis of E in some way. (In fact, of course, these first two steps could be collapsed into one by use of TREAT UP as a pseudovariable.) Step 3 then checks to see whether the *a* and *b* semiaxes of E are now equal. If they are, then E denotes a real-world circle, and Step 4 therefore sets its current most specific type to CIRCLE

---

*Since noncircles also inherit the constraint $a \geq b$ from type ELLIPSE, they are actually subject to the more specific constraint $a > b$.

(by converting it to that type); otherwise, Step 5 sets its current most specific type to NONCIRCLE (again, by converting it to that type). Note that the TREAT UP in Step 1 could be replaced by a CAST, if a CAST from circles to ellipses has been defined (but such a CAST has probably *not* been defined—see the discussion of OO Very Strong Suggestion 1 in Chapter 11). However, the CASTs in Steps 4 and 5 *cannot* be replaced by TREAT DOWNs (why not?).

It would obviously be possible (and in practice it might be desirable) to provide some kind of "update and change type" operator as a shorthand for the foregoing sequence of operations.

We should not leave this example without making another (important) point. In the real world, of course, every ellipse is either a circle or a noncircle. However, the system is not aware of this fact (because we have not told it). To be specific, we have told the system that every ellipse has $a \geq b$ and every circle has $a = b,$ and we might also have told it that every noncircle has $a > b,$ but we have not told it that $a = b$ means the ellipse is a circle and $a > b$ means it is a noncircle. Suppose now that we do inform the system of these latter facts (i.e., that every ellipse is actually either a circle or a noncircle). Then ELLIPSE becomes a dummy type! (Refer back to the section on IM Proposal 10 if you need to refresh your memory regarding this notion.) An immediate consequence is that the TREAT UP operation shown in our "change type" example now *will not work*—because, if no value has ELLIPSE as its most specific type, it is clearly not possible to TREAT UP some value to that type (recall that TREAT UP returns a value that has the specified target type as its most specific type).* In other words, our "change type" example now fails.

One possible way to work around this problem—not very elegant, we admit— is to introduce some kind of artificial but regular type FAKE_ELLIPSE as a proper supertype of ELLIPSE, with the same possible representation as ELLIPSE (and hence the same THE_ operators) but *without* the constraint that every "fake ellipse" is really a circle or a noncircle. Now we can modify our "change type" example to TREAT UP to FAKE_ELLIPSE instead of ELLIPSE, and the code will then work after all. *Note:* Once again it might be possible to define an "update and change type" operator as a shorthand for some such sequence of operations; alternatively, of course, we could define an "update and change type" *primitive* (but we prefer not to invent new primitive operators unless absolutely necessary). Overall, we feel this question requires further investigation.

Let us return to the topic of TREAT (UP or DOWN) *vs.* CAST. It is instructive to consider some of the differences between these operators a little further. Assume for the sake of the discussion that CASTs have indeed been defined (and given "sensible" semantics) both from ellipses to circles and—the remarks on this possibility under OO Very Strong Suggestion 1 in Chapter 11 notwithstanding—from

---

*IM Proposal 18 proposes that TREAT UP be supported "for every type T"—but if dummy types are supported, it will clearly have to be revised to say "for every *nondummy* type T."

circles to ellipses. Let variables E and C be of declared types ELLIPSE and CIRCLE, as usual. Then:

- TREAT_DOWN_AS_CIRCLE(E) succeeds if MST(E) is some subtype of CIRCLE, but gives a run-time type error otherwise, even if THE_A(E) = THE_B(E).
- CAST_AS_CIRCLE(E) succeeds if THE_A(E) = THE_B(E), even if MST(E) is ELLIPSE, but gives a run-time error (constraint violation) if THE_A(E) ≠ THE_B(E).
- TREAT_UP_AS_ELLIPSE(C) and CAST_AS_ELLIPSE(C) always succeed; in fact, they are logically equivalent.

In other words, treating (up or down), if successful, is equivalent to converting a given value to *a type that it already has*. Note, however, that for CAST and TREAT UP (but not TREAT DOWN), the result will "lose" any types—loosely speaking!—the original value might have had that are proper subtypes of the target type. One consequence of this fact is that while the expression

```
CAST_AS_CIRCLE ( TREAT_UP_AS_ELLIPSE ( C ) )
```

succeeds (producing a result of most specific type CIRCLE), the expression

```
TREAT_DOWN_AS_CIRCLE ( CAST_AS_ELLIPSE ( C ) )
```

fails on a run-time type error (or—better—a compile-time type error, if the compiler is alert). Of course, the expression

```
CAST_AS_CIRCLE ( CAST_AS_ELLIPSE ( C ) )
```

succeeds (in fact, it is effectively a no-op).

We remark that it would probably prove convenient in practice to support a new kind of relational expression* of the form

```
RX TREAT_UP_AS_T ( A )
```

Here *RX* is a relational expression, *A* is an attribute of the relation denoted by that expression, and *T* is a type. The overall expression is defined to be shorthand for the following:

```
( ( EXTEND ( RX ) ADD ( TREAT_UP_AS_T ( A ) ) AS A' )
                           { ALL BUT A } ) RENAME A' AS A
```

(where *A'* is an arbitrary name not already appearing as an attribute name in the result of evaluating *RX*).

---

*And a tuple expression analog, too, and corresponding tuple and relational pseudovariables.

We remark that a slightly more general form of TREAT UP could prove useful in practice:

```
TREAT_UP_TO_SAME_TYPE_AS ( SY, SX )
```

(where *SX* and *SY* are scalar expressions such that $DT(SY)$ is a supertype of $DT(SX)$). We define the semantics of this expression to be identical to those of the expression

```
TREAT_UP_AS_T ( SX )
```

where *T* is $DT(SY)$. The obvious relational expression analog should be supported too:

```
RX TREAT_UP_TO_SAME_TYPE_AS ( SY, A )
```

Two final points to close this section:

- Note first that there is a logical difference between TREAT UP and TREAT DOWN, even in the degenerate case in which the declared type $DT(SX)$ and the target type *T* are identical. To be specific, TREAT DOWN preserves $MST(SX)$ while TREAT UP does not.

- Second, note that the expression TREAT_UP_AS_ELLIPSE(*c*), where *c* is an expression denoting a value of type CIRCLE—i.e., $MST(c)$ is some subtype of CIRCLE—is logically equivalent to (and can thus be regarded as shorthand for) the following selector invocation:

```
ELLIPSE ( THE_R ( c ), THE_R ( c ), THE_CTR ( c ) )
```

As a consequence, the comparison (e.g.)

```
TREAT_UP_AS_ELLIPSE ( E ) = TREAT_UP_AS_ELLIPSE ( C )
```

is equivalent to the comparison

```
ELLIPSE ( THE_A ( E ), THE_B ( E ), THE_CTR ( E ) ) =
ELLIPSE ( THE_R ( C ), THE_R ( C ), THE_CTR ( C ) )
```

Likewise, the assignment (e.g.)

```
THE_A ( TREAT_UP_AS_ELLIPSE ( E ) )  := LENGTH ( 5.0 ) ;
```

is equivalent to the (multiple) assignment

```
E  :=  ELLIPSE ( THE_A ( E ), THE_B ( E ), THE_CTR ( E ) ) ,
THE_A ( E )  :=  LENGTH ( 5.0 ) ;
```

Note: A small issue arises in connection with this question of treating TREAT UP as a shorthand. Suppose type ELLIPSE has two distinct possible representations and hence two distinct selectors, *ES1* and *ES2,* say. Then an expression of the form TREAT_UP_AS_ELLIPSE (…) can be regarded equally well as shorthand for a certain *ES1* invocation or as shorthand for a certain *ES2* invocation. From the point of view of the model, of course, the point is of no concern (it makes no difference which invocation we choose to regard it as shorthand for); from the point of view of the implementation, however, it could conceivably be of concern (in particular, if the TREAT UP is actually implemented as a selector invocation).

IM PROPOSAL 19: LOGICAL OPERATOR IS_*T*(*SX*)

For every type T, *a logical operator of the form*

```
IS_T ( SX )
```

(or logical equivalent thereof) should be supported, where SX *is a scalar expression.* DT(*SX*) *must be a supertype of* T *(this is a compile-time check). The overall expression is defined to yield* true *if* SX *is of type* T, false *otherwise.*

———— ♦♦♦♦ ————

The general intent here is simply that defining a given scalar type should cause automatic definition of an operator for testing scalar values to see whether they are of the type in question. Note that (as stated) the declared type of the argument must be a supertype of the type in question; thus, for example, if E is a variable of declared type ELLIPSE, the expression

```
IS_SQUARE ( E )
```

is illegal (it will fail on a compile-time type error).

We note that a slightly more general form of this operator could prove useful in practice:

```
IS_SAME_TYPE_AS ( SY, SX )
```

(where *SX* and *SY* are scalar expressions such that *DT*(*SX*) is a supertype of *DT*(*SY*)). We define the semantics of this expression to be identical to those of the expression

```
IS_T ( SX )
```

where *T* is *DT*(*SY*).

IM PROPOSAL 20: RELATIONAL OPERATOR *RX*:IS_*T*(*A*)

For every type T, *a relational operator of the form*

```
RX : IS_T ( A )
```

(or logical equivalent thereof) should be supported. Here RX *is a relational expression and* A *is an attribute of the relation—r, say—denoted by that expression.*

The declared type DT(A) *of* A *must be a supertype of* T *(this is a compile-time check). The value of the overall expression is defined to be a relation with:*

a. *A heading the same as that of* r, *except that the declared type of attribute* A *in that heading is* T;

b. *A body consisting of those tuples of* r *in which attribute* A *contains a value of type* T, *except that the declared type of attribute* A *in each of those tuples is* T.

The intent of this proposal is illustrated by the following example. Suppose relvar R includes an attribute A of declared type ELLIPSE. Then (assuming the obvious operator precedence) the expression

```
R : IS_CIRCLE ( A ) WHERE THE_R ( A ) > LENGTH ( 2.0 )
```

returns those tuples of the current value of R in which the A value is a circle with radius greater than two—or, more precisely, it returns a relation with (a) the same heading as R, except that the declared type of attribute A in that result is CIRCLE instead of ELLIPSE, and (b) a body consisting of just those tuples from R in which the A value is of type CIRCLE and the radius for the circle in question is greater than two.

By contrast, the expression

```
R WHERE THE_R ( A ) > LENGTH ( 2.0 )
```

is illegal (it fails on a compile-time type error), since THE_R is not defined for type ELLIPSE, the declared type of attribute A of relation R.

Note that the (legal) expression

```
R : IS_CIRCLE ( A ) WHERE THE_R ( A ) > LENGTH ( 2.0 )
```

is almost but not quite equivalent to the following (also legal) expression:

```
R WHERE CASE
          WHEN IS_CIRCLE ( A ) THEN
              THE_R ( TREAT_DOWN_AS_CIRCLE ( A ) )
                                          > LENGTH ( 2.0 )
          WHEN NOT ( IS_CIRCLE ( A ) ) THEN FALSE
        END CASE
```

The difference is that this latter expression yields a relation with the same heading as R, rather than one in which the declared type of attribute A is CIRCLE instead of ELLIPSE.

More generally, however, the expression

```
RX : IS_T ( A )
```

is equivalent to—and is therefore shorthand for—the following expression:

```
( RX WHERE IS_T ( A ) ) TREAT_DOWN_AS_T ( A )
```

Moreover, this latter expression is itself shorthand for a longer one (see the remarks at the end of the section on IM Proposal 17).

We note finally that a slightly more general form of the "*RX*:IS_*T(A)*" operator could prove useful in practice:

```
RX : IS_SAME_TYPE_AS ( SY, A )
```

(where *SY* is a scalar expression such that *DT(A)* is a supertype of *DT(SY)*). We define the semantics of this expression to be identical to those of the expression

```
RX : IS_T ( A )
```

where *T* is *DT(SY)*.

IM PROPOSAL 21: LOGICAL OPERATOR IS_MS_*T(SX)*

For every type T, *a logical operator of the form*

```
IS_MS_T ( SX )
```

(or logical equivalent thereof) should be supported, where SX *is as under IM Proposal 19.* DT(SX) *must be a supertype of* T *(this is a compile-time check). The overall expression is defined to yield* true *if the current most specific type of* SX *is* T, false *otherwise.*

———— ♦♦♦♦♦ ————

The comments under IM Proposal 19 apply here also, *mutatis mutandis* (though it might help to observe that, e.g., whereas the operator IS_ELLIPSE is perhaps best rendered into natural language as "is an ellipse," the operator IS_MS_ELLIPSE is probably better rendered as "is *most specifically* an ellipse"). Here is an example:

```
VAR E ELLIPSE ;

IF IS_MS_ELLIPSE ( E )
   THEN ... ;      /* apply some ellipse-specific update to E */
                   /* (see IM Proposal 26)                    */
   ELSE ... ;      /* do something else                       */
END IF ;
```

Once again, a slightly more general form of this operator could prove useful in practice:

```
IS_SAME_MS_TYPE_AS ( SY, SX )
```

(where *SX* and *SY* are scalar expressions such that *DT(SX)* is a supertype of *DT(SY)*). We define the semantics of this expression to be identical to those of the expression

```
IS_MS_T ( SX )
```

where *T* is *MST*(*SY*). Here is an example to show one possible use of this latter form:

```
OPERATOR EQ ( E1 ELLIPSE, E2 ELLIPSE ) RETURNS ( BOOLEAN ) ;
    RETURN ( IS_SAME_MS_TYPE_AS ( E1, E2 ) AND
             THE_A ( E1 )   = THE_A ( E2 ) AND
             THE_B ( E1 )   = THE_B ( E2 ) AND
             THE_CTR ( E1 ) = THE_CTR ( E2 ) ) ;
END OPERATOR ;
```

EQ is the required "=" comparison operator for type ELLIPSE.

IM PROPOSAL 22: RELATIONAL OPERATOR *RX*:IS_MS_*T*(*A*)

For every type T, *a relational operator of the form*

```
RX : IS_MS_T ( A )
```

(or logical equivalent thereof) should be supported, where RX *and* A *are as under IM Proposal 20, and (also as under IM Proposal 20)* r *is the relation denoted by* RX. *The declared type* DT(A) *of* A *must be a supertype of* T *(this is a compile-time check). The value of the overall expression is defined to be a relation with:*

   a. *A heading the same as that of* r, *except that the declared type of attribute* A *in that heading is* T;

   b. *A body consisting of those tuples of* r *in which attribute* A *contains a value of most specific type* T, *except that the declared type of attribute* A *in each of those tuples is* T.

———— ♦♦♦♦♦ ————

The comments under IM Proposal 20 apply here also, *mutatis mutandis.* Note in particular that the expression

```
RX : IS_MS_T ( A )
```

is really just shorthand for the following expression:

```
( RX WHERE IS_MS_T ( A ) ) TREAT_DOWN_AS_T ( A )
```

Moreover, this latter expression in turn is itself shorthand for a longer one (see the remarks at the end of the section on IM Proposal 17).

A slightly more general form of the "*RX*:IS_MS_*T*(*A*)" operator could prove useful in practice:

```
RX : IS_SAME_MS_TYPE_AS ( SY, A )
```

(where *SY* is a scalar expression such that *DT*(*A*) is a supertype of *DT*(*SY*)). We define the semantics of this expression to be identical to those of the expression

```
    RX : IS_MS_T ( A )
```

where *T* is *MST(SY)*.

IM PROPOSAL 23: THE_ PSEUDOVARIABLES

For every component of every declared possible representation of every type, a THE_ pseudovariable (or logical equivalent) should be supported.

IM Proposal 23 essentially just repeats part of RM Prescription 5 (see Chapters 3 and 6), and of course we have made extensive use of THE_ pseudovariables in the examples in this chapter already. However, there are some important implications of the concept that come into play if subtyping is in effect, which we now discuss.

First, recall that we saw in our discussion of RM Prescription 5 in Chapter 6 that THE_ pseudovariables were logically unnecessary (at least in the absence of subtyping). For example, given variable E of declared type ELLIPSE, the assignment

```
    THE_CTR ( E )  :=  POINT ( X, Y ) ;
```

(which uses a THE_ pseudovariable) is logically equivalent to the assignment

```
    E  :=  ELLIPSE ( THE_A ( E ),
                     THE_B ( E ),
                     POINT ( X, Y ) ) ;
```

(which does not). However, we went on in Chapter 6 to say that pseudovariables did "seem intuitively more attractive than the alternative, and become even more so—though still not *logically* necessary—if type inheritance is supported." It is time to examine this latter claim.

For the sake of the example, therefore, let us add another type to the type hierarchy of Fig. 14.1, thus:

```
    TYPE COLORED_CIRCLE
         POSSREP ( R LENGTH, CTR POINT, COLOR COLOR )
         SUBTYPE_OF ( CIRCLE ) ;
```

(in fact, of course, we have already made use of this type in certain earlier examples). Suppose too that variable C is of declared type CIRCLE (not COLORED_CIRCLE):

```
    VAR C CIRCLE ;
```

We initialize C to some circle:

```
    C  :=  CIRCLE ( LENGTH ( 3.0 ),
                    POINT ( 0.0, 0.0 ) ) ;          /* for example */
```

Now suppose we "add some color to circle C":

```
C   :=  COLORED_CIRCLE ( THE_R ( C ),
                         THE_CTR ( C ),
                         COLOR ('Blue') ) ;
```

C now denotes "the same circle as before," but that circle is now colored (loosely speaking, its most specific type has changed—C has been *further specialized* to type COLORED_CIRCLE).

Now suppose the end user tells the system that the circle denoted by variable C (regardless of whether or not it is colored) is to have its radius increased to five. We might try the following:

```
C   :=  COLORED_CIRCLE
              ( LENGTH ( 5.0 ),
                THE_CTR ( C ),
                THE_COLOR
                  ( TREAT_DOWN_AS_COLORED_CIRCLE ( C ) ) ) ;
```

However, the TREAT DOWN here will give a run-time type error if the current value of C is only a circle, not a colored circle. (In general, of course, we cannot say for sure ahead of time which of the two possibilities is the case.)

Alternatively, we might try the following:

```
C   :=  CIRCLE ( LENGTH ( 5.0 ),
                 THE_CTR ( C ) ) ;
```

But now, if the previous value of C was in fact a colored circle, its color will be lost (the expression on the right hand side of the assignment returns "just a circle," not a colored circle). Indeed, an attempt to TREAT DOWN the variable C as a colored circle will fail after this assignment, even if it succeeded before.

We might of course try something like this:

```
C   :=  CASE
            WHEN IS_COLORED_CIRCLE ( C ) THEN COLORED_CIRCLE
                      ( LENGTH ( 5.0 ),
                        THE_CTR ( C ),
                        THE_COLOR
                          ( TREAT_DOWN_AS_COLORED_CIRCLE ( C ) ) )
            WHEN IS_CIRCLE ( C ) THEN CIRCLE
                      ( LENGTH ( 5.0 ),
                        THE_CTR ( C ) )
        END CASE ;
```

The drawbacks to this approach are surely obvious, however; thus, the pseudovariable equivalent

```
THE_R ( C )  :=  LENGTH ( 5.0 ) ;
```

does seem preferable.*

---

*We are making a tacit but reasonable assumption here that the pseudovariable THE_R that applies to variables of type CIRCLE applies to variables of type COLORED_CIRCLE too. See IM Proposal 26.

We must stress, however, that we are only talking about syntax here (the pseudovariable version is really just shorthand for the longer version, and there are no *logical* differences involved). But it is probably fair to say that THE_ pseudovariables, or something logically equivalent to them, are effectively required in practice in order to support inheritance and subtyping properly.

IM PROPOSAL 24: READ-ONLY OPERATOR INHERITANCE AND VALUE SUBSTITUTABILITY

Let Op *be a read-only operator, let* P *be a parameter to* Op, *and let* T *be the declared type for* P. *Then the most specific type of the argument value* v *corresponding to parameter* P *in some invocation of* Op *can be **any subtype** T′ of* T. *In other words, the read-only operator* Op *applies to values of type* T *and therefore, necessarily, to values of type* T′—The Principle of **(Read-only) Operator Inheritance.** *It follows that such operators are* polymorphic, *since they apply to values of several different types*—The Principle of **(Read-only) Operator Polymorphism.** *And it further follows that wherever a value of type* T *is permitted, a value of any proper subtype* T′ *of* T *is also permitted*—The Principle of **(Value) Substitutability.**

———— ♦♦♦♦ ————

Result Covariance

As we have already seen, subtyping implies that a reference to a *variable* of declared type *T* can in fact denote a value of any subtype of *T*. What we have not explicitly mentioned prior to this point is that it also implies that an invocation of a *read-only operator* with declared result type *T* can likewise denote a value of any subtype of *T*. This latter fact is an immediate consequence of *The Principle of Value Substitutability,* as can be seen from the following example:

```
OPERATOR EORC ( B BOOLEAN ) RETURNS ( ELLIPSE ) ;
   RETURN ( IF B THEN ELLIPSE ( ... )
                 ELSE CIRCLE ( ... )
            END IF ) ;
END OPERATOR ;
```

Because of value substitutability, we are acting within our rights when we specify a circle instead of an ellipse in the ELSE clause here; thus, an invocation of the read-only operator EORC returns either a circle or just an ellipse, depending on the value of its BOOLEAN argument B.

Here is a simpler example that illustrates much the same point:

```
OPERATOR COPY ( E ELLIPSE ) RETURNS ( ELLIPSE ) ;
   RETURN ( E ) ;
END OPERATOR ;
```

An invocation of COPY returns either a circle or just an ellipse, depending on the value of its ELLIPSE argument E.

This property—that if *Op* is a read-only operator, then the most specific type of the value returned from an invocation of *Op* can be any proper subtype *RT'* of the declared type *RT* of the result—is sometimes referred to as *result covariance* (although we dislike this term for several reasons and do not use it much ourselves).* Note carefully that the property can apply:

- Even if *Op* is not explicitly specialized as described in the subsection "Explicit Specialization" below (see both EORC and COPY for examples), and

- Even if no argument has a most specific type that is a proper subtype of the declared type of the corresponding parameter (see EORC for an example).

Now we can explain the remark we made in the section on IM Proposal 14, to the effect that (a) the fact that the user might have to know which version of a given polymorphic operator *Op* is invoked does not undermine (b) our claim that the user's perception is still that there is really just a single operator. The point is, the semantics of *Op* can and should be explained to the user in such a way as to take into account any variations in the most specific types of its arguments (if necessary). For example, the semantics of COPY are simply that it returns a copy of its argument; thus, if it is passed a circle, it returns a circle, and if it is passed "just an ellipse," it returns "just an ellipse." And the semantics of EORC are that it returns either a circle or "just an ellipse," depending on the value (TRUE or FALSE) of its argument B.

Note incidentally that the "result covariance" property does not apply to selector operators—see RM Prescriptions 1 and 4 in Chapters 3 and 6—which must, by definition, return a value whose most specific type is exactly the specified type, not some proper subtype of that type. By contrast, the property does apply to THE_ operators, in general.

Argument Contravariance

Another concept, related (somewhat) to result covariance, is also described in the literature: *argument contravariance*. We do not wish to incorporate this concept into our own inheritance model; in fact, we believe it stems from a confusion over the

---

*To elaborate briefly: The property is presumably called *covariance* on the grounds that the type of the result "covaries" with the type of the argument (which is exactly what happens in the COPY example). But there seems to be a tacit assumption that there is exactly one argument! In the case of the operator MOVE, for example (discussed in the subsection "Argument Contravariance" later), the result type covaries with the type of the first argument but not with that of the second. And the result type can "covary" even if the argument type remains fixed (see the EORC example), or even if there are no arguments at all (imagine an operator that returns a circle on weekdays but just an ellipse at weekends).

model *vs.* implementation distinction, and quite possibly from a flawed definition of the very concept of *subtype.** However, we do think it worth trying to explain what the concept is, in order to be able to explain exactly why we reject it. By way of an example, therefore, consider the operator MOVE defined as follows:

```
OPERATOR MOVE ( E ELLIPSE, S SQUARE ) RETURNS ( ELLIPSE )
   VERSION ES_MOVE ;
   /* "moves" E so that it is centered on center of S; */
   /* more precisely, returns an ellipse just like E   */
   /* except that it is centered on the center of S    */
   ... ;
END OPERATOR ;
```

The VERSION specification in the second line here introduces a distinguishing name, ES_MOVE, for this particular *version* of the MOVE operator. *Note:* You might well be wondering what exactly that MOVE operator is that ES_MOVE is "a version of." The discussion that follows is aimed, in part, precisely at answering this question.

Now let us assume an *explicit specialization*—i.e., another version—of MOVE has been defined that moves circles instead of ellipses:

```
OPERATOR MOVE ( C CIRCLE, ... ) RETURNS ( CIRCLE )
   VERSION C_MOVE ;
   /* this explicit specialization of MOVE to circles might */
   /* not be needed in practice -- see IM Proposal 26        */
   ... ;
END OPERATOR ;
```

Now suppose variables E and S are of declared types ELLIPSE and SQUARE, respectively. Suppose further that the current value of E is of type CIRCLE. Now consider the MOVE invocation

```
MOVE ( E, S )
```

The system performs a compile-time type check on this expression; that check succeeds, of course. Then, at run time, it discovers that the current most specific type of E is CIRCLE and therefore invokes the version of MOVE that applies to circles (i.e., the version called C_MOVE). Moreover, it also discovers that the current most specific type of the other argument S is SQUARE. It follows that the declared type of the *parameter* corresponding to that other argument, in that version C_MOVE of MOVE, can be *any proper supertype* of SQUARE—RECTANGLE, for example, as here:

---

*The definition in question is flawed because it is circular (not recursive!): "A type T' is a subtype of a type T if … for each method M of T there is a corresponding method M' of T' such that … the ith argument type of M is a subtype of the ith argument type of M' *(rule of contravariance in arguments)* …" (paraphrased from reference [9]). In other words, the concept of some type being a subtype of another relies on the concept of some type being a subtype of another. Note too that the definition seems to be saying that T' is a subtype of T if substitutability applies, whereas we would say the opposite (i.e., that substitutability applies if T' is a subtype of T).

```
OPERATOR MOVE ( C CIRCLE, R RECTANGLE ) RETURNS ( CIRCLE )
   VERSION CR_MOVE ;
   /* explicit specialization of MOVE to circles,      */
   /* now renamed and showing declared type of second */
   /* parameter as RECTANGLE                           */
   ... ;
END OPERATOR ;
```

This property—that if the declared type of one parameter to operator *Op* (in some version of *Op*) is further specialized, then the declared type of another parameter (in that same version of *Op*) can be further generalized—is the *argument contravariance* property (although we dislike this term for several reasons and do not use it much ourselves).* Note carefully that, unlike "result covariance," "argument contravariance" *must* be made explicit (by defining explicit specializations of the operator in question), because it refers to the *declared* types of parameters to such specializations.

In any case (and as already indicated), we prefer not to talk very much about "argument contravariance," as such, at all; it seems clearer to us to talk in terms of *restrictions on argument type combinations.* Consider the operator MOVE once again. Presumably what the MOVE definer will do is tell the user that MOVE is an operator that takes two arguments, of types ELLIPSE and RECTANGLE respectively, and returns a result of type ELLIPSE (after all, to the user there is just one MOVE operator). Then, because of value substitutability, the user knows that:

- The arguments to any given MOVE invocation can be of *any subtypes* of ELLIPSE and RECTANGLE, respectively.
- The result can be of *any subtype* of ELLIPSE.[†]

However, *certain combinations of most specific argument types are illegal.* To be precise, the combination ELLIPSE-SQUARE (which gives a result of most specific type ELLIPSE) and the combination CIRCLE-RECTANGLE (which gives a result of most specific type CIRCLE) are both legal, but the combination ELLIPSE-RECTANGLE is not.

So the obvious question arises: Why did the MOVE definer impose such a strange restriction in the first place? Does it not constitute a violation of value substitutability? (After all, ELLIPSE is a subtype of ELLIPSE and RECTANGLE is a subtype of RECTANGLE, so we should surely be able to invoke the operator and pass it an ellipse *per se* and a rectangle *per se*.) In fact, the restriction might be

---

*To elaborate briefly: The property is presumably called *contravariance* on the grounds that the type of one parameter "contravaries" with that of another. But there seems to be a tacit assumption that there are exactly two parameters! In the case of MOVE, there are indeed two parameters, which "contravary"; but what if there had been three? Also, of course, it is really *parameters* that "contravary," not *arguments,* so at the very least the term should be *parameter* contravariance.

[†] Though it must have the same most specific type as the first argument, because of the semantics of the operator. More generally, of course, the user must be aware of the exact logical effect of *any* combination of most specific argument types on *any* invocation of *any* operator (as already mentioned in the previous subsection).

regarded as a violation of *orthogonality* too, because there is an unpleasant—and un-explained—interdependence between the two arguments to any given invocation.

For such reasons, we reject the "argument contravariance" concept. In its place, we propose simply that read-only operators always be defined in such a way as to allow the most specific type of any given argument to be the same as the declared type of the corresponding parameter. Indeed, it seems perverse to us to do otherwise.

Explicit Specialization

Although the point is not strictly part of the model *per se,* it is important to under-stand that if the code that implements a given operator *Op* needs access to some pos-sible representation* of some argument value *v* that is defined only if *v* is of type *T'* and not just of type *T,* then—as explained under IM Proposal 13—two versions of that code will have to exist under the covers. As already mentioned several times, we refer to the requisite definition of the second version in such a situation as an *ex-plicit specialization* of *Op.* (More precisely, we refer to the definition of the version of the code to deal with the case where the argument corresponding to parameter *P* is of type *T'* as "an explicit specialization of *Op* to deal with the case where the ar-gument corresponding to parameter *P* is of type *T'.*")

As also explained under IM Proposal 13 earlier, explicit specialization might also be desirable, even if logically unnecessary, if improved efficiency is required and can be achieved by such means. Moreover, it is never logically wrong to define an explicit specialization, regardless of whether it is logically necessary. *Note:* If no explicit specialization is needed and none is defined, then (as mentioned under IM Proposal 13) we have *code reuse:* The very same implementation code can operate upon arguments of different types. Observe, however, that here we are talking about reuse of "under the covers" code, not reuse of some program that merely *invokes* that "under the covers" code.

Now, the fact that explicit specialization is always at least legal has a very im-portant consequence: Namely, it opens up the possibility of *changing the semantics* of the operator in question. Moreover, such a change might even be claimed to be desirable. For example, let type TOLL_HIGHWAY be a proper subtype of type HIGHWAY, and let TRAVEL_TIME be an operator that computes the time it takes to travel between two specified points on a specified highway. For a toll highway, the formula is $(d/s) + (n*t),$ where d = distance, s = speed, n = number of tollbooths, and t = time spent at each tollbooth; for a nontoll highway, by contrast, the formula is just $d/s.$[†]

---

*Or (worse) some actual representation.

[†]Indeed, the explicit specialization of TRAVEL_TIME for TOLL_HIGHWAY could be defined by "treating up" the toll highway as a highway, invoking TRAVEL_TIME for HIGHWAY on the result (thereby determining the travel time as if the toll highway were just a regular highway), and then adding in the time spent at tollbooths.

By way of a counterexample—i.e., an example of a situation in which such a change is definitely *un*desirable—consider ellipses and circles once again. Presumably we would like the AREA operator to be defined in such a way that the comparison

```
AREA ( C ) = AREA ( TREAT_UP_AS_ELLIPSE ( C ) )
```

(where C is of declared type CIRCLE) always gives *true*. However, this would-be requirement is not enforceable; that is, there is little or nothing to stop AREA from being explicitly specialized for circles in such a way as to return, e.g., the circumference instead of the area (though careful type design might help to alleviate such problems somewhat).

We return to the TRAVEL_TIME example to make another point. The fact is, we find that example unconvincing (unconvincing, that is, as an example of a situation in which changing the semantics of an operator might be thought desirable). For consider:

- If TOLL_HIGHWAY is truly a subtype of HIGHWAY, it means by definition that every individual toll highway is in fact a highway.

- Thus, some highways (i.e., some values of type HIGHWAY) are indeed toll highways—they do indeed have tollbooths. So type HIGHWAY is not "highways without tollbooths," it is "highways with *n* tollbooths" (where *n* might be zero).

- So the operator TRAVEL_TIME for type HIGHWAY is not "compute the travel time for a highway *without* tollbooths," it is "compute the travel time for a highway *ignoring* tollbooths" (another logical difference here!).

- The operator TRAVEL_TIME for type TOLL_HIGHWAY, by contrast, is "compute the travel time for a highway *with* tollbooths." So we have found another logical difference—the two TRAVEL_TIMEs are logically different operators. Confusion arises because those two different operators have been given the same name (and so we have *overloading* polymorphism instead of *inclusion* polymorphism).

Thus, we are still not convinced that changing operator semantics is ever a good idea. We would prefer to insist that, in general, if *v* is a value of type *T′*, then the two expressions *Op* (...,*v*,...) and *Op* (...,TREAT_UP_AS_*T*(*v*),...) always give the same result. As we have seen, this requirement is unenforceable; however, we can certainly define our inheritance model to say that if the two expressions do *not* give the same result, then the implementation is in violation—i.e., it is not an implementation of the model, and the implications are unpredictable.* Indeed, it could be argued that the ability to change operator semantics (or, rather, the fact that some

---

*Of course, our "hard line" position on this matter does not preclude support for genuine overloading polymorphism. The **Tutorial D** COUNT operator provides an example, since it can be used to obtain the cardinality either of an array or of a relation.

writers seem to regard that ability as a virtue) is—like "argument contravariance" earlier—a case of the implementation tail wagging the model dog.

Observe that our position here does mean that, regardless of whether any explicit specializations of operator *Op* are defined, the user perception remains the same: namely, that (a) there exists a read-only operator—a *single* read-only operator—called *Op,* and (b) that operator *Op* applies to argument values of type *T* and hence, by definition, to argument values of any proper subtype of *T*.

One last point on explicit specialization: As already indicated, we propose that it be possible, as part of the definition of any version of a given operator, to introduce a unique *version name*. For example:

```
OPERATOR AREA ( E ELLIPSE ) RETURNS ( AREA )
   VERSION E_AREA ;
      ... ;
END OPERATOR ;

OPERATOR AREA ( C CIRCLE ) RETURNS ( AREA )
   VERSION C_AREA ;
      ... ;
END OPERATOR ;
```

Now, e.g., the operator

```
DROP OPERATOR VERSION C_AREA ;
```

can be used to drop a particular version, while the operator

```
DROP OPERATOR AREA ;
```

can be used to drop the operator entirely (i.e., all versions).

As noted in Chapter 5, it might even be desirable to allow the definition of the specification signature for a given operator and the definitions of *all* of the implementations (i.e., versions) of that operator to be completely separated. For example:

```
OPERATOR AREA ( E ELLIPSE ) RETURNS ( AREA )
END OPERATOR ; /* definition of specification signature only */

OPERATOR AREA VERSION E_AREA ( E ELLIPSE ) RETURNS ( AREA ) ;
                  /* ellipse version -- note version signature */
   RETURN ( 3.14159 * THE_A ( E ) * THE_B ( E ) ) ;
END OPERATOR ;

OPERATOR AREA VERSION C_AREA ( C CIRCLE ) RETURNS ( AREA ) ;
                   /* circle version -- note version signature */
   RETURN ( 3.14159 * ( THE_R ( C ) ** 2 ) ) ;
END OPERATOR ;
```

See the subsection immediately following for further explanation.

Signatures

We can define the term *signature* (or, rather, *operator* signature), somewhat loosely, as the combination of the name of the operator in question and the types of the operands to that operator. As you have probably come to expect by now, however, we need to be very careful once again over (a) the difference between arguments and parameters, (b) the difference between declared types and actual types, and (c) the difference between operators as seen by the user and operators as seen by the system (i.e., explicit specializations or versions under the covers). In fact, we need to distinguish at least three different kinds of signatures for any given operator *Op:**

- A single *specification signature,* which consists of the operator name *Op* together with the declared types, in order, of the parameters to *Op* as specified to the user by the *Op* definer. This signature corresponds to operator *Op* as understood by the user.

- A set of *version signatures,* one for each explicit specialization or implementation version of *Op,* each consisting of the operator name *Op* together with the declared types, in order, of the parameters defined for that version. These signatures correspond to the various pieces of implementation code that implement *Op* under the covers.

- A set of *invocation signatures,* one for each possible combination of most specific argument types, each consisting of the operator name *Op* together with the corresponding combination of most specific argument types, in order. These signatures correspond to various possible invocations of *Op.*

Different invocation signatures involving the same operator thus correspond, at least potentially, to different implemented versions under the covers of the operator in question (i.e., different specializations). Thus, if several versions of "the same" operator do in fact exist under the covers, then which version is invoked on any given occasion will depend on which version signature is the best match for the applicable invocation signature. The process of deciding that best match (i.e., the process of deciding which version to invoke) is known variously as—among many other things—*run-time binding* (our own preferred term) or *dynamic binding* or *dynamic dispatch* or *subject routine determination* or *function resolution.*

Let *Op* be a polymorphic operator, then, and let *OpI* be some invocation of *Op.* As we have just seen, the specific version of *Op* to be invoked for *OpI* will be determined on the basis of consideration of the most specific types of the arguments to that invocation *OpI. We suggest that every argument should be able to participate equally in this process.* In other words (and as in fact previously indicated under OO Very Strong Suggestion 2 in Chapter 11), we do not much care for the notion, supported by certain object systems, that an operator might have a special "distinguished" or "receiver" or "target" parameter that plays some special role in the run-time binding process.†

Note: There is a well-known practical—though not unsolvable—problem here. Suppose, for example, that (a) operator *Op* has a specification signature

---

*We should note too that different writers and different languages ascribe slightly different meanings to the term "signature" anyway. For example, the result type is sometimes regarded as part of the signature; so too are operand and result names.

† In fact we find that notion somewhat illogical. However, we should point out that the issue is primarily one of syntax and implementation, of little significance to the model as such.

involving two parameters, both of declared type ELLIPSE; (b) explicit special-izations (versions) are defined for the most specific argument type combinations ELLIPSE-ELLIPSE, ELLIPSE-CIRCLE, and CIRCLE-ELLIPSE (only); and (c) *Op* is invoked with the most specific argument type combination CIRCLE-CIRCLE. Note that the invocation signature in this example does not exactly match *any* of the corresponding version signatures. Clearly, rules are needed in order to de-termine which particular version should be invoked. (Observe carefully, however, that once again this is an implementation issue, not a model issue. See the subsec-tion immediately following.)

Implications for the Model

To conclude this section, we remark that many of the concepts that we have been discussing at such length—*inclusion polymorphism, value substitutability, result covariance, argument contravariance, explicit specialization (versions), code reuse, version signatures, invocation signatures,* and *run-time binding*—are not really fea-tures of the *model,* as such, at all (despite the fact that you do need to understand them in order to appreciate what inheritance and subtyping are all about). The only relevant concept that is truly part of the model is this: "To say that T' is a subtype of T means, by definition, that read-only operators that apply to values of type T apply to values of type T' also"—and the rest follows.

IM PROPOSAL 25: READ-ONLY PARAMETERS TO UPDATE OPERATORS

> *Let* Op *be an update operator and let* P *be a parameter to* Op *that is not subject to update. Then* Op *behaves as a* read-only *operator so far as* P *is concerned, and all aspects of IM Proposal 24 therefore apply,* mutatis mutandis *(except for the prop-erty of "result covariance"—update operators do not return a result).*

——— ♦♦♦♦♦ ———

This proposal does not seem to require any further explanation.*

IM PROPOSAL 26: UPDATE OPERATOR INHERITANCE AND VARIABLE SUBSTITUTABILITY

> *Let* Op *be an update operator, let* P *be a parameter to* Op *that is subject to update, and let* T *be the declared type for* P. *Then it might or might not be the case that the*

---

*Except to note that we have revised the wording from Chapter 13 in a very minor way, as you might have noticed.

current most specific type of the argument variable V *corresponding to parameter* P *in some invocation of* Op *can be a proper subtype* T′ *of type* T. *It follows that for each such update operator* Op *and for each parameter* P *to* Op *that is subject to update, it is necessary to state explicitly for which subtypes* T′ *of the declared type* T *of parameter* P *operator* Op *is inherited*—The Principle of **(Update) Operator Inheritance.** *Update operators are thus only conditionally polymorphic*—The Principle of **(Update) Operator Polymorphism.** *If* Op *is an update operator and* P *is a parameter to* Op *that is subject to update and* T′ *is a subtype of the declared type* T *of* P *for which* Op *is inherited, then by definition* Op *can be invoked with an argument variable* V *corresponding to parameter* P *that is of current most specific type* T′—The Principle of **(Variable) Substitutability.**

First of all, let us explain why update operators cannot always be inherited unconditionally. Let variables S and R have declared types SQUARE and RECTANGLE, respectively (where SQUARE is a proper subtype of RECTANGLE, of course). Then—speaking *very* loosely!—it might be possible to change the height of R without changing its width; more precisely, it might be possible to perform an update operation on R that replaces the current value, *r* say (where *r* is a rectangle, by definition), by a new value *r′* that is a rectangle with the same width but a different height. However, it is certainly not possible to do the same thing to S, because squares must always have equal height and width. In other words, a certain update operator ("change height") might be defined for type RECTANGLE but not for type SQUARE.

For a more probing example, we return to the MOVE operator from our discussion of IM Proposal 24 two sections back. Previously, we defined two versions of that operator, one for moving ellipses and one for moving circles. Here are those two definitions, now shown complete:

```
OPERATOR MOVE ( E ELLIPSE, R RECTANGLE ) RETURNS ( ELLIPSE )
   VERSION ER_MOVE ;
   RETURN
      ( ELLIPSE ( THE_A ( E ), THE_B ( E ), THE_CTR ( R ) ) ) ;
END OPERATOR ;

OPERATOR MOVE ( C CIRCLE, R RECTANGLE ) RETURNS ( CIRCLE )
   VERSION CR_MOVE ;
   RETURN
      ( CIRCLE ( THE_R ( C ), THE_CTR ( R ) ) ) ;
END OPERATOR ;
```

Note: In accordance with our rejection of the notion of "argument contravariance," we now show the declared type of the second parameter as RECTANGLE in both cases. We also assume that an operator THE_CTR ("the center of") is defined for that type. (Observe, therefore, that THE_CTR is overloaded!—it applies to both type RECTANGLE and type ELLIPSE, neither of which is a subtype of the other. Also, types ELLIPSE and RECTANGLE have no common supertype to which

THE_CTR could sensibly apply, so they cannot be regarded as inheriting that operator from any common supertype, either.)

Now, we also remarked in our earlier discussion of MOVE, in a comment on the explicit specialization for circles, that that explicit specialization might not be needed in practice. Now we can explain that comment. Recall that the purpose of MOVE is to "move" its first argument so that it is centered on the center of the second; more precisely, an invocation of MOVE returns a result that is just like its first argument except that it is "located somewhere else" (it is, to repeat, centered on the center of the second argument). Note that the operator is defined to be read-only and therefore does indeed return a result. What we could do instead, however, is define MOVE to be an *update* operator, thus:

```
OPERATOR MOVE ( E ELLIPSE, R RECTANGLE ) UPDATES ( E )
   VERSION ER_MOVE ;
   THE_CTR ( E )   :=   THE_CTR ( R ) ;
END OPERATOR ;
```

Observe that—quite apart from the obvious fact that the code is now a little more compact—an invocation of this version of MOVE *updates its first argument* (loosely, it "changes the center" of that argument; note the UPDATES specification, which replaces the RETURNS specification from the read-only versions). Note further that the update works *regardless of whether that first argument is of most specific type ELLIPSE or most specific type CIRCLE.* In other words, the explicit specialization for circles is no longer needed!

We see, therefore, that one advantage of update operators in general is that they save us from having to write out certain explicit operator specializations. In particular, note the implications for program maintenance. Suppose, for example, that once again we introduce the type COLORED_CIRCLE as an immediate subtype of CIRCLE. If we treat MOVE as we did originally, as a read-only operator, we would now have to write out another explicit specialization, thus:

```
OPERATOR MOVE ( C COLORED_CIRCLE, R RECTANGLE )
   RETURNS ( COLORED_CIRCLE )
   VERSION CCR_MOVE ;
   RETURN
     ( COLORED_CIRCLE ( THE_R ( C ), THE_CTR ( R ),
                                     THE_COLOR ( C ) ) ) ;
END OPERATOR ;
```

If we treat MOVE as an update operator, by contrast, no such explicit specialization is needed. *Note:* We remind the reader in passing, however, that explicit specialization might be desirable, or even necessary, if the operator code needs access to a possible—or actual—representation component that exists only at the subtype level, or if more efficiency is desired and can be achieved by means of such explicit specialization.*

———————————

*Or (we add, grudgingly) if either "argument contravariance" or a change in semantics is desired.

The net of the foregoing is this: Although (as we should perhaps remind you) assignment is the only update operator that is logically necessary, it is highly convenient in practice to allow others as well, like our MOVE operator. In other words, it is probably fair to say that update operators are effectively required in practice in order to support subtyping and inheritance properly.

Note: For completeness, we observe that (as noted under IM Proposal 25) the property of "result covariance" does not apply to update operators, since update operators do not return a result. The property of "argument contravariance" does apply, but we reject that concept anyway. The remarks regarding explicit specialization (versions), code reuse, signatures, and run-time binding in the section on IM Proposal 24 apply to update operators also, *mutatis mutandis*.

We would like to stress the point that (to repeat) update operator inheritance is *not* unconditional in our model. Essentially, what this means is that *which update operators are inherited by which subtypes must be specified explicitly*. For example, the following update operators apply to variables of current most specific type ELLIPSE:

- assignment to THE_A, THE_B, THE_CTR
- MOVE (update version)

The following update operators apply to variables of current most specific type CIRCLE:

- assignment to THE_CTR and THE_R but *not* to THE_A and THE_B
- MOVE (update version)

That is, the definer of type CIRCLE will specify that MOVE (update version) and pseudovariable THE_CTR are inherited by type CIRCLE from type ELLIPSE, while pseudovariables THE_A and THE_B are not.

In order to illustrate some of the consequences of the foregoing, let us assume once again that variables E and C are of declared types ELLIPSE and CIRCLE, respectively. Then:

- The system *will* probably be aware that THE_A(C) and THE_B(C) must return the same value (as noted earlier, this is just a constraint on type CIRCLE).
- An attempt to assign to THE_A(C) or THE_B(C) will give a compile-time type error, because these pseudovariables are not available for variables of (declared) type CIRCLE.
- An attempt to assign to THE_A(E) or THE_B(E) will give a run-time type error if the most specific type of E is CIRCLE, because these pseudovariables are not available for variables of (current) type CIRCLE.

As already noted under IM Proposal 17, this last point unfortunately does mean that now we can incur some additional run-time type errors (run-time type errors, that is, that do not arise in the context of a TREAT DOWN). The general rule is as follows:

■ Let *Op* be an update operator, let *P* be a parameter to *Op* that is subject to update, let the declared type of *P* be *T,* and let *T′* be a subtype of *T* for which *Op* is not inherited for parameter *P*. If *Op* is invoked with an argument variable *V* corresponding to parameter *P* that is of current most specific type *T′*—a state of affairs that could arise because of value substitutability—then a run-time type error occurs.

There are some implications for code reuse here, of course. For example, we said in Chapter 12 that a program *P* that works for ellipses might work for circles too, even if type CIRCLE had not even been defined at the time program *P* was written. However, we now see that if *P* includes an update of the form (say)

```
THE_A ( E )  :=  ... ;
```

then *P* will fail at run time if the current most specific type of variable E is CIRCLE. But this problem is intrinsic! Reuse is, by definition, easier to achieve for read-only operators than it is for update operators, and in certain circumstances it *cannot* be achieved.

Of course, we can avoid the run-time error in this particular example by replacing the assignment shown by the following one:

```
THE_A ( TREAT_UP_AS_ELLIPSE ( E ) )  :=  ... ;
```

The message once again is: Code defensively!

We close this section by admitting that this issue of update operator inheritance is one in which our thinking might be regarded as a little heretical. Other writers disagree with us on this issue; more specifically, they feel that update operators, like read-only operators, should be inherited *unconditionally,* whereas we want them to be inherited only where they make sense.

Now, it is true that unconditional inheritance of such operators might allow a program that updates ellipses to "work" for circles too, and hence that the approach might provide more reuse than ours does. But what does it mean to say that such a program "works"? In all probability, it will produce a nonsensical result, involving (e.g.) "nonsquare squares" or "noncircular circles." In other words, those other writers run into a variety of logical problems and other undesirable consequences that we avoid (see, e.g., references [98] and [116]). For example:

■ They require update operators to return a value, thereby allowing retrieval operations to have the side effect of updating the database (see the discussion of RM Prescription 3 in Chapter 6);

■ Or they allow (e.g.) a value of type SQUARE to have sides of different lengths, thereby violating its own "squareness," undermining the database "as a model of reality," and causing programs to produce nonsensical results such as "nonsquare squares" or "noncircular circles";

- Or they simply do not support type constraints at all (see Appendix C for a detailed discussion of this particular—and important—issue);

and so on. But the common thread running through all such thinking is—it seems to us—*a failure to make a clear distinction between values and variables.* To us, by contrast, that distinction is both crucial and fundamental; indeed, as explained in Chapter 1, we regard it as one of the great *logical differences*—one that underlies and buttresses our thinking throughout the entire *Manifesto,* including of course the inheritance proposals discussed in this chapter specifically.

WHAT ABOUT SPECIALIZATION BY CONSTRAINT?

In this, the final section of the chapter, we offer a few observations on the topic of "specialization by constraint." Just to remind you, we use this term to refer to the notion that the system might be aware after all that (e.g.) an ellipse with equal semi-axes *a* and *b* should really be of type CIRCLE. In the body of this chapter we have presented—in considerable detail—a model of type inheritance that excludes this concept (in large part because other inheritance models mostly seem to have done the same thing). We are, however, actively exploring the possibility of swimming against the tide of convention here and adjusting our model to include the concept after all. Details of that possibility are presented in the final section of Appendix C; here we simply note a number of benefits that seem to be direct consequences of such support, if it can indeed be achieved.

- The model becomes "more faithful to reality" and more intuitively acceptable. For example, it is no longer the case that values of most specific type ELLIPSE might correspond to real-world circles.

- Noncircular circles and similar nonsenses cannot occur.

- More compile-time type checking can be done.

- Fewer run-time type errors can occur; in fact, they can occur solely on an attempt to TREAT DOWN a value to a type it does not possess, as originally intended. (In particular, the type errors identified in connection with Assignments 2 and 3 under IM Proposal 17 can no longer occur.)

- Assignments become simpler (especially assignments to THE_ pseudovariables, which no longer involve a complicated CASE expression in their expansion).

- Changing types is easy. That is, given (say) types ELLIPSE, CIRCLE, and NONCIRCLE, in order to "change the type" of variable E from CIRCLE to NONCIRCLE, it is sufficient just to update the variable E appropriately. There is no need to use "TREAT UP to ELLIPSE" as a preliminary step, and there is no need for the type FAKE_ELLIPSE (in the case where ELLIPSE is a dummy type).

- Comparisons no longer need TREAT UP. In fact, TREAT UP becomes completely unnecessary and can be dropped (of course, it was only shorthand anyway).

- The rules regarding inheritance of update operators now apply to declared types only, instead of most specific types.

- More code reuse is achievable; programs are more immune to the introduction of new subtypes (e.g., a program that assigns to THE_A(E) will now still work after type CIRCLE is introduced).

- There is never any logical need to CAST (e.g.) a value of type ELLIPSE to type CIRCLE (and so the operator itself is unnecessary).

It should be clear that support for specialization by constraint seems highly desirable! Refer to the final section of Appendix C for further discussion.

Multiple Inheritance

INTRODUCTION

In this chapter we consider what is involved in extending our model of subtyping and inheritance as described in the last two chapters to include support for multiple inheritance as well. Loosely, multiple inheritance means that a given subtype might have more than one supertype, and might therefore inherit operators (and constraints) from more than one supertype. As noted in Chapter 12, we do believe that support for multiple inheritance is desirable. To quote reference [112]: "Most modern . . . systems allow [multiple inheritance]. . . . A generally accepted view is that a modern . . . language should support [multiple inheritance], despite the fact that [it] introduces many conceptual and technical intricacies." We will be examining some of those "conceptual and technical intricacies" in the body of this chapter.

THE RUNNING EXAMPLE

As a running example, we use a simple variation on our geometric example from the previous chapter, involving parallelograms, rectangles, rhombi, and squares. (Just to remind you, a *rhombus* is a parallelogram in which all four sides are of equal length.) Fig. 15.1 shows a graph—a *directed acyclic graph,* to be precise—of the

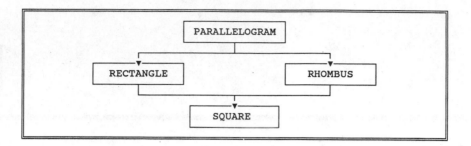

Fig. 15.1   Sample type graph

subtype/supertype relationships in this example; observe in particular that type SQUARE has two immediate supertypes, RECTANGLE and RHOMBUS.

To see that the subtype/supertype relationships in the figure are indeed reasonable, consider the following facts:

- Every parallelogram has a "long" diagonal of length ld and a "short" one of length sd, where $ld \geq sd$.

- Every parallelogram also has two "long" sides of length ls and two "short" ones of length ss, where $ls \geq ss$.

- A rectangle is a parallelogram for which $ld = sd, = d$ (say). Also, every rectangle has a unique circumscribed circle (i.e., a circle that passes through each of the rectangle's four vertices).

- A rhombus is a parallelogram for which $ls = ss, = s$ (say). Also, every rhombus has a unique inscribed circle (i.e., a circle that touches each of the rhombus's four sides). *Note:* We remark in passing that a parallelogram that is not a rhombus is sometimes called a *rhomboid.*

- A square is a rectangle for which $ls = ss = s$ (say); it is also a rhombus for which $ld = sd = d$ (say). Unlike rectangles and rhombi in general, every square has a unique associated *annulus* that is the difference between the corresponding circumscribing and inscribed circles; hence, every square has a property, unique to squares alone among rectangles and rhombi, that is exactly that annulus.

- Finally, every parallelogram, and therefore every rectangle and every rhombus, and therefore every square, has an area.

Thus, we might imagine a set of operator definitions as follows. *Note:* We will not actually be using all of these operators in the rest of this chapter—we show them here merely by way of illustration.

```
OPERATOR AREA ( P PARALLELOGRAM ) RETURNS ( AREA ) ... ;
   ... ;
END OPERATOR ;

OPERATOR THE_LD ( P PARALLELOGRAM ) RETURNS ( LENGTH ) ... ;
   /* "the long diagonal of" */ ... ;
END OPERATOR ;

OPERATOR THE_SD ( P PARALLELOGRAM ) RETURNS ( LENGTH ) ... ;
   /* "the short diagonal of" */ ... ;
END OPERATOR ;

OPERATOR THE_LS ( P PARALLELOGRAM ) RETURNS ( LENGTH ) ... ;
   /* "the long side of" */ ... ;
END OPERATOR ;

OPERATOR THE_SS ( P PARALLELOGRAM ) RETURNS ( LENGTH ) ... ;
   /* "the short side of" */ ... ;
END OPERATOR ;

OPERATOR THE_D ( R RECTANGLE ) RETURNS ( LENGTH ) ... ;
   /* "the diagonal of" */ ... ;
END OPERATOR ;

OPERATOR CIR_CIRCLE ( R RECTANGLE ) RETURNS ( CIRCLE ) ... ;
   /* "the circumscribed circle of" */ ... ;
END OPERATOR ;

OPERATOR THE_S ( R RHOMBUS ) RETURNS ( LENGTH ) ... ;
   /* "the side of" */ ... ;
END OPERATOR ;

OPERATOR IN_CIRCLE ( R RHOMBUS ) RETURNS ( CIRCLE ) ... ;
   /* "the inscribed circle of" */ ... ;
END OPERATOR ;

OPERATOR ANNULUS ( S SQUARE ) RETURNS ( ANNULUS ) ... ;
   /* "the annulus of" */ ... ;
END OPERATOR ;
```

Note in particular that types RECTANGLE and RHOMBUS both inherit the operator AREA from their immediate supertype PARALLELOGRAM, and hence that type SQUARE inherits that operator from *both* of its immediate supertypes. We will return to this point in the final section of this chapter.

Here then are the corresponding type definitions. Note (a) the type constraints, (b) the SUBTYPE_OF specification for type SQUARE.

```
TYPE PARALLELOGRAM
    POSSREP ( ... )
    CONSTRAINT
    ( THE_LD ( PARALLELOGRAM ) ≥ THE_SD ( PARALLELOGRAM ) AND
      THE_LS ( PARALLELOGRAM ) ≥ THE_SS ( PARALLELOGRAM ) ) ;

TYPE RECTANGLE
    POSSREP ( ... )
    SUBTYPE_OF ( PARALLELOGRAM )
    CONSTRAINT ( THE_LD ( RECTANGLE ) = THE_SD ( RECTANGLE ) ) ;
```

```
TYPE RHOMBUS
     POSSREP ( ... )
     SUBTYPE_OF ( PARALLELOGRAM )
     CONSTRAINT ( THE_LS ( RHOMBUS ) = THE_SS ( RHOMBUS ) ) ;

TYPE SQUARE
     POSSREP ( ... )
     SUBTYPE_OF ( RECTANGLE, RHOMBUS ) ;
```

IM PROPOSALS 1–26 REVISITED

Here once again is a list, repeated from Chapter 12, of our 26 original IM Proposals:

1. Types are sets	15. Comparison with inheritance
2. Subtypes are subsets	16. Join etc. with inheritance
3. "Subtype of" is reflexive	17. TREAT DOWN
4. Proper subtypes	18. TREAT UP
5. "Subtype of" is transitive	19. Logical operator IS_$T(SX)$
6. Immediate subtypes	20. Relational operator RX:IS_$T(A)$
7. Single inheritance only	21. Logical operator IS_MS_$T(SX)$
8. Global root types	22. Relational operator
9. Type hierarchies	RX:IS_MS_$T(A)$
10. Subtypes can be proper subsets	23. THE_ pseudovariables
11. Types disjoint unless one a subtype of the other	24. Read-only operator inheritance and value substitutability
12. Scalar values (extended definition)	25. Read-only parameters to update operators
13. Scalar variables (extended definition)	26. Update operator inheritance and variable substitutability
14. Assignment with inheritance	

We now proceed to revisit these proposals in an attempt to discover what changes are needed to them in order to support multiple inheritance. It turns out that several (in fact, the majority) need no change at all. To be specific, the only ones that seem to need some attention are Numbers 7–9, 11–12, 15–16, 24, and 26.* Of these,

---

*In particular, we make no changes to IM Proposals 19–22. We should perhaps point out one consequence of this fact, however: namely, that although (e.g.) certain values of type RECTANGLE are also of type RHOMBUS, the expression IS_RHOMBUS(R), where R is of type RECTANGLE, is illegal (it fails on a compile-time type error). By contrast, the expression IS_SQUARE(R) is legal, of course, and returns *true* if and only if the current value of R is of type SQUARE—which is to say, if and only if it is of type RHOMBUS (see the revised version of IM Proposal 12, later), Thus, it is still possible to test a rectangle to see whether it is also a rhombus, in a slightly indirect fashion.

moreover, Number 8 really just requires a slightly extended interpretation (the wording is still accurate); thus, the only ones requiring serious attention are as follows:

7. Single inheritance only

9. Type hierarchies

11. Types disjoint unless one a subtype of the other

12. Scalar values (extended definition)

15. Comparison with inheritance

16. Join etc. with inheritance

24. Read-only operator inheritance and value substitutability

26. Update operator inheritance and variable substitutability

For the remainder of this chapter, therefore, we concentrate on just these eight. In fact we will argue, after due consideration, that Numbers 24 and 26 do not need any change either, so Numbers 7, 9, 11–12, and 15–16 are really the important ones.

MANY SUPERTYPES PER SUBTYPE

The original version of IM Proposal 7 ("single inheritance only") ran as follows:

7. *Every proper subtype* T′ *has exactly one immediate supertype* T.

We propose the following simple generalization:

7. *Every proper subtype* T′ *has at least one immediate supertype* T.

Thus, e.g., the situation shown in Fig. 15.1, in which proper subtype SQUARE has the two distinct immediate supertypes RECTANGLE and RHOMBUS, is legal.

Note: An obvious question arises—namely, could we also define PARALLELOGRAM as an immediate supertype of SQUARE? In terms of Fig. 15.1, such a definition would involve an additional directed arc from type PARALLELOGRAM to type SQUARE. Could we add such an arc?

Well, observe first of all that—by definition!—type PARALLELOGRAM is *not* an immediate supertype of type SQUARE, because there does exist at least one type that is both a proper supertype of SQUARE and a proper subtype of PARALLELOGRAM (check the wording of IM Proposal 6 if you wish to confirm this observation). At the very least, therefore, we would have to revise our definition of "immediate supertype" (and/or our definition of "type hierarchy") if we wanted to permit the additional arc. So do we want to permit it?

We answer this question in the negative. It seems to us that permitting such an additional arc does not lead to any useful additional functionality; to be specific, all of the operators and constraints that type SQUARE would then inherit "immediately" from type PARALLELOGRAM by means of such an arc it already does inherit anyway, transitively, by means of the arcs via the intermediate types RECTANGLE and RHOMBUS. Furthermore, permitting such an extension to our understanding of the term "immediate supertype" certainly has the potential to complicate some of our later concepts and definitions unduly. We therefore invoke *The Principle of Cautious Design* [49] and prohibit such an extension at this time. As already indicated, we do not need to introduce any new rule to achieve this effect—IM Proposal 6 already takes care of matters for us.

TYPE GRAPHS

IM Proposal 9 ("type hierarchies") obviously requires extension, too. We propose the following generalization:

9. *Let* TG *be a directed acyclic graph of nodes and directed arcs from one node to another in which:*

   a. *Each node is given the name of a type.*

   b. *Let* T *and* T′ *be two nodes. Then there is at most one directed arc from node* T *to node* T′*; in fact, there is such an arc if and only if type* T *is an immediate supertype of type* T′.

   c. *If there is a directed arc from node* T *to node* T′*, then node* T′ *is not reachable from node* T *via any other path.* Note: *A* path *is a sequence of zero or more directed arcs. A node* T′ *is* reachable *from a node* T *if and only if there is a path to node* T′ *from node* T.

   d. *If* TG *includes any nodes at all, then—because it is directed and acyclic—it necessarily contains at least one node with no immediate supertype node. Such a node is called a **global root** node, and the type corresponding to that node is called a **global root** type, with respect to graph* TG.

   e. *If nodes* T1 *and* T2 *are distinct global roots with respect to graph* TG, *then— in accordance with our revised IM Proposal 11,* q.v.—*no node* T *is reachable from both* T1 *and* T2.

   f. *If nodes* T1, T2, T′, *and* T″ *are such that there exist paths from both* T1 *and* T2 *to both* T′ *and* T″*, then—in accordance with our revised IM Proposal 12,* q.v.—*there must exist a node* T *that is common to all of those paths.*

   Then TG *is said to be a **type graph.***

   Points arising from this definition:

   ■ Parts a. and b. are self-explanatory.

   ■ Part c. simply reflects the fact that no type *T* can be both an immediate and a nonimmediate supertype of the same type *T′*.

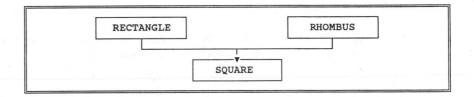

Fig. 15.2   A graph that is not a valid type graph (nonunique root)

- Part d. is an obvious generalization of the corresponding portion of the "type hierarchy" definition for the single inheritance case. We observe, however, that whereas in the single inheritance case it makes sense to regard various subhierarchies of a given hierarchy as type hierarchies in their own right, an analogous remark does not apply to type graphs in general. As a consequence, the concept of "local roots" does not really apply to type graphs in general—all roots are global, by definition (and so we could drop the "global" modifier without ambiguity, and often do, though we also permit it for consistency with the single inheritance case).

  A global root can be regarded as an entry point into the overall type graph. As already indicated, we do not assume that there is exactly one such root; if there is more than one, however, we can always invent some kind of "system" root that is an immediate supertype for all of them, and so there is no loss of generality in assuming just one (though such an assumption would make our revised IM Proposal 11—see the next section below—vacuous).*

- Part e. implies that, e.g., the situation shown in Fig. 15.2—in which proper subtype SQUARE has two distinct proper supertypes, RECTANGLE and RHOMBUS, that are both global root types with respect to the graph in question—is illegal (i.e., it is not a valid type graph). In other words, any given type graph can be divided into a set of *partitions,* one per global root, such that (a) within any such partition every node is connected to every other but (b) no node in one partition is connected to any node in another (see the next section for further discussion). *Note:* When we say that some node A is *connected* to some node Z, what we mean is that there exists a sequence of zero or more nodes B, C, ..., Y such that there is a directed arc from A to B or *vice versa,* a directed arc from B to C or *vice versa,* ..., and a directed arc from Y to Z or *vice versa.*

  Observe that partitions are always *fully connected,* in the sense that every node in a given partition is connected to every other node in that partition.[†]

---

*As mentioned in the previous chapter, we will be discussing an important special case of such a system root, called *alpha,* in Chapter 16.

[†]In mathematical terms, in fact, a type graph partition is a *lattice,* and the overall graph is a set of such lattices.

- Part f. is discussed in the next section but one.

Note finally that type graphs (like type hierarchies before them) are still not part of our model *per se,* of course—they are just a convenient way of depicting subtype/supertype relationships. Also, of course, a type hierarchy is a special case of a type graph.

LEAST SPECIFIC TYPES UNIQUE

What about IM Proposal 11 ("types disjoint unless one a subtype of the other")? In its original form, that proposal ran as follows:

11. *If* T1 *and* T2 *are distinct global root types, or distinct immediate subtypes of the same supertype, then they are disjoint (in other words, no value* v *is of both type* T1 *and type* T2*).*

As stated, this proposal obviously does *not* still apply. For example, types RECTANGLE and RHOMBUS in Fig. 15.1 are distinct immediate subtypes of the same supertype (PARALLELOGRAM), yet they are certainly not disjoint (also, neither is a subtype of the other, because some rectangles are not rhombi and some rhombi are not rectangles; in other words, we really are talking about "distinct immediate subtypes" as such). Of course, those values that are both rectangles and rhombi are, precisely, squares; note, however, that until such time as we actually introduce SQUARE as a subtype of both RECTANGLE and RHOMBUS, we still do not have multiple inheritance *per se.* Thus, in order to support multiple inheritance, it is *necessary* but not *sufficient* that we relax our type disjointness requirement.*

However, we do not have to relax that requirement completely, nor do we wish to. Rather, we proceed as follows. First, we introduce the concept of **least specific type:** If value *v* is of type *T* and not of any proper supertype of *T,* then we say that *T* is the *least specific type* of *v* (note that *T* here must be a root type in the applicable type graph). Then we go on to insist that the least specific type of any given value be unique.† Thus, we propose replacing IM Proposal 11 by the following simplified version (a version that implies the original one):

11. *If* T1 *and* T2 *are distinct global root types, then they are disjoint (in other words, no value* v *is of both type* T1 *and type* T2*).*

---

*More precisely, if we relax it for leaf types only, we do not have multiple inheritance; if we relax it for nonleaf types, we do.

†Our reasons for insisting on this property should become clear in the next two sections. Note that the property is certainly satisfied if we limit our attention to single inheritance only.

MOST SPECIFIC TYPES UNIQUE

We also need to revise IM Proposal 12 ("scalar values"). Here is the original version:

12. *Let scalar value* v *be of type* T. *If and only if no proper subtype* T' *of type* T *exists such that* v *is also of type* T', *then* T *is said to be the **most specific** type for (or of)* v.

Now, with single inheritance, it is clear that every value does logically (and necessarily) have just one most specific type. With multiple inheritance, by contrast, we need to impose an additional rule to ensure that the same is still the case. Why do we want it still to be the case? Well, suppose it were not; suppose (e.g.) that a given value *v* could be both a rectangle and a rhombus, and suppose further that type SQUARE has not (yet) been defined. Then the expression "the most specific type of *v*" would be ambiguous. One undesirable consequence would be that, if an operator named *Op* had been defined for rectangles and a distinct operator with the same name *Op* had been defined for rhombi, an invocation of *Op* with argument *v* would be ambiguous. The (partial) solution to this problem is, of course, to insist that type SQUARE in fact be defined after all.*

We therefore propose the following replacement for IM Proposal 12:

12. *Let types* T1 *and* T2 *(neither of which is a subtype of the other) be distinct and nondisjoint. Then* T1 *and* T2 *must have a common subtype* T' *(not necessarily immediate), such that scalar value* v *is of type* T' *if and only if it is of both type* T1 *and type* T2.

Note that to say that scalar value *v* is of type *T'* if and only if it is of both type *T1* and type *T2* means, precisely, that the set of values constituting type *T'* is the intersection of the sets of values constituting types *T1* and *T2*. We can therefore refer to type *T',* informally, as an *intersection type.*

By way of example, consider the type graph shown in Fig. 15.3 (type EQUILATERAL in that figure is meant to stand for polygons whose sides are all the same length). Note that, for example, types QUADRILATERAL and EQUILATERAL fulfill the conditions of our proposed replacement for IM Proposal 12: They are distinct, they overlap (i.e., they are nondisjoint), and neither is a subtype of the other. But they do have a common subtype, RHOMBUS, such that it is indeed the case that a polygon that is both quadrilateral and equilateral must be, precisely, a rhombus. Thus, RHOMBUS is the intersection type for types QUADRILATERAL and EQUILATERAL.† *Note:* SQUARE is also a common sub-

---

*The other part of the solution is discussed in the final section of this chapter.

†We should perhaps point out that the only way a given value can be of both type QUADRILATERAL and type EQUILATERAL in our model is, precisely, if it is obtained by an invocation of a selector for type RHOMBUS (or for some proper subtype of RHOMBUS). There is no way of, e.g., taking a value of type QUADRILATERAL and somehow "adding" type EQUILATERAL to it. On the other hand, we observe that if we were to extend our model to support *specialization by constraint* along the lines sketched in the final section of Appendix C, then such "addition of types" could and would be performed automatically.

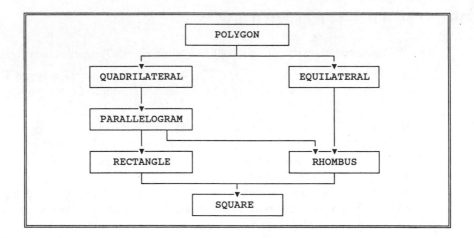

Fig. 15.3   Overlapping types must have an intersection subtype

type for types QUADRILATERAL and EQUILATERAL, of course, but it is not the intersection type *per se* (see the discussion of the fourth "important logical consequence" in the subsection immediately following).

For completeness, we give the intersection type for every pair of types in the example that fulfill the specified conditions:

```
QUADRILATERAL   and   EQUILATERAL   :   RHOMBUS
PARALLELOGRAM   and   EQUILATERAL   :   RHOMBUS
RECTANGLE       and   EQUILATERAL   :   SQUARE
RECTANGLE       and   RHOMBUS       :   SQUARE
```

Note that our new IM Proposal 12 is satisfied trivially if we drop the requirement that neither *T1* nor *T2* is allowed to be a subtype of the other, and/or the requirement that they be distinct. In fact, we can simplify the wording to the following final version:

12. *If types* T1 *and* T2 *overlap, they must have a common subtype* T' *such that scalar value* v *is of type* T' *if and only if it is of both type* T1 *and type* T2.

Now, we do recognize that this proposal is a little stronger than might be strictly necessary. To be precise, it might be sufficient to require merely that types *T1* and *T2* have a *set* of common subtypes such that (a) scalar value *v* is of some type in that set if and only if it is of both type *T1* and type *T2,* and (b) no scalar value *v* is of more than one type in that set. For example, suppose every value of type RECTANGLE is either a red rectangle or a blue one, and every value of type RHOMBUS is either a red rhombus or a blue one. Then we can imagine two types RED_SQUARE and BLUE_SQUARE, with the obvious interpretations; these two types are disjoint, their *union* is the intersection of types RECTANGLE and

RHOMBUS, and it is still the case that every individual rectangle or rhombus has exactly one most specific type.

It should be clear, however, that relaxing the requirements of our new IM Proposal 12 along such lines causes additional complexity—complexity that is probably unnecessary and certainly undesirable. We therefore choose to invoke *The Principle of Cautious Design* once again [49] and go with the version of IM Proposal 12 as stated.

Some Important Logical Consequences

Our revised version of IM Proposal 12 has a number of very important consequences, which we now proceed to explain.

- The first is that, as already indicated, it is indeed still the case (as it was with single inheritance) that every value does have a well defined, unique most specific type. Note, however, that our existing IM Proposal 10 still applies—i.e., we do not require every value to have a leaf type as its most specific type. For example, values can exist whose most specific type is RECTANGLE and not SQUARE.

- It is also still the case that leaf types are disjoint. For suppose, contrariwise, that types *T1* and *T2* are distinct but overlapping leaf types. Then *T1* and *T2* must have a common subtype, by our revised IM Proposal 12, and so they cannot be leaf types after all.

- It follows from the foregoing points that our model of a scalar variable as defined in IM Proposal 13—i.e., as a named ordered triple of the form *<DT,MST,v>*—is still valid.

- Next, observe that the *intersection* type *T'* of IM Proposal 12 must be unique. That is, given overlapping types *T1* and *T2*, there cannot exist two different types *T'* and *T''* both of which are common subtypes of *T1* and *T2* and both of which satisfy the conditions of our new IM Proposal 12. For if they both satisfy those conditions, they are both, precisely, the intersection of *T1* and *T2*; hence they are identical. In other words, if *T1* and *T2* overlap, they have precisely one **least specific common subtype**—and so, e.g., the situation shown in Fig. 15.4 makes no sense, and we propose that it be outlawed. (The arcs in that figure are broken in order to indicate that, e.g., *T'* and *T''* are not necessarily *immediate* subtypes of *T1* and *T2*.)

  Note: Of course, type *T'* in turn can have a proper subtype of its own—*T3*, say—and that type *T3* will certainly be a common subtype of *T1* and *T2*, but it will not be the specific intersection type that the revised IM Proposal 12 requires. (As pointed out in the previous subsection, type SQUARE is a common subtype of types QUADRILATERAL and EQUILATERAL, but it is not the required intersection type *per se*.)

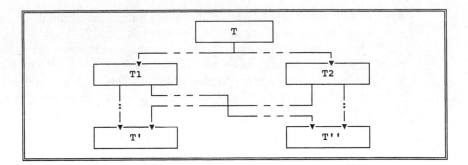

Fig. 15.4   Another graph that is not a valid type graph

- Next, we remark that IM Proposal 12 does *not* need any extension to cater for the case where we have *n* types ($n > 2$) that all overlap each other. For example, let types *T1, T2,* and *T3* be such that they overlap pairwise, and let the intersection types required by IM Proposal 12 be *Ta* (for *T2* and *T3*), *Tb* (for *T3* and *T1*), and *Tc* (for *T1* and *T2*). Then types *Ta, Tb,* and *Tc* also overlap pairwise; however, the three intersection types required for these types *Ta, Tb,* and *Tc* are in fact all the same type. Development of a concrete example to illustrate this point is left as an exercise for the reader.

- Finally, not only do any given pair of overlapping types *T1* and *T2* have exactly one least specific common subtype (as already explained), they also have exactly one **most specific common supertype,** as we now show. First of all, they certainly have at least one common supertype, *viz.* the (unique) applicable root type. Suppose, therefore, that they have two distinct common supertypes *Ta* and *Tb,* say, neither of which is a subtype of the other. Note that *Ta* and *Tb* also overlap, since they have a common subtype (actually, at least two common subtypes, namely *T1* and *T2*). Suppose further that *Ta* and *Tb* do not have a common proper subtype *T* that is a common proper supertype of *T1* and *T2* (i.e., *Ta* and *Tb* are both "most specific common supertypes" of *T1* and *T2,* loosely speaking). Now rename the types as follows: Rename *T1* and *T2* as *T′* and *T″,* respectively; rename *Ta* and *Tb* as *T1* and *T2,* respectively. Then we have exactly the invalid situation shown in Fig. 15.4! It follows that the original types *Ta* and *Tb* cannot be distinct after all—they must in fact be the same type. Hence, as stated, *T1* and *T2* have precisely one most specific common type.

It is our experience that the full implications of all of the foregoing points are far from immediately apparent. We therefore present a couple more examples, rather more complicated than the one given in Fig. 15.3, that repay careful study (refer to Figs. 15.5 and 15.6). The first example probably requires a few words of explanation (the second is meant to be self-explanatory, more or less):

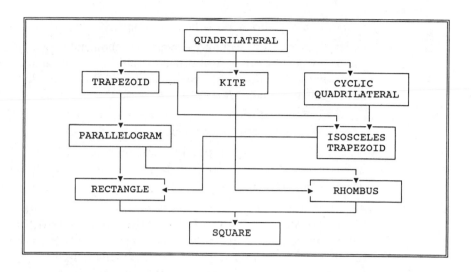

Fig. 15.5 Overlapping types must have a common subtype (a more complicated example)

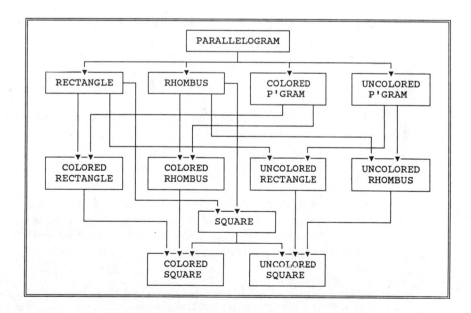

Fig. 15.6 Overlapping types must have a common subtype (yet another example)

- A *trapezoid* is a quadrilateral with at least one pair of opposite sides parallel.*

- A *kite* is a quadrilateral with mirror symmetry about a diagonal, none of whose angles is greater than 180° (if this latter condition is not satisfied, the quadrilateral is not a kite but a *dart*). Note that if *ABCD* is a kite that is symmetric about diagonal *AC,* then *AB = AD* and *CB = CD.*

- A *cyclic* quadrilateral is one whose vertices lie on a circle. Note that a quadrilateral is cyclic if and only if its opposite angles add up to 180°.

- An *isosceles* trapezoid is a trapezoid whose base angles are equal. Note that if *ABCD* is an isosceles trapezium with *AD* parallel to *BC,* then the base angles are *BAD* and *CDA,* and *AB = DC.*

With regard to Fig. 15.6, incidentally, we remark that types PARALLELOGRAM, RECTANGLE, RHOMBUS, and SQUARE are all *dummy types*† (refer to the discussion of IM Proposal 10 in Chapter 14 if you need to remind yourself of the meaning of this term). Every parallelogram, for example, is either colored or uncolored; what is more, no parallelogram is both. It follows that type PARALLELOGRAM is subject to a certain slightly complicated type constraint. Now, the constraint in question can certainly be stated in **Tutorial D**—meaning, of course, **Tutorial D** extended with inheritance support along the lines suggested in the previous chapter—but not very elegantly (exercise for the reader); it might be nice to introduce some special shorthand for the purpose, along the lines of "type PARALLELOGRAM is *partitioned* by types COLORED_PARALLELOGRAM and UNCOLORED_PARALLELOGRAM," perhaps.

COMPARISON WITH MULTIPLE INHERITANCE

IM Proposal 15 ("comparison with inheritance") requires a very slight generalization. The new version looks like this.

15. *Consider the comparison*

```
SY = SX
```

(where SX *and* SY *are scalar expressions).* DT(SX) *and* DT(SY) *must have a common subtype, otherwise the comparison is illegal (this is a compile-time check). If the comparison is legal, its effect is to return true if* MST(SX) *is equal to* MST(SY) *and* v(SX) *is equal to* v(SY), false *otherwise.*

---

*You might or might not be interested to learn that in researching this example we discovered that a quadrilateral with two parallel sides is called a *trapezoid* in the US and a *trapezium* in the UK, while a quadrilateral with no parallel sides is called a *trapezium* in the US and a *trapezoid* in the UK. But we digress.

†At least, they will be dummy types so long as the system is informed of the relevant constraints.

The slight generalization is as follows: Under single inheritance, $DT(SX)$ had to be a subtype of $DT(SY)$ or *vice versa;* now we require merely that $DT(SX)$ and $DT(SY)$ have some common subtype (the subtype in question could be either $DT(SX)$ or $DT(SY)$, of course, so this new version includes the old one as a special case). Here is an example:

```
VAR RE RECTANGLE ;
VAR RH RHOMBUS ;

IF RE = RH THEN ... ;
END IF ;
```

The comparison here will give *true* if and only if (a) the current values of variables RE and RH have type SQUARE—or some proper subtype of SQUARE, of course, if any such proper subtype exists—as their common most specific type, and (b) those current values are equal.

Further elaboration seems unnecessary,* except to note that of course the rules regarding less-than comparisons, greater-than comparisons, and so on—for types where those comparisons are defined—follow the same general pattern as those for equality comparisons (except that it might not be necessary to insist that the most specific types be the same for the comparison to give *true*).

IM Proposal 16 (regarding join etc.) requires a somewhat similar generalization, as follows:

16. *Let* rx *and* ry *be relations with a common attribute* A, *and let the declared types of* A *in* rx *and* ry *be* DT(Ax) *and* DT(Ay), *respectively. Consider the join of* rx *and* ry *(necessarily over* A, *at least in part).* DT(Ax) *and* DT(Ay) *must have a common subtype, otherwise the join is illegal (this is a compile-time check). If the join is legal, the declared type of* A *in the result is the **most specific common supertype** of* DT(Ax) *and* DT(Ay).

    Analogous remarks apply to union, intersection, and difference operators: In every case, (a) corresponding attributes of the operands must be such that their declared types have a common subtype, and (b) the declared type of the corresponding attribute in the result is the corresponding most specific common supertype.

The (unique) most specific common supertype of two types with a common subtype is as defined in the previous section. For example (referring back to Fig. 15.1 once again), if the declared type of attribute *A* in relation *rx* is RECTANGLE and the declared type of attribute *A* in relation *ry* is RHOMBUS, then the declared type of attribute *A* in the join of *rx* and *ry* is PARALLELOGRAM.

---

*Though you might like to meditate on just why our existing IM Proposal 14 ("assignment with inheritance") does not require a generalization analogous to that for IM Proposal 15.

OPERATOR INHERITANCE

Finally we turn our attention to IM Proposals 24 and 26. There are two separate problems that need to be addressed. First, consider types RECTANGLE and RHOMBUS from Fig. 15.1 once again. As noted earlier in this chapter, both of these types inherit the read-only operator AREA from type PARALLELOGRAM, and hence type SQUARE inherits that operator from *both* of its immediate supertypes. What are the implications of this fact?

Well, if AREA is *reimplemented* ("explicitly specialized") for type SQUARE, there is no problem: An invocation AREA(*s*), where *s* is of most specific type SQUARE, will be unambiguous. But, of course, we want to avoid explicit specializations as much as we reasonably can. Suppose, therefore, that AREA is *not* reimplemented for type SQUARE. Now there are two possibilities:

- If the semantics of the RECTANGLE and RHOMBUS versions of the AREA operator are the same—i.e., if the expressions

```
AREA ( TREAT_UP_AS_RECTANGLE ( s ) )
```

and

```
AREA ( TREAT_UP_AS_RHOMBUS ( s ) )
```

give the same result—then again there is no problem. (No problem so far as the model is concerned, that is. There will still have to be a way of telling the system which of the two versions, the RECTANGLE version or the RHOMBUS one (or maybe even the PARALLELOGRAM one?), is to be invoked under the covers for a square. But this fact is of no concern to someone who is merely *making use of* type SQUARE; it is an implementation issue, not a model issue.)

- However, if the semantics of the RECTANGLE and RHOMBUS versions of the AREA operator differ, then it matters very much which version is inherited by type SQUARE. But now we face a logical absurdity! To say that SQUARE is a subtype of both RECTANGLE and RHOMBUS is to say that any given square is both a rectangle and a rhombus. To go on and say "yes, but the area of that square depends on whether we think of it as a rectangle or as a rhombus" is surely nonsense.

As with our discussion of the TRAVEL_TIME operator in Chapter 14, therefore, we will set a stake in the ground here and insist that, in our model at least, if (a) T' is a subtype of T and (b) v is a value of type T' and (c) Op is a read-only operator that applies to values of type T, then (d) invoking Op on v and invoking Op on a version of v that has been "treated up" to type T must always give the same result. And if this position is accepted, then IM Proposal 24 is applicable as it stands.

It should be clear that remarks analogous to the foregoing apply to update operator inheritance and IM Proposal 26 also.

Now we turn to the second problem. Suppose some operator *Op* has been defined for rectangles and another operator with the same name *Op* has been defined for rhombi; suppose further that these operators are *not* inherited from parallelograms (i.e., there is no operator *Op* for type PARALLELOGRAM). Suppose still further that the two operators named *Op* are really different operators (i.e., *Op* is "overloaded"). What do we do about the inheritance of *Op* by type SQUARE?

The solution to this problem is to recognize that, since we really are dealing with two different operators, we need to give them two different names. We therefore propose, first, that there be a way of introducing a *synonym* for either the RECTANGLE operator or the RHOMBUS operator (or both). For example, we might introduce the synonym *Op'* for the RECTANGLE operator (the names *Op* and *Op'* will then be effectively interchangeable so far as type RECTANGLE is concerned). Then we can specify that type SQUARE inherits operator *Op* from type RHOMBUS, but operator *Op'* from type RECTANGLE. Note in particular that now the expressions

```
Op' ( ..., s, ... )
```

and

```
Op' ( TREAT_UP_AS_RECTANGLE ( ..., s, ... ) )
```

(where *s* is of most specific type SQUARE) will give the same result, as our model requires. Note too that the second of these expressions could equally well have been written as

```
Op ( TREAT_UP_AS_RECTANGLE ( ..., s, ... ) )
```

16

Tuple and Relation Types

INTRODUCTION

In the last three chapters we have presented, described, and illustrated a series of proposals for a model of subtyping and inheritance for *scalar* types. Now we turn our attention to the question of what might be involved in extending that model to take tuple and relation types into account as well—as indeed we really must, since we explicitly permit domains (in the usual relational sense) to be tuple or relation types in addition to the more traditional scalar types.

The style of presentation in what follows resembles that of Chapter 14 (we choose not to use quite the same firm "IM Proposal" format, however, but it would be a simple matter to revise the material to fit that format if desired). To be specific, most of the sections consist of (a) a fairly formal definition, followed by (b) an informal discussion, with examples, of the concepts involved in that definition; in other words, they do indeed follow the same general pattern as most of the sections in Chapter 14. And once again we often use the symbols T and T' generically to refer to a pair of types such that T' is a subtype of T (equivalently, such that T is a supertype of T'); but now, of course, those types might be tuple or relation types instead of scalar types, as previously.

One last introductory remark: It might have been thought better, at least from a pedagogic viewpoint, to treat tuple types exclusively first, and then to extend the treatment to include relation types subsequently. In practice, however, tuple and relation inheritance are so intricately interwoven that it is virtually impossible to treat them separately. Indeed, it turns out that many of the concepts and definitions to be discussed:

- Come in pairs (a tuple version and a relation version); and
- Are both recursive (they refer to themselves) and mutually recursive (they refer to each other).

Indeed, this state of affairs is not really surprising, given that tuples can contain relation- and tuple-valued attributes and relations can contain tuple- and relation-valued attributes.

TUPLE AND RELATION SUBTYPES AND SUPERTYPES

Let types T *and* T$'$ *be both tuple types or both relation types, with headings*

```
{ <A1,T1>,   <A2,T2>,   ..., <An,Tn>  }
{ <A1,T1'>,  <A2,T2'>,  ..., <An,Tn'> }
```

respectively. Then type T$'$ *is a **subtype** of type* T *(equivalently, type* T *is a **supertype** of type* T$'$*) if and only if for all* i *(i = 1, 2, ..., n), type* Ti$'$ *is a subtype of type* Ti *(equivalently, type* Ti *is a supertype of type* Ti$'$*). And if type* T$'$ *is a subtype of type* T *and* v *is a tuple or relation (as applicable) of type* T$'$*, then* v *is also a tuple or relation (as applicable) of type* T.

———— ♦ ♦ ♦ ♦ ♦ ————

As we know, a scalar variable of declared type ELLIPSE might have a current value of type CIRCLE, because CIRCLE is a subtype of ELLIPSE; likewise, a scalar variable of declared type RECTANGLE might have a current value of type SQUARE, because SQUARE is a subtype of CIRCLE. It should be clear, therefore, that if we have a *tuple* variable, TV say, defined thus—

```
VAR TV TUPLE { E ELLIPSE, R RECTANGLE } ;
```

—then TV might have a current value whose E value is of type CIRCLE, or whose R value is of type SQUARE, or both. What are the implications of this fact? Well, let us consider the following tuple types:

```
TUPLE { E ELLIPSE, R RECTANGLE }        /* tuple type "ER" */

TUPLE { E CIRCLE,  R RECTANGLE }        /* tuple type "CR" */

TUPLE { E ELLIPSE, R SQUARE    }        /* tuple type "ES" */

TUPLE { E CIRCLE,  R SQUARE    }        /* tuple type "CS" */
```

Let us agree to refer to these types by the names ER, CR, ES, and CS, respectively, as the comments suggest. Note that they all have the same attribute names; clearly, then, tuples of any of these four types can all be legal values of the tuple variable TV. Note too that all four types are at least implicitly available, even though no variables have been explicitly defined to be of those types in the last three cases. (Recall that, in **Tutorial D** at least, tuple types can be defined only implicitly—typically as part of the operation that defines a tuple variable, as in the case of tuple variable TV.)

Now let us concentrate, for a moment, on just the two "extreme" types ER and CS. Does it make sense to regard type CS as a "subtype" of "supertype" ER? Well, it should be clear that:

- Every type constraint that applies to values of type ER also applies to values of type CS, while the converse is not true, in general. (We remind you that the only type constraints, as such, that apply to tuple types in our model are constraints that are a logical consequence of the ones that apply to the scalar types in terms of which those tuple types are ultimately defined. Thus, there is no way tuple type ER could be subject to any type constraint that did not also apply to tuple type CS.)

- Hence, every value of type CS is certainly a value of type ER, while the converse is not true, in general.

- Every operator that applies to values of type ER also applies to values of type CS, while the converse is not true, in general. The operators in question are (a) the builtin tuple operators of **D** (tuple comparisons, tuple rename, tuple join, and so on), together with (b) whatever user-defined tuple operators have been defined for tuple type ER. *Note:* We are assuming here that RM Very Strong Suggestion 7 is in effect (see Chapter 10). If it is not, then the operators that apply to values of type CS will be exactly the same as those that apply to values of type ER—they will be just the builtin tuple operators. Even in this case, however, it is still true that (as stated) every operator that applies to values of type ER also applies to values of type CS.

Now, all of these observations are in accord with our usual understanding of what it means for one type to be a subtype of another, so there does seem to be a *prima facie* case for regarding CS as a subtype of ER (equivalently, ER as a supertype of CS). But is it *useful* to do so? The answer is, of course, *yes*. In particular, the concept of *value substitutability* is applicable (meaning that wherever the system expects a tuple of type ER, we can always substitute a tuple of type CS instead). Among other things, therefore, we can assign a tuple of type CS to a variable of declared type ER, and we can test a variable of declared type CS and a variable of declared type ER for equality.

In a similar manner, we can say that types CR and ES are both subtypes of type ER and both supertypes of CS (note, however, that neither of CR and ES is a subtype of the other). And so CS is a subtype with two immediate supertypes, and we are dealing with *multiple* inheritance (which is why we wanted to discuss multiple inheritance first, in Chapter 15, before considering tuples and relations).

With the foregoing example in mind by way of motivation, therefore, let us try to define exactly what it means for tuple type *TT′* to be a subtype of tuple type *TT*. First of all, of course, *TT′* and *TT* must certainly have the same attribute names (for otherwise there is no way that a value of type *TT′* could be a value of type *TT*). Thus, we might attempt a definition along the following lines:

- Let tuple types *TT* and *TT′* have headings

```
{ <A1,T1>,   <A2,T2>,   ..., <An,Tn>  }

{ <A1,T1'>, <A2,T2'>, ..., <An,Tn'> }
```

  respectively. Then tuple type *TT′* is a **subtype** of tuple type *TT* (equivalently, tuple type *TT* is a **supertype** of tuple type *TT′*) if and only if for all *i* (*i* = 1, 2, ..., *n*), type *Ti′* is a subtype of type *Ti* (equivalently, type *Ti* is a supertype of type *Ti′*).

And this definition is acceptable, *provided* we understand that, for any given *i,* types *Ti* and *Ti′* might themselves be tuple or relation types in turn (because, of course, tuples can have tuple- and relation-valued attributes). In other words, our definition of what it means for one tuple type to be a subtype of another:

- Is recursive (a fact that should not cause any problems, of course), but also
- Relies on a definition of what it means for one *relation* type to be a subtype of another—a possibility we have not yet considered.

So let us now turn our attention to this latter possibility. Suppose we have a relation variable (relvar) RV, say, defined thus:

```
VAR RV ... RELATION { E ELLIPSE, R RECTANGLE } ... ;
```

Then it should be clear that the current relation value of RV might include tuples of any of the four tuple types ER, CR, ES, and CS discussed above. Thus, that current relation value might reasonably be of any of the following *relation* types:

```
RELATION { E ELLIPSE, R RECTANGLE }    /* relation type "ER" */

RELATION { E CIRCLE,  R RECTANGLE }    /* relation type "CR" */

RELATION { E ELLIPSE, R SQUARE    }    /* relation type "ES" */

RELATION { E CIRCLE,  R SQUARE    }    /* relation type "CS" */
```

Without going through the detailed analysis (it parallels that already given for the tuple case above), it should be clear that we can regard (e.g.) relation type CS as a subtype of relation type ER (equivalently, relation type ER as a supertype of relation type CS). Here then is a definition of what it means for relation type *RT′* to be a subtype of relation type *RT*.

- Let relation types *RT* and *RT'* have headings

```
{ <A1,T1>,  <A2,T2>,  ...,  <An,Tn> }
{ <A1,T1'>, <A2,T2'>, ...,  <An,Tn'> }
```

respectively. Then relation type *RT'* is a **subtype** of relation type *RT* (equivalently, relation type *RT* is a **supertype** of relation type *RT'*) if and only if for all *i* (*i* = 1, 2, ..., *n*), type *Ti'* is a subtype of type *Ti* (equivalently, type *Ti* is a supertype of type *Ti'*).

Again, however, it must be understood that, for any given *i*, types *Ti* and *Ti'* might themselves be tuple or relation types. In other words, our definition of what it means for one relation type to be a subtype of another:

- Is recursive, and also
- Relies on a definition of what it means for one *tuple* type to be a subtype of another (but this latter is a possibility we have already discussed).

To sum up, therefore: The definitions of "tuple subtype" and "relation subtype" are each both recursive (they refer to themselves) and mutually recursive (they refer to each other); ultimately, however, they each rely on the notion of a *scalar* subtype, a notion that has already and independently been defined in earlier chapters.

IM PROPOSALS 1–11 STILL APPLY

Given the definitions of tuple and relation types from the previous section, it turns out that the first eleven of our *scalar* IM Proposals, as defined in Chapters 13 and 14 (and refined, in the case of Numbers 7, 9, and 11, in Chapter 15) apply essentially unchanged to tuples and relations. For convenience, we list those proposals once again here:

1. Types are sets
2. Subtypes are subsets
3. "Subtype of" is reflexive
4. Proper subtypes
5. "Subtype of" is transitive
6. Immediate subtypes
7. Multiple inheritance
8. Global root types
9. Type graphs
10. Subtypes can be proper subsets
11. Root types disjoint

IM Proposals 12 and 13 consider the effects of inheritance on scalar values and variables. Clearly, we need some tuple and relation analogs of these proposals; such analogs are the subject of the next three sections.

TUPLE AND RELATION VALUES (EXTENDED DEFINITIONS)

Let H *be a tuple heading or relation heading, defined as follows:*

```
{ <A1,T1>, <A2,T2>, ..., <An,Tn> }
```

Then:

a. t *is a tuple that* **conforms** *to heading* H *if and only if* t *is of the form*

```
{ <A1,T1',v1>, <A2,T2',v2>, ..., <An,Tn',vn> }
```

where, for all i (i = *1, 2, ...,* n), *type* Ti' *is a subtype of type* Ti *and* vi *is a value of type* Ti'.

b. r *is a relation that* **conforms** *to heading* H *if and only if* r *consists of a heading and a body, where:*

- *The heading of* r *is of the form*

```
{ <A1,T1'>, <A2,T2'>, ..., <An,Tn'> }
```

where, for all i (i = *1, 2, ...,* n), *type* Ti' *is a subtype of type* Ti;

- *The body of* r *is a set of tuples, all of which conform to the heading of* r.

You might have noticed two sections back that, although we defined what it meant for (tuple or relation) type *T'* to be a subtype of (tuple or relation) type *T,* we did not really pin down just what it meant for a given *value* to be of a given tuple or relation type; in fact, we deliberately ducked the issue in that section, because it is not quite as straightforward as might at first be thought (especially in the relational case). Now we turn our attention to that issue.

First, tuples. Let tuple type *T* have heading

```
{ <A1,T1>, <A2,T2>, ..., <An,Tn> }
```

Then we define *t* to be a tuple that **conforms** to the heading of type *T*—equivalently, we say that *t* is **of** type *T*—if and only if it is of the form

```
{ <A1,T1',v1>, <A2,T2',v2>, ..., <An,Tn',vn> }
```

where, for all *i* (*i* = 1, 2, ..., *n*), type *Ti′* is a subtype of type *Ti*—equivalently, type *Ti* is a supertype of type *Ti′*—and *vi* is a value of type *Ti′*. And, of course, the legal values of type *T* are precisely the tuples that are of type *T*.

Example: The tuple returned by the tuple selector invocation

```
TUPLE { E CIRCLE (...), R SQUARE (...) }
```

(note the nested CIRCLE and SQUARE selector invocations) is of all four of the tuple types ER, CR, ES, CS discussed two sections back.

Once again, of course, type *Ti′* in the foregoing definition might be a tuple or relation type in turn. Hence, that definition:

- Is recursive again (it relies on a definition of what it means for a value to be of a given tuple type), and also

- Relies on a definition of what it means for a value to be of a given *relation* type.

  So let us now consider this latter question. Let relation type *T* have heading

  ```
  { <A1,T1>, <A2,T2>, ..., <An,Tn> }
  ```

Then we define *r* to be a relation that **conforms** to the heading of type *T*—equivalently, we say that *r* is **of** type *T*—if and only if it consists of a heading and a body, where:

- The heading is of the form

  ```
  { <A1,T1'>, <A2,T2'>, ..., <An,Tn'> }
  ```

  where, for all *i* (*i* = 1, 2, ..., *n*), type *Ti′* is a subtype of type *Ti* (equivalently, type *Ti* is a supertype of type *Ti′*);

- The body is a set of tuples, all of which conform to the heading of *r*.

And, of course, the legal values of type *T* are precisely the relations that are of type *T*.

Example: Consider the following relation type ("relation type ER") once again:

```
RELATION { E ELLIPSE, R RECTANGLE }    /* relation type "ER" */
```

Fig. 16.1 shows a few legal relations of this type. *Note:* We adopt the convention in that figure that values of the form E*i* are ellipses that are not circles, values of the form R*i* are rectangles that are not squares, values of the form C*i* are circles, and values of the form S*i* are squares. The most specific types for all such values—they are, of course, all *scalar* values—are shown in lower case italics.

It follows from the foregoing definitions that:

- If tuple *t* is of type *TT*, it is also of all supertypes of *TT;*

- If relation *r* is of type *RT,* it is also of all supertypes of *RT.*

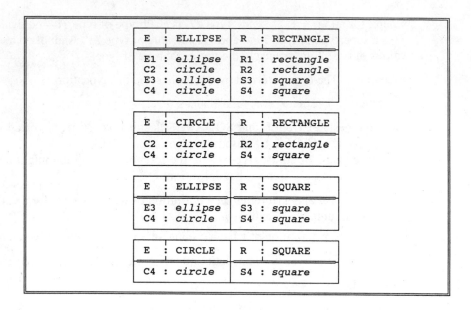

Fig. 16.1   Some relations of type RELATION { E ELLIPSE, R RECTANGLE }

TUPLE AND RELATION MOST SPECIFIC TYPES

Let H *be a tuple heading or relation heading, defined as follows:*

```
{ <A1,T1>, <A2,T2>, ..., <An,Tn> }
```

Then:

a. *If* t *is a tuple that conforms to* H—*meaning* t *is of the form*

```
{ <A1,T1',v1>, <A2,T2',v2>, ..., <An,Tn',vn> }
```

where, for all i *(i = 1, 2, ..., n), type* Ti′ *is a subtype of type* Ti *and* vi *is a value of type* Ti′—*then the **most specific** type of* t *is that unique tuple type with heading*

```
{ <A1,MST1>, <A2,MST2>, ..., <An,MSTn> }
```

where, for all i *(i = 1, 2, ..., n), type* MSTi *is the most specific type of value* vi.

b. *If* r *is a relation that conforms to* H—*meaning the body of* r *is a set of tuples, each of which has as its most specific type a type that is a subtype of the type*

TUPLE{H}, and meaning further that each such tuple can be regarded without loss of generality as being of the form

```
{ <A1,T1',v1>, <A2,T2',v2>, ..., <An,Tn',vn> }
```

where, for all i *(i = 1, 2, ..., n), type* Ti′ *is a subtype of type* Ti *and is the most specific type of value* vi *(note that distinct tuples in the body of* r *will be of distinct most specific types, in general; thus, type* Ti′ *varies over the tuples in the body of* r*)—then the* **most specific** *type of* r *is that unique relation type with heading*

```
{ <A1,MST1>, <A2,MST2>, ..., <An,MSTn> }
```

where, for all i *(i = 1, 2, ..., n), type* MSTi *is the most specific common supertype of those most specific types* Ti′, *taken over all tuples in the body of* r.

——— ♦♦♦♦♦ ———

The concept of *most specific type* does apply to tuples and relations, though the situation is considerably more complicated than it is for scalars (at least in the case of relations, where the terminology of "most" specific type is unfortunately a trifle inapt; by contrast, the tuple case is comparatively straightforward). Once again, it turns out that the definitions are both recursive and mutually recursive.

As usual, we treat tuples first. Let t be a tuple of the form

```
{ <A1,T1,v1>, <A2,T2,v2>, ..., <An,Tn,vn> }
```

Then we define the **most specific** type of t to be that unique tuple type with heading

```
{ <A1,MST1>, <A2,MST2>, ..., <An,MSTn> }
```

where, for all i ($i = 1, 2, ..., n$), type *MSTi* is the most specific type of value *vi*. *Note:* Once again the definition is recursive (because Ai can be tuple-valued), and it relies on the analogous definition for relations (because Ai can be relation-valued).

Example: Let t be the tuple

```
TUPLE { E EX, R RX }
```

and let the most specific types of EX and RX be CIRCLE and SQUARE, respectively. Then the most specific type of t is tuple type CS.

Now let r be a relation with heading

```
{ <A1,T1>, <A2,T2>, ..., <An,Tn> }
```

Then the body of r is a set of tuples, each of which has as its most specific type a type that is a subtype of the tuple type with the same heading as r. In other words, each such tuple can be regarded without loss of generality as being of the form

```
{ <A1,T1',v1>, <A2,T2',v2>, ..., <An,Tn',vn> }
```

where, for all i ($i = 1, 2, \ldots, n$), type Ti' is a subtype of type Ti, and is in fact the most specific type of value vi; that is, each tuple t in the body of r is replaced, conceptually, by a tuple t' obtained from t by "treating down" each component value of t to its most specific type. Note that distinct tuples in the body of r will be of distinct most specific types, in general; thus, type Ti' varies over the tuples in the body of r. Then we define the **most specific** type of r to be that unique relation type with heading

```
{ <A1,MST1>, <A2,MST2>, ..., <An,MSTn> }
```

where, for all i ($i = 1, 2, \ldots, n$), type $MSTi$ is the most specific common supertype of the types Ti', taken over all tuples in the body of r—see the explanation of *most specific common supertype* (for a set of types) immediately following. *Note:* Yet again the definition is recursive (because Ai can be relation-valued), and it relies on the analogous definition for tuples (because Ai can be tuple-valued).

*Definition of **most specific common supertype:**** First, let T and T' be two scalar types. Then the most specific common supertype of T and T' is as defined in the previous chapter (in the section "Most Specific Types Unique").

Second, let $T1, T2, \ldots, Tn$ and $T1', T2', \ldots, Tn'$ be two sets of types, where for all i ($i = 1, 2, \ldots, n$) Ti and Ti' (a) are both scalar types or both tuple types or both relation types, and (b) have a common supertype. Now:

- Consider tuple types T and T', with headings

```
{ <A1,T1>,  <A2,T2>,  ..., <An,Tn>  }
{ <A1,T1'>, <A2,T2'>, ..., <An,Tn'> }
```

respectively. Then we define the most specific common supertype of types T and T' to be the unique tuple type with heading

```
{ <A1,MSC1>, <A2,MSC2>, ..., <An,MSCn> }
```

where, for all i ($i = 1, 2, \ldots, n$), $MSCi$ is the most specific common supertype of Ti and Ti'.

- Consider relation types T and T', with headings

```
{ <A1,T1>,  <A2,T2>,  ..., <An,Tn>  }
{ <A1,T1'>, <A2,T2'>, ..., <An,Tn'> }
```

---

*The definitions that follow are a generalization of the definition given for scalar types in Chapter 15. Note that in these definitions we break for once with our convention that type T' is always a subtype of type T.

respectively. Then we define the most specific common supertype of types T and T' to be the unique relation type with heading

```
{ <A1,MSC1>, <A2,MSC2>, ..., <An,MSCn> }
```

where, for all i ($i = 1, 2, …, n$), $MSCi$ is the most specific common supertype of Ti and Ti'.

The definition of *most specific common supertype* for a set of N types ($N > 2$), all scalar types or all tuple types or all relation types and all having a common supertype, follows by pairwise application of the foregoing definition to the set in question. But what about $N < 2$? Well, the case $N = 1$ is straightforward; the set of types contains just one type, T say, and we define the "most specific common supertype" for that set to be simply T itself. *However, we also need to address the case $N = 0$*—in particular, we need to consider what the most specific common supertype is for the (empty) set of types corresponding to some attribute *in an empty relation.*

We approach this question by noting that the type graph can always be regarded (conceptually) as including two extreme types, *alpha* and *omega,* defined as follows:

- Type *alpha* is **the universal type:** It contains all possible values and is a supertype of every type (more precisely, it is a supertype of every scalar type, every tuple type, and every relation type)—in fact, it is a *proper* supertype of every type except itself, and an *immediate* supertype of every type that would otherwise be a root type (and of no others). Note that type *alpha* is probably a dummy type in the sense of Chapter 14; note too that the effect of introducing it is to make the entire type graph into a single partition, in the sense of Chapter 15.

- Type *omega* is **the empty type:** It contains no values at all and is a subtype of every type (more precisely, it is a subtype of every scalar type, every tuple type, and every relation type)—in fact, it is a *proper* subtype of every type except itself, and an *immediate* subtype of every leaf type (and of no others). Note that type *omega* is a dummy type, by definition.

We then go on to define the most specific common supertype of an empty set of types to be, precisely, *omega** (analogously, the least specific common subtype of an empty set of types is, of course, *alpha*). Note, incidentally, that TREAT DOWN to *omega* will always fail and IS_*omega* (…) will always give *false* (as will

---

*In an earlier paper [31], we said we were unable to find a use for the concept of an empty domain; we are naturally delighted to have found such a use in connection with our proposed inheritance model.

IS_MST_*omega* (…)). By contrast, TREAT UP to *alpha* will always succeed, unless *alpha* is indeed a dummy type (but it probably is), and IS_*alpha* (…) will always give *true.* Note too that *alpha* might possibly have no operators other than "=" and ":=", while *omega* has all possible operators (but vacuously so, since they can never be invoked on any value or variable of the type). Note finally that the membership predicates—i.e., the predicates that a value must satisfy to be a value of the types in question—for *alpha* and *omega* are simply *true* and *false,* respectively.

Here then are some "most specific common supertype" examples. First, the most specific common supertype of the scalar types POLYGON, RECTANGLE, and SQUARE is POLYGON; likewise, the most specific common supertype of the scalar types PLANE_FIGURE and RECTANGLE is PLANE_FIGURE; and the most specific common supertype of CIRCLE and SQUARE is again PLANE_FIGURE. (All of these examples refer to Fig. 14.1 from Chapter 14, of course.)

Second, consider once again the tuple types

```
TUPLE { E ELLIPSE, R RECTANGLE }          /* tuple type "ER" */

TUPLE { E CIRCLE,  R RECTANGLE }          /* tuple type "CR" */

TUPLE { E ELLIPSE, R SQUARE     }          /* tuple type "ES" */

TUPLE { E CIRCLE,  R SQUARE     }          /* tuple type "CS" */
```

Then:

- The most specific common supertype of CR and CS is CR; likewise, the most specific common supertype of ES and CS is ES.

- The most specific common supertype of CR and ES is ER.

- The most specific common supertype of all four types is also ER.

Of course, we have only to replace the four tuple types above by four analogous relation types to obtain a set of relation "most specific common supertype" examples.

Now we turn to the real point of this section and consider the question of the *most specific type* of a given value. The scalar case has already been dealt with in the previous chapter, of course, and the tuple case is an obvious generalization of the scalar case—but the relation case is a little more complicated, as we now explain.

We begin by considering some examples. Take another look at the four relations in Fig. 16.1. The most specific types of those four relations are (from top to bottom) relation types ER, CR, ES, and CS, respectively. Note further that, e.g., the top relation in that figure would still have relation type ER as its most specific type even if we deleted the only tuple (*viz.,* the E1-R1 tuple) that is actually of *tuple* type ER. If we deleted the C2-R2 tuple as well, however, that relation would then have relation type ES as its most specific type.

Now, you might feel something counterintuitive is going on here (and so it is, in a way). For example, look again at the top relation in Fig. 16.1 (call it *TopRel*). For relation *TopRel*, it almost seems as if we have defined the *most* specific type (*viz.,* relation type ER) to be the *least* specific type of the tuples in that relation!—and indeed so we have, in this particular example. Why then did we not define the most specific type of *TopRel* to be relation type CS (the other "extreme" type) instead? A moment's thought should serve to answer this question. Suppose we *had* defined that most specific type to be CS instead of ER. Then certain of the attributes in certain of the tuples in *TopRel* would contain values that were not of the "right" type. The E1-R1 tuple, for example, contains a value of type ELLIPSE (not CIRCLE) and a value of type RECTANGLE (not SQUARE), and thus certainly does not conform to type CS.* It follows that we *must* define the most specific type for relation *r* in the way we have done— namely, in such a way that the type corresponding to attribute *A* is the *most specific common supertype* of the most specific types of all of the A values in *r*. As noted earlier, the terminology is (unfortunately) perhaps a little inappropriate in the relational case.†

In an attempt to help you understand better exactly what is going on here, we show in Fig. 16.2 another set of relations, based on the multiple inheritance example shown in Fig. 15.1 in Chapter 15. The most specific types of these relations (from top to bottom) are as follows. Note the last one in particular!

- RELATION { PX PARALLELOGRAM, PY RECTANGLE }

- RELATION { PX RHOMBUS,   PY RECTANGLE }

- RELATION { PX RECTANGLE,   PY SQUARE   }

- RELATION { PX SQUARE,   PY SQUARE   }

- RELATION { PX *omega,*   PY *omega*   }

---

*More accurately, it does not conform to *tuple* type CS, and so a relation that contains it does not conform to *relation* type CS.

†We remark that computation of the most specific type of a given relation might be too time-consuming to be a practical proposition, except when the relation in question is of low cardinality. One implication is that the implementer of an operator that has a parameter of some relation type might well want to avoid having special versions of that operator to deal with special subtypes of that relation type.

```
┌─────────────────────────────────────────────────────────────┐
│   ┌─────────────────────────┬─────────────────────────┐      │
│   │ PX  :  PARALLELOGRAM    │ PY  :  PARALLELOGRAM    │      │
│   ├─────────────────────────┼─────────────────────────┤      │
│   │ X1  :  rectangle        │ Y1  :  rectangle        │      │
│   │ X2  :  rhombus          │ Y2  :  rectangle        │      │
│   │ X3  :  rectangle        │ Y3  :  square           │      │
│   │ X4  :  square           │ Y4  :  square           │      │
│   └─────────────────────────┴─────────────────────────┘      │
│                                                               │
│   ┌─────────────────────────┬─────────────────────────┐      │
│   │ PX  :  PARALLELOGRAM    │ PY  :  PARALLELOGRAM    │      │
│   ├─────────────────────────┼─────────────────────────┤      │
│   │ X2  :  rhombus          │ Y2  :  rectangle        │      │
│   │ X4  :  square           │ Y4  :  square           │      │
│   └─────────────────────────┴─────────────────────────┘      │
│                                                               │
│   ┌─────────────────────────┬─────────────────────────┐      │
│   │ PX  :  PARALLELOGRAM    │ PY  :  PARALLELOGRAM    │      │
│   ├─────────────────────────┼─────────────────────────┤      │
│   │ X3  :  rectangle        │ Y3  :  square           │      │
│   │ X4  :  square           │ Y4  :  square           │      │
│   └─────────────────────────┴─────────────────────────┘      │
│                                                               │
│   ┌─────────────────────────┬─────────────────────────┐      │
│   │ PX  :  PARALLELOGRAM    │ PY  :  PARALLELOGRAM    │      │
│   ├─────────────────────────┼─────────────────────────┤      │
│   │ X4  :  square           │ Y4  :  square           │      │
│   └─────────────────────────┴─────────────────────────┘      │
│                                                               │
│   ┌─────────────────────────┬─────────────────────────┐      │
│   │ PX  :  PARALLELOGRAM    │ PY  :  PARALLELOGRAM    │      │
│   ├─────────────────────────┴─────────────────────────┤      │
│   └─────────────────────────────────────────────────────┘      │
└─────────────────────────────────────────────────────────────┘
```

Fig. 16.2   Some relations of type RELATION { PX PARALLELOGRAM,
PY PARALLELOGRAM }

TUPLE AND RELATION VARIABLES (EXTENDED DEFINITIONS)

Let (tuple or relation) variable V *be of declared type* T, *and let the heading of* T *have attributes* A1, A2, ..., An. *Then we can model* V *as a set of named ordered triples of the form* <DTi,MSTi,vi>, *where:*

- *The name of each triple is the name of the corresponding attribute.*

- DTi *is the name of the declared type of attribute* Ai.

- MSTi *is the name of the **most specific type**—also known as the **current** most specific type—for, or of, attribute* Ai. Note: *If* V *is a relation variable, then* MSTi *is defined to be the name of the most specific common supertype of the most specific types of the* m *values in* vi *(see the explanation of* vi *below).*

- *If* V *is a tuple variable,* vi *is a value of most specific type MST—the **current value** for, or of, attribute* Ai. *If* V *is a relation variable, then let the body of the current value of* V *consist of* m *tuples; label those tuples (in some arbitrary* *sequence) "tuple 1," "tuple 2," ..., "tuple m"; then vi is a sequence of m values (not necessarily all distinct), being the Ai values from tuple 1, tuple 2, ..., tuple m (in that order); note that all of those values are of type MSTi.*

We use the notation DT(Ai), MST(Ai), v(Ai) to refer to the DTi, MSTi, vi components, respectively, of attribute Ai of (our model of) tuple or relation variable V. We also use the notation DT(V), MST(V), v(V) to refer to the overall declared type, overall current most specific type, and overall current value, respectively, of tuple or relation variable V. Note that in fact MSTi(Ai) is implied by v(Ai) and MST(V) is implied by v(V).

Now (at last!) we are in a position to give the necessary extended definitions for *tuple variable* and *relation variable* (relvar). Yet again, it turns out that the definitions are both recursive and mutually recursive.

Basically, **a tuple variable of declared type *TT*** is a variable whose permitted values are tuples of type *TT,* and **a relation variable (relvar) of declared type *RT*** is a variable whose permitted values are relations of type *RT.* (In fact, these definitions are essentially the same as in Chapter 3—see RM Prescriptions 12 and 13—but the concept of a tuple or relation value being of a given type has been given a considerably extended interpretation.)

We need to be a little more specific than this, however. In fact, what we really need is a *model* for tuple and relation variables, analogous to the model we already have for scalar variables (see Chapters 13 and 14). So let us examine this question. As usual, we consider tuples first.

Let tuple variable *V* be of declared type *T,* and let the heading of *T* have attributes *A1, A2, ..., An.* Then we can model *V* as a set of named ordered triples of the form *<DTi,MSTi,vi>,* where:

- The name of each triple is the name of the corresponding attribute.

- *DTi* is the name of the declared type of attribute *Ai.*

- *MSTi* is the name of the **most specific type**—also known as the **current** most specific type—for, or of, attribute *Ai.*

- *vi* is a value of most specific type *MST*—the **current value** for, or of, attribute *Ai.*

We use the notation *DT(Ai), MST(Ai), v(Ai)* to refer to the *DTi, MSTi, vi* components, respectively, of attribute *Ai* of (our model of) tuple variable *V.* Note that it must always be the case that *MST(Ai)* is some subtype—not necessarily a proper subtype—of *DT(Ai).* Note too that *MST(Ai)* and *v(Ai)* change with time, in general; in other words, the phrase "most specific type of attribute *Ai*" refers to the most specific type of the value of *Ai* within the *current value* of tuple variable *V,* not to the most specific type that such *Ai* values are ever permitted to have.

Note: We also use the notation $DT(V)$, $MST(V)$, $v(V)$ to refer to the overall declared type, overall current most specific type, and overall current value (respectively), of tuple variable V. In other words (using **Tutorial D** notation):

- `DT(V)` ≡ `TUPLE { A1 DT1,   A2 DT2,   ..., An DTn }`

- `MST(V)` ≡ `TUPLE { A1 MST1, A2 MST2, ..., An MSTn }`

- `v(V)`   ≡ `TUPLE { A1 v1,   A2 v2,    ..., An vn }`

Turning now to relation variables (relvars): Let relation variable V be of declared type T, and let the heading of T have attributes $A1$, $A2$, ..., An. Let the body of the current value of V consist of m tuples; label those tuples (in some arbitrary sequence) "tuple 1," "tuple 2," ..., "tuple m." Then we can model V as a set of named ordered triples of the form $<DTi,MSTi,vi>$, where:

- The name of each triple is the name of the corresponding attribute.

- DTi is the name of the declared type of attribute Ai.

- $MSTi$ is the name of the **most specific type**—also known as the **current** most specific type—for, or of, attribute Ai (it is in fact the most specific common supertype of the most specific types of the m values in vi—see below).

- vi is a sequence of m values (not necessarily all distinct), being the Ai values from tuple 1, tuple 2, ..., tuple m (in that order); all of those values are of type $MSTi$.

We use the notation $DT(Ai)$, $MST(Ai)$, $v(Ai)$ to refer to the DTi, $MSTi$, vi components, respectively, of attribute Ai of (our model of) relation variable V. Note that it must always be the case that $MST(Ai)$ is some subtype—not necessarily a proper subtype—of $DT(Ai)$. Note too that $MST(Ai)$ and $v(Ai)$ change with time, in general; in other words, the phrase "most specific type of attribute Ai" refers to the most specific common supertype of the most specific types of all of the Ai values within the *current value* of the relation variable V, not to the most specific type that such Ai values are ever permitted to have.

Note: We also use the notation $DT(V)$, $MST(V)$, $v(V)$ to refer to the overall declared type, overall current most specific type, and overall current value (respectively), of relation variable V. In other words (using **Tutorial D** notation):

- `DT(V)` ≡ `RELATION { A1 DT1,   A2 DT2,   ..., An DTn }`

- `MST(V)` ≡ `RELATION { A1 MST1, A2 MST2, ..., An MSTn }`

- `v(V)`   ≡ `RELATION`
  ` { TUPLE { A1 v11,  A2 v12,  ..., An v1n },`
  `   TUPLE { A1 v21,  A2 v22,  ..., An v2n },`
  `   ...............................`
  `   TUPLE { A1 vm1,  A2 vm2,  ..., An vmn } }`

Here the symbol vij denotes the value of attribute Aj in tuple i, of course ($i = 1$, 2, ..., m; $j = 1, 2, ..., n$).

We close this section by repeating that (as indicated three sections back) the definitions in this section and its two immediate predecessors together constitute the tuple and relation analogs of our scalar IM Proposals 12 and 13 ("extended definitions of scalar values and variables").

TUPLE AND RELATION ASSIGNMENT

Let X be a tuple expression or relational expression. The notation DT(V), MST(V), v(V) introduced in the previous section can be extended in an obvious way to refer to the declared type DT(X), the current most specific type MST(X), and the current value v(X), respectively, of X—where "declared type" is as explained in RM Prescriptions 12 and 13 and is known at compilation time, and "current most specific type" and "current value" refer to the result of evaluating X and are therefore not known until run time, in general. Now consider the assignment

```
V   :=  X ;
```

(where V is a tuple or relation variable, as appropriate). DT(X) must be a subtype of DT(V), otherwise the assignment is illegal (this is a compile-time check). If the assignment is legal, its effect is to set MST(V) equal to MST(X) and v(V) equal to v(X).

—— ♦♦♦♦♦ ——

The definitions above are the tuple/relation analog of our scalar IM Proposal 14 ("scalar assignment with inheritance"). The extensions (extensions to the scalar version, that is) are straightforward—essentially, all that is needed is to replace "scalar" by "tuple or relation" (twice). Here is a slightly nontrivial example to illustrate tuple assignment:

```
VAR V1 TUPLE { P POINT, ER TUPLE { E ELLIPSE, R RECTANGLE } } ;
VAR V2 TUPLE { P POINT, ER TUPLE { E CIRCLE,  R SQUARE     } } ;

V2   :=  TUPLE { P POINT (...),
                 ER TUPLE { E CIRCLE (...), R SQUARE (...) } } ;

V1   :=  V2 ;
```

After the second assignment here:

- *DT*(V1) is unchanged (it is the tuple type specified in the definition of V1).
- *MST*(V1) is the same as *MST*(V2) (it is in fact the tuple type specified in the definition of V2, but only because that type happens to be the most specific type of the current value of V2).
- *v*(V1) is the same as *v*(V2).

Suppose now that V2 had been defined slightly differently:

```
VAR V2 TUPLE { Q POINT, ER TUPLE { E CIRCLE, R SQUARE } } ;
```

(the difference is that the point-valued attribute is now called Q instead of P). The assignment of V2 to V1 will now fail, because the declared type of V2 is no longer a subtype of that of V1 (this is a compile-time check). However, the following assignment is legal:*

```
V1  :=  V2 RENAME Q AS P ;
```

It should be clear that relational assignments obey the same general rules, and we therefore leave the provision of examples as an exercise for the reader. However, we should perhaps remind you that *The Third Manifesto* also requires support for operators to extract attribute values from tuples and tuple values from relations (see RM Prescriptions 6 and 7), and we need to consider the implications of subtypes and supertypes on those operations also. Here is an example involving extraction of an attribute value from a tuple:

```
VAR Z POINT ;

Z  :=  P FROM V1 ;
```

Let us use the symbol X to denote the expression P FROM V1. Then the declared type $DT(X)$, the current most specific type $MST(X)$, and the current value $v(X)$ are defined to be equal to the declared type $DT(P)$, the current most specific type $MST(P)$, and the current value $v(P)$, respectively, of attribute P of tuple variable V1.

Here is an example involving extraction of a tuple from a relation:

```
VAR RV ... RELATION { E CIRCLE,  R RECTANGLE } ... ;

VAR TV     TUPLE    { E ELLIPSE, R RECTANGLE }      ;

TV  :=  TUPLE FROM ( RV WHERE E = ... AND R = ... ) ;
```

Let us use the symbol Y to denote the expression on the right hand side of this assignment. Then we define the declared type $DT(Y)$ to be

```
TUPLE { E CIRCLE, R RECTANGLE }
```

("tuple type CR"); the current most specific type $MST(Y)$ to be the most specific type of the extracted tuple (which is some subtype of tuple type CR); and the current value $v(Y)$ to be that extracted tuple.

---

*It is only fair to point out a minor oddity here. Given scalar variables E and C of declared types ELLIPSE and CIRCLE, respectively, we can legally assign C to E. Yet if ET and CT are *tuple* variables, of tuple types TUPLE {E ELLIPSE} and TUPLE {C CIRCLE}, respectively, we *cannot* legally assign CT to ET; we have to assign CT RENAME C AS E to ET instead. The reason for this seeming anomaly, of course, is that tuple types have attributes, and the attribute names are part of the type; scalar types, by contrast, have no attributes, and so the question of the names of such attributes being somehow part of the type does not arise.

TUPLE AND RELATION COMPARISON

Consider the comparison

```
Y = X
```

(where Y *and* X *are both tuple expressions or both relational expressions).* DT(X) *and* DT(Y) *must have a common subtype, otherwise the comparison is illegal (this is a compile-time check). If the comparison is legal, its effect is to return* true *if* MST(Y) *is equal to* MST(X) *and* v(Y) *is equal to* v(X), false *otherwise.*

—— ◆ ◆ ◆ ◆ ◆ ——

The definition above is the tuple/relation analog of our scalar IM Proposal 15 ("scalar comparison with inheritance"), as extended in Chapter 15 to handle multiple inheritance. As in the previous section, the extensions to the scalar version are straightforward—essentially, all that is needed is to replace "scalar" by "tuple or relation" (once). Here is an example:

```
VAR V1 TUPLE { E ELLIPSE, R SQUARE } ;    /* tuple type "ES" */
VAR V2 TUPLE { E CIRCLE,  R RECTANGLE } ; /* tuple type "CR" */

IF V1 = V2 THEN ... ;
END IF ;
```

The comparison here will give *true* if (a) the current values of tuple variables V1 and V2 have tuple type CS* as their common most specific type, and (b) those current values are equal. (Recall that tuple type CS is defined as follows—

```
TUPLE { E CIRCLE, R SQUARE }
```

—and observe that this type is indeed a subtype of both the declared type ES of V1 and the declared type CR of V2.)

Further elaboration seems unnecessary, except to note that of course the rules regarding comparison operators other than equality ("is a subset of," etc.) can be derived in an obvious way from the rules for equality—though it is perhaps worth pointing out that relation *ry* can be a subset of relation *rx* only if *MST(ry)* is a subtype of *MST(rx)*.

As for IM Proposal 16 ("join etc. with inheritance"), the revised version given in Chapter 15 applies to tuple and relation types unchanged. For example, if the declared type of attribute *A* in relation *rx* is tuple type ES and the declared type of attribute *A* in relation *ry* is tuple type CR, then the declared type of attribute *A* in the join of *rx* and *ry* is tuple type ER.

---

*Or some proper subtype of type CS, of course, if any such proper subtype exists.

TUPLE AND RELATION TREAT DOWN

For every tuple or relation type T, *a tuple or relational operator (as applicable) of the form*

```
TREAT_DOWN_TO_SAME_TYPE_AS ( Y, X )
```

(or logical equivalent thereof) should be supported, where X *and* Y *are tuple or relation expressions (as applicable),* DT(Y) *is* T, *and* T *is a subtype of* DT(X) *(this is a compile-time check). We refer to such operators generically as "TREAT DOWN" operators; their semantics are as follows. First of all,* MST(X) *must be a subtype of* T *(this is a run-time check, in general). Assuming this condition is satisfied, then:*

   a. *If the TREAT DOWN invocation appears in a "source" position (in particular, on the right hand side of an assignment), then the invocation yields a result,* R *say, with* DT(R) *equal to* T, MST(R) *equal to* MST(X), *and* v(R) *equal to* v(X).

   b. *If the TREAT DOWN invocation appears in a "target" position (in particular, on the left hand side of an assignment), then, first, the invocation acts as a pseudovariable, which means that it actually* designates *its argument* X *(more accurately, it designates a version of* X *in which* DT(X) *is equal to* T *but* MST(X)) *is unchanged; second, that argument* X *must be specified as a variable specifically, not as an arbitrary expression.*

——— ♦♦♦♦♦ ———

The definitions here, of course, constitute a tuple/relation analog of our scalar TREAT DOWN operator (see IM Proposal 17). Consider the following example:

```
VAR V1 TUPLE { E ELLIPSE, R RECTANGLE } ;
VAR V2 TUPLE { E CIRCLE,  R SQUARE    } ;

V2   :=   TUPLE { E CIRCLE (...), R SQUARE (...) } ;

V1   :=   V2 ;
```

After the second assignment here, the current value of V1 consists of a circle and a square, not an ellipse and a rectangle (speaking rather loosely!). Suppose now that we want to assign that value back to V2. Then the following assignment will not work:

```
V2   :=   V1 ;                     /* COMPILE-TIME TYPE ERROR !!! */
```

(it fails because the declared type of V1 is not a subtype of the declared type of V2). Instead, what we have to say is something like this:

```
V2   :=   TREAT_DOWN_TO_SAME_TYPE_AS ( V2, V1 ) ;
```

The expression on the right hand side here is defined to have declared type the same as that of variable V2, so the compile-time type checking now succeeds. At run time:

- If the current value of V1 is indeed of that type, then the expression yields a result, VV say, with (a) $DT(VV)$ equal to $DT(V2)$, because of the V2 argument, (b) $MST(VV)$ equal to $MST(V1)$, which is the same as $DT(V2)$ in the example, and (c) $v(VV)$ equal to $v(V1)$.

- However, if the current value of V1 is only of the (declared) type of V1, not of V2, then the expression fails on a run-time type error.

In other words, the TREAT_DOWN_TO_SAME_TYPE_AS operator is indeed a tuple analog of TREAT DOWN as discussed under (scalar) IM Proposal 17 in Chapters 13 and 14.* (Note that we have to use the slightly more general "SAME AS" format because our tuple type naming conventions do not lend themselves to the simpler format available in the scalar case.)

Without going into further specifics, we hope it is clear that we can (and do) also propose:

- A relational version of TREAT_DOWN_TO_SAME_TYPE_AS

- Tuple and relation TREAT_DOWN_TO_SAME_TYPE_AS pseudovariables

- Tuple and relational operators of the form

```
X TREAT_DOWN_TO_SAME_TYPE_AS ( Y, A )
```

(where X is a tuple expression or a relational expression, A is a tuple- or relation-valued attribute of the tuple or relation denoted by X, and Y is an expression such that $DT(Y)$ is some proper subtype of $DT(A)$).

Together, these operators constitute a complete tuple/relation counterpart to the scalar facilities discussed under IM Proposal 17 in Chapters 13 and 14.

IM PROPOSALS 18–26 REVISITED

Thus far in this chapter, we have considered the impact of tuple and relation subtyping on our scalar IM Proposals 1–17 from Chapters 13–15. In particular, in the section immediately preceding, we showed tuple and relation counterparts to the

---

*It is worth noting in passing that the particular TREAT DOWN invocation in the example is logically equivalent to the following tuple selector invocation:

```
TUPLE { TREAT_DOWN_AS_CIRCLE ( E FROM V1 ),
        TREAT_DOWN_AS_SQUARE ( R FROM V1 ) }
```

scalar TREAT DOWN operator and related scalar facilities. Without going into too much detail, it should be clear that we can (and do) make proposals—where applicable—for tuple and relation counterparts to the remaining scalar IM Proposals (Numbers 18–26) also. We therefore conclude this chapter by summarizing those remaining proposals very briefly (retaining the numbering from those previous chapters).

18. *TREAT UP*

    We propose:

    - Tuple and relation TREAT_UP_TO_SAME_TYPE_AS operators and pseudovariables

    - Tuple and relational operators and pseudovariables of the form

      ```
      X TREAT_UP_TO_SAME_TYPE_AS ( Y, A )
      ```

      where X is a tuple or relational expression, A is a tuple- or relation-valued attribute of the tuple or relation denoted by X, and Y is an expression such that $DT(Y)$ is some proper subtype of $DT(A)$.

19. *Logical operator IS_T(SX)*

    We propose operators of the form

    ```
    IS_SAME_TYPE_AS ( Y, X )
    ```

    where X and Y are both tuple expressions or both relational expressions.

20. *Relational operator RX:IS_T(A)*

    We propose relational operators of the form

    ```
    X : IS_SAME_TYPE_AS ( Y, A )
    ```

    where X is a relational expression, A is an attribute of the relation denoted by X, and Y is an expression such that $DT(Y)$ is some subtype of $DT(A)$.

21. *Logical operator IS_MS_T(SX)*

    We propose operators of the form

    ```
    IS_SAME_MS_TYPE_AS ( Y, X )
    ```

22. *Relational operator RX:IS_MS_T(A)*

    We propose relational operators of the form

    ```
    X : IS_SAME_MS_TYPE_AS ( Y, A )
    ```

23. *THE_ pseudovariables*

    This IM Proposal is not applicable, because tuple and relation types have no declared possible representations other than those implied by their attributes.

24. *Read-only operator inheritance and value substitutability*

    No change necessary.

25. *Read-only parameters to update operators*

    No change necessary.

26. *Update operator inheritance and variable substitutability*

    No change necessary.

APPENDIXES

The appendixes that follow cover a somewhat mixed bag of topics. Appendix A presents an alternative version of **Tutorial D,** one that is based on relational calculus instead of relational algebra. Appendix B discusses a database design issue that—some people have suggested—might arise in a system that conforms to the prescriptions (especially the *type* prescriptions) laid down in *The Third Manifesto.* Appendix C addresses an important issue having to with type inheritance, known as *specialization by constraint.* Appendix D discusses "subtables and supertables." Appendix E presents a detailed comparison of the SQL3 proposals [87–89,100–101] with the ideas of the *Manifesto,* and Appendix F performs the analogous task for the ODMG proposals [15]. Appendix G contains the text of an interview the present authors gave in 1994 on the subject of the *Manifesto.* Finally, Appendix H provides an annotated list of references and suggestions for further reading.

A Relational Calculus Version of Tutorial D

INTRODUCTION

In this appendix we sketch the principal features of an alternative version of **Tutorial D,** one for which the "data sublanguage" portion—see Chapter 5—is based on relational calculus instead of relational algebra (tuple relational calculus, to be precise). In terms of the BNF grammar of Chapter 5, the main syntactic categories that need revision are *<bool exp>* ("boolean expression") and *<builtin relation op inv>* ("builtin relational operator invocation"). *Note:* The *<relation update>* and *<relation delete>* shorthands, if supported, will need some minor revisions too, but the revisions in question are essentially similar to those for *<builtin relation op inv>*. For brevity, we omit extended discussion of those shorthands in this appendix, though we do give some syntax and a couple of examples.

The first thing we need to do is introduce the concept of a **range variable,** which we do forthwith:

```
<range var def>
    ::=   RANGEVAR <range var name>
          RANGES OVER <ne relation exp commalist>
```

The *<relation exp>*s must not mention any variables except relvars, and possibly other range variables—but range variables are not really variables at all as we normally use that term, which is why we use the keyword RANGEVAR instead of simply VAR. In Chapter 1, when we were discussing the distinction between values and variables, we said that the kind of variable we were interested in was a variable "in the usual programming language sense." Range variables, however, are *not* variables in the usual programming language sense, they are variables in the sense of logic; in fact, they are analogous, somewhat, to the *placeholders* discussed in Chapter 4 (the difference is that the placeholders of Chapter 4 stood for domain values, while our range variables stand for tuples).

A *<range var def>* is a new form of *<statement body>*. Here are some examples (expressed in terms of the usual suppliers-and-parts database):

```
RANGEVAR SX  RANGES OVER S ;
RANGEVAR SY  RANGES OVER S ;
RANGEVAR SPX RANGES OVER SP ;
RANGEVAR PX  RANGES OVER P ;
RANGEVAR SU RANGES OVER
        ( SX WHERE CITY FROM SX = 'London' ) ,
        ( SX WHERE EXISTS SPX ( S# FROM SPX = S# FROM SX AND
                                P# FROM SPX = P# ('P1') ) )
```

Range variable SU in this last example is defined to range over the *union* of the set of supplier tuples for suppliers who are located in London and the set of supplier tuples for suppliers who supply part P1. Note that the definition of range variable SU makes use of the range variables SX and SPX.

We also need two new syntactic categories, *<range var ref>* and *<range attribute ref>*. First, *<range var ref>:*

```
<range var ref>
    ::=    <range var name>
```

A *<range var ref>* is a special case of a *<tuple exp>*. Unlike *<tuple exp>*s in general, however, a *<range var ref>* can appear only in certain limited contexts. To be specific, a *<range var ref>* can appear:

- As the FROM operand in a *<range attribute ref>*—see below;
- Immediately following the quantifier in a *<quantified bool exp>*—see the next section;
- As an operand within a *<bool exp>* (or as an operand within certain kinds* of *<exp>* within a *<bool exp>*)—see the next section;
- As a *<proto tuple>* (or as an operand within certain kinds of *<exp>* within a *<proto tuple>*)—see the next section but one.

Here now is the syntax for *<range attribute ref>:*

```
<range attribute ref>
    ::=    <attribute ref> FROM <range var ref>
```

---

*As this wording suggests, we are not trying to be 100 percent precise in this appendix.

A *<range attribute ref>* is a special case of an *<exp>;* more precisely, it is a special case of a *<scalar exp>, <tuple exp>,* or *<relation exp>,* depending on whether the attribute in question is scalar-, tuple-, or relation-valued. Unlike *<exp>*s in general, however, a *<range attribute ref>* can appear only in certain limited contexts. To be specific, a *<range attribute ref>* can appear:

- As an operand within a *<bool exp>* (or as an operand within certain kinds of *<exp>* within a *<bool exp>*)—see the next section;
- As an operand within certain kinds of *<exp>* within a *<proto tuple>*—see the next section but one;
- As the *<exp>* (or as an operand within an *<exp>*) on the right hand side of an *<attribute update>* in a *<relation update>*, if *<relation update>* is supported.

BOOLEAN EXPRESSIONS

We extend the definition of *<bool exp>* as follows:

```
<bool exp>
    ::=   ... all previous possibilities, together with:
        | <quantified bool exp>

<quantified bool exp>
    ::=   EXISTS <range var ref> ( <bool exp> )
        | FORALL <range var ref> ( <bool exp> )
```

We assume the semantics of the **quantifiers** EXISTS and FORALL are well understood.

BUILTIN RELATION OPERATOR INVOCATIONS

We replace the definition of *<builtin relation op inv>* by the following revised definition:

```
<builtin relation op inv>
    ::=   <proto tuple> [ WHERE <bool exp> ]

<proto tuple>
    ::=   <tuple exp>
```

Note: In order to stay within the relational calculus spirit of this appendix, we had originally intended not to avail ourselves of any of the builtin tuple operators (tuple project, tuple rename, tuple join, and so on) within a *<tuple exp>* that was acting in the capacity of a *<proto tuple>* ("prototype tuple"). We observe, however, that relational calculus has traditionally used "." as a kind of tuple projection operator, "," as a kind of tuple join—or at least Cartesian product—operator, and AS as a kind of tuple rename operator, within its analog of our *<proto tuple>*; we therefore decided (reasonably enough, we feel) to allow the use of tuple project, join, and rename operators within our own expressions in the same kind of way.

Certain additional details regarding the syntax of *<builtin relation op inv>*s are explained in the next section. The semantics are meant to be both orthodox and obvious; basically, the *<builtin relation op inv>* evaluates to a relation containing every possible value of the *<proto tuple>* for which the *<bool exp>* specified in the WHERE clause evaluates to *true*. Omitting the WHERE clause is equivalent to specifying "WHERE *true*." See, e.g., reference [56] for a more detailed explanation.

FREE AND BOUND RANGE VARIABLE REFERENCES

Every reference to a range variable is either **free** or **bound** (in some context). The rules are as follows. Let *r* be such a range variable reference. Then:

- The sole reference to *r* in the *<range var ref>* "*r*" is free within that *<range var ref>*.

- The sole reference to *r* in the *<range attribute ref>* "*A* FROM *r*" is free within that *<range attribute ref>*.

- The sole reference to *r* in the *<tuple rename>* "*r* RENAME ..." is free within that *<tuple rename>*.

- The sole reference to *r* in the *<tuple project>* "*r* {...}" is free within that *<tuple project>*.

- The sole reference to *r* in the *<tuple join>* "*r* JOIN *s*" is free within that *<tuple join>*.

- References in the *<bool exp>* "NOT *x*" are free or bound within that *<bool exp>* according as they are free or bound in *x*. References in the *<bool exp>*s "(*x* AND *y*)" and "(*x* OR *y*)" are free or bound in those *<bool exp>*s according as they are free or bound in *x* or *y*, whichever is applicable.

- References to *r* that are free in the *<bool exp>* "*x*" are bound in the *<bool exp>*s "EXISTS *r* (*x*)" and "FORALL *r* (*x*)." Other references in "*x*" are free or bound in those *<bool exp>*s according as they are free or bound in "*x*".

- Let the *<relation exp>* argument in some *<agg op inv>* be a *<builtin relation op inv>* of the form "*pt* WHERE *x*." Then references to *r* in the *<proto tuple>* "*pt*" (which are necessarily free in that context—see below) are bound in that *<agg op inv>*.

- If a reference to *r* is free in some expression *exp,* that reference is also free in any expression *exp'* that immediately contains *exp* as a subexpression, unless *exp'* introduces a quantifier that makes the reference bound instead.

All range variable references appearing immediately—i.e., not within some inner nested *<proto tuple>*—within a given *<proto tuple>* must be free within that *<proto tuple>*. Range variable references appearing within a *<bool exp>* can be free only if both of the following are true:

- The *<bool exp>* appears immediately within a *<builtin relation op inv>* (i.e., following the keyword WHERE), and
- A reference (necessarily free) to that very same range variable appears immediately within the *<proto tuple>* immediately contained within that very same *<builtin relation op inv>* (i.e., preceding the keyword WHERE).

RELATION UPDATE AND DELETE OPERATORS

We need to revise *<relation update>* and *<relation delete>* slightly. As noted in the introduction to this appendix, we content ourselves with simply presenting the revised syntax without further comment (the semantics should be obvious).

```
<relation update>
    ::=   UPDATE <range var name> [ WHERE <bool exp> ]
                <ne attribute update commalist>

<relation delete>
    ::=   DELETE <range var name> [ WHERE <bool exp> ]
```

EXAMPLES

We conclude this appendix with a series of examples to lend credibility to our contention that this alternative form of **Tutorial D** does indeed provide all of the relational functionality of its algebraic counterpart.* We assume the existence of range variables as defined in the introductory section.

Rename: Get all suppliers, renaming CITY to SCITY.

```
SX RENAME CITY AS SCITY
```

Restriction: Get suppliers in London.

```
SX WHERE CITY FROM SX = 'London'
```

Or:

```
SX WHERE SX { CITY } = TUPLE { CITY 'London' }
```

This alternative form makes use of a tuple comparison instead of a scalar one.

---

*We omit one major feature of the algebraic version, however—*viz.,* transitive closure. In principle, transitive closure could be supported by (e.g.) allowing the relational expression used in the definition of a range variable *R* to refer to that very same range variable *R* itself.

Projection: Get all supplier-number/supplier-city pairs.

```
SX { S#, CITY }
```

Union: Get suppliers who are located in London or supply part P1 or both.

```
SU
```

Intersect: Get cities in which both a supplier and a part are located.

```
SX { CITY } WHERE EXISTS PX ( PX { CITY } = SX { CITY } )
```

Minus: Get cities in which a supplier is located, but not a part.

```
SX { CITY } WHERE NOT EXISTS PX ( PX { CITY } = SX { CITY } )
```

Join: Get suppliers and matching shipments.

```
SX JOIN SPX
```

Note that the JOIN here is a *tuple* join; it yields a result tuple if and only if the tuples to be joined have common values for their common attributes.

Join (Cartesian product): Get all supplier-number/part-number pairs.

```
SX { S# } JOIN PX { P# }
```

Compose: Get all supplier-number/part-number pairs where the supplier and part are located in the same city.

```
( SX { S# } JOIN PX { P# } ) WHERE SX { CITY } = PX { CITY }
```

The parentheses surrounding the *<proto tuple>* here are included only for clarity—they are not essential (nor are they wrong).

Semidifference: Get suppliers who do not supply part P1.

```
SX WHERE NOT EXISTS SPX ( SPX { S# } = SX { S# } AND
                          P# FROM SPX = P# ('P1') )
```

Semijoin: Get suppliers who do supply part P1.

```
SX WHERE EXISTS SPX ( SPX { S# } = SX { S# } AND
                      P# FROM SPX = P# ('P1') )
```

Divide: Get suppliers who supply all parts.

```
SX WHERE FORALL PX ( EXISTS SPX ( SPX { S# } = SX { S# } AND
                                  SPX { P# } = PX { P# } ) )
```

Note: The foregoing illustrates the Small Divide. The Great Divide is left as an exercise for the reader.

Extend: Get all parts, together with their weight in grams (weights in relvar P are given in pounds).

```
PX JOIN TUPLE { GMWT ( WEIGHT FROM PX ) * 454 }
```

GMWT here is an introduced attribute name.

Summarize: For each part supplied, get the part number and the corresponding total quantity, TOTQ.

```
PX { P# } JOIN
TUPLE { TOTQ SUM ( SPX WHERE SPX { P# } = PX { P# }, QTY ) }
```

Wrap: "Wrap" shipment attributes P# and QTY into a single tuple-valued attribute, PQ.

```
SPX { S# } JOIN
TUPLE { PQ SPX { P# } JOIN SPX { QTY } }
```

Or:

```
TUPLE { S# S# FROM SPX,
        PQ TUPLE { P# P# FROM SPX, QTY QTY FROM SPX } }
```

Unwrap: Let R be the result of the foregoing "wrap" operation and let RX be a range variable ranging over R. "Unwrap" attribute PQ of R.

```
TUPLE { S# S# FROM RX,
        P# P# FROM PQ FROM RX, QTY QTY FROM PQ FROM RX }
```

Group: "Group" shipments by supplier number.

```
TUPLE { S# S# FROM SPX,
        PQ ( SPY { P#, QTY } WHERE SPY { S# } = SPX { S# } ) }
```

SPY here is another range variable ranging over SP. The parentheses are included only for clarity.

Ungroup: Let R be the result of the foregoing "group" operation. "Ungroup" attribute PQ of R.

Here we need to extend the syntax and semantics of *<range var def>* slightly:

```
RANGEVAR RX RANGES OVER R ,
RANGEVAR RY RANGES OVER PQ FROM RX ;

RX { S# } JOIN RY { P#, QTY }
```

The idea here is that the definition of range variable RY depends on that of RX (note that the two definitions are separated by a comma, not a semicolon, and are thereby bundled into a single operation).

UPDATE: Double the status of all suppliers in London.

```
UPDATE SX WHERE CITY = 'London'
         STATUS := 2 * STATUS FROM SX ;
```

DELETE: Delete all shipments from Paris suppliers.

```
DELETE SPX WHERE EXISTS SX ( SX { S# } = SPX { S# } AND
                             S# FROM SX = 'Paris' ) ;
```

The Database Design Dilemma ·

INTRODUCTION

It is sometimes suggested that to treat relational domains as fully fledged data types, as *The Third Manifesto* does, is to introduce a design dilemma. For example, suppose we need to deal with employees, where each employee has an employee number (EMP#), a name (ENAME), a department number (DEPT#), and a salary (SALARY). Consider the following **Tutorial D** definitions:

```
TYPE EMP                                      /* Design T */
POSSREP ( EMP#  CHAR, ENAME  CHAR,
          DEPT# CHAR, SALARY MONEY ) ... ;

VAR EMP REAL                                  /* Design R */
RELATION { EMP#  CHAR, ENAME  CHAR,
           DEPT# CHAR, SALARY MONEY } ... ;
```

Clearly, we could choose to define an EMP **type** ("Design T") or an EMP **relvar** ("Design R").* So the obvious question is: Which design is better? What grounds are there for choosing one over the other?

---

*We could also opt for various in-between arrangements, of course.

ENCAPSULATION

One immediate difference between Design T and Design R is that the EMP *type* is **encapsulated,** while the EMP *relvar* is not. Now, *encapsulation* is a term much used in the object world (and you might already be familiar with it); however, you might also have noticed that we have not used it at all in this book prior to this point— largely because we do not find much need for it (see below). Be that as it may, we now explain it.

Briefly, to say that some value or variable is "encapsulated" is simply to say that it has no user-visible components, no matter how complex its actual representation (i.e., its internal encoding) might be. Note immediately, therefore, that in *The Third Manifesto* all scalar values and variables are encapsulated by definition. Tuple and relation types, by contrast, are not encapsulated in this sense, because they both involve a set of user-visible attributes. In fact, **a type is encapsulated if and only if it is scalar** (in our sense of "scalar"—see Chapter 6). And this is essentially why we find little use for the term; after all, it really just means that users do not need to worry about what they *should* not need to worry about—namely, internal encodings. In fact, the idea that scalar values and variables must be encapsulated is a logical consequence of the distinctions we draw between model and implementation in general, and between type and representation in particular.

To return to the example: The fact that the EMP type in Design T is encapsulated means that values and variables of type EMP are scalar (they have no internal structure so far as the user is concerned). Of course, we do have a set of operators— THE_EMP#, THE_SALARY, etc.—available that allow us to "get and set" certain employee properties, but the availability of those operators says *nothing* about any internal structure employees might possess. *Note:* If you are having difficulty with this idea, recall the POINT examples from Chapter 6 and elsewhere. The fact that operators THE_X and THE_Y are available for points says nothing about the actual representation of points, which might be, e.g., polar coordinates instead of Cartesian coordinates.

By contrast, the EMP relvar in Design R is of course not encapsulated. That is, the user certainly does know with Design R that employees have a component that is the EMP# attribute, a component that is the SALARY attribute, and so on. Furthermore, of course, access to those components is not by means of THE_ operators but is more direct (or what might be thought of as more direct, at any rate).

DISCUSSION

We now proceed to argue that, at least in the particular case under discussion (*viz.,* employees), the "choice" is really no choice at all. First of all, observe that Design

T gives us no way to hire and fire! Type EMP is the set of *all possible employees,** and there is no way to "insert" new employees into that set or "delete" existing ones. That is, the set in question contains *all possible* values of the form "EMP (*e#,en,d#,sal*)"—where *e#, en, d#,* and *sal* are values of types CHAR, CHAR, CHAR, and MONEY, respectively—regardless of whether any employee actually exists with the indicated properties. In other words (loosely): Types are *static. Note:* Again, if you are having difficulty with this idea, consider the simpler example of type INTEGER. This type is the set of *all possible* integers, and it is clearly not possible to insert new ones or delete existing ones.

It follows from the foregoing that Design T *additionally* requires an accompanying relvar—for example:

```
VAR EMPL REAL RELATION { EMP EMP } KEY { EMP } ;
```

Relvar EMPL contains a tuple for every employee currently of interest, and now of course we do have a way to hire new employees and fire existing ones. Note carefully, however, that relvar EMPL has just one attribute, not four (because of encapsulation).

One implication of the Design T approach is thus that it tends to suggest that the database will wind up containing a large number of single-attribute relvars—a fact that should perhaps give us some pause (see later).

Anyway, note that now not only can we "hire and fire employees," we can also perform operations analogous to the usual relational operations that we would have performed on the *relvar* EMP if we had opted for Design R. Here are a couple of examples:

Restriction: Get employees with salary greater than $50,000.

```
EMPL WHERE THE_SALARY ( EMP ) > MONEY ( 50000 )
```

Projection: Get all employee-name/employee-salary pairs.

```
( EXTEND EMPL ADD THE_ENAME  ( EMP ) AS ENAME,
                  THE_SALARY ( EMP ) AS SALARY )
                                   { ENAME, SALARY }
```

But the result in this second example has (obviously) two attributes, not one! It should thus be clear that:

- Given the single-attribute relvar EMPL required by Design T, we can create the four-attribute relvar EMP required by Design R (as a "view," perhaps);

---

*More accurately, the set of all possible employee *surrogates* or *representatives*. The type EMP does not contain actual employees, of course, but rather *symbols*—symbols that can be used to serve as surrogates or representatives (inside a database, for example) that stand for employees *per se.*

- Furthermore, we would probably want to do exactly that in practice, because—
for a variety of reasons—the four-attribute relvar is considerably more convenient than the single-attribute one.

Here is the definition of that four-attribute "view":

```
VAR EMPL_UNENCAPSULATED VIRTUAL
        ( EXTEND EMPL ADD THE_EMP#   ( EMP ) AS EMP#,
                          THE_ENAME  ( EMP ) AS ENAME,
                          THE_DEPT#  ( EMP ) AS DEPT#,
                          THE_SALARY ( EMP ) AS SALARY )
        { EMP#, ENAME, DEPT#, SALARY } KEY { EMP# } ;
```

In other words, we can start off with Design T, the type design, if we like, which
means we also need an associated single-attribute relvar; but we quickly find that in
effect we have created Design R (the relvar design) as well. So Design T implies that
we wind up with everything in Design R, *plus* the type EMP, *plus* the single-attribute
relvar EMPL as well. So what was the point of opting for Design T in the first place?
And what purpose is served, exactly, in Design T by the type EMP and the single-
attribute relvar EMPL?

FURTHER CONSIDERATIONS

What then is the criterion for making something a type and not a relvar? (We must
have *some* types, of course, for the obvious reason that relvars cannot be defined
without them.) In our opinion, this question is still somewhat open. However, we
offer the following points for consideration.

- In conventional database design terms, types correspond—loosely!—to *properties* and relvars—again loosely—to *entities* (or *sets* of properties and *sets* of
entities, rather). Hence, if something is "only" a property, it should map to a type
and not a relvar.

  The trouble with this idea, of course, is that one person's property is another
person's entity [55]. For example, consider colors. We would usually tend to
think of (say) the color red as a property, not an entity, and we would therefore
usually tend to map colors into a *type*. But some users might be very interested
in the color red as an entity, with further properties of its own (shade, for example)—in which case we might want to map colors into a *relvar*. Perhaps this
is an example of a situation in which we need both (i.e., the type and the relvar).

- Another important general point that can be made is that if "hire and fire" (or
something analogous to "hire and fire") is a requirement, then we are definitely
talking about entities rather than properties, and we should definitely be aiming
for a relvar design.

Given this state of affairs, incidentally, it is odd that so many presentations, especially "object" ones, do tend to use employees, departments, and so forth as examples of *object classes.* An object class is a type, of course, and so those presentations are typically forced to go on to define a "collection" for those employees, a "collection" for those departments, and so on. What is more, those "collections" typically omit the all-important attribute names, so they are not relations (or relvars). As a consequence, they do not lend themselves very well to the formulation of *ad hoc* queries, declarative integrity constraints, and so forth—a fact that advocates of the approach themselves often admit, apparently without being aware that it is precisely the lack of attribute names that causes the problems.*

Overall, we suspect that the most appropriate design choices will emerge if careful consideration is given to the distinction between (a) declarative sentences in human language and (b) the vocabulary used in the construction of such sentences. As we saw in Chapter 2, it is unencapsulated tuples in relations that stand for those sentences, and it is encapsulated domain values in attributes in those tuples that stand for particular elements—typically nouns—in that vocabulary. To say it slightly differently (and to repeat what we have said in Chapter 2 and elsewhere): Domains (types) give us values that represent things we might wish to refer to; relations give us ways of referring to those things in utterances about them.

Consider once again the EMP relvar of Design R. Suppose that relvar includes the tuple

```
TUPLE { EMP# 'E7', ENAME 'Amy', DEPT# 'D5', SALARY MONEY(20000) }
```

The existence of this tuple in the relvar means, by definition, that the database includes something that asserts the fact that the following declarative sentence is true:

Employee E7, named Amy, is currently assigned to department D5 and receives a salary of $20,000.

By contrast, consider the EMP *type* of Design T. Where the relvar of Design R allowed us to insert the tuple just shown (with the effect just described), the type of Design T allows us instead to execute the *selector invocation*

```
EMP ( 'E7', 'Amy', 'D5', MONEY(20000) )
```

This invocation does not of itself assert or deny the truth of *anything*. Rather, it constitutes nothing more than a certain rather heavy-duty noun, something like "an E7-numbered, Amy-named, D5-assigned, $20,000-earning employee." Now, we can

---

*As a trivial example, consider the class (type) INTEGER and a corresponding collection of "currently interesting" integers. Does that collection have a name for its sole attribute? Probably not. And if not, it cannot be joined to some other collection.

"wrap" that noun—i.e., that EMP value—into a 1-tuple and then insert that 1-tuple into the single-attribute relvar EMPL that Design T additionally requires; to do so, however, is effectively just to add a "There exists" in front of that noun, to make a declarative sentence, the truth of which is thereby asserted.

Of course, the fact asserted by the 4-tuple in Design R is exactly the same as that asserted in different "words" by the 1-tuple in Design T; however, database designers might profitably reflect on which of the two ways of asserting that fact is the more economical, the more communicative, and the more tractable to further reasoning.

Specialization by Constraint

INTRODUCTION

In Chapter 14, we used the term *specialization by constraint* to refer to the idea that the system should be aware of the fact that (e.g.) an ellipse whose semiaxes a and b are equal is really a circle. As noted in that chapter, our inheritance model does not currently support that idea, and in the first two sections of this appendix we explain why. As also mentioned in Chapter 14, however, there do seem to be some good reasons for at least attempting to support it after all; we are therefore currently investigating the possibility of adjusting our model to do so, and we discuss that possibility in this appendix also, in the final section. Before we get to that section, however, we briefly consider a related issue known as the "3 out of 4" rule.

We begin by observing that specialization by constraint—hereinafter abbreviated to *S by C*—has the fundamental consequence that a selector invocation might return a value of some proper subtype of the specified "target" type. For example, the selector invocation

```
ELLIPSE ( LENGTH (...), LENGTH (...), POINT (...) )
```

will return a value of most specific type CIRCLE, not ELLIPSE (under S by C), if the two LENGTH invocations happen to return the same value. (In our inheritance model, by contrast, at least as currently defined, we insist that a selector invocation must always return a value whose most specific type is *precisely* the specified type, as explained—under the heading "Result Covariance"—in the discussion of IM Proposal 24 in Chapter 14.) One immediate implication of this fact is that every time we define a new proper subtype *T'*, we might have to reimplement the selector(s) for every proper supertype *T* of *T'* (because they might now return values of that new type *T'* as their most specific type). Another possible implication is illustrated by the following code fragment:

```
VAR E ELLIPSE ;

E  :=  ELLIPSE ( LENGTH ( 3.0 ), LENGTH ( 3.0 ), ... ) ;
THE_A ( E )  :=  ... ;              /* RUN-TIME TYPE ERROR !!! */
```

The assignment to THE_A(E) here fails at run time, even though it passes the compile-time type checks, because the current value of E is of type CIRCLE, and—in accordance with IM Proposal 26 as explained in Chapter 14—assignment to THE_A is not legal for circles.

S by C has the further implication that if X is an expression of type CIRCLE, then the TREAT UP invocation

```
TREAT_UP_AS_ELLIPSE ( X )
```

will effectively be a no-op, because the system will immediately specialize the result back down to a circle again.* In fact, of course, the TREAT UP invocation just shown is logically equivalent to the selector invocation

```
ELLIPSE ( THE_A ( X ), THE_B ( X ), THE_CTR ( X ) )
```

The expressions THE_A(X) and THE_B(X) here certainly return the same value and so S by C comes into play, with the effect already explained.

All of the foregoing points constitute a significant departure from our inheritance model, of course—at least as currently defined.

A CLOSER LOOK

As already indicated, assignment to THE_A or THE_B is legal in our model only for variables whose current value is of most specific type ELLIPSE, not for variables whose current value is of most specific type CIRCLE (or some proper subtype thereof). So consider the following code fragment:

```
VAR E ELLIPSE ;

E  :=  ELLIPSE ( LENGTH ( 4.0 ), LENGTH ( 3.0 ), ... ) ;
THE_A ( E )  :=  LENGTH ( 3.0 ) ;   /* MST(E) now CIRCLE ??? */
```

---

*As a consequence, we cannot use the defensive coding technique suggested under IM Proposal 26 in Chapter 14 to get around the problem (already noted) that assignment to THE_A(E) might give a runtime type error. That is, replacing THE_A(E) in that assignment by THE_A(TREAT_UP_AS_ELLIPSE(E)) will still give rise to such an error because, to repeat, the TREAT UP invocation will effectively be a no-op.

If S by C is supported, the second assignment here has the side effect of setting the most specific type of E to CIRCLE. Now consider the assignment:

```
THE_A ( E )   :=   LENGTH ( 4.0 ) ;
```

This assignment will fail at run time, because the current value of E is a circle and assignment to THE_A is not legal for circles. So we apparently cannot undo the update we did just a moment ago!—i.e., that update was *irreversible.*

Now, it is true that some updates in the real world are indeed irreversible—the cat might knock your beer over—but updates that are purely internal to the computer are surely not (indeed, ROLLBACK would make no sense otherwise). So let us examine the possibility of accepting the assignment to THE_A(E) after all, thereby permitting the update to be undone. Note that:

- First of all, of course (to spell it out), permitting the update to be undone means that assignment to THE_A for variables of declared type ELLIPSE whose current value is of type CIRCLE has to be legal after all (and after such an assignment, the current most specific type of the variable will be ELLIPSE again, not CIRCLE, in general).

- And hence assignment to THE_A for variables of *declared* type CIRCLE presumably has to be legal too. (It would be rather odd otherwise!—it would mean, loosely speaking, that we could use assignment to THE_A to update ellipses that the system knew at *run* time were really circles, but not ellipses that the system knew at *compile* time were really circles. However, see the final section of this appendix for further discussion of this particular issue.)

- And hence, after such an update, the CIRCLE variable in question would contain a "noncircular circle"—i.e., a value c of type CIRCLE* for which THE_A(c) ≠ THE_B(c), or in other words a "circle" that violates the type constraint on circles (a point we will return to in just a moment).

Note that the net effect of the first of these three points is what we might call *generalization* by constraint (hereinafter abbreviated to *G by C*); that is, the assignment to THE_A(E) has the side effect of setting the most specific type of E back to ELLIPSE again. Indeed, it seems obvious with hindsight that if S by C is supported, then (by symmetry) G by C should be supported as well.

Now we turn to the second and third points. Consider the following example:

```
VAR C CIRCLE ;

C   :=   CIRCLE ( LENGTII ( 3.0 ), ... ) ;
                /* now THE_R(C) = THE_A(C) = THE_B(C) = three */

THE_A ( C )   :=   LENGTH ( 4.0 ) ;
```

---

*It obviously cannot be of most specific type ELLIPSE—a variable of declared type CIRCLE cannot hold a value of most specific type ELLIPSE.

After the second assignment here:

- THE_A(C) = four (obviously).

- THE_B(C) = three (presumably, since we have not changed it—unless assignment to THE_A for circles is redefined to have the side effect of assigning to THE_B too; but we reject this possibility for reasons to be discussed in the next section).

- So, as already noted, the current value of C is now a "noncircular circle"—i.e., to repeat, a value c of type CIRCLE for which THE_A(c) $\neq$ THE_B(c).

- So the type constraint on circles (namely, that THE_A(c) = THE_B(c)) is meaningless, and there is thus no point in informing the system of that constraint in the first place!

So S by C apparently undermines the concept of type constraints. (More precisely, S by C appears to imply *either* that type constraints make no sense or that some updates are irreversible, but we reject this latter alternative.) In other words, S by C and type constraints appear to be conflicting concepts. Note carefully too that the conflict in question implies that we cannot support type constraints even if we do *not* support inheritance, just in case we might ever want to add inheritance support (with S by C) at some future time. In our opinion, this argument should be sufficient to reject S by C (and hence G by C as well) out of hand—*unless* we adopt the approach sketched in the final section of this appendix, *q.v.*

THE "3 OUT OF 4" RULE

In the foregoing sections we have presented arguments in support of the notion that the system should *not* be aware of the fact that, e.g., an ellipse whose semiaxes a and b are equal is really a circle. By contrast, we have generally assumed throughout most of this book that the inverse notion—i.e., that the system *should* be aware of the fact that, e.g., if the ellipse is really a circle then a and b must be equal—is desirable; in fact, of course, what we are talking about here is just a constraint on type CIRCLE. (If $a \neq b$, an attempt to CAST the ellipse to a circle will fail at run time on a type constraint violation.)

Not everyone agrees with us on this question, however. Consider the following excerpt from reference [116]:

We can list four features of a subtyping mechanism that all seem to be desirable, yet . . . it is not possible to combine them in a single type system. The four features are:

- Substitutability
- Static type checking

- Mutability*
- Specialization via constraints†

All four of these properties seem to be desirable . . . We submit, however, that it is impossible to have all four of them in the same type system. This conflict can be illustrated with the following example. [*Note: We have replaced the original example by one that is essentially similar but conforms to our own notation and our own running example.*]

```
VAR  E  ELLIPSE ;
VAR  C  CIRCLE ;

C   :=   CIRCLE ( LENGTH ( 3.0 ), ... ) ;
E   :=   C ;
THE_A ( E )   :=   LENGTH ( 4.0 ) ;
```

[The first assignment initializes C to a circle of radius three.] The [second] assignment must be allowed . . . if we have substitutability and mutability . . . The [third assignment] would type-check at compile time . . . Of course, [that assignment] . . . will fail [at run time] even though the compile-time check determined that it was all right.

"We observe that any three of the four features seem to work just fine. No one of them is obviously the one that must be discarded, but in any type system, at least one of them must be sacrificed to achieve consistency with the others.

Let us analyze these claims one by one.

- *Substitutability:* As explained in Chapter 14, type inheritance *implies* (value) substitutability, so this feature cannot possibly be discarded. The second assignment in the example appeals to the value substitutability feature.

- *Static type checking:* Reference [116] defines static type checking to mean that "there is no need to insert expensive run-time [type] checks [into the compiled] code, and also the coder can be assured that [run-time type] errors can never occur." In our inheritance model, by contrast, run-time type errors certainly can occur (at least in the context of TREAT DOWN), even though static type checking is performed. So perhaps it can be claimed that static type checking—*full*

---

*"Mutability" just means *updatability;* as mentioned in Chapter 6, "mutator" is just another term, much used in the object world, for what we call an update operator (the corresponding term for a read-only operator, you will recall, is "observer").

†Note carefully that the authors of reference [116] use this term to mean *type constraint enforcement,* not what we use it to mean, though this fact is not readily apparent. Here is their definition: "*Specialization via constraints* happens whenever the following is permitted:

B subtype_of A and T subtype_of S and
$f(\ldots b{:}T, \ldots)$ returns $r{:}R$ in $\mathrm{Ops}(B)$ and
$f(\ldots b{:}S, \ldots)$ returns $r{:}R$ in $\mathrm{Ops}(A)$

That is, specialization via constraints occurs whenever the operation redefinition on a subtype constrains one of the arguments to be from a smaller value set than the corresponding operation on the supertype."

static type checking, that is, in the sense of reference [116]— is the feature we have discarded.

However, we would argue that to insist that everything be fully type-checkable at compilation time is to throw the baby out with the bathwater. For example, consider the following code fragment:

```
VAR L LENGTH ;

E   :=   C ;
L   :=   THE_R ( E ) ;
```

The expression THE_R(E) will fail on a compile-time type check, of course. So we have no way to obtain the radius of the circle that is the current value of E (we cannot use TREAT DOWN, because TREAT DOWN *intrinsically* cannot be fully type-checked at compilation time). So there is really no point in saying that the current value of E is of type CIRCLE; we might as well have converted that circle to an ellipse when we assigned C to E. So we have lost substitutability!—and therefore the whole idea of type inheritance, in fact.

- *Mutability:* As noted in a footnote on the previous page, mutability is just a synonym for updatability. Updatability in turn implies support for variables and assignment (and the example does involve variables and assignments, of course). Now, we did say in Chapter 1 that a functional-style language would not need variables or assignment as such, so we might possibly be persuaded that mutability could be discarded (though we suspect this interpretation is not what the authors of reference [116] had in mind). And even if the language is imperative in style, as **Tutorial D** is, and therefore does require variables and assignment, we could certainly be persuaded that assignment is the only update operator (or "mutator") that is logically necessary. But that still leaves us with mutability as a *sine qua non.*

  Note: It is possible (though it is hard to be sure) that what reference [116] means by the term "mutability" is not merely assignment as such, but rather the fact that certain "mutator" operators work in such a way as to assign to *some component of* their target variable while leaving other components unchanged (as in the third assignment in the example). If so, then we have already argued in Chapter 14 (under IM Proposal 23) that such operators are very desirable in practice, despite the fact that in the final analysis they are also logically unnecessary.

- *"Specialization by constraint":* We agree with reference [116] that the third assignment fails at run time. The reason it fails, of course, is that assignment to THE_A is illegal for a variable of declared type ELLIPSE if the current value of that variable is of type CIRCLE. And the reason, in turn, why that assignment is illegal is that if it were permitted, it would (in general) violate a type constraint on circles. In other words, for the assignment to succeed, *the system must not be informed of the type constraint on circles* (and, *a fortiori,* must not *enforce* that constraint). This option seems to us completely unacceptable; surely, the more constraints the system is aware of and can enforce, the better (we surely want our data to be as correct as possible at all times).

As already indicated, therefore, what the authors of reference [116] call "specialization by constraint" is really a matter of *type constraint enforcement;* indeed, their example does not involve S by C at all, in our sense of that term. In fact, we feel bound to say that we find the term "S by C" quite unhelpful as a characterization of the true nature of the problem at hand. For consistency with other publications in this area, however, especially reference [116] and also reference [98] (see below), we will continue to use "S by C" in the sense of reference [116] in the remainder of this section.

Now, in reference [98], Mattos and DeMichiel examine the foregoing "3 out of 4" rule and conclude that what reference [116] and they both call "S by C"—i.e., type constraint enforcement—is the feature that should be discarded. Their analysis goes somewhat as follows:

- *Can we discard substitutability?* Well, no: As we have already seen, substitutability—*value* substitutability, that is—cannot possibly be thrown away without undermining the whole point of type inheritance.

- *Can we discard static type checking?* Well, no: Discarding static type checking is highly undesirable, of course, and in any case it solves nothing—in the example, the third assignment will still fail at run time.

- *Can we discard mutability?* Well, no: We *must* have assignment, at least (assuming the language is imperative in style), and "component-level" update operators are highly desirable too in practice. (We note in passing that in fact Mattos and DeMichiel do assume that the term *mutability* here refers specifically to the idea of "component-level" updating, not just to assignment *per se.*)

Reference [98] therefore concludes that "the most appropriate [solution to the problem] is to not permit specialization via constraints" (meaning, to remind you once again, that they advocate not declaring or enforcing type constraints!). They claim that to do otherwise would mean "[forcing] the overloading of all functions defined on supertypes." We should immediately explain that by "overloading" here, they really mean *explicit specialization,* in the terminology of Chapter 14;* in terms of our example, that is, they are claiming that S by C would require that assignment to THE_A be "overloaded"—i.e., explicitly specialized—for a circle in such a way

---

*Note, therefore, that they are not using the term "overloading" as we did in Chapters 6 and 14 to mean something that is properly part of the model; rather, they are using it to mean something that is of concern to the implementation merely.

as to have the side effect of assignment to THE_B too, so that the circle still satisfies the constraint $a = b$ after the update. And they go on to say:

> This option [i.e., of forcing "overloading" or explicit specialization] seems to be unacceptable because we believe that . . . users are not likely to define type hierarchies themselves, but to buy them as class libraries from third party vendors. It is an important requirement that users be able to define . . . subtypes of these type hierarchies [*sic*] . . . If we force all operators to be overloaded, users will have to redefine every [operator] provided by the class libraries whenever they need to [define such a subtype].

We agree that forcing such "overloading" is unacceptable. In fact, we would argue, and have argued, that the semantics of assignment to THE_A in particular are (for good reasons) prescribed by the model and *must not* be "overloaded" in the manner suggested. And even if those semantics were not prescribed by the model, we would also argue that (a) changing the semantics of an operator in arbitrary ways is a bad idea in general, and (b) changing the semantics of an operator in such a way as to cause arbitrary side effects is an even worse one; it is a good general principle to insist that operators have exactly the requested effect, no more and no less. Furthermore, we observe that the option of changing the semantics in the manner suggested is not always available, anyway. For example, let type ELLIPSE have another immediate subtype NONCIRCLE; let the constraint $a \neq b$ (more precisely, $a > b$) apply to noncircles; and consider an assignment to THE_A for a noncircle that, if accepted, would set a equal to b. What would an appropriate "overloading" be for that assignment? Exactly what side effect would be appropriate?

On the face of it, then, the conclusion of reference [98] that "specialization by constraint"—i.e., type constraint enforcement—should be rejected does seem inescapable. But note the following implications of adopting that position:

- Assignment to THE_A is (as already explained) *not* explicitly specialized for circles.

- The fact that the current value of E in the example is a circle does *not* cause the assignment to THE_A to fail.

- Hence, the net result is that after that assignment, variable E contains a "noncircular circle"!—that is, it contains a value of type CIRCLE for which $a \neq b$.

- In fact, type constraints cannot be enforced (and therefore cannot even be stated) *even if inheritance is currently not supported at all.*

To us, these implications—the last two in particular—seem even more unacceptable than the option of "forcing overloading."

So what is to be done? Well, let us step back a moment and take stock. It seems to us that the system *should* support all four of the features substitutability, static type checking, mutability, and "specialization by constraint" (i.e., type constraint enforcement). More precisely, it seems to us that:

- The system should support *The Principle of Value Substitutability* 100 percent.

- The system should support static type checking to the maximum extent possible. Certain important cases where it is *not* possible are identified and explained in detail in Chapter 14.

- The system should support mutability—meaning not only that it should support assignment *per se,* but also that it should support "component-level" update operators.

- The system should support what reference [116] calls "specialization by constraint" (i.e., type constraint enforcement)—meaning that it should be aware of the fact that circles are subject to the constraint that $a = b,$ and meaning further that assignment to THE_A(E) fails at run time if the current value of E is of type CIRCLE.

In other words, the one feature we are prepared to give up is the idea that run-time type checking is unnecessary (though we do try to minimize the amount of such checking, as explained in Chapter 14, by drawing a careful boundary around situations in which it must be done).

Of course, the foregoing analysis does raise a major issue: Namely, what does inheritance really *mean?* Does a sensible model even exist? We have just proposed that assignment to THE_A for a circle must fail. It therefore does not seem reasonable to talk of the operator "assignment to THE_A" being inherited by type CIRCLE from type ELLIPSE. It therefore does not seem reasonable to regard type CIRCLE as being a subtype of type ELLIPSE!—after all, to say that type CIRCLE is a subtype of type ELLIPSE is to say that all operators that apply to type ELLIPSE apply to type CIRCLE too, does it not?

Well, no, it does not. To repeat from Chapter 12:

> . . . it is important in this context (as in all others!) to distinguish carefully between *values* and *variables*. When we say that every circle is an ellipse, what we mean, more precisely, is that every circle *value* is an ellipse *value*. We certainly do not mean that every circle *variable* is an ellipse *variable*—i.e., that a variable of declared type CIRCLE is a variable of declared type ELLIPSE, and hence can contain a value that is an ellipse and not a circle. In other words, **inheritance applies to values, not variables.**

Thus, it seems to us that the key to the problem is to recognize:

- The logical difference between values and variables, and hence

- The logical difference between read-only and update operators, and hence

- The logical difference between *The Principle of Value Substitutability* and *The Principle of Variable Substitutability*

(and, of course, to act appropriately upon such recognition).

It appears to us that references [98] and [116] (and a variety of other similar writings) are confused over these crucial distinctions. It seems further that such confusions are at least partly responsible for the lack of consensus (noted several times earlier in this book) on a formal, rigorous, and abstract—"clearly defined and generally agreed"—inheritance model. For example:

- The Object-Oriented Database System Manifesto [1] states that "[there] are at least four types of inheritance: *substitution* inheritance, *inclusion* inheritance, *constraint* inheritance, and *specialization* inheritance. . . . Various degrees of these four types of inheritance are provided by existing systems and prototypes, and we do not prescribe a specific style of inheritance."

- Reference [18] states that "[inheritance can be] based on [a variety of] different criteria and there is no commonly accepted standard definition"—and proceeds to give eight (!) possible interpretations.*

- Reference [3] states that "a programming language [merely] provides a set of [inheritance] mechanisms. While these mechanisms certainly restrict what one can do in that language and what views of inheritance can be implemented [in that language], they do not by themselves validate some view of inheritance or other. [Types,] specializations, generalizations, and inheritance are only concepts, and . . . they do not have a universal objective meaning. . . . This [fact] implies that how inheritance is to be incorporated into a specific system is up to the designers of [that] system, and it constitutes a policy decision that must be implemented with the available mechanisms." In other words, there is no model!

It is, however, relevant to mention that the authors of reference [3] draw their conclusion after analysis of an example that is essentially isomorphic to the example discussed earlier of assignment to THE_A for a circle—and their analysis is essentially isomorphic to that of reference [98], too. For these reasons, we reject their conclusion.

CAN THE IDEA BE RESCUED?

We now revert to our original interpretation of the term "S by C"—i.e., we use it to refer to the idea that the system should know that (e.g.) an ellipse with $a = b$ should really be a circle. The arguments in the first two sections of this appendix notwithstanding, we have to admit that S by C in this sense does seem to be an intuitively attractive idea; to be specific, it is more faithful to reality, and it is consistent with the general principle (usually a good one) that the more the system knows the better. In this final section, therefore, we explore the possibility of revising our model (slightly) to support S by C after all.

---

*Reference [102] gives *twelve*.

One way we might try to be "more faithful to reality" would be to specify the following type constraint on type ELLIPSE:

```
CONSTRAINT ( IF THE_A ( ELLIPSE ) = THE_B ( ELLIPSE )
             THEN IS_CIRCLE ( ELLIPSE )
           END IF )
```

Let us call this constraint *Constraint EC*. Constraint EC ensures that the only legal values of type ELLIPSE for which $a = b$ are values that are also of type CIRCLE. Note carefully, however, that Constraint EC is not S by C as such: It says only that if $a = b$ then the ellipse had better be of type CIRCLE, not that if $a = b$ then the ellipse is somehow to be *forced* to be of type CIRCLE.

However, Constraint EC also means that an ELLIPSE selector invocation of the form

```
ELLIPSE ( a, b, ctr )
```

will fail if $a = b$, since it will be trying to return an ellipse with $a = b$ that is not of type CIRCLE. As a consequence, "mutating an ellipse" such that the new value has $a = b$ will also fail. That is, the assignment

```
THE_A ( E )  :=  new_a ;
```

might violate Constraint EC, because it is really just shorthand for the following (the notation is meant to be self-explanatory)—

```
E  :=  ELLIPSE ( new_a, old_b, old_ctr ) ;
```

—and will therefore fail if *new_a = old_b*. Of course, we can get around this particular problem by rewriting the assignment as follows:

```
E  :=  IF new_a = old_b
          THEN CIRCLE  ( new_a, old_ctr )
          ELSE ELLIPSE ( new_a, old_b, old_ctr )
       END IF ;
```

Note, incidentally, that this latter assignment effectively constitutes a hand-coded version of S by C. Such hand-coding is always logically possible, of course, but what we are interested in here is the possibility of somehow automating the process.

Now, the fact that certain ELLIPSE selector invocations—namely, those for which $a = b$—now fail might be felt to contravene RM Prescription 4. That prescription states, in part, that if T is a type and S is a corresponding selector, then every value of type T shall be produced by some invocation of S. In fact, of course, that prescription was originally defined without concern for the possibility of inheritance support; however, we could easily (and compatibly) extend it to cater for such support, by requiring only that every value of *most specific* type T shall be produced by some invocation of S. In terms of our example, an ellipse that is really a circle cannot be obtained by an invocation of the ELLIPSE selector, but it can be obtained by means of an invocation of the CIRCLE selector instead.

However, we now observe that—as you might already have realized—Constraint EC also implies that *any attempt to TREAT UP a value of type CIRCLE to type ELLIPSE will now fail.* And in any case, as already pointed out, Constraint EC is still not S by C as such; i.e., we have still not achieved our objective of "automatic" support for S by C. So let us now drop the idea of constraints like Constraint EC and concentrate instead on the possibility of explicitly telling the system that (e.g.) an ellipse with $a = b$ must be forced to be of type CIRCLE. To invent some syntax on the fly, we might say:

```
SPECIALIZE ( IF THE_A ( ELLIPSE ) = THE_B ( ELLIPSE ) THEN
             ELLIPSE := CIRCLE ( THE_A ( ELLIPSE ),
                                 THE_CTR ( ELLIPSE ) ) ;
        END IF ; )
```

This SPECIALIZE clause would appear as part of the ELLIPSE type definition. Conceptually speaking, the IF statement included in this clause will now have to be incorporated into the code that implements the ELLIPSE selector. Thus, we do have to face up to the possibility that (as noted near the beginning of this appendix) certain selector invocations will now produce results of most specific type some proper subtype of the specified target type.

As a consequence of this SPECIALIZE clause, then, no value of most specific type ELLIPSE ever has $a = b$ (and so values of most specific type ELLIPSE do now correspond to real-world ellipses that are not circles, not to real-world ellipses that might be circles; thus, the model does now seem to be a little more acceptable, intuitively speaking).

Here are some further important implications of S by C, expressed for the most part in terms of our usual variables E and C, with definitions as follows:

```
VAR E ELLIPSE ;
VAR C CIRCLE ;
```

Consider first our usual comparison example:

```
IF E = C THEN ... ;
END IF ;
```

If E contains a value of most specific type ELLIPSE, there is now no possibility of that value happening to be "equal" to the value of type CIRCLE in C. There is therefore no point in using TREAT UP in such a comparison, thereby writing (e.g.)

```
IF TREAT_UP_AS_ELLIPSE ( E ) = TREAT_UP_AS_ELLIPSE ( C )
    THEN ... ;
END IF ;
```

In fact, this lengthier version is now semantically identical to the short one: It returns *true* in exactly those cases where the short one does and *false* in exactly those cases where the short one does.

Next, observe that assignment to THE_A(E) is now always legal, even if *MST*(E) is currently CIRCLE. If *MST*(E) is ELLIPSE before the assignment but

$a = b$ afterward, *MST*(E) becomes CIRCLE ("S by C"). If *MST*(E) is CIRCLE before the assignment but $a \neq b$ afterward, *MST*(E) becomes ELLIPSE ("G by C").

Note: These effects occur because the assignment

```
THE_A ( E )   :=   ... ;
```

is defined (under S by C) to be shorthand for

```
E   :=   ELLIPSE ( ... ) ;
```

—i.e., it is specifically the *ELLIPSE* selector that is invoked on the right hand side, precisely because the declared type of E is ELLIPSE.* Note in particular, therefore, that there is no need to specify any kind of "G by C" rule explicitly; the effect of G by C "just happens," automatically.

Suppose, however, that (as in several examples in Chapter 14) type CIRCLE has a proper subtype COLORED_CIRCLE. Then, if variable E contains a colored circle, assignment to THE_A(E) will—according to the foregoing definition of the semantics of such an assignment—cause the most specific type of E to become just CIRCLE, not COLORED_CIRCLE (i.e., the color will be lost). So have we found a flaw in our S by C scheme?

Well, perhaps we should remind you that, as noted in Chapter 14, we find the idea of COLORED_CIRCLE being a subtype of CIRCLE somewhat suspect anyway. Observe in particular that there is no way to obtain a colored circle by simply applying S by C; i.e., there is no type constraint that, if satisfied by some given circle, means the circle in question is really a colored circle. Thus, we think it would be more reasonable to regard COLORED_CIRCLE and CIRCLE as completely separate types, and to regard type COLORED_CIRCLE in particular as having a possible representation in which one component is of type CIRCLE and another is of type COLOR. In fact, we would like to argue that if *T'* **is a subtype of** *T,* **then such subtyping should always be via S by C!** We justify this position as follows:

- *T* and *T'* are both basically *sets* (named sets of values), and *T'* is a subset of *T*.

- Thus, *T* and *T'* both have *membership predicates*—predicates, that is, that a value must satisfy in order to be a value of the type in question. Let those predicates be *P* and *P'*, respectively.

- Since we are dealing with finite sets only, we can for simplicity regard predicates *P* and *P'* as effectively just enumerating the values of types *T* and *T'*, respectively.

- Note in particular that since every value of type *T'* is also a value of type *T*, the predicate *P'* can be formulated in terms of values of type *T* (not *T'*) only.

---

*In other words, we no longer define assignment to THE_A(E) as shorthand for an assignment in which the right hand side involves a complicated CASE expression, as we did under IM Proposal 23 in Chapter 14.

- And that predicate *P′*, formulated in terms of values of type *T,* is precisely the type constraint that values of type *T* have to satisfy in order to be values of type *T′*. In other words, a value of type *T* is specialized to type *T′* precisely if it satisfies the constraint *P′*.

Thus, we see S by C as the *only* conceptually valid means of defining subtypes. And we reject examples like the one involving COLORED_CIRCLE as a subtype of CIRCLE (despite the fact that we made fairly extensive use of that example, and others like it, in Part IV of this book).

Here is another (more complicated) example of assignment:

```
THE_R ( TREAT_DOWN_AS_CIRCLE ( E ) )   :=   LENGTH ( 5.0 ) ;
```

This assignment is defined to be shorthand for the following—

```
TREAT_DOWN_AS_CIRCLE ( E )   :=
CIRCLE ( LENGTH ( 5.0 ), THE_CTR ( TREAT_DOWN_AS_CIRCLE ( E ) ) ;
```

—and it will fail, of course, if *MST*(E) is ELLIPSE, not CIRCLE.

Still on the question of assignment, we now observe that (of course) assignment to THE_A(C) is always illegal.* Noncircular circles are always illegal. In other words, our rules for inheritance of update operators are still conditional, as explained in Chapter 14 under IM Proposal 26—but now those rules apply only to *declared* types, not *most specific* types. As a consequence, we have fewer run-time errors. In fact, the only run-time errors that can now possibly occur are those *intrinsic* ones that arise in the context of TREAT DOWN.

Yet another consequence of our revised rules for assignment is that using TREAT UP as a pseudovariable is now no longer necessary. In fact, a program that assigns to THE_A(E) will now still work after type CIRCLE is introduced—and so we can introduce new subtypes with impunity (existing programs will still work, and code reuse is enhanced).

Now suppose type ELLIPSE has an additional immediate subtype, NONCIRCLE, with the obvious semantics. Then, in order to "change the type" of variable E from (say) CIRCLE to NONCIRCLE, it is sufficient just to do the update! There is no need to use "TREAT UP to ELLIPSE" as a preliminary step, and there is no need for the artificial type FAKE_ELLIPSE (in the case where ELLIPSE is a dummy type). Of course, we are assuming here that the SPECIALIZE clause for type ELLIPSE has been extended to include the necessary S by C rules for NONCIRCLE, as follows:

---

*We said earlier in this appendix that this state of affairs might be regarded as "rather odd"—but not so odd as the alternative, which is to permit "noncircular circles."

```
SPECIALIZE ( CASE ;
            WHEN THE_A ( ELLIPSE ) = THE_B ( ELLIPSE )
            THEN ELLIPSE := CIRCLE ( THE_A ( ELLIPSE ),
                                     THE_CTR ( ELLIPSE ) ;
            WHEN THE_A ( ELLIPSE ) > THE_B ( ELLIPSE )
            THEN ELLIPSE := NONCIRCLE ( THE_A ( ELLIPSE ),
                                        THE_B ( ELLIPSE ),
                                        THE_CTR ( ELLIPSE ) ;
      END CASE ; )
```

Moreover, there is now never any logical need to CAST a value of type ELLIPSE to type CIRCLE, and so that CAST operator itself becomes unnecessary. (If the value was of *most specific* type ELLIPSE, the CAST would fail anyway; otherwise the value would already be of type CIRCLE.)

Next we observe that TREAT UP is now no longer needed at all (as noted earlier, it effectively becomes a no-op). Of course, TREAT UP was admittedly only shorthand anyway, but any simplification is generally to be desired.

And one last point: S by C has the happy implication that it makes the question of *intersection types* (see Chapter 15) more intellectually respectable (perhaps) and more intuitively satisfying. For example, if a certain RECTANGLE selector invocation returns a RECTANGLE value *r* that has equal sides, that value *r* will automatically be recognized as being of type SQUARE, and hence of type RHOMBUS as well.

The net of all of the foregoing is that the idea of supporting S by C certainly seems attractive, and quite possibly feasible. On the other hand, such support does have numerous implications, some of them serious, not all of which are readily apparent or fully understood at the time of writing. We therefore invoke *The Principle of Cautious Design* [49] once again and exclude S by C from our model—at least for the time being.

Subtables and Supertables

INTRODUCTION

In Part IV of this book, we proposed a detailed model for what in relational terms might be called *domain* inheritance. When approached regarding the possibility of inheritance in a relational context, however, many people (perhaps most) immediately jump to the conclusion that it is some kind of *table* inheritance that is under discussion. The section "Relvars *vs.* Object Classes" in Chapter 2 provides an example; so too do the SQL3 specifications [87–89,101], which currently include proposals for something called "subtables and supertables," according to which some table *B* might inherit all of the columns of some other table *A* and then add some more of its own. An example is shown in Fig. D.1.

The intuitive idea underlying the example is that every employee has an employee number EMP#, a name ENAME, a department number DEPT#, and a salary SALARY; in addition, some employees are programmers and are proficient in a certain programming language LANG. (For simplicity, we assume each programmer has just one programming language in which he or she is proficient. This assumption is somewhat unrealistic, of course, but the point is not important for present purposes.) Thus, nonprogrammers have a row in table EMP only, while programmers have a row in both tables—so every row in PGMR has a counterpart in EMP, but the converse is not true. However, the properties EMP#, ENAME, DEPT#, and SALARY are not recorded twice for programmers; rather, the PGMR table "inherits" those properties from the EMP table.

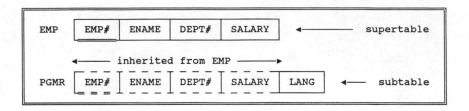

Fig. D.1   Subtable/supertable example

Here then are the table definitions (hypothetical syntax):

```
CREATE TABLE EMP ( EMP# ..., ENAME ..., DEPT# ..., SALARY ... )
      PRIMARY KEY ( EMP# ) ;

CREATE TABLE PGMR ( LANG ... )
      UNDER ( EMP )
      PRIMARY KEY ( EMP# ) ;
```

Note: You will observe that we are departing here from our preferred terminology of relations, tuples, etc., to use the "fuzzier" terminology of tables, rows, etc. One reason for this departure is to enable you more easily to relate the discussion that follows to other writings on this subject. Another is that the subject seems to be inherently fuzzy anyway . . .

The semantics of the EMP-PGMR example are as follows:*

- *Retrieval:* Retrieval from EMP behaves normally. Retrieval from PGMR behaves as if PGMR actually contained the columns EMP#, ENAME, DEPT#, and SALARY.

- *Insert:* INSERT into EMP behaves normally. INSERT into PGMR effectively causes new rows to appear in both EMP and PGMR.

- *Delete:* DELETE from EMP causes rows to disappear from EMP and (if the rows in question happen to correspond to programmers) from PGMR too. DELETE from PGMR causes rows to disappear from both EMP and PGMR.

- *Update:* Updating EMP# or ENAME or DEPT# or SALARY updates both tables (conceptually). Updating LANG updates PGMR only.

Note, incidentally, that the INSERT/DELETE behavior sketched above means that we are not dealing with a mere conventional foreign-to-primary-key relationship from PGMR to EMP, with conventional "referential actions"; for if we were,

---

*We are guessing here. It is hard to find a coherent account of subtables and supertables in the literature.

then, e.g., deleting a row from PGMR could not possibly cause deletion of a row from EMP. Note too that we have overlooked a couple of complicating factors in our brief explanations. For example:

- Suppose an existing nonprogrammer employee becomes a programmer. If we simply try to insert an appropriate row into PGMR, the system will attempt to insert a corresponding row into EMP as well—an attempt that will presumably fail on some kind of uniqueness violation. Thus, it looks as if we will need an additional form of INSERT ("INSERT ONLY"?) that will let us insert a row into the subtable only.

- Conversely, suppose an existing programmer becomes a nonprogrammer. If we simply try to delete the appropriate row from PGMR, the system will delete the corresponding row from EMP as well—a side effect that will presumably not be desired. Thus, it looks as if we will need an additional form of DELETE ("DELETE ONLY"?) that will let us delete a row from the subtable only.

Anyway, the obvious question is: What (if anything) do the foregoing ideas have to do with our inheritance model? Well, it should be immediately clear that they have nothing to do with the relation type inheritance proposals described in Chapter 16. In those proposals, if RT' and RT are relation types such that RT' is a subtype of supertype RT, there is no notion that RT' somehow "inherits columns" from RT; rather, RT' and RT have the *same* columns (loosely speaking). In fact, the subtype/supertype relationship is actually *implied* (in part) in our model by the fact that types RT' and RT "have the same columns" (recall that we have no way of defining tuple and relation types explicitly, and hence no way of stating explicitly that one such type is a subtype of another). To repeat, therefore: What does the "subtables and supertables" idea have to do with our inheritance model?

SOME GENERAL OBSERVATIONS

The fact that our inheritance model deals exclusively with *type* (or domain) inheritance does not of itself rule out the possibility of some kind of table inheritance, of course. Indeed, it should be the case that our model provides a framework for understanding whether some sense might be made of such a notion; after all, that model is quite general and does necessarily address the implications of inheritance for values and variables in general—including relation values and variables in particular—and of course "tables" in the present context are really just relation variables (i.e., relvars).

But herein lies a crucial point. "Tables" are indeed variables; thus, to talk of "subtables and supertables" is to talk of what might perhaps be called "subvariables and supervariables" . . . whatever that might mean! (How can two distinct *variables* possibly be such that one is a "subvariable" of the other?) This insight immediately suggests that:

- First, whatever "subtables and supertables" might be all about, the one thing they are definitely *not* about is type inheritance; the tables in question are variables, and variables are not types.

- Second, the idea seems a little suspect right away. We explained in Part IV of this book that inheritance applies to values, not variables. ("To say a circle is an ellipse is to say that every circle *value* is an ellipse *value,* not that a circle *variable* is an ellipse *variable*.") What then can it mean to say that relation *variable* PGMR is a "sub"-*anything* of relation *variable* EMP?

Thus, it might be possible to make some kind of sense out of the "subtables and supertables" idea, but (as we will show) it is a completely different phenomenon, one that has essentially nothing to do with type inheritance as such.*

THE TERMINOLOGY IS EXTREMELY BAD

The next point to be made is this: When we talk of PGMR being a "subtable" of EMP (and inheriting columns from EMP), what we really mean is that each PGMR *tuple* inherits certain properties from the corresponding EMP *tuple*. (We now deliberately revert to our own preferred terminology of tuples, relations, and so forth.) In other words, we should really be talking about "subtuples and supertuples," not "subtables and supertables" at all.

Next, we observe that this latter terminology is *really* bad, because the "*sub*tuples" have a superset of the attributes of the "*super*tuples"! A PGMR tuple, for example, has all of the attributes of an EMP tuple, plus one additional one (LANG).

Next, it follows that, whatever else they might be, "subtables and supertables" are *not* an application of our inheritance ideas in which the variables are relation variables specifically. Nor are they an application of our inheritance ideas in which the variables are tuple variables specifically, because the only tuple variables we deal with in our model are "free-standing" ones—there is not, nor can there be, any notion of a tuple variable somehow being contained within a relation variable or "table" (see reference [72] if you wish to see this point elaborated).

All in all, it begins to look as if "subtables and supertables" involve some very strange notions indeed . . . Never mind: We struggle on.

---

*In view of this conclusion, it is interesting to observe that in SQL3 specifically, the "subtables and supertables" idea—at least in its present incarnation—is tightly interwoven with (some people might say *confused* with) the concept of type inheritance. See Appendix E, especially the final section, for further explanation.

THE CONCEPT IS NOT TYPE INHERITANCE

Relvars EMP and PGMR each have a type, of course (a *relation* type). The types in question have headings as follows:

```
{ EMP#  ..., ENAME  ..., DEPT# ..., SALARY ... }
{ EMP#  ..., ENAME  ..., DEPT# ..., SALARY ..., LANG ... }
```

For simplicity, let us agree to refer to the corresponding *tuple* types as types EMP and PGMR, respectively: tuple types, not relation types, since (as we saw in the previous section) if there is any inheritance going on here at all—in itself a dubious proposition—it really has to do with tuples, not relations.

It should immediately be obvious, then, that:

- Neither of the two types is a subtype of the other, in the sense of our inheritance model (nor in the sense of any other inheritance model we are aware of, either); thus, we are not talking about subtyping, as such, at all. (Recall that, in our model at least, tuple type TT' can be a subtype of tuple type TT only if TT' and TT have exactly the same attribute names.)

- No EMP tuple is a PGMR tuple; more importantly, no PGMR tuple is an EMP tuple, either.

- Hence, if *Op* is an operator that is defined to work for EMP tuples, it is not possible (in general) to invoke it with an argument that is a PGMR tuple instead. In other words, the property of polymorphism does not apply, and there is no value substitutability either.

- Thus, **we are not really talking about type inheritance, as such, in any sense at all.**

So can the idea be rescued? Well, we might try pretending that:

- There is some kind of *abstract, scalar* type—not a tuple type as such—EMP, with associated operators THE_EMP#, THE_SALARY, etc.

- There is another such abstract type, PGMR, that is defined to be a subtype of EMP (and therefore inherits operators THE_EMP#, THE_SALARY, etc.— note, however, that it must inherit these operators for update purposes as well as read-only purposes), and adds another operator THE_LANG.

- Relvar EMP contains the "currently interesting" set of values of type EMP, and relvar PGMR contains the "currently interesting" set of values of type PGMR.

    However:

- Relvars EMP and PGMR would then have to be single-attribute relvars (because, as already noted, types EMP and PGMR are now scalar types, not tuple types; in the jargon of Appendix B, those types are *encapsulated*). This point by itself is sufficient to make this proposed approach a logical nonstarter.

- Some people would argue that with this approach relvar EMP should contain just tuples for those employees who are not programmers, instead of for all employees. If so, then the semantics of relvar EMP have changed (and the insert/delete semantics will have to change accordingly). Moreover, they have changed in a rather unpleasant way, because they involve a *database constraint*—one that did not exist previously—that interrelates the two relvars (refer to Chapter 6 if you need to refresh your memory regarding database constraints).

- Even if the semantics of relvar EMP are not changed as suggested in the previous paragraph, the usual relational INSERT and DELETE operations will have to be *overloaded* for relvar PGMR in order to achieve the desired insert/delete semantics.

We therefore feel this pretense should be recognized for what it is, and rejected.

WHY?

Why then might "subtables and supertables" be a good idea? What are the advantages? As you might have noticed, we have not yet addressed these questions at all.

The sole advantage we can see (and it is a pretty minor one) is this: Informing the system that, e.g., PGMR is a "subtable" of "supertable" EMP might be regarded as constituting a shorthand for stating certain new kinds of referential actions declaratively. To be specific, it could allow:

- Insertion of a tuple into PGMR to cause automatic insertion of the corresponding tuple into EMP;

- Deletion of a tuple from PGMR to cause automatic deletion of the corresponding tuple from EMP.

But observe now that there is no need to pretend that certain attributes are "inherited" by PGMR from EMP in order to achieve these effects!* Indeed, it begins to look as if the whole business of "attribute inheritance" is nothing but a syntactic shorthand—it simplifies the formulation of certain queries (by avoiding certain explicit joins), and it allows the attributes in question to be defined once instead of twice. *Note:* We are, of course, not talking about the possibility of *storing* those attributes once instead of twice. The relational model has nothing to say concerning physical storage matters.

---

*In fact, we could achieve these effects very simply by (a) defining two real relvars, EMP {EMP#, ENAME, DEPT#, SALARY} and EMP_LANG {EMP#, LANG}, and then (b) defining PGMR as the "view" (virtual relvar) EMP JOIN EMP_LANG. Note that such an approach also gets around the "INSERT ONLY" and "DELETE ONLY" problem (trivially so, in fact). What is more, this approach could serve as a convenient and simple basis for *implementing* the subtables/supertables idea. (Thanks to Spencer Olson of State Street Bank, Boston, Mass., for these observations.)

A Comparison with SQL3

INTRODUCTION

Naturally we believe the ideas of *The Third Manifesto* are valuable in and of themselves. However, we also believe they can be useful as a *yardstick* or *framework*—i.e., as a basis against which alternative proposals, and indeed concrete implementations, can be carefully analyzed, criticized, evaluated, and perhaps judged.* In this appendix, we use that framework to examine the SQL3 proposals specifically. Appendix F then performs the analogous function for the proposals of the Object Data Management Group, ODMG.

First we should explain what SQL3 is. It is not a standard (not yet, anyway, though the phrase "the SQL3 standard" is frequently encountered in the trade press and elsewhere). Rather, the SQL standard at the time of writing (April 1998) is *Database Language SQL:1992,* known informally as SQL-92 or SQL/92 [76,87–89]. In addition to its normal maintenance work on SQL/92 *per se,* however, the ISO Database Languages committee (which is the body responsible for international SQL standards) has been at work for some considerable time on a proposed SQL/92 follow-on, and it is that proposed follow-on that is referred to, again informally, as

---

*However, we should stress the fact that we do not want our ideas to be used as a basis for any kind of "checklist" evaluation. To repeat, we do think those ideas can serve as a convenient framework for structuring discussions, but they are *not* meant to serve as some kind of scoring scheme. We are not interested in scoring schemes.

SQL3. The working draft of SQL3 is currently in a fairly advanced state of production [87–89].

Note: In principle, SQL3 includes the whole of SQL/92 as a proper subset. In this appendix, however, we follow the conventional path of taking the name "SQL3" to refer primarily (though informally) to those features that are not already part of SQL/92.

As explained in the annotation to reference [87] in Appendix H, the original single-volume SQL/92 specification has since been expanded into a series of separate documents, called *Parts.* Most of the SQL3 material is defined in Part 2, *SQL/Foundation;* other relevant material is to be found in Part 4, *SQL/PSM,* and Part 5, *SQL/Bindings.* At the time of writing, these three parts have all been presented to ISO national bodies as *Final Committee Drafts* for ballot. Despite having reached this advanced stage in the ISO publication procedure, however, SQL3 must nevertheless still be regarded as a moving target, for there are certainly some remaining important issues to be resolved and some fairly major parts of the specification to be completed or clarified. It follows that certain portions of this appendix might be slightly out of date (not seriously, we hope) by the time the aforementioned Parts 2, 4, and 5 are formally published.

Before going any further, we should acknowledge the fact that one of the present authors has been actively involved in the production of SQL standards for several years (since 1988, in fact). Therefore—just in case any reader, possibly seeing some conflict of interest in that involvement, might think of raising an eyebrow at some of the stark differences to be observed between SQL3 and *The Third Manifesto*—we would like to take a moment to point out some of the ways in which we as independent manifesto writers enjoy certain freedoms that SQL standardizers do not.

- First and foremost, we do not have to deal with the *Shackle of Compatibility.* SQL standardizers at large might very well share our regrets over (e.g.) nulls and duplicate rows, but they are powerless to remove them from the standard, just as vendors are powerless to remove them from products already shipped and perhaps widely used.

- Second, the design and implementation of established products might have an adverse effect on the feasibility and cost-effectiveness of proposed SQL extensions.

- Third, an SQL standardizer whose participation is funded by an employer, say, might sometimes feel obliged to place the commercial interests of that employer above his or her own personal opinions, should there be any conflict.

- Fourth, an SQL standardizer has to make compromises within a large group of people with perhaps widely differing opinions and interests. By contrast, coauthors with closely shared opinions and interests have to make hardly any compromises at all, and certainly none on matters considered by both to be very important.

It follows from the foregoing that our criticisms of SQL3 are definitely not intended as, nor should they be taken as, criticisms of the individuals involved. Nor do we necessarily mean to suggest that we think SQL3 could and should have been more closely aligned with *The Third Manifesto*. Indeed, it is our recognition of the inevitability of misalignment that makes us advocate serious consideration of something that might supersede SQL in the long term.

Comparison format: We should explain the style and content of the point-by-point comparisons that follow. First, we aim to make each individual comparison a bald statement of fact; except on rare occasions, we do not restate opinions, give value judgments, or comment on the relative severity of various points. Second, we use the terms **conforms** and **fails,** in **boldface,** to indicate our general finding in connection with each point. Very often these terms have to be qualified, and sometimes both terms are used in connection with the same point. For example, SQL3 sometimes conforms to the *Manifesto* in certain respects but fails in others; sometimes it conforms as far as it goes but does not go far enough; sometimes it fails not because of specifics of the SQL3 feature at hand, but rather because it depends on some other feature on which it fails in turn. Such dependencies are appropriately indicated.

We now proceed with our point-by-point comparisons.

RM PRESCRIPTIONS

1. Scalar types

SQL3 **conforms,** mostly. *User-defined* scalar types can be defined and destroyed by means of appropriate CREATE TYPE and DROP TYPE statements. *Builtin* scalar types (BOOLEAN, INTEGER, REAL, DECIMAL, CHARACTER, BIT, DATE, TIME, TIMESTAMP, etc.) are also supported, of course. All such types are named sets of scalar values and are mutually distinct.* Values and variables of such types can be operated upon solely by means of the operators defined for the type in question. *Note:* We should mention that SQL3 does not use the term "operator" in the same generic way the *Manifesto* does but reserves it for builtin functions like "+" that make use of some special infix notation.

SQL3 also meets our requirement for operators whose purpose is to "expose the possible representation" for each declared possible representation for a given type. For user-defined types, it requires exactly one representation to be specified, and it automatically provides appropriate operators for each component of that representation. For builtin types, it provides appropriate literals.

---

*Actually there is some confusion here. Certain builtin types—REAL and FLOAT, for example—seem to be regarded as both distinct and not distinct, depending on context. If they are distinct, they are certainly not *disjoint* as required by RM Prescription 2. If they are not distinct, they violate the requirement of RM Prescription 1 that two types that are identical in all respects except for their names are different types.

SQL3 **fails** in that it is possible for a user-defined type to have nothing corresponding to a *selector* operator; that is, no such operators are provided automatically (though it is always possible to provide a user-defined one to serve the purpose). It is true that certain operators *are* provided automatically for user-defined types, including something called a *constructor function*. However, every invocation of such a function always returns the same value (*viz.,* a value specified explicitly or implicitly by the type definer). In other words, what such a function really does is *allocate storage* and initialize it—it does not support the selection of an arbitrary value of that type, as RM Prescription 1 requires.

SQL3 also fails in that it does not really meet our requirement for a builtin *truth value* type. To be specific, its BOOLEAN type (which might have been thought to fit the bill) suffers from certain anomalies arising from its idiosyncratic concept of nulls and its foundation in three-valued logic. That type does include just the two values we prescribe, *true* and *false*—but we make that prescription precisely because we require **D** to be based on two-valued logic! We would naturally expect a language based on three-valued logic, as SQL is, to support *three* "BOOLEAN" values (*true, false,* and *unknown*), not two. But SQL3 represents the *unknown* truth value not by a value at all but by means of an SQL-style *null.* Null is not a value in SQL because it does not have all the properties that we require of values.* Specifically, it is not always treated as equal to itself and unequal to all other values, though it is sometimes so treated.

2. *Scalar values are typed*

SQL3 **conforms** (except for the possible overlap among certain builtin types noted under RM Prescription 1).

3. *Scalar operators*

SQL3 **conforms** with respect to our prescribed user-defined *update* operator support, via its CREATE PROCEDURE statement. It also conforms to our prescription for a method of destroying user-defined operators, via certain DROP statements.

SQL3 also **conforms** with respect to our prescribed user-defined *read-only* operator support, in that the output parameters that can be declared in CREATE PROCEDURE statements are prohibited in CREATE FUNCTION statements. However, we would argue that this conformance is sullied by the fact that the body of a function is allowed to include invocations of operators that modify the database (INSERT, UPDATE, DELETE) or the database definition (CREATE, ALTER, DROP).

---

*There is a major logical difference, in fact, (a) between nulls and values in general, and (b) between null and "the third truth value" (i.e., *unknown*) in particular.

4. *Actual* vs. *possible representations*

SQL3 **conforms** in that it does require a representation to be specified in connection with each user-defined type, and such a specification does involve components as assumed in RM Prescription 4.

SQL3 **fails** in that it does not clearly distinguish between possible representations and actual representations. It further fails in that (as already noted) it does not automatically provide selector operators.

5. *Expose possible representations*

SQL3 **conforms** (at least for user-defined types, though arguably not for builtin ones). The components of a representation are called *attributes* (not to be confused with tuple and relation attributes as defined in *The Third Manifesto*). Each attribute definition automatically causes definition of one *observer* function and one *mutator* function. An SQL3 observer function is a read-only operator, of course—but an SQL3 mutator function is *not* the corresponding update operator that might have been expected (and the term is thus being used in a somewhat unconventional manner). However, assignment of the result of invocation of such a function back to the applicable variable can achieve the "mutation" effect we require. For example, let T be a type, let V be a variable of type T, let C be a component of the representation of type T, let TC be the type of that component, and let X be an expression of type TC. Then the assignment

```
SET V = C ( V, X ) ;
```

updates V such that its C component is set to the value of X and all other components remain unchanged. Further, a shorthand is available that permits the foregoing assignment to be abbreviated to just

```
SET V.C = X ;
```

Nesting is supported on the left hand side, too, as in the following example:

```
SET LS.BEGIN.X = Z ;
```

(see the discussion of nested THE_ pseudovariables in Chapter 6).

Note: Throughout our examples in this appendix we use semicolons as statement terminators, as in "direct SQL" [76,87].

6. *Type generator TUPLE*

SQL3 **conforms** to the following extent. First, it supports a ROW type constructor, which is the obvious analog of our TUPLE type generator (SQL3 uses the term *constructor* rather than our preferred *generator*). The components of a row type are called *fields* (the corresponding *Manifesto* term is *attribute*); thus, the SQL3 analog of our tuple heading is an ordered list (not a set—see below) of $<F,T>$ pairs, where F is a field and T is the corresponding type (not necessarily scalar). A row type can be used for all of the purposes mentioned in RM Prescription 6.

SQL3 **fails** in that it assigns significance to the left to right order of $<F,T>$ pairs (in other words, those pairs form an *ordered list,* not a *set,* as already noted). Thus, for example, the row types

```
ROW ( F1 T1, F2 T2 )
```

and

```
ROW ( F2 T2, F1 T1 )
```

are different types in SQL3.

7. *Type generator RELATION*

SQL3 **fails,** having nothing that corresponds to our RELATION type generator.* *Note:* A TABLE type constructor was included in earlier SQL3 drafts, but it ran into difficulties and was shelved in the hope of speeding up the overall SQL3 standardization process. The type constructors SET, LIST, and MULTISET were also shelved along with TABLE. Among the problems with TABLE was that it was defined as a shorthand for the composite type constructor MULTISET(ROW(...)), whereas it is clear that some SQL tables, at least, contain *sets* of rows, not *bags* (or multisets). Indeed, TABLE(...) would have to have been equated to SET(ROW(...)), not MULTISET(ROW(...)), in order to meet RM Prescription 7 fully.

8. *Equality*

SQL3 **fails.** To repeat an example from Chapter 6, it is possible in SQL3 for the comparison

```
'AB' = 'AB '
```

to give *true,* while the comparison

```
CHAR_LENGTH ( 'AB' ) = CHAR_LENGTH ( 'AB ' )
```

gives *false* (the left comparand evaluates to two and the right to three). Likewise, the comparison

```
'AB '||'AB' = 'AB'||'AB'
```

also gives *false. Note:* These examples are all illustrations of a more general phenomenon—namely, that SQL3 regards certain data values as "equal but distinguishable." For further discussion, see reference [76].

---

*Except for "created temporary tables," which are not tables at all but table type constructors of a very special and restricted kind [76,87–89].

We further remark that it is possible in SQL3 for the expression $X = Y$ not to return *true* and yet for X and Y to be otherwise indistinguishable. This is the case, for example, when X IS NULL and Y IS NULL are both *true*.

Yet another failure occurs here in connection with user-defined types; the definer of such a type can specify the algorithm by which the system is to determine equality of values of the type, and there is no requirement for that algorithm to abide by RM Prescription 8.

We remark finally that several of today's SQL DBMSs (though not SQL3 *per se*) further fail on RM Prescription 8 in that they support certain builtin types—usually called BLOBs or something similar—for which the "=" operator is not defined and cannot be used.

9. Tuples

SQL3 **conforms** to the extent that its row concept is a counterpart to our tuple concept.

SQL3 **fails** by attaching significance to the ordinal positions of row components (i.e., field values). Also, we require tuple components to have names; row components in SQL3 have names only when those names can be, and are, provided by the context in which the row in question is used. In particular, the *row value constructor* of SQL3—its analog of our *tuple selector invocation*—takes the form

```
[ ROW ] ( <ne exp commalist> )
```

(to use the BNF conventions of Chapter 5), and thus provides no way of specifying field names.

SQL3 further fails in that a field "value" can be null, which, as we have already observed in connection with RM Prescription 1, does not have all the properties required for it to qualify as a value.

10. Relations

SQL3 **conforms** to the extent that its table concept is a counterpart to our relation concept. An SQL3 table has:

- A counterpart to our *heading,* in the form of an ordered list of $<C,T>$ pairs, where C is a column and T is the corresponding type (not necessarily scalar);

- A counterpart to our *body,* in the form of a bag (sometimes a set) of rows.

It narrowly escapes failure to conform to our requirement for every attribute (column) to have a name, even though it does allow the user to write an expression that yields a table that contains columns for which no name is specified explicitly. It does so, somewhat suspectly, by requiring the system to *generate* a name for each such column. Such names are required to be unique within the entire scope of the outermost containing statement (an obvious case of overkill, especially since SQL3 does permit two distinct columns of the same table to have the same name!).

The VALUES construct of SQL3 provides a counterpart to our prescribed relation selector operator, though of course it suffers from the failures we observe here in connection with relations in general.

SQL3 **fails** in the following respects:

- Significance is attached to the left to right order of columns;
- Two or more distinct columns of the same table can have the same name;
- The collection of rows corresponding to our *body* is, in general, a bag, not a set;
- Rows do not fully conform to our prescription for tuples (as already noted under RM Prescription 9).

We observe too that, in its nomenclature at least, SQL3 does not adequately distinguish between table *values* and table *variables.*

11. Scalar variables

SQL3 **conforms** (apart from its support for nulls).

12. Tuple variables

SQL3 **conforms** insofar as it conforms to RM Prescriptions 6 and 9 concerning tuple types and tuples.

13. Relation variables (relvars)

SQL3 **conforms** (to a greater extent than that to which it conforms to RM Prescriptions 7 and 10), thanks to its support for *base tables,* its counterpart to our real relvars. Although (as noted under RM Prescription 7) there is no counterpart in general to our RELATION type generator, a base table definition does make use of a construct that is somewhat analogous: namely, an ordered list of $<C,T>$ pairs, where C is a column and T is a type (not necessarily scalar). Further, no two columns of a given base table are permitted to have the same name. *Note:* This latter fact notwithstanding, SQL3 still attaches significance to the left to right order of the columns.

SQL3 also **fails,** because it permits a base table to have a special type *in addition to* the type it acquires from its heading (see the final section of this appendix for detailed discussion of this point). It also fails inasmuch as, at any isolation level other than SERIALIZABLE, updating a base table is not logically equivalent to a simple (relational) assignment.

SQL3 also fails to provide any counterpart to our *global application relvars.*

14. Real vs. *virtual relvars*

SQL3 **conforms,** insofar as it conforms to RM Prescription 13, by providing a facility to define *updatable views* (its counterpart to our virtual relvars). However, it also **fails,** because not all "views" that we require to be updatable can in fact be updated in SQL3; it also fails because it permits both (a) some "views" that are not logically updatable at all to be updated and (b) some "views" that are logically updatable to be updated in logically incorrect ways.

15. *Candidate keys*

SQL3 **fails.** It permits but does not require keys to be defined for a base table, and does not even permit them to be defined for a view.

We further remark that SQL3 permits one key to be a proper superset of another, in which case it is blatantly not a candidate key but a proper superkey.

16. *Databases*

Strictly speaking, there is no such thing as a database in SQL3. Instead, there is something called *SQL-data,* which is "any data described by schemas that is under the control of an SQL-implementation in an SQL-environment" [87]. However, some might say that SQL3 does **conform** to the general intent of RM Prescription 16, inasmuch as "SQL-data" really means relvars, loosely speaking. Others might say it **fails** . . . Its support for *REF values* (see the final section in this appendix) is the bothersome feature; as we have argued elsewhere [72], it is a logical consequence of such support that the database does *not* contain relvars only, but tuple (or rather row) and/or scalar variables as well.

17. *Transactions*

SQL3 **conforms.**

18. *Relational algebra*

SQL3 **conforms** in that (a) all of the prescribed operators are directly or indirectly available, and (b) it is possible to ensure—by judicious use of the language—that the operands to invocations of these operators are effectively true relations (i.e., they are tables whose columns have distinct names, whose bodies are sets, and whose rows contain no nulls). However, it **fails** in some cases, notably DIVIDEBY PER and SUMMARIZE PER, to provide these operators "without excessive circumlocution."

That said, we should note that at the time of writing:

- Almost nobody seems to have implemented NATURAL JOIN or JOIN with the USING option. As a result, the SQL analog of our own JOIN operation sometimes involves a very great deal of "excessive circumlocution" indeed (specifically, when tables of very large degree are involved).

- Nobody seems to have implemented the CORRESPONDING version of UNION, INTERSECT, and EXCEPT. As a result, there is often no direct SQL analog of our UNION, INTERSECT, and MINUS operations (which place no significance on left to right column ordering, of course).

- The most important feature of all so far as expressive completeness is concerned—namely, the ability to specify table expressions* of arbitrary complexity in the FROM clause—is still absent from some implementations.

---

*The standard SQL term is *query* expression.

We stress the point that none of these features is new in SQL3 (they were all present in SQL/92).

19. Relvar names, relation selectors, and recursion

SQL3 **conforms** with respect to relation selector invocations and recursion. First, a VALUES invocation is a legal table expression. Second, the WITH clause (new in SQL3) permits a table expression to be given a name and for that very name to be referenced in that very table expression, thereby supporting what are commonly known as "recursive queries."

SQL3 **fails** to permit a table name to be a legal table expression. The current value of a named table can be referenced by writing the word TABLE, or alternatively SELECT * FROM, in front of the name in question; however, we do not regard these features as meeting this part of RM Prescription 19.

20. Relation-valued operators

SQL3 **conforms** to some extent, with its support for nonupdatable views. However, it **fails** in that its view definitions cannot be parameterized.

21. Assignments

SQL3 **conforms** (more or less) with respect to scalar and tuple assignment, subject to failures already noted in connection with tuples. However, it **fails** with respect to relational assignment, because "relvars"—base tables and updatable views, in SQL3 terms—cannot be directly assigned to; they can only have their current values "modified" via INSERT, UPDATE, and DELETE. SQL3 also fails to support our *multiple* assignment.

We observe too that there is a certain anomaly in the SQL3 provisions for assignment, arising from its support for nulls. The observation is that immediately following the assignment SET $X = Y$ it is not always the case that the comparison $X = Y$ gives *true*. Further, when this anomalous circumstance arises, it is not necessarily the case in SQL3 that Y is *null* (though it *is* necessarily the case in SQL/92). For example, Y could be a value of some user-defined type T such that $Y.C$ IS NULL is *true* for some component (attribute) C of Y, while Y IS NULL is *false*.

22. Comparisons

SQL3 **conforms** to this prescription with respect to scalar comparisons. It also conforms with respect to tuple comparisons, subject to failures already noted in connection with tuples, and subject also to the failure that it expressly does support "tuple"—or, rather, row—comparison operators other than "=" and "≠" (e.g., it supports "<"). It also conforms to our prescription for an operator to test membership of a tuple in a relation, via that version of its IN operator that takes a row expression on the left hand side and a table expression on the right.

SQL3 **fails** completely with respect to relation comparison, lacking all of the operators in question and any circumlocutory means of achieving the same effects.

Note: To see that this latter claim is justified, consider the following expression, which might be proposed as an "equivalent" for the relation comparison T1 = T2. Assume for simplicity that tables T1 and T2 each have two columns only, C1 and C2.

```
NOT EXISTS ( SELECT * FROM T1
             WHERE NOT EXISTS ( SELECT * FROM T2
                                WHERE T1.C1 = T2.C1
                                AND   T1.C2 = T2.C2 ) )
AND
NOT EXISTS ( SELECT * FROM T2
             WHERE NOT EXISTS ( SELECT * FROM T1
                                WHERE T2.C1 = T1.C1
                                AND   T2.C2 = T1.C2 ) )
```

Observe that in order to be able to write this expression in the first place, we obviously need to be aware of all of the applicable column names. Furthermore, the expression gets increasingly harder to write as the number of columns increases. We remark too that the expression does not take into account the possibility, occasioned by the fact that SQL tables can contain duplicate rows, that some row occurs m times in T1 and n times in T2, where $m \neq n$.

Note: Not surprisingly, the situation is further complicated if any column of either T1 or T2 can contain nulls. A *scalar* comparison such as V1 = V2 can return the truth value *unknown* in SQL3. To be faithful to its own concepts, therefore, the SQL3 analog of T1 = T2 should surely be able to do the same, whereas the workaround we have suggested can only ever return either *true* or *false*. You might like to consider what additions are needed to that workaround if T1 = T2 is to be regarded as *true* in the case where T1 and T2 contain exactly the same collection of rows, taking into account the fact that (in view of our observations under the previous item, "Assignments") it is not necessarily sufficient to replace T1.C1 = T2.C1 by the following—

```
T1.C1 = T2.C1 OR ( T1.C1 IS NULL AND T2.C2 IS NULL )
```

—and similarly for the other three scalar comparisons in that workaround.

23. Integrity constraints

SQL3 **conforms** with respect to our attribute, relvar, and database constraints (though its classification scheme for constraints is nothing like as clearcut and straightforward as that required by the *Manifesto*). It also supports a certain degree of constraint inference, via functional dependency analysis.

SQL3 **fails** completely with respect to type constraints.* *Note:* SQL/92 does support something it calls "domains," and such "domains" do have associated constraints. However, those "domains" are not true types—they are nothing to do with true relational domains—and those "domain constraints" are not true type constraints.

---

*We speculate that the reason it fails has to do with the "3 out of 4" rule (see the discussion of this "rule" in Appendix C).

Rather, they are attribute, relvar, or database constraints, in *Manifesto* terms, that happen to have been specified in a rather unorthodox way. We should add that this feature of SQL/92 is now recognized as problematical and might conceivably be dropped when SQL3 is finally published.

24. *Relvar and database predicates*

SQL3 **conforms** with respect to database predicates being satisfied at transaction boundaries.

SQL3 **fails** with respect to relvar predicates being satisfied at statement boundaries, on two counts: its support for deferred constraints, which are checked only when the user "switches on" the necessary checking (transaction termination at the latest) by means of SET CONSTRAINTS, and its support for updatable views that are specified without WITH CASCADED CHECK OPTION.

25. *Catalog*

SQL3 **conforms** in that its catalogs are themselves collections of tables (meaning table *variables,* of course).

SQL3 **fails** to support assignment to those tables for two reasons. First, the tables in question are nonupdatable views (so they are not *really* table variables!); second, SQL3 in any case has deficient support for relation assignment, as already noted under RM Prescription 21.

26. *Language design*

SQL3 **fails** to some considerable extent by most, if not all, of the generally agreed yardsticks of good language design. More specifically, it fails with respect to at least the following measures: conceptual integrity, syntactic consistency, parsimony, and orthogonality [33].

- It fails with respect to *conceptual integrity* in its treatment of nulls, for example. The originally intended interpretation of nulls when they were first added to SQL was "value unknown," and this interpretation accounts for the behavior of nulls in (e.g.) comparisons. Yet SQL3 sometimes generates nulls in circumstances where such an interpretation is utterly inappropriate. The nulls that result from OUTER JOIN, for example, might perhaps signify "not applicable"; the null that results from attempting to compute the average of an empty set of numbers surely signifies "undefined"; and the null that results from an attempt to sum that same set is just a perverse way of indicating zero. We remind you too that null is also used in SQL3 to signify "the third truth value" (see the discussion of RM Prescription 1, earlier).

  On another front, SQL3 claims that its tables, in general, are *multisets* (bags) of rows; yet the normal *union* operator on bags is not directly provided, and considerable circumlocution is required to obtain its effect.

In any case, SQL3 concepts are not agreeably few, and they include many that are not agreeable at all—for example, nulls, three-valued logic, left to right column ordering, duplicate rows, and so on.

■ SQL3 fails with respect to *syntactic consistency* in the various ways it uses AS to give a name to an expression. In some contexts, such as the SELECT and FROM clauses, the expression comes before the AS and the name after. In others, such as the CREATE VIEW statement and the WITH clause, the name comes before and the expression after.

By way of another example (taken from reference [76]), consider the following SQL3 expressions:

```
A NATURAL JOIN B

A UNION B

TABLE A UNION TABLE B

TABLE A NATURAL JOIN TABLE B

SELECT * FROM A UNION SELECT * FROM B

SELECT * FROM A NATURAL JOIN SELECT * FROM B

( TABLE A ) UNION ( TABLE B )

( TABLE A ) NATURAL JOIN ( TABLE B )

( TABLE A ) AS AA NATURAL JOIN ( TABLE B ) AS BB
```

Some of these expressions are syntactically legal and some not, and it is a nontrivial exercise to figure out which are which.

■ SQL3 fails with respect to *parsimony* in the remarkable degree of redundancy—different ways, that is, sometimes radically different ways, of achieving the same effect—that has been noted by the present authors among others (see, e.g. reference [73]). For example, the plugging of those "holes" in the original SQL language that rendered it relationally incomplete has made all of the following features theoretically redundant: GROUP BY, HAVING, subqueries, and correlation names. And of these, we venture to suggest that HAVING, at least, is positively undesirable.

■ With respect to *orthogonality,* SQL/92 has already addressed many of the complaints that made SQL quite notorious among computer languages. However, a few violations remained in SQL/92 (and at the time of writing SQL3 is introducing a few more). For example:

• Table variables are supported "in the database" but (mostly) not as local variables in applications or the bodies of user-defined functions and procedures.

• The availability of the CASCADE option of DROP depends on the kind of object being dropped.

- It is not possible to define subtypes of builtin types. It could be argued that as it is possible to specify that a given user-defined type is not permitted to have any subtypes, that option is merely implied for all system-defined types. Alternatively, it could be argued that as subtype prohibition is only an option on user-defined types, it ought to be an option on builtin types too.

- The new VALUES ARE SYSTEM GENERATED feature in column definitions is available only for base tables created using OF (i.e., having a user-defined type—see the final section in this appendix). On the face of it, at least, it would appear that these two features, OF and VALUES ARE SYSTEM GENERATED, should be orthogonal.

The foregoing list of criticisms is not meant to be exhaustive.

RM PROSCRIPTIONS

1. *No attribute ordering*

SQL3 **fails.** Examples of where SQL attaches significance to the left to right order of columns include:

- SELECT *
- UNION, INTERSECT, EXCEPT (without CORRESPONDING in each case)
- INSERT (if no column names specified)
- Row comparisons
- IN (of rows and tables)

2. *No tuple ordering*

SQL3 **conforms.**

3. *No duplicate tuples*

SQL3 **fails.** Duplicate rows can arise in at least the following ways:

- SELECT without DISTINCT
- INSERT into a base table for which no candidate key is specified
- UNION ALL
- Specifying the same row more than once in an invocation of VALUES

4. *No nulls*

SQL3 **fails.**

5. No nullological mistakes

SQL3 **fails.** Examples:

- Requiring at least one column in every base table
- Requiring at least one expression in the SELECT clause
- Requiring at least one column in every key

RM Proscription 5 specifically addresses only tables and keys, but we additionally note here certain other nullological mistakes in SQL3:

- Requiring at least one table reference in the FROM clause
- Requiring at least one item in GROUP BY and ORDER BY (though in these cases case the required effect can be obtained by omission of the clause in question)
- Several errors in the handling of empty tables (for example, treating such a table as a *null* in the context of a scalar subquery)

6. No internal-level constructs

SQL3 **conforms.**

7. No tuple-level operations

SQL3 **fails.** Its FETCH operation (not to be confused with our TUPLE FROM operator!) retrieves an individual row. Worse, its UPDATE and DELETE WHERE CURRENT OF CURSOR operations update individual rows.

8. No composite attributes

SQL3 **conforms.**

9. No domain check override

SQL3 **conforms.**

10. Not SQL

SQL3 **fails.** The language defined in the SQL3 specification is called SQL.

OO PRESCRIPTIONS

1. Compile-time type checking

SQL3 **conforms.**

2. Single inheritance (conditional)

SQL3 **fails** in that its support for subtypes and supertypes is in accordance with a model that, though acceptably clear so far as its single inheritance features are concerned, is not at the time of writing clear overall (i.e., when its multiple inheritance features are taken into account too).

SQL3 further **fails** in that the model in question is not yet generally agreed (in the community at large, that is). In particular, it is not fully acceptable to the present authors, because it requires, in the case where CIRCLE is defined as a subtype of ELLIPSE, CIRCLE to include values that are not true circles (specifically, values that have semiaxes that are not equal). By contrast, our own inheritance proposals permit type definers to ensure that such anomalies do not arise.

3. Multiple inheritance (conditional)

SQL3 **fails.** As already noted, it does currently include support for multiple inheritance, but the model is not clear, nor generally agreed, nor fully acceptable.

4. Computational completeness

SQL3 **conforms** (via its Persistent Stored Modules feature, SQL/PSM).

5. Explicit transaction boundaries

SQL3 **conforms** (almost) with respect to transaction termination, but **fails** with respect to transaction initiation, which is allowed to be implicit (see the discussion of this issue in Chapter 8).

6. Nested transactions

SQL3 **fails.** It does provide some analogous and useful functionality by means of its *savepoint* mechanism, but establishing a savepoint is not the same as starting a transaction [85].

7. Aggregates and empty sets

SQL3 **fails,** because SUM, AVG, MAX, and MIN all return *null* if invoked on an empty argument.

OO PROSCRIPTIONS

1. Relvars are not domains

SQL3 **conforms,** but in view of our reservations in connection with RM Prescription 13 (to the effect that a base table can have a second type, over and above the one it acquires from its heading) we feel compelled to add that it does so only by the skin of its teeth. The final section of this appendix contains an extended discussion of this issue.

2. No object IDs

SQL3 perhaps **conforms,** but once again only by the skin of its teeth. Its system-generated REF values look very much like object IDs, though they do manage not quite to violate the letter of OO Proscription 2.

RM VERY STRONG SUGGESTIONS

1. System keys

SQL3 to some extent **conforms,** but only via the VALUES ARE SYSTEM GEN-ERATED feature which, as we have already observed under RM Prescription 26, is not as generally available as we suggest it should be. It has no analog of the TAG operator we suggest in Chapter 10.

2. Foreign keys

SQL3 **conforms.**

3. Candidate key inference

SQL3 **conforms** insofar as it conforms to RM Prescription 15. *Note:* Although SQL3 does require candidate keys to be inferred for query results, those inferred keys are put to only rather limited use.

4. Transition constraints

SQL3 **fails.** It might be possible to use CREATE TRIGGER to achieve some—not all—of the same functionality as a general declarative transition constraint, but CREATE TRIGGER is at least partly procedural in nature. In particular, it speci-fies when the triggered action is to be invoked; as a result, it might be possible (e.g.) to subvert an UPDATE triggered action by executing a DELETE followed by an INSERT instead of executing an UPDATE *per se.*

5. Quota queries

SQL3 **fails** to provide the suggested shorthand. However, quota queries can of course be expressed with some circumlocution, so at least it does avoid the neces-sity to convert a relation into (e.g.) an array for this purpose.

6. Generalized transitive closure

SQL3 **conforms,** via its support for recursion in WITH clauses and view definitions (though the support in question is unfortunately subject to a very complex set of rules and restrictions).

7. Tuple and relation parameters

SQL3 **fails.** It does permit parameters to user-defined operators to be of some specific row type, but not of some specific table type; it also does not permit the definition of "generic" operators, with "generic" parameters.

8. Special ("default") values

SQL3 **fails.** It does support a weak form of defaults as such, but that support is very far from being the kind of "special values" support intended by our suggestion here.

9. SQL migration

Not applicable. Further research would be needed to say whether SQL3 conforms to this suggestion. For it to do so, it would have to be possible to implement SQL in SQL3. However, as the purpose of the suggestion is to provide "a painless migration route . . . for current SQL users," and such a migration route is available in SQL3 because SQL3 has been deliberately designed to be compatible with SQL, it would be churlish to record a failure here if further research did in fact show SQL not to be implementable in SQL3.

OO VERY STRONG SUGGESTIONS

1. Type inheritance

SQL3 **conforms** to the spirit of this suggestion. However, some coercions are supported in connection with builtin types, to which type inheritance is not applicable.

2. Types and operators unbundled

SQL3 partly **conforms** and partly **fails.** Some operators (namely, those specifically designated as "methods") *must* be bundled, other operators must not.

3. Collection type generators

SQL3 **conforms,** but only just: It supports an ARRAY type constructor (as noted earlier in this appendix, SQL3 uses the term "type constructor" in place of our "type generator").

4. Conversion to/from relations

SQL3 **fails** *a fortiori,* since it does not support a TABLE type constructor. However, we note that the earlier draft that included such a constructor did also include the conversion operators we suggest here.

5. Single-level store

SQL3 **conforms** to some extent, through its PSM feature, but **fails** through its lack of full support for local table variables. It also fails when used as an "embedded data sublanguage."

IM PROPOSALS (SCALAR TYPES, SINGLE INHERITANCE)

1. Types are sets

SQL3 **conforms.**

2. Subtypes are subsets

SQL3 **conforms.**

3. "Subtype of" is reflexive

SQL3 **conforms.**

4. Proper subtypes

SQL3 **conforms.**

5. "Subtype of" is transitive

SQL3 **conforms.**

6. Immediate subtypes

SQL3 **conforms** (we note, however, that it uses the term "direct" in place of the more apt "immediate").

7. Single inheritance only

SQL3 **fails,** because it (currently) supports multiple inheritance. Such a failure is desirable, of course!—so long as the multiple inheritance support in question is based on a model that is "clearly defined and generally agreed" (but we would argue the SQL3 support is not).

8. Global root types

SQL3 **conforms** (the SQL3 term is "maximal supertype").

9. Type hierarchies

The remarks under IM Proposal 7 above apply here also, *mutatis mutandis.*

10. Subtypes can be proper subsets

SQL3 **conforms.** *Note:* In our discussion of this IM Proposal in Chapter 14, we also introduced and briefly described the concept of *dummy types.* What seems to be an analogous concept, *noninstantiable* types, has recently been added to SQL3; however, it does not yet seem to be adequately specified, and so it is hard to be sure if the concepts are really the same.

11. Types disjoint unless one a subtype of the other

For multiple inheritance, SQL3 (desirably) **fails,** of course. For single inheritance, it **conforms.**

12. Scalar values (extended definition)

SQL3 **conforms.**

13. Scalar variables (extended definition)

SQL3 **conforms.**

14. Assignment with inheritance

SQL3 **conforms.**

15. Comparison with inheritance

Not clear. In terms of our usual example, the SQL3 specification does currently appear to allow a comparison between a variable of declared type ELLIPSE and one of declared type CIRCLE, but it does not define the semantics of such a comparison.

16. Join etc. with inheritance

Not clear. No doubt matters will be clarified before publication, but we cannot yet tell whether that clarification will yield conformance to IM Proposal 16.

17. TREAT DOWN

SQL3 **conforms** inasmuch as it does support a "TREAT DOWN" *operator* (in fact the operator in question is called TREAT). However, it **fails** to support a "TREAT DOWN" pseudovariable.

18. TREAT UP

SQL3 **fails.** It does have an operator that provides "TREAT UP" functionality, but that operator can be used only in function invocations, to generalize the declared type of an argument in order to force invocation of a "less specific" version of the operator in question. We remark that the provision of this functionality tends to suggest some confusion over model *vs.* implementation.

19. Logical operator IS_T(SX)

SQL3 **conforms.** Here is the SQL3 analog of our IS_*T(SX)*:

```
TYPE ( SX ) [ IS ] IN ( T )
```

The optional IS is a noiseword. The expression following IN is a parenthesized commalist of type specifications (possibly including specifications of the form TYPE (*<exp>*), so SQL3 also supports an analog of our IS_SAME_TYPE_AS (*SY,SX*)). Analogous remarks apply to IM Proposals 20–22 as well, *q.v.*

20. Relational operator RX:IS_T(A)

SQL3 **conforms.** However, its support is clumsy. Let *RX* denote a relation with attributes *A, B,* and *C.* Then the SQL3 analog of our *RX*:IS_T(*A*) looks like this:

```
( SELECT DISTINCT TREAT A AS T AS A, B, C
  FROM    RX
  WHERE   TYPE ( A ) IS IN ( T ) )
```

Such expressions become increasingly cumbersome as the number of attributes increases.

21. Logical operator IS_MS_T(SX)

SQL3 **conforms.** Here is the SQL3 analog of our IS_MS_*T*(*SX*):

```
TYPE ( SX ) [ IS ] IN ( ONLY T )
```

Note: SQL3 also provides an operator that returns the type of its argument as a character string.

22. Relational operator RX:IS_MS_T(A)

SQL3 **conforms.** However, its support is clumsy. Let *RX* denote a relation with attributes *A, B,* and *C.* Then the SQL3 analog of our *RX*:IS_MS_*T*(*A*) looks like this:

```
( SELECT DISTINCT TREAT A AS T AS A, B, C
  FROM    RX
  WHERE   TYPE ( A ) IS IN ( ONLY T ) )
```

Such expressions become increasingly cumbersome as the number of attributes increases.

23. THE_ pseudovariables

SQL3 **fails.** It does have something a little similar to the pseudovariable THE_*C*(*V*), namely the construct *V.C;* as already noted under RM Prescription 5, however, assigning *X* to *V.C* is just shorthand for assigning *C*(*V,X*) to *V*—and SQL3 requires the function *C* here to be inherited by all subtypes of *T,* where *T* is the declared type of *V.* The consequence is that type CIRCLE, for example, has to include values that do not represent genuine circles, as we now explain.

   Suppose variable E, of declared type ELLIPSE, is assigned a circle of radius three (consequently having A and B semiaxes both three). Suppose we now assign the value four to E.A, implying (among other things) that we invoke the function A on E. That function is required to be what SQL3 calls *type preserving,* meaning (in the case at hand) that it returns a result of the same most specific type—*viz.,* CIRCLE—as its argument E. Thus, the overall effect is that the variable E now contains a value of type CIRCLE with A semiaxis four and B semiaxis three—so it is not *really* a circle!

24. Read-only operator inheritance and value substitutability

SQL3 **conforms.** *Note:* In our discussion of IM Proposal 24 in Chapter 14, we suggested that every argument to a given invocation of a given operator should participate in the run-time binding process. SQL3 currently conforms on this point of detail too, but the issue is controversial and moves are afoot at the time of writing to change the specification in this respect. The reason for the controversy is that C++ and Java, the two most likely candidates to be host languages for applications using the "object" portions of SQL3, do *not* conform to the feature in question; rather, they perform run-time binding on the basis of the first argument only. Even some of those who advocate our approach here are having to admit that mismatch with C++ and Java is likely to prove problematical. As a result, we might yet see something more akin to the so-called *selfish methods* of C++ and Java (and several other object languages) in SQL3, in place of the current so-called *multifunctions.* *

25. Read-only parameters to update operators

SQL3 **conforms.**

26. Update operator inheritance and variable substitutability

SQL3 **fails.** It requires update operators to be inherited unconditionally. However, we should add that the SQL3 *mutator* concept does seem to include the germ of an approach, more general than the one described in the body of Chapter 14, to the "application immunity" problem (the problem, that is, of ensuring that a program that updates, say, the a semiaxis of a variable of declared type ELLIPSE will still work after type CIRCLE has been introduced). SQL3 mutators are a special case of a more general feature, mentioned in passing under IM Proposal 23 above, called *type preserving functions.* Such functions explicitly rely on the notion of result *covariance* (though that terminology is not used); to be more specific, their result type covaries with that of the argument corresponding to a certain designated parameter. We can explain this idea (for mutators specifically) as follows:

- Suppose type *T* has an attribute *A* (using "attribute" in the SQL3 sense, not the *Manifesto* sense). Then the system automatically defines a mutator for type *T* with the same name *A* and with two parameters, the first of declared type *T* and the second of declared type the same as that of attribute *A*. Invoking that mutator returns a result of most specific type the same as that of the argument

---

*"Selfish methods" were added to SQL3 just as this book was going to press. Thus, SQL3 now supports both (a) C++- and Java-style methods and (b) "nonmethod" operators, for which the binding process is performed at compilation time (necessarily on the basis of declared types only).

corresponding to the first parameter (so it is the type of that argument that is "preserved," loosely speaking).

- Let $A(v1,a)$ be such an invocation and let $v2$ be the corresponding result. Then $v2$ is identical to $v1$ (in particular it has the same most specific type), except that its A attribute has value a. Note carefully that no updating has occurred here (the operator A is read-only). However, if we now assign the result $v2$ back to $v1$, the net effect would be as if the assignment

```
THE_A ( v1 )   :=   a ;
```

(**Tutorial D** notation) had been executed.

Despite their reliance on the concept of result covariance—a concept that, as explained in Chapter 14, we do not ourselves much care for—we do believe (as already stated) that the foregoing ideas might possibly be of use in the development of a more general approach to the application immunity problem. On the other hand, we also believe that a better approach might be found in extending our model of inheritance to include support for *specialization* (and *generalization*) by *constraint,* along the lines sketched in the final section of Appendix C. If we do decide to follow this latter path, of course, SQL3 and our own inheritance model will be that much further apart.

IM PROPOSALS (SCALAR TYPES, MULTIPLE INHERITANCE)

7. Many supertypes per subtype

SQL# **conforms,** subject to the reservations regarding multiple inheritance mentioned in the previous section.

9. Type graphs

SQL3 **conforms,** more or less. It supports a concept it calls a "subtype family," defined as follows:

> Let T be a maximal supertype and let T' be a subtype of T. The set of all subtypes of T (which includes T itself) is called a *subtype family* of T' or (equivalently) of T. The subtype family is not permitted to have more than one maximal supertype.

(We have edited this definition very slightly.) This concept appears to be the same as what in Chapter 15 we called a type graph *partition.*

11. Least specific types unique

SQL3 **conforms.**

12. Most specific types unique

SQL3 **conforms.**

15. Comparison with multiple inheritance

Not clear. In terms of our example from Chapter 15, the SQL3 specification does currently seem to allow a comparison between a variable of declared type RECTANGLE and one of declared type RHOMBUS, but it does not define the semantics of such a comparison.

16. Join etc. with multiple inheritance

The situation in SQL3 is not clear at the time of writing. It is documented as an outstanding problem.

IM PROPOSALS (TUPLE AND RELATION TYPES)

SQL3 **conforms** with respect to tuple types. Having no relation type generator at all, it obviously **fails** with respect to relation types.

HISTORY OF THE WRONG EQUATION IN SQL3

What we call the wrong equation—i.e., "relvar = class"*—has been (and indeed still is) so widespread in the industry that it has inevitably shown up from time to time in proposals for SQL3. Such proposals have been the subject of much debate, sometimes painful, in the ISO Database Languages committee. Since that wrong equation was the strongest single factor in our original motivation for writing *The Third Manifesto,* we thought it worth taking a few moments here to review the somewhat checkered history of SQL3 in this connection; hence this final section (which is a kind of appendix to the appendix). *Note:* An interestingly different account of this history can be found in reference [100].

As it nears formal publication, SQL3 looks as if it is probably going with the right equation ("domain = class") and thereby conforming to OO Proscription 1. But even now the clear distinctions we prescribe in this area are at least partly muddied in SQL3; in fact, it might even be argued that SQL3 is going with both equations at once.

We have given some thought to the question of why the wrong equation has been so widely advocated. We suspect that (as noted in the annotation to reference [10] in Appendix H, *q.v.*) the root of the problem is closely connected with the concept of entity/relationship (E/R) modeling, which became widely used in the 1980s as an early stage in database design. For consider:

- E/R modeling typically leads to a situation in which each entity type in the E/R diagram maps to precisely one database table (or relvar, as we would now prefer to call it).

------

*Or even, sometimes, "*relation* = class."

- Critics of this approach have often mildly observed—though users of it have usually overlooked—the fact that the entity types *per se* disappear in that mapping to tables (i.e., the database contains tables, not entity types). And that disappearance is a necessary consequence of the fact that relational operators apply to relations (tables), not to entities or collections of entities.

- Thus, for example, the database designer might come up with an entity type EMPLOYEE, with properties EMPLOYEE NUMBER, HIRE DATE, SALARY, and so on. That entity type might then map to a table that looks like this:

```
EMP { EMP# CHAR, HIREDATE DATE, SALARY MONEY, ... }
```

- Now, the designer might *think* of this table, psychologically, as being "of type EMPLOYEE." The fact remains, however, that so far as the DBMS is concerned the type in fact *is*

```
RELATION { EMP# CHAR, HIREDATE DATE, SALARY INTEGER, ... }
```

(no more and no less).

Two further developments then occurred:

- E/R modeling grew into *object-oriented analysis.*
- *Object-oriented DBMSs* began to become available.

The idea of mapping entity types—now called *object classes*—directly into constructs in the database of the same name and connotation thus became an alluring possibility. Moreover, it was a possibility that DBMS implementers on both sides of the object/relational divide found themselves in a position to comply with. To be specific, many implementers, both of SQL systems with "object-like" extensions and of object systems with "SQL-like" extensions, were able to equate object classes with relations (meaning relvars, usually) by pursuing certain alluring, albeit vague, analogies. For example:

- There is an apparent analogy between (a) the components of the representation specified for objects of a class and (b) the attributes of a relation (in SQL, columns of a table). Indeed, those object class components are sometimes even called attributes, though we prefer the term *instance variables* [81].

- There is an apparent analogy between (a) the object IDs of object systems and (b) the internal "row IDs" used—for performance reasons—in many SQL systems (though it should be noted that such row IDs are not part of the SQL language itself).

These analogies are attractive to implementers because they seem to provide a relatively quick and easy way of making their SQL systems object-like or their object systems SQL-like. However, we find both of them inappropriate. To elaborate:

- With regard to the first analogy: Of course, a tuple is a value; therefore it is a value of some type (i.e., it is "an instance of some class"). However, it is a value with a very special meaning, a meaning that lies at the very heart of relational theory. We have explained that special meaning in detail in Chapter 2, and we remind you in particular of the parallel we draw between the domains and relations of relational theory and the nouns and sentences of human language. Under that parallel, a tuple in a relation is interpreted as a sentence: specifically, a *true proposition.* And such tuples are explicitly visible *as* tuples by users of the system, and are to be understood by those users as such propositions.

  Of course, tuples can be used at the internal level of the system too, as the hidden internal representation for certain other values. For example, the ellipse whose *a* semiaxis is four, whose *b* semiaxis is three, and whose center is the origin might be represented internally by such a tuple; however, in no way does *that* tuple represent a proposition! (If you feel somehow tempted to try to make it into one, might we suggest that you try making one out of the value "3"?) Equating components of a hidden representation to attributes of a user-visible tuple is tantamount to confusing a noun with a sentence.

- With regard to the second analogy: Here we simply claim that to equate row IDs to object IDs is to bring into the model something that is not needed there. It should stay where it belongs, in the implementation. (We note too that even in those SQL systems that support row IDs, it is typically the case that not all rows have such IDs; usually, only rows in base tables do.)

Back to the two equations. Actually, SQL3 has always subscribed to the *right* equation, inasmuch as it has always acknowledged, noncontroversially, the fact that user-defined types should be available as types for columns. In the checkered history we referred to above, however, there have been various attempts to make user-defined types somehow available as types for tables, too. *Note:* Perhaps we should stress the point here that the user-defined types we are talking about are not types generated by means of something like our RELATION type generator; rather, they are what the *Manifesto* calls *scalar* types—also known as encapsulated types, as explained in Appendix B. So any table having such a type would apparently have to be a single-column table specifically.

The 1992 SQL3 draft did in fact attempt to embrace the equation of object classes and *relations*—not relvars—via a concept that became known as "tables of ADT" (ADT standing for *abstract data type*). The material in connection with this concept was eventually removed from the draft; however, it was removed not so much because of the theoretical arguments of its opponents, but merely because it gave rise to certain technical problems. Those problems in turn were largely caused by the difficulty (we would say *impossibility*) of devising a system in which every table has some additional "encapsulated" scalar type, over and above the unencapsulated table type it already has thanks to the pertinent column definitions. *Note:* We are departing from SQL3 terminology here; SQL3 does not talk in terms of scalar *vs.* table types as such, nor indeed of encapsulation *vs.* unencapsulation.

In 1994 another attempt was made to introduce something arising from equating object classes to relvars, when a concept called "extent tables" was proposed. The proposal was defeated, but again it was technical problems rather than theoretical arguments that prevailed. The proposal included a counterpart to our *selector* operators, called "constructor functions" (not the same as the constructor functions of the current SQL3 draft—see the discussion of RM Prescription 1 earlier in this appendix). Every invocation of such a function was to have the side effect of inserting a row into the applicable extent table, and it was that technical flaw (i.e., the side effect that every such invocation caused the database to be updated) that contributed more than anything else to the demise of the idea.

In 1996, yet another attempt to associate scalar or "encapsulated" types with tables was proposed, this time as a separate Part, Part 8, known as *SQL/Object*. SQL/Object introduced three new concepts—"named row types," "reference types," and "system-generated REF values"—but otherwise stayed much closer to existing SQL than the previous attempts. It also did not seem to suffer from the same technical flaws that had spelled the end of those previous attempts. Indeed, supporters of the new proposal were careful to point out the extent to which *syntactic substitution* [33] was used in their specification. In SQL/Object:

- A row type could be given an explicit name. (Prior to this proposal, row types in SQL3—like tuple types in the *Manifesto*—had no such explicit name.)

- A base table could be defined in terms of such a named row type, instead of in terms of explicit columns. That table then effectively had two types: the named row type (loosely speaking), and the type specified by the columns of that named row type.

- The named row type in question could have named subtypes.

- The base table in question could have "subtables," a concept already present in SQL3 when SQL/Object was proposed (see Appendix D). Those subtables corresponded to subtypes of the supertable's named row type (though we remind you that, as explained in detail in Appendix D, the "supertables and subtables" concept is *not* type inheritance as such).

- The base table in question could also have a special column whose definition carried the specification VALUES ARE SYSTEM GENERATED. That column would then contain "REF values," analogous to object IDs. The rows in such tables became referred to, informally, as "row objects" in some circles.

- Other base tables could then have columns containing REF values that referred to rows in the base table in question.

But SQL/Object was by no means universally accepted in the SQL standards community. First, people rightly complained at having so many apparently distinct concepts all somehow connected with user-defined types: ADTs, named row types, and something else called "distinct types" (not discussed in this appendix)—not to mention the extra confusion caused by the feature known as "domains" hanging over from SQL/92. Second, the development of SQL/Object as a separate Part, for which the justification was perhaps never very strong, ran into technical difficulties. As a result, 1997 saw two further developments of some significance:

- The concepts of ADT, named row type, and distinct type were "unified," yielding just *user-defined* types, UDTs ("unified" in quotes, because some might argue that the unification is more one of syntax than of concepts).

- The SQL/Object material was merged into Part 2 (SQL/Foundation) and Part 8 was discarded, as was the "SQL/Object" name.

The net effect of the foregoing is that SQL3 does currently permit a table to be defined on a user-defined type (note, however, that the table in question must be a base table). For example:

- We might define a type EMPLOYEE, with certain "attributes" (EMP#, HIREDATE, and so on).

- We might then define a base table EMP thus:

```
CREATE TABLE EMP OF EMPLOYEE ;
```

As noted earlier, base table EMP now effectively has two types.

- Let *emp* be a row occurring in (the current value of) base table EMP. Then *emp* (of course) includes an EMP# value, a HIREDATE value, and so on; in other words, it conforms to the structure of the type EMPLOYEE. However, it does *not* conceptually carry with it the type EMPLOYEE,* in the same way that every value always conceptually carries its own type(s) with it (see RM Prescription 2 of the *Manifesto*); rather, it carries only the (unnamed) row type defined by its component column values.

- Moreover, we might define several distinct base tables on the same type—e.g.:

```
CREATE TABLE EMPX OF EMPLOYEE ;

CREATE TABLE EMPY OF EMPLOYEE ;

CREATE TABLE EMPZ OF EMPLOYEE ;
```

(though the "new database design principle" described in reference [58]—later christened *The Principle of Orthogonal Design*—would militate against such a state of affairs). And, of course, these distinct tables will typically have distinct current values (table values, that is) at any given time.

These concepts will very likely appear strange and confusing to many users. For example, how do users, provided with a type such as EMPLOYEE, decide when to use it as a type for base tables and when as a type for columns? (See Appendix B for

---

*Despite the fact that the containing table effectively does.

a discussion of this particular issue.) And how do users decide when to define a base table in terms of such a type and when to define it in the old-fashioned way? Indeed, it is far from clear just what problem overall is being addressed by these proposals. We conjecture that it might be an attempt to extend SQL to support the object maxim "persistence orthogonal to type" (see, e.g., references [1–2] and [111])—in which connection the original name "SQL/Object" is certainly suggestive—but it is hard to be sure.

Be that as it may, base tables defined in terms of a type such as EMPLOYEE still *are not* types as such, and so we have no good grounds for stating that SQL3 fails to meet OO Proscription 1. However, we can still express our concern about such tables by noting a deviation from RM Prescription 13, concerning relation variables. To be specific, RM Prescription 13 requires every variable to have *one* declared type, not two.

A Comparison with ODMG

INTRODUCTION

The term *ODMG* is used, loosely, to refer to the proposals of the Object Data Management Group, a consortium of representatives from "member companies [covering] almost the entire object DBMS industry."* At the time of writing, those proposals consist of an *Object Model,* an *Object Definition Language* (ODL), an *Object Interchange Format* (OIF), an *Object Query Language* (OQL), and *bindings* of these facilities to the programming languages C++ [80], Smalltalk [81], and Java [84]. *Note:* The first two of these components are based, respectively, on the Object Model and Interface Definition Language of the Object Management Group, OMG [108]. Observe that there is no "Object Manipulation Language" component; instead, object manipulation capabilities are provided by whatever language ODMG happens to be bound to (C++, Smalltalk, Java, possibly others as well).

The following definition is worthy of note:

[We] define an *object DBMS* to be a DBMS that integrates database capabilities with object-oriented programming language capabilities. An object DBMS makes

---

*All otherwise unattributed quotes in this appendix are taken from Cattell and Barry (eds.), *The Object Database Standard: ODMG 2.0* (Morgan Kaufmann, 1997), hereinafter referred to as "the ODMG book" [15]. They are reprinted here by permission of Morgan Kaufmann. We should make it clear that reference [15] is the third edition of the book and thus represents the third version of the ODMG proposals (the previous two were Releases 1.0 and 1.2, respectively).

database objects appear as programming language objects . . . [it] extends the language with transparently persistent data, concurrency control, data recovery, associative queries, and other database capabilities.

We—i.e., the authors of the present book—agree with the implication here that "one language, not two" is a desirable goal. However, we do not agree with the further implication that "persistence orthogonal to type" is another, for reasons explained in reference [70] and sketched in the annotation to that reference in Appendix H.

Incidentally, reference [15] refers repeatedly, both in its title and throughout the text, to "the ODMG standard." While it is certainly possible or even likely that ODMG will someday become a *de facto* standard ("the ODMG . . . member companies are committed to support this standard . . . by the end of 1998"), it is not a *de jure* one, since the ODMG committee has no official standardization authority; the bodies that do have such authority are the International Organization for Standardization, ISO (for worldwide standards) and national bodies such as the American National Standards Institute, ANSI (for standards in the USA). On the other hand, it is at least true that the ODMG committee has been working with the ANSI SQL committee to try to achieve some level of compatibility between their proposals and those of SQL3 (see Appendix E).

The following quote give some idea of the ODMG committee's *modus operandi* and its own assessment of the significance of its work:

We have worked outside of traditional standards bodies for our efforts in order to make quick progress . . . The intense ODMG effort has given the object database industry a "jump start" toward standards that would otherwise have taken many years . . . It is to the personal credit of all participants that the ODMG standard has been produced and revised [so] expeditiously. All of the contributors put substantial time and personal investment into the meetings and this document. They showed remarkable dedication to our goals.

And elsewhere: "[Object DBMSs] are *a revolutionary rather than an evolutionary development*" (italics added). Observe the contrast here with *The Third Manifesto*, which is intended very specifically to be evolutionary, not revolutionary, in nature.

It must be said too that the ODMG book includes many remarks that seem either to display a poor understanding of the relational model or to mix matters that are of concern to the model with ones that are more properly of concern to the implementation. Here are some examples (some of which we choose to comment on, though not all):

■ "Analogous to the ODMG Object Model for object databases is the relational model for relational databases, as embodied in SQL."

SQL and the relational model are *not* the same thing. SQL is merely a flawed attempt to realize in concrete syntactic form some (not all) of the components of the abstract relational model.

- "The [ODMG] query language [OQL] is more powerful [than a relational query language]."

    OQL is more *complicated,* certainly, but it is not more *powerful.* The added complication derives from the fact that ODMG in general, and OQL in particular, both expose many different data structures to the user—a consequence, in our opinion, of a failure to appreciate the advantages of keeping model and implementation rigidly separate. Analogous remarks apply to most of the next few quotes also.

- "The scope of object DBMSs is more far-reaching than that of relational DBMSs."

- "We have used the relational standard SQL as the basis for OQL, where possible, though OQL supports more powerful capabilities."

- "We go further than relational systems, as we support a unified object model for sharing data across programming languages."

    Surely it might reasonably be argued that the *relational* model is precisely a unified model for sharing data across programming languages?

- "The ODMG Object Model . . . includes significantly richer semantics than does the relational model, by declaring relationships and operations explicitly . . . Relationships in the Object Model are similar to relationships in entity-relationship data modeling."

    Now this one does demand a response. The point is, the relational model *deliberately* does not "declare relationships explicitly"—instead, it represents both "entities" and "relationships" in the same uniform way.* (Incidentally, it is not really true that ODMG relationships are "similar to relationships in entity-relationship data modeling," because (a) they are binary only, and (b) they cannot have properties. See later in this appendix for further discussion.) As for "declaring *operations* explicitly," we have tried to make it clear in the present book that while the relational model has nothing explicit to say regarding such a capability, it certainly implies it as a requirement, as part of its domain support.

- "The ODMG data model encompasses the relational data model by defining a TABLE type to express SQL tables. The ODMG TABLE type is semantically equivalent to a collection of structs." (See the next section for an explanation of "structs." We remark that, at the very least, the term *collection* here should be replaced by *set* if we are truly talking about the relational model, or *bag* if we are talking about SQL. We note too that those "structs" have object IDs, whereas relational tuples or rows do not.)

---

*Some might feel that relational foreign key definitions constitute explicit relationship declarations. We would argue rather that foreign keys are really just shorthand for certain pragmatically important integrity constraints.

One major problem with this particular claim is that it ignores the relational operators. For example, it is hard to see how we could use the ODMG Object Model to implement a generic join operation—i.e., one that would work on arbitrary "SQL tables."* *Note:* OQL does provide such an operation, but the Object Model *per se* does not.

OVERVIEW

We did not bother to present any kind of overview of the SQL3 proposals in Appendix E because we suspect that most readers will probably have at least a general knowledge of SQL *per se*. By contrast, it is probably fair to say that comparatively few readers have much familiarity with ODMG. In this section, therefore, we present a general overview of the most important features of the ODMG proposals. We concentrate on the Object Model component specifically, for the most part.

Caveat: The descriptions that follow are, of course, based on our own reading and interpretation of the ODMG book. Naturally we believe them to be accurate, but it is only fair to warn you that we might have misunderstood (and hence misrepresented) some points of detail; this appendix should thus not be taken as a definitive statement of the ODMG proposals *per se* (that definitive statement is reference [15] itself, of course).

Objects

ODMG supports atomic, structured, and collection objects. It is possible to draw some loose (very loose!) analogies between these various kinds of objects and certain constructs in *The Third Manifesto,* as follows:

- An ODMG *atomic* object corresponds roughly to a scalar variable, in *Manifesto* terms. (We note that the ODMG book also talks about variables on occasion, but an ODMG variable and an ODMG object seem to be different things. It also talks—fairly ubiquitously, in fact—about *instances,* which it uses as a synonym for *objects.* For consistency with the ODMG book, therefore, we will do the same ourselves in what follows.)

- An ODMG *structured* object corresponds roughly to a tuple variable, in *Manifesto* terms. (Tuples are called "structs" in ODMG; STRUCT is the ODMG counterpart to the *Manifesto's* TUPLE type generator—see later.)

---

*It is worth pointing out too that even if we could implement such an operation, we would then have succeeded only in writing a lot of code that in a relational DBMS would have been provided by the system itself.

- An ODMG *collection* object is a set, bag, list, or array of other objects, all of which must be of the same type.* Collections have no precise *Manifesto* counterpart. (It is true that relation variables—i.e., relvars—might be thought of as "collections" of a kind, but they are one the Object Model does not directly support.) *Note:* ODMG also supports another kind of collection called a dictionary (defined in the ODMG book as "an unordered sequence [*sic*] of key-value pairs with no duplicate keys." We ignore dictionaries in this appendix, for simplicity.

  Every object has a unique object ID.

Atomic Objects

The analogies in the previous subsection notwithstanding, there is at least one major difference between ODMG's atomic objects and the *Manifesto's* scalar variables, and that is that, to use object terminology, the former have structure (the ODMG term is *properties*) as well as behavior, while the latter have behavior only. Just why "atomic" objects should have any structure at all—user-visible structure, that is—is never explained; it seems clear, however, that such a state of affairs violates encapsulation and undermines data independence.

Note: ODMG does not draw the clear distinction the *Manifesto* does between actual and possible representations. To quote: "[Each] property [maps to] an *instance variable* [in the representation]" (and the context makes it clear that *representation* here means the actual representation specifically). At the same time, the book also states that "separation between [object definition and object implementation] is the way that the Object Model reflects encapsulation." (These two quotes—taken from the same page, though slightly paraphrased here—seem to contradict each other.) And then on a later page we find: "While it is common for [properties] to be implemented as data structures, it is sometimes appropriate for an attribute to be implemented as a method." This quote seems to contradict the first of the previous two. The true situation is thus not really clear.

Be that as it may, ODMG properties fall into two categories, *relationships* and *attributes.* A relationship is an association between two objects (and is in fact represented by a *pair* of properties, one for each of the objects involved); an attribute is a property that is not part of any such pair. More precisely:

- A *relationship* is, very specifically, a *binary* association (involving, therefore, exactly two objects); it is realized in the Object Model by two properties (one

---

*More accurately, the *value* of such a collection object at any given time is a set, bag, list, or array. ODMG is sometimes a little imprecise regarding value *vs.* variable distinctions (and value *vs.* variable *vs.* type distinctions, come to that).

for each of the objects involved), each of which names the other as its *inverse*. The two properties are said to define *traversal paths* between the two objects. For example, a given employee object might have a traversal path to a certain department object, and that department object might have a traversal path to a certain set of employee objects—a set that includes the original employee object, of course. (Note the redundancy here; to be specific, the fact that a given employee is in a given department is represented twice, at least from the user's point of view.) Operators are provided to create, destroy, and traverse relationships (more precisely, relationship "members"). Moreover, those operators "vary according to the traversal path's cardinality"; to be specific, different operators are used depending on whether the relationship is one-to-one or not.

It has to be said that ODMG's relationships look a lot like a throwback to the days of prerelational systems (and in any case, why the binary limitation?). The only justification for the idea—and it is a fairly weak one, in our opinion—to be found in reference [15] seems to be this: "The object DBMS is responsible for maintaining the referential integrity of relationships. This means that if an object that participates in a relationship is deleted, then any traversal path to that object must also be deleted." (Some people might feel there is more to referential integrity than this brief characterization might suggest.)

Relationships are not objects and have no properties (in particular, no user-defined "behavior") of their own, a fact that in itself constitutes a major argument against the idea, one might have thought. (Note that while it is true that *entities* and *relationships* have been useful concepts for many years in database design, the relational model—as noted earlier in this appendix—deliberately does not make a logical distinction between the two, because as noted in Appendix B the very same object can quite legitimately be regarded as an entity by one person and as a relationship by another.)

■ An *attribute* is any property that is not part of a pair that defines a relationship in the foregoing sense. There are two kinds of attributes: those whose legal values are *object IDs,* and those whose legal values are *literals.*

  ▪ An attribute whose legal values are object IDs "enables one object to reference another, without expectation of an inverse traversal path or referential integrity." *Note:* Attributes whose legal values are object IDs are often described—somewhat confusingly, in our opinion—as if their values were in fact those objects *per se,* instead of pointers to those objects.

  ▪ An attribute whose legal values are "literals" is simply an attribute that contains values that are not pointers but are of some "literal" type (e.g., character strings). See later in this section for a discussion of "literals"—in particular, for an explanation of why we often place the term in quotation marks in an ODMG context.

Structured Objects

A structured object is basically just a tuple variable (it is not encapsulated). The components of such an object—the ODMG term is *elements* or *members*—can be objects (of any kind), "literals" (of any kind), or a mixture. Operators are provided for accessing such components (typically using dot qualification syntax). ODMG does not, however, seem to provide analogs of all of the tuple operators required by *The Third Manifesto* (see RM Prescription 6). On the other hand, ODMG does prescribe support for certain *builtin* structured object types, *viz.* DATE, TIME, TIMESTAMP, and INTERVAL, with semantics "as in the ANSI SQL specification" (this latter claim is unfortunate if true, because the relevant features of "the ANSI SQL specification" are both incomplete and self-contradictory [76]).

Collection Objects

The ODMG terminology in this area is not used consistently.* We therefore choose not to use it, although we recognize that our attempt to explain the concepts might therefore be a little incorrect. Be that as it may, it seems to us that ODMG supports certain *collection type generators*—SET, BAG, LIST, and so on—which can be used (of course) to define certain *generated collection types*. Let T be such a generated type; to fix our ideas, assume until further notice that T is defined using the type generator LIST. Then objects of type T are variables, the value of which at any given time is a list: either a list of object IDs or a list of "literals," depending on how T is defined (that is, either it is true for all time that every object of type T has a value that is a list of object IDs, or it is true for all time that every object of type T has a value that is a list of "literals").

- In the former case, every object whose object ID can appear in any such list must be of the same type (a type specified in the definition of T); in the latter case,

---

*For example, the ODMG book says: "In the ODMG Object Model, instances of *collection objects* are composed of distinct elements, each of which can be an instance of an atomic type, another collection, or a literal type . . . An important distinguishing characteristic of a collection is that *all* the elements of the collection must be of the *same* type. They are either all the same atomic type, or all the same type of collection, or all the same type of literal." The word *collection* occurs five times in this extract. The first occurrence is in the phrase "instances of collection objects," which seems to mean *all objects of any given generated collection type.* The second is in the phrase "another collection," which seems to mean *an object of some distinct generated collection type.* The third occurrence seems to mean *any given generated collection type.* The fourth seems to mean *any object of the given generated collection type.* The fifth occurrence is in the phrase "the same type of collection," which might mean *of a generated collection type defined by means of the same collection type generator,* or it might mean *of the same generated collection type.* (And by the way: What exactly does it mean for two elements of a "collection"—no matter how that term is interpreted—to be "distinct"? Especially when the elements in question are objects, not literals, and hence are represented in the collection by their object IDs?)

every "literal" that can appear in any such list must be of the same type (again, a type specified in the definition of *T*).

■ In the former case, the objects whose object IDs appear in a given list are regarded as the elements of that list; in the latter case, the "literals" that appear in a given list are regarded as the elements of that list.

As noted earlier, there is no ODMG "Object Manipulation Language" component as such. However, the Object Model does prescribe support for the following builtin operators (most of which should be self-explanatory) for operating on objects—i.e., lists—of type *T:*

```
IS_EMPTY
IS_ORDERED
ALLOWS_DUPLICATES
CONTAINS_ELEMENT
INSERT_ELEMENT
REMOVE_ELEMENT
CREATE_ITERATOR
CREATE_BIDIRECTIONAL_ITERATOR
REMOVE_ELEMENT_AT
RETRIEVE_ELEMENT_AT
REPLACE_ELEMENT_AT
INSERT_ELEMENT_AFTER
INSERT_ELEMENT_BEFORE
INSERT_ELEMENT_FIRST
INSERT_ELEMENT_LAST
REMOVE_FIRST_ELEMENT
REMOVE_LAST_ELEMENT
RETRIEVE_FIRST_ELEMENT
RETRIEVE_LAST_ELEMENT
CONCAT      /* concatenate two lists without changing either */
APPEND      /* append list L2 to list L1 (changing list L1)  */
```

Remarks analogous to the foregoing apply to all of the other ODMG collection type generators (SET, BAG, and so on). *Note:* We remark that the builtin operators defined for sets in the Object Model are strictly weaker—*much* weaker—than those defined for relations in the relational model. This fact gives the lie to claims to the effect that the Object Model "is more powerful than" or "encompasses" the relational model. Also, serious questions arise regarding the type of the object that results from (e.g.) set operators such as CREATE_UNION. We remark too that ODMG's collection type generators are really examples of what in Chapter 14 we called *dummy types.* As a consequence, it appears that if we define (say) two distinct specific list types, one in which the list elements are integers and one in which they are rectangles, we have to construct two distinct implementations of every single one of the operators prescribed for lists.

Literals

ODMG uses the term "literal" in what seems to the present writers to be a rather unconventional way. In most conventional languages, if *T* is a type, then *variables* can be defined that are of that type *T*, and legal *values* of those variables are values of that type *T;* further, every such value can be denoted by some *literal* of that type *T*. Note in particular, therefore, that it is normal to distinguish between:

- *Literals,* which are symbols that denote values (usually in some kind of self-explanatory way), on the one hand, and
- The *values* that are denoted by such symbols, on the other.

For example, the symbol 3.5 might be a literal denoting the value "three and a half." Note in particular that different literals can denote the same value (a fact that points up the distinction we are emphasizing here); for example, the literals TIME ('10:00 am PST') and TIME ('6:00 pm GMT') might very well both represent the same value of some TIME type.

The foregoing distinction, which we might as well call the symbol *vs.* denotation distinction (or, more simply, just the literal *vs.* value distinction) is certainly made in *The Third Manifesto*. ODMG, however, does not seem to make the same distinction, but instead uses the term "literal" to include both meanings (which is why we often place the term in quotation marks). And yet we note that ODMG also frequently talks about values *per se;* thus, it is not really clear whether an ODMG value and an ODMG "literal" are the same thing or not.

Be that as it may, ODMG does then go on to distinguish between *literal types* and *object types* (implying among other things that an object and a literal can never be of the same type). Apparently, instances of a literal type are literals (values?), while instances of an object type are objects (variables?). In fact, LITERAL_TYPE and OBJECT_TYPE are defined as two distinct global roots, in two distinct builtin type hierarchies (*Third Manifesto* terminology); thus, for example, there is a builtin LONG (integer) literal type, but no builtin LONG object type. However, the user could define an "atomic" object type with just one attribute, X say, of literal type LONG; it might then be possible to perform, e.g., comparisons between values of that attribute X and LONG literals.* We note in passing that, like *The Third Manifesto,* ODMG does not support implicit conversions between types (i.e., coercions).

ODMG supports three kinds of literals—atomic, structured, and collection literals—which we now proceed to describe. First, *atomic* literals. Atomic literals seem to be the ODMG version of the *scalar value* concept, as we defined that concept earlier in this book: "[Atomic literals] are not explicitly created by applications, but rather implicitly exist." ODMG prescribes support for certain builtin atomic literal types. Without going into details, we note merely that in addition to the types that one might expect (BOOLEAN, FLOAT, CHAR, etc.), the list includes ENUM ("enumeration"), which is in fact a type generator. (Actual enumerated types that

---

*Reference [15] actually states that "literals . . . are embedded in objects and cannot be individually referenced," thereby implying that, e.g., even a simple comparison such as "X = 3" is illegal (though the OQL chapter includes plenty of examples of such comparisons).

are generated by means of that type generator, by contrast, might perhaps be said to be "atomic.")

Next, *structured* literals. As noted earlier, ODMG supports a STRUCT type generator, analogous to the TUPLE type generator of *The Third Manifesto;* hence, "struct" or tuple types can be generated, and instances of such types then seem to be called "structured literals," regardless of whether (in *Manifesto* terms) they are values or variables. "A structured literal . . . has a fixed number of elements, each of which has a . . . name and can contain either a literal value [*sic!*] or an object [i.e., an object ID]." The idea of a *literal* including a component that is an *object* (i.e., variable) seems to mix together some very basic notions that would surely be better kept separate. *Note:* ODMG requires support for certain builtin structured literal types, *viz.* DATE, TIME, TIMESTAMP, and INTERVAL (not to be confused with the structured *object* types of the same names).

Finally, *collection* literals. Here again the situation seems unnecessarily confusing. Collection literals are *collection type generators.* "The ODMG Object Model supports collection literals of the following types [*sic!*]: SET, BAG, ... (etc.). These type generators [*sic*] are analogous to those of collection objects . . . Their elements . . . can be of literal types or object types." Apparently, therefore, we can have, e.g., a list *object* whose elements are *literals,* and a list *literal* whose elements are *objects*—? *Note:* The ODMG book also mentions a user-defined UNION literal type, the semantics of which it does not explain (we suspect it refers to heterogeneous collections, however, although collections are elsewhere stated to be homogeneous). It does not say whether there is an analogous UNION object type.

In sum, we agree wholeheartedly that there is a vast and important logical difference between *values* and *variables,* but that particular difference does not seem to be the one that ODMG draws between *literals* and *objects*—nor is the precise nature of the difference that ODMG does draw in this connection very clear to us. At the same time, ODMG also makes use of the value *vs.* variable terminology, but it does not give definitions of these latter concepts.

We conclude this subsection by noting that:

- An ODMG literal (of any kind) is not an object and does not have an object ID.
- Although as noted earlier the Object Model prescribes certain operators for certain *objects* (especially collection objects), it does not appear to prescribe any such operators for *literals.*
- Indeed, if it is really true that object types and literal types are different kinds of things, it would seem that (e.g.) if operator *Op* is defined to work on, say, integer *objects,* it cannot be invoked on integer *literals*—?
- ODMG also supports a special *null literal.* "For every literal type . . . there exists another literal type supporting a null value [*sic*] . . . This nullable type is the same as the literal type augmented by the . . . value *nil.* The semantics of null are the same as those defined by [the SQL standard]." (This last sentence is contradicted later, in the chapter on OQL.)

Types, Classes, and Interfaces

On the face of it, it might have seemed more sensible to explain these concepts prior to this point. We deliberately did not do so, however, because (a) the concepts are not as clear as they might be, and (b) it therefore seems necessary to have some appreciation of the material discussed in the foregoing subsections in order to understand them. Consider the following series of quotes:

- "A type has an external *specification* and one or more *implementations.* The specification defines the external characteristics of the type. These are the aspects that are visible to users of the type: the *operations* that can be invoked on its instances [and] the *properties* . . . whose values can be accessed . . . By contrast, a type's implementation defines the internal aspects of the objects of the type [*or literals of the type, presumably, if the type in question is a literal type instead of an object type*]: the implementation of the type's operations and other internal details."

- "An external specification of a type consists of an abstract, implementation-independent description of the operations . . . and properties that are visible to users of the type. An *interface* definition is a specification that defines only the abstract behavior of an object type. A *class* definition is a specification that defines the abstract behavior and abstract state of an object type. A *literal* definition defines only the abstract state of a literal type."

Observe, therefore, that the terms *type* and *class* are being used here in a somewhat unusual way: *Class* is being used to refer to what in the body of this book, following more orthodox usage, we called a *type,* and *type* is being used to refer to the combination of *class* in this unorthodox sense together with the *implementation* of the class in question.* *Note:* We will come back to "literal definitions" in a few moments, and to "interface definitions" in the next subsection.

But then what are we to make of the following, which appears a couple of pages later?

- "Classes are types . . . Interfaces are types . . . "

Most of the rest of the ODMG book either ignores the distinction between types and classes or observes it in inconsistent ways. In what follows, we will stay with the term "type" (mostly).

As for the assertion that "a literal definition defines only the abstract state of a literal type": This statement seems to suggest that no operations can be performed on literals, which cannot be correct. We suspect that what the ODMG book really

---

*In fact the ODMG terminology derives from that of OMG [108]. Other object texts and systems use the terms the other way around—i.e., they use *type* in our sense and *class* to mean the implementation of a type (see, e.g., references [10] and [90]).

means here is that a "literal definition" that is actually *an application of some type generator* (see the previous subsection) defines the unencapsulated logical structure of some generated type but does not define any operators that apply to instances of that generated type (the only operators that do apply being inherited builtin ones).

Inheritance

ODMG includes support for both multiple and (*a fortiori*) single inheritance, though the semantics are not very clear. In fact, it supports both behavioral inheritance (which it calls *subtyping*) and structural inheritance (which it calls *extension* or "the EXTENDS relationship"). We will return to these two kinds of inheritance in a moment; first, however, it is necessary to say something about the difference between interfaces and classes.

ODMG's "interfaces" correspond to what in Chapter 14 we called *dummy types*. In other words, an ODMG interface is a type that is not—in fact, is not allowed to be—the most specific type of any value at all. Such a type *must* have proper subtypes, and every value of the type *must* be a value of one of those subtypes. For example, consider the types ELLIPSE, CIRCLE, and NONCIRCLE, where type CIRCLE and type NONCIRCLE are both proper subtypes of type ELLIPSE (and the usual semantics apply). Clearly, every instance of type ELLIPSE is also an instance of one of the other two types, and so ELLIPSE is not the most specific type of anything at all.

In ODMG, then, a type like ELLIPSE in this example can be defined by means of an *interface* definition instead of a *class* definition; an interface definition defines behavior (or at least what we called in Chapter 14 a *specification signature*) but no structure.* The general intent seems to be that, as we travel down any given path in the type graph, operations *must* be explicitly specialized at the point where we first encounter a class instead of an interface. Observe in passing, therefore, that ODMG assigns a very special meaning to what is more usually a very general term (*viz.,* interface).

Reference [15] then goes on to say: "Subtyping pertains to the inheritance of behavior only; thus interfaces may inherit [behavior] from other interfaces and classes may inherit [behavior] from interfaces . . . [but] interfaces may not inherit [behavior] from classes, nor may classes inherit [behavior] from other classes. . . . The EXTENDS relationship is a single inheritance relationship between two classes[†]

---

*And yet later in the ODMG book we find an extensive example (of an interface definition specifically) that includes several attribute and relationship—i.e., "structure"—definitions as well as operator definitions as such (?).

[†]It could hardly be a *multiple* "inheritance relationship," since it is "between two classes." More to the point, the two sentences quoted here contradict each other—the first says classes cannot inherit behavior from other classes, the second says they can.

whereby the subordinate class inherits all of the properties [i.e., structure] and all of the behavior of the class that it extends." In other words, if T is a global root type and T' is a leaf type (*Third Manifesto* terminology), then the path from T to T' consists of zero or more *interfaces* followed by one or more *classes* (i.e., once we meet the first class, the rest are all classes). Note too that if every such path contains just one class (i.e., all inheritance is via subtyping, not extension), then all instances are instances of leaf types.

As already noted, ODMG does support multiple inheritance, but only for interfaces, not for classes (speaking a little loosely). More precisely, a type can have any number of proper supertypes, but at most one of them can be a class, not an interface. Also, note the following: "The ODMG Object Model supports multiple inheritance of object behavior [only]. Therefore it is possible that a type could inherit operations that have the same name, but different parameters, from two different interfaces. The model precludes this possibility [*so in fact the "possibility" is not really a possibility after all*] by disallowing name overloading during inheritance."

While we are on the subject of inheritance, incidentally, the ODMG book includes a nice example of how difficult it can be to get the type hierarchy right: "For example, ASSOCIATE_PROFESSOR is a subtype of PROFESSOR . . . Where an object of type PROFESSOR can be used, an object of type ASSOCIATE_PROFESSOR can be used instead, because ASSOCIATE_PROFESSOR inherits from PROFESSOR." But surely professors have properties (perhaps *tenure*) that associate professors do not? In other words, is not the hierarchy (at best) upside down?

ODMG does not appear to distinguish between value and variable substitutability.

Object Definition Language

The foregoing subsections summarize the major aspects of the Object Model (though we have skipped over features that we regard as secondary, such as details of the catalog or "metadata" and details of recovery and concurrency control). Now we turn to the Object Definition Language, ODL. ODL is basically a language that provides a concrete syntax for "the specification of object types that conform to the ODMG Object Model." *Note:* ODL supports the definition of operator "specification signatures" (*Manifesto* terminology)—including the names of any *exceptions* that might be raised by the operation in question—but does not provide a means of writing the code to implement such operations. Presumably that code must be written in a language such as C or C++.

The chapter of the ODMG book that discusses ODL gives a number of examples, together with a complete definition of ODL syntax (a BNF grammar), but has almost nothing to say about semantics. Possibly the reader is supposed to read the *OMG* specifications (on which ODL is based) first. In any case, we omit the details of ODL here since (as indicated in Chapter 1) we do not regard matters of mere syntax as being very important.

Object Interchange Format

To quote the ODMG book, the Object Interchange Format (OIF) is "a specification language used to dump and load the current state of an object database to or from a file or set of files." As such, it is not very germane to the present book, and we therefore skip the details here.

Object Query Language

The Object Query Language OQL might be characterized as a large superset of a small subset of SQL, with incompatibilities. It is *not* the ODMG "Object Manipulation Language" (as noted in the introduction to this appendix, no such language exists); rather, it is, specifically, a *query* language that supports nonprocedural retrieval (only)* of data stored in an ODMG database. As such, it supports a variety of operators that are not part of the Object Model *per se*. It is not computationally complete.

   We choose not to provide anything close to a complete description of OQL here. Suffice it to say that:

- OQL provides SQL-style SELECT–FROM–WHERE queries against sets, bags, lists, and arrays.
- It also provides analogs of the SQL GROUP BY, HAVING, and ORDER BY constructs.
- It also supports union, intersections, and differences, and special operations for lists and arrays (e.g., "get the first element").
- It also supports "path expressions" for traversing relationships.

There appear to be quite a few detail-level incompatibilities, of both style and substance, between OQL and the Object Model. For example, "[certain] expressions yield objects without identity" (but surely objects *always* have identity in the Object Model?); "OQL allows us to call a method" (but methods are defined earlier in the book to be part of the implementation, not part of the model); "[we can retrieve] the ith element of an indexed collection" (the term *indexed* here does not mean what it means earlier in the book); and so on. It should be noted too that the semantics of nulls and certain query constructs are—presumably unintentionally—different from those of their SQL analogs.

---

*What happens if an OQL query invokes an *update* operator does not seem to be defined.

Summary

The basic idea behind ODMG, in a nutshell, is (of course) to allow many different data structures—sets, bags, lists, arrays, and so on—to be used for data in the database *and to expose them all to the user* ("persistence orthogonal to type"). We reject this idea for reasons explained in detail in references [70] and [72] and sketched in the annotation to those references in Appendix H.

We now proceed to consider the question of how ODMG measures up to the various prescriptions, proscriptions, suggestions, and inheritance proposals defined formally and explained in the body of the present book. We begin with the RM Prescriptions.

RM PRESCRIPTIONS

1. Scalar types

ODMG **conforms,** partly. However, (a) the distinction between "atomic" literal and object types seems unnecessary and confusing;* (b) there does not appear to be a way of destroying user-defined scalar types; (c) ODMG's objects have object IDs; (d) ODMG objects have structure as well as behavior; (e) instead of supporting *Manifesto*-style selectors, ODMG requires "new object instances" (apparently uninitialized) to be "created" by means of a prescribed NEW operator. *Note:* OQL (as opposed to the Object Model as such) does include something it calls a "type name constructor" that seems to be more akin to our selector, however.

2. Scalar values are typed

ODMG **conforms,** subject to the reservations indicated under RM Prescription 1.

3. Scalar operators

ODMG **conforms,** partly. However, (a) there does not appear to be a way of destroying user-defined operators; (b) it is not clear whether ODMG conforms to the *Manifesto's* many prescriptions regarding the distinction between read-only and update operators.

4. Actual vs. possible representations

ODMG **fails** (it does not clearly distinguish between actual and possible representations).

---

*In fact, it looks like a serious violation of orthogonality. At best, it requires many specifications—regarding legal operations, for example—to be duplicated; at worst, it introduces undesirable rules and distinctions. (In fact, it seems to us that the ODMG distinction between literals and objects has something to with another ODMG distinction that is also unnecessary and confusing: namely, that between structure and behavior.)

5. *Expose possible representations*

ODMG **fails** *a fortiori*. However, it does expose *actual* representations. It is not clear whether it supports anything analogous to the *Manifesto's* nestable THE_ pseudovariables.

6. *Type generator TUPLE*

ODMG **conforms,** partly. However, (a) the distinction between literal and object tuple types seems unnecessary and confusing; (b) there does not appear to be a way of destroying user-defined tuple types; (c) ODMG's "tuple objects" have object IDs; (d) instead of supporting tuple selectors, ODMG requires "new object instances" (apparently uninitialized) to be "created" by means of a prescribed NEW operator; (e) ODMG does not support tuple-valued possible representation components (because it does not support the concept of possible representations at all); (f) ODMG tuple types have names; (g) it is not clear when two ODMG tuple types are regarded as equal; (h) most of the *Manifesto's* required tuple operators are not supported in the Object Model (though it might be possible to simulate them in OQL). *Note:* OQL (as opposed to the Object Model as such) does include a construct that seems to be somewhat more akin to our tuple selector.

7. *Type generator RELATION*

ODMG **fails.** The comments under RM Prescription 6 apply here also, *mutatis mutandis.* Note in particular that most of the operators of the relational algebra are not supported in the Object Model (though they can probably be simulated in OQL).

8. *Equality*

ODMG **fails** (probably). First, it distinguishes between *identity* and *equivalence* (sometimes called deep equality and shallow equality, though authorities disagree as to which is which); second, it distinguishes between literals and objects. Both of these facts muddy the picture considerably. In addition, there does not appear to be any way to prevent users from defining an "=" operator with any semantics they please (note that no "=" operator, as such, is actually prescribed). However, it is least true that support for a SAME_AS operator, with prescribed semantics, is required for objects (though apparently not for literals); SAME_AS tests to see whether two objects are "identical" (i.e., have the same object ID).

9. *Tuples*

See RM Prescription 6.

10. *Relations*

See RM Prescription 7.

11. Scalar variables

ODMG **conforms,** partly. At least, it supports *objects* of (user-defined) "atomic" type T, and ODMG objects seem to be something like variables and ODMG "atomic" types seem to be something like scalar types. But the values of those "scalar variables" are not exactly values of type T, owing to the distinction ODMG draws between literal and object types (in fact, it is quite difficult to say *what* they are). Also, "defining"—i.e., creating, via NEW—a scalar variable (atomic object) does not appear to initialize that variable (atomic object).

12. Tuple variables

The comments under RM Prescription 11 apply here also, *mutatis mutandis*.

13. Relation variables (relvars)

ODMG **fails** in all respects.

14. Real vs. virtual relvars

ODMG **fails** in all respects.

15. Candidate keys

ODMG **fails** *a fortiori*, because it does not support relation values or variables (in the full sense of the relational model) at all. However, it does support something it *calls* candidate keys: "The *extent* of a type is the set of all instances of the type within a particular database . . . [The] object database designer can decide whether the object DBMS should automatically maintain the extent of [any given] type. Extent maintenance includes inserting newly created instances in the set . . . In some cases the individual instances of a type can be uniquely identified by the values [*sic*] they carry for some property or set of properties . . . A *simple key* consists of a single property. A *compound key* consists of a set of properties. The scope of uniqueness is the extent of the type; thus a type must have an extent to have a key." Points arising:

- The extent notion does not exist in the relational model at all. The closest we might come to it would be something like the following: "Let T be a type and let R be a relvar with an attribute A defined on T; then the extent of T would be the union of all projections of all such relvars R over all such attributes A." Note that (a) that extent is itself a relvar (a virtual relvar, in fact), and (b) in general, it does not seem to be particularly useful.

- "Automatic maintenance" of such an extent implies that "creating a new object" of the type in question via NEW has the side effect of updating the database (for indeed the extent is a variable in the database). It also implies that support for a "constructor" operator (like NEW) is required, a notion that the *Manifesto* rejects.

- It is not "instances of a type" that are identified by keys, it is "instances within an extent." The ODMG book does say that "a type must have an extent [*meaning, presumably, an extent that is explicitly defined and automatically maintained—after all, all types have an extent, by definition*] to have a key," but the ODL syntax does not enforce this rule.

- We would not draw the distinction ODMG does between simple and compound keys. Keys *always* consist of sets of "properties." If the set has cardinality one, then we might say the key is "simple."

16. Databases

ODMG **conforms,** partly. However, ODMG databases are not "named containers for relvars," they are named containers for *objects* (of any type); also, ODMG database definition and destruction are not done "outside the ODMG environment."

17. Transactions

ODMG **conforms,** more or less.

18. Relational algebra

The Object Model **fails** in almost all respects. However, OQL does support analogs of most of the operators of the relational algebra. Unfortunately, it supports many other things as well.

19. Relvar names, relation selectors, and recursion

The comments under RM Prescription 18 apply here also, *mutatis mutandis*. Also, OQL apparently does not support recursion.

20. Relation-valued operators

ODMG **fails.**

21. Assignments

ODMG **fails.** It does require support for a large number of operators of an updating nature—for example, NEW, DELETE, INSERT_ELEMENT, REMOVE_ ELEMENT, REMOVE_ELEMENT_AT, REPLACE_ELEMENT_AT, INSERT_ ELEMENT_AFTER, INSERT_ELEMENT_BEFORE, INSERT_ELEMENT_ FIRST, INSERT_ELEMENT_LAST, REMOVE_FIRST_ELEMENT, REMOVE_ LAST_ELEMENT, and APPEND in the case of lists, and analogous operations in the case of sets, bags, arrays, relationships, and so on—but it does not seem to support assignment *per se* (presumably, assignment support is to be provided by whatever language ODMG is bound to). It also does not support multiple assignment, *a fortiori*.

22. Comparisons

ODMG mostly requires type definers to provide comparison operators. Almost no such operators (not even "=") are builtin, with prescribed semantics.

23. Integrity constraints

ODMG **fails** in all respects.

24. Relvar and database predicates

ODMG **fails** in all respects.

25. Catalog

ODMG **conforms,** partly (it does define a catalog, but that catalog consists of objects, not relvars).

26. Language design

Not directly applicable. The ODMG analog of **D** is a combination of ODL and whatever language ODMG is bound to, plus OQL (which is really rather separate). OQL in particular is hamstrung by its goal of being "SQL-like"; hence, it cannot possibly "be constructed according to well-established principles of good language design," by definition.

RM PROSCRIPTIONS

1. No attribute ordering

Not clear. OQL presumably **fails.**

2. No tuple ordering

ODMG **conforms** for sets and bags (of tuples).

3. No duplicate tuples

ODMG **conforms** for sets (of tuples).

4. No nulls

ODMG **fails.** What is more, ODMG nulls and SQL nulls are different.

5. No nullological mistakes

The Object Model probably **fails** (it is hard to tell). OQL definitely **fails.**

6. No internal-level constructs

ODMG **fails.**

7. *No tuple-level operations*

ODMG **fails** (it expressly prescribes "iterators" over collections).

8. No composite attributes

ODMG **conforms.**

9. *No domain check override*

ODMG **conforms.**

10. *Not SQL*

The Object Model **conforms.** OQL **conforms** (just).

OO PRESCRIPTIONS

1. Compile-time type checking

ODMG allows, e.g., a parameter type to be specified as ANY, a fact that might possibly undermine the system's ability to perform compile-time type checking. Otherwise, it probably **conforms.**

2. Single inheritance (conditional)

ODMG **fails** (it does support single inheritance, but the underlying model is scarcely defined at all, let alone being "clearly defined and generally agreed").

3. Multiple inheritance (conditional)

The comments under OO Prescription 2 apply here also, *mutatis mutandis.*

4. Computational completeness

OQL **fails.** Not applicable to the Object Model *per se;* however, we note that ODMG does share our distaste for the "embedded data sublanguage" approach adopted in SQL: "Note that unlike SQL in relational systems, object DBMS data manipulation languages are tailored to specific application programming languages, in order to provide a single, integrated environment for programming and data manipulation." And: "It is possible to read and write the same database from C++, Smalltalk, and Java, *as long as the programmer stays within the common subset of supported data types*" (italics added). *Note:* The reference here to "the programmer" seems to suggest that ODMG is aimed specifically at application programmers. What about shared access via OQL?

5. Explicit transaction boundaries

ODMG **conforms.**

    6. Nested transactions

ODMG **fails.**

    7. Aggregates and empty sets

Not applicable to the Object Model. OQL **fails.**

OO PROSCRIPTIONS

    1. Relvars are not domains

ODMG **conforms,** inasmuch as it does at least distinguish between types and collections (where by "collections" we mean both collection values and collection variables, in *Manifesto* terms).

    2. No object IDs

ODMG **fails** (of course).

RM VERY STRONG SUGGESTIONS

    1. System keys

ODMG **fails** on both parts of this suggestion. *Note:* An argument might be made that object IDs make system keys unnecessary. Even if this argument is accepted, however, object IDs are still not keys in the relational sense, because:

- Unlike keys, object IDs are represented differently (at the *logical* level) from other data; as a consequence,
- Unlike access via keys, access to data via object ID is different from access via other properties.

    2. Foreign keys

ODMG **fails.**

    3. Candidate key inference

ODMG **fails.**

    4. Transition constraints

ODMG **fails.**

    5. Quota queries

ODMG **fails.**

6. *Generalized transitive closure*

ODMG **fails.**

7. *Tuple and relation parameters*

ODMG **conforms,** partly.

8. *Special ("default") values*

ODMG **fails.**

9. *SQL migration*

ODMG **conforms,** partly (at least for query operations, via OQL).

OO VERY STRONG SUGGESTIONS

1. *Type inheritance*

ODMG **conforms,** in that it does at least support behavioral inheritance. However, it supports structural inheritance as well . . . and ODMG's behavioral inheritance "model," at least, is not exactly "clearly defined," let alone being "generally agreed."

2. *Types and operators unbundled*

ODMG **fails.** "An operation is defined on [and bundled with] only a single type . . . [We] had several reasons for choosing to adopt this single-dispatch model rather than a multiple-dispatch model. The major reason was for consistency with the C++ and Smalltalk programming languages . . . Another reason to adopt the classical object model was to avoid incompatibilities with the OMG . . . object model, which is classical rather than general."

3. *Collection type generators*

ODMG **conforms.**

4. *Conversion to/from relations*

ODMG **fails.**

5. *Single-level store*

ODMG **conforms.**

IM PROPOSALS (SCALAR TYPES, SINGLE INHERITANCE)

1. *Types are sets*

ODMG presumably **conforms** (though *object* types seem to be sets of variables, not sets of values—?).

2. Subtypes are subsets

ODMG **conforms,** subject to the reservations indicated under IM Proposal 1.

3. "Subtype of" is reflexive

Not clear. Certainly the ODMG book never explicitly mentions the fact that every type is both a supertype and a subtype of itself.

4. Proper subtypes

Not clear. Certainly the ODMG book never explicitly mentions the concept.

5. "Subtype of" is transitive

ODMG **conforms**—but note the class *vs.* interface distinction, not part of our inheritance model.

6. Immediate subtypes

Not clear. Certainly the ODMG book never explicitly mentions the concept.

7. Single inheritance only

ODMG **fails,** because it supports multiple inheritance. Such a failure is desirable, of course—so long as the multiple inheritance support in question is based on a model that is "clearly defined and generally agreed" (but we would argue that the ODMG support is not).

8. Global root types

Not clear (even if we limit our attention to single inheritance only). The ODMG book never discusses the issue of cycles in the type hierarchy.

9. Type hierarchies

ODMG **conforms,** subject to the reservations indicated under IM Proposals 7 and 8, and subject too to the reservation that type "subhierarchies"—i.e., hierarchies with a local root that is not a global root—are never discussed.

10. Subtypes can be proper subsets

ODMG **conforms.**

11. Types disjoint unless one a subtype of the other

For multiple inheritance, ODMG (desirably) **fails,** of course. For single inheritance, the situation is not clear; certainly the ODMG book never explicitly discusses the issue.

12. Scalar values (extended definition)

ODMG **conforms** (in fact, it uses the same "most specific type" terminology as we do).

13. *Scalar variables (extended definition)*

Not clear. Certainly the ODMG book never discusses the issue of an abstract *model* of a scalar variable, with its *DT, MST,* and *v* components, nor does there seem to be an ODMG term corresponding to our "declared type."

14. *Assignment with inheritance*

Not clear. First of all, the reservations under IM Proposal 13 apply here *a fortiori*. Second, the Object Model does not support assignment as such anyway. However, the book does say (in connection with the example mentioned earlier involving types PROFESSOR and ASSOCIATE_PROFESSOR) that "where an object of [most specific] type PROFESSOR can be used, an object of [most specific] type ASSOCIATE_PROFESSOR can be used instead," but the semantic implications (for assignment in particular) are left unspecified.

15. *Comparison with inheritance*

Not clear. The comments under IM Proposal 14 apply here also, *mutatis mutandis.* In addition, OQL provides some rules regarding comparisons, but they seem to be (a) incomplete and (b) both less and more than what is required by IM Proposal 15.

16. *Join etc. with inheritance*

Not clear. Again, the comments under IM Proposal 14 apply here also, *mutatis mutandis.* However, OQL provides some rules regarding joins and similar operations that do seem to **conform** to IM Proposal 16.

17. *TREAT DOWN*

The Object Model **fails** (it never mentions the concept at all). OQL probably **fails** too; it does seem to have something analogous to TREAT DOWN, but it is not fully specified and it cannot be used as pseudovariable (since OQL is a retrieval-only language).

18. *TREAT UP*

The Object Model **fails.** OQL probably **conforms** (though what happens if an object is "treated up" to a type that corresponds to an interface rather than a class is not specified).

19. *Logical operator IS_T(SX)*

ODMG **fails.**

20. *Relational operator RX:IS_T(A)*

ODMG **fails.**

21. Logical operator IS_MS_T(SX)

ODMG **fails.**

22. Relational operator RX:IS_MS_T(A)

ODMG **fails.**

23. THE_ pseudovariables

ODMG **fails.** However, it does expose *actual* representations, which can presumably be assigned to (in whatever language ODMG is bound to). It is not clear whether it supports anything analogous to the *Manifesto's* nestable THE_ pseudovariables.

24. Read-only operator inheritance and value substitutability

ODMG **conforms.**

25. Read-only parameters to update operators

ODMG **conforms.**

26. Update operator inheritance and variable substitutability

ODMG probably **fails.** Although the book never discusses the issue, it can safely be assumed that unconditional inheritance of update operators is required; further, ODMG does not seem to distinguish between value substitutability and variable substitutability.

IM PROPOSALS (SCALAR TYPES, MULTIPLE INHERITANCE)

7. Many supertypes per subtype

ODMG **conforms,** subject to all of the reservations regarding multiple inheritance mentioned in the previous section.

9. Type graphs

ODMG **conforms,** subject to the reservations mentioned under the revised version of IM Proposals 11 and 12 below.

11. Least specific types unique

Not clear (the ODMG book never discusses the issue).

12. Most specific types unique

Not clear (the ODMG book never discusses the issue).

15. Comparison with multiple inheritance

The Object Model **fails** (it never mentions the issue). OQL probably **conforms.**

16. Join etc. with multiple inheritance

The Object Model **fails** (it never mentions the issue). OQL **conforms.**

IM PROPOSALS (TUPLE AND RELATION TYPES)

ODMG **fails** (the entire topic is simply not addressed in the ODMG book).

The Next 25 Years of the Relational Model?

REMARKS ON REPUBLICATION

This appendix consists of a lightly edited version of an interview conducted by Rick van der Lans* with the present authors in 1994 [37]. The original abstract (the original English language abstract, that is—the first published version of the interview was in Dutch) reads as follows:

> For the past [several years] Hugh Darwen and Chris Date have been working on a document with the intriguing title: *The Third Manifesto* . . . The objective of this document is (to quote the authors) to "present a manifesto for the future direction of data and database management systems." It can be seen as an attempt to give a reasonably complete definition of a new version of the relational model; it can also be seen, more specifically, as an alternative to two previous manifestos on database systems. In this interview the authors clarify certain aspects of [their *Manifesto*] and explain why they wrote it.

---

*Rick F. van der Lans is an independent consultant, author, and lecturer specializing in database technology, development tools, and information modeling. He is Managing Director of R20/Consultancy, a company based in The Netherlands. He served for over six years on the Dutch committee responsible for developing the international (ISO) standard for SQL.

What follows is basically the English language version of the original interview [39], with just a few revisions (all very minor). The footnotes are new.

Note: Since Codd's first paper on the relational model [19] appeared in 1969, 1994 was the relational model's Silver Jubilee. It thus seemed appropriate at the time of the interview to give some thought to the *next* 25 years; hence our choice of title (for both the interview itself and this appendix). We are grateful to Rick van der Lans, also to InfoIT Inc., publishers of *InfoDB* (where the English language version first appeared), for permission to republish the material in the present book.

INTRODUCTION

As indicated in the abstract, *The Third Manifesto* has been written by Hugh Darwen and Chris Date, two well-known names in the database world. Why did they write it? What are its goals? Why the "third" manifesto? To enable the reader to understand the following interview better, we first discuss why there are now three manifestos related to database technology. We also briefly describe the objectives and backgrounds of the first two, for the benefit of readers who might not be familiar with them.

As we all know, relational technology has always been under attack. From its birth it has been criticized. In the first few years the main objection was that it was "just theory"—it was "just plain impossible" to build a commercial system on relational concepts. Then, when the first relational products came on the market, they were considered to be too slow for building OLTP systems. Now that relational products have proven that they can support hundreds of users on multi-gigabyte databases, the latest cry is that relational technology is not suitable for new application requirements. The application of the future wants to store so-called unstructured data (images, sound, free text), and wants to perform complex operations, such as scanning images or compressing sound. The question is: Are these criticisms truly valid? In other words, has relational technology finally met its Waterloo? Is it really not suitable for new application requirements?

Some people believe we need a new type of database system, based not on relational concepts but on object-oriented concepts (such as inheritance, classes, polymorphism, etc.). This is why object-oriented (OO) DBMSs have received so much attention recently. However, one disadvantage of commercial OO systems has been (and still is) that they use a variety of different terminology. Partly for this reason, in 1989 a manifesto was written entitled *The Object-Oriented Database System Manifesto* [1]. This manifesto listed rules to which a system should conform in order to be called an object-oriented DBMS. It was intended to bring some order and structure to the confusing world of OODBMSs. Because the authors all had an OO background, their assumption was that the database of the future needs an OO foundation, not a relational one.

One year later, in 1990, a second manifesto was published with the title: *Third Generation Database System Manifesto* [111]. In a way this document was a response to the first manifesto. It was written by another group of database experts, mainly people with a relational background, including Michael Stonebraker (at that time with Ingres) and James Gray (at that time with DEC). The opinion of these authors was that no new data model was needed—extending the relational model with new concepts could do the job. Their aim was to define a set of required characteristics for all future DBMSs. Those characteristics (defined through a set of *tenets* and *propositions*) were based on new application and business requirements.

Note that neither of the first two manifestos tried to define new database models or new languages; they simply listed requirements, or in other words minimal characteristics, that DBMSs really ought (in the authors' opinions) to adhere to.

The Third Manifesto [38] has a different standpoint. It tries to give a reasonably formal and complete definition of a new version of the relational model. This new version, which the authors call **D**,* is still compatible with the classic relational model as originally defined by Dr. E. F. Codd. However, by defining certain concepts, especially domains, more precisely, the authors believe they can show that the relational model is suitable for the new application requirements referred to above.

The main body of *The Third Manifesto* is divided into six sections: Relational Model Prescriptions, Proscriptions, and Very Strong Suggestions, and OO Prescriptions, Proscriptions, and Very Strong Suggestions.† By the way, OO here stands for Other Orthogonal!—it includes, but is not limited to, features that are commonly regarded as part of object orientation. A small amount of new terminology is introduced, such as *relational variable (relvar),* in order to clarify certain aspects of the relational model. The document is still in draft form; however, the authors feel it is stable enough to serve as a basis for an interview such as the one that follows.

BACKGROUND

van der Lans: **Let's start with some background. Could you explain what your goal was in writing *The Third Manifesto*? Why did you write it? What do you hope or expect will happen to it?**

---

*This characterization of our objectives is not really accurate. First, **D** is just a language (any language) that realizes the ideas of *The Third Manifesto* in some concrete form. Second, *The Third Manifesto* does attempt to define the relational model very precisely—as noted in Chapter 1, in fact, we would like it to be seen in part as a definitive statement of that model—but we would never claim that it constitutes "a new version" of that model.

†In the interview as originally published the various prescriptions, proscriptions, and "very strong suggestions" were summarized in a sidebar. That sidebar is omitted from this appendix.

Darwen: Our goal was to alert "the market" to the possibility of a future in which users could:

- Control and enjoy their own data;
- And be able to ask any questions of that data that might arise;
- And have sufficient confidence in the answers provided by the system to take actions that might be suggested by those answers, even bold actions.

We wrote the *Manifesto* because current database products do not, in our opinion, hold out such promise; because neither of the two previous manifestos, in our opinion, clearly shows the right way forward; and because we think we can see a clear way forward, solidly based on a theory that has already stood the test of time—namely, the relational model of data.

What will happen to the *Manifesto?* Very likely, "the market," in its complacency, will continue to embrace either SQL or the current OODBMSs, in the mistaken belief that our goals will be met that way. Alternatively, we might find that "the market" doesn't share our goals. Less pessimistically, we would like somebody to be inspired to define the language we have generically called **D,** and we would like that effort in turn to inspire somebody to implement that language (even if initially just in a standalone, single-user environment suitable for domestic, scientific, or small enterprise use).

If this last situation materializes, people will be able to see and touch something that really is a Prince [24] in comparison with what's currently available. Put it another way: Let's agree that, say, Pascal, or Ada, or *<your own favorite language>* is a Prince alongside the much derided but very widely used COBOL, FORTRAN, or BASIC; we want there to be a *database* Pascal, or Ada, or *<your own favorite language>,* too.

van der Lans: What are the two or three main deviations from or extensions to the classical relational model as defined by Codd? Are there areas of the *Manifesto* that are not "compatible" with the relational model?

Date: Well, first of all it's important to understand that "the classical relational model" itself has evolved over time. Or perhaps it would be more accurate to say that our own understanding of it has evolved over time, so that we now have a clearer notion of what domains really are, what candidate keys really are, even what relations themselves really are (and so on). In the newest (6th) edition of my book *An Introduction to Database Systems,* I've tried to describe our current understanding of the model as carefully as I can [56]. I must emphasize, however, that we are indeed talking about evolution here, not revolution; the relational model as we currently see it is not wildly different from Codd's original vision, it's just more carefully pinned down in certain respects, and slightly extended here and there (e.g., with additional operators).

Having said all that, I would now like to state categorically that there are *NO* "deviations" in our *Manifesto* from the relational model as we now understand it (i.e., as documented in reference [56]). And the sole "extension"—which isn't in fact an extension at all!—is that domains are seen for what they really are, which is *data types:* possibly system-defined data types, more generally user-defined data types, of potentially arbitrary complexity.

You see, people tend to think of the relational model as dealing only with very simple data types, like numbers and strings. In fact, however, the model nowhere states what data types are allowed. The question as to what data types are allowed *IS COMPLETELY ORTHOGONAL TO* the relational model. So you can have a data type (or domain—they're the same thing) of engineering blueprints, or books, or time series, or architectural drawings, or videos, or X-rays, or absolutely anything else you like.

Of course, you must understand that support for user-defined data types includes support for user-defined operators, and most likely support for data type inheritance too (subtypes and supertypes). I'm sure we'll come back to these topics later.

No, there are no areas of the *Manifesto* that are incompatible with the relational model.

Darwen: Chris is right, we don't deviate from the relational model, nor do we extend it. A language that conforms to our *Manifesto* is entirely compatible with the classical relational model. By contrast, we do deviate a great deal from SQL, but that is (of course) because SQL deviates a great deal from the relational model, as well as being a rather poorly designed language by any measure.

Some might say that our demand for support for data types of arbitrary complexity is a deviation from or extension to the relational model. We think that those who interpret the relational model's insistence on "atomicity" as meaning that the only data types you can have are numbers, strings, dates, and times are those who have axes of their own to grind and *want* there to be weaknesses in the relational model.

van der Lans: **What is the history of the** *Manifesto?* **How did it evolve? When did you start thinking about it? Why the decision to publish a draft first?**

Darwen: The idea of writing a manifesto first entered my mind when the other two came to my attention, in about 1991 I suppose. I just couldn't bear the idea of leaving the last word with them. Also, Chris and I had been talking about devising a proper relational language ever since 1988 or so, when we started to collaborate on various database writings (including our attempt—at once hilarious and depressing—to produce a clarifying guide to the 1992 SQL standard [76]). However, we both really knew that such talk was idle and dreamy, for we both lead very busy professional lives that leave little time for such backroom work. One day, over a beer somewhere, I turned to Chris and said "Oh, by the way, I know what the language is called: **D**," and he nodded his immediate comprehension and assent. However, I keep the joke (that it stands for "Date and Darwen's Database Dream") for my lectures: We don't see any need for an explanation in the *Manifesto* itself.

Things came to a head after the publication of the 1992 SQL standard, when I, as a member of the ISO SQL committee SC21, turned my attention to the evolving SQL3 proposals. I discovered that people were proposing to use the new "abstract data type" facility for defining *tables,* as well as for the obviously theoretically correct purpose of defining *columns;* and I discovered that, as might be expected of such a peculiar idea, it just didn't hold water, technically. (It was eventually abandoned in SQL3, at the summer 1993 SC21 meeting in Yokohama.)*

Worse, I discovered that those OODBMSs that were attempting to provide *ad hoc* query and declarative integrity support, *à la* relational, were making the same fatal mistake. The mooted manifesto could wait no longer, and I promised Chris that I would deliver an initial draft in early 1994—which I did, in February of that year. That draft was five pages long; our current draft is (regrettably) 30 pages[†] . . . However, the first draft's structure and style have survived this expansion, I'm glad to say. Since that first draft, there have been countless faxes, phone calls, and consultations with other people, not to mention numerous weekend slogs over Chris's computer at his home in California.

Date: As Hugh says, we'd been thinking for several years about the idea of trying to design the "ideal" database language (well, if not ideal, then at least a language that was much more faithful than SQL to the principles of the relational model). Certainly I remember discussing such an idea many times in the mid to late 1980s. But it was the increasing emphasis in the marketplace on OO database technology, and especially the recent (mostly flawed) attempts to marry OO and relational ideas together, that finally got us moving . . . I guess it was the fact that the industry seemed to be on the brink of making what was arguably an even bigger mistake than the original SQL decision that spurred us to get something down on paper at last. As Hugh has explained, he wrote the first draft early this year [i.e., 1994] (so the structure of the document as a series of prescriptions, proscriptions, and "very strong suggestions" is due to him), and we have collaborated on every iteration since then.

I wouldn't say we've exactly "published" the draft yet. All we've done is distributed it to a fairly wide group of technical people (both in Europe and in the USA—elsewhere too as a matter of fact), in order to get feedback that will help us feel more comfortable about whatever the final version looks like. By the way, I'd like to mention that the feedback so far has been almost entirely positive; no one has shown that the complete project is misguided!—so we're beginning to get a fairly

---

*But see Appendix E!

[†]The expansion was due mainly to the addition of clarifying commentary. As you can see from Chapter 3 of this book, the final version of the *Manifesto* as such—not counting the inheritance proposals, which were added later anyway—is still only some ten or so pages.

warm feeling about the whole idea. We'd like to have the final version ready some-time before the end of this year.* As for actual publication of that version, we're still examining our options.

van der Lans: **What is Codd's opinion on *The Third Manifesto,* if he has read it?**

Date: I don't know if Codd has read the document yet. We look forward to hear-ing his opinion in due course.

van der Lans: **Have the DBMS vendors already shown interest in the lan-guage D?**

Darwen: The language **D** doesn't yet exist! In any case, we didn't really expect the vendor community to display any immediate interest in either **D** *per se* or the *Man-ifesto* in general (though in fact it would already be not quite right to say there's been no interest at all). After all, the vendors are heavily committed to SQL; they're not going to risk huge amounts of venture capital on an alternative until a clear demand emerges for such a thing. From their perspective, a self-proclaimed "manifesto" by a couple of pundits who've been getting up the vendors' collective nose for many years does not by itself constitute such a clear demand, obviously. Our most realis-tic hope is that interest is aroused in the more aware sections of the user and acade-mic communities. Somebody has to define a **D,** and then somebody has to persuade some vendor to make a **D** implementation.

van der Lans: **Isn't your *Manifesto* too late, since we already have products on the market that try to combine relational and OO technology, such as UniSQL and Illustra (previously known as Montage)[†]—especially since you've chosen a different approach for integration? And what about the OO support in SQL3?**

Date: We feel it's important to try to lay down what we think is the right way to move forward, even if there are huge obstacles to overcome in making such a move. After all, what's the alternative? If you just accept the *status quo,* progress is im-possible (this is true in all walks of life!). Furthermore, we're very concerned that—as I've already mentioned—the industry seems to be about to make a very big mistake: We MUST speak out, if only as a matter of professional honesty and tech-nical credibility. And at the very least we'd like to influence the way database prin-ciples are taught in universities and the like—perhaps get university prototypes built too. Of course, we'd be delighted if some vendor saw fit to build an actual product, and we're still lobbying . . .

---

*We did have a "final" version ready by the end of 1994 [38,40]. The *Manifesto* as documented in the present book is a considerably—but compatibly!—refined and extended version of that 1994 original.

[†] Illustra was subsequently purchased by Informix Software Inc. and the technology incorporated (as the *Universal Data Option*) into Informix's own Online Dynamic Server DBMS product.

Darwen: The existence of COBOL, FORTRAN, and BASIC (not to mention C) didn't make it too late for Pascal, Ada, and *<your own favorite language that is not COBOL, FORTRAN, or BASIC>*. True, SQL3 will have user-defined data type support and inheritance (and you can call this "OO support" if you think those two things are sufficient to justify the use of the term)—but SQL3 will also have SQL. With or without "OO support," SQL is not a suitable foundation for the future of data. "Different approach for integration?" Well, our approach is the same as that part of SQL3's abstract data type support ("value ADTs") that is generally agreed to be reasonably sound and likely to survive and appear in the next published SQL standard. However, I believe at least one of the products you mention treats object classes as relations, instead of or as well as treating them as data types, and that's something we expressly forbid in our *Manifesto*. [*Ed:* More on these matters later.]

THE THIRD MANIFESTO AND SQL

van der Lans: **The next question is probably for Hugh: Is *The Third Manifesto* compatible with the working draft of SQL3? If not, do you think the committee has chosen the wrong path to extend SQL with OO concepts?**

Darwen: I presume you're talking about our approach of using the relational domain concept as the point of *rapprochement* with OO, since compatibility with SQL is otherwise the *Manifesto's* most obvious *pro*scription! As I just mentioned, the *Manifesto* in its general approach is compatible with SQL3's "value ADTs"; however, we expressly forbid anything like SQL3's so-called "object ADTs" (a part of SQL3 that is in any case in an immature state of development). Also, our *Manifesto* expressly forbids nulls; currently, SQL3 permits nulls to appear among the secret components of an encapsulated complex value, adding a Whole New Dimension to the profusion of strange effects caused by these unpleasant creatures.*

van der Lans: **The document says "We do not believe that the database language SQL is capable of providing a firm foundation for the future." Does this mean we should get rid of SQL? Or what do you want the market to do with their SQL investment?**

Date: Well, the document also says ". . . we do pay some attention to the question of what to do about today's SQL legacy." Of course SQL data and SQL applications are going to be with us for many, many years—to think otherwise would be quite unrealistic. So what we have to do is provide a way to migrate SQL data to **D** databases. And we have to provide a way of implementing SQL operations via a **D** interface against that migrated data. We do have some ideas as to how to do this. [*Ed:* Hugh will be elaborating on these ideas later.]

---

*Refer to Appendix E for an extended discussion of the current state of affairs *vis-à-vis* SQL3.

TECHNICAL CONTENT

van der Lans: **In the document you make a distinction between pre- and pro-scriptions. What's the difference?**

Date: Well, you're right, there's really no *logical* difference at all, in the sense that it's often a little arbitrary as to whether a given requirement should be expressed as a prescription or a proscription. For example, the *pro*scription that there be no tuple-at-a-time relational operations could equally well have been expressed as a *pre*-scription that all relational operations be set-at-a-time (or, rather, relation-at-a-time). It was our general intent, however, that the proscriptions would add little or no technical substance to the overall proposal; rather, they're supposed to be implied by the prescriptions already stated. But we felt quite strongly that it was necessary to state certain proscriptions explicitly by way of clarification, in order to avoid some of the mistakes that have been made in the past—especially since they (the proscriptions) are often not *obviously* implied by the prescriptions.

van der Lans: **Why did you introduce a distinction between relvars and relations? What are the advantages of doing this?**

Darwen: It's obvious when you think about it. The distinction is exactly the distinction that's made in normal programming languages between variables and values. A relation is a value—for example, the value currently assigned to the relvar named EMPLOYEE. When some employee gets a salary raise, we might say that we update some EMPLOYEE tuple; whether or not we say that, the result is that the relvar EMPLOYEE now has a value (a relation) that is not the same as the value (another relation) that it had before the update.

Before we introduced the term "relvar," people tended to say "relation" when they meant the value and also "relation" when they meant the variable, and that usage frequently led to dreadful confusions that really should never have arisen at all. We'll be very happy, of course, if those who prefer to use the term "table" for "relation" will follow our example and use "table variable" ("tablevar"? "tabvar"?) for "relvar."

Date: We didn't introduce the distinction, we merely clarified it. The concepts definitely *are* distinct, but they've been very much confused over the past 25 years. The advantages of stressing the distinction are thus *precision* and *clarity of thinking.*

I'd like to repeat here something I said in another interview recently, for *Data Base Newsletter* [53]. If I say, in some programming language, "DECLARE N INTEGER," then N is a variable whose values are integers—different integers at different times. Likewise, if I say, in SQL, "CREATE TABLE T," then T is a variable whose values are relations (or tables)—different relations at different times. We say loosely that T is a relation, but it really isn't. It's a relation-valued variable.

In mathematics, if the value 4 is inserted into the set {1,2,3}—I'm speaking very loosely here!—the result is a different set, namely the set {1,2,3,4}. It's not an "updated version" of the old set, it's a *different set.* Similarly, if I insert a row into T, the original relation value of T is replaced by another relation that includes the additional row. The value of the relation-valued variable T is now a *different relation.* In other words, a relation is a value, not a variable. A relation-valued variable— we call it a *relvar* for short—is a variable whose values are different relations at different times.

Having said all that, I must also say that it's very difficult to get out of the habit of saying "relation" when we really mean "relvar"! But I think in future we really ought to try to be a little bit more careful.

van der Lans: In the *Manifesto,* you say that relations are not object classes. You categorically reject this equation. For a lot of people relations and object classes are both "things you can populate," and therefore they are the same kind of thing. Could you explain what you mean when you say they're not the same?

Date: Actually, we've revised the *Manifesto* to say that *relvars* (not relations) aren't classes, and I'll interpret your question in this light.

First of all, let me say that it's always difficult to debate matters sensibly when there's no consensus on what even the most basic terms mean. In the case of OO specifically, there's still no universally agreed abstract "OO model" (indeed, part of what we're trying to achieve with our *Manifesto* is precisely to define such a model, or at least to start to do so). Thus, different people have different understandings of different OO terms. In particular, different people attach different meanings to the term "object class."

So we have to put a stake in the ground and say what we mean by the term. So far as we're concerned, an object class is a *data type* (with all that that entails). In other words, it's a domain—since we've already said that a domain is a data type. And domains and relvars simply *aren't* the same thing. A relvar, by definition, is a *variable,* not a type.

Of course, when I put it like that, it sounds obvious. It hardly seems worth fussing about. But the point is, so many people are getting this one wrong! This is exactly the Big Mistake that some of the "object/relational" products have already made. And the implications of having such a massive confusion at the absolute foundation of the system are highly nontrivial.

(As an aside, I should probably mention that while many OO people would agree with us that a class is a type, others would use the term "type" to mean "type" *per se,* and then would use "class" to mean the set of all currently existing instances of a given type.* For these latter people, I suppose the term "class" is closer to our relvar notion. At least their "class" is a variable. But there are still major differences having to do with encapsulation and related matters, which I'm sure we'll get to later in this interview.)

---

*Still others use "class" to mean an *implementation* of a type.

Darwen: I don't understand why relations (and classes) are characterized as "things you can populate." Like many database people, I use the term "populate" when speaking informally, but I apply it to what we now call relvars, not relations (the thing that populates a relvar is a relation). However, I'd like to return to this point in a moment, for the justification for our position is actually independent of whether we're talking about variables or just sets of values, and it goes like this:

First, we agree that a relation is in a certain sense a set and that an object class is in a certain sense a set—this much they do have in common. However:

- A relation is a set of symbol-arrangements (in other words, tuples), each of which is to be interpreted as a statement concerning certain things—a *proposition* (more precisely, a proposition that is held to be true). The symbols in the symbol-arrangement represent the things the statement is about. Such a symbol-arrangement has all and only the "properties" (or "behavior" or "functionality"—feel free to choose your term, the concept is the same) prescribed for tuples by the relational model. And in this prescription—some might even call it a restriction—lie the strength and the generality of the relational model.

- An object class, by contrast, is a set of symbols, not symbol-arrangements. Those symbols represent just *things,* things whose properties are not prescribed by some general model but rather are prescribed individually for each class. (Don't be confused by the fact that the symbols in some object classes—not all!—might in fact be tuples; such tuples constitute the *secret, encapsulated* representation of the values in the object class in question, and that representation is permitted to change, under the covers, without affecting external interfaces.)*

The other issue—and here I return to the point about "things you can populate"—is orthogonal to the issue of whether object classes are domains or relations, but I'll have to address it now because not everybody realizes it is orthogonal. It's the question of whether the object class POLYGON (for example) is the set of all polygons imaginable or just the variable containing "all the polygons we happen to be interested in at the moment." It's my observation that many OO people talk in a very fuzzy way about this distinction (one that is so easily and clearly made in the relational model that one can only lament the poor teaching, or lack of teaching, of the relational model in recent times).

---

*We were a little confused over encapsulation in 1994! It is true that, as stated here, some object classes might contain values (i.e., *scalar* values) whose secret, encapsulated representation is tuples. More to the point, however, some classes might contain values that are *known to the user* to be tuples—i.e., *nonsecret, nonencapsulated* tuples (see RM Prescription 6).

Some of our other remarks in this appendix on the subject of encapsulation are (we now realize) slightly off base too; we decided not to change them, however, because (a) to do so smacked too much of rewriting history, and in any case (b) they are mostly not *very* incorrect. But it is only fair to warn you to be a little careful in interpreting the remarks in question.

Anyway, it matters not which view of "object class" you take, I say in both cases that it's not the same as "relation," and my reason is the same in both cases:

- In the case where class POLYGON is the set of all imaginable polygons, well, this concept *obviously* corresponds to the relational concept of "domain" or "data type."
- In the case where the object class POLYGON is some finite set of judiciously (or injudiciously!) chosen polygons that varies from database to database, well, we have no directly corresponding concept in the relational model, and it's another of the relational model's strengths that we need no such concept. The only "variable sets" we deal in are sets of tuples. If you wish to reason in relational style about your arbitrary set of polygons, you'll just have to make that set into a unary relation—in SQL terms, a table with a single column of data type POLYGON (and don't forget to name the column!).

Now I've shown a way in which one of the various interpretations of "object class" can become close enough to the concept of "relation" to perhaps be useful; but this is precisely the one correspondence between object class and relation that I don't see mentioned by OO people or products!

Actually, I'd much prefer our jingle on this matter to be "a row is not an object," clearly covering both of the foregoing possible meanings of "object class." However, we've gone for the consequence of that jingle, namely the jingle "an object class is not a relation" (and hence, *a fortiori,* not a relvar). We opted for this latter version because "object class = relation" is the manner in which "row = object" is expressed, or so we observe, by those OO people seeking *rapprochement* but going about it the wrong (according to our thesis) way.

van der Lans: Why is it necessary to distinguish between relvars and domains? Why not make domains queryable too?

Darwen: Domains are there *before* the database is there, *while* the database is there, and they're still there *afterwards,* when the database has gone away. What's more, they remain—in principle—constant throughout this time. The elements of domains are not propositions,* and therefore they do not represent truths from which further truths can be concluded by logical reasoning. That—concluding further truths from given truths—is what queries do. Thus, it doesn't make sense to "query a domain."

Now, you might say it would be handy to be able to derive, say, from the domain that is the set of all polygons imaginable, the set of all pairs of regular polygons where both members of the pair have the same number of sides. Well, if you really want to do that, you'll have to treat the domain as a unary relation (otherwise,

---

*More accurately, they are *usually* not propositions (a domain of propositions is certainly a legal domain).

how can the required *binary* relation result?), and now you aren't looking at a domain any more. What's more, you should ask yourself the interesting question "What's the domain of the single attribute of this unary relation?" Furthermore, you should note that the relational model has no objection to infinite domains, such as the domain of all imaginable polygons; but it certainly does object to infinite relations (though that objection might not be due to any fundamental reason, but might merely be a useful and safe restriction in practice).

Of course, the foregoing should not be interpreted as a prohibition of support for adding new domains or dropping domains or changing the definition of existing domains. If you add a domain, for example, you can imagine that you're saying that this domain was "there" all the time, really, only there wasn't a need to say so before. If you drop a domain, you're saying that there is no longer any need, after all, to say anything about the existence of this domain (which is a reasonable thing to say only if you no longer make any use of the domain). And changing the definition of a domain is like dropping and adding at the same time, carrying with it an opportunity, in some circumstances, for the domain to be kept in use throughout the change without loss of integrity.

Date:　Relvars and domains certainly are distinct. Here are a couple of very important differences between them:

- *Domains are static, relvars are dynamic* (loosely speaking). The domain CITY, for example, consists of *all possible cities*—its value is static, it doesn't change over time (or rather, if it does change, then that's what you might call a "meta-level" change, a change to the "metadata," a definitional change; it's like changing employee numbers from three digits to five). The value of a relvar, by contrast, certainly does change over time (i.e., it's dynamic); a relvar is a *variable,* and that's what "variable" means. But changing the value of a relvar is not a big deal, it happens all the time; it's certainly not a "definitional" change.

- *Domains encapsulate, relations don't.* Values from domains, which is to say values in row-and-column cells in relations, can be operated upon *solely* by means of the operators defined for the domain in question.* When a domain is defined, the operators that act upon values from that domain have to be defined as well (this is true even for system-defined domains such as INTEGER, where the operators are "+", "–", "<", and so on). The "innards" of the domain values are not exposed (except to the code that implements the operators); in other words, the representation is hidden. So domain values are encapsulated.

  Relations, by contrast, expose their innards to the user, which makes it possible to perform operations that get at those innards—doing joins and other

---

*This sentence is correct, but it does not follow that "domains encapsulate"; for example, as noted in an earlier footnote, a domain might contain values that are nonencapsulated tuples. But the paragraph is still broadly correct overall.

operations that depend on the structure of the relation. The structure of the relation is not hidden, whereas the structure of values inside the relation *is* hidden.

Of course, when I talk about exposing the structure of a relation to the user, I'm talking about the *logical* structure. What the relation looks like physically is both undefined and irrelevant, so far as the model is concerned.

I could sum up the foregoing by saying: *A domain IS a type; a relation HAS a type.* They're not the same thing!

MORE ON SQL

van der Lans: **In your presentations in London and Amsterdam in April 1994 you stated that SQL should be definable on top of D. Can this be done if D doesn't support "sets" with duplicate rows (i.e., bags)?**

Darwen: I'm glad you said *definable*—we don't absolutely insist on it being actually defined, and we'd be delighted if it weren't, if "the market" could see its way into the future without needing such an SQL implementation (but of course it can't).

In any case, several reviewers have raised what is essentially an extended form of your question—"How can SQL be implementable in **D,** when **D** is expressly prohibited from supporting (a) duplicate rows and (b) nulls?"—and I'm glad to have the opportunity to address it here. Although duplicates and nulls must indeed be absent from **D,** they could be simulated by a frontend layer of code on top of **D** as follows:

- An SQL base table for which no candidate keys are declared could be implemented as a **D** database relvar with a system-supplied key. The frontend could make sure that the extra attribute needed for this key didn't appear as a column visible to the SQL user. Similarly, when an SQL query requires generation of duplicate rows, the frontend would use a special **D** operator to generate a "keying" attribute which would be discarded (by the frontend, not by the **D** implementation) so that it doesn't appear as a column in the SQL result. UNION ALL can be simulated by generating an extra distinguishing attribute in each operand. Again, the frontend would discard this attribute so that it didn't appear as a column in the SQL result.

- Nulls can be simulated by devising domains that include special values to be interpreted as null *in addition to* all the regular values. For example, the domain INTEGER_WITH_NULL would include (perhaps) the symbol "?" in addition to the usual symbols representing integers. The frontend would support the definition of suitable operators in connection with this domain, in order to allow the idiosyncratic behavior of SQL nulls to be simulated.

van der Lans: **The NULL value has not been included. Does that mean that if you don't know the value for a certain attribute, you'll assign an empty set?**

Date: This question requires a rather careful response, or rather sequence of responses.

- First of all, I wish you wouldn't use the term "null value." Part of the point about nulls is precisely that they're not values. Some of the SQL mistakes in this area stem from exactly this confusion. (I'm assuming, of course, that you're referring to the kind of null that SQL tries—but fails—to support, namely the kind that requires a logic with more than two truth values. I'll leave discussion of a different kind of null to Hugh.)

- Once you understand that nulls aren't values, you're led inevitably to the conclusion that "relations" that contain nulls aren't relations (check the formal definition of "relation" if you don't believe me). So you've abandoned the relational model, and all bets are off! This is the fundamental reason why we reject nulls in our *Manifesto* . . . though we can get much more specific about the problems that nulls cause, if we really have to.

- Your question implies, correctly, that we permit relations to contain values that are sets. Please note carefully, however, that we allow relations to contain sets in such a way as *not to violate the requirements of first normal form*. Specifically, we insist that any such contained sets be *encapsulated.** We explicitly do not espouse the concept of "NF^2 relations," in which such sets are not encapsulated. We believe we can achieve the functionality we desire without the complexities that the NF^2 notion seems to imply.

- We would represent a missing value by an empty set if an empty set correctly represented the desired semantics. For example, if relation DEPT has attributes DEPT# (department number) and EMPS (set of employee numbers for employees in the relevant department), the EMPS value for a department with no employees would indeed be correctly represented by an empty set of employee numbers. But other types of missing information are better represented in other ways. For example, the best "middle initial" value for a person with no middle initial is an empty string. The best "birthdate" value for an employee with an unknown birthdate is "?" or "UNKNOWN." And so on.

Darwen: "[Do you] mean that if you don't know the value for a certain attribute, you'll assign an empty set?" No. In any case, the empty set could be placed at a row/column intersection only if the relevant domain is set-valued. If the value for a certain attribute, in a certain tuple to be inserted in a certain relvar, is literally not known, then the tuple in question cannot be constructed and therefore cannot be inserted.

I'm interested in your choice of terminology here: "NULL value." We don't have a problem with the concept we would infer from such terminology! A value,

---

*This statement is incorrect. See the earlier footnotes on encapsulation.

by definition, is a member of some domain. If you have a domain one of whose elements you choose to represent by the symbol NULL, that's fine. You must, of course, define all the operators that are available in connection with this domain, and the definitions of the operators might or might not involve some special treatment of the element for which you chose the symbol NULL. But there's one thing you're absolutely prohibited from doing, and that's to say that NULL and NULL are anything other than the same symbol; that is, that the comparison NULL = NULL ever returns anything but *true* (nor, for that matter, is "anything but *true*" ever permitted to be anything but *false!*).

I'd like to mention here my conjecture that user-defined domains could provide a basis for a sound, consistent, and noncounterintuitive treatment of the thorny old "missing information" problem, without getting involved in abstruse and unpleasant areas such as 3-or-more-valued logic (I touched on this point in the second part of my answer to the previous question). Some will scoff at this notion, and I admit that I don't see a way of treating null marks orthogonally with respect to data types (as SQL attempted to do); but we've been waiting for more than 20 years for somebody, scoffer or not, to come up with a better approach, and nobody, in our well-documented opinion (Chris has written extensively on this subject, and I've pitched in, too), has yet done so.

MISCELLANEOUS QUESTIONS

van der Lans: **You say that a transaction can interact with one database only. Does this imply that multisite updates are not allowed?**

Date: Certainly not. "Database" is a logical concept. How a given database maps to physical data is not defined in the model (nor should it be). We certainly do not preclude the possibility that it maps to physical data stored at several distinct sites.

van der Lans: **Why did you exclude triggers? In the Stonebraker manifesto this feature was classified as important.**

Darwen: We don't prohibit triggers. We see no reason to demand them, either, in our *Manifesto*. They're not an essential part of the firm foundation for the future that we propose.

Date: We did suggest that referential actions such as cascade delete might be supported, and these are a special kind of "trigger." But note that cascade delete and suchlike are *declarative*. As an article of faith, we prefer declarative solutions to procedural ones, and of course triggers are usually procedural in nature. So we need to be convinced further of a genuine need for them.

By the way, I think "trigger" is a silly term. *Why* is our field (database technology, or computer technology in general, I suppose) so bad at choosing appropriate terminology? A more accurate term would be "triggered action" (the trigger *per se* then being the event that triggers the action). But I digress.

van der Lans: **Why no inheritance on the relvar level, but only on the domain level? Did I miss something?**

Darwen: Presumably you mean something along the lines of SQL3's subtables and supertables. We don't prohibit such a thing, if somebody can come up with a good model for it; at this time, however, we don't see any need to demand or even strongly suggest it.*

Date: Our principal concern was to figure out what the concept of inheritance means in relational terms, and *that's* domain inheritance, not relvar inheritance. I might mention that even with domain inheritance we're having extraordinary difficulty in coming to grips with a good model . . . As Bruce Lindsay of IBM remarked in this regard (in a recent presentation), there aren't any good models out there, there are only various people's favorite methodologies. We're doing our best to come up with a good model, but the *Manifesto* still says only that *IF* inheritance is supported, *THEN* it must be in accordance with "some clearly defined and generally agreed model." In an appendix to the *Manifesto,* we've begun to sketch our own idea of what such a model might look like.†

van der Lans: **About the naming of the *Manifesto* and the language D: First of all, I would rename *The Third Manifesto;* it looks too much like the Third Generation DBMS Manifesto. I have already talked to people about this, and it certainly confuses them. Second, the name D sounds as if it is the sequel to C. And why do you call it a language? Isn't it database logic, like predicate and propositional logic?**

Darwen: We struggled to find a title for the paper. It had to include the word "manifesto," as we do very much want it to be judged alongside the other two. We considered something like "*A Manifesto for Rapprochement,*" but decided that that put too much emphasis on just one of its themes, albeit an important one. Eventually the short, neutral title took our fancy more than anything else, in spite of its using a word already used in the title of one of our predecessors.

As for **"D,"** well, the modishness of single-letter names was certainly something to do with the choice, but I've already given the main explanation in an earlier response. Do note, though, that it's not actually proposed as a name of a database language—it's merely a symbol we use, in the document, to refer generically to whatever conforming language(s) might arise from the *Manifesto.*

Date: As Hugh has explained, the name **"D"** is meant to denote one or more languages, so in a sense **D** certainly is—or, rather, will be—a language, just as (e.g.) SQL is a language. (Well, no, not just as SQL is a language; it's our hope and intent that **D** will be much better than SQL, of course!) I'd just like to add that, in my

---

*See Appendix D.

†That appendix grew into Part IV of the present book, of course. We hope it is obvious that we now feel we are much closer to that desirable "good model" than we were back in 1994.

opinion, "database logic" (in other words, the relational model) is a language too (rather abstract, to be sure, inasmuch as it doesn't prescribe a specific syntax).

van der Lans: **You say that each base relvar should have a candidate key. Should you not define "candidate key"? And what if the relvar has no columns?**

Darwen: Hmm. You're not the first to suggest that we include a definition of the term "candidate key"; in that case, aren't there any other well-known terms from relational theory that we should also define?

Regarding columnless relvars, I've already pointed out, in my writings about TABLE_DEE and TABLE_DUM [27,31], that the only subset of the empty set is the empty set itself, from which it follows that the only candidate key—and hence the primary key—for a relvar with no attributes is the empty set. In fact, empty candidate keys are mentioned in the *Manifesto* in the same proscription that mentions relations with no columns.

A moment's reflection shows that an empty candidate key has all the usual properties of candidate keys. Indeed, it's perhaps the smallest of my own contributions to the current SQL3 draft that empty primary keys are now supported. However, although my proposal was readily accepted by the majority of the ISO SQL committee, I understand that many of the *vendor* representatives still think it was really some sort of joke on my part. Of course TABLE_DEE and TABLE_DUM are funny, but they're deadly serious, too.*

van der Lans: **What happens to attributes if a domain is destroyed?**

Darwen: No need to spell anything out in the *Manifesto,* here. If you say a certain set of things you once wanted your database to include statements about is no longer required, it had better be the case that your database no longer has anything to say about those things. No, I would not subscribe to a "cascaded delete" idea in this context; even less would I subscribe to SQL's scatty handling of dropped "domains" (domains in the SQL sense, not the relational sense), where a column defined on a dropped domain suddenly becomes defined on the underlying data type of that domain instead!

van der Lans: **Why are your prescriptions regarding computational completeness and explicit transaction boundaries "OO Prescriptions" and not "RM Prescriptions"? They're not specific to OO, or are they?**

Date: Don't forget that for the purposes of the *Manifesto* OO stands for "Other Orthogonal"!—as explained in the introduction to the document. I agree that these prescriptions are not specific to object-oriented, but they're not specific to relational either. They're orthogonal.

---

*That the vendors did not accept the importance of empty keys is perhaps indicated by the fact that the feature in question got moved into *SQL4* (see Appendix F of reference [76]) in 1994, and then into oblivion when SQL4 itself became empty in early 1997.

van der Lans: **Maybe you should explain why certain things are forbidden, such as cursor updates (or at least give some references to articles that include such explanations).**

Darwen: SQL-style cursors are not needed at all in **D.** However, we don't rule out the possibility that applications will sometimes need to iterate over some collection of rows in some order; we just insist that such a collection be treated as what it is, a list or array (and not a relation).

Date: We do state in the introduction that we intend "to follow this *Manifesto* with further publications describing various aspects of our ideas in more depth." We didn't want the document to get any bigger than it already is. On the specific point you mention, we prohibit cursor updates because such operations are by definition row-level, and the relational model is set-level. Some set-level operations simply cannot be simulated by a sequence of row-level updates. For example, consider a relvar called EMPS that is subject to the constraint that the salaries of employees E1 and E2 must always be the same. Then any attempt to change the salary of employee E1 (only) must necessarily fail.

van der Lans: **Maybe you should emphasize that physical storage aspects should not lead to restrictions on the update side. For example, in some products you can't delete rows from a table with a statement if that same delete statement refers to the table from which it tries to delete.**

Date: We originally said that **D** shall include no constructs that "relate to" physical storage. We've since strengthened this statement to include the requirement that nothing in **D** *shall be logically affected by* physical storage matters.

Your example, incidentally, I think is an example of a *logical* limitation (it's the well-known "Halloween problem"). It's just that the system is too lazy to make a copy of the table in question. I don't see that it has anything to do with physical storage matters. A better example would be a rule that says you can't update the partitioning column of a partitioned base table. This really is a case of "physical storage aspects" causing update restrictions.

van der Lans: **Where do you say that NULL is not allowed?**

Darwen: In one of our RM Proscriptions (which is really little more than a reiteration of the precise definition we offer for "tuple"). In SQL, NULL is stated to be a "value" ("symbol" would be a better term) that belongs to no data type. We'll allow that symbol you suggest ("NULL") so long as it *does* belong to the data type of the column in which you want it to be permitted.

van der Lans: **By the way, is the difference between a domain and a relvar that a domain has a fixed (nonupdatable) value, while the value of a relvar can always change (i.e., it can be assigned another value)?**

Darwen: That's one of the differences. Another is that a domain is a set of symbols representing things that are talked about in the enterprise, while a relation is a set of tuples representing true statements about such things. Another is that the members of a domain don't have to be tuples, while the members of a relation certainly do.

Date: As I said earlier, domains are static, relvars are dynamic (this is another way of saying what you're saying). Another difference is that domains *are* types, while relvars *have* types. And another is: Domains encapsulate, relvars don't!*

---

*See the earlier footnotes on encapsulation.

APPENDIX H

References and Bibliography

This appendix provides a consolidated and annotated list of references for the entire book. We should immediately apologize for the embarrassingly large number of references to publications by ourselves; such a state of affairs is unavoidable, however, given the nature of the book and of our subject.

1. Malcolm Atkinson *et al.:* "The Object-Oriented Database System Manifesto," Proc. First International Conference on Deductive and Object-Oriented Databases, Kyoto, Japan (1989). New York, N.Y.: Elsevier Science (1990).

   The following comments are based on a draft dated August 10th, 1989. Like our own *Manifesto,* the paper proposes a foundation for future DBMSs. As noted in Chapter 1 of the present book, however, it virtually ignores the relational model; in fact, it does not seem to take the idea of a model, as such, very seriously at all. Here is a direct quote: "With respect to the specification of the system, we are taking a Darwinian approach: We hope that, out of the set of experimental prototypes being built, a fit model will emerge. We also hope that viable implementation technology for that model will evolve simultaneously." In other words, the authors are suggesting that the code should be written first and that a model *might* possibly be developed later by abstracting somehow from that code. By contrast, we believe it would be better to develop a model first (which is what happened in the relational case, of course).

Be that as it may, the paper goes on to propose the following as *mandatory* features—i.e., features that (in the authors' opinion) must be supported if the DBMS in question is to deserve the label "object-oriented"):

1. collections
2. object IDs
3. encapsulation
4. types or classes
5. inheritance
6. late binding
7. computational completeness
8. user-defined types
9. persistence
10. large databases
11. concurrency
12. recovery
13. *ad hoc* query

It also discusses certain *optional* features, including multiple inheritance and compile-time type checking; certain *open* features, including "programming paradigm" ("we see no reason why we should impose one programming paradigm more than another: the logic programming style, the functional programming style, or the imperative programming style could all be chosen"); and certain features on which the authors could reach no consensus, including—a little surprisingly, considering their importance—views and integrity constraints.

Here in a nutshell are our own positions on the proposed mandatory features (only):*

■ We agree that Numbers 8 and (almost certainly) 5 are important. Number 4 is implied by Number 8. Number 6 is implied by Number 5 (and therefore probably important too), but it is really an implementation matter, not part of the model (it is what we referred to as run-time binding in Chapter 14). We also agree with Number 7.

■ We agree that Numbers 10–13 are important, but they are orthogonal to the question of whether the system is object-oriented, or relational, or something else entirely. (The point is worth repeating from Chapter 6, however, that *ad hoc* query support in particular can be difficult to provide in a pure object system, because it clashes with the object system goals of encapsulation and predefined methods. We note too that providing many different data structures at the logical level, as object systems typically do, inevitably makes the query interface more complex. See OQL [15] for an example illustrating this latter point.)

---

*Our assessment here is based on the premise that the object of the exercise is to define features of a good, genuine, general-purpose DBMS. We do not deny that the features in question might be useful for a highly specialized DBMS that is tied to some specific application such as CAD/CAM, with no need for (say) integrity constraint support—but then we would question whether such a system is truly a DBMS, as that term is usually understood. See the annotation to references [10] and [90].

- With regard to Numbers 1 and 9, the only kind of "collection" we really want, and certainly the only kind of data we want to possess the property of "persistence," is, very specifically, the database relvar. Reference [1], by contrast, argues for the "persistence orthogonal to type" idea.
- We think the emphasis on encapsulation (Number 3) is slightly off base. What is important is to distinguish between *type* and *representation* (and hence, in database terms, to achieve data independence [77–78]). After all, unencapsulated relations can provide just as much data independence, in principle, as encapsulated objects can.
- We reject Number 2 outright [72,74].

We should add that—and it is to the credit of the authors that at least they recognized as much—reference [1] was never really more than a straw man: "We have taken a position, not so much expecting it to be the final word as to erect a provisional landmark to orient further debate."

2. Malcolm P. Atkinson and O. Peter Buneman: "Types and Persistence in Database Programming Languages," *ACM Comp. Surv. 19,* No. 2 (June 1987).

One of the earliest papers, if not *the* earliest, to articulate the position that persistence should be orthogonal to type. This paper is a good starting point for reading in the area of database programming languages in general ("database programming languages" being perceived by many people as the *sine qua non* of object database systems—see, for example, references [14] and [15]).

3. Kenneth Baclawski and Bipin Indurkhya: Technical Correspondence, *CACM 37,* No. 9 (September 1994).

This short paper is discussed in Appendix C.

4. Douglas K. Barry: *The Object Database Handbook: How to Select, Implement, and Use Object-Oriented Databases.* New York, N.Y.: John Wiley and Sons (1996).

The principal thesis of Barry's book is that we need an object system, not a relational one, if we have to deal with "complex data." Barry characterizes complex data as (a) ubiquitous, (b) often lacking unique identification, (c) involving numerous many-to-many relationships, and (d) often requiring the use of type codes "in the relational schema" (because of the lack of direct support for subtypes and supertypes in today's SQL products).

The author is executive director of the Object Database Management Group, ODMG [15], and it follows that we are probably going to disagree with much of what he has to say (see Appendix F). Prejudice aside, however, it does seem to us that his book exhibits many of the confusions that we find permeate object thinking. For example: "An ODBMS differs from an RDBMS in that an ODBMS directly supports relationships" (page 8). We would suggest that that "directly" should really be *differently* (an RDBMS certainly supports relationships directly too—supporting relationships directly is *exactly* what relations do). And then we would have to question the wisdom of representing "relationships" differently from "entities," as object systems do (understand that we are talking about the *logical level* here). It is relevant to remark that representing relationships differently at the logical level was what the old hierarchic and network systems used to do, too.

The book also contains repeated assertions that RDBMSs "store tuples" (as opposed to ODBMSs, which "store objects"). There is also a very misleading example regarding many-to-many relationships and normalization (pages 33–40). There are contentious claims to the effect that object schemas are simpler than relational ones (in fact the book contains no *schemas,* as such, at all; it does, however, contain several diagrams that could be used to explicate the structure of *any* database, object-oriented or relational or something else entirely). "A *base table* is the way the data is stored physically using an RDBMS" (page 183). "A configuration is versioning of versions. This allows for versioning a group of versioned objects" (page 330). And so on.

5. David Beech: "A Foundation for Evolution from Relational to Object Databases," in J. W. Schmidt, S. Ceri, and M. Missikoff (eds.): *Extending Database Technology.* New York, N.Y.: Springer-Verlag (1988).

This paper is one of several to propose an approach to extending SQL to become some kind of "Object SQL" or "OSQL" (see also reference [97], which gives more detail on this particular proposal). In common with most such papers, it has little or nothing to say regarding such crucial concepts as *domains,* the relational *closure* property, or relational *operators* such as join; i.e., it falls into the "relvar = class" trap (see Chapter 2 of the present book). OSQL "types" (i.e., tables) are not encapsulated.

The paper also makes a number of somewhat debatable claims regarding— among other things—the "smooth adaptation" of SQL to the world of objects. Here, for example, is an OSQL CREATE FUNCTION statement (taken from reference [97]):

```
CREATE FUNCTION RaiseAllSalaries (Integer incr) AS
     UPDATE Salary(e) = newsal
     FOR EACH Employee e, Integer newsal
     WHERE newsal = Salary(e) + incr ;
```

The following might have been thought to be more in keeping with the style of conventional SQL:

```
CREATE FUNCTION RaiseAllSalaries (Integer incr) AS
     UPDATE Employee
     SET Salary = Salary + incr ;
```

One interesting aspect of OSQL is that (in contrast to some other object languages) functions are themselves regarded as objects.

6. David Beech: "Collections of Objects in SQL3," Proc. 19th International Conference on Very Large Data Bases, Dublin, Ireland (August 1993).

See the annotation to reference [57].

7. Catriel Beeri and Philip A. Bernstein: "Computational Problems Related to the Design of Normal Form Relational Schemas," *ACM TODS 4,* No. 1 (March 1979).

8. Jon Bentley: "Little Languages," in *More Programming Pearls.* Reading, Mass.: Addison-Wesley (1988).

This paper illustrates and discusses the following "yardsticks of language design":

1. orthogonality   5. similarity
2. generality   6. extensibility
3. parsimony   7. openness
4. completeness

The term *parsimony,* incidentally, is nicely defined in *Chambers Twentieth Century Dictionary* as "praiseworthy . . . avoidance of excess." Parsimony is of course related to Occam's Razor ("entities should not be multiplied beyond necessity").

9. Elisa Bertino and Lorenzo Martino: *Object-Oriented Database Systems: Concepts and Architectures.* Reading, Mass.: Addison-Wesley (1993).

Many publications from the object world try to draw a distinction (as we do not) between *type* and *class,* and this book is one of them: "Object-oriented systems can be classified into two main categories—systems supporting the notion of *class* and those supporting the notion of *type* . . . [Although] there are no clear lines of demarcation between them, the two concepts are fundamentally different [*sic!*] . . . Often the concepts type and class are used interchangeably. However, when both are present in the same language, the *type* is used to indicate the specification of the interface of a set of objects, while class is an implementation notion [*so why is it "in the language" at all?*]. Therefore . . . a type is a set of objects which share the same behavior . . . [and] a class is a set of objects which have exactly the same internal structure and therefore the same attributes and the same methods [*but if all objects in a "class" have the same attributes and the same methods, is not that class a type, by the authors' own definition?*]. The class defines the implementation of a set of objects, while a type describes how such objects can be used." (Contrast reference [15], which uses the terms *type* and *class* in exactly the opposite way.)

The authors then go on to say: "With inheritance, a class called a *subclass* can be defined on the basis of the definition of another class called a *superclass.*" Surely—in accordance with their own earlier definitions—they should be talking in terms of types here, not classes? And then they add: "The specification hierarchy (often called *subtype hierarchy*) expresses . . . subtyping relationships which mean that an instance of the subtype can be used in every context in which an instance of the supertype can correctly appear (*substitutability*)." Observe that they do now speak of types, not classes. Observe too that we now have two new terms for the type hierarchy . . . Finally, observe the failure to distinguish properly between values and variables (note the talk of "instances"), and the consequent failure to distinguish between value substitutability and variable substitutability.

Of course, it is precisely because of confusions (terminological and otherwise) such as those just illustrated that we felt free—or compelled, rather—to introduce our own terms in *The Third Manifesto* and to define them as carefully as we could.

10. Michael Blaha and William Premerlani: *Object-Oriented Modeling and Design for Database Applications.* Upper Saddle River, N.J.: Prentice-Hall (1998).

This book is not really concerned with the kinds of issues that are the principal concern of *The Third Manifesto;* rather, it is concerned with a particular *design methodology* called Object Modeling Technique (OMT for short). Nevertheless, we do have our reasons for mentioning it here, which we will get to in just a moment.

OMT is a variant of the well-known "entity/relationship model" [17]; like most such, therefore, it relies extensively on the use of graphical symbols ("boxes and arrows" and a great deal more). Blaha and Premerlani's book consists primarily of an indepth description of OMT, with emphasis on its relevance to the design of databases in particular (OMT is claimed to be "especially helpful with database applications").* An OMT database design does not, or at least should not, depend on the capabilities of any particular DBMS; the book therefore also includes a detailed discussion of how to map such a design to a design that *is* specific to a particular object or SQL DBMS.

One reason we mention this book here is because it provides a good example of a point we made in Chapter 1: namely, that even the term *object* itself has a variety of different meanings in the object world. In the present context, it clearly means what the database community usually calls an *entity*—implying among other things that it is not encapsulated—whereas in object-oriented programming languages it generally means something that definitely *is* encapsulated. *Note:* These remarks are not meant as a criticism of reference [10], of course; we are only using it to illustrate a point.

---

*Actually this remark is a little puzzling, because databases are generally supposed to be designed, as far as possible, in a way that is independent of the applications that will use them. However, it is possible—especially given OMT's object-oriented "look and feel"—that Blaha and Premerlani are principally concerned with the design of *application-specific* databases (in this connection, see the annotation to reference [70]).

Following on from this point, we now observe that—presumably because OMT objects are really entities—OMT maps them to tuples in relvars instead of to values in domains. (More precisely, it maps *classes* to *relvars* instead of to domains.) OMT is not alone in this regard, of course (many other design methodologies do exactly the same thing); however, we speculate—and this is the crux of the matter—that it is this state of affairs (i.e., that "object modeling" is really just "entity/relationship modeling" by another name) that is the source of the infamous "relvar = class" mistake that we discussed at length in Chapter 2 (see also the final section in Appendix E).

We note in passing that reference [10] uses several other terms apart from "object" and "class" in ways that are at odds with the way we use them in the *Manifesto*. For example, on page 46 we find: "Do not confuse a domain with a class." At this point reference [10] is certainly using *class* to mean what we definitely *would* call a domain or—preferably—type (though elsewhere it seems to use it to mean a *collection* instead), so its use of *domain* does not accord with ours. And it uses *inheritance* to mean not *type* inheritance as discussed in Part IV of this book, but rather something akin to the rather suspect "subtables and supertables" notion discussed in Appendix D. *Polymorphism* is mentioned only in passing, and *substitutability* not at all.

Reference [10] also includes one or two other rather startling remarks. For example (page 273): "We see normal forms [*i.e., third normal form, etc.*] as an anachronism, largely irrelevant to OMT modeling" (they might be irrelevant to OMT as such, but they are most definitely *not* an "anachronism"). Another example (page 15): "Object is to class as value is to attribute." This latter quote suggests that an object is a value and a class is a collection; yet on the next page we find "Do not confuse values with objects."

Finally, the book also contains an interesting observation regarding code reuse. Recall from Chapter 14 that code reuse is one of the objectives of type inheritance. Of course, reuse does not imply inheritance, but the kinds of reuse that are *not* related to inheritance are not new. And in this connection, reference [10] makes the following point regarding DBMS code specifically: "DBMSs are intended to provide generic functionality for a wide variety of applications . . . *You are achieving reuse when you can use generic DBMS code, rather than custom-written application code*" (italics added). We agree, and observe that such reuse is supported very well by relational DBMSs, less well by object DBMSs.

11. Declan Brady: "Relational *vs.* Object-Oriented Database Systems: An Approach to Rapprochement," M.Sc. thesis, School of Computer Applications, Dublin City University, Ireland (January 1997).

Brady's thesis builds on an earlier version of *The Third Manifesto* to offer some interesting arguments and proposals of its own regarding, among other things, (a) possible coexistence of objects and relations and (b) what we called the "database design dilemma" in Appendix B.

12. Frederick P. Brooks, Jr.: *The Mythical Man-Month* (20th anniversary edition). Reading, Mass.: Addison-Wesley (1995).

The source of our "conceptual integrity" guiding principle.

13. Luca Cardelli and Peter Wegner: "On Understanding Types, Data Abstraction, and Polymorphism," *ACM Comp. Surv. 17,* No. 4 (December 1985).

14. R. G. G. Cattell: *Object Data Management* (revised edition). Reading, Mass.: Addison-Wesley (1994).

The first book-length tutorial on the application of object technology to database management. The following edited extract suggests that the field is still a long way from any kind of consensus: "Programming languages may need new syntax . . . swizzling, replication, and new access methods also need further study . . . new end-user and application development tools [are] required . . . more powerful query-language features [must be] developed . . . new research in concurrency control is needed . . . timestamps and object-based concurrency semantics need more exploration . . . performance models are needed . . . new work in knowledge management needs to be integrated with object and data management capabilities . . . this [will lead to] a complex optimization problem [and] few researchers have [the necessary] expertise . . . federated [object] databases require more study."

And another quote (this one illustrates terminological problems once again): "Generalization is also called inheritance, subtyping, or subclassing." Surely that *generalization* should be, rather, *specialization?*

Note: Reference [109] is another good tutorial on the same general subject.

15. R. G. G. Cattell and Douglas K. Barry (eds.): *The Object Database Standard: ODMG 2.0.* San Francisco, Calif.: Morgan Kaufmann (1997).

See Appendix F.

16. Donald D. Chamberlin: "Relations and References—Another Point of View." *InfoDB 10,* No. 6 (April 1997).

See the annotation to reference [72].

17. Peter Pin-Shan Chen: "The Entity-Relationship Model—Toward a Unified View of Data," *ACM TODS 1,* No. 1 (March 1976). Republished in M. Stonebraker (ed.): *Readings in Database Systems.* San Mateo, Calif.: Morgan Kaufmann (1988).

This is the paper that introduced the "entity/relationship model" (E/R model) and entity/relationship diagrams (E/R diagrams). *Note:* The E/R model has been revised and refined considerably over time; certainly the explanations and definitions given in this first paper were quite imprecise, so that such revisions were definitely needed. *Caveat lector.*

18. J. Craig Cleaveland: *An Introduction to Data Types.* Reading, Mass.: Addison-Wesley (1986).

19. E. F. Codd: "Derivability, Redundancy, and Consistency of Relations Stored in Large Data Banks," IBM Research Report RJ599 (August 19th, 1969).

    Codd's very first paper on what became the relational model of data (it is essentially a preliminary version of reference [20]).

20. E. F. Codd: "A Relational Model of Data for Large Shared Data Banks," *CACM 13,* No. 6 (June 1970). Republished in "Milestones of Research," *CACM 26,* No. 1 (January 1982).

    The first widely available description of the original relational model, by its inventor (the first *published* description was reference [19]).

21. E. F. Codd: "Relational Completeness of Data Base Sublanguages," in R. Rustin (ed.): *Data Base Systems:* Courant Computer Science Symposia 6. Englewood Cliffs, N.J.: Prentice-Hall (1972).

22. E. F. Codd: *The Relational Model for Database Management Version 2.* Reading, Mass.: Addison-Wesley (1990).

    Codd spent much of the late 1980s revising and extending the original relational model (which he now refers to as "the Relational Model Version 1" or RM/V1), and this book is the result. It describes "the Relational Model Version 2" or RM/V2. *Note:* We include this reference primarily in order to make it clear that the version of the relational model on which *The Third Manifesto* is based is *not* "RM/V2," nor indeed "RM/V1" as Codd currently defines it. Rather, it is (as noted in Chapter 1) the version described in references [51] and [56].

23. O. J. Dahl, B. Myhrhaug, and K. Nygaard: *The SIMULA 67 Common Base Language.* Pub. S-22, Norwegian Computing Center, Oslo, Norway (1970).

    SIMULA 67 is often cited as the very first object programming language.

24. Hugh Darwen (writing as Andrew Warden): "Adventures in Relationland," in reference [47].

25. Hugh Darwen (writing as Andrew Warden): "The Keys of the Kingdom," in reference [24].

26. Hugh Darwen (writing as Andrew Warden): "A Constant Friend," in reference [24].

27. Hugh Darwen (writing as Andrew Warden): "TABLE_DEE and TABLE_DUM," in reference [24].

28. Hugh Darwen: "The Askew Wall: A Personal Perspective," in reference [75].

29. Hugh Darwen: "The Duplicity of Duplicate Rows," in reference [75].

30. Hugh Darwen: "The Role of Functional Dependence in Query Decomposition," in reference [75].

31. Hugh Darwen: "The Nullologist in Relationland; *or,* Nothing Really Matters," in reference [75].

32. Hugh Darwen: "Outer Join with No Nulls and Fewer Tears," in reference [75].

33. Hugh Darwen: "Valid Time and Transaction Time Proposals: Language Design Aspects," in O. Etzion, S. Jajodia, and S. Sripada (eds.): *Temporal Databases: Research and Practice.* New York, N.Y.: Springer-Verlag (1998).

This paper includes and discusses a set of language design principles that are similar but not identical to those of reference [8]. The principles in question are:

1. precise specification
2. encouragement of Good Practice
3. generality
4. semantic consistency
5. syntactic consistency
6. orthogonality
7. parsimony
8. syntactic substitution
9. conceptual integrity

Regarding *syntactic substitution,* this paper has this to say: "A language definition should start with a few judiciously chosen primitive operators . . . Subsequent development is, where possible, by defining new operators in terms of . . . previously defined [ones]. Most importantly, syntactic substitution does not refer to an imprecise principle such as might be expressed as '*A* is something like, possibly very like, *B*,' where *A* is some proposed new syntax and *B* is some expression using previously defined operators. If *A* is close in meaning to *B* but cannot be specified by true syntactic substitution, then we have a situation that is disagreeable and probably unacceptable, in stark contrast to true syntactic substitution, which can be very agreeable and acceptable indeed." As should be clear from Chapters 4 and 5 (and 10) of the present book, we applied the principle of true syntactic substitution liberally in the design of **Tutorial D.**

34. Hugh Darwen and C. J. Date: "Relation-Valued Attributes; *or,* Will the Real First Normal Form Please Stand Up?", in reference [75].

35. Hugh Darwen and C. J. Date: "Into the Great Divide," in reference [75].

36. Hugh Darwen and C. J. Date: "Introducing . . . *The Third Manifesto,*" *Database Programming & Design 8,* No. 1 (January 1995).

An earlier (and, to be frank, slightly confused) version of reference [42].

37. Hugh Darwen and C. J. Date: "Een Tweede Leven voor het Relationale Model" (interview by Rick van der Lans, Dutch language version). Part 1, *DB/M Magazine (Netherlands) 1,* January/February 1995; Part 2, *DB/M Magazine (Netherlands) 2,* March/April 1995.

The original (Dutch language) version of the interview presented in Appendix G. Note the somewhat different title ("A Second Life for the Relational Model").

38. Hugh Darwen and C. J. Date: *The Third Manifesto. ACM SIGMOD Record 24,* No. 1 (March 1995).

The first "official" version. The *Manifesto* as described in the present book consists of a considerably extended (but, of course, compatible) version.

39. Hugh Darwen and C. J. Date: "The Next 25 Years of the Relational Model?" (interview by Rick van der Lans, English language version), *InfoDB 9,* No. 4 (August 1995).

The English language version of reference [37].

40. Hugh Darwen and C. J. Date, "The Third Manifesto," in reference [58].

A preliminary version of reference [38]. Unlike reference [38], it does include an appendix detailing a set of proposals for type inheritance (in fact, this was the first published version of those proposals). It should be made clear that those proposals were really only preliminary, however; they are completely superseded by Part IV of the present book.

41. Hugh Darwen and C. J. Date: "Les 25 Ans à Venir du Modèle Relationnel" (interview by Rick van der Lans, French language version), *Databases Journal 1,* January/February 1996.

A French language version of reference [37].

42. Hugh Darwen and C. J. Date: *"The Third Manifesto:* Foundation for Object/ Relational Databases," in C. J. Date: *Relational Database Writings 1994–1997.* Reading, Mass.: Addison-Wesley (1998, to appear). A version of this paper can also be found on the World Wide Web at *http://www.alternativetech.com.*

Chapter 2 of the present book is heavily based on this article.

43. C. J. Date: "An Architecture for High-Level Language Database Extensions," Proc. ACM SIGMOD International Conference on Management of Data, Washington, D.C. (June 1976). A revised version of this paper entitled "An Introduction to the Unified Database Language (UDL)" can be found in reference [44].

44. C. J. Date: *Relational Database: Selected Writings.* Reading, Mass.: Addison-Wesley (1986).

45. C. J. Date: "Some Principles of Good Language Design," in reference [44].

46. C. J. Date: "A Critique of the SQL Database Language," in reference [44].

47. C. J. Date: *Relational Database Writings 1985–1989.* Reading, Mass.: Addison-Wesley (1990).

48. C. J. Date: "What's Wrong with SQL?", in reference [47].

49. C. J. Date: "The Principle of Cautious Design," in reference [75].

To quote: "The Principle of Cautious Design says, in effect, that whenever we are faced with a design choice, say between alternative *A* and alternative *B* (where *A* is upward-compatible with *B*), and the full implications of alternative *B* are not yet known, then the recommendation is to go with alternative *A.*" Our decision in the *Manifesto* to prohibit coercions can be seen as an application of this principle. By contrast, the decision to permit duplicate rows in SQL can be seen as a case in which the principle was flouted.

50. C. J. Date: "What Is a Relation?", in reference [75].

51. C. J. Date: "Notes Toward a Reconstituted Definition of the Relational Model Version 1 (RM/V1)," in reference [75].

52. C. J. Date: "The Default Values Approach to Missing Information," in reference [75].

    See reference [71].

53. C. J. Date: "Marrying Objects and Relational" (interview), in *Data Base Newsletter 22,* No. 3 (May/June 1994, Part 1); *Data Base Newsletter 22,* No. 4 (July/August 1994, Part 2). Republished in reference [58].

    This interview covers much of the same territory as reference [39].

54. C. J. Date: "Oh Oh Relational . . .," *Database Programming & Design 7,* No. 10 (October 1994). Republished in C. J. Date: *Relational Database Writings 1994–1997.* Reading, Mass.: Addison-Wesley (1998, to appear).

    A less formal presentation—really just a summary and sequence of position statements—of some of the material from reference [57].

55. C. J. Date: *An Introduction to Database Systems* (6th edition). Reading, Mass.: Addison-Wesley (1995).

56. C. J. Date: "The Relational Model," Part II of reference [55].

57. C. J. Date: "Toward an OO/Relational Rapprochement," in reference [55].

    Explains in detail why "domain = class" is right and "relvar = class" is wrong, and describes the benefits that would accrue from a true rapprochement between relational and object principles as advocated in *The Third Manifesto.* References [6] and [91–93] are examples (not the only ones) of publications that advocate the wrong equation.

58. C. J. Date: *Relational Database Writings 1991–1994.* Reading, Mass.: Addison-Wesley (1995).

59. C. J. Date: "Nothing in Excess," in reference [58].

60. C. J. Date: "Tables with No Columns" and "More on DEE and DUM," in reference [58].

61. C. J. Date: "Empty Bags and Identity Crises," in reference [58].

62. C. J. Date: "How We Missed the Relational Boat," in reference [58].

63. C. J. Date: "The Importance of Closure," in reference [58].

64. C. J. Date: "Domains, Relations, and Data Types" (in two parts), in reference [58].

    Lays the groundwork for understanding why "domain = class" is the right equation.

65. C. J. Date: "The Primacy of Primary Keys: An Investigation," in reference [58].

66. C. J. Date: "It's All Relations!" *Database Programming & Design 8,* No. 1 (January 1995). Republished in C. J. Date: *Relational Database Writings 1994–1997.* Reading, Mass.: Addison-Wesley (1998, to appear).

67. C. J. Date: "Say No to Composite Columns," *Database Programming & Design 8,* No. 5 (May 1995). Republished in C. J. Date: *Relational Database Writings 1994–1997.* Reading, Mass.: Addison-Wesley (1998, to appear).

68. C. J. Date: "Objects and Relations: Forty-Seven Points of Light," *Data Base Newsletter 23,* No. 5 (September/October 1995). Republished in C. J. Date: *Relational Database Writings 1994–1997.* Reading, Mass.: Addison-Wesley (1998, to appear).

A blow-by-blow response to reference [93].

69. C. J. Date: "Quota Queries," *Database Programming & Design 9,* Nos. 7–9 (July-September 1996). Republished in C. J. Date: *Relational Database Writings 1994–1997.* Reading, Mass.: Addison-Wesley (1998, to appear).

70. C. J. Date: "Why 'The Object Model' Is Not a Data Model," *InfoDB 10,* No. 4 (August 1996). Republished in C. J. Date: *Relational Database Writings 1994–1997.* Reading, Mass.: Addison-Wesley (1998, to appear).

This paper argues among other things that object and relational systems are more different than is usually realized. The following excerpt summarizes the argument:

"Object databases grew out of a desire on the part of object application programmers—for a variety of application-specific reasons—to keep their application-specific objects in persistent memory. That persistent memory might perhaps be regarded as a database, but the important point is that *it was indeed application-specific;* it was not a shared, general-purpose database, intended to be suitable for applications that might not have been foreseen at the time the database was defined. As a consequence, many features that database professionals regard as essential were simply not requirements in the object world, at least not originally. Thus, there was little perceived need for:

1. Data sharing across applications
2. Physical data independence
3. *Ad hoc* queries
4. Views and logical data independence
5. Application-independent, declarative integrity constraints
6. Data ownership and a flexible security mechanism
7. Concurrency control
8. A general-purpose catalog
9. Application-independent database design

These requirements all surfaced later, after the basic idea of storing objects in a database was first conceived, and thus all constitute add-on features to the original object model . . . One important consequence of all of the foregoing is that there really is a *difference in kind* between an object DBMS and a relational DBMS. In fact, it could be argued that an object DBMS is not really a DBMS at all—at least, not in the same sense that a relational DBMS is a DBMS. For consider:

- A relational DBMS comes *ready for use*. In other words, as soon as the system is installed, users (application programmers and end users) can start building databases, writing applications, running queries, and so on.

- An object DBMS, by contrast, can be thought of as a kind of *DBMS construction kit*. When it is originally installed, it is *not* available for immediate use by application programmers and end users. Instead, it must first be *tailored* by suitably skilled technicians, who must define the necessary classes and methods, etc. (the system provides a set of building blocks— class library maintenance tools, method compilers, etc.—for this purpose). Only when that tailoring activity is complete will the system be available for use by application programmers and end users; in other words, the result of that tailoring will indeed more closely resemble a DBMS in the more familiar sense of the term.

- Note further that the resultant "tailored" DBMS will be *application-specific;* it might, for example, be suitable for CAD/CAM applications, but be essentially useless for, e.g., medical applications. In other words, it will still not be a general-purpose DBMS, in the same sense that a relational DBMS is a general-purpose DBMS."

The paper also argues against the "persistence orthogonal to type" idea, as follows:

"The object model requires support for a full complement of *type generators* . . . Examples include STRUCT (or TUPLE), LIST, ARRAY, SET, BAG, and so on. These generators can be combined in arbitrary ways; thus, for example, an array of lists of bags of arrays of [integers] might constitute a single object in suitable circumstances. Along with object IDs, the availability of these type generators essentially means that *any data structure that can be created in an application program can be created as an object in an object database*—and further that the structure of such objects is *visible to the user*. For example, consider the object, EX say, that is (or rather denotes) the collection of employees in a given department. Then EX might be implemented either as a linked list or as an array, and users will have to know which it is (because the access operators will differ accordingly).

"This 'anything goes' approach to what can be stored in the database is a major point of difference between the object and relational models, of course, and it deserves a little further discussion here. In essence:

- The object model says we can store anything we like—any data structure we can create with the usual programming language mechanisms.

- The relational model effectively says the same thing, but goes on to insist that whatever we do store be presented to the user in pure relational form.

"More precisely, the relational model—quite rightly—says *nothing* about what can be physically stored . . . It therefore imposes no limits on what data structures are allowed at the physical level; the only requirement is that whatever structures *are* in fact physically stored must be mapped to relations at the logical level and hence be hidden from the user. Relational systems thus make a clear distinction between logical and physical (data model *vs.* implementation), while object systems do not. One consequence is that—contrary to conventional wisdom—object systems might very well provide less data independence than relational systems. For example, suppose the implementation in some object database of the object EX mentioned above (denoting the collection of employees in a given department) is changed from an array to a linked list. What are the implications for existing code that accesses that object EX?"

71. C. J. Date: "Faults and Defaults," *Database Programming & Design 9,* Nos. 11–12 and *10,* Nos. 1–2 and 4 (November 1996–April 1997). Republished in C. J. Date: *Relational Database Writings 1994–1997.* Reading, Mass.: Addison-Wesley (1998, to appear).

A detailed examination of the "default" or special values approach to dealing with missing information. *Note:* An earlier discussion of the same subject (couched, however, in terms of attributes instead of domains) appears in reference [52]. The proposals in the series of articles referenced here [71] should be regarding as superseding that earlier discussion.

72. C. J. Date: "Don't Mix Pointers and Relations!" *InfoDB 10,* No. 6 (April 1997); "Don't Mix Pointers and Relations—*Please!*" Republished in C. J. Date: *Relational Database Writings 1994–1997.* Reading, Mass.: Addison-Wesley (1998, to appear).

The first of these two articles argues strongly against the proposal—characterized in Chapter 2 of the present book as *The Second Great Blunder*—that relational databases should be allowed to include pointers to data as well as data *per se.* (In particular, therefore, it attacks SQL3 [87–89,100–101], which currently includes something very close if not identical to such a proposal.) In reference [16], Chamberlin offers a rebuttal to some of the arguments of that first article. The second article was written as a direct response to Chamberlin's rebuttal.

The crux of the argument is worth spelling out here. The basic point is simply that—by definition—pointers point to *variables,* not *values* (variables have addresses, values do not). Thus, if relvar *R1* is allowed to have an attribute whose values are pointers "into" relvar *R2,* then—by definition—those pointers point to tuple *variables,* not to tuple *values.* **But there is no such thing as a tuple variable in the relational model.** The relational model deals with relation values, which are (loosely speaking) sets of tuple values, which are in turn (again loosely speaking) sets of scalar values. It also deals with relation variables, which are variables whose values are relations. However, it does *not* deal with tuple variables (which are variables whose values are tuples) or scalar variables (which are variables whose values are scalars).* In other words, the *only* kind of variable included in the relational model is, very specifically, the *relation* variable. *It follows that the idea of mixing pointers and relations constitutes a MAJOR departure from the relational model, introducing as it does an entirely new kind of variable.* Indeed, we would argue that it **undermines the conceptual integrity of the relational model** (and the two articles [72] present numerous detailed arguments in support of this position).

Given the foregoing, it is sad to see that (as indicated in Chapter 9 of the present book) most—possibly all—of the current crop of so-called "object/ relational" products do indeed mix pointers and relations in exactly the manner discussed and objected to above. This flaw is beginning to look at least as serious as **The First Great Blunder,** discussed at length in Chapter 2, of embracing the wrong equation "relvar = class."

73. C. J. Date: "Grievous Bodily Harm." Part 1, *Database Programming & Design 11,* No. 5 (May 1998); Part 2, *Database Programming & Design 11,* No. 6 (June 1998).

One strong criticism of SQL is that it is an extremely redundant language; that is, for all but the most trivial of queries, it provides many different ways of formulating the query in question (and some of the differences between formulations are quite radical). Such redundancies do not make the language more general, they just make it more complicated—with significant negative consequences for documentation, teaching, learning, remembering, applying, and (last but not least) implementation. This two-part paper describes some major SQL redundancies in detail and discusses some of the consequences of such redundancies.

74. C. J. Date: "Object Identifiers *vs.* Relational Keys," in C. J. Date: *Relational Database Writings 1994–1997.* Reading, Mass.: Addison-Wesley (1998, to appear).

Presents arguments in support of the position that object IDs are first and foremost a performance feature and should not be part of the model as seen by the user. To elaborate briefly, the paper argues that (a) object IDs do perform some of the same functions as relational keys, but they're certainly not just "keys pure and simple"—they carry a lot of additional baggage with them; (b) the

---

The Third Manifesto does support tuple and scalar variables, of course, but they are not allowed *in the database* (only relvars are allowed in the database). By the way, we hope it is clear that it makes no sense to think of relvars as somehow "containing" tuple or scalar variables; relvars contain relation *values,* and no value (of any kind) can possibly contain a variable (of any kind).

baggage in question is strongly motivated by performance considerations and does not belong in the model. *The Third Manifesto* proscribes object IDs precisely because of that extra baggage.

75. C. J. Date and Hugh Darwen: *Relational Database Writings 1989–1991*. Reading, Mass.: Addison-Wesley (1992).

76. C. J. Date and Hugh Darwen: *A Guide to the SQL Standard* (4th edition). Reading, Mass.: Addison-Wesley (1997).

This book is a tutorial reference and guide to the current (1998) version of the SQL standard, "SQL/92" [87–89]. It contains numerous examples of violations of good language design principles. In particular, it includes an appendix, Appendix D, that documents "many aspects of the standard that appear to be inadequately defined, or even incorrectly defined, at this time."

77. C. J. Date and P. Hopewell: "Storage Structures and Physical Data Independence," Proc. 1971 ACM SIGFIDET Workshop on Data Definition, Access, and Control, San Diego, California (November 1971).

78. C. J. Date and P. Hopewell: "File Definition and Logical Data Independence," Proc. 1971 ACM SIGFIDET Workshop on Data Definition, Access, and Control, San Diego, California (November 1971).

79. C. J. Date and David McGoveran: "Updating Union, Intersection, and Difference Views" and "Updating Joins and Other Views," both in reference [58].

Note: These two papers are undergoing a certain amount of revision at the time of writing.

80. Margaret A. Ellis and Bjarne Stroustrup: *The Annotated C++ Reference Manual*. Reading, Mass.: Addison-Wesley (1990).

81. Adele Goldberg and David Robson: *Smalltalk-80: The Language and its Implementation*. Reading, Mass.: Addison-Wesley (1983).

According to reference [106], object-oriented programming has its roots in Smalltalk, and "the phrase *object-oriented programming* originated with the development of the Smalltalk language" (though Smalltalk was surely influenced in turn by SIMULA 67 [23]). And in their book on Smalltalk [81], Goldberg and Robson state categorically that "an object consists of some private memory and a set of operations . . . An object's public properties are the messages that make up its interface . . . An object's private properties are a set of *instance variables* that make up its private memory." In other words, it is indeed the case that *pure* objects have no public instance variables, and further that many so-called object-oriented systems are not pure.

82. Nathan Goodman: "Bill of Materials in Relational Database," *InfoDB 5,* No. 1 (Spring/Summer 1990).

83. Nathan Goodman: "Can Objects and Relational Work Together?" (interview), *Data Base Newsletter 24,* No. 2 (March/April 96).

A couple of interesting quotes from this interview:

- "Designing for database sharing and reuse are not part of the training for object-oriented developers. Object-oriented rhetoric talks about reuse, but it is reuse of *programs*—not databases—that they have in mind."
- "In actual practice, it is very difficult to create reusable *business* objects."

84. James Gosling, Bill Joy, and Guy Steele: *The Java Language Specification.* Reading, Mass.: Addison-Wesley (1996).

85. Jim Gray and Andreas Reuter: *Transaction Processing: Concepts and Techniques.* San Mateo, Calif.: Morgan Kaufmann (1993).

The standard and definitive text on transaction management.

86. Peter Henderson: *Functional Programming Application and Implementation.* Englewood Cliffs, N.J.: Prentice-Hall (1980).

87. International Organization for Standardization (ISO): *Database Language SQL.* Document ISO/IEC 9075:1992. Also available as American National Standards Institute (ANSI) Document ANSI X3.135-1992.

The original definition of the current (1992) version of the ISO/ANSI SQL standard (but see also references [88–89]). *Note:* The original single-part document has since been expanded into an open-ended series of separate parts, under the general title *Information Technology—Database Languages—SQL.* At the time of writing, the following parts have been defined (though certainly not all completed):

1. Framework (SQL/Framework)
2. Foundation (SQL/Foundation)
3. Call-Level Interface (SQL/CLI)
4. Persistent Stored Modules (SQL/PSM)
5. Host Language Bindings (SQL/Bindings)
6. XA Specialization (SQL/Transaction)
7. Temporal (SQL/Temporal)

The SQL3 proposals discussed in Appendix E of the present book logically belong (for the most part) in Part 2, *SQL/Foundation.* As yet unpublished documents (working drafts) describing those proposals can be found on the World Wide Web at *ftp://jerry.ece.umassd.edu/isowg3/dbl/BASEdocs/public.*

88. International Organization for Standardization (ISO): *Information Technology–Database Languages–SQL–Technical Corrigendum 1.* Document ISO/IEC 9075:1992/Cor.1:1994(E).

Contains a large number of revisions and corrections to reference [87]. *Note:* This document is subsumed by reference [89].

89. International Organization for Standardization (ISO): *Information Technology–Database Languages–SQL–Technical Corrigendum 2.* Document ISO/IEC 9075:1992/Cor.2:1996(E).

An expanded version of reference [88].

90. Ivar Jacobson *et al.: Object-Oriented Software Engineering* (revised printing). Reading, Mass.: Addison-Wesley (1994).

A widely respected book on software engineering. It presents a methodology called OOSE (Object-Oriented Software Engineering), a simplified version of a more extensive approach called *Objectory.* From a database perspective, however, we have to say that we find it a little confused, especially over encapsulation and type *vs.* class (in fact, over model *vs.* implementation in general). For example: "The behavior and information are **encapsulated** in the object" (page 48, boldface in the original), but "each . . . attribute [of the class] will become one column in the table" (page 277). Tables are not encapsulated. And: "A type is defined by the manipulations you can do with the type. A class is more than that. You can also look inside a class . . . to see its information structure. . . . [A] class is [an] *implementation* of a type" (page 50, italics in the original). These statements are clear enough, of course, but the book then goes on to talk almost exclusively in terms of classes where types would seem more appropriate.

Many of the comments in the annotation to reference [10] apply here too, *mutatis mutandis.* In particular, as the previous paragraph suggests, OOSE objects (like OMT objects) seem to correspond for the most part to what the database community would call *entities*—and we remind you of our speculation that this state of affairs is the source of the "relvar = class" mistake.

One last quote: "Most of the methods used in the industry today, for both information and technical system development, are based on a functional and/or data-driven decomposition of the system. These approaches differ in many ways from the approach taken by object-oriented methods where data and functions are highly integrated." It seems to us that here Jacobson puts his finger on a significant mismatch between object and database thinking. Databases are *meant* to be somewhat divorced from "functions"; as noted in a footnote under reference [10], databases are usually supposed to be designed separately from the applications that use them. Thus, it seems to us once again that the term "database" as used in the object community really means a database that is *application-specific,* not (as is more usual in the database community) one that is general-purpose.

91. William Kelley and Won Kim: "Observations on the Current SQL3 Object Model Proposal (and Invitation for Scholarly Opinions)," available from UniSQL, Inc., 9390 Research Blvd., Austin, Texas 78759 (1994).

See the annotation to reference [57].

92. Won Kim: "Object-Oriented Database Systems: Promises, Reality, and the Future," Proc. 19th International Conference on Very Large Data Bases, Dublin, Ireland (August 24th–27th, 1993).

93. Won Kim: "On Marrying Relations and Objects: Relation-Centric and Object-Centric Perspectives," *Data Base Newsletter 22,* No. 6 (November/December 1994).

See reference [68].

94. Won Kim: "Bringing Object/Relational Down to Earth," *Database Programming & Design 10,* No. 7 (July 1997).

In this article, Kim claims that "confusion is sure to reign" in the object/relational database marketplace because, first, "an inordinate weight has been placed on the role of data type extensibility," and, second, "the measure of a product's object/relational completeness . . . is a potentially serious area of perplexity." He goes on to propose "a practical metric for object/relational completeness that can be used as a guideline for determining whether a product is truly [object/relational]" (an idea that inevitably invites comparison with the approach taken in reference [1] to the question of whether a DBMS is truly object-oriented).

Kim's scheme (*metric* is really not the *mot juste,* since there is nothing quantitative about it) involves the following criteria:

1. data model
2. query language
3. mission-critical services
4. computational model
5. performance and scalability
6. database tools
7. harnessing the power

With respect to Criterion Number 1 here, Kim takes the position (very different from that of *The Third Manifesto*) that the data model must be "the Core Object Model defined by the Object Management Group" [108], which "comprises the relational data model as well as the core object-oriented modeling concepts of object-oriented programming languages." According to Kim, it thus includes all of the following concepts: *class* (Kim adds "or type"—?), *instance, attribute, integrity constraints, object IDs, encapsulation, (multiple) class inheritance, (multiple) ADT inheritance, data of type reference, set-valued attributes, class attributes, class methods* (and more besides).

(By the way, note that relations—which of course we regard as both crucial and fundamental—are never explicitly mentioned. Kim claims that the OMG Core Object Model includes the entire relational model in addition to everything in the foregoing list of concepts, but in fact it does not [108].)

As for Criterion Number 2 ("query language"), Kim's position (again very different from that of *The Third Manifesto*) is that the language must be some kind of "Object SQL"—i.e., a version of SQL that has been extended to deal with all of the various constructs just listed.

Criteria Numbers 3–6 all have to do with the implementation rather than the model. In other words, they might be important in practice—they might very well make the difference between a good object/relational system and a bad one—but they cannot, by definition, make the difference between a system that is object/relational and one that is not. In other words, it is not clear exactly what Kim's "metric" is supposed to be measuring.

The final criterion ("harnessing the power") constitutes an interesting, and major, point of difference between Kim's position and our own. It is our opinion that user-defined types constitute the primary justification—the *raison d'être,* the *sine qua non,* the absolutely essential ingredient—for object/relational systems (as opposed to systems that are "just relational"), as explained at length in Chapter 2. Kim's opinion, by contrast, is that user-defined types are merely a secondary feature (indeed, they have been "oversold"), and they constitute just one aspect of "harnessing the power." (The other is the claimed ability of an object/relational DBMS to act as the basis for "heterogeneous database fusion"—i.e., to serve as a unified frontend to a variety of disparate databases "including RDBs, OODBs, hierarchical databases, CODASYL databases, and even flat files.")

95. Bruce Lindsay: "Object/Relational: Separating the Wheat from the Chaff" (presentation), in reference [114].

96. Claudio L. Lucchesi and Sylvia L. Osborn: "Candidate Keys for Relations," *J. Comp. and Sys. Sciences 17*, No. 2 (1978).

This paper presents an algorithm for inferring candidate keys from functional dependencies.

97. Peter Lyngbaek *et al.*: "OSQL: A Language for Object Databases," Technical Report HPL-DTD-91-4, Hewlett-Packard Company (January 15th, 1991).

See the annotation to reference [5].

98. Nelson Mattos and Linda G. DeMichiel: "Recent Design Trade-Offs in SQL3," *ACM SIGMOD Record 23*, No. 4 (December 1994).

See Appendix C for a discussion of this paper.

99. James D. McCawley: *Everything That Linguists Have Always Wanted to Know about Logic (but were ashamed to ask).* Chicago, Ill.: University of Chicago Press (1981).

100. Jim Melton: "A Shift in the Landscape (Assessing SQL3's New Object Direction)." *Database Programming & Design 9*, No. 8 (August 1996).

101. Jim Melton: "ANSI SQL3: New Directions for the SQL Standard" (presentation), in reference [114].

102. Bertrand Meyer: "The Many Faces of Inheritance: A Taxonomy of Taxonomy," *IEEE Computer 29*, No. 5 (May 1996).

103. Bertrand Meyer: *Object-Oriented Software Construction* (2nd edition). Upper Saddle River, N.J.: Prentice-Hall (1997).

104. R. Morrison: *S-Algol Reference Manual,* Internal Report CSR-80-81, Dept. of Computer Science, University of Edinburgh (February 1981).

105. Mark A. Roth, Henry F. Korth, and Abraham Silberschatz: "Extended Algebra and Calculus for Nested Relational Databases," *ACM TODS 13,* No. 4 (December 1988).

106. Robert W. Sebesta: *Concepts of Programming Languages.* Redwood City, Calif.: Benjamin/Cummings (1989).

107. Richard T. Snodgrass (ed.): *The Temporal Query Language TSQL2.* Dordrecht, Netherlands: Kluwer Academic Pub. (1995).

108. Richard Mark Soley and William Kent: "The OMG Object Model," in Won Kim (ed.): *Modern Database Systems: The Object Model, Interoperability, and Beyond.* New York, N.Y.: ACM Press. Reading, Mass.: Addison-Wesley (1995).

The ODMG Object Model [15] is based on the "core object model" of the Object Management Group, OMG. OMG (like ODMG) has no formal standardization authority, but it "is developing standards in the form of wholesale agreements among member companies" (of which there were "about 340" at the time this paper was written).

The OMG core object model is based on "a small number of basic concepts: objects, operations, types, and subtyping." Note that *values* and *variables* are not included in this list; however, reference [108] does also recognize something it calls *nonobjects,* and gives as examples of "nonobject types" such things as CHAR and BOOLEAN, suggesting that "nonobjects" might perhaps be values (or perhaps a "nonobject type" is just a primitive builtin type?). Moreover, objects are certainly variables, although the term *variable* is not used. But then the paper goes on to say that objects and nonobjects together "represent the set of denotable *values* in the core object model" (our italics).

Objects have object IDs, nonobjects do not. Further, objects have behavior and no user-visible structure: "In the core object model, operations are used to model the external interface to state" (*state* here meaning the object's current *value*). But the paper then adds, somewhat confusingly, that "*attributes* and *relationships* . . . can be used to model the externally visible declarations of state more succinctly."

Another puzzle concerns the distinction between read-only *vs.* update operators (to use *Third Manifesto* terminology). OMG expressly does not make any such distinction; in fact, it "defines a pass-by-value argument passing semantics," implying that operators are always read-only. However, it clearly also allows operations that produce "side effects, manifested in changes of state." There seems to be a contradiction here.

OMG draws a distinction between *subtyping* and *inheritance:* "*Subtyping* [can be intuitively defined thus:] . . . one type is a subtype of another if the first is a specialization or refinement of the second . . . if *S* is a subtype of *T,* an object of type *S* may be used wherever an object of type *T* may be used [*note the lack of distinction between value and variable substitutability*] . . . *Inheritance* is a notational mechanism for defining a type *S* in terms of another type *T* . . . Intuitively, *inherit* means that the operations defined for *T* are also defined for . . . *S*." So far, the distinction does not seem very clear! Anyway, the paper continues: "Subtyping is a relationship between interfaces (types). Inheritance can apply to both interfaces and implementations; that is, both interfaces and implementations can be inherited. The core object model is concerned with . . . interfaces, . . . not . . . implementations." So why is the distinction even mentioned?

The paper then goes on to muddy the picture still further—irretrievably?—by saying: "Whether [the set of operations defined for *S*] is a superset of [the set of operations defined for *T*] or the two are disjoint sets is an implementation issue and does not affect the core object model semantics" (!).

It has to be said too that the OMG model of subtyping and/or inheritance appears to be considerably underspecified. Many of the features of our own inheritance model (see Part IV of this book)—for example, TREAT UP, TREAT DOWN, the semantics of assignments, the semantics of comparisons, notions such as "most specific common supertype," and numerous other aspects—seem to have no counterpart at all.

Note finally that objects in OMG can never change their type; they cannot even be further specialized, implying that (e.g.) an object of type *employee* can never subsequently acquire the more specific type *manager.* Such restrictions surely constitute grounds for rejecting the frequently heard claims to the effect that objects—at least, OMG-style objects—are "a good model of reality"; real-world objects certainly do acquire and lose types dynamically (for example, an employee can become or cease to be a manager). By contrast, we believe our own model of inheritance is not subject to such criticisms, precisely because it embraces the value and variable concepts instead of some kind of "object" concept. See in particular the discussion of IM Proposals 18 and 23 in Chapter 14.

Note: The singular nature of the book that contains Soley and Kent's paper should not go unremarked. Its overall title is *Modern Database Systems*—yet it contains almost nothing on relational theory, which (in our opinion) is certainly relevant to "modern database systems" and will remain so for future systems too, for as far out as anyone can see. The book in fact consists of two parts: "Next-Generation Database Technology" (512 pages) and "Technology for Interoperating Legacy Databases" (188 pages). Part I in turn consists entirely of a single subpart, "Object-Oriented Database" (Part Ia; there is no Part Ib). In other words, the book subscribes to the position—a position in stark contrast to our own—that object DBMSs are the "next generation"; it therefore also subscribes to the position that we need to deal with the problem of "legacy databases" (by which the book clearly means *SQL* databases specifically)—a position we might agree with, though we have a different interpretation of what it really means.

109. Jacob Stein and David Maier: "Concepts in Object-Oriented Data Management," *Database Programming & Design 1,* No. 4 (April 1988).

A good early tutorial on the basic concepts of object database systems.

110. Michael Stonebraker (with Dorothy Moore): *Object-Relational DBMSs: The Next Great Wave.* San Francisco, Calif.: Morgan Kaufmann (1996).

This book is a tutorial on object/relational systems. It is heavily—in fact, almost exclusively—based on Illustra, a commercial product that Stonebraker himself was instrumental in developing. *Note:* As mentioned in Appendix G, the Illustra company was subsequently purchased by Informix Software Inc. and large portions of the Illustra technology incorporated into Informix's own Online Dynamic Server product (under the name *Universal Data Option*).

The book begins by presenting Stonebraker's by now well known "DBMS classification matrix" (see Fig. H.1). Quadrant 1 of that matrix represents applications that deal only with rather simple data and have no requirement for *ad hoc* query (a traditional word processor is a good example). Such applications are not really database applications at all, in the classical sense of that term; the "DBMS" that best serves their needs is just the native file system of the underlying operating system.

Quadrant 2 represents applications that do have an *ad hoc* query requirement but still have only rather simple data. Most of today's business applications fall into this quadrant, and they are fairly well supported by today's relational (or at least SQL) DBMSs.

Quadrant 3 represents applications with complex data and processing but no *ad hoc* query requirement. For example, CAD/CAM applications typically fall into this quadrant. Current object DBMSs are primarily aimed at

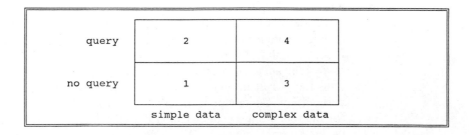

Fig. H.1   Stonebraker's DBMS classification matrix

this segment of the market (today's SQL products tend not to do a very good job on Quadrant 3 applications).

Finally, Quadrant 4 represents applications with a need for both complex data and *ad hoc* queries against that data. Stonebraker gives an example of a database containing digitized 35mm slides, with a typical query being "Get pictures of sunsets taken within 20 miles of Sacramento, California." He then goes on to give arguments in support of his position that (a) an object/relational DBMS is required for applications that fall into this quadrant, and (b) over the next few years, the majority of applications will move over into this quadrant—hence the "next great wave" of the book's title.* For example, even a simple human resources application might expand to include employee photographs, sound recordings (spoken messages), and the like.

Stonebraker himself summarizes the overall message of the book by stating that a "good" object/relational DBMS must possess the following four "cornerstone characteristics," with features as indicated:

1. Base type extension
   - Dynamic linking of user-defined functions
   - Client or server activation of user-defined functions
   - Secure user-defined functions
   - Callback in user-defined functions
   - User-defined access methods
   - Arbitrary-length data types

2. Complex objects
   - Type constructors
   - User-defined functions
   - Arbitrary-length data types
   - SQL support

3. Inheritance
   - Data and function inheritance
   - Overloading
   - Inheritance of types, not tables
   - Multiple inheritance

4. Rule system
   - Events and actions are retrieves as well as updates
   - Integration of rules with inheritance and type extension
   - Rich execution semantics for rules
   - No infinite loops

---

*As a practical matter, we agree that object/relational systems are likely to be the "next great wave." However, Stonebraker nowhere seems to come right out in reference [110] and agree with our position (articulated in Chapter 2) that (a) a true "object/relational" system would be nothing more nor less than a true **relational** system, and that (b) today's "relational" systems (which he would presumably say represent the *current* "great wave") are not true relational systems at all, but SQL systems merely.

To elaborate:

1. *Base type extension:* Stonebraker uses this term to mean that users must be able to define their own scalar types and operators (he uses the term "functions," however, reserving "operators" for functions like "+" that make use of some special infix notation; he also—very unfortunately, in our opinion—asserts that "a data type is both information and operations [whereas] the relational notion of a domain includes only the stored representation, and there is no behavior associated with a domain"*). *Dynamic linking* is self-explanatory. *Client or server activation* means it must be possible to execute user-defined functions in the same address space as the DBMS (at the server) and also in other address spaces (at the client); moreover, such executions must be *secure*—i.e., they must not be allowed to read or (worse) write any data that is supposed to be protected. (For obvious reasons, this problem is particularly severe if the execution occurs at the server.) *Callback*—not a very apt term, in our opinion—just means that user-defined functions must be allowed to perform database operations. *User-defined access methods* means that type definers or implementers must be permitted to extend the system by introducing new storage structures (e.g., quadtrees) and corresponding access code. *Arbitrary-length data types* should be self-explanatory.

   Note: The Third Manifesto suggests that function definitions and type definitions are better kept separate instead of being bundled together (see OO Very Strong Suggestion 2). Stonebraker agrees with this position.

2. *Complex objects:* Stonebraker uses this term to mean that certain type generators—he uses the term "type constructors"—must be supported. (A "complex object" is presumably either a value or a variable of such a generated type.) According to Stonebraker, the following type generators "must" be supported:
   - Composites (records)
   - Sets
   - References

   Composites correspond to our TUPLE type generator (though there seems to be some confusion over whether or not the generated "composite" values and variables are encapsulated). *Sets* should be self-explanatory (note, however, that they are not the same as our RELATION type generator). As for *references,* our *Manifesto* categorically prohibits them, of course (see OO Proscription 2); in fact, we find here, regrettably, a certain amount of confusion over the values *vs.* variables distinction and the model *vs.* implementation distinction once again. We also find confusion over *The Principle of Interchangeability* (see the discussion of RM Prescription 14 in

---

*This claim cannot be correct (if taken literally, "no behavior" implies no operators at all, not even "=").

Chapter 6). To quote: "The Illustra system allows a column in a table to contain . . . a pointer to a [row] . . . in a table . . . References make use of the fact that all [*sic*] Illustra rows have a unique identifier, called an object identifier (OID) . . . that is guaranteed to never change." See reference [72], also Chapter 2 of the present book, for a detailed critique of such ideas.

The *user-defined functions* and *arbitrary-length data types* features just mean that (of course) generated types are indeed types; hence, users must be able to define functions that operate on values and variables of such generated types, and there must not be any implementation restrictions on the physical size of (the internally encoded versions of) such values and variables.

Last, we agree with the *SQL support* feature, but only as an aid to migration (see the discussion of RM Very Strong Suggestion 9 in Chapter 10).

3. *Inheritance:* We agree with the need for inheritance. Unfortunately, Stonebraker uses this term to refer not to *type* inheritance as we understand that term, but rather to the business of "subtables and supertables"—a very different notion, as we tried to explain in Appendix D. While we do not necessarily reject that notion, we do claim that it is not true type inheritance, and it does not provide very much of the functionality that we feel is truly needed. We also note that Stonebraker does not really address the question of an inheritance *model,* nor does he mention most of the intrinsic complexities that seem to arise with inheritance in general (see Part IV of this book).

For the record, however, we offer a few comments on the features Stonebraker lists under his inheritance heading. *Data and function inheritance* means that the "subtable" inherits both columns and (user-defined) functions from the "supertable." *Overloading* means polymorphism (though it is surely not inclusion polymorphism as such). *Inheritance of types, not tables* means—to use the terminology of *The Third Manifesto*—that relation type definitions and relvar definitions are kept separate, and hence that several relvars can be defined to be of the same (named) relation type. (The *Manifesto* takes the exact opposite approach, for reasons explained under RM Prescription 7 in Chapter 6.) *Multiple inheritance* is self-explanatory (at least, the basic idea is—the consequences are not, as we tried to show in Chapter 15).

4. *Rule system:* We agree that a rule system might well be desirable in practice, but rule systems are orthogonal to the question of whether the system is object/relational or something else. We therefore choose not to discuss them here.

It is noteworthy that Stonebraker nowhere discusses the "equation wars" (domain = class *vs.* relvar = class). Indeed, his examples tend to suggest that relvar = class is the right equation, though he never comes out to say as much explicitly.

111. Michael Stonebraker *et al.*: "Third Generation Database System Manifesto,"
     ACM SIGMOD Record 19, No. 3 (September 1990).

In part, this paper is a response to—i.e., counterproposal or rebuttal to—the
proposals of reference [1]. We should explain the title. Basically, *first* generation database systems are the old hierarchic and network (CODASYL) systems, such as IMS and IDMS; *second* generation systems are relational (or at
least SQL) systems; and *third* generation systems are whatever comes next. A
direct quote: "Second generation systems made a major contribution in two
areas, nonprocedural data access and data independence, and these advances
must not be compromised by third generation systems." (We would argue that
relational systems made many more than two "major contributions.") In other
words, third generation systems—whatever else they might do—must certainly support the relational model. Unfortunately, the authors then go on to
say that supporting the relational model really means supporting *SQL* . . .

The following features are claimed as essential requirements of a third
generation DBMS (we have paraphrased the original somewhat):

1. Provide traditional database services plus richer object structures and rules
   - Rich type system
   - Inheritance
   - Functions and encapsulation
   - Optional system-assigned tuple IDs
   - Rules (e.g., integrity rules), not tied to specific objects

2. Subsume second generation DBMSs
   - Navigation only as a last resort
   - Intensional and extensional set definitions [meaning collections that are
     maintained automatically by the system and collections that are main-
     tained manually by the user]
   - Updatable views
   - Clustering, indexes, etc., hidden from the user

3. Support open systems
   - Multiple language support
   - Persistence orthogonal to type
   - SQL (characterized as "intergalactic dataspeak")
   - Queries and results must be the lowest level of client/server communi-
     cation

Again we offer our own comments and reactions:

1. *Traditional database services and richer object structures and rules:* Of
   course we agree with "traditional database services." We also agree with
   "rich type system" and "inheritance," so long as it is understood that
   (a) *type* is just another word for *domain,* and (b) the sole use made of such
   types insofar as the database is concerned is as the domains over which

database relations and relvars are defined. "Functions"—we prefer the term *operators*—are implied by "rich type system." Regarding "encapsulation," see Appendix B. Regarding "tuple IDs," there seems to be some confusion here between tuples and "objects," a point that might be the cause for some alarm; we reject object IDs, of course, but we are prepared to entertain the idea of system keys, and such keys might possibly be thought of as (user-visible) "tuple IDs." As for rules: We certainly support integrity rules specifically, of course; further, we do not preclude support for other kinds of rules (but we regard such support as a secondary matter).

2. *Subsume second generation DBMSs:* If "subsume" here means that the relational model must be subsumed, then we reject the suggestion (but perhaps it does not mean that). "Navigation only as a last resort": We take a firmer stand and reject navigation entirely, believing that it is incumbent on anyone who thinks that navigation is ever necessary to show *first* that a nonnavigational (relational) solution is logically—or at least effectively—impossible. We also reject "extensional set definitions" (in the sense meant here), because much of the meaning of such a set is hidden in some application instead of being exposed in the database. We certainly agree with support for updatable views (and we have some concrete proposals to offer in this regard). Finally, we also agree that access mechanisms—i.e., indexes, etc.—should be hidden from the user (they are *not* hidden in certain object systems, but they were always supposed to be hidden in relational systems).

3. *Support open systems:* We agree with this objective in principle, but we reject the idea of "persistence orthogonal to type," and of course we also reject SQL, firmly (we are in this business for the long haul). We do agree with the general sense of "queries and results being the lowest level of client/server communication," but note that this objective seems to be in conflict with the earlier objectives concerning "extensional set definition" and "navigation."

112. Andrew Taivalsaari: "On the Notion of Inheritance," *ACM Comp. Surv. 28,* No. 3 (September 1996).

113. Stephen Todd: Private communication (1988).

114. Various authors: Proc. 2nd Annual Object/Relational Summit, Boston, Mass. (August 4th–6th, 1997). San Mateo, Calif.: Miller Freeman Inc. (1997).

115. Stanley B. Zdonik and David Maier (eds.): *Readings in Object-Oriented Database Systems.* San Francisco, Calif.: Morgan Kaufmann (1990).

116. Stanley B. Zdonik and David Maier: "Fundamentals of Object-Oriented Databases," in reference [115].

Index

1. Types are sets
2. Subtypes are subsets
3. "Subtype of" is reflexive
4. Proper subtypes
5. "Subtype of" is transitive
6. Immediate subtypes
7. Single inheritance only
8. Global root types
9. Type hierarchies
10. Subtypes can be proper subsets
11. Types disjoint unless one a subtype of the other
12. Scalar values (extended definition)
13. Scalar variables (extended definition)
14. Assignment with inheritance
15. Comparison with inheritance
16. Join etc. with inheritance
17. TREAT DOWN
18. TREAT UP
19. Logical operator IS_$T(SX)$
20. Relational operator RX:IS_$T(A)$
21. Logical operator IS_MS_$T(SX)$
22. Relational operator RX:IS_MS_$T(A)$
23. THE_ pseudovariables
24. Read-only operator inheritance and value substitutability
25. Read-only parameters to update operators
26. Update operator inheritance and variable substitutability